COERCIVE CONTROL

INTERPERSONAL*VIOLENCE*

Series Editors
Claire Renzetti, Ph.D.
Jeffrey L. Edleson, Ph.D.

Parenting by Men Who Batter: New Directions
for Assessment and Intervention,
Edited by Jeffrey L. Edleson and Oliver J. Williams

Coercive Control: The Entrapment of Women in Personal Life,
Evan Stark

COERCIVE CONTROL
The Entrapment of Women in Personal Life

Evan Stark

OXFORD
UNIVERSITY PRESS

OXFORD
UNIVERSITY PRESS

Oxford University Press, Inc., publishes works that further
Oxford University's objective of excellence
in research, scholarship, and education.

Oxford   New York
Auckland   Cape Town   Dar es Salaam   Hong Kong   Karachi
Kuala Lumpur   Madrid   Melbourne   Mexico City   Nairobi
New Delhi   Shanghai   Taipei   Toronto

With offices in
Argentina   Austria   Brazil   Chile   Czech Republic   France   Greece
Guatemala   Hungary   Italy   Japan   Poland   Portugal   Singapore
South Korea   Switzerland   Thailand   Turkey   Ukraine   Vietnam

Copyright © 2007 by Oxford University Press, Inc.

Published by Oxford University Press, Inc.
198 Madison Avenue, New York, New York 10016

www.oup.com

First issued as an Oxford University Press paperback in 2009

Oxford is a registered trademark of Oxford University Press

Library of Congress Cataloging-in-Publication Data
Stark, Evan.
Coercive control : the entrapment of women in personal life / Evan Stark.
   p. cm.
Includes bibliographical references and index.
ISBN 978-0-19-538404-8
1. Wife abuse—United States.   2. Abused women—United States.
3. Psychological abuse—United States.   4. Control (Psychology)
I. Title.
HV6626.2.S67   2007
362.82'920973—dc22   2006025765

Printed in the United States of America
on acid-free paper

Cooking is hard work, but cooking to music eases your fatigue and makes you lose track of time. Cook slowly and patiently for the best results, and let the beat of the music be the pulse of your soul.

—Bonnie Jean Foreshaw,
York Correctional Facility,
Niantic, Connecticut.

ACKNOWLEDGMENTS

I began *Coercive Control* in 1995 and have been at it so long that my wife, Anne Flitcraft, describes it as my "mistress," my friends simply as "the book," and Al Roberts, a colleague at Rutgers who brought my proposal to Oxford and stuck with me during the writing almost as closely as my wife, resorted to one-word questions on our answering machine. The debt I owe others naturally increased with the length of the writing process. But the passage of time has also erased some of these obligations from my memory, for which I sincerely apologize.

Two of those to whom I'm most indebted died before I could express my appreciation, leaving a hole in my heart as well as my intellectual life. The late Susan Schechter introduced me to the concept of coercive control as well as to David Adams, who was using coercive control as a model for his work with Emerge, the innovative program for abusive men he cofounded in Boston. A founding mother of the battered women's movement and its political conscience and historian, Susan taught me to reframe even the darkest experiences of battered women to locate their agency, an approach I apply to the cases in this book. I learned the same lesson from Sharon Vaughan and Enid Peterson, two other activist thinkers and friends. Jack Sternbach had been my mentor and brother since our days as student radicals at the University of Wisconsin in the 1960s and the work he put into maintaining our friendship was as much the source of my understanding of men and masculinity as his many publications on the topic. I owe my clinical education to Susan and Jack as well as to Jean Hay, Jack's wife, my sister Joyce Duncan, and Laurie Harkness, my supervisor at the U.S. Veteran's Hospital, social workers all.

Andrew Klein, Joan Zorza, Al Roberts, and Donald Downs went far beyond what is normally expected from outside reviewers, providing detailed criticism of earlier drafts and continuing to respond to my always urgent queries. Elizabeth Schneider's *Battered Women and Feminist Lawmaking* (2000) and Downs's book, *More Than Victims* (University 1996) said many of the things I had intended to say about the "syndrome" defense, making it unnecessary for me to say them, and deepened my appreciation of the ethical and practical dilemmas posed by the dominant victimization narrative. Because much of the information I draw on is from unreported legal cases, uncataloged agency documents, training curricula, and unpublished reports to state and federal agencies, communication within the network of researchers and practitioners is vital. For facilitating this communication, I owe special thanks to Joan Zorza, Nancy Lemon, Jill Zuccardy, Eve Buzawa (who also published my early work on coercive control), and particularly Barbara Hart. Virtually all the information I present on women's unprecedented gains since the 1960s as well as on persistent inequalities is drawn from the work of Heidi Hartmann, Amy Ciazza, and the extraordinarily talented research staff Heidi directs at the Institute of Women's Policy Research, a group on whose board I was privileged to sit for more than a decade.

There are still considerable costs paid by faculty who include advocacy and political engagement in their activities, as I do. In the Rutgers School of Public Affairs and Administration, I have been fortunate to find an academic home that views public service and improving the responsiveness of government as part of its mission; a chair, Marc Holzer, with a strong commitment to this mission; and administrators who support my work on behalf of women and children, particularly Gary Roth, vice provost for Academic Programs at Rutgers–Newark, and Ray Caprio, vice president for Continuous Education. I am indebted to scores of graduate students from Public Administration, Public Health, and Women's Studies who took my class on Violence in the United States over the years, challenged and refined my case analyses, and shared their own experiences as victims and service providers. The diversity and multinationalism of the student body at Rutgers–Newark made this an ideal environment in which to teach as well as to weigh program innovations against the needs of the least advantaged. Using political theory as the medium, the doctoral students in the seminar "Public Administration in Democratic Society" have engaged me in an ongoing conversation about the nature of liberty, rights claims, citizenship, social justice, and the construction of social problems in liberal market societies. Without this forum, it would have been much more difficult to think outside the box about the status of rights in personal life, the paradoxical role of sexual equality, the importance of narrative in setting the tone of a field, or how the subordination of women bears on liberty, citizenship, or personhood.

As a doctoral student at Rutgers, Cynthia Lischick put the coercive control model to its first empirical test. Cynthia started as my student but became a close friend and colleague and continues to mentor me as often as I do her. Throughout the writing, Jill Zuccardy also remained a steadfast ally and friend. As a legal advocate for immigrant and low-income women at the Sanctuary for Families and in the path-breaking class action suit *Nicholson v. Williams*, Jill set a stellar example of what it means to talk truth to power, steeling my own courage to do so, even when this meant criticizing the battered women's movement with which we both identify.

For direct assistance with the manuscript, I am grateful to Alicea Schatteman, a PhD student who served as my assistant in 2004–2005, and particularly to Carol Marci, who provided months of assistance in identifying and preparing bibliographic material. A retired police woman who was the Officer in Charge of the Sexual Assault and Bias Crimes Unit at the New Haven Police Department, Carol's counsel on substantive issues was as invaluable as her technical expertise.

As my editor at Oxford, Maura Roessner was a supportive guide, keeping me on task while instilling the confidence that I was up to finishing. That I came close to the timelines she set is due in large part to my being given a sabbatical by Rutgers and an International Fellowship by the School of Policy Studies at the University of Bristol for spring 2006. Gill Hague, head of the Violence Against Women Research Group (VAWRG) at the school, extended herself in every way to make my stay in Bristol comfortable, as others did as well, particularly Lesley and Len Doyal, Jane Dennis, Dave Merrick, Jacqui Dalley, Geraldine Ringham, Paul Burton, Hillary Abrams, Hillary Land, Elaine Farmer, George Davey-Smith, Helen Lambert, Ian Gough, and Carolyn Roth. It would be hard to exaggerate how invigorating it felt to work in an environment with activist feminist scholars like Hilary Saunders, Ellen Malos, Nicole Westmarland, and Melanie McCarry. Among the many persons who provided forums in the United Kingdom where I could air my work, three stand out: Janette deHaan, who convened an exciting group of activist practitioners in Glasgow, and Gene Feder and psychologist Roxanne Agnew-Davies, who did the same in London. Dr. Agnew-Davies generously shared the raw data she and her colleagues had collected on the frequency with which coercive and controlling tactics were used against women who came to refuge. Brilliant feminist scholar Marianne Hester was the ideal colleague at Bristol, as challenging and stimulating as she was generous with her time and resources.

When I began testifying in criminal and custody cases in the late 1980s, I faced two dilemmas: how to do justice to the strength and courage of battered women without minimizing the harms they had suffered, and how to convey the importance of structural constraints (like the denial of money) and micro-regulation in settings where these tactics were either invisible or treated as insignificant compared to violence. I am indebted to Susan Schechter, Ann Jones, Joan Meier, Sally Goldfarb, Lewis Okun, Cynthia Lischick, Lee Bowker, Ellen Pence, and Lundy Bancroft for addressing similar concerns by delineating elements of coercive control and to Phyllis Frank, Shamita DasGupta, Michael Johnson, and Suzanne Swan for helping me differentiate women's violence from coercive control.

The major sources for my depiction of coercive control are the stories told to me by Bonnie Jean Foreshaw, Lavonne Lazarra, and the several hundred other women who have shared the most intimate details of their experience with abusive men over the years, most while incarcerated. The privilege of hearing their stories, for which I also thank their attorneys, and of bearing witness to a record of evil and of unparalleled courage in the face of this evil that has no counterpart in the official transcripts of our lives, is the reason I do this work. Because I met these women primarily in the forensic context, and the reports and testimony I provide are part of the public record, nothing they tell me is confidential in the usual sense. But out of respect for their privacy, unless I have explicit permission to do otherwise or the subject was killed or has died or her case was widely publicized, I have changed the names, places, and identifiable circumstances of the stories I recount. I appreciate the irony of "speaking in the name" of battered women whose names I cannot speak and whose voices were silenced for so long by their partners. If I am still haunted by the cases that turned out badly, this is less because I feel guilt about my role—I did what I could—than because it is incomprehensible to me that a good society would hold women subjected to these horrors legally accountable.

I leave for last the appreciation that is so much part of my everyday life that it is easily taken for granted. As my wife, Anne Flitcraft has stood by my side both literally and figuratively for more than 30 years, a comrade, sister, caretaker, lover, colleague, critic, and far and away the best friend I have ever had. She and I have raised three beautiful children and helped raise a fourth. In their own way, as support or critic or inspiration, each has played a vital role in this project. Our confidence in them is unbounded. Until we turn the world over to them, to paraphrase Bonnie, we will let "the beat of the music . . . be the pulse of our soul."

CONTENTS

Introduction   *1*

I The Domestic Violence Revolution: Promise and Disappointment

1 The Revolution Unfolds   *21*
2 The Revolution Stalled   *50*

II The Enigmas of Abuse

3 The Proper Measure of Abuse   *83*
4 The Entrapment Enigma   *112*
5 Representing Battered Women   *133*

III From Domestic Violence to Coercive Control

6 Up to Inequality   *171*
7 The Theory of Coercive Control   *198*
8 The Technology of Coercive Control   *228*

IV Living With Coercive Control

9 When Battered Women Kill   *291*
10 For Love or Money   *314*
11 The Special Reasonableness of Battered Women   *339*

Conclusion: Freedom Is Not Free   *362*
Notes   *402*
Index   *441*

INTRODUCTION

The Estate of Terry Traficonda v. the Town of Waterford, CT

On a June evening in 1989, Philip Traficonda chased his wife, Terry, across their yard to a neighbor's house, where she took refuge with their infant son. Philip had been drinking all afternoon. He approached the modified mobile home to which his wife had escaped, peered through a window, walked around the house several times, and then burst through the screen door into the kitchen. "Get the f—k home," he ordered. When Terry failed to move, Philip grabbed their son from her arms, carried the boy to his pickup truck, and peeled out of the driveway. Terry called 911.

By the time Philip went on trial for her murder, police had "lost" the tape of Terry's call. But the neighbor testified that Terry told the dispatch operator her husband had "kidnapped" their child, was drunk, and was driving at a dangerous rate of speed and that she wanted the child returned. Two officers were sent to the address.

The police knew the Traficondas. Two weeks earlier, in response to a neighbor's complaint, the senior officer dispatched to the house had arrested Philip for beating Terry. Shortly afterward, Terry called to ask that a loaded shotgun be removed, and the same officer responded. Confused about his authority to take the weapon, he gave the gun to a buddy of Philip's for safe-keeping who had come over to the house when he saw the police car.

Terry and the dispatch operator were still talking when Philip returned to the driveway. He got out of the truck and carried the child into their house. Fearing he might hurt their son, Terry became "hysterical" and

1

begged the operator to call off the police. "If they come, he'll kill me," she said. The officers were recalled.

Shortly after 2 a.m., Terry Traficonda was fatally shot in the head. She was found on the couch, naked from the waist down.

At his trial, Philip claimed they were watching a TV film about hunting, Terry asked how it was done, and the shotgun went off accidentally while he was showing her. In addition to two bullet wounds, the coroner identified numerous bruises on Terry's arms, legs, and back. Philip was convicted of murder and sentenced to life in prison. Even so, during the sentencing, the judge lectured Terry in absentia for "staying with the brute so long."

Terry Traficonda was killed in Connecticut, one of the many states that mandates that police make an arrest in domestic violence cases if there is probable cause that such a crime occurred. Following Philip's trial, Terry's sister brought a wrongful death suit against the town, arguing the death would have been prevented had police responded appropriately. I was hired as an expert on the appropriate police response.

The main facts were undisputed. But the wrongful death case hinged on whether, given the known history of domestic violence and the 911 conversation, police should have recognized Terry's risk. Because victims are often too afraid to identify abuse, a basic tenet of police training is that they must respond to a domestic violence call even if a victim countermands a previous request. But the lawyer representing the town raised an additional issue. Had they come to the house, he asked, what could police have done to prevent Terry's death?

I recounted the results of my investigation. Philip's assaults on Terry were well known to the woman's family, neighbors, and workmates as well as to the police. The recent arrest and the autopsy confirmed that domestic violence was ongoing. Most impressive was Philip's behavior after his earlier arrest. In the week before the killing, he had locked his wife out of their bedroom and forced her to sleep on the living room couch. She was limited to one meal a day, such as the slice of cold pizza found in the refrigerator. Philip had taken the toilet paper from the downstairs bathroom and forbidden her to use the upstairs bathroom. He had taken her money and her car keys. He had forbidden her to go to work, speak to friends or family members on the phone, or watch TV. He had also kept her from touching her baby, except to breastfeed, and he had repeatedly threatened to kill her. When she took her son and ran across the lawn, Terry was a hostage in her own home. Police could have learned this with minimal probing.

The lawyer looked perplexed. "What would police have done that night that would have made a difference?" he asked again. I suddenly realized he wanted me to concede that there was little the officers could have done under Connecticut's Family Violence Prevention Act even had they learned about the deprivations, threats, restraints on Terry's movement, and the prior violence. Philip could have been arrested for minor offenses. But because there was no evidence that Terry had been seriously injured on that night, he would be released the next day, almost certainly angrier than before. Connecticut's statute is typical of domestic violence laws generally. Until he shot his wife, Philip Traficonda had not committed a serious crime.

The town settled the lawsuit on a technicality. The officers involved had not completed the legally required domestic violence training, and the civilian dispatcher had received none at all. But the attorney's question continued to gnaw.

Some months later, the same issue resurfaced.

To battered women's advocates, myself included, the killing of Nicole Brown Simpson and Ronald Goldman in June 1994 was the logical culmination of O. J. Simpson's repeated assaults, threats, obsessive jealousy, and attempts to control Nicole's life, including his use of a woman friend to follow her. Simpson had been arrested only once for domestic violence. But his letters to Nicole, her terrified 911 call, as well as other evidence documented nine abusive incidents, including one in which he had smashed her car windows with a baseball bat. Experience told me there had probably been dozens of unreported incidents. In its initial brief, the prosecutors called the homicide "the ultimate act of control." But at trial they decided to downplay the abuse evidence because they were convinced jurors would not grasp its seriousness. They never called their domestic violence experts and relied instead on physical evidence. Their hunch was confirmed after Simpson's acquittal. One juror called the domestic violence a "smokescreen" and asked, "what did all the talk about domestic abuse have to do with homicide?" Another juror was more candid. "If they wanted to talk about domestic violence," she said, "they should have gone down the hall to domestic violence court."[1]

I had been working on various facets of woman battering since the early 1970s. But these cases crystallized my growing sense that a huge chasm separated the experiences of abused women from the prevailing approach to domestic violence. The danger faced by Terry Traficonda and Nicole Brown Simpson was not taken seriously because neither woman had been severely injured and because the hostage-like components of their abuse had no legal standing. Another point struck home. Along with hundreds of like-minded researchers, advocates, and counselors, I shared responsibility for this divide. Ironically, focusing on incidents of severe violence trivialized the strategies used to entrap Terry, Nicole, and millions of women in similar situations, leaving them unprotected.

An Overview

This book attempts to bridge the gap between how men subjugate women in personal life and the domestic violence model that guides the response. I compare the current approach to the life experiences of battered women, assess the effectiveness of interventions based on this approach, provide an alternative model of abuse, and show how adapting this alternative could improve our response. The domestic violence model was first made explicit by researchers. But it is also the cornerstone of an unprecedented revolution in how society treats partner violence. Critiquing the dominant framework entails deciphering where this revolution went wrong and how to put it back on course.

Part I tracks the domestic violence revolution from its incredible promise in the early shelter movement to its current stagnation, describes the range of reforms the revolution instigated, and documents its limited success in realizing its goals, safety, justice, and empowerment for victims and accountability for offenders. Part II traces the limits of the domestic violence revolution to three major fault lines in the current approach, its failure to provide a usable picture of abuse, the failure to explain the durability of abusive relationships ("why women stay" with violent men), and failure to devise a credible strategy to win justice for battered women in the legal system. These enigmas are rooted in the equation of abuse with violent incidents, the application of a "calculus of physical harms" to assess how men hurt women in personal life, and reliance on a "battered woman's defense" built around a psychological narrative that links the harms victims suffer to violence-induced trauma. To resolve these enigmas requires an alternative model of how women are entrapped in personal life.

Parts III and IV outline and apply this new model. Drawing on cases encountered in my 30-year experience as an advocate, counselor, and forensic social worker, I argue that most abuse victims are propelled to seek help by coercive control, the pattern of oppression that led to the death of Terry Traficonda and Nicole Brown Simpson, not by domestic violence. I sketch the historical, theoretical, and strategic dimensions of coercive control and argue that it as an offense to liberty that prevents women from freely developing their personhood, utilizing their capacities, or practicing citizenship, consequences they experience as *entrapment*. Part IV applies the model to the experience of Donna Balis, who shot her husband, Frank, while he slept; Laura Ferucci, who embezzled a large sum of money from the company where she worked; and Bonnie Foreshaw, a battered woman who shot at a man she had met only once and accidentally killed the pregnant woman he used as a shield.

The fundamental premises of this book are that women deserve an equal chance to become persons with men, that this right extends to their personal lives, and that we are obligated to employ every means at our disposal, including the coercive power of the state, to protect and support these rights. The conclusion considers the practical implications of applying these premises to coercive control, providing both the rationale for refocusing interventions on the liberty harms inflicted by abuse and identifying the challenges this poses. I propose a three-pronged approach: criminalize coercive control, revise intervention to highlight women's liberty rights alongside their safety, and enter the law through a reinvigorated political movement that brings their real equality in line with their formal rights through what I call "the dance of justice."

This book reframes woman battering from the standpoint of its survivors as a course of calculated, malevolent conduct deployed almost exclusively by men to dominate individual women by interweaving repeated physical abuse with three equally important tactics: intimidation, isolation, and control. Assault is an essential part of this strategy and is often injurious and sometimes fatal. But the primary harm abusive men inflict is political, not physical, and reflects the deprivation of rights and resources that are critical to personhood and citizenship. Although coercive control can be devastating psychologically, its key dynamic involves an objective state of subordination and the resistance women mount to free themselves from domination. Women's right to use whatever means are available to liberate themselves from coercive control derives from the mode men use to oppress them, not from the proximate physical or psychological harms they may suffer because of abuse.

Coercive control shares general elements with other capture or course-of-conduct crimes such as kidnapping, stalking, and harassment, including the facts that it is ongoing and its perpetrators use various means to hurt, humiliate, intimidate, exploit, isolate, and dominate their victims. Like hostages, victims of coercive control are frequently deprived of money, food, access to communication or transportation, and other survival resources even as they are cut off from family, friends, and other supports. But unlike other capture crimes, coercive control is personalized, extends through social space as well as over time, and is gendered in that it relies for its impact on women's vulnerability *as women* due to sexual inequality. Another difference is its aim. Men deploy coercive control to secure privileges that involve the use of time, control over material resources, access to sex, and personal service. Like assaults, coercive control undermines a victim's physical and psychological integrity. But the main means used to establish control is the microregulation of everyday behaviors associated with stereotypic female roles, such as how women dress, cook, clean, socialize, care for their children, or perform sexually. This is accomplished by exploiting the benefits women derive from their newfound equality—taking the money they earn, for instance—and the disadvantages they suffer because of persistent sexual discrimination in the market and their consignment to default domestic roles. These dynamics give coercive control a role in sexual politics that distinguishes it from all other crimes.

I approach women's entrapment in personal life from a feminist perspective that stresses their rights as sexual beings and the means used to suppress these rights. I do not downplay women's own use of violence either in fights or to hurt or control men or same-sex partners. Numerous studies in the United States indicate that women of all ages assault male and female partners in large numbers and for many of the same reasons and with much the same consequences as men. However, there is no counterpart in men's lives to women's entrapment by men in personal life due to coercive control. Why this is so and how this bears on this conspicuous form of subjugation are among the questions this book addresses.

The Domestic Violence Revolution

Society's response to male violence against women has been revolutionized in the past three decades. If the long-term basis for this revolution is women's unprecedented gains in every sphere of life, its immediate expressions are the proliferation of community-based services for victims of rape, battering, and sexual abuse; the development of a knowledge base documenting various forms of abuse; the changed professional response; and a growing sensitivity to these problems in popular culture.

The age-old prerogative for men to physically subjugate their female partners has been radically curtailed since the first battered women's shelters opened in the early 1970s. On the ground in virtually every corner of the globe, the revolution consists of the proliferation of battered women's shelters, a burgeoning research and popular advice literature, a dramatic shift in how the media portray violence against women, a range of policies to combat the problem, and a broad spectrum of frequently innovative programs to protect, counsel, or otherwise support abused women and/or to arrest, sanction, or counsel the men who abuse them.[2] Countries that fail to recognize wife abuse as a human rights issue are now the exception and most of these, with the United States, Great Britain, and Canada as leaders, have developed a specialized response grounded in the criminal justice and refuge systems that extends across a broad spectrum of services and policies. In the United States alone, shelters or other services for battered women in over 2,000 communities serve over 3 million women and children annually. Reforms in the U.S. legal system include extending the definition of rape to wives, removing discretion in deciding whether to arrest or prosecute persons who assault their partners, providing a range of new protections for victims, implementing specialized and integrated domestic violence courts and prosecution approaches (called dedicated or evidence-based), creating counseling programs for batterers, consolidating and coordinating the justice and service responses, and allowing women accused of crimes against abusive partners to use a battered woman's defense based on their victimization. The rationale for these reforms in the United States is straightforward: under the equal protection clause of the Fourteenth Amendment to the Constitution women assaulted by present or former partners are entitled to the same protections as persons assaulted by strangers. Whether the autonomous women's movement, the government, or some combination play the key roles in responding to partner abuse depends on the special circumstances in each country.[3] But the basic contours of the response to violence against women—protection and service for victims and punishment for offenders—are similar worldwide. Never before has so broad a spectrum of resources and interventions been brought to bear on men's oppression of women in relationships.

The Revolution Is Stalled

Hundreds of thousands of women and children owe the fact that they are alive to the availability of shelters and to criminal justice and legal reforms. What is less clear is whether women as a group are safer today or are less likely to be beaten, controlled, or killed by their partners than they were before the domestic violence revolution began.

Partner violence against women is no longer just life. But anyone with reasonable sympathies and a passing acquaintance with interventions to stem men's abuse of woman will sense the failure of a range of systems to mount an adequate response, the justice system included. Among the conclusions supported in chapter 2 are these:

- Partner homicides have dropped precipitously. But this change has benefited men far more than women. The prevalence of violence against women has not changed significantly in 30 years.
- The number of men arrested for partner violence has increased dramatically. But assaults against partners are treated as a second-class misdemeanor. The chance that a perpetrator will go to jail in any given incident is just slightly better than the chance of winning a lottery.
- The battered woman's defense has kept some abuse victims from going to jail. But it has not helped the vast majority of victims charged with crimes against the men who beat them or who have committed crimes in the context of being abused.
- Hundreds of thousands of service professionals have been trained to identify and respond to domestic violence. Yet rates of institutional identification have improved only very slightly, and intervention may actually "normalize" the most devastating forms of abuse.
- Batterer intervention programs (BIPs) are widely offered as an alternative to incarceration. But these programs are little more effective than doing nothing at all. Regardless of intervention, the vast majority of perpetrators continue their abuse.
- Shelters are the core response to abused women. But in hundreds of communities, shelters today are indistinguishable from the traditional, paternalistic service system they arose to challenge.

Unfortunately, the vast research establishment that has developed around family violence offers little help in getting out of this quagmire. A report from the National Research Council suggests why. Although "various disciplines have contributed to the development of research on violence against women," it tells us, "each brings different theoretical models, databases, instrumentation, and problem definitions to its work. As a result, it is often extremely difficult to generalize from a cluster of studies or to build on earlier work."[4] This critical assessment is too kind. In reality, family violence research has been atheoretical to the extreme, beholden to outdated conceptual models, and often seems more concerned with footnotes and professional reputations than with generating a synthetic core of common knowledge rooted in the experience of those on whose behalf the work is presumably conducted. Tens of millions of public dollars have been spent to measure virtually every facet of violence among adult intimates. Yet we still lack a definition of the problem that allows us to accurately determine its significance in the general population, its duration or dynamics, or whether the steps we have taken to limit or prevent the problem are working. Researchers have yet to provide satisfactory answers to such basic questions as whether abuse by male and female partners is similar, how many victims require assistance, why abusive relationships last as long as they do, or why so many battered women—but not men assaulted by female partners—develop medical, psychosocial, and behavioral problems that compromise their physical and mental health. The size, dimensions, and outcome of the problem are almost as opaque today as they were when domestic violence was "discovered" in the early 1970s. Lost beneath a mountain of words is the vision of empowerment that initially motivated thousands of volunteers—many former victims of abuse—to construct one of the most extensive and successful movements for change in history.

Our key finding is that the domestic violence revolution appears to have had little effect on coercive control, the most widespread and devastating strategy men use to dominate women in personal life. Refocusing research, advocacy, law, policy, and institutional services on coercive control would be a giant step toward changing this situation. The domestic violence movement began with a vision, to provide women worldwide with a safety net that protected them against harm in personal life. Such a net is in place in most countries. But long-term protection still eludes us.

Where Do We Go From Here?

The domestic violence revolution is stalled. The question is "why?"

One answer is political. Domestic violence will persist so long as sexual inequalities persist. Reflecting on women's current status in private life, legal theorist Isabel Marcus suggests that the practice of coverture is alive and well in the United States.[5] Others feel it is premature to question efforts on behalf of battered women. The problem is simply too great and the movement to challenge age-old habits of male dominance too young for us to rush to judgment. Besides, some say, criticizing the achievements of the domestic violence revolution fuels opponents of sexual equality. A less global explanation for why such a huge investment of resources has yielded diminished returns is that sexist bias in law, criminal justice, medicine, and government remains pervasive. By contrast, "conservative feminists" like Linda Mills, Christa Hoff Sommers, Camille Paglia, and Kate Rophie blame "mainstream" feminists for exaggerating the extent and severity of male violence, portraying women primarily as victims, and relying on state interventions, which are as likely to hurt as help women.[6] The result, they claim, is that men's victimization is discredited, women's disempowerment is enhanced, and the legitimate problems of the small minority of women who genuinely deserve assistance are masked.

These explanations are ultimately unsatisfactory. True, much remains to be done to achieve full sexual equality, and sexist bias remains widespread. But the skeptics conceal the most important fact about women's lives in modern liberal societies: despite the significant forces arrayed against their liberation, since the 1960s, women have made greater progress toward full equality in economic, political, civic, and cultural life than in all previous centuries combined. It is against the momentum of this progressive project that the present struggle to end one of the most archaic vestiges of male dominance—the rule of men over women in personal life—must be understood and judged. Gender bias remains deeply ingrained in the current service response. But the course of abuse remains largely unaffected *even when services are delivered as intended.* The conservatives are right to challenge movement rhetoric that denies the reality of women's violence and exaggerates their victimization. But they are wrong on all other counts—the size of the problem, the similarity of male and female abuse, and on the harms caused by state intervention to stop partner violence. Their call to return abuse to the private sphere for solution in the name of intimacy is regressive in the extreme.

But should we wait to challenge the current course lest we jeopardize the progress we've made? Law professor Jane Maslow Cohen has wisely observed that initial legal victories by the battered women's movement depended less on "the crude moral power of the arguments in favor of change" than on "the ludicrous weakness of the reasons that were mustered to support the status quo."[7] The lack of a coherent opposition meant that the images of battering presented in the courts and other public arenas could be helpful even when they were improvised, internally inconsistent, and lacked external validity. But receptivity to this patchwork can no longer be assumed. It is simply a matter of time before the conservative and religious backlash against the hard-won gains of oppressed minorities extends to what defense attorney Allan Dershowitz dubs "the abuse excuse" and other protections currently available for battered women.[8] Initially set back on their heels in defense by the moral power of the movement against woman abuse, so-called men's rights and father's rights groups have formed around the globe and are moving aggressively to recapture lost ground. Change cannot wait.

Having let domestic violence pass without much notice for centuries, it is hardly surprising that society hesitates before enforcing zero tolerance as a norm. Nor should we be shocked to find the same legal system that was unimpressed by partner violence only moments ago (historically speaking) resisting the mandate to harshly sanction this behavior or that piecemeal reforms have failed to dislodge long-running patterns of abuse. Even so, the fact that women have made such unprecedented gains in other areas compels us to look for proximate explanations for why the domestic violence revolution has not led to greater improvements than it has, particularly given its initial promise. Having expended billions of public dollars and hundreds of thousands of life-years attempting to stem woman battering, activists, their supporters, and those in whose name we proceed have a right to an accounting.

A New Model

The limits of current interventions can be directly traced to a failure of vision, not of nerve. Conservatives attack the advocacy movement for exaggerating the nature and extent of abuse. In fact, because of its singular emphasis on physical violence, the prevailing model minimizes both the extent of women's entrapment by male partners in personal life and its consequences.

An old joke has it that one psychiatrist can change a light bulb, but only if it really wants to change. Challenging the prevailing approach is difficult because it is tied to a vast institutional network that supports thousands of careers and is the basis on which foundations distribute research funds, journals identify what will be published, universities grant promotion, politicians garner support, and service providers attract clients and their fees. Only when its internal contradictions escalate to the point of challenging the very legitimacy of a model that dominates a field is the stage set to mold anomalous evidence into an alternative way of seeing the problem, what Thomas Kuhn called a "scientific revolution."[9] The domestic violence field is on the brink of such a sea change.

Viewing woman abuse through the prism of the incident-specific and injury-based definition of violence has concealed its major components, dynamics, and effects, including the fact that it is neither "domestic" nor primarily about "violence." Failure to appreciate the multidimensionality of oppression in personal life has been disastrous for abuse victims. Regardless of its chronic nature, courts treat each abuse incident they see as a first offense. Because well over 95% of these incidents are minor, no one goes to jail. This is a classic instance of ineffective demand: cases accumulate and are processed, but the system fails to produce its expected outcomes, sanctions in this case. BIPs are revolving doors. As calls to the police or visits to the emergency room are repeated over time, the helping response becomes more perfunctory and may actually contribute to making abuse routine, the process called normalization. Everyone involved views the fact that abuse will continue as tragic but somehow inevitable.

The Triumph of the Violence Approach

Things were not always this way. Women sought refuge in the early shelters for a variety of oppressive conditions, not merely physical abuse, and many early shelters targeted economic and political injustices as well as violence. A number of the seminal articles and books in the domestic violence field highlighted isolation and control strategies such as taking money or enforcing household tasks alongside violence, portrayed battered women as aggressive help seekers, and supported retaliatory violence by victims as a just response rather than as a byproduct of trauma.[10] But by the late 1980s a consensus had emerged that abuse meant domestic violence, that injury and psychological deterioration were the principal consequences of violence that required attention, that "ending violence against women" was the goal of our movement and that, therefore, victim safety and offender accountability were the appropriate measures of shelter and related work, not systems' change. Only slightly less universal were the psychological theories associated with the model, the belief that trauma was the primary mechanism by which violence was converted into psychological dependence and that this dependence was typically manifest in some variant of posttraumatic stress disorder (PTSD) or battered woman's syndrome (BWS). When nonviolent forms of oppression were discussed, they were described as psychological abuse, as if their primary dynamic involved mental processes rather than concrete deprivations and structural restraints.

The domestic violence model has been an incredible success by conventional standards of intellectual productivity, funding, political credibility, or acceptance by courts and the general public. Embracing the core imagery of violence and victimization has allowed politicians across a broad spectrum to retain support from women without antagonizing law and order or religious constituencies opposed to abortion or equal rights for women.[11] Passage of the Violence Against Women Act (VAWA) in 1994 and its reauthorization in 2000 and 2005 in the United States and the Domestic Violence, Crime and Victims Act of 2004 in the United Kingdom are merely a few of the more prominent initiatives in a funding pattern that extends in many countries across the range of justice, health, service, and research departments and agencies. Just as telling is an increasing sensitivity to the portrayal of abused women by the mass media.

Coercive Control

A true revolution requires that a credible alternative be put in place of what is torn down. I start from the anomalous evidence generated by adherents to the current approach. But I construct the alternative model primarily from prior conceptual and empirical work on the nature, extent, and dynamics of coercive control and the real-life experiences of perpetrators and victims of abuse

The most important anomalous evidence indicates that violence in abusive relationships is ongoing rather than episodic, that its effects are cumulative rather than incident-specific, and that the harms it causes are more readily explained by these factors than by its severity. Among these harms, the dominant approach identifies two for which it fails to adequately account: the entrapment of victims in relationships where ongoing abuse is virtually inevitable and the development of a problem profile that distinguishes abused women from every other class of assault victim. That these differences reflect the unique dynamics associated with abuse rather than predisposing factors is indicated by their emergence in the context of ongoing violence. But what dynamics? The prevailing view is that women *stay* and develop a range of mental health and behavioral problems because exposure to severe violence induces trauma-related syndromes, such as PTSD or BWS that can disable a woman's capacity to cope or escape. This view is the basis for defending women who retaliate against abusive partners. In fact, however, only a small proportion of abuse victims evidence these syndromes. Most victims of abuse do not develop significant psychological or behavioral problems. Abused women exhibit a range of problems that are unrelated to trauma, the vast majority of assault incidents are too minor to induce trauma, and abuse victims can be entrapped even in the absence of assault. The duration of abusive relationships is made even more problematic when we appreciate that abuse victims are aggressive help seekers and are as likely to be assaulted and even entrapped when they are physically separated as when married or living together. Thus, whatever harms are involved can cross social space as well as extend over time and appear to persist regardless of how women respond. But if violence doesn't account for the entrapment of millions of women in personal life, what does?

The answer is *coercive control*, a strategy that remains officially invisible despite the fact that it has been in plain sight at least since the earliest shelter residents told us in no uncertain terms that "violence wasn't the worst part." Cognitive psychologists in the late 1970s and 1980s tried to capture what these women were experiencing by comparing it to "coercive persuasion," brainwashing, and other tactics used with hostages, prisoners of war, kidnap victims, and by pimps with prostitutes. Although this view was largely ignored by academic researchers, the understanding of abuse as coercive control was developed in popular literature and incorporated at least implicitly into how various practitioners approached the problem. In its early educational campaign for doctors, the American Medical Association identified abuse with "coercive behavior that may include repeated battery and injury, psychological abuse, sexual assault, progressive social isolation, deprivation, and intimidation perpetrated by someone who was or is involved in an intimate relationship with the victim."[12] Working on men's control skills provides one template for BIP. A range of child welfare, health, and advocacy organizations have added questions about isolation and control to the protocols used to identify abuse. Prosecutors are increasingly charging batterers with stalking, or harassment as well as domestic violence, crimes that typically involve a course of intimidating and controlling conduct as well of violence. Scotland and Canada are examples of countries that now define violence against women or abuse from a human rights perspective that includes a range of coercive and controlling behaviors in addition to assault. The U.S. Armed Forces include economic abuse in its definition. The most widely used graphic representation of abuse is the Power and Control Wheel introduced by the Domestic Violence Intervention Project (DAIP) in Duluth, Minnesota. Although violence is the hub of the original wheel, its spokes depict isolation, economic control, emotional and sexual abuse, and other facets of coercive control. The Sanctuary for Families and Children in New York City is only one of the hundreds of advocacy programs that employ the wheel in assessment or to help women identify unrecognized facets of their abuse. This attention is merited. The several dozen studies that attempt to measure control and psychological abuse suggest that coercive control accounts for 50% to 80% of all help seeking by abused women and that the majority of these victims have been subjected to multiple control tactics, among which the denial of money, the monitoring of time, and restricted mobility and communication are prominent.[13]

Despite these inroads, coercive control remains marginal to mainstream thinking. It is rarely acknowledged in policy circles, has had almost no impact on domestic violence policing or criminal law, and commands no special funding. Although providers and advocates may ask about elements of coercive control, I know of no programs or interventions that address it. Everyone acknowledges that domestic violence is about power and control. But we have yet to incorporate this truism into our understanding of abuse or our response. As for Terry Traficonda and Nicole Brown Simpson, so for the millions of other victims: absent injurious assault, the entrapment of women in personal life goes unnoticed.

The major source for the model of coercive control are the victims and perpetrators of abuse with whom I and others have worked. I detail a range of harms caused by tactics other than violence. But the women in my practice have repeatedly made clear that what is done to them is less important than what their partners have prevented them from doing for themselves by appropriating their resources; undermining their social support; subverting their rights to privacy, self-respect, and autonomy; and depriving them of substantive equality. These harms highlight a key conclusion of this book: that coercive control is a liberty crime rather than a crime of assault. Preventing a substantial group of women from freely applying their agency in economic and political life obstructs overall social development

Violence remains critical. The women whose stories I recount suffered appalling physical harm. But it is notable that most of those who suffered *only* violence retained their autonomy in key areas of their lives. Importantly, the most devastating effects were as likely to result from routine but minor violence as from life-threatening assaults.

The new model is rooted in the same tenets that gave birth to the battered women's movement—that the abuse of women in personal life is inextricably bound up with their standing in the larger society and therefore that women's entrapment in their personal lives can be significantly reduced only if sexual discrimination is addressed simultaneously. In the early shelters, the interrelatedness of these tenets was grounded in the practice of empowerment, whereby the suffering of individual victims was mollified by mobilizing their collective power to help one another and change the institutional structures that caused and perpetuated women's second-class status, an example of women doing for themselves. Our challenge is to resurrect this collective practice and broaden its political focus to the sources of coercive control.

The material and social benefits men garner through coercive control provide its proximate motive. But I cannot explain why men choose this course rather than seek the same or even greater benefits by respecting their partners' autonomy, accepting their equality, cultivating their love, and honoring their creativity and power. Those who insist on understanding why a substantial subset of men deploy coercive control would be best served by following the lead of Princeton professor of religion Cornel West, who urges his students to pursue evil into the dark recesses of men's soul.

Control: Invisible in Plain Sight

Like Philip and Terry Traficonda and O. J. Simpson and Nicole Brown Simpson, the perpetrators and victims of woman battering described in this book are easily identified. Many of the rights violated in battering are so fundamental to the conduct of everyday life that is hard to conceive of meaningful human existence without them. How is it possible then, that, taken together, the men who committed the thousands of assaults and other oppressive acts described in this book suffered virtually no official sanctions as a result? If coercive control has been in plain sight for decades, why has it attracted so little notice?

I have already pointed to the prominence of the domestic violence model. Another explanation is the compelling nature of violence. Once injury became the major medium for presenting abuse, its sights and sounds were so dramatic that other experiences seemed muted by comparison. The radical feminists who led the fight against rape and pornography also inadvertently contributed to the invisibility of coercive control. Placing so much political currency on violence against women as the ultimate weapon in men's arsenal made it a surrogate for male domination rather than merely one of its means. It was a short step to replacing political discourse with the current economy of victims and perpetrators.

Another explanation for why coercive control has had such little impact is that no one knows what to do about it.

The entrapment of women in personal life is also hard to discern because many of the rights it violates are so basic—so much a part of the taken-for-granted fabric of the everyday lives we lead as adults, and so embedded in female behaviors that are constrained by their normative consignment to women—that their abridgement passes largely without notice. The following chapters will introduce women who had to answer the phone by the third ring, record every penny they spent, vacuum "till you can see the lines," and dress, walk, cook, talk, and make love in specific ways and not in others, always with the "or else" proviso hanging over their heads. What status should we accord Terry Traficonda's right to have toilet paper in the downstairs bathroom or to Laura's right to go to the gym without being beeped home? Given the prominence of physical bruising, how can we take these little indignities seriously or appreciate that they comprise the heart of a hostage-like syndrome against which the slap, punch, or kick pale in significance? Most people take it for granted that normal, healthy adults determine their own sleep patterns or how they drive or laugh or make love. The first women who used our home as her safe house described her partner as a tyrant. We thought she was speaking metaphorically.

Violence is easy to understand. But the deprivations that come packaged in coercive control are no more a part of my personal life than they are of most men's. This is true both literally, because many of the regulations involved in coercive control target behaviors that are identified with the female role, and figuratively, because it is hard for me to conceive of a situation outside of prison, a mental hospital, or a POW camp where another adult would control or even care to control my everyday routines.

What is taken from the women whose stories I tell—and what some victims use violence to restore—is the capacity for independent decision making in the areas by which we distinguish adults from children and free citizens from indentured servants. Coercive control entails a malevolent course of conduct that subordinates women to an alien will by violating their physical integrity (domestic violence), denying them respect and autonomy (intimidation), depriving them of social connectedness (isolation), and appropriating or denying them access to the resources required for personhood and citizenship (control). Nothing men experience in the normal course of their everyday lives resembles this conspicuous form of subjugation.

Some of the rights batterers deny to women are already protected in the public sphere, such as the rights to physical integrity and property. In these instances, law is challenged to extend protections to personal life. But most of the harms involved in coercive control are gender-specific infringements of adult autonomy that have no counterpart in public life and are currently invisible to the law. The combination of these big and little indignities best explains why women suffer and respond as they do in abusive relationships, including why so many women become entrapped, why some battered women kill their partners, why they themselves may be killed, or why they are prone to develop a range of psychosocial problems and exhibit behaviors or commit a range of acts that are contrary to their nature or to basic common sense or decency.

In the late 1970s, we reached into the shadows to retrieve physical abuse from the canon of "just life." Now it appears, we did not reach nearly far enough.

The gender specificity of the liberty crime of coercive control means that equal outcomes for men and women—what legal theorist Martha Fineman calls "result equality"—can be achieved only when "rule equality" is abandoned in favor of an approach that recognizes—and responds aggressively to—women's special vulnerability to domination in personal life, largely due to their positioning within the social structure.[14] Shifting from equal protection as a principle for framing intervention to a "special rules" approach raises the vexing policy dilemma of how to win support from the class of actors (mainly men) whose privileges are being defended with coercive control without reproducing the paternalistic stereotypes that legitimate these privileges. The emphasis on a special vulnerability is itself problematic. Persistent sexual inequalities make women more vulnerable than men to the deprivation of liberty in personal life. Still, as batterers themselves have pointed out to me over the years, there would be no need for so many men to deploy elaborate means to control female partners if women still accepted subordination as a fate bestowed by nature. If coercive control can only be widely implemented because women are not in the same social position as men, it is executed by repressing and/or exploiting the capacity for self-realization in personal life that corresponds to the larger historical movement toward women's full equality, as philosopher Drucilla Cornell puts it, toward "recognition of the equivalent value of the feminine within sexual difference."[15] This dialectic demands that the law extend women's rights and opportunities even as it defends them against victimization.

Neither the law nor other institutional service systems are neutral arbiters in interpersonal relationships, but instead exercise considerable power in shaping these affairs. If these systems currently prefer to weigh in against partner violence but not against the exercise of male domination in personal life and insist that women can be protected from harm only if they concede they are victims rather that free persons entitled to a liberatory response, this is not merely because state actors are misinformed about the true nature of women's oppression. It is also because this approach to woman battering accommodates an obvious social wrong—violence against women—without threatening, indeed by reproducing the prevailing sexual hierarchy. An important message in this book is that attempts to protect women that do not simultaneously expand the space where they can act as fully entitled citizens are forms of disguised betrayal that fail both in practical terms (as means of enhancing long-term safety) and in moral terms. I rest my case on the transparent premise that the wrong done to women's liberty by coercive control is greater, and hence more deserving of legal redress, than the wrong done to men by constraining their (nonviolent) right to maintain their privileged social position. In the current political climate, this position may seem naive. But I direct this appeal less to an abstract legal rationality—in which I do not believe— than to the historical forces, including those that currently support women's liberation, that shape legal practice.

The women whose stories form the heart of this book mustered incredible courage to resist the tyrannies to which they were subjected. Some did so directly and others by taking their resistance underground. The greatest challenge in representing these experiences is how to accurately portray the strategy used to subordinate these women without losing sight of their indomitable spirit. Imagining the women whom this book is about as what historian Linda Gordon called "heroes of their own lives" is made even more difficult by sex stereotypes that equate heroism with actions in public arenas to which men have historically enjoyed privileged access.[16] If the ordeals my clients endured had occurred on a battlefield, sports stadium, or in the political arena, their courage would have been publicly celebrated. But there is little recognition afforded to women who survive the ordeals of personal life.

Working with people who have endured what Conrad's Kurtz called "the horror of it all" requires a personal buffer. The victimization narrative serves this function. Picturing battered women as pathetic, tragic, and helpless allows us to act sympathetically, while remaining at a safe distance. But these sympathies also prevent us from relating to Nate Parkman, a woman who confronted and stabbed her ex-boyfriend in the street. Nor do they provide a vantage on what propelled Donna, Lisa, Bonnie Foreshaw, Tracy Thurman, Francine Hughes, and the dozens of other battered women who people this book through an often paralyzing fear to draw on a reservoir of courage and capacity for self-emancipation that had no objective confirmation in their immediate situations. This is no mystical allusion. Despite the seeming totality of their oppression, battered women nonetheless are able to maintain a sense of control—even if it is only "control in the context of no control"—because they are in touch with a larger social context in which their right to safety and freedom is affirmed. Readers may be alternately depressed by the devastating harms recounted here or enraged by the indifference with which these crimes were met. But attend, too, to this. The spirit that continually resurfaces in these lives indicates that each of us is capable of remaking the worlds we are given, even against impossible odds. Hopefully, witnessing this spirit will provide the vantage, what Hannah Arendt called the "Archimedean point," needed to go down among women whose struggles excite impotence, rage, and exaltation.

Part I

The Domestic Violence Revolution: Promise and Disappointment

1

THE REVOLUTION UNFOLDS

Sara Buell mounted a podium in the Green Room at the White House. A strong-willed prosecutor known for her "get tough" policies with domestic violence perpetrators in Quincy, Massachusetts, Buell is a Harvard Law School graduate and a dynamic public speaker. Along with a San Diego prosecutor, Casey Quinn, she pioneered evidence-based or "no drop" prosecution, the controversial practice of proceeding with charges against perpetrators irrespective of a victim's wishes. Advocates disagree about the wisdom of this approach. But these differences were no more evident in the room than the gulf that normally separated champions of women's rights from the conservative Republicans present. Buell introduced President Bill Clinton, who would publicly sign the Violence Against Women Act (VAWA), Title IV of the Violent Crime Control and Law Enforcement Act. Moments before the president entered with Attorney General Janet Reno and Secretary of Health and Human Services Donna Shalala, a line of women's advocates stolidly embraced Senator Orrin Hatch, the bane of reproductive rights, as well as liberal Senator Joseph Biden, a key architect of VAWA. The president needed this alliance to protect a crime bill that contained death penalty and sentencing provisions opposed by liberals along with a prevention agenda opposed by the Right. The makeup of the group also symbolized a growing propensity to define violence against women as a crime problem. But the main thought on our mind was the unprecedented national audience we had garnered.

The president identified Buell as a survivor of abuse and former welfare mom as well as a justice pioneer and pronounced domestic violence "the most important criminal justice issue in the United States." Next, he introduced Bonnie Campbell. A former attorney general in Iowa who had lost a reelection bid because of her outspoken views on rape and woman battering, she would oversee the expenditure of the approximately $1.62 billion appropriated to combat domestic violence and sexual assault over the next 6 years. Twenty-five percent of the funds would support community-based shelters and sexual abuse programs, and 25% would be spent at a state's discretion. The rest would go to law enforcement.

First introduced in the Senate in 1990, passage of VAWA was the culmination of a growing consensus between advocates and lawmakers that the prevention of domestic violence and rape merited a nationally coordinated effort focused on safety, prosecution, and increasing the responsiveness of community-based and traditional services. VAWA provides for the interstate enforcement of restraining orders (so-called full faith and credit provisions), makes it a federal offense to cross state lines to violate a restraining order or injure an intimate party, and outlaws the possession of ammunition and firearms by persons subject to restraining orders. The act also provides significant penalties for a defendant found guilty of the new federal crimes of domestic violence and allows victims to seek restitution in federal court for the full amount of losses, including medical expenses; physical therapy expenses; lost income; attorney fees; and travel, child care, and temporary housing expenses. VAWA also establishes education and prevention grants to reduce sexual assaults against women and a national domestic violence hotline. Based on the premise that these crimes are motivated by "animus" toward a victim's gender, a provision added by Senator Biden (and subsequently found unconstitutional) defined violence against women as a civil rights violation and allowed victims to sue for damages as a remedy. It was assumed that states would use VAWA funding to expand training programs for criminal justice personnel, refine criminal justice data collection and processing, and build bridges between law enforcement and domestic violence services.

As we rose to applaud, I looked over at Lucy Freidman, longtime director of Victims' Services Inc. in New York City, the nation's largest provider of shelter. She winked knowingly. We had come a long way. Perhaps too far, her look suggested.

The Beginning

In August 1975, on our way back from an idyllic summer in La Jolla, my wife, Anne Flitcraft, and I decided to stop in St. Paul to see our friend Sharon Vaughan. After phone messages went unanswered, a mutual acquaintance produced an address. The large Victorian house sat on a quiet residential street that had seen better days. In response to our knocks, the door was opened a crack, then shut abruptly. Aaron, who was three at the time, started to cry. I picked him up and knocked again. This time, we were admitted.

The place was in a state of frenetic activity. Women and children were everywhere. Two women were on the phones in a converted walk-in-closet while another woman talked at them, oblivious that her audience was pre-occupied. Six women sat in a semicircle in an open dining area, listening intently to an older, heavy-set black woman. Sobbing was audible from a stairwell where a squat Native American woman held a much taller white woman who could have stepped out of a Depression photo by Margaret Bourke-White. Everyone was smoking. In the 10 minutes we waited, several pairs of women left the house through a back door in the kitchen and another pair entered with several children in tow, carrying groceries. Children ran up, then down the stairs, or disappeared into the basement. Someone yelled at her children; we heard the telltale music of a TV soap opera, and the whirring of a washing machine. "She's in the attic," someone told us in passing. As if waiting for this cue, Sharon descended from the top of the stairs, her long skirt swinging in front of her like Katharine Hepburn in *Philadelphia Story*, managing to dodge the children and the clutter while staring straight ahead, her eyes sparkling. "I was working on a grant," she apologized. "What do you think?" Then, she told us about Woman House in that understated Minnesota drone parodied in the film *Fargo*.

In 1972, with the help of Susan Ryan, a Vista volunteer from New York, Sharon's consciousness-raising group, Women's Advocates, developed a do-it-yourself divorce handbook for women who called legal services in Ramsey County, Minnesota. To their surprise, many of the callers needed emergency housing or to get away from their partners. It was unclear what had precipitated these crises. Sharon invited a particularly desperate caller to stay at her apartment, but her two-year-old wreaked havoc on her files. His mother didn't talk about being battered; she said she wanted to go to secretarial school to make a life for her and her son. Sharon's children were perplexed. The women were sad, broke, and disheveled. Sharon compared their house to the Underground Railroad. But her children wanted their family time back. Her son asked, "Are we poor like these women?"

Similar scenes were enacted at the homes of other volunteers. The group rented a small apartment as a retreat, but frequent turnover led to eviction. In the meantime, they purchased the five-bedroom Victorian house, a short bus ride from downtown St. Paul, using the home of one of the volunteers as collateral for the $24,000 down payment and securing $600 a month in pledges to pay the monthly mortgage. Other members of Women's Advocates went on to alternative projects. But in October 1974, Sharon Vaughan and Susan Ryan formally opened Woman House.

The shelter took in 39 women and children in the first month and was always full far beyond capacity. In 1975, 500 women and children were housed: 60% of the women had been physically abused; the rest had suffered from a broad range of indignities and tyrannies. Money from donations and the women's welfare checks barely covered operating expenses. When the loan came due and foreclosure threatened, letters and cards began to arrive, as if carried by an invisible wind, most with only a few dollars. The bank was paid.

Despite its secret location, shortly after the shelter opened, a man threw a rock through the window, terrifying the residents. Several weeks later, another man broke into the house with a knife, necessitating collective safety planning complete with a complex warning system built around kitchen pots and bells. But the house survived. Volunteers and residents operated as a collective, and no limits were set on the length of stay. Sharon was the only paid staff. Residents provided advocacy and support for one another.

"They have one like this in England," Sharon concluded.

Several months later, Anne and I hid our first family in the back bedroom our New Haven home, a woman and her nine-year-old daughter who had been hiding from her husband in a car for a week in nearby Waterbury, eating little more than cold cereal.

This seemed like yesterday. Now a battered woman was speaking at the White House and receiving the standing applause of some of the most powerful—and most conservative—men in the land.

Generations of theatergoers will recall Billy Bigelow, the hero of the Rodgers and Hammerstein musical *Carousel*. A wife-beater who is punished for his life of depravity by being killed in a botched robbery attempt, Billy is given a last chance at redemption by returning to Earth to keep his daughter from going astray. They meet, argue about her independence, and Billy slaps her face, just as he had slapped her mother's. Then he disappears, though whether God realizes the experiment has failed is unclear. As the girl is describing what happened to her mother, she puts her hand on the spot where she was hit, but there is no pain. She smiles knowingly, and mother and daughter gaze into a space colored with filtered light. The audience sighs. True love makes the pain men inflict bittersweet. This scene and the girl's high school graduation that follows are vehicles for an endless rendition of "You'll Never Walk Alone." Despite the song's soporific evocation to "walk on, walk on, with hope in your heart," the context lends the romantic fantasy an eerie undertone of desperation. The return of men from the dead to love, protect, or pester their wives is a common theme in film. But abuse victims do not need fiction to remind them that an abuser's imago endures after death. Kathy K. was in jail for 6 months before she realized that the abusive husband she hired a man to kill could no longer hurt her. Escaping from male authority—presumably like *His* authority—is easier said than done.

For century on century, force was so intrinsic to relationships with men that it was officially invisible. Its ordinariness made wife-beating "just life." Chris, a 24-year-old battered woman, describes the dilemma posed by her father's abuse of her mother.

Where would my mother have gone? Yes, he was awful to her and to us. She was beaten so badly that she would have black eyes all the time. He'd tie her to a chair and if she cried, he'd stuff a rag in her mouth. We'd try and help but then he'd beat us too. She'd try to make us not get involved, but we were the only ones who could have saved her at that time. . . . She didn't have any family or friends . . . he made sure of that. For her, I guess staying was the only option she thought she had. There was no such thing as a battered woman those days. . . . Only some women had bad home lives, that's all.[1]

Because those who endured it lacked full status as persons, neither the community nor the courts recognized victims as credible witnesses to their own abuse.

There were repeated attempts to criminalize wife-beating in the United States from the sixteenth through the early twentieth centuries. In the 1880s, feminist reformers working with the poor in Chicago opened a shelter for battered women and provided court advocacy for victims, but the shelter idea didn't take hold.[2] Public opposition to wife-beating resurfaced again after the turn of the century, when Temperance Leaguers were joined by law-and-order elites who favored using the whipping post for wife-beaters, "unruly" immigrants, and "uppity" blacks. These laws atrophied as enthusiasm for Prohibition and other puritanical reforms waned. Half a century later, in 1968, an Alanon chapter in Pasadena, California, opened a shelter for the battered wives of recovering alcoholics. Then, in the 1970s, the movement took off. The domestic violence revolution had begun.

Feminist Prequels

The U.S. women's movement that blossomed in the late 1960s and 1970s was part of an international groundswell of protest that targeted civil and national rights. In Europe, feminism emerged from left-leaning political parties and intellectual circles attempting to update Marxism and psychoanalytic theory. In the United States, other activist movements were an important source of feminism, in part because of how badly women were treated by left-wing, peace, and civil rights organizations. First-wave feminists (such as those involved in Prohibition) had recognized the importance of male violence. But the campaigns to legalize abortion and support victims of rape and battering were the first to combine activism; the local organization of women-run services; efforts to reform the legal, criminal justice, and service establishments; and bipartisan political pressure to revamp the policy response.

Starting in 1969 with what would become the National Abortion Rights Action League (NARAL), feminist collectives in the United States used a number of media, including demonstrations, alternative newspapers, "speak outs," hotlines, and self-help groups to voice women's personal experiences of illegal abortions and support women seeking to terminate pregnancies. These same means were extended to rape in the early 1970s. By 1980, there were rape squads, Women Against Rape (WAR) groups that operated 24-hour hotlines to provide emergency counseling and information to victims, or Rape Crisis Centers staffed largely by volunteers that provided self-defense courses, support, and counseling in more than 400 cities. Activists succeeded in extending the assault statutes to rape in marriage and protecting the integrity of rape victims in the criminal justice and legal systems. Using a rape defense, Joan Little, Inez Garcia, and Yvonne Wanrow were found innocent of killing men who raped them or who they believed were rapists.[3]

Against Our Will: Men, Women and Rape (1976), Susan Brownmiller's relentless historical record of sexual violence by men, argued that rape, harassment, and pornography were linchpins in the system of male domination designed to instill fear in women's consciousness, reinforce their dependence on men, and limit their activity in public space.[4] A multicity survey provided empirical proof for this claim. Even women who had not been assaulted were found to be severely inhibited by fears of sexual violence. Women were many times more likely than men to stay home at night, not venture out alone in the evening, travel by car rather than walk, and take care not to dress "provocatively" when they went out.[5] The researchers emphasized behavioral constraints. But by forcing women to conceal and/or protect their sexual personae rather than use it as a vehicle to express their capacities and desires, the rape culture also reinforced sexual hierarchy, a political effect. This was true even when men were raped in prison, where victims often become the perpetrator's "bitch," a degraded status akin to a female possession.

Feminism and the Battered Woman's Movement

According to its historians, advocates, and critics of the domestic violence revolution, the shelter movement was the byproduct of the organized women's movement. The reality was more complicated.

From its start in the early 1970s, activism by radical feminists to combat rape, pornography, and sexism in the media and professional life threatened to undermine the more traditional women's rights agenda by alienating the male support on which it depended. Even more intimidating was the insistence that sexual politics begins "at home," that what goes on in personal relationships is deeply political. Because of its connection to the largely white and middle-class consciousness-raising groups that were common in the period, this message initially appeared to stem from the sort of angst in women's everyday lives dramatized by Betty Friedan's *Feminine Mystique*. But its far more radical implications became clear as it was extended to marital rape and domestic violence, problems that affected women irrespective of their class or race and for which changing awareness was an insufficient antidote.

Despite its connection to militancy, antiviolence activism had the unintended effect of inverting the relative importance of coercion and male domination in feminist rhetoric. Rape was initially described as among the many "weapons of the patriarchy" in Kate Millet's phrase. In January 1978, the U.S. Civil Rights Commission sponsored a Consultation on Battered Women: Issues of Public Policy attended by a broad range of antiviolence activists, researchers, and service professionals. Del Martin, the meeting chair, firmly linked domestic violence to the institution of marriage, male domination, and female subordination.[6] But by the early 1980s, the means had replaced the end as the focus of activism: rape, pornography, sexual harassment, and wife abuse were portrayed as components of what was called the unitary phenomenon of male violence and the focus of protest had shifted from the institutional and structural sources of male dominance to acts of power and control by individual men. The new economy of victimization highlighted concrete harms and demanded protection and punishment, goals that were indisputably more tangible than sexual equality or women's liberation. But they were also further removed from the basic sources of women's vulnerability.

The emphasis on violence and safety was a retreat from a core principle inherited from nineteenth-century feminists—that freedom and equality matter. But the radical feminists had a credible reply to this charge, that this principle had already been downsized in the 1970s to fit the limited ideas of liberation advanced by a women's movement that was overwhelmingly young, educated, heterosexual, white, and middle class. They also argued persuasively that the potential benefits of "speak outs," marches to "Take Back the Night," and other direct actions to advance abortion and oppose rape, pornography, and sexual harassment transcended class, race, and cultural boundaries. Women who identified with the traditional Left, like Ann Braden and Angela Davis, attacked Susan Brownmiller, Diana Russell, Andrea Dworkin, and other early antiviolence activists for the racism implicit in their antimale politics.[7] In fact, answered the radicals, because male violence constrains mobility, security, autonomy, and social development, it is the bread-and-butter equivalent in women's lives of the economic concerns that drive trade unions and much of the Left.

Amidst this debate, national survey data were published showing that women in almost a third of all marriages had suffered physical abuse by the men with whom they were intimate.[8] In addition to confirming the importance of violence against women, the data lent material substance to the radical critique of misogyny. The prevalence and frequency of woman battering in particular and the clear identity of its perpetrators and victims gave it a political currency that was lacking in other antiviolence campaigns.

The battered women's movement developed in temporal proximity to antirape activism and appropriated the hotline, speakout, and other tools used by pro-abortion and WAR groups. Prominent U.S. feminists like Robin Morgan, Andrea Dworkin, and Laura X gave eloquent public testimony about their experiences with violent partners, whereas Jan Peterson, Del Martin, Dorchen Leidholdt, and other rape activists extended their critique to battering and linked it to the marriage contract and other dimensions of sexual inequality. The first hospital-based response to battered women built on the rape crisis intervention teams staffed by volunteer nurses and social workers. And early opponents of battering in the criminal justice and legal communities had cut their eye teeth on sexual assault. Despite these connections, the larger women's movement generally kept its distance from activism to combat partner abuse, and many early shelters developed with little or no support from local women's groups.

Feminist organizations often helped start local shelters. The Red Stockings, a Danish women's liberation organization, opened a shelter in Copenhagen in 1971. Shortly after Woman House was founded in 1974 in St. Paul and Transition House opened in Boston, feminists in Toronto, Vancouver, Australia, and the Netherlands opened refuges for battered women. In April 1975, the Ann Arbor (Michigan)–Washtenaw County Chapter of the National Organization of Women (NOW) started the first Wife (Spouse) Abuse Task Force and established a volunteer network of safety havens for the emergency housing needs of battered women and their children. Activists in the U.S. women's movement were critical in forming the National Coalition Against Domestic Violence (NCADV) in 1978.[9] Openly lesbian ("radical") feminists had been initially marginalized by traditional women's organizations such as NOW. But they played critical leadership roles in the early battered women's movement, staffed many shelters, and helped maintain the organizational integrity of woman-on-woman services.

Every woman-led grassroots initiative in the 1970s and 1980s was publicly identified with women's liberation. But local women's activists were often ambivalent about the formation of shelters and provided little or no support. By the mid-1970s, even as popular interest in feminism was peaking, many local women's organizations had been rendered moribund by internal disputes, much as had many left-wing organizations in the 1930s. Moreover, many activists felt their antirape and pro-abortion initiatives had been co-opted by free-standing "women's health services" or hospital-based "rape teams." As services were professionalized, radical politics got lost. They were skeptical about investing their energy to make yet another service "political." One result of this ambivalence was that dozens of early shelters drew their primary supporters from traditional progressive, human service, and religious constituencies, even in cities with a substantial core of feminist activists, such as St. Paul, Minnesota, or New Haven, Connecticut.

The first modern refuge exclusively for battered women was Chiswick Women's Aid, started in London in 1971 by Erin Pizzey. Comprised largely of immigrant women, the Goldhawk Road group had been struggling for economic justice in their neighborhood, against racial discrimination, and to secure housing. Chiswick was initially opened as an advice center for women exclusively. But Pizzey was an outspoken antifeminist. She circulated a letter opposing the formation of the explicitly feminist-oriented National Women's Aid Federation (NWAF; now called WAFE) in

February 1975 that urged the Social Service and Housing Departments in Britain to "look very carefully at the groups in their areas who are offering to set up a refuge."[10] By contrast with Chiswick, in its founding principles, WAFE linked "the violence women suffer" to "the general position of women in our society," a political position that threatened its charitable status.[11] Some of the 70 refuge organizations that belonged to NWAF in 1976 emerged from women's action groups on college campuses or community-based women's liberation groups. But other refuges, those in York or Norwich for instance, were formed by professional social workers (e.g., the Shield refuge in Manchester) or housewives with little if any connection to women's liberation.[12] The National Women's Liberation Conference in Britain had been meeting annually since 1970. But only in 1978 did it adapt a platform that included the demand for "freedom from intimidation by threat or the use of violence or sexual coercion, regardless of marital status."[13]

Simply opening a woman's space from which male authority has been cleared could be considered a feminist initiative. Many of those who had been beaten for signs of independence grasped the subversive nature of a woman-run refuge even when explicit feminist content was lacking. That *men* were the problem rather than a particular man was also apparent. As shelter residents listened to one woman after another recount similar experiences of assault, humiliation, and control, it seemed as if their partners had followed a shared script. But the battered women's movement drew from a broad array of civil rights, antiwar, welfare rights, and religious activists; attracted persons who embraced the countercultural emphasis on "self-help" and "alternative" institutions; and relied heavily on women for whom starting a shelter was an initiation into grassroots politics rather than the extension of prior political commitments.

Many early organizers came from disadvantaged groups and/or were survivors of abuse themselves. Sandy Ramos, a single mother with no previous movement history, opened her house in Hackensack to other single mothers in 1971, the same year Chiswick started. By 1976 she was housing 23 people, many of them battered, and leading demonstrations to secure public funding for Save Our Sisters. Sharon Vaughan had been a peace activist. Transition House in Boston was founded by Chris Mendez and Chris Jimenez, welfare recipients who had left abusive husbands. La Casa de las Madres, one of California's first shelters, was started by Marta Segovia Ashley, a Chicana from a poor family, and Marya Grambs, the daughter of a college professor. Shelters appealed to poor, black, Latina, lesbian, and older women because they provided jobs to survivors as well as emergency housing, responded to broad range of oppressions, accommodated women as "persons with problems" rather than as "problem persons," and because their service ethic converged with religious and cultural traditions in African American, Latina, and working-class white communities.

A side effect of its class and race diversity was distrust of feminist talk in the battered women's movement. As one woman in Britain complained in an early shelter newsletter,

> The criticism I have was of the people who spoke at the (battered woman's) Conference. I found it very boring due to the fact that I couldn't understand a lot of it. Mainly because the speakers sounded as if they'd eaten a dictionary for breakfast.[14]

The experience of Betsy Marple Mahoney illustrates the complex interplay of social class, race, and feminist practice in the early shelter movement. A white working-class mother from the South End of Boston, Betsy dropped out of high school and married at age 17, had a child, and then left her husband after he abused her. Alienated by how women were treated by the Communist Party and other left-wing groups with whom she flirted, she helped found the Female Liberation Front, a group that subsequently was called Cell 16 (after the address of Abbie Rockefeller's Boston apartment where they met). She first signed her writing Betsy Lethuli, after the African chief, then changed her name permanently to Warrior. She worked briefly at Transition House in Boston, then declined to join the board of the newly formed NCADV because she disliked the bureaucracy and personal wrangling. Instead, while employed as a janitor, and with advocate Lisa Leghorn, she compiled a *Battered Women's Directory*, a seminal source of practical and conceptual work on battering that continued publication until 1985.

In the United States, domestic violence programs were as likely to be organized by the YWCA, the Salvation Army, or unaffiliated individuals who came together for the first time as they were by activists in the women's movement. Only a handful of the numerous publications from the early battered women's movement in my files link abuse to male dominance in any sphere other than personal life or discuss (let alone endorse) political or economic reforms favored by the women's movement. Discussions of abuse are conspicuously absent from the feminist journals of the period such as *Signs, Feminist Review* (England), and *Feminist Studies* (United States). The first White House meeting between advocates and policy makers was convened in July 1977 by Midge Costanza and Jan Peterson, special liaisons to President Carter and longtime activists in the women's movement. Although the meeting focused broadly on "the problems and challenges posed by violence in the family," participants targeted service-related issues exclusively, including the eligibility of shelter residents for welfare, day care for children coming out of violent situations, and the use of federal funds via the Comprehensive Employment and Training Act (CETA), ACTION (Vista), and the Law Enforcement Assistance Administration (LEAA) to provide shelter employment, outreach workers, and training. Advocates at the meeting stressed the local autonomy of each shelter, "confidentiality," shelter control by "community women," and the role of victims in training and policy making.[15] Sexism, sex discrimination, equal rights, or other items on the women's agenda were not mentioned.

The movement's broad appeal and its innovative mix of service and idealism are inconceivable apart from the multiple strains of political activism and community concerns from which it drew. But its eclectic roots also made it difficult to develop a coherent conceptualization of abuse, instill feminist consciousness in the second generation of advocates, provide strong national leadership to the shelter movement, vocalize women's concerns beyond violence, or provide a principled framework with which to resolve the dilemmas created by its "success" or its "partnership" with law enforcement.

The Promise of Emancipation

Empowering women was as important to the early shelters as safety. An aim of NWAF in England was "to encourage women to determine their own futures and to help them achieve them, whether this involves returning home or starting a new life elsewhere."[16] After a heated debate, Women's Advocates in St. Paul determined to provide advocacy rather than advice, a position rooted in the view that the women seeking assistance were the real experts on their situation. The absence of paid staff at most shelters made resident and volunteer involvement critical to day-to-day operations, including house governance, and gave antihierarchical organizational politics special meaning. By contrast with the client dependence required for assistance at conventional services, the shelter's supportive milieu allowed women to be assertive, examine their predicament realistically, and use their real-life experience to negotiate on behalf of themselves and others. In the context of mutual recognition and support, women learned to join their capacity for independence to the experience of community.[17]

In Britain, the debate about refuge took place amidst a broad crisis in housing that included opening emergency housing for the homeless to men and concerned whether structural change or employing individual case work was the best way for the welfare state to confront the effects of economic crisis among the urban poor. Debate in the United States focused on whether domestic violence was a family problem or a problem of women's rights, whether women's lib was its cause or its consequence, and whether criminal justice intervention or just stepped-up counseling was required. Concerns with economic justice, housing, or social welfare programs prominent in Britain were secondary in the United States to civil rights issues and problems in violence management. Despite these different political contexts, the shelters in Britain and the United States initially operated in similar ways.

What Shelters Do

A majority of women who sought shelter were in the throes of a crisis precipitated by a violent incident. Today, virtually all shelter residents have been physically abused; many have been referred by police, child welfare, or other community agencies; paid staff are the mainstay of daily operation rather than volunteers; and programs offer an array of services in addition to emergency housing. In the United States, where the availability of guns makes secrecy a greater concern than in Britain or Canada, women who call the 24-hour hotline are checked out by an advocate at a neutral location (like Dunkin' Donuts) who explains house rules such as no drugs, alcohol, or contact with the abuser. Often in an appalling physical state and ashamed because she is "damaged goods" and has left her home, the woman enters a world surrounded by a diverse group of strangers. Crossing the threshold to ask for help is an enormous step, particularly if her autonomy has been quashed or she has been threatened with even more serious harm if she leaves. Most shelters are still located in deteriorating neighborhoods where housing is cheap, reinforcing women's worst fears about the consequences of separating from her breadwinner. A woman describes the original accommodation in Glasgow (circa 1974):

> (It) consists of three rooms, kitchen and bathroom in a slum tenement, which houses three other families. The exterior of the building is in very poor condition; the backcourt stores garbage for several tenements, and the close (small yard) is dingy and depressing. The tenement is only a few yards from a busy road and it is not safe to allow children to play outside.[18]

At Woman House in St. Paul, for the first 48 hours, the new arrival got around-the-clock support from another resident, her advocate. Then she "joined."

The transformation after the crisis passes can be profound. This may be the first space in some time which *he* cannot invade at will. This realization is brought home slowly, less because others reassure her she is safe than because she experiences moments of autonomy without dire consequence—flashes of independence when choosing what to have for breakfast, what clothes to wear, whom to talk to, what to reveal in a meeting, or which shows to watch. Any pretense of privacy is lost because the shelter facility—indeed, her room—may be literally overflowing with women and children. But the space feels psychologically expansive compared to the constricted world she has left.

Sophie

Sophie arrived at a New Jersey shelter with her hair matted hard against her head and impossible to comb. After a minor infraction, she had been forbidden to cut or wash her hair for 3 years. Ashamed to be seen, she rarely left her house or went to church and now retreated to her room with her children immediately after she ate. Several nights into her stay, she was invited downstairs. There, four women gave her a surprise party and a collective haircut during which each "strand of courage" was applauded as it fell to the floor.

Few of the early refuges in Britain or the United States had more than one paid employee, resident warden, or housekeeper, and many had none at all. Volunteers did most of the support work, staffing the hotline, providing public education, painting, renovating, and fundraising, and shelter residents managed daily operations and provided interpersonal support. Residents screened new admissions, shopped, cooked, provided child care, settled disputes, made and enforced house rules, and accompanied other victims to service sites. Although lack of money was a prime reason to emphasize self-help, its rationales ranged from confidence building to the belief that survivors of abuse were best able to empathize with other battered women. The disarray at the early shelters could be overwhelming. This was certainly our impression of Chiswick Women's Aid, a five-bedroom facility that was occupied by 90 women and children when we visited in 1976. Sensing our discomfort, Pizzey waved her arm in the air and pronounced, "If they can manage this, they can manage anything." She called her approach "therapeutic chaos." The courage rather than pathos that dominated women's spirit was evident that night when we joined a group of residents who left the shelter with a portable toilet and rolls of wall paper, squatted in an old railroad hotel on the other side of town, and opened another refuge.

Children in the shelters are often as anxious as their moms, having been removed not merely from the cacophony of noise and disorder attendant on the abuse at home but also from their defensive repertoire, the friends, rooms, dolls, covers, and closets they used to block out the terror. Behind the character armor of indifference or bravado they don for their peers, they experience the same range of emotion as the adults, including shame, rage, self-blame, anxiety, and ever so slowly, a sense of relief that allows them to be children once again and make the mistakes that children make without their world caving in.

At Woman House, the transition from crisis to community was symbolized by a contract in which residents identified their goals for the stay and agreed to support and advocate for other residents. An agreement among equals, the contract was premised on the belief that the provision of safety removed the major obstacle to self-development, that change ultimately derived from immersion in the community of women, and that the survivor was the sole decision maker, not the advocate or another professional, even when the woman was "wrong." As one director put it:

> We have never called women needing help "clients" or "cases" and this has not prevented effective communication with the professional community. When we were told that only trained and certified professionals could run the house, we insisted that professional credentials not be included as job requirements. We asserted our belief that women in need of shelter were not sick . . . emphasizing instead their need for safety, support and help with practical problems.[19]

The Growth of the Shelter Movement

There were barely two dozen emergency services for battered women at the end of 1976. But a year later, the Department of Health and Human Services received replies to a survey of shelter services from 163 programs, and Rutgers social work professor Albert Roberts analyzed responses from 89 of the 110 service providers he surveyed, more than half of which (45) had been operating less than a year and almost three-quarters (65) of which had been open for less than 2 years.[20] These surveys give an excellent picture of the nature, structure, support for, and evolution of community based shelter services.

Almost 80% of the responding programs operated shelters, and over half of these (53.9%) located their crisis intervention services in free-standing facilities, 20% used private homes, and the rest used varying combinations of YWCA space, motels, hospitals, mental health centers, often relying on private homes to house overflow. The facilities surveyed serviced 110,000 women and provided emergency housing to over 6,000 women and children in 1977. This was possible, many respondents admitted, only because staff could be provided through the CETA, the locally administered federal program that offered job slots to agency "sponsors" that were to be filled by the "hard-core unemployed." Fully 65% of the shelters received CETA funds, and CETA workers, most with no prior experience in service or the women's movement, soon comprised the majority of paid staff. The shelters also relied heavily on volunteers, including those supported by Vista, a domestic poverty program, maintaining an average ratio of three volunteers to each paid staff person. Rules governing admission and readmission varied, with most shelters prohibiting women with substance use or mental health problems as well as male teens, and many requiring special permission to house repeaters. The average shelter capacity was 15, and the average length of stay 2 weeks, with a maximum of 1 month. Shelters usually charged a nominal fee for room and board, ranging from the $2.75 "requested" by a Boston shelter for food and utilities per family to $5 a day for women and $2 a day for children in Athens, Ohio. But the majority of funds came from local government, private foundations, charitable organizations, and personal donations.[21]

Program sponsorship reflected the diverse base of the battered women's movement: if the YWCA was the single largest sponsor, affiliations extended from NOW though local church societies. Interestingly, only 15% of the shelters operating in 1978 originated in feminist groups such as NOW, rape crisis programs, consciousness-raising groups, or the newly formed NCADV or followed the so-called activist model. To maintain their facilities and staff, the majority of shelters in the United States had incorporated as nonprofit organizations and/or formed boards of directors or advisory boards. Although these boards often included former victims, they were heavily weighted toward professionals. An estimated 10% of shelters closed shortly after opening, a failure rate that compared favorably to parallel programs started from a community base, such as alternative schools or food pantries. As a result, the expansion of the shelter movement slowed only in the late 1980s. By this time, there were approximately 1,200 shelters in the United States housing 300,000 women annually.

Shelters lacked a coherent philosophical mission and differed markedly in the quality of the facility, funding source, admission criteria, length of stay, volunteer involvement, rules or other internal regulations, and the extent to which residents were responsible for governance. La Casa de las Madres refused entry to substance-abusing women as well as to sons of battered women over age 16 and "women who were not honorable and honest." Chiswick had a separate facility for young men. Women's Survival Space in Brooklyn accepted all comers, including women with mental health, and behavioral problems. The cultural climate in the house was set by the ethnic makeup of the organizers, the surrounding community, and whether racism and/or homophobia were tolerated. Whatever their differences, in the three decades following the opening of Woman House, several thousand U.S. towns and cities developed similar shelters and local women, women's groups, or government agencies opened shelters in every major city and most countries in the world. By 1994, when the VAWA was signed, shelters in the United States were serving more than 1 million women annually, states had devised mechanisms to fund and coordinate their services, and programs in dozens of communities had extended services to children and were providing support beyond the shelter's walls. The numbers of women and children served continue to grow.

Debate about whether to partner with law enforcement began in the early 1970s, when several U.S. shelters rejected funds from the LEAA. But equal protection for abuse victims through more aggressive law enforcement was the key theme advocates emphasized at hearings on domestic violence by the U.S. Commission on Civil Rights in 1978. Although LEAA was defunded by the Carter administration in 1980, federal support for shelters remained important. As of February 1981, 40% of the 460 shelters for battered women in the United States received some form of federal assistance, and a third of the 325 projects providing services other than shelter to battered women also received federal support, most often in the form of legal assistance from the Legal Services Corporation.[22]

Despite its multiple sources of inspiration, the NCADV we formed at the 1978 Civil Rights Commission hearings had no funding and lacked the authority and the technical resources to provide anything more than a communication link for state shelter organizations. With few models to work from, minimal outside guidance, and constant pressure to devote all attention to day-to-day operation and survival, shelter development was bound to be uneven. This fact remains: in less than three decades, a woman-run, community-based response to violent relationships had been created worldwide that compared favorably to more conventional approaches to personal troubles, whether judged by crude recidivism, cost-effectiveness, or by immediate benefits to those served. Shelters remain the heart of the domestic violence revolution. Without their growth, its progress is unthinkable.

Changing Professional Response

The unprecedented proliferation of community-based shelters stimulated an equally dramatic change in the professional response to abused women.

Criminal Justice

From the start, the U.S. battered women's movement turned to police to arrest or at least remove abusers, ensure safe escort to the shelter, and to protect staff and victims from irate partners. A working relationship with courts as well as police was also critical to the enforcement of protection orders. Yet no system appeared more alien to the victim's interests or to the shelter philosophy of empowerment through mutual decision making.

The legal and police response when shelters opened has been widely criticized.[23] By the mid-1960s, "domestics" were a more common source of police calls than all other violent acts combined.[24] To manage these complaints, calls were lumped into a very low-status category with other family trouble calls, and callers were often diverted to other services. Police viewed violence as normal behavior among low-income or minority city dwellers and hence as an inappropriate matter for law enforcement.[25] Among the impediments to an aggressive police response was the distaste for social work among officers, ambiguity about men's prerogatives in these situations, the mixed response their arrival elicited, and the belief that responding officers faced serious risks. Because most domestic violence incidents were classified as misdemeanor or simple assaults, and police had to actually witness a misdemeanor to make an arrest without a warrant, they understood their role in these situations as peripheral as well as distasteful. Even a violation of a restraining order, taken as a high-risk indicator by most advocates, is by statute a misdemeanor in most states, merely a civil violation in other states, and left to the judge's discretion elsewhere.[26] Research from the period also indicated that a variety of personal and situational characteristics, including the victim-offender relationship, were more important than the severity of the crime in determining whether police made an arrest or prosecutors proceeded to bring charges in court. Arrest was least likely when the victim called for help instead of a neighbor or bystander. As a result, unless the perpetrator was present when police arrived and insulted or otherwise threatened police authority, police saw their function as defusing tension and imposing order rather than making an arrest. Studies in Washington, D.C., Boston, and Chicago revealed that police were about four times more likely to arrest strangers for assault than partners.[27] Overall, between 3% and 13.9% of reported abuse resulted in an arrest, and almost no one went to jail.[28]

To ease the frustration beat officers felt in responding to what they viewed as frequent but relatively minor disturbances, New York psychiatrist Morton Bard and psychologist Sydney Berkowitz established an experimental Family Crisis Intervention Unit in a Harlem police precinct in 1967, and their model was replicated in 10 cities.[29] While psychologists targeted training to a select group of officers, overall training in domestic violence—averaging four to eight hours for all disturbance calls in the 1970s—emphasized that the officer should restore and maintain control, employ conflict resolution or mediation techniques, and exit quickly. Arrests declined and referrals to social and mental health agencies increased. But repeat calls to police also increased, a response that Bard interpreted as indicating victim satisfaction with the new response. Courts took a similar approach. In the Rapid Intervention Program (RIP) adapted in New York City in 1972, a team of community health workers acted as the emergency room of the family court to evaluate domestic violence cases and advise the court on disposition. The RIP staff was specifically directed to view family members as a unit rather than as adversaries, even where domestic violence was extreme, and was sensitized to accept what various ethnic groups "considered to be 'appropriate' violence or the socially accepted norm."[30]

As the harms caused by domestic violence became more widely known, mediation was viewed with extreme skepticism. Disillusionment with crisis intervention also reflected a broader trend away from "penal welfarism," where rehabilitation is emphasized, toward more punitive approaches.[31] In 1984, after holding public hearings in each region that included prominent advocates, a U.S. attorney general's Task Force on Family Violence appointed by President Reagan stressed the need for a uniform policy of sanctions and concluded that domestic violence was a crime, not a conflict situation; that culpability should be assigned; and that police failure to take this approach could contribute to escalation of the violence.[32] The Task Force recommended that police departments make arrest mandatory in domestic violence cases.

A concurrent influence on criminal justice reform was litigation brought against police departments in New York City, Los Angeles, and other major cities alleging the denial of equal protection under the law when police failed to respond appropriately to assaults against women by their husbands or boyfriends.[33] In a landmark Connecticut case, Tracy Thurman successfully sued the city of Torrington for the paralyzing injuries she suffered when her husband, Buck, beat and kicked her with an officer actually present.[34]

Law and Prosecution

Between the opening of the St. Paul shelter and the president's announcement of the VAWA in 1994, the legal response to partner violence changed more profoundly than in the preceding three centuries. Legal reform was premised on a two-pronged approach, adaptation of domestic violence laws under the equal protection guarantee in the Fourteenth Amendment and allowing victims to initiate action in family or civil courts to obtain and/or enforce the legal relief needed to terminate abusive relationships. Between 1974 and 1994, most states amended their laws to specifically identify domestic violence as a form of criminal assault, and every state expanded women's access to criminal and civil remedies from battering, including court orders restraining offenders from contacting their victims.[35] Today, in all but two states, the arrest of batterers is mandatory; a number of states require that a primary aggressor be identified if both sides claim they are victimized; and a majority of states authorize their courts to order the abuser into treatment. To better support victims as well as respond to the increased workload created by the more aggressive response, numerous jurisdictions have also implemented specialized domestic violence response teams, dockets, or courts; integrated family violence courts (which hear civil as well as criminal charges); prosecutorial units dedicated to domestic violence (so-called vertical prosecution); no drop or evidence-based prosecution policies; court or prosecution-based advocacy procedures to assess future dangerousness of domestic violence offenders; and justice centers where victims can access a range of services in "one-stop shopping."[36] Domestic violence education is now required to a greater or lesser extent for police, probation and parole, judges, and other court personnel.[37]

Emphasis in the civil arena has been on relief, primarily through protection orders, and on making domestic violence a consideration in the award of custody and alimony. A criminal act (though not necessarily an arrest) is the usual ground for securing civil orders. But which acts defendants are ordered to cease differ markedly from one jurisdiction to another and can encompass threats, harassment, stalking, and emotional abuse. Some states have issued protection orders based on acts of coercion or control that are not covered by criminal statute but infringe on the person's liberty, such as physically preventing a person from leaving the home or calling police or locking them out of their home and threatening to physically remove the person from the property. Violations of these orders can lead to further civil or criminal sanctions for contempt and, under a provision of VAWA, violation of a protection order is itself a crime that can be prosecuted in federal court.[38] All but two states require courts to at least consider allegations of abuse in awarding custody.

The Battered Woman's Defense

In the past, women who killed abusive partners often concealed their abuse, fearful that it would provide evidence of their motive. One result is that a large proportion of women in prison for murder or manslaughter killed partners who physically assaulted them, most in direct retaliation or to protect themselves and/or a child.[39] In civil proceedings, battered women were frequently denied custody or relief in divorce, particularly if they abandoned the marital home, otherwise neglected their marital obligations, or suffered from medical, mental health, or behavioral problems, even if these were direct results of abuse.

Feminist lawmakers responded to these dilemmas in the 1970s by constructing a battered woman's defense designed to mitigate liability for acts prompted by or linked to abuse. A closely related development is the widespread use of expert testimony on behalf of battered women to correct for the general lack of lay knowledge about the nature of domestic violence, its dynamics, consequences, or its significance for children.[40] The use of experts also reflects the dearth of evidence to support a claim of abuse in these cases, the corresponding reluctance to give victims full credibility as witnesses to their own experience, and the frequent need to counteract other psychological assessments that fail to consider domestic violence or mistakenly view reports of abuse as symptomatic of a woman's mental problems.[41] Discussed in detail in chapter 5, the new defense strategy relies heavily on a relatively neglected line of research and clinical practice that emphasizes the importance of violence and other extreme external events in eliciting psychological dysfunction as the result of trauma. Thousands of women have benefited from its use.

Programs for Batterers

Shortly after the first shelters opened in the United States, small groups of men who wanted to support the antiviolence movement began free-standing counseling programs primarily directed at the abusive partners of women who sought refuge. Some of the early programs followed a leaderless, self-help format, and all the early clientele attended voluntarily. But neither their founders (like David Adams of Emerge in Boston or Ellen Pence of The Domestic Violence Intervention Project in Duluth) nor the shelter movement as a whole saw them as a long-term solution to domestic violence. Mary Morrison, a spokeswoman for the NCADV, explained:

> Because the Coalition has a systematic analysis of woman abuse, we do not believe that therapy for abusers is the solution. Battering is not an individual problem that can be solved with therapy or drug and alcohol abuse counseling. What we need to do is change the system that allows woman abuse.[42]

There is continued skepticism about the rationale of counseling men for behavior widely considered volitional, instrumental, and criminal. Still, just 20 years after the initial programs were started, BIPs have become a mainstay of the domestic violence response in the United States and elsewhere.[43] BIPs are generally locally administered by a shelter, mental health center, or a similar agency and are typically state funded (though they many charge a sliding fee). They may follow a standard curriculum (like the Duluth Model) or be more eclectic. Although some BIPs still accept voluntary clients, most attendees are court-mandated as part of a pretrial diversion program, as an alternative to incarceration, a condition of probation, or as a precondition for custodial rights or unsupervised visitation. BIPs have helped the justice system manage the fiscal/administrative challenges created by the sharp increase in caseload following the transformation of domestic violence from a nuisance offense into a distinctive crime. Apart from their practical function as an economical alternative to jail, enormous ambiguity remains about whether the primary aim of BIPs is prevention, punishment, antisexist education, treatment, support for intimate relationships, or merely to provide information about the impropriety of abuse. Many BIPs attempt to meet a number of these goals simultaneously by packaging messages about accountability, techniques to change violent behavior, and cultural messages about the value of sexual equality.

Health Care

Because courts and police departments are governmental agencies, their policies are dictated by a central authority, allowing for relative standardization within geographical regions. By contrast, the U.S. health system is comprised of a decentralized array of largely free-standing government, nonprofit, and private facilities and private practices. As a result, its response to abuse has been far less consistent.

Two things were clear by the mid-1980s: that battered women utilized health facilities of all types for a range of problems related to abuse and that health personnel neither identified the problem nor treated its victims appropriately.[44] Shortly after Anne Flitcraft and I reported that domestic violence was the leading cause of injury for which women sought medical attention, the American Medical Association (AMA) estimated that 1.5 million women nationwide seek medical treatment for injuries related to abuse each year.[45] Looking only at the most severe cases, a National Crime Victimization Survey for 1991 concluded that partner assaults cost medicine more than $44 million annually and resulted in 21,000 hospitalizations with 99,800 patient days, 28,700 emergency department visits, and 39,900 visits to physicians each year.[46] A more realistic cost assessment was provided by the Centers for Disease Control (CDC) in 2003. The CDC estimated the direct costs of medical and mental health services for intimate partner rape, assault, and stalking exceeded $4.1 billion annually and that lost productivity and life-time earnings lost due to partner homicide cost another $1.8 billion, most of it due to health care for battered women.[47] These costs reflected a related finding. To a large extent, the disproportionate utilization of health services by battered women was prompted by systematic failure of health personnel to identify or respond appropriately to abuse. Women rated medicine the last effective of all interventions.[48] Indicative of the reigning level of ignorance, a 1985 survey, *Injury in America*, conducted under the joint auspices of the National Research Council and the National Academy of Medicine failed to mention domestic violence and disposed of other forms of "deliberate injury" in a few sentences.[49]

The earliest medical responses relied on individual, hospital-based initiatives by nurses and social workers. In 1977, building on the success of hospital-community collaborations in establishing rape crisis teams, the Ambulatory Nursing Department of the Brigham and Women's Hospital in Boston formed a multidisciplinary committee to develop a "therapeutic intervention" for abuse victims. The intervention at Brigham, like a parallel program at Harborview Hospital in Seattle, relied on a Social Service Trauma Team composed initially of volunteer social workers who met weekly with nursing staff. Although these largely volunteer efforts proved difficult to sustain, over the next decade, domestic violence services were introduced at hundreds of hospitals, most centered in their emergency departments.

Most major organizations of health professionals in the United States have identified domestic violence as a priority.[50] In 1992, the AMA Council on Ethical and Judicial Affairs suggested that domestic violence intervention be rooted in the principles of beneficence (doing good) and nonmalfeasance (doing no harm).[51] In the same year, the Joint Commission on the Accreditation of Health Care Organizations (JCAHO) required emergency and ambulatory care services to develop domestic violence protocols, and in 1996, the standards were upgraded to include objective criteria to identify, assess, and refer victims of abuse. Other high points in the health response included the formation of National Center for Injury Prevention and Control at the CDC; a major commitment to health research in rape and domestic violence by the National Institutes of Mental Health (NIMH); the dissemination of educational materials by state medical associations; major commitments of research dollars by private foundations, including the March of Dimes and the Commonwealth Fund; the development and funding of training curriculum and special medical training units in New York, New Jersey, Connecticut, and other states; the formation of the National Coalition of Physicians Against Family Violence with institutional membership from more than 75 major medical organizations; funding to the San Francisco Family Violence Prevention Fund to establish a national center to disseminate information on domestic violence related health issues; the creation of the Nursing Network on Violence Against Women to pressure the American Nursing Association to make domestic violence a priority; and the creation of a comprehensive medical response to domestic violence by a collaborative effort of the American Medical Women's Association, the American Academy of Family Practice, and the American College of Emergency Physicians.[52] Conferences for providers have played a particularly important role in legitimating domestic violence as a health issue. The most important of these were an unprecedented Workshop on Violence and Public Health convened by U.S. Surgeon General C. Everett Koop in 1985 and followed by regional conferences on the same theme; a conference convened in Washington, D.C., by the AMA and co-sponsored by 50 medical, legal, and social service organizations; and annual conferences of health researchers sponsored by the U.S. Department of Health and Human Services and the San Francisco Family Violence Prevention Fund. The success of these efforts is indicated by the fact that by 1993, 101 of the 126 U.S. medical schools responding to a survey had incorporated material on domestic violence into required course material.[53] By contrast, in England, where health initiatives on domestic violence have been few and far between, education about woman abuse is conspicuously absent from medical training.

Child Welfare

Next to the law, the child welfare system has the greatest influence on battered women, particularly in low-income, immigrant, and minority communities. Domestic violence is the single most common context for child abuse and neglect, with estimates of the overlap ranging from 6.5% to 82%, and the number of children affected from 3.3 million to 10 million.[54] The proportion of abuse and neglect cases where battering is a background factor in cases ranges from 16% to 49% and is a function of whether the local child welfare agency has a screening tool in place, whether the organization supports intervention, and whether the host community perceives it as responsive to their safety concerns.[55]

Despite its importance for children's well-being, domestic violence was officially invisible to the child welfare system when the shelter movement began.

Children comprise as many as two-thirds of the estimated 3 million persons receiving shelter services annually in the United States. The laissez-faire philosophy at many early shelters left children with little counseling or structure. Advocates took the sensible position that women became better mothers when they were treated as women with needs of their own first, rather than as transmission belts to the problems of others. But this view was anathema to the child welfare system and so confrontations between shelter advocates and the state-based Child Protective Services (CPS) were common. An important finding from the Yale Trauma Studies was that for any given claim of abuse or neglect, the children of battered women were significantly more likely to be placed in foster care than other children.[56]

Women typically access child welfare services along the quasi-judicial continuum that extends from an initial complaint of abuse or neglect through the termination of parental rights. The punitive response to mothers in the Yale system reflected a gender bias that extends across the entire spectrum of CPS services, combines with the race and class bias reflected in the fact that clientele of the child welfare system are disproportionately poor and black, and puts them in a double bind. They fear they will lose their children if they reveal their victimization to CPS, but they or their children may be seriously hurt or killed if they do not. In the face of what

I call the battered mother's dilemma, women may take steps to protect their children that place themselves at extreme risk, as Terry Traficonda did. A similar dilemma is posed when CPS demands that women end all contact with their abusive partner, often regardless of the immediate risks of doing so, while the family court grants him visitation.

Early twentieth-century child savers often worked closely with police to remove abusive men from the home or have them arrested. But by the 1920s, the view that "brutal men" were the center of a matrix of power that harmed women and children in similar ways had been replaced by the current emphasis on prescriptive parenting for "inadequate" or "neglectful" mothers, and domestic violence had disappeared as a concern along with the men responsible for a disproportionate share of serious and fatal violence against children.[57] The child welfare system we confronted in the 1970s viewed the emphasis on the criminal law as a "regression" from its "humanistic" approach, feared that acknowledging domestic violence would open a political Pandora's box, and worried that funding to help battered women would diminish support for children's services. These attitudes changed when federal and state dollars became available through VAWA, a growing body of literature highlighted how domestic violence harmed children, and shelters introduced a range of services for children.

Not all changes were positive, however. In dozens of jurisdictions, when the news that exposure to abuse could harm children was filtered through the child-centered mission of CPS, the response to battered mothers actually became more punitive. With New York as the leader, many state child welfare agencies joined with family courts to charge nonoffending mothers who had been abused with neglect, for "engaging in domestic violence" in front of the children, and to temporarily remove their children to foster care. In June 2000, a class action suit against the city of New York and its child protection agency—the nation's largest—was brought in federal court to stop this practice, and in December 2001, after months of evidentiary hearings, Judge Jack Weinstein found that it was unconstitutional to remove children and charge their mother with neglect solely because she had been abused, an opinion with which New York's highest court concurred.[58] Parallel changes in family court followed the passage of the Morella resolution by Congress (named after its sponsor, Maryland Republican Representative Connie Morella) advising state courts to give a presumption of custody to victims of domestic violence. All but two states have enacted legislation recognizing the importance of domestic violence in custody disputes. Meanwhile, advocates now play multiple roles in the child welfare system. They help train CPS workers or develop curriculum for training, provide technical assistance, counsel mothers in "dual victim" families, and even conduct "safety audits" to monitor the efficacy of the CPS response. In hundreds of communities, child welfare and domestic violence services collaborate as part of a "coordinated community response" to domestic violence.

The Expanded Knowledge Base

The third prong of the domestic violence revolution is the mobilization of the family sciences to target violence in the home. Before 1970, the professional and scholarly literature was silent about domestic violence. Then, as if an invisible wall had been removed, social, mental health, and medical scientists rushed into the caverns of family life to document every detail of sexual abuse, child abuse, incest, rape, marital rape, date rape, spouse abuse, "granny bashing," "victim-precipitated homicide," and a number of these events in combination. Federal agencies, private foundations, and companies have expended hundreds of millions of dollars to support this work. Outside the physical sciences, specialists in interpersonal violence occupy prominent posts in every major academic field. In the years since the first shelters opened, an estimated 15,000 research monographs, reports, and books have appeared on the problem, and it is the subject of numerous specialized journals and of several hundred professional, service, or academic conferences annually.[59]

The research grounding the current approach is the subject of subsequent chapters. Suffice it to say here that if domestic violence research owes much of its current prestige to the battered women's movement, the reverse point is equally important. Had the revolution not embraced the new knowledge about abuse, its access to public agendas would have been much more limited.

Feminist Influence on Public Policy

Despite a consensus that partner violence is the problem at hand, in the United States as well as in many other countries, partisans of a catholic approach to family violence competed for attention with proponents of the "violence against women" approach. The family violence school emphasized two facets of abuse that appealed to policy makers: that once initiated violence circulates among all family members and across generations and that it overflows into and breeds civil violence. In the annals of competitive victimization, indignation about violence against women is hard to sustain against the more profound sympathies reserved for abused children, the elderly, and other groups whose dependence for care is based on age or disability. Even if women are the prime targets of abuse as advocates contend, once we accept the premise that any and all violence in families is morally repugnant, differences regarding how hard people hit, whom they hit, why they use force, or with what physical consequences become secondary variations on a common theme. From the standpoint of mainstream social science, there is no logical reason why male violence against women should command more attention than coercion directed at other family members. Meanwhile, the claim that violence at home crosses the generational divide to excite violence in the street offers professionals a new rationale to police broken or dysfunctional families. From the first meetings at the White House in July 1977 through the lobbying efforts for VAWA II and III, proponents of the violence against women approach have supported a package of interventions that promote safety for women and accountability for men through shelter, supportive services, court protections, and criminal justice interventions. By contrast, although they are less proscriptive than the advocates, the family violence researchers have advanced the humanist approach adapted from child welfare, preferring administrative, therapeutic, or service remedies to legal solutions, which they feel are insensitive to the moral and practical realities of family life.[60]

Given their catholicism, it was inevitable that adherents of the family violence school would command a disproportionate share of research support, media attention, and publication opportunities. In some countries (Finland and Denmark are examples), the belief that partner violence is a family issue has led governments to support counseling as the frontline response.[61] But the advocates have carried the day in the United States, England, Scotland, Canada, and Australia, largely because they command a broad and vocal political base and because their goals converge with the state's interest in expanding the legitimacy of justice institutions. Although opponents of the advocacy movement include powerful men's rights groups and prominent figures in journalism and government, they have consistently failed to block aggressive intervention to halt abuse, including mandatory arrest laws, the diffusion of no drop prosecution, and changes in criminal and family law that favor female victims. These victories are even more impressive when we consider that shelters lack central organization, have never mounted a national grassroots campaign, have no independent source of financing, lack the unified professional constituency who identify their self-interest with child welfare, addiction services, or mental health services, and have no nationally visible spokespersons. Congress could easily have stonewalled domestic violence legislation, as it did in the past or has done with other women's issues such as abortion or child care. Or, it could have given the funds to the child welfare establishment instead of creating a distinct funding stream.

Changes in Popular Culture

Perhaps the most significant change accompanying the domestic violence revolution involves the portrayal of male violence against women in the media, particularly on TV, the ultimate family medium. As women made unprecedented gains in economic, political, and cultural status, the hazards men pose to their wives became a moral compass for the integrity of relationships generally. Violence continued to be glamorized as the penultimate test of manhood (the ultimate test remains sexual conquest) well into the 1980s, as illustrated by the popularity of the James Bond, Rocky, and Rambo films. But male violence has increasingly been forced to share the stage with images of women as equally capable of using force and of abusive men as purposeful, obsessive, and cruel.

Women who are footloose, aggressive, and clever like Clara Bow played key roles in the films of the 1920s and in comic strips like *Blondie*, whose madcap antics as a flapper captured that era's spirit of economic independence. But Blondie's marriage to Dagwood in 1933 reflected a general trend during the Depression for assertive personalities to redirect their energies to make things work at home and to endure hard times, including abuse, the character trait that defined Ma Joad in Steinbeck's classic *Grapes of Wrath*. Women entered basic industry in large numbers during World War II, a trend that was complemented by their move into the services and administration afterward. The pronatalist ideology disseminated by media portrayals of women only as wives and homemakers during the 1940s and 1950s masked this reality, discouraged their efforts to translate economic independence into autonomy in personal life, and reinforced sex segregation in employment and the discriminatory wage structure that had been given legitimacy by the National Labor Board under Franklin Roosevelt. Doris Day's portrayal of Frank Sinatra's wife in the 1955 Otto Preminger film *Man with the Golden Arm* symbolized the era's fascination with women who could heal the significant men in their lives even while suffering the consequences of their depravities—heroin addiction as well as abuse in this instance. Whether women chose a course of psychotherapy or an equally costly divorce, it is now apparent that much of what the family sciences of the period treated as marital discord actually consisted of a loveless barrage of passivity, rage, violence, and control. Getting children to dance lessons or sporting contests was one thing; compromising physical and moral integrity to keep the peace at home quite another.

Following the family sciences, the media of the 1960s and 1970s sharply distinguished marital aggression from criminal violence. The imagined disconnect between anger, conflict, and literal violence was epitomized in the 1950s sitcom *The Honeymooners*, where Ralph Kramden's raised fist famously stops just short of Alice's face when he threatens to send her "to the moon." We can laugh at this pretext of self-control—just as we did at the blustering oaf played earlier by William Bendix in *Life of Riley*—because we see the vulnerability of these men through the eyes of TV wives who face their husbands fearlessly, reassuring the female audience that the threatened blows will never materialize, using a combination of humor, insults, manipulation, and emotional distance to manage. The outbursts and implied terror are slightly muted in the comic bravado of Archie Bunker a decade later. *All in the Family* is an intergenerational conversation about how to treat women that takes place largely among men. Archie's wife, Edith, is a carryover from stoic sufferers like Ma Joad and lacks even the hint of hysteria evident in the Doris Day character. But Archie's anger is an update: elicited by the claims of women, blacks, gays, and other emerging minorities for rights and recognition, its immediate target is his "meathead" son-in-law who refuses to adapt an autocratic pose with his own wife. Archie expresses the dilemma posed to traditional manhood by a new woman who works and has a mind (if a small one) of her own. The meathead talks the talk of the new man, complete with racial tolerance and sexual equality. But he is also indolent, dependent, and passive to his fate, suggesting that the cost of abandoning the search-and-destroy Rambo philosophy of life Archie advocates is the loss of manhood. The show suggests that the choice men face is to change with the times or become trapped in a loser's personality like Riley, Ralph, and Archie. Abusive men in my clinical practice described a similar dilemma. They wanted their fathers' "control" over their wives, but despised themselves for being "like them."

Homer Simpson is the Archie Bunker for the 1980s. He presents a similar composite of bluster, pettiness, ignorance, and rage that is transparent to everyone but himself, but without the social location provided by Archie's race, sex, and class biases. In an early episode of *The Simpsons*, a therapist asks the family to pictorially represent the image they associate with anger in their household. Mother, son, daughter, and baby draw Homer, while Homer draws a fighter plane. In marked contrast to ever-loyal Edith, Homer's wife joins the rest of the Simpson clan in a defensive alliance against him. Where it was common for men to identify with Ralph or Archie as well as with their propensity to scapegoat, only the most paranoid can identify with Homer's isolation.

An older generation can still watch reruns of *The Honeymooners* and *All in the Family*. But by the 1990s, domestic terrorism was no longer funny. Paralleling the trend in research, the media focus had shifted from the comic machismo of the father/husband to the realistic pain of the victim. In *Public Enemy* (1931), the prototypical male anger film, director William Wellman shot James Cagney squashing a grapefruit in his girlfriend's face from the gangster's standpoint, openly inviting his audience to identify with the aggressor. By contrast, in an episode of an evening medical drama in the mid-1990s, *Chicago Hope*, a young black woman is hospitalized after being beaten by her white boyfriend. The camera moves from a close-up of the woman's battered and swollen face to a physician (the woman's brother) and nurse—regulars on the show—who are formulating a strategy to protect the girl against the bully. More exacting is the portrayal on NBC's *ER* a few years later, one of the most widely viewed dramatic shows ever. After a battered woman is admitted to the hospital, a social worker pressures an attending physician to call the police, which he does reluctantly, not wanting to be drawn into "private troubles." When the physician returns to the hospital room, a policeman is present, he assumes in response to his call. In a chilling moment, the officer puts his arm around the woman, and leaves with his wife. The emotive dynamic in the Cagney film is inverted: we identify with the epiphany experienced by the stunned physician, thereby admitting—and so penetrating—our own naiveté. The seminal female image for the 1990s is Julia Roberts's portrayal of a battered woman in *Sleeping with the Enemy* (1991). In place of Doris Day's codependent pursuit of Sinatra, it is Roberts's husband who pursues and is eventually killed by her; the Roberts character is portrayed as victimized and heroic, a marked contrast to Depression-era films like *Craig's Wife* (1936) where women with similar stealth are pictured as selfish and sinister. The mass media remain misogynist in many respects. By the late 1990s, however, in large part as a byproduct of the domestic violence revolution, battering had replaced substance abuse, illegitimacy, infidelity, and terminal illness as the interpersonal problem of choice. By putting Sara Buell on a stage at the White House, President Clinton was acknowledging a reality with which the millions who watch daytime soaps, talk shows, or nightly police, law, and medical dramas were already familiar.

The passage and reauthorizations of VAWA signaled that the battered woman's movement in the United States had outflanked its opponents, turning the traditional prerogative of men to forcibly discipline their partners into the core image of female mistreatment, just as lynching epitomizes the excesses of racism.

The reasons why male violence against women took so deep a hold on the American psyche after 1970 are not entirely clear. Even less clear is why the domestic violence revolution was so quickly embraced by the professional and research establishment.

The simplest explanation is that domestic violence increased. Recent Justice Department data support this conclusion. Between 1974, the year the domestic violence revolution began in the United States, and 1994, the year VAWA was passed, the proportion of all assaults directed against women increased from two of every six to two in five and most of these assaults (more than 75%) were committed by relatives, friends or intimates.[62] In fact, however, this proportional increase in partner assaults against women reflected a decline in stranger and male-male violence, not an increase in woman abuse. Some forms of partner violence did increase sharply during the period. But the forms of violence that were most closely watched—partner homicides and severe partner assaults against women—declined sharply.

The dissemination of research on abuse certainly contributed to its visibility. An obvious example was the importance of a Minneapolis experiment showing the deterrent effect of arrest on the adaptation of mandatory arrest policies.[63] As economist Charles Lindblom argues, however, the primary role of information in policy making is to exert control in partisan negotiations.[64] The Minneapolis results were only accepted because they provided a rationale for justice officials to placate widespread political pressure to respond more aggressively to batterers. Several years later, a series of government-funded experiments failed to replicate the dramatic results of the Minneapolis study. Absent political sentiment to reverse direction in policing, however, these findings were largely disregarded.

A more plausible explanation for "why now?" is that a focus on women's problems followed their growing importance in political and economic life. The Democratic setbacks in the 1994 elections and Republican control of Congress led to renewed interest in a crime bill. On their side, advocates recognized that the VAWA could only succeed if it appealed to conservatives as well as liberals. Eyeing the upcoming election, President Clinton believed domestic violence legislation would garner female votes without his having to take a position on more controversial issues such as abortion, affirmative action, and gay rights. The strategy worked. In the 1996 election, he secured unprecedented electoral support from women. By contrast, Democratic candidate for president, John Kerry, ignored these issues in 2004 until his belated support for a right to abortion in the third and last presidential debate. He lost, largely because he failed to win the support women had given Clinton and Al Gore.

VAWA I was opposed by pro-family conservatives, the religious Right, and a national media campaign. VAWA II and III were enacted with little debate or public notice. In 2006, responding to violence in women's personal lives has become a fact of life.

What was new in the 1970s and 1980s was not the incidence of male violence directed at women, nor its discovery by researchers or helping professionals. What was new was its selection as a prism through which to assess women's experience with men in personal life. This construction reflects the confluence of political, economic cultural, and social currents set in motion by a grassroots women's movement—the battered women's movement in the United States and parallel movements in dozens of countries—that was joined in ascribing a peculiar form of female suffering to male violence by a range of radical, academic, cultural, professional, and political elites.

It is hard to exaggerate the importance of the domestic violence revolution. Unlike my grandmother, mother, and even my sister, our children understand that if a partner uses violence to hurt or control them, our community will treat this as a criminal act rather than as their prerogative. If we can, we will protect them. If they protect themselves, they have our support. And the state will also act on their behalf. No other cohort of women in history could say this.

Have we been here before? Absolutely not. Apart from the sheer magnitude of the current effort, the narratives of domestic violence victims have made unprecedented inroads into mainstream culture, academic research and teaching, a spectrum of service institutions, and even into the less fickle professions of law and medicine. Never before has domestic violence been the target of a worldwide social movement, let alone of a movement with roots in a direct action and community-based service. Domestic violence may yet slide back into the morass of problems we enumerate when thinking about poverty, as it did earlier in the century. But women's unprecedented power in economic and political arenas should be sufficient to prevent this.

2

THE REVOLUTION STALLED

The domestic violence revolution far surpassed initial expectations. But it has gone as far as current strategies can take it.

In 1977, during one of the many incidents when Mickey Hughes assaulted his wife, Francine, their 12-year-old daughter, Christy, called police. When the police arrived, Mickey threatened to kill Francine. But this seemed like "idle talk," an officer testified. "He hadn't killed her before, he wouldn't do so now." After the police left, Francine set fire to the bed in which her husband was sleeping and he was fatally burned.[1]

Things have changed dramatically since 1977. Mickey was never arrested, though he had raped Francine on several occasions and assaulted her dozens of times. Not until 1979, as the result of lawsuits in a number of cities were police required to replace their arrest-avoidance strategy. Marital rape was not a crime in 1977 and in New York and a number of other states was not even considered grounds for divorce. In several states, Francine could have gotten an injunction, though police had no role in enforcing these orders, and only if she was married, and only pursuant to a divorce.

Farrah Fawcett portrayed Francine in a TV film version of *The Burning Bed*. In the mid-1990s, when her boyfriend slammed Fawcett to the ground and choked her after an argument at a restaurant, he was arrested, tried, and convicted.[2] By this time, most states had abolished the marriage rape exemption and mandated police to presumptively arrest if they had probable cause to believe domestic violence had occurred. Around the globe, courts provided a range of new protections for abuse victims. On the two occasions when Francine left Mickey to return to her parents, he stalked and harassed her without consequence. Today, stalking is a crime, and harassment is widely recognized as a facet of abuse. Aside from her family, Francine had no recourse, no shelter to enter, and no support services. Francine pled temporary insanity. A woman faced with a burning bed situation today would mount a battered woman's defense. The forces of law and order that protected a man's right to "physically correct" his wife in 1977 now target this bastion of male authority for destruction.

These changes are impressive. But have they brought us significantly closer to ending the condition of suffering whose public exposure gave birth to the domestic violence revolution? This concern is hardly academic. Apart from the unprecedented commitment of resources to help battered women are the enormous costs of not addressing woman battering effectively. Battering threatens the dignity, autonomy, and liberty of tens of millions, not just their physical integrity, and so inhibits social and political progress in the same way that slavery in the United States constrained a huge mass of labor power within an obsolete form of private dependence. Woman battering is decidedly not slavery: women are the formal equals of men in most modern societies, men are neither their masters nor owners, and the sexist ideology that justifies woman battering is less coherent and devastating in its effects than the racialist dogma that justified the plantation system. But if the systemic qualities of battering are less dramatic than slavery, battering affects a much larger population and compromises liberty in ways that can be just as degrading. The widespread entrapment of women in personal life puts our collective future at risk in much the same way as would have been the case had the plantation economy survived the Civil War.

The revolution advanced two basic goals: safety for battered women and accountability for offenders. As we saw in chapter 1, the specialized institutional means developed to realize these goals extend across a broad spectrum. A third goal grew out of shelter practice: supporting women's empowerment. This meant two things: restoring the capacity for victims to make critical decisions about their futures through mutual assistance and expanding their larger options as women by using their experience as a springboard to system change. "Off our backs," the name of an important feminist newspaper in the 1960s, would be an apt slogan for the long-term aims of sheltering. Though only recently made explicit, a fourth goal, justice for abused women in the criminal and civil courts, is implied by the efforts of hundreds of feminist lawmakers on behalf of battered women and their children.

This chapter asks how well the major strategies adapted by the domestic violence revolution have met the goals of safety, accountability, and empowerment. Chapter 5 weighs the utility of the strategies currently used to win justice for women like Francine Hughes.

Safety: Is Domestic Violence Decreasing?

Are women safer in personal life now than when the domestic violence revolution began? The answer starts by examining whether partner violence has declined. Oddly, few observers have considered this issue, let alone whether changes in abuse rates are due to intervention. But the few assessments are positive. Richard Gelles, a pioneer in the field, reports that family homicides and wife beating have dropped dramatically. He cites data from the U.S. Department of Justice and population surveys showing an 18% decline in spousal homicide by husbands between 1976 and 1992 and a remarkable 48% drop in rates of wife beating, from 38 per 1,000 women to 19 per 1,000, a figure that translates into 600,000 fewer female victims in a span of approximately 15 years. The same sources suggest even more dramatic changes since 1992. In early June 2005, the U.S. Department of Justice announced that family violence had declined by approximately half from 1993 to 2002, mirroring the overall drop in violent crime.[3] Indeed, despite population growth, the absolute number of persons killed by a partner has also dropped sharply in the United States from 2,957 murders in 1976 to just 1,590 in 2002, a 46% decline.[4] Because these declines began after the first shelters opened and became marked after the introduction of mandatory arrest, aggressive prosecution policies, court reforms and the passage of the Violence Against Women Act (VAWA) in 1994, it seems sensible to join Gelles, the National Coalition Against Domestic Violence (NCADV), researchers at the Centers for Disease Control (CDC), and a range of columnists in attributing these improvements to the domestic violence revolution.[5]

Data Sources

The first problem with these conclusions is their source. Data on homicides are fairly reliable because they are based on the Federal Bureau of Investigation (FBI)'s Uniform Crime Reporting System (UCR) that captures an estimated 92% of all homicides.[6] However, the UCR classifies boyfriends or girlfriends as "nonfamily members" and reports their offense and victimization data separately from family violence crimes. This means that comparisons between family and nonfamily homicides exclude the large proportion of abuse-related deaths caused by unmarried partners. When it comes to nonfatal partner assaults, the best federal source of information is the National Crime Victimization Survey (NCVS) (formerly called the National Crime Survey), which relies on self-reports by victims. Under the auspices of the Bureau of Justice Statistics, the NCVS collects data annually from a representative panel of some 80,000 individuals representing approximately 43,000 households. The NCVS captures victimizations that are not reported to police. But as a source of data on abuse, it presents a number of special problems. Prior to 1992, the NCVS had no specific questions about violence by a partner. Moreover, it relies on telephone survey techniques, directs respondents to report only the most serious crimes they have suffered, and classifies reports of six or more violent incidents in a year as one incident.[7] This approach seriously minimizes the number of persons who acknowledge partner victimization and discounts the experiences of the estimated 40% of persons who experience multiple attacks or serial victimization over a relatively short time period.[8]

The limits of federal sources have led researchers to assess trends by relying on the only other major source of longitudinal data on partner violence: the National Family Violence Survey (NFVS), a series of population-based studies conducted in four waves, 1976, 1985, 1992, and as part of a national alcohol survey in 1995.[9] The NFVS uses a Conflict Tactics Scale (CTS) to measure the forceful means deployed by family members in the previous year (and "ever") to resolve disagreements or arguments.[10] Respondents choose from options ranging from "pushing" through attacks with knives or guns and these tactics are classified as either "severe" ("spouse abuse," "wife beating") or "minor" ("not abuse, "ordinary violence") according to the probability that a given act will cause injury. These acts are then aggregated to produce prevalence rates of family violence by gender and family status. The CTS is the most widely used measure in domestic violence research, is easy to administer, and has been employed at hundreds of service sites as well as in numerous population surveys. According to the NFVS, wife beating declined over 10% between 1976 and 1985, from 38 to 34 per 1,000 women a year, and declined another 19% during the next decade.[11]

Partner and Nonpartner Homicide

All types of homicides have declined significantly in the United States over the past three decades, largely because of demographic changes like the aging of the baby boom generation. Partner and nonpartner homicides are influenced by many of the same factors, such as jealousy, the availability of guns, and trends in marriage and employment, though these factors affect males and females differently and blacks differently from whites. One hint that domestic violence reforms had an independent effect is that family homicide rates followed a different path than overall homicides. Partner homicides dropped between 1976 and 1980, when overall homicides rose most sharply; leveled off in the next decade while overall rates were rising; and have declined since then, though more slowly than overall homicide, increasing the proportion of all homicides caused by partners.

Professor Gelles is technically correct. Fewer wives were killed by husbands in 1992 (the date of the third NFVS survey) than in 1976. But this claim is mitigated by two facts: during this period, changes in marriage and divorce made wives a decreasing proportion of female partners and the proportion of femicides (killings of women) committed by ex-husbands, boyfriends, and ex-boyfriends increased sharply, going from one in four in 1976 to approximately one in two today.[12] Another problem is that much of the change Gelles reported is accounted for by a 10% drop in the single year, 1976–1977, before domestic violence intervention was widespread. In fact, the absolute number of women killed by male partners in 1992 ($N = 1,445$) was virtually identical to the number killed in 1977 ($N = 1,430$) and the modest declines occurring since 1993 have been far smaller than the decline in homicide overall.

Gender and Race Differences in Intimate Homicide Trends

Intervention has affected partner homicide, but in very different ways than we expected. Since 1976, there has been an historically unprecedented drop in the number of men and particularly of black men killed by female partners, a drop that far outpaced the decline in overall homicide.[13] The only credible interpretation for this is that shelters and other domestic violence interventions have protected men far better than they have women.

To be sure, the number of women killed by partners declined after 1993, reaching the lowest level recorded in 2004. Even so, the overall drop since the first shelters opened is just 30% and is less than 20% if we exclude the outlier year of 1976–1977, which is less than 1% annually. By contrast, the number of men killed by their partners in this period dropped 70%, more than 3 times as much, from 1,288 to 385 in 2004, a change that accounts for almost three-fourths of the total decline in intimate homicide since the first shelters opened. In other words, domestic violence interventions appear to have saved the lives of 3.5 men for every woman's life they saved. In 1976, male and female partners were equally likely to be killed in a violent confrontation (1:1.2). Today, a woman's risk of being killed by her partner is three times as great as his.[14] See figure 2.1.

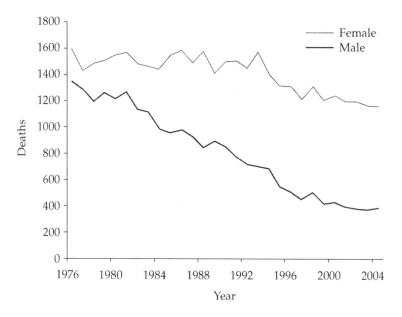

Figure 2.1 Intimate homicide deaths by gender, 1976–2004. *Source: Uniform Crime Reports.* Adapted from "Homicide Trends in the United States" (Washington, DC: U.S. Department of Justice). Available at http://www.ojp.usdoj.gov/bjs/homicide/homtrnd.htm. Accessed July 15, 2006.

Just as important, the changes that have occurred are race-specific. In 1976, black husbands were 16 times as likely and black boyfriends 20 times as likely as white men to be killed by their female partners. By 2004, these ratios had dropped to approximately 5:1 for spouses and 6:1 for boyfriends. Meanwhile, the absolute number of black males killed by intimates dropped an astounding 82% (from 844 to 152) between 1976 and 2004, the number of black females by 56%, and the number of white males by 55%. But for the largest group of victims, white females, the number killed by an intimate dropped by only 5% in this period, and the risk to never-married white women actually increased after 1976 and has only declined very slightly since 2003. The risk to spouses of both races was higher than to boyfriend/girlfriends in 1976. But this pattern had been reversed by 2004, when the risk to boyfriend/girlfriends was considerably higher than for spouses.[15] Since the domestic violence revolution began, black men have accounted for 88% of the male lives saved and black women for 90% of the female lives saved. This information is summarized in figure 2.2.

Woman Battering

Any life saved is an achievement. But these trends fly in the face of what everyone expected from the domestic violence revolution, including those

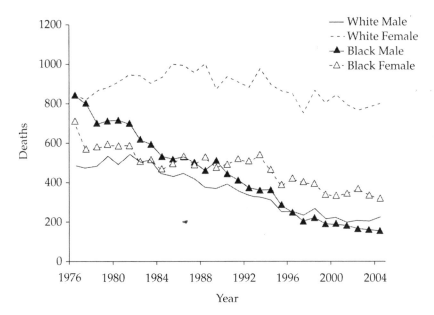

Figure 2.2 Intimate homicide deaths by gender and race, 1976–2004. *Source: Uniform Crime Reports.* Adapted from "Homicide Trends in the United States" (Washington, DC: U.S. Department of Justice). Available at http://www.ojp.usdoj .gov/bjs/homicide/homtrnd.htm. Accessed July 15, 2006.

conservatives who predicted that providing services to female victims primarily would give women a license to kill. Still, homicide is a rare outcome in partner violence. Because most killings of acquaintances or partners start out as assaults and are not premeditated, we would expect serious and fatal assaults to follow the same pattern as homicide. This is not what has happened. Instead of remaining stable, severe violence by male partners in the United States reported to the NCVS has dropped by almost half (49.3%) since 1976, whereas women's violence against men, which was relatively rare to start, remained stable at about 160,000 assaults annually.[16] A majority of partner femicides are committed by husbands. But the majority of severe assaults on women are committed by men who are single, separated, or divorced, making the risk of partner violence to divorced or separated women (31.9/1,000) three times greater than the risk for never married women (11.3/1,000) and 12 times higher than for married women (2.6/1,000).[17] These data underscore why it is misleading to think of woman abuse as domestic or intimate.

Similar declines in severe violence against women are reported by the NFVS, which records acts that are likely to cause injury, such as kicking or attacking with a knife or gun. The 10% drop in severe violence recorded by the NFVS between 1976 and 1985 lacked statistical significance. But the decline between 1985 and 1992 was real, suggesting an overall drop of 48% since 1976, a trend that is identical to the decline reported by the NCVS.

The NFVS also gives us a vantage point on the less serious forms of violence that are more typical of abuse. After 1985, acts of minor violence reported to the NFVS increased so sharply that the overall level of male-female violence in 1992 was identical to the level reported in 1976.[18] Much of this minor violence involves fights rather than abuse. Still, in fully 40% of these cases, the incidents were sufficiently frequent to constitute serial abuse. Gelles and other family violence researchers dismiss the significance of this increase, attributing it to a growing sensitivity among women to even very minor violence. As we will see shortly, however, it is this pattern of routine but minor violence that lies at the heart of women's entrapment in abusive relationships.

In sum, the domestic violence revolution appears to have caused dramatic declines in fatal violence by female partners and in severe violence by male partners as well as a much smaller drop in fatal violence by black men. At the same time, reforms probably contributed to a sharp increase in frequent and minor violence against women. Wives are safer today than they were when the shelters opened. But the risk of fatal and nonfatal partner violence against women who are single, separated, or divorced has increased

Explaining Trends in Partner Violence

Those who argue that woman abuse has declined point to structural changes in the family that reduced exposure to partners (such as a tendency to delay marriage), and alleviated stress (such as economic prosperity), or to changing attitudes, increased sanctions, and other factors attributable to the domestic violence revolution.[19] But how should we explain what actually happened? Why did shelters, arrest, and other interventions protect men more than women? Why did femicide resist the downward pattern in severe violence? And why didn't the same protective factors that reduced severe violence against women lead to a parallel declines in minor violence?

Exogenous factors affected the risk to men and women differently because partner violence by men has a different dynamic than partner violence by women. Women typically kill male partners after a prolonged history of abuse and when they fear for their own or their children's safety.[20] Interventions led to a sharp drop in fatal violence by female partners because shelters, arrest, and court orders gave them an immediate option to retaliatory violence and allayed their fears of suffering proximate harm. However, because virtually all current interventions are rationed according to a calculus of injury, with injurious assaults eliciting the most protection, the major change has been in severe violence. An unanticipated consequence of rationing intervention according to the severity of a violent incident is to send the message to perpetrators that lower levels of violence against women are acceptable, causing so-called minor violence to rise, an example of normalization. Protecting women from severe assaults has also led many men to supplement physical abuse with coercive control, the issue we turn to in subsequent sections of the book. Suffice it to say here that this strategy effectively neutralizes the benefits of separation by substituting stalking, surveillance, and other tactics to extend subjugation through social space. This helps explain why the abuse of women living separately from abusive men has increased so sharply.

Some men kill women in response to an assault. But men commit femicide in two situations primarily: impulsively, when they are jealous or when women threaten to leave or actually try to do so, and during a separation, when they despair they will lose everything, the dynamic captured by the warning, "If I can't have you, no one will."[21] Shelter, protection orders, and arrest interrupt these dynamics, reducing severe violence against women. Because current interventions are crisis-oriented, short-term, predicated on a calculus of harms, and based on the expectation that separation is itself protective, however, they leave victims and perpetrators in the same social orbit even after a man is arrested and/or partners are living apart. This is why the long-term benefit of intervention for women's safety has been minimal.

Explaining Racial Trends

In 1976, overall spousal homicide rates were higher in the black than in the white community, as were the proportional rates of homicide generally. Racial bias in policing led to the disproportionate arrest of black men for crimes committed in public spaces. But police rarely intervened to protect black victims in their homes. Sociologist Darnell Hawkins attributed this failure to the belief among police that blacks were "normal primitives" for whom violence came naturally.[22] On their side, black victims were historically reluctant to "go to the man" when they were attacked and subject their private lives to the scrutiny and control of a police force that was frequently hostile. This view was immortalized in the song "Ain't Nobody's Business if I Do," where Billie Holiday assured an imaginary male partner "I swear I won't call no copper / If I'm beat up by my poppa." Black women are more likely to be employed than white women when they enter abusive relationships, less likely to be isolated from family and kin, and less likely to expect their partner to take care of them. By contrast, although abusive black males are more flexible about domestic roles than white males, they are also more prone to exploit their partner's role as provider, presumably because of their own economic disadvantage due to discrimination.[23] The combination of relative economic independence and a paucity of alternatives due to real and perceived bias explains why so many black women killed male partners when the domestic violence revolution began.

Racial bias remains a major issue in service delivery, and the number of shelter beds in inner-city areas is far below what is needed. But black women were attracted to shelters by their empowerment philosophy, their rejection of demeaning models of service delivery, and by the offer of safe housing and employment. Mandatory arrest policies also had two effects that led to increased use of police and other services by black women: they substantially increased the absolute number of persons arrested, including the number of black perpetrators, and brought the proportion of black men arrested in line with their proportion in the general population. In 1981, when police in Duluth, Minnesota, had full discretion in arrest, African Americans and Native Americans comprised 32% of those arrested for domestic violence crimes, though they were less than 5% of the population. Domestic violence arrests for all races increased sharply when pro-arrest policies were introduced and again when arrest was mandated. But the proportion of minority men arrested dropped to 13.3% when arrest was encouraged and to 8.5% when it was mandated.[24] The proportion of minority arrests for domestic violence also dropped sharply after the adoption of a pro-arrest policy in New York City.[25] The result of aggressive and more equitable enforcement was that, by the late 1980s, black and Latina women were calling police for help with partner violence in larger numbers than any other groups.[26] For a variety of reasons, including the propensity for police to intervene in fights, mandatory arrest policies also increased dual arrests.[27] But young, unmarried white women suffer most from dual arrests, not women of color.[28]

Sexual Equality or Inequality?

Observers agree that trends in abuse are shaped by broad improvements in women's status as well as by more proximate factors. But they disagree about whether these improvements protect women or make them more vulnerable. One view is that women's subordinate status makes them "appropriate victims" of sexual violence and that greater sexual equality reduces violence against women by giving them the resources needed to escape abusive relationships.[29] This ameliorative hypothesis is supported by data showing an inverse relationship between measures of equality and both the general prevalence of wife abuse and its expression in particular relationships. The alternative "backlash" hypothesis holds that women's gains threaten male privilege, causing violence to escalate. Because women mainly kill male partners who have assaulted them, this hypothesis also predicts that greater equality will increase women's violence against male partners.[30] A third explanation is that men abuse and control women in the household in response to their lack of power in the workplace, the compensation hypothesis.[31] If there is little support for the compensation hypothesis, evidence for the others is mixed: though the lowest rates of domestic violence are reported by states where women's status relative to men is highest, supporting the ameliorative view, men are significantly more likely to kill female partners in cities where women experience relatively high economic status compared to men, a seeming example of backlash.[32]

All of these accounts downplay the rational or instrumental nature of abuse and the extent to which decisions to abuse or control women are shaped by societal and individual responses. If men already have power over women, as the ameliorative hypothesis implies, their use of violence to subdue women would seem superfluous. Meanwhile, the backlash hypothesis explains men's motive for using violence—namely, to protect their privileges—but not how abuse can remain widespread in the face of substantial gains in women's economic and political power. In the first view, female equality nullifies partner violence in much the same way that civil rights legislation nullifies racial discrimination by proprietors of public facilities. The antidote to abuse is less clear in the second view: even if women's equality increases men's violence, compromising women's gains for family peace is not a credible option.

Empirical assessment of these hypotheses is complicated because different markers of status (such as education, income, or employment) affect violence differently, there are different results when women's absolute gains are used as a gauge rather than their status relative to men, and because the distribution of rights, resources, and opportunities to which women are equally entitled (such as the right to attend professional school or own property) are stratified by class, race, and other demographic characteristics. To illustrate: although the median annual earning of employed women and of minority women is higher in Washington, D.C., than anywhere else in the United States and the differential between the earnings of men and women is smaller, the earnings ratio between African American women and white men in Washington, D.C., is 50%, larger than in all but one other city.[33] If women's gains are unequally distributed based on preexisting intrasexual differences by race or class, so are the threats posed by women's improved status and men's opportunities to do something effective in response. The resource differences between men and women are greatest at the top of the class pyramid, not at the bottom. Affluent or professional white women have far greater access to rights and resources than their less advantaged sisters. But they are actually more disadvantaged than poor women relative to the men in their pool of probable partners, a difference that is starkly apparent in divorce or custody disputes.[34] Women in my home state of Connecticut rank third nationally in median annual earnings, seemingly a mark of equality. But if this makes them better off than other women, because of its proportion of high earning white males, Connecticut ranks 43rd in the ratio of female to male earnings, indicating that women in Connecticut are less likely than other women to be equal to their partners.[35]

Culture also shapes how equality bears on abuse. In many societies and cultures, women continue to be subordinated to their partners by law, lore, or religion regardless of their familial status or personal income. White men appear to be more threatened by a partner's economic independence than black men, for instance, whereas the latter are more threatened by a partner's perceived social independence and dominance in the domestic setting, views that are linked to violence by what psychologist Tameka Gillum calls the "matriarch" and "Jezebel" stereotypes.[36]

Equality and inequality matter, but they are neither mutually exclusive conditions nor linked to violence in a one-dimensional way. I argue in chapter 6 that women's equality made violence less effective as a means through which men could control them as the ameliorative hypothesis predicts. But in response to this dilemma, a significant subgroup of men chose to protect their privileges by devising coercive control, a strategy that complimented violence with other tactics. This backlash can succeed in quashing women's new found independence only because persistent inequalities continue to make women vulnerable to male control in personal life. Greater equality has reduced severe partner violence against women, allowed them to resist abuse more effectively, and made it easier for victims to separate from abusive men. But the overall probability that a woman will be abused or killed by her partner has not changed. This is because men have expanded their oppressive repertoire in personal life, and governments have tolerated their doing so.[37]

The Criminal Justice Response: From Closed to Evolving Door

So long as the tide is receding, a child carrying water away from the ocean in a pail may think she is working a miracle. When the tide turns, her efforts are futile, no matter how furiously she loads and bails. Violence trends have little to do with the lunar gravitational field. But the general principle is the same. Few interventions are likely to succeed unless converging social forces are pushing events in a similar direction.

By 1994, when he signed VAWA, President Clinton could affirm it was national policy to get tough with batterers. Arrest has been the linchpin in this response. Supported by VAWA, the American Bar Association, and every major law enforcement body, pro-arrest or mandatory arrest policies in abuse cases are now almost universal in the United States. According to a 1998 study of the nation's largest police departments, almost 99% of officers make arrests "the usual response" if domestic violence occurred in the officer's presence, 81% if it occurred before police arrived, and 28% if violence was threatened but had not occurred.[38] Between 1984 and 1989, local arrests for minor assaults in the United States increased 70%, largely due to a sevenfold rise in domestic violence arrests.[39] Of course, the starting point was very low.[40]

The seriousness of battering justifies this response. According to research in Quincy, Massachusetts, men arrested for domestic violence are chronic offenders, averaging almost 14 prior criminal charges on their record for all crimes, a little less than half of these for assault.[41] Similar histories typify domestic violence offenders in England.[42] Many of the violent acts that prompt domestic violence arrests would be classified as felonies if committed against strangers, and most of the men arrested resemble the worst class of felons: they are repeat offenders, are typically unrepentant, and frequently retaliate against, threaten, or otherwise intimidate their victims after an arrest. Many perpetrators proceed to abuse other women, particularly if they have longer criminal histories and/or prior restraining orders.[43] All of these facets suggest a high-profile crime worthy of an aggressive criminal justice response.

Change in criminal justice policy has been dramatic. Arrest reduces subsequent violence better than any other intervention.[44] If it has had little effect on women's long-term safety, this is because so small a proportion of domestic violence incidents is reported, offenders are arrested in only a small proportion of these cases, few of these cases are prosecuted, and almost no offenders go to jail. The result is that men who batter their partners are only slightly more likely to be held accountable for their actions today than when the domestic violence revolution began.

Domestic Violence Reporting

A majority of female victims of partner violence who seek outside assistance have called police, many multiple times. In Connecticut, all of the women seeking protection orders had called police at least once and a third had done so from 5 to 10 times.[45] Police have been called in almost half of the domestic violence crimes reported to the NCVS.[46] But studies that have tried to estimate the proportion of actual incidents that are reported provide much lower estimates, ranging from 2% in a Scottish study of 35,000 incidents to 14% of the most serious forms of assault identified by the 1985 NFVS, with most estimates hovering at or below 10%.[47] This paradox—that most victims call, but only a small proportion of incidents is reported—is explained by the fact that abuse is typically frequent but noninjurious. In Memphis, Tennessee, 89% of the female victims interviewed at the scene of police calls reported previous assaults by the current assailant, and 35% reported being assaulted on a daily basis by this assailant.[48] Only two of the several thousand assaults suffered by the women whose case histories are summarized in part IV resulted in a police call. Even so, "domestics" are sufficiently numerous to comprise the largest category of police complaint.

Does Arrest "Work"?

Police are called to respond to a specific incident. But because abuse is so frequent, its harms cumulative, and calling is a function of the opportunity to do so (not necessarily of the severity of an incident), it is imperative for women's long-term safety that law enforcement be positioned to open the narrow window afforded by a police call to assess the larger danger a victim faces from a particular perpetrator. At present, this window of opportunity remains largely shut.

Starting with the U.S. Civil Rights Commission hearings in 1978, the premise behind police reform was that victims of domestic violence were being denied the same protection as victims of stranger assault guaranteed by the U.S. Constitution. Police rationalized the wide variability in their response to partner violence by pointing to everything from the scarce resources available for policing and the lack of cooperation by victims through the supposed fact that intervention has little impact. Advocates countered by pointing to sexist bias among officers and their propensity to define involvement in domestics as low-status work. In eliminating officer discretion in arrest decisions, policy makers hoped to sidestep these problems.

Depending on how calls are screened before they are classified as domestic and on whether low-level abuse offenses are classified as domestic violence crimes, the proportion of calls that result in arrest is variously estimated at from 3% to 77%.[49] One problem with accurately measuring attrition is that many domestic violence calls are screened out based on departmental priorities before they are recorded as domestic or an officer is dispatched. Even where mandatory arrest policies are tightly enforced, only a small proportion of those arrested are prosecuted, and only a small proportion of these offenders are convicted, though proportions are considerably higher in jurisdictions like Quincy that only arrest in more serious cases. Data from Milwaukee indicate that 95% of the men arrested for domestic assault were not prosecuted, and only 1% were convicted.[50] In England, the attrition from a police call to imprisonment is 99.50%.[51]

Charlotte, North Carolina

Evidence about policing in Charlotte, North Carolina, was collected with funds from the National Institute of Justice (NIJ) as part of the attempt to assess the efficacy of arrest against domestic violence. The mandatory arrest policy in Charlotte is considered exemplary. Despite this, out of 47,687 calls classified by Charlotte police under the city's domestic violence code, mandatory arrest policies were applied to just 785 (.016%) either because the case was misclassified, no "spouse-like" situation was found at the scene, a domestic violence crime could not be verified, or the perpetrator had fled. Moreover, fewer than 1% (.9%) of the men in Charlotte who were arrested, convicted, and sentenced for domestic violence actually served time in jail.[52] Thus, even if we make the highly unlikely assumption that all of the 785 men arrested in Charlotte were tried and convicted, this would mean that a mere 7 of the 47,687 perpetrators about whom victims complain, about 1 in 7,000, went to jail. In Connecticut, one of the first states to make arrest mandatory, 80% of the domestic violence cases are nollied or dismissed in court, and almost none result in felony charges or jail time.[53]

The odds that a given act of abuse will result in imprisonment are infinitesimal. They are better than the odds of winning a lottery, but not by much. For every 10,000 incidents of abuse uncovered by the NFVS, 6.7% (670) are reported to the police, though 14% of the most serious incidents is reported, where persons are shot, stabbed, choked, burned, or "beaten up." An extremely optimistic projection would be that the perpetrator would be arrested in half of these cases, a percentage of arrests that is even higher than in Quincy. This would mean that between 335 and 700 perpetrators would be arrested, presumably cases deemed most serious. In Charlotte, where the attrition from call to arrest was 98%, fewer than 13 arrests would result. If we assume that 10% (between 35 and 70) of the men arrested are prosecuted (in Milwaukee, the figure was only 5%), that half of this group (18 to 35) is convicted of a crime (approximately the conviction rate in New Jersey), and that 5% of those convicted (between 1 and 2) get jail time (again many times higher than the conviction and imprisonment rate in Charlotte), this would mean that there is just a bit better than 1 in 10,000 chance that the perpetrator of any given incident of partner abuse will go to jail. And this is the most optimistic scenario. A more realistic estimate is that about 1 incident in 100,000 ends with imprisonment.

The Police Response

Key factors that shape the police response include the social class and marital status of the partners; victim preference; whether the victim or a neighbor initiates the complaint; whether the victim requires medical attention; whether the victim has a protection or restraining order; whether the offender is present when the officer arrives; whether the offender (or the victim) is drunk or abusive to the officer; and whether the officer believes violence is normal for a specific subgroup.[54] But the single thread that runs through the justice response involves reliance on a calculus of harms to decide whom to arrest, prosecute, and punish. In terms of state statutes, the physical harms required for a probable cause arrest run the gamut from Wisconsin, where only a complaint of pain is required, to Nebraska, which requires visible injuries. Regardless of statutory differences, along with the offender's presence and demeanor at the scene, police consistently report that injury is their most important consideration in arrests. Even so, in actual practice only 10% to 20% of offenders are arrested even when victimized women suffer serious injuries.[55] In Canada, police made an arrest in only one of every seven cases in which they advised victims to seek medical help because of their injuries.[56] These findings are particularly disturbing because criminal justice involvement is a key portal to resources for victims in hundreds of communities.

Even the small proportion of domestic violence arrests has flooded courts and police blotters. Rising demand is a common stimulus to resources in the public as well as the private sector. But demand is considered ineffective unless the resources expended lead to credible outcomes. As we've seen, attempts to manage the flow of domestic violence cases include an array of specialized police and prosecution teams, domestic violence courts, and integrated courts where civil and criminal matters are heard in the same venue. The incident-specific focus of law enforcement renders these responses ineffective, however, largely because it generates high proportions of dual arrests, arrests for fights, and other instances of "false positives," where persons are brought in for the wrong offense or no real offense seems to have occurred. In 2002, women comprised 31% of domestic violence arrests in Connecticut, 28% in Arizona, 18% in California, and 17% in Rhode Island and the proportion appears to be increasing.[57] Most of these arrests reflect police frustration or failure to collect appropriate evidence. In Connecticut, New Jersey, and many other states, no sanctions or other outcomes the system is designed to produce result in 80% to 90% of the cases in which police are deployed, victims interviewed, and offenders arrested, booked, charged, and assigned for trial. Adding more resources in this situation merely aggravates inefficiency by increasing the disproportion between cases processed and sanctions. The result is a negative feedback loop, where failed intervention at one point on the service line inhibits the delivery of effective service at other points. When police arrest for minor offenses that prosecutors are reluctant to pursue, or prosecutors proceed with cases that judges fail to punish, police lose patience, withhold arrest, fail to gather appropriate evidence, or announce at a scene that "everyone is going to jail." These responses further stretch administrative tolerance at other levels of the system, diminishing overall confidence in justice interventions. Reoffending is a near certainty in domestic violence cases. Thus, returning so many offenders to the street increases a sense of powerlessness among police, greatly lowering morale. As commitment wanes throughout the system, street-level bureaucrats become reluctant to intervene, their response becomes more arbitrary, and tensions between advocates and providers escalate.

This evidence should give pause both to those who view criminal justice intervention as the answer to domestic violence as well as to the growing number who claim that the police response to abuse is too aggressive.

But it does not necessarily mean criminal justice has failed abused women or that mandatory arrest policies should be rescinded. Despite a paucity of new resources to support their implementation, legal reforms have led domestic violence arrests to skyrocket and heightened sensitivity among a range of justice actors to the needs of battered women. Even when perpetrators remain at large, arrest provides access to a range of supports that victims can access in no other way and sends a strong message about the moral disrepute in which we hold offenders. What arrest does not do is substantially improve women's overall safety or long-term prospects to be free of abuse. As we shall see, the problem here is not the administrative mandate for an aggressive justice response, but the framework that guides intervention.

Specific and General Deterrence

This evidence will not surprise students of criminal justice. Few of those who commit any type of crime are arrested. Criminal justice is a scarce resource that impacts crime through selective enforcement of laws that encompass a universe of criminal acts that is far larger than the capacity of police, prosecution, or courts to interdict or punish wrongdoing. The United States has consistently had one of the highest proportions of its population in prison. The fact remains that most serious crimes are never reported; most persons who break the law are never arrested; anywhere from a third to half of those arrested never go to court; another third have their cases dismissed; and, of those who are convicted, typically as a result of a plea bargain, only a small proportion end up in jail. In this respect, the response to domestic violence is typical and may not reflect a particular bias related to crimes among intimates.[58] As Ferraro and Boychuk pointed out with only slight sarcasm, "Trying to make the justice system work for battered women as it works for other victims overlooks the difficulties of the system for everyone."[59]

If deterrence was the sole criterion for criminal law, statute books could fit onto postage stamps.

Still, although punishment is not the constitutional purpose of arrest, advocates and policy makers nonetheless hoped it would deter specific offenders as well as potential offenders from committing further domestic violence crimes, the effect referred to as general deterrence. If we take the proportion of cases where violence is repeated after an arrest or related intervention as a crude measure of effectiveness, the specific deterrence picture is dismal. Returning to Charlotte, we find that almost a third (31.0%) of the offenders arrested for domestic violence committed another assault on their initial victim within two weeks of arrest, and that almost two-thirds (61.5%) had done so within six months after their initial contact with police.[60] This figure reflects the lower limit of failure because it excludes offenders who substituted nonviolent forms of coercion and control for physical assault, who waited more than six months before their next assault, who left their victims after the arrest (and might have done so without police intervention), and those who abused new partners. From the standpoint of the communities that host these interventions, the failure rate is probably closer to 80%. Nor does criminal justice intervention appear to have a general deterrent effect on nonoffenders or abusers who are not arrested. In the United States, repeat assaulters who have not been arrested perceive the probability of arrest as around 2 in 10; in Canada, the perceived risk is just 1 in 10.[61] Although this is far higher than the actual probability of arrest, it is probably insufficient to deter law breaking.

The impact of aggressive prosecution may be greater. Although some studies show that the backlog of cases created by no-drop or evidence-based prosecution can actually increase pretrial violence, when a specialized court was introduced in Milwaukee that cut processing time in half, convictions were up by 25%, pretrial crime declined, and there was a nonsignificant reduction in new felony arrests.[62]

Protection or restraining orders (TROs) that prohibit an offender from contacting his partner are among the most important legal innovations prompted by the domestic violence revolution, both as a supplement to calling police and as an alternative. Ninety percent of the victims in a recent study obtained TROs without police involvement.[63] Conversely, police in a number of jurisdictions are more responsive to women who have sought a TRO. Prosecutors rely heavily on protection orders, though they harbor grave doubts about their utility.[64] If significant barriers continue to prevent ready access to TROs in many communities, they appear to limit physical abuse, verbal threats, and harassment in the short term, at least by men with little or no prior criminal justice involvement.[65] There is a growing trend toward permanent orders of protection. But when researcher and former probation head Andrew Klein tracked 663 victims who sought restraining orders in the Quincy District Court, he found no differences in reabuse among victims who maintained their orders and those who dropped them prior to the 1-year termination date. Almost half of the abusers reabused their victims within a 2-year period, and whether a woman had or had not dropped the restraining order made no difference in the reabuse rate.[66] In Colorado, almost a third (29%) of the victims suffered severe violence in the year after they obtained the restraining order.[67] Importantly, the probability of reabuse was directly related to the severity and persistence of prior abuse but not to the severity of the episode that prompted the immediate intervention. In both Quincy and Colorado, reabuse remained an enormous problem despite the fact that many of the women had divorced or physically separated from their partners.

Counseling for Batterers: The Paradox of Treating a "Normal" Pathology

Once domestic violence was identified as a misdemeanor assault, a combination of court-based supervision and counseling or education for men appeared a more appropriate response than incarceration. Instead of going to jail, in many jurisdictions, most of those arrested for domestic violence are now diverted to the batterer intervention programs (BIPs).

The battered women's movement initially opposed batterers' treatment. Advocates feared it would drain critical funds from shelters and endanger victims by deceiving them into believing their partners could be "fixed" and by leaving abusive partners at large. They also worried that BIPs sent the inappropriate message that abuse stemmed from educational, moral, or personality deficits rather than from the systemic benefits derived from controlling women. Today, most domestic violence advocates take the more pragmatic position that something must be done to change perpetrator behavior and that BIPs are preferable to the alternative, traditional forms of therapy or couples' counseling that can damage victims. Though their duration varies widely, BIPs generally last between 10 and 14 weeks, are larger than traditional counseling programs, target short-term behavioral change, and vary markedly in their design. They also vary in the quality of their direction, the degree to which attendance and compliance with nonviolence are monitored, and in the extent to which nonattendance or other violations of court orders are punished. Even observers familiar with their limits generally believe that BIPs are preferable to no justice response at all.

The best known of the early BIPs—EMERGE in Boston, Brother-to-Brother in Providence, AMEND (Abusive Men Exploring New Directions) in Denver, and the Domestic Abuse Intervention Project (DAIP) in Duluth— were free-standing community-based educational efforts for voluntary clients that confronted men's control skills and sent a clear message that battering was a crime of power and control rooted in sexism for which men alone were responsible. Today's BIPs typically combine elements of the psychoeducation approach pioneered in these early efforts with cognitive-behavioral techniques developed in the substance abuse field to manage errors in thinking and judgment believed to be associated with abuse, such as an inability to identify mood changes or to end confrontation before violence erupts, so-called anger management.[68] A smattering of BIPs use more traditional group practice or couples counseling techniques.

By the early 1990s, court-mandated batterers accounted for 80% of all offenders attending counseling, and the rest were socially mandated by partners who threatened separation unless the man entered a program.[69] Apart from the felt need to "do something for 'the men,'" this largely untested response to abuse was so rapidly adapted because it offered a relatively economical solution to a political dilemma, how to satisfy the demand for offender accountability without overresponding to the minor nature of most partner assaults. In New Jersey, Colorado, Illinois, and other states, battered women's coalitions have attempted to regulate the quality and/or content of services delivered by BIPs. But the size of such programs (including 40 or more men in Connecticut, for example) and the paucity of resources available to those who deliver the service make it virtually impossible to do preadmission screening, effectively monitor repeat violence by participants, or follow offenders after program completion. Noncompliance with court-ordered counseling is a formal violation in many jurisdictions, but sanctions are rare.

The Aims of Counseling for Perpetrators

A program's effectiveness is measured against its goals. The program goals of BIPs can extend from a reduction in violent behavior ("statistically significant changes in a desired direction by all participants") and a general insistence that men be accountable to preparing men "to take social action against the woman-battering culture."[70] Social work professor Jeffrey Edleson argues that the most pragmatic goal of short-term intervention should be the creation of an environment where women can "make choices that best meet [their] . . . needs and the needs of . . . [their] children."[71] But this goal is hard to measure. Nor is it clear why counseling is a better mechanism to expand women's choices than incarcerating men and providing enhanced advocacy and resources to women.

Is "Battering" a Treatable Problem?

BIPs are not designed as treatment. Still, counseling makes sense only if abuse stems from a remediable deficit in personality, knowledge, or belief. BIPs are often compared to DWI programs or interventions with sexual predators with which criminal justice has extensive experience. But these analogies are weak. Woman battering is not an addiction. Moreover, where the harms-to-benefits ratio of substance abuse clearly favors abstinence, battering offers offenders a number of tangible as well as intangible benefits.

Batterers and sexual offenders share such characteristics as an obsession with power or sexuality, extreme narcissism, and fear of a hostile outside world from which they crave protection. A growing body of literature emphasizes other types of psychiatric comorbidity among batterers, including borderline personality and schizoidal disorders, narcissistic/antisocial personality and passive/dependent compulsive disorders, and a quasi-genetic configuration called intermittent explosive disorder or IED, the same acronym used for improvised explosive devises in Iraq.[72] Still, perpetrators are most commonly diagnosed with personality disorders, a class of problems that is unresponsive to the short-term regimens typical of BIPs. Moreover, many studies find batterers psychologically indistinguishable from nonviolent men and men in distressed relationships. In a large assessment of perpetrators in treatment, Edward Gondolf found that only one in four had serious psychological problems. Even among repeat assaulters, the group considered the principal candidates for specialized psychiatric care, 60% showed no serious personality dysfunction or psychopathology.[73]

Psychological models based on very different profiles can predict future abusive behavior in almost 20% of cases. By contrast, simply knowing whether a man has assaulted his partner in the past explains 50% of the variance in physical violence by men.[74] Prediction is enhanced even further when previous violence is combined with asking victimized partners if they feel safe or whether abuse is likely to reoccur. By contrast, personality and risk factors widely thought to identify high-risk offenders have little predictive value.[75]

The most detailed evidence that batterers share a distinctive psychiatric profile comes from Canadian psychologist Donald Dutton. In a comparative study of batterers and nonbatterers in treatment, Dutton established a strong correlation between abusive behavior (as measured by the Conflict Tactics Scale) and elevated scores on a measure of what he calls "Borderline Personality Organization" or BPO. Dutton and others interpret his research as evidence that woman battering is the result of psychopathology and as "casting serious doubt on the theory that all or most sexual violence against women is gender-motivated."[76] On close examination, the profile Dutton identifies turn out not to be a psychiatric condition at all but a spectrum of personality or behavioral traits that are widely found in the general population. For example, the borderline traits he measures include "demandingness," "manipulation," "intense anger," and other characteristics that have a baseline prevalence in the general population of up to 15%. These traits correlate closely with dominance and isolation, but not with violence. As Dutton admits, these traits are likely to be "strongly attuned to aspects of the culture that direct and justify abuse," rather than the byproduct of mental processes, let alone of mental illness.[77]

Dutton has identified what I call a normal pathology, a set of personality characteristics that are integral to the use of violence and control to establish dominance, and so have pathological consequences, particularly for women and children, but are rooted in the normative construction of masculinity rather than in a mental defect. Classifying perpetrators based on their personality types might help clinicians target their services. But serious ethical questions are raised by treating traits like demandingness, manipulation, and control as personality problems once they are actualized in criminal strategies to dominate, hurt, and isolate women.

Are Batterers' Programs Effective?

Because the probability of punishment is so low, the main incentive for perpetrators to recover is the secondary gains they might derive from replacing their self-interested and harmful behavior with care and respect for their partner. In my experience, this incentive works with men whose abuse is limited to violence; who use violence primarily to resolve conflicts rather than to extract material, sexual, or other tangible benefits; and who are in relationships that their partners want to continue. Unfortunately, by the time they are arrested and referred to counseling, few men meet these criteria.

Counseling for perpetrators might make sense if it significantly reduced women's immediate pain and suffering. Dramatic claims are made about the effectiveness of BIPs. Dutton reported that 2.5 years following their arrest, only 4% of the men who had undergone court-mandated treatment had been rearrested for assault compared to 40% of the untreated offenders.[78] The mainstream view is more tempered, holding that counseling is more likely than incarceration to effect behavioral change after an arrest and is a more appropriate intervention than prison for cases of misdemeanor domestic violence or where couples want to remain together. The most widely replicated model of batterer's counseling is the Domestic Abuse Intervention Project (DAIP) developed in Minnesota by Ellen Pence, a 12-session program designed primarily for arrested offenders. More sophisticated than most other programs, yet accessible to counselors without formal training in psychology or social work, the DAIP focuses on gender equity issues, teaches behaviors to control violence, maintains a close working relationship with a range of supportive services, and holds the threat of prison over men who fail. A study of the DAIP by Jeffrey Edleson indicated that 69% of its graduates (for whom data were available) remained nonviolent at 6- and 18-month follow-ups, an impressive achievement.[79]

Even if all such programs could claim similar success, a major problem with BIPs is that only about a third of the men who contact them show up. Of those who attend, the drop-out rate in the Duluth program is 46%, about the national norm.[80] Thus, such programs fail to engage the vast majority of offenders. Even if we accept the outcome data reported by Edleson, this means that for every 100 arrested offenders who are referred to a BIP, 35 will attend, 18 will finish the program, and 12 will stop their violence for up to 18 months. This is no small accomplishment. Still, making the dubious assumption that the success of the Duluth program is replicated by programs elsewhere, and attributing all of the success reported by the DAIP to the intervention (which assumes no men would have stopped on their own), we may still feel uneasy about relying on a program as an alternative to prison that leaves anywhere from 50% to 80% of the small minority of victims who get the law's attention at extreme risk.

If their limited scope makes batterers' programs impractical as a general antidote, are they nevertheless successful with those served as intended? If graduates stop their violence far more readily than offenders who don't attend or complete a program, we could concentrate on improving retention, particularly because retention rates are much higher in integrated programs that deal with substance abuse as well as violence.[81] The ideal test of program effectiveness would be a control trial where perpetrators are randomly assigned to treatment or no treatment, variance in program design and delivery is minimized, drop-outs are compared to completers to eliminate selection bias, victim reports and other records are used to detect abuse during and after intervention, the period of follow-up is sufficient to capture long-term change, and information about the types and frequency of pretreatment abuse is collected to properly assess post-treatment changes. In the real world where BIPs operate, these conditions are hard to meet. Nonetheless, five of the many published evaluations of BIPs use quasi-experimental designs that approach this ideal.

In a large study comparing men sentenced to a 26-week BIP plus a year of probation to men only sentenced to probation in Broward County, Florida, researchers found no significant differences between the two groups in attitude changes, victim perception of changes, or in rearrests or probation violations, though the men who completed the BIP were less likely to be rearrested than drop-outs.[82] A Brooklyn study compared men attending a 26-week BIP, men attending a more intensive 8-week program, and men simply assigned to community service. Whereas the men attending the longer group generated the fewest criminal complaints, there were no differences in victim reports of abuse for the three groups or in attitude change.[83] The best designed study to show positive effects followed 614 men for 48 months who had been arrested for domestic violence and court assigned to BIPs of varying lengths in four geographically dispersed cities. Approximately 47% of all men who entered the programs (both drop-outs and completers) reassaulted their partners during the 48-month period, and fully 25% did so repeatedly throughout the follow-up. Still, the probability of reassault declined significantly after the first 9 months and by the 30-month and 48-month follow-up, 85% of the women felt "very safe" and believed it was "very unlikely" that they would be hit again. The study also found lower rates of assault against new than against the initial partners (28% versus 39%), though this is likely to reflect the shorter exposure time of the new relationships.[84] These findings suggest that treatment may reduce abusive violence in the long term if not lead to its immediate cessation.

Another well-designed study was conducted in the Bronx Misdemeanor Domestic Violence Court. Between July 2002 and February 2004, researchers followed 420 misdemeanor defendants randomly assigned to four groups: batterer programs plus monthly court monitoring; batterer programs plus graduated monitoring (less frequent monitoring in response to compliance); monthly court monitoring only; and graduated monitoring only. There were no statistically significant differences in the probability of rearrest between men assigned to batterer programs (16%) and men who were only monitored (12%). Just as important, men who were monitored were no less likely to be rearrested than men who received no court monitoring. Despite the lack of effect on repeat violence, the study found that victims were more satisfied with the outcomes of their cases if batterers were assigned to a BIP (77%) than those who were not (52%).[85]

These studies share a number of methodological weaknesses, including high rates of sample attrition, high percentages of victim noncooperation, and little or no standardization of program delivery, making it impossible to know whether and which program design elements accounted for observed changes. Some of these pitfalls were avoided in a natural experiment conducted in a Baltimore court by Adele Harrell, a researcher with the Urban Institute. Without any prescreening, domestic violence cases at the court were assigned to two judges, one who used BIPs as an option and one who did not. Those ordered into counseling (both pre- and postprosecution) attended three differently designed 8- to 12-week programs. Data gathering ranged from interviews 6 months after treatment through a review of court records across a period of 15–29 months following case disposition.

The results of the Urban Institute experiment are sobering. Treated offenders felt their self-understanding and acceptance of responsibility for their violence improved. But their coercive behavior was unchanged. Between 80% and 85% of all offenders abstained from severe violence during the treatment period, far more than in the Gondolf study, and almost half (47%) abstained from threats. But abstention rates declined sharply afterward, particularly among the men who had been counseled. Fifteen months after counseling, 88% of the men who received no counseling remained nonviolent, but only 57% of counseled men had not pushed, shoved, kicked, or hit their partners. After 29 months, half of the partners of men in the treated group had called police for an assault, but only 30% of the partners of men in the untreated groups had done so, and counseled offenders were also three times as likely as untreated men to face new domestic violence charges (19% compared to 7%). Despite these differences, wives in the two groups differed little in their overall assessment of safety. Treated offenders were more likely than nontreated offenders to understand the legal ramifications of domestic violence. Significantly, however, both groups rated the likelihood of experiencing legal sanctions as low.[86]

Despite important strengths, the single well-designed study showing that counseling reduces violence used neither a random sample nor a control group. When I asked Harrell why she thought the counseled men in her Baltimore study were more violent than those who received no postarrest intervention, she blamed "the parking lot syndrome," where men get together informally and seek support after a session. Three other factors may explain the poor outcomes. In Baltimore, the same offenders who claimed that the program improved their communication and conflict resolution skills also admitted it reinforced their belief that coercion was justified under certain circumstances. Despite the insistence that domestic violence is criminal behavior, assignment to counseling rather than prison sends the implicit message that sanctions are unlikely. Finally, abuse may be more likely after a perpetrator attends a BIP because a victim is more likely to stay with or return to a violent partner if he enters a program.[87]

Their exclusive focus on repeat violence is another important limit to these outcome studies. Even in relationships where violence stops, many women report high levels of fear and continued entrapment. This is illustrated by a national survey from Finland that found the highest levels of fear, depression, hatred, guilt, low self-esteem, and other emotions associated with exposure to repeated violence among a population of older women (age 54–64) whose partners had not been physically violent for an average of 10 years. In these relationships, physical abuse had been replaced by mental torment and other forms of coercive control.[88] A case from my practice illustrates this pattern.

Carl and Joanne

Carl was an elementary school teacher in a small Connecticut town. When his authority was questioned, he would lift his much smaller wife, Joanne, by the throat, then drop her, breaking several of her ribs on one occasion. After several months of group psychotherapy, his violence stopped and he became a model of reform, challenging new group members to take responsibility for their violence and to accept female equality. But Joanne was deteriorating. She was increasingly depressed, withdrew from friends, and admitted a deep-seated rage about which she felt guilty. Along with the other women in our support group, we wondered what was going on. The answer became clear one night, when Carl tried to illustrate how he had changed to a new member of our men's group. He described his reaction when a friend of his wife's whom he disliked came to town. In the past, he would have thrown a fit, demanded Joanne choose between the two of them, and become assaultive. Instead, he negotiated a compromise, that the three meet at a nearby pizza parlor. As soon as he sat down in the restaurant, Carl's feelings of abandonment returned. Instead of giving in to his mounting anger, however, he put his new skills to work. He announced he would take time out, leave the restaurant, and walk home . . . along the interstate. Joanne panicked, left her friend, returned home. When Carl appeared, miraculously unhurt, she reassured him she would not disrespect him like this again. Carl recited similar agreements he had negotiated about child care, cooking, and time off on the weekend. Ironically, the larger lesson he intended to convey was how he could get what he wanted from Joanne without violence. To Joanne, Carl's quiet rage was even more intimidating than his assaults. Only now, she was isolated as well and had neither a name for nor the space to explore her feelings of entrapment.

The Battered Woman's Shelter: Challenges to Empowerment

As the cornerstone of the domestic violence revolution, shelters can be distinguished from traditional services by their grassroots base, their incorporation of clients into day-to-day operations, their juxtaposition of advocacy and service, and their rapid acceptance worldwide as a victim-centered, nonhierarchical, community-based response to violence against women. Shelters prevent hundreds of deaths and thousands of assaults annually. As we've seen, they also protect men. Nothing in what follows discounts these achievements.

Early on, we realized that shelters could provide only limited protection once women returned to their communities, particularly in lieu of credible sanctions for perpetrators. This was one reason why the activist shelters focused on empowerment, emphasized mutual support and resident self-governance, and focused resident anger at system change and leveraging resources. Most of the women sheltered by Women's Aid in England returned to their abusive partners. Even so, according to a follow-up study, 18 months after they left the refuge, they highly valued the experience for offering a respite from violence, an end to isolation, and an atmosphere of mutual support, sharing, and assisted self-help.[89] African American battered women utilizing shelter in the United States also found that they retained their self-confidence and satisfaction with their lives after they left, although their objective situation changed little.[90] Although the activist model defined the overall direction of the battered women's movement in the United States, a large number of shelters followed what Russell and Rebecca Dobash call a "therapeutic" model. As illustrated by Rainbow Retreat in Phoenix, Arizona, these were hierarchically organized facilities that often grew out of halfway houses, residential treatment programs for alcoholics, or sheltered workshops of the sort managed by the Salvation Army and other religiously oriented organizations. Backed by a small core of clinicians, nonprofessional staff set out to break the cycle of abuse by providing residents with information about appropriate behaviors (staying away from violent men, nonabusive parenting) and organized individual recovery through a highly regimented format that combined individual case management (also called advocacy) and mandated services with group work oriented toward changing ways of behaving and thinking thought to be habitual. Because of their institutional setting and experience with multiproblem clientele, therapeutic shelters could serve a broad range of women. But their emphasis on recovery and coping left little room for activism, let alone identification with the larger women's movement.

Domestic Violence Services, Inc.

The British shelters affiliated with the National Women's Aid Federation (now called WAFE) generally sustained the activist model through the 1990s, when many refuges replaced the congregate living so critical to activism with housing in self-contained apartments. In the United States, however, one cost of their relative success in garnering governmental support was that by the mid-1980s, many of the activist shelters had abandoned their overtly confrontational stance toward traditional institutions and moved well along the continuum toward a therapeutic model.

The rapid spread of shelters in the United States forced local organizers to reach far outside the initial pool of committed activists for staff, volunteers, and monetary support, challenging even the most idealistic advocates to accommodate their organizational principles to the political realities of a competitive service market. Woman House in St. Paul was able to secure outside funding without compromising its commitment to social change. But the equally activist Transition House in Boston saw its support dwindle and finally closed. By the mid-1980s, the surviving activist shelters in the United States were firmly embedded in a "third sector" of independent, nonprofit organizations that were formally controlled by local boards or institution like the YWCA that had not been directly involved in their creation.

Without a consistent source of funds or political support, program survival in the service marketplace required a flexible entrepreneurial discourse that could accommodate diverse audiences of employees, funders, state policy makers, and local supporters. Militant feminism was incompatible with this requirement. Even in shelters operated under the auspices of a free-standing or university-based women's center or feminist-oriented organization, the imperatives of funding, political negotiation, and crisis management fostered a pragmatic approach that offered little space for long-term planning or political advocacy. By the mid-1980s, medium-sized U.S. shelters housing 20 women and children often had annual program budgets in excess of $250,000. Expanding budgets led to the selection of entrepreneurially minded governing boards and a growing dependence on federal, state, and charity funding sources (such as the United Way) that took a dim view of activism. Safety and confidentiality, important values from the start, were given exaggerated importance by the new risks of liability, and the threat that public exposure, particularly if interpreted as adversarial, could lead to a loss of funding. Shelters were pressured to replace the volunteer base whose sweat equity had been critical to early economies with "professional" staff, management procedures, and personnel practices, though usually without significant improvements in salaries, benefits, or opportunities for upgrading. The need to integrate CETA workers into permanent positions, the availability of state dollars targeting specific programs or functions (such as child care or court advocacy), and the increasing need to support management functions in development and outreach transformed the shelter director from a facilitator to an executive and widened the gap in salaries and decision-making power, often along racial lines. One result was that staff responsible for education, development, and administration often moved out of the shelter facility and away from front-line operations, insulating it from resident influence. Meanwhile, the policy imperatives created by a growing interdependence with law, policing, medicine, and child welfare institutions pushed advocacy toward traditional forms of case management, complete with a standard package of mandated services.[91]

Despite remaining formally independent, shelters increasingly mimic the language, fundraising strategies, and apolitical style of a host of parallel agencies that primarily serve poor and minority populations, such as drug and alcohol treatment programs, shelters for the homeless, and community counseling centers. By the late 1980s, many states were funding shelters through distinct budgetary lines that could be maintained only through continual lobbying at state capitals; competition with other needy constituencies such as welfare recipients, the homeless, foster parents, or the mentally ill; and public relations campaigns designed to at least neutralize interests traditionally hostile to women's concerns. Because VAWA funds went to the states rather than directly to shelter organizations, federal policy reinforced this trend, even as it strengthened the bargaining power of state coalitions in most (but not all) states. State coalitions redefined the common ground shared with other women-oriented service organizations as contested terrain to be parsed through negotiation. The isomorphism fostered through local collaboration and competition for scarce service dollars increasingly found expression in how the problem was represented, first at public forums where victim imagery was far more effective than tales of courage and resistance, and then to internal audiences, including members of the board, funders, staff, and residents.

Victim stories are critical to charity work because they allow audiences to join in the helping effort without linking the problem to their own experience. But this approach also masks the continuum of oppression around which diverse elements of the women's community once joined as relative equals. What Almeida and Hudak call the "myth of activism" remains part of the shelter aura: advocates continue to use "the power and control wheel" and shelters to evoke the pioneering efforts of their founders at awards dinners and other exercises in fundraising and self-congratulation.[92] But actual militancy in pursuit of women's liberation is a luxury shelters can no longer afford. By 1993, when Jeff Edleson published his survey of 379 advocacy programs in the United States, the majority emphasized counseling, information, and referral, meeting immediate needs for clothing or shelter, helping women get protection orders, and other direct services rather than systems change, although many understood that structural change was a precondition for effective help.[93] Today's advocates have learned to only parse what they can handle, salve, or fix, an approach made easier by focusing on a woman's dependency rather than her rage. Leaders of most statewide coalitions are better known by the legislative subcommittees charged with managing their funds than by the public at large or, for that matter, by their own constituencies of shelters or residents.

Worthy and Unworthy Victims

By the mid-1990s, hundreds of shelters had been transformed from resident-run, radical alternatives into staff-dominated players in a social service game that deploy restrictive definitions of victims to discourage inappropriate utilization and highlight individual correction, albeit around an empathic core. Sociologist Donileen Loseke's *The Battered Woman and Shelters* provides a microscopic look at how this process affected victims of abuse. As images of victimization initially devised for outside consumption were imported into the shelter experience, they were used to exclude as unworthy applicants for shelter who threatened to disrupt operations.[94]

To support its claims for public support, Loseke argues, the battered women's movement publicized extreme instances of abuse, described the battered woman as someone who had suffered severe injury, had no place to turn when she called the shelter, and as morally pure or "innocent, hence with no complicity in her plight."[95] But what began as public relations imagery soon came to define the reality of battering for advocates, recruits to the battered women's movement, and shelter residents. In the California shelter Loseke studied, staff used this profile as an interpretive device (or frame) to determine which women were worthy (i.e., really needed to be safe), and who should be excluded from the emergency service. As collective self-help gave way to individual case management, staff were left with new responsibilities for keeping the peace at the shelter, managing children, coping with such organizational limits of shelters as lack of needed space, and negotiating to secure resident access to traditional services. Moreover, without a political understanding of male domination, there was little to salve the emotional tensions inherent in work with clients who appeared to become "stuck" with abusers out of choice, habit, or because they had no options. Images of victims that joined their appalling physical injuries with a sense of dependence and fatalism appealed to new recruits who had come to shelter work without being socialized in the women's movement. But the imagery did more: it also gave shelter workers a handle on the organizational and emotional challenges they faced day-to-day.

Even at best, the safety shelters afford is of limited duration, particularly since most women return to the social world where they've been harmed, if not always to the same relationship. The belief that authentically battered women had been beaten into passivity and helplessness rationalized staff frustration at this situation and kept it from overflowing into defensive anger at shelter residents. But log entries from the shelter also reveal that basing admission on stereotypes of acceptable and inappropriate clients discriminated against a range of battered women whose character, physical state, or emergency situation failed to fit the stereotype. Gloria is defined as worthy for admission. According to the shelter log: "She had just been very beaten up and requested shelter. Met her and brought her in—a very classical case and nice woman."[96]

But Daniele is excluded because her aggressive response to abuse proves she was not really a victim. Wrote the shelter worker, "she is an extremely young woman with 'ruff attitude'—if he hits me I always hit him back."

Amy is similarly unsuited for shelter. "She was talking so fast that I could barely understand. She said she needed shelter because someone she knows is beating her. She sounded real spacey—I suggested friends, relatives. She said everybody hates her. I followed my instincts and said we were full."

Amy is not visibly injured and fails to fit the stereotype in other ways as well because she is agitated, confused, and refuses to name her assailant, all typical signs that she has been isolated and intimidated as well as beaten. By contrast, Toni is clear, obviously desperate, and the "hopeless creature" the stereotype demands. But her sense of immediate danger derives from intimidation and humiliation rather than a beating.

"Toni called the shelter twice. The second time, she reported that her husband threatened to throw her out at midnight. . . . She sounds dippy to me but states she is a verbally abused woman. . . . She really sounds like a strange woman. I think she is looking for a shoulder to cry on."[97]

The pop mental health diagnoses—Amy is "spacey," Toni is "dippy"—reiterate the sexist stereotypes undoubtedly used by the perpetrators in these cases. The main point, however, is that in suggesting these women lack a credible claim to assistance, the labels help staff avoid the special challenges posed to the smooth functioning of shelter life by women who are agitated, aggressive, terrified, and emotionally demanding (e.g., looking "for a shoulder to cry on").

The early shelters afforded a space in which women could use safety as a springboard to recapture the sense of purpose, reciprocity, and the capacity for independent decision making their partners had usurped. Shelters were not for everyone. At least at the core of activist shelters, the notion was that through continual dialogue with relative strangers, women could better understand their predicament and what to do about it. A famous quip in the movement was that we knew we had done a good job when women were allowed to make their own mistakes, something for which they would have been punished by their partner. Whether or not this was always true, we assumed that women's innate survival skills remained relatively intact, including their capacities for reasoned judgment, listening to others, working cooperatively, seeking help aggressively, and challenging conventional norms and structures. Within the chaos of sheltering as well as outside in the community, collectivity aimed at social transformation presented itself as a credible antidote to a deadening isolation and as the most viable context for long-term safety.

Loseke fails to situate the dilemmas she identifies in the larger context of women's struggle for liberation and so cannot distinguish the political challenge represented by the shelter movement from the careers of more conventional social problems, such as alcoholism. Nevertheless, she captures how rigid images of victimization helped transform an activist vision into a remedial service orientation. Few in the early shelter movement would have agreed with the shelter director who insisted that a battered woman can only be reconstituted through the shelter experience after she accepts her "nothingness."[98] But by the mid-1980s, it was common to hear advocates insist that women in shelter have to be deprogrammed in the same way as prisoners of war.[99] The imagery behind this approach does more to manage troublemakers than to help women make trouble for abusive partners or for the service institutions that fail to protect them. The shelter remains orderly. But the existing sexual order remains undisturbed.

To appreciate this process of devolution, there is no need to exaggerate the radicalism of the early shelters. If we took women's capacity for change for granted rather than as something they had to prove, this often had less to do with a philosophical commitment to their liberation than with the view of refuge as a transitional support so women could get on with business as usual. Even at best, only a small proportion of residents used the moments of autonomy forged in the makeshift community of survivors as a springboard to change institutional practice. Although what empowerment meant was hotly debated, our reliance on collective self-help also reflected the practical reality that shelters were overcrowded, underfunded, and maintained largely by volunteers. Hundreds of shelters are still starved for resources, and the demand for shelter beds still far exceeds capacity. But most shelters today are modest, reasonably staffed facilities with a funding base that compares favorably to community-based organizations that serve the homeless, the mentally ill, or substance abusers. Even if the construction of Domestic Violence Inc. was a wrong turn politically, it was amazingly successful in institutionalizing a grassroots movement that could easily have been relegated to the historical dust bin.

The changes installed by the domestic violence revolution have touched every area of public life. What is equally clear is that the domestic violence revolution is stalled.

Spousal homicide is down. But men, and particularly black men, are the main beneficiaries of this change. As the risk that a wife will be killed by her partner has decreased, the risk to women who are single, separated, or divorced has risen.

Severe partner violence against women has also declined significantly. But the total number of violent attacks on women by their partners is about the same today as when the domestic violence revolution began. Moreover, the frequent but minor violence that has increased so rapidly has a cumulative effect on women's entrapment that can be more devastating than injurious assault.

Due to mandatory arrest laws, arrests for domestic violence are now commonplace. Still, the chance that any given incident will result in an arrest is small, and the probability that it will lead to a prison sentence is virtually nil. Although men arrested for domestic violence crimes resemble the most serious felons, assaults against partners have been turned into a second-class misdemeanor.

Counseling of batterers is widely offered as an alternative to incarceration. But the weight of evidence indicates that BIPs make little difference in the likelihood that violence will continue. At worst, these programs may increase reabuse, deceive women into remaining with abusive men, and lead men to control tactics for violence.

Shelters were opened as a resident-run, community-based alternative in which safety was a means to empowerment and collective empowerment was an instrument to challenge systemic sexual inequality, an approach called "transformational" feminism.[100] Today, most shelters are active players in a social service game that employs restrictive definitions of victims, highlights individual service rather than collective empowerment, utilizes stereotypes of worthy victims to discourage utilization, and marginalizes battered women.

The entrapment of women in personal life appears almost as intractable as it did when we opened the first shelters for battered women three decades ago. The domestic violence revolution is stalled. The question is why?

The explanation, I believe, lies at the heart of the revolution, in the very images of violence and victimization on which our current success depends. Absent these images, it is hard to conceive how the revolution could have happened. So long as we continue to embrace these images, our aims—safety, accountability, empowerment, and justice—will remain elusive.

Part II

The Enigmas of Abuse

3

THE PROPER MEASURE OF ABUSE

No sooner had the first shelters opened than a consensus emerged about what brought women through their doors. However much advocates and mainstream academics disagreed, it seemed self-evident that violence was our central concern.

Twenty-five years have passed. A woman's face is prominently displayed on a poster in Marshall's Department Store. Her eyes are blackened, and her cheeks swollen. Without him being pictured, everyone understands that the woman's husband or boyfriend is responsible. "There's No Excuse for Abuse," reads the market-tested slogan at the bottom of the poster. A sign tells us a portion of what we spend goes to domestic violence services, though not what portion or which services. The *New York Times* identifies a similar woman, whose bruised face appears on the cover of its Sunday Magazine, as a victim of "Bad Love."[1]

In the two decades that separated the founding of the first battered women's shelters and the president's declaration that October is Domestic Violence Month, violence against women was framed as the penultimate expression of male power, an irreducible fact of women's social world: "victims" and "perpetrators" could be recognized, counted, and serviced or held accountable. Whether one believes exposure to the facts about violence against women stimulates the young to model or to inhibit their own sexual aggression, the diffusion of images of women hurt by their partners has unquestionably made the use of force a litmus test in male-female relations, defining the boundary of male authority wherever sexual intimacy occurs, from the campus to the storefront church. Today, education, research, and deterrence convey the same messages: violence against women originates in the microdynamics of human relationships, emanates from individual men, is supported by widely accepted norms to which boys are socialized, is replicated across generations, and produces physical and psychological harms that can be captured by scales, surveys, and in eloquent testimony by those who have been victimized.

The equation of woman battering with domestic violence and of violence with masculinity is so pervasive that when survey researchers headquartered at the University of New Hampshire unearthed what they believed was a hidden population of battered men, the resulting critical barrage forced them to publicly retreat from the implications. Authors of a Harris poll of Kentucky housewives merely suppressed findings about women's violence. So palpable are the injuries women suffer because of their partner's power, so pressing is the need to intervene, so broad is the professional commitment to identifying and managing these injuries, so widely have the media promoted the images of psychological deterioration that accompanies physical abuse, so quickly have these images circulated internationally, that it seems callous to impugn their political value by questioning their validity. To ask whether the prevailing images of male violence actually contribute to the condition they purport to describe is to an act of heterodoxy.

Defining Abuse

Everything starts with the definition.

Summarizing the dominant view in the field, Richard Gelles defines violence as an "act carried out with the intention or perceived intention of causing physical pain or injury to another person."[2] With this definition in hand, identifying domestic violence should be a simple matter of determining whether partners or former partners are responsible for assaults. In one form or another, this is the definition that is incorporated in domestic violence statutes, guides research in the field, and provides the framework used by service providers to identify and intervene with victims and offenders.

In its application, the definition is meant to include a broad range of aggressive acts. "Our view," write its two leading proponents, "is that it is impossible to differentiate between force and violence. Rather, all violent acts from pushing and shoving to shooting and stabbing properly belong under a single definition of violence."[3] As a practical matter, this approach puts research on a collision course with popular sentiment because it includes fights, which most people would consider personal business unless someone is seriously hurt or the force used is grossly disproportionate to the issues in dispute. In a concession to this view, the family violence researchers classify the "commonplace slaps, pushes, shoves . . . that frequently are considered a normal or acceptable part of raising children or interacting with a spouse" as "normal" violence or as "not abuse."[4] Still, they insist such acts are part of a continuum of violence and that classifying these acts by anything other than a calculus of injury introduces political bias.

The equation of abuse with physical force in relationships has helped the domestic violence revolution access a range of professional and political agendas. But it has failed victimized women in critical ways. Billions have been spent to apply this definition to study and manage domestic violence in the population at large and at thousands of service points. Yet the most basic dimensions of woman battering still elude us. There is little more agreement today than when the domestic violence revolution began about the actual incidence, prevalence, duration, or dynamics of the problem. Although everyone purports to be measuring the same phenomenon, the picture that emerges from population data differs dramatically depending on whether persons are asked about conflict, crime, or safety concerns. Population surveys identify large numbers of male victims and female perpetrators. But studies conducted at service points show the population in need to be overwhelmingly female. One source of confusion is indecision about whether any and all use of force in relationships should be counted as violence. But the discrepancies remain even after we eliminate low levels of violence. One reason for this has already been suggested, that minor violence is used in fights, which rarely prompt help seeking, as well as in the most devastating strategy used to dominate partners.

How we resolve the problem of the definition matters. In the last chapter, we saw the widely touted decline in partner violence evaporate when we added so-called minor violence to the picture. But which is the right approach? Does the upward trend in minor violence mean that fights have increased, perhaps because women are increasingly standing up for their rights in relationships? In this case, disputing claims that violence against women has declined is splitting hairs. But if the trend signals the spread of a coercive and controlling pattern that is being missed or trivialized, stepped-up assistance is urgent. The current definition is no help in settling this question. The enigma addressed in this chapter is why a definition that is ostensibly so straightforward has created more problems than it has resolved. The answer is that neither the definition nor the picture of abuse it supports captures the strategies men use to entrap women in personal life.

Definitional Stretching

One explanation for why the definition has failed is that its focus on *physical* violence is too narrow. In this view, violence should be broadened to encompass the range of tactics and harms referred to as psychological or emotional abuse. This approach is called definitional stretching, and its official aim is to incorporate dimensions of a problem whose significance was appreciated after its core elements were delineated. But stretching also plays a political role in social problem work. It protects the status quo by accommodating powerful claimants whose interests are not reflected in the prevailing approach. The growing influence in the domestic violence field of psychologists, social workers, advocates, and a range of actors whose expertise lies in facets of abuse other than violence made the definition's exclusive focus on assault and injury untenable. One result was that government agencies convened a workshop in 1998 to forge a consensus around definition and measurement issues. The workshop concluded that the definition of violence should be expanded to encompass "a broad range of maltreatment against women," including sexual violence, threats of physical or sexual violence, stalking, and psychological/emotional abuse. Violence against women, conveners conceded, is a "complex and multidimensional problem" that cannot be captured by "one number" or measured by a "single tool."[5]

Incorporating competing views in a broadened definition leaves funding streams uninterrupted. But has it helped us better understand, measure, or manage the problem? Gelles makes a persuasive case that including a long list of abusive behaviors in the definition of violence so "muddies the waters" that it is "impossible to determine what causes abuse" or delineate targets for intervention.[6] Without one number that approximates how many people are suffering abuse, there is no basis to rationally allocate resources or determine whether our investments are doing any good. Violence is a distinctive behavior with a special link to injury, pain, and other forms of suffering. By subsuming all forms of abuse to violence, we conflate the multiple layers of women's oppression in personal life, making nonviolent abusive acts seem highly subjective or soft core. A metaphorical sleight of hand sidesteps the hard work of delineating where these acts fall empirically on what Stanko calls the "continuum of unsafety" in women's lives.[7]

The violence definition of abuse has much to recommend it. It is easy to apply, lends itself readily to measurement and comparison, appeals to audiences beyond the women's movement, can be used across cultural and national boundaries, and bridges multiple disciplines. The focus on injury is also a useful rationing tool. It is simple to adjust the bar of injury required for real abuse so that intervention can match available resources. Given these benefits, it is a pity that it has been so hard to apply the definition to real life. The convening of a government workshop to consider this embarrassing morass is encouraging. It would be more encouraging if it had found a way out.

The Battered Data Syndrome

The conventional definition of domestic violence is adapted from criminal justice. With a few marked exceptions, crimes are conceived as discrete acts. The definition also highlights a stated or perceived intention to cause harm, though this is almost always inferred from the acts themselves or their consequence. It is also neutral with respect to sex, age, power, and other sociodemographic or situational factors and highlights injury, implying that a calculus of harms alone can be used to assess how seriously an incident should be treated.

Everything we know about woman battering is based on the huge amount of information collected on discrete episodes of physical abuse. Ask "how common is battering?" or who is responsible, and you will be deluged. Each year, I ask students in my class on interpersonal violence to determine the size of the problem and whether it is increasing or decreasing. Using the Internet and sometimes the library, they locate surveys, fact sheets, articles, and reports from dozens of nonprofit programs and local, state, and federal agencies like the Centers for Disease Control (CDC) or the National Institute of Justice. The students take the raw numbers as self-explanatory. A punch is a punch, after all. But their self-assuredness dissolves when other students muster an equally impressive array of sources to support the opposite conclusion.

Early in the domestic violence revolution, there were few negative consequences to using unreliable sources of information. Statistics served mainly as a political tool to help advocates access public agendas and garner resources. This meant disseminating the highest estimates available, regardless of who produced them or why. Conservative opponents of the Violence Against Women Act (VAWA) dubbed this approach "the battered data syndrome" and responded by citing equally unreliable but much lower estimates.[8] The fuzzy math that helped promote our cause has now become a distinct liability. Accurate numbers are imperative not merely to retain support from an increasingly skeptical public but because a vast service infrastructure is in place that cannot function properly without them. If before it made little difference if we were standing in empirical quicksand or whether the population of battered women was estimated at 50% (psychologist Lenore Walker) or at just over 1% (sociologists Murray Straus and Richard Gelles), today accurate numbers are needed to determine how many personnel to enlist, what resources to allocate, whom to target for service and interdiction, and when, where, and how to intervene to maximize effectiveness. No one is harmed more seriously by the absence of agreement on the what, who, and how much of battering than its victims. If we were once talking about an anonymous mass, we now bear responsibility for millions of real people for whom a range of public or quasi-public institutions must be held accountable, billions in public and private dollars that could arguably be spent with greater effect elsewhere, and the investment of millions of person hours annually by real advocates, police, judges, physicians, psychologists, and social workers.

The Definition Applied

Using the commonsense definition to measure battering has been difficult, to put it mildly. Statistical information on domestic violence comes from two sources, points of service like courts, police, hospitals or shelters, and population surveys, some of which have already been described.

Why Service Research Is Unreliable

Because the violence definition guides intervention, to appreciate the significance of abuse, we turn first to those who victims ask for help. Police regularly collect information on calls and arrests, and these data are publicly available. Counting emergency room visits or shelter calls is only somewhat less straightforward. These statistics are an important source of information. But it is impossible to determine the size of the problem from service-related information because there is no agreement on what proportion of total abusive incidents result in police calls, health visits, or shelter stays; whether those who seek outside assistance are typical; or what proportion of victims who call police or show up at the hospital, for instance, are accurately identified. Survey estimates of the proportion of domestic violence incidents reported to police range from 2% (the National Family Violence Survey [NFVS]) to 60% (the most recent National Crime Victimization Survey [NCVS]) and the proportion of "true positives" who are identified in the hospital population hovers between 1 in 11 and 1 in 20.[9] As we saw in the discussions of the police and shelter response, the culture of particular service institutions influences who is counted as a victim and who is turned away. Estimates of service utilization are functions of whether screening for domestic violence is routine, what tool is used, whether the organizational culture supports identification, and whether the agency asking is perceived as responsive. To illustrate, an initial record review revealed that approximately 32% of child welfare cases in Massachusetts involved domestic violence. Yet when case workers included a stated goal of protecting adult victims, the proportion of cases identified jumped to 48.2%.[10] Service data give a very general idea of where victims go for help and how they are received, but not how many actually use the service or would do so if access was expanded.

Population Surveys: Estimating the Extent of the Problem

This leaves nationally representative population surveys as the only usable source of information on the extent and demographic makeup of the problem. I described the two sources of longitudinal data in chapter 2, the Bureau of Justice Statistics (BJS) NCVS and the NFVS, which was conducted in 1975, 1985, 1992, and 1995. There are also about a dozen cross-sectional surveys that provide state- or national-level data on domestic violence. The most important of these was a Harris poll sponsored by the Commonwealth Fund in 1993 and the National Violence Against Women Survey (NVAWS), a telephone survey conducted from November 1995 through May 1996 with a nationally representative sample of 8,000 women and 8,000 men.[11] The NVAWS focused respondent attention on safety concerns raised by partner violence, rape, and stalking during the previous 12 months and "ever." All but the NCVS use the behavioral lists taken from the Conflict Tactics Scale (CTS) to measure violence.

These surveys show that respondents report low rates of abuse when they are asked about crimes, moderate rates when asked about safety concerns, and very high rates when they are asked to catalog any instances of force used to resolve conflicts in their relationships.[12] The Commonwealth Fund (which asked about conflict tactics) estimates annual female victimization rates at 84 women per 1,000, approaching the estimates of 100, 116, 91, and 136 per 1,000 women offered, respectively, by the NFVS for 1976, 1985, 1992, and 1995.[13] At the other extreme, the NCVS reported that the combined rate of simple and aggravated assault against women by an intimate was just 7.6 per 1,000 women in 1992, a tiny fraction of the Commonwealth and NFVS estimates for the same period, and the gap had closed only slightly by 1995.[14] Thus, "conflict" surveys produce estimates of abuse that are 13 times higher than "crime" surveys. The NVAWS—which asked about safety—reported an annual female victimization rate due to rape and assault of 1.5% (15/1,000) for all women and of 1.1% (11/1,000) for women who were married or cohabiting, the group originally targeted for interviews by the NFVS. Although this is twice as many victims as are identified by the NCVS, it is still a fraction of the estimates from the NFVS and the Commonwealth-funded Harris poll.[15]

The magnitude of these discrepancies is dramatized when we consider the actual numbers involved. Based on projections from the 2000 U.S. Census to the population in 2006, the respective estimates of women assaulted annually by their partners are 851,000 (NCVS), 1.7 million (NVAWS), 9.5 million (Commonwealth), and 15 million (NFVS). Estimates of how many men are abused by female partners are even more discrepant.

One explanation for this divergence is that asking about crimes or safety picks up only the relatively few cases that involve serious injury. By contrast, insist the family violence researchers, asking about conflict uncovers a "hidden epidemic," particularly of battered men, relatively few of whom are identified when couples are questioned about crimes or safety concerns. The trouble with this explanation is that the vast majority of incidents reported to all of the surveys were noninjurious. Thus, if persons are reporting only domestic violence they think is serious to crime or safety surveys, which seems likely, this reflects something other than the mechanical properties of the acts or their physical consequences.

From the start, shelter advocates were concerned with women whose safety was jeopardized by their partners, regardless of the circumstance in which this occurred or whether they regarded abuse as a crime. This is what the NVAWS measured. So its estimates come closest to approximating the problem as advocates and service providers see it. By asking about sexual assault and stalking as well as partner violence, the NVAWS also afforded a broader picture than other surveys of the range of coercive tactics used in abuse. Even so, it missed three important groups of victims: those in abusive relationships where violence is infrequent and has not occurred in the previous 12 months; where it is frequent, but too minor in any given case to pose a safety concern; and where the main expression of abuse is intimidation and control rather than assault, rape, or stalking.

Abuse Over the Life Course

One strategy used to get a more accurate picture of abuse than is afforded by cross-sectional data on discrete incidents is to ask about abuse experiences that have occurred at any time during adulthood. This approach captures women whose abuse has continued over many years, but who may not have been seriously assaulted in the past 12 months, as well as those who are suffering what the Finnish survey identified as mental torment from their partners rather than violence. Interestingly, estimates of lifetime victimization from the NVAWS, the Commonwealth Harris poll, and a Commonwealth Fund Survey of Women's Health converge at between 210 (Harris Poll) and 221 of every 1,000 women, a proportion that supports the most widely quoted international statistic, that one woman in five is abused.[16] Using census projections to extrapolate from the 8,000 women surveyed, the authors of the NVAWS estimate that 25,677,735 women in the United States have been assaulted, raped, and/or stalked by an intimate partner as an adult, a number that is almost 15 times higher than the estimated 1,812,546 women who have been victimized in these ways during the past 12 months. This dramatic finding should be considered the upper limit of woman battering in the United States. Even so, as a measure of prevalence or current service need, it has limited utility because there is no way to know how many of the 23,865,189 adult women in the United States who have been abused in the past, but not assaulted, raped, or stalked in the previous year remain in coercive and controlling relationships.

In sum, estimates of abuse based on random population surveys range from almost 1 in 3 (the lifetime prevalence identified by the Commonwealth survey) to 1 in 140 (the figures offered by the NCVS). Do we need to make a commitment of resources equivalent to the use of U.S. and UN troops during the Korean War, called a "mopping-up exercise," or to World War II, when the resources of entire societies were mobilized?

Is Domestic Violence "Domestic?"

Based on the beliefs that "the family is a cradle of violence," "the marriage license is a hitting license," and that abused women are "hostages at home," early surveys targeted only intact couples. In fact, however, every study that has looked at the status of abusive relationships finds that married women have a lower risk than all other groups except widows. In the Yale Trauma Studies, husbands were responsible for only 26% of the abuse-related episodes presented by women to the emergency room.[17] The Yale studies relied on medical records. So the 73% of victims who identified themselves as single, separated, or divorced could have been cohabiting with the abusive partner. But two recent studies suggest otherwise. At the time they assaulted their partners, 75% of the male perpetrators in a sample of child welfare cases and a majority of the men arrested for domestic violence in Quincy, Massachusetts, were *not* living with the women they victimized.[18] The NVAWS also found that women living apart from their partners were more likely than married or cohabiting women to be abused.[19] Men are also more likely to be assaulted by female partners if they are living separately rather than cohabiting, though the absolute numbers are relatively small. Despite these findings, the field continues to view abuse as intimate and to view separation as a major goal of intervention.

Is Abuse Gender-Neutral?

The definition of abuse is gender-neutral. But none of the thousands of studies conducted at points of service identify a substantial number of male victims. Even in Connecticut, where the rate of dual arrests is among the nation's highest, men are the sole offenders and women the primary victims in more than four of every five domestic violence arrests.[20] An even more sharply skewed ratio emerges from victimization surveys. Although the ratio of female to male victims reported by the NCVS dropped from 10:1 to 7:1 after it introduced a specific question about abuse in 1992, the proportion was still far closer to rape, which is widely considered a gendered crime, than to mugging, which is not. In 1998, for instance, 85% of the approximately 1 million reported cases of victimization by partners were against women.[21] Other federal crime data, evidence from the Department of Defense, state surveys, and studies in other countries all point to the same conclusion. For instance, a large-scale study of police data from Scotland found that only 1% of intrafamily assault cases involved a male victim.[22]

This evidence would seem to settle the question of whether abuse should be considered "violence against women." But it does not. In 1976, a year in which only 3 men in every 1,000 reported being assaulted by female partners to the NCVS, more than 15 times this number (46/1,000) reported to the NFVS that their wives had used what researchers classified as abusive violence, prompting the counterintuitive conclusion that the percentage of women who assault their partners is as high or higher than the proportion of men who do so. These and related findings indicated that 2.2 million men were being abused nationwide, even more than the number of abused women. Both the 1992 and 1995 surveys found that the percentages of wives who used severe violence against their husbands was more than twice as high as the comparable rates of husband-to-wife violence.[23]

Not all population-based surveys have similar findings. The NVAWS found the lifetime difference in male versus female domestic violence was

3:1 and that women were 17 times more likely than men to have been "badly beaten."[24] Still, the annual domestic violence ratio reported by the NVAWS was only 1.4:1, an important difference, but not nearly as dramatic as the differences reported by crime surveys or from service sites, where ratios run as high as 17:1. Moreover, the findings from the NFVS are not unique. Dozens of population studies find sex parity in partner violence, including the National Survey of Families and Households (NSFH), studies of high school students, college students, young married couples, and community-based samples.[25] The National Youth Survey, a longitudinal study of 1,725 youth that assessed relationship violence at different ages found that between the ages of 27 and 33, fully 27.9% of women but only 20.2% of men reported using violence against their partners.[26] These findings are widely cited by conservative journalists and the fathers' rights groups who fill right-wing Web sites with complaints about the "feminist" bias that dominates family courts and the criminal justice system when it comes to abuse. However uncomfortable this may make feminist-oriented researchers, it is incontrovertible that large numbers of women use force in relationships, including the types of force classified as severe or abusive.

Getting a handle on the gender dynamics in abuse is also complicated by another finding from the surveys, that the most common dynamic in couples is *mutual* violence. Compared to the 49% of couples who reported mutual violence to the NFVS and other surveys, 27% reported it was used exclusively by husbands, and 24% reported it was exclusively used by wives.

The current definition is no help in resolving the question of whether abuse is gendered.

Is Domestic Violence a Discrete Event?

Following the definition, measurement and intervention proceed from the assumption that abuse consists of discrete acts that can be sharply delineated and so managed within a tight temporal frame, like stranger assaults. Safety planning, risk assessment, and work with offenders are all predicated on the belief that perpetrators and victims possess decisional autonomy *between* episodes. Thus the former can be persuaded not to repeat their violence and the latter to leave.

The Frequency of Abusive Assaults

The problems with this approach start with the frequency of partner assaults. Illustrated by police data, every study that has considered the issue reports that partner assaults are repeated in a minimum of three out of every four cases and, in a majority, are also frequent. A classic study conducted in Detroit and Kansas City found that police had responded to a domestic disturbance at least once in 90% of the households where a homicide or aggravated assault occurred and five or more times in 50% of the cases.[27] In the preceding chapter, I reported evidence from a Memphis police study that 35% of the victims where an arrest was made were experiencing physical abuse daily.[28] A Canadian study found that women who charged their husbands with assault had suffered an average of 35 previous assaults.[29] Offender data affords another angle on the frequency of violent episodes. We saw in chapter 2 that perpetrators who were arrested averaged approximately 14 prior criminal complaints. Although many of these offenses involved drunk driving or drugs, almost half of the offenders also had been charged with violence against persons (men as well as women) and the average number of prior crimes against persons complaints was 4.5.[30] Because only a small proportion of incidents result in police reports, these frequencies are merely a fraction of actual partner assault rates.

As we would expect, cross-sectional population data suggest lower frequency rates. But they are still impressive. According to the NFVS, NVAWS, and the National Youth Survey, persons who report a previous episode of abuse average between 3.5 and 8 assaults annually. Remarkably, 25% to 30% of the abuse victims identified by a general population survey in Texas report serial abuse, many beaten once a week or more, the same proportion identified by the NCVS.[31] The burden repeat assaults place on the larger community of women can be gleaned from a London survey that revealed that victims of domestic violence suffered an average of 7.1 assaults during the previous 12 months resulting in an average of 4.3 injuries and an annual assault incidence rate of 85 per 100 women.[32] Because of recall problems and the propensity of victims to downplay minor assaults, particularly if they were severely injured at some point, these studies also dramatically underestimate the actual frequency of partner violence. The method used to calculate average frequencies in population surveys also underestimates actual abuse. Yearly averages are derived by dividing the number of assaults reported for the previous year by the total of victims without adjusting for the length of a relationship. To illustrate, a woman who was beaten three times during the target year would be given an annual rate of three assaults even though her relationship may have ended after a month, making the actual annual rate 36 assaults. Taken together, the three women whose cases are summarized in part III suffered several thousand assaults. For them, as for many of my forensic clients, abuse happened "all the time" or "whenever we were together" and was so frequent that they were better able to recall times when they were *not* hurt than when they were.

The emphasis on discrete incidents has survived this evidence by borrowing yet another concept from criminal justice. Repeated criminal acts are treated as instances of recidivism rather than as intrinsic to abuse and assumed to be a function of how a particular type of offender behaves because of his psychological makeup. Researchers alternately subdivide offenders into "pit-bulls" and the far more violent "cobras"; into "sociopathic," "antisocial," and "typical" abusers; or into those that are "generally violent" or "chronic" batterers and those who limit their violence to "family only."[33] These typologies can be clinically useful in selecting a mode of treatment. But because they are based on descriptive, cross-sectional and retrospective evidence and no causal link has been demonstrated between patterns of abuse and individual psychology, they have neither predictive nor explanatory power. As we've seen, barring speedy and effective intervention, abuse is repeated in almost all cases irrespective of an offender's personality, background, or predilection for violence. Thus, the treatment of abuse as a series of discrete acts rather than as a unitary phenomenon, like the distinction of repeaters as a unique subtype, is an ideological strategy that should be assessed like any other political choice, by whether its consequences are benign or harmful, rather than as an objective reflection of reality. Distinguishing perpetrators by the number or type of assaults they commit or whether they harm strangers as well as their partners is somewhat akin to differentiating kidnappers by the type of rope they use to bind their victims, whether they steal or pay for the rope, or by the make of getaway car they drive.

Sheer repetition is not the issue. Even though pickpockets, muggers, or car thieves typically commit dozens of similar offenses, because each harm is inflicted on a different person, the law is compelled to treat each act as discrete. But the single most important characteristic of woman battering is that the weight of multiple harms is borne by the same person, giving abuse a cumulative effect that is far greater than the mere sum of its parts. As British sociologist Liz Kelly has pointed out in her work on sexual predators, a victim's level of fear derives as much from her perception of what *could* happen based on past experience as from the immediate threat by the perpetrator.[34] In subsequent chapters, we will see that the cumulative harms inflicted by male partners explain why women are so much more likely to be entrapped by abuse than men and, as a consequence, develop a problem profile found among no other class of assault victims. The current definition ignores this reality. One result is that women are assumed to be lying or exaggerating if they claim a level of fear or danger than seems disproportionate to the proximate incident.

Measuring Harms: The Limits of Injury

The Yale Trauma Studies confirmed the importance of injury as a signpost of abuse in health settings. Based on a random sample that included almost 4,000 hospital patients, Anne Flitcraft and I found that domestic violence caused twice as many injuries to women in the hospital population as auto accidents, then thought to be the most common source of adult injury (18% versus 11%). Subsequent research proved our estimates conservative.[35] But as a window to women's overall experience of partner assault, injury is misleading.

Serious injury due to abuse is common enough. But survey and point of service research indicate that the vast majority of domestic violence is either noninjurious or causes injuries that are minor from a medical or criminal justice standpoint. Of the 2,500 women surveyed for the Commonwealth Harris poll, not a single one reported they had been shot, stabbed, choked, or beaten up.[36]

The minor nature of abusive violence holds even at the emergency room, the scene of arrests, and in the military, sites where we would expect to find the most serious cases. In the Yale studies, of 2,123 visits by abused women who complained that they were injured, 9% involved no injury at all and the largest proportion, 58%, involved "contusions, abrasions or blunt trauma," "lacerations," and "sprains or strains." These are mechanisms of injury that in themselves reveal little about the severity of trauma. In a blunt trauma, for instance, the blow does not break the skin. More significant, just 2 of every 100 of these injuries required hospitalization or major medical care. Even among the incidents presented by those with the longest and most severe histories of abuse, only 4 in 100 prompted hospitalization. Nine percent of the injury episodes were fractures or dislocations, 3% involved human bites, and 2% involved rapes—problems that are serious regardless of whether the patient was hospitalized. But with these problems included, the emergency data still show that somewhere between 85% and 90% of the injuries battered women presented to the hospital would be classified as minor or moderate.[37] Police data are even clearer. Connecticut is typical in reporting that victims required medical attention in fewer than 3% of cases where police made a domestic violence arrest, obviously a serious class of cases.[38] Of more than 11,000 substantiated abuse cases reported to the military in 2001, 57% involved mild abuse (i.e., no injury or medical care), 36% moderate abuse (usually one visit to outpatient care), and 7% involved abuse classified as severe (requiring more than one visit or hospitalization).[39]

To critics of the battered data syndrome, the fact that most abusive violence is minor means that most abuse is minor and that justice intervention is only merited in a small proportion of cases.[40] A similar conclusion is implied by how rarely perpetrators are punished. In fact, the appearance of abuse as minor is the direct byproduct of applying a definition that disaggregates frequent assaults into discrete incidents, measures abuse by incident-specific harms, and ignores the cumulative impact of multiple assaults on individual victims. When the radar that guides decisions to arrest, prosecute, sentence, or treat is tuned to discrete, injurious incidents, as it is at hundreds of helping sites, somewhere between 85% and 97% of all abuse is missed and/or turned into a second-class misdemeanor.

Normalization

Another effect of targeting discrete, injurious episodes of violence against a background of frequent, noninjurious abuse is normalization, a defensive strategy by which helping professionals rationalize their failure to stem abuse by building the assumption that nothing will change into their response. Nineteenth-century feminist Frances Power Cobbe recognized the effects of normalization on a systems level, predicting that, if courts only responded to the most violent incidents, the average level of abuse seen as acceptable would rise. In fact, this is what happens today, when courts, hospital emergency departments, or Child Protective Services (CPS) agencies only intervene in injurious assaults.[41] On an individual level, normalization can turn intervention from the antidote to abuse to a predictable element in its evolution. On a systems level, it describes the paradoxical fact that intervention becomes more perfunctory, hence less effective, as abuse escalates.

Donald and Hazel Collins: A Case of Normalization

Prior to fatally stabbing Donald, her live-in boyfriend, Hazel Collins had called police on about 30 occasions, always after a beating. Police arrived at the house more than a dozen times, although often an hour or two after the call—a high response rate. On different occasions, they advised Hazel to go to her sister's, took her to the hospital for treatment, talked to Donald, told him to leave, or took him downtown. He was only charged twice, when he threatened a neighbor for "interfering in my business" and when he violated a protection order. On a third occasion, when her manager from the salon called, Donald was arrested for not letting Hazel go to work, but he was not charged. Because of jealousy, Donald locked Hazel in the bedroom if friends were coming over as well as after a beating. Before the second arrest, she called police from the locked bedroom. They found him in the kitchen playing cards with three friends in violation of a stay-away order. Instead of removing Donald or freeing Hazel, they waited until the next day, when they arrested him at his mother's house. On two occasions, Hazel was arrested along with Donald, though she was never charged.

For Hazel and so many other women in my practice, calling police, going to the emergency room, entering a shelter, or taking refuge with a neighbor or family member became part of the battering routine. Donald often resumed his assaults when police left. After the card playing incident, he tied Hazel's hands to the bed so she couldn't call again from the locked room. Often, the police came two or three times in one evening. Over time, the ritual of calling police, waiting, then dealing with the aftermath of their response aggravated Hazel's sense of being trapped, contributed to Donald's belief that his behavior would elicit few consequences, and supported Hazel's decision to end the abuse with one desperate act—by killing him.

Professional bias, incompetence, and inadequate training contribute to normalization. But its principal source is the narrow focus professionals take to the field. Even as the inconsistent and ineffectual police response normalized Donald's abuse and Hazel's reactions, suggesting she was the powerless victim he was trying to make her, so was the police response normalized in turn, as Donald's abuse and Hazel's calls became an expected part of policing in this South Carolina town. When abuse escalated and Hazel called more frequently, police "recognized" her as the type of person who would call police, and then be crying or bleeding when they arrived.

Gender Redux

No question in the domestic violence field excites more passionate disagreement than whether there is gender symmetry in partner violence. Dispute peaked early in the domestic violence revolution when Suzanne Steinmetz, a family sociologist and a codeveloper of the original NFVS, warned Congress that an epidemic of "battered husbands" remained hidden because men were too ashamed to report. Steinmetz's exaggerated claims were based on only two cases of supposed husband abuse reported to a local Delaware police department. But subsequent surveys bore out two of her claims, that a large number of women use force with their male partners and that almost none of these men seek help. Reticence is unlikely to explain why so few men ask for outside assistance. These same men freely report being hit to survey researchers, fill court records with complaints about mistreatment in divorce and custody proceedings, and insist they are the "real" abused persons in counseling.

Sociologist Murray Straus, another proponent of the battered husband thesis, offers a more plausible explanation for why so few abused men seek help, that women's assaults are less serious than men's.[42] There is solid evidence that men injure women far more often than women injure men and use the most severe forms of violence much more frequently. According to the NFVS, both the proportion of injury-causing assaults committed by men and their frequency are roughly six to eight times greater than those committed by women.[43] Meanwhile, the 1988 NSFH found women reported domestic violence related injuries five times as often as men.[44] According to the NVAWS, with the marked exception of knives, which both partners use equally, men are likely to use every other means of serious assault more often, including kicking, biting, choking, trying to drown, hitting with an object, "beating up," and threatening with a knife or a gun, with the ratios extending from 2:1 (for kicking and biting) to more than 14:1 (for beating up).[45]

These differences are impressive. But they do not account for sexual differences in reporting. First, a number of studies show little or no differences in severity or frequency. Among the 495 couples interviewed for the NFVS in 1985 in which at least one assault was reported by a female respondent, there were no significant differences between the mean number of assaults committed by men and women, in the number of assaults classified as severe (punching, kicking, attack with weapons, etc.) or in the likelihood of initiating an assault with a high probability of causing injury.[46] But even if *all* severe or injurious assaults were carried out by men and none by women, this would not explain the sex gap in reporting. This is because the vast majority of reported abuse incidents, fully 9 of every 10,

are neither severe nor injurious. At best, the greater severity of male violence may explain 10% of the huge discrepancy in help seeking.

Feminist Arguments

Feminist accounts of how men and women's violence differ are somewhat
more satisfying. As evidence of partner violence by women mounts, feminist authors have shifted from denying its significance to targeting its
specific contexts, motives, and meaning.[47] One theme is that men use violence instrumentally to gain an external end such as money or control,
whereas women use it expressively to discharge feelings of jealousy or rage
or are reacting to men's abuse. But what little research there is on partner
violence by women suggests that, although they are much more likely to
have a childhood history that includes sexual or physical abuse than men,
they assault partners in much the same context as men and with similar
motives and consequences.

The notion that only men use violence proactively reinforces paternalistic
stereotypes that discount women's capacity for self-interested aggression.
Virtually every perpetrator claims they were provoked, whether male or
female. According to reports from the 446 wives interviewed by the 1985
NFVS, however, their husbands struck first in 42.3% of the violent encounters
and they struck first in 53.1%. Even if we make the unlikely assumption
that all of the women are being defensive in the 49% of cases where violence is mutual, we are still confronted with the 25%–30% of cases where
women themselves report they were the sole party that used force.[48]
Critics rightly point out that the NFVS and similar population surveys
greatly overestimate female violence by including a range of behaviors
that women endorse on the survey but that neither they nor their partners
consider abusive. But this speaks to the meaning of male and female violence, not to its mechanical properties or dynamics.

The instrumental/expressive dichotomy is also simplistic. All partner
violence combines expressive with instrumental elements. Even when
men use violence to effect a particular end such as sexual conquest or getting a woman to hand over her money, it is also an expression of their sexual identity, a way to enact masculinity, and a response to the deeply felt if
culturally installed sense of loss, impotence, or emptiness excited by signs
of women's independence. Conversely, expressive explanations for violence
such as "I lost control" or was "overwhelmed" with frustration or anger
conceal the extent to which the contexts in which persons "let go" are
carefully selected to maximize gains and minimize punishment, the instrumental process counselors call "losing control to gain control." Similarly,
studies of women's motives show they use violence as often because "it
works" to affect some end as to express anger or frustration.[49] Women
who use force are slightly less likely than men to identify jealousy or a
desire to control or hurt their partner as their motive.[50] But given the fact
that the rationales persons offer for their behavior are selected to conform

to culturally endorsed roles, it is remarkable that women acknowledge these motives as frequently as they do.

Unless they use weapons, most women will get the worst of physical fights with men, though this is by no means inevitable. But even if they are hurt more seriously than their partner, like the men, many of my female clients see violence as a legitimate way to stand up for themselves, maintain their self-respect, and to demonstrate that assaulting them has a cost. This is a lesson some have learned in inner-city schools and communities where fighting is thought to be a better way to reduce the probability of subsequent conflict and violence, even if you lose, than letting it be known you can be had. Still, however similar violence talk by men and women may seem, female violence against partners is unintelligible apart from its leveling intent and effects in the face of relationships structured around sexual inequality. Oddly, this reality has been ignored even by researchers who study women's violence in relationships.

The Proper Measure of Abuse

The Continuous Nature of the Battering Experience

The cumulative effect of frequent but relatively minor assaults occurring over many years is that victims experience abuse as continuous or ongoing. A prior assault predicts subsequent assault better than all other risk factors combined and the near certainty that abusers will reoffend is the basis for shelter, safety planning, the issuance of protection orders, batterer intervention programs (BIPs), and numerous other interventions. Because this predictable course of conduct is reframed as recidivism, however, the justice and helping systems treat each incident de novo, an approach that fragments, trivializes, and confounds what is actually happening. As we've seen, when institutions interpret the repeated calls for help prompted by escalating abuse as the re-enactment of earlier events, their response becomes more perfunctory, reinforcing both the abusive dynamic and the view that the continuation of abuse in this relationship is inevitable and little can be done to stop it. The absurdity of the incident-specific approach is illustrated in communities where police assess an offender's risk by judging the severity of each incident, as they do in a number of English communities, identifying the same man as high risk on Monday and as low risk a week later. In states like Arizona and Connecticut, BIPs have become revolving doors through which the same perpetrators pass an average of five times or more. The most serious consequence of the incident-specific approach is the reduction of woman battering to a second-class misdemeanor for which no one is punished.

Starting with women's experience turns the prevailing definition on its head, replacing its emphasis on discrete, gender-neutral acts of injurious violence with a picture of an ongoing and gender-specific pattern of coercive and controlling behaviors that causes a range of harms in addition to injury. This reconceptualization has far-reaching implications for intervention.

Psychologist Paige Hall-Smith opened an empirical door to this new approach when she developed a reliable method to identify abuse based on how women experienced it rather than on its behavioral dimensions. Through in-depth interviews and focus groups with self-identified survivors, she found that battered women see abuse as a continuous experience that over time leads to disruptions in five areas of their lives which she summarized as (1) perceived threat, (2) managing, (3) altered identity, (4) entrapment, and (5) disempowerment.[51] Based on these dimensions, she constructed and validated the Women's Experience with Battering (WEB) Scale. Hall-Smith made no attempt to identify the objective correlates of these experiences. But simply treating physical abuse as ongoing rather than as repeated or recidivist completely changes how the problem is understood.

It is easy to see how women who suffer repeated assaults might experience it as ongoing. Interestingly, however, Hall-Smith found that women's experience of *continuous* abuse was independent of the frequency of abusive episodes and was shared by women who had suffered relatively few assaults (e.g., the two-thirds who view their abuse as a crime but who have not experienced serial victimization) as well as by those who had suffered hundreds. One implication of this finding was that women's sense of being entrapped in these situations was being elicited by something other than violence.

This possibility was first assessed in an ingenious experiment by psychologist Cynthia Lischick. For her doctoral research at Rutgers, Lischick questioned a representative multicultural sample of 106 young, unmarried women about their most difficult, hurtful heterosexual relationship, classifying women as battered only if they scored in the top third of the WEB scale, a cut-off point suggested by Hall-Smith. Next, she classified the partners of these women, using questions from the CTS to assess the use of violence and a Coercive Partner Profile (CPP) she devised to measure their use of control. The CPP highlighted isolation, intimidation, and control with questions about restricting access to friends, possessiveness, threats to friends, forced sexuality, and forcing a partner to account for her time. But it contained no questions about domestic violence. As the designers of the CTS would predict, partners of the 41 women whom the WEB scale identified as battered used more physical abuse than the partners of women in the other groups. Remarkably, however, where 29% of these abusive men used minor and severe violence and 15% used only minor violence, the majority of the abusive partners (56%) had used no violence of any kind. Because it relied on the presence of physical assault to identify someone as battered, the CTS correctly identified fewer than half of the battered women. By contrast, because both the violent and nonviolent partners of battered women used tactics to isolate, intimidate, and control their partners, the CPP could distinguish these women from women who had simply been hurt or had been in a bad relationship.[52]

Earlier, I described a population of older women identified by the Finnish National Survey as victims of mental torment. These women exhibited higher levels of fear, depression, and other problems than any other group even though they had not been assaulted by their partners for an average of 10 years. Although these problems might have been caused by their earlier physical abuse, Lischick showed that a similar profile of entrapment could be elicited even in the absence of violence and even in a population of younger women whose exposure to abuse had been of relatively short duration. The Finnish survey did not identify the etiology of mental torment. But Lischick's work pointed to the use of tactics to isolate, intimidate, and control women as key.

For decades, domestic violence researchers have approached violence as the independent means whose outcomes for victims had to be studied and managed. Prominent among these outcomes were injury, psychological dependence, and "power and control." But the work of Lischick and Hall-Smith and her colleagues suggested that a pattern of structural controls might be as much the context within which violence developed in abusive relationships, and so contribute to its emergence, as its consequence.

The shift in emphasis from repeated assault to understanding abuse as a continuous process that includes structural elements and has cumulative effects is more than a rhetorical sleight of hand. Jumping ahead for just a moment, consider how such a reframing might have helped to protect Danielle DiMedici, a young woman from Brooklyn, who was murdered by her abusive boyfriend.

The Murder of Danielle DiMedici

In September 1996, Danielle DiMedici was killed in her Borough Park, Brooklyn, home by James Parker, her former boyfriend. Parker's long history of domestic violence included documented incidents where he had cut her, punched her, beaten her with a club, and burned her feet with cigarettes. A recent, but noninjurious assault had prompted Brooklyn prosecutors to ask for $25,000 bail. Instead, acting Supreme Court Justice Joseph Bruno released Parker on $7,500 bond. On August 29, Parker abducted DiMedici from her home at gun point and held her captive for 8 days. In contrast to the earlier incidents, DiMedici claimed Parker was affectionate during the abduction and did not physically abuse her. This account frustrated the FBI and local law enforcement officials and they blamed the delay in the kidnapping prosecution on DiMedici's "ambivalence." After his release on bond, Parker called DiMedici nightly, threatening her and her family. In response, the Brooklyn District Attorney's Office provided her with extraordinary protection and even considered moving the entire family for safety. But when police withdrew protection based on mistaken information about Parker's whereabouts, he was able to break into her house and kill her and wound several others before killing himself. After the murder, New York Mayor Rudolph Giuliani and others harshly criticized Judge Bruno for not taking DiMedici's abuse more seriously. In his defense, Judge Bruno explained that he was following the widely accepted procedure of basing disposition on the degree of injury involved.

With the current framework, law enforcement officials behaved as well as could be expected, and the response by the Brooklyn prosecutor's office was exemplary. Even the low bond was reasonable from this perspective, because DiMedici suffered no serious injuries in the target assault as Judge Bruno pointed out. Parker's prior assaults on DiMedici were not before the court. Nor was the fact that he had served time for assaulting a previous girlfriend. To the contrary, lacking an appreciation of the ongoing nature of his abuse, officials interpreted DiMedici's claim that Parker had not used force when he kidnapped her or during her confinement as evidence that she was ambivalent about ending the relationship. Even though she and her mother had called the police frequently in the past, gotten a protection order, and cooperated fully in Parker's prosecution on other charges, the FBI projected its own frustration onto her by drawing on a well-worn stereotype.

This case exemplifies a number of core issues in this book, including how victims are blamed when they suffer the consequences of institutional failure. But the issue at hand is that the justice system could have responded far more aggressively had Parker's conduct been evaluated as a continuous course of malevolent behavior with a cumulative impact on DiMedici's level of fear and entrapment. From this vantage point, the current assault would be understood as an extension of Parker's prior bad acts against DiMedici, raising the level of crime with which he was charged. Focusing on entrapment and fear as cumulative effects of an ongoing course of conduct would also explain why DiMedici "cooperated" with his demands during the kidnapping without his having to use violence. Instead of being frustrated with DiMedici, the FBI and other authorities would now recognize the nonviolent nature of the kidnapping as proof positive that she had been deprived of autonomy as well as liberty by Parker. Because the kidnapping charge was pending when the assault occurred, the assault was also an attempt at witness intimidation, another serious crime. This connection was obvious to Danielle and her family, but was invisible to the authorities.

At this point, I ask readers to take two things on faith: that the pattern of intimidation, isolation, and control Lischick measured is unique to men's abuse of women and that it is critical to explaining why women become entrapped in abusive relationships in ways that men do not and experience abuse as ongoing. These tactics do not typify all forms of abuse. But if we assume this pattern is gender-specific, is used by a large number of men to coerce and control their partners, causes a range of harms independently of assault, and can set the stage for an escalation of violence, this would explain the principal enigma addressed by this chapter: why a seemingly straightforward definition of domestic violence has failed to provide a coherent picture of abuse or help us measure or manage it. The existence of a gender-specific pattern could also explain why population surveys that focus on violence produce a different picture of partner abuse than surveys that focus on crime, safety, or service delivery. The most influential school of survey researchers points to sex parity in partner violence. Feminist researchers insist the problem requiring public attention involves female victims almost exclusively. Could both groups be right?

Toward a Typology of Force in Relationships

Imagine a raging dispute between researchers and clinicians about why most persons who report chest pain to telephone interviewers never show up at the hospital and have a very different profile than those who do. The telephone interviewers describe chest pain sufferers as young, slightly overweight, but otherwise healthy working men and women whose complaints tend to be transient. These people are hypochondriacs say the clinicians. "Real" chest pain, they insist, can signal a life-threatening chronic illness that primarily afflicts older people and is associated with smoking, a familial history of heart disease, and a sedentary lifestyle. The researchers chide the doctors for generalizing from a small sample of extreme cases, an example of what is termed the clinical fallacy. A few persons might require high-tech treatment, they admit. But most chest pain can be relieved with a few over-the-counter pills, slightly raising the head of the bed, and cutting back on fast food.

Focusing on the single symptom, chest pain, makes it hard to distinguish heartburn from coronary heart disease, a problem with a very different etiology and consequence. Knowing more about the pain involved helps some, but not much.

A similar quandary confronted the domestic violence field. So long as abuse was equated with the use of force, the only credible way to explain why "clinical" cases that involved police calls and visits to the ER or shelters looked so different from the cases depicted by general population surveys was to refer to the level of force applied and its consequence. Ignoring the fact that the severity of violence predicted very little, each side assailed the other's methods and occasionally their motives. The debate shared elements of medieval disputes about the nature of God.

Then, like the child in "The Emperor's New Clothes," sociologist Michael Johnson pointed to a reality that was obvious as soon as he noticed it, that point-of-service research and population surveys generated different pictures of abuse because they were tapping different phenomenon.[53] Surveys like the NFVS or the Commonwealth Harris poll captured what he called "common couple violence," primarily where force is used to address situationally specific stressors, express grievances or other feelings, or resolve disputes. But crime, safety, and service-based research was identifying "patriarchal terrorism," the pattern described as mental torment by the Finnish survey, and shown by Lischick to include a range of tactics to control, isolate, and intimidate as well as injure partners. Johnson subsequently renamed his categories "situational violence" and "intimate terrorism."[54]

Because research in the field focused only on violence, Johnson had to piece together empirical support for his distinction from studies of physical abuse. Even so, he found that although men and women engaged in common couple violence in similar numbers, what little evidence there was of control suggested it was used almost exclusively by men. Johnson crystallized observations I and others had been making since the early 1980s. But he added a key point. Set within their proper frame of reference, the conflicting claims about the nature of force in relationships were equally valid, even with respect to women's use of violence.

Johnson's typology offered a gracious exit from two decades of methodological back-biting. But it did more. By suggesting that the presence of control distinguishes an important class of abusive behavior, his work swept aside the major tenet on which the domestic violence model relies: that the only significant variation in abuse that really matters involves the quantity of force applied. A key implication of Johnson's terminology is that situational violence and intimate terrorism have different dynamics and qualitatively different outcomes and so should be judged by different moral yardsticks. They also require a different response. Abuse should no more be considered a simple extension of using force than a heart attack should be treated as an extreme instance of heartburn

Redefining the Object of Concern: Distinguishing Fights, Assaults, and Coercive Control

Johnson's typology retains certain aspects of the dominant behaviorism. He believes that the violence used in intimate terrorism is consistently more severe than in situational violence. Moreover, his category of situational violence confounds two dynamics with very different significance, the ordinary fights that many couples view as legitimate ways to settle differences, and frank assaults where violence is used to hurt, frighten, or subordinate a partner, but control tactics are not. In fact, the force involved in fights, assaults, and intimate terrorism often has identical mechanical properties. As we've seen, moreover, the vast majority of violent acts in all forms of abuse are relatively minor. To distinguish abuse from fights, therefore, it is necessary to know not merely *what* a party does—their behavior—but its context, its sociopolitical as well as its physical consequence, its meaning to the parties involved, and particularly to its target(s) and whether and how it is combined with other tactics.

As we've seen, most partner assaults occur when couples are physically estranged. This reality is masked by terms like *intimate, domestic,* or *couple* violence that suggest abuse occurs in intact couples primarily or in relationships to which both parties share a comparable commitment. At the same time, what I term *the presumption of intimacy* affords former partners a type of access to and knowledge of their victim that is not normally available to strangers.

I use the phrase "coercive control" to describe the configuration Johnson calls intimate terrorism in part because the term was used by others several decades before Johnson's articles appeared to describe a similar situation (see chapter 7) and in part because it more accurately captures the tactics being deployed in this type of abuse, which are not intimate and have little to do with the tactics normally used by terrorists. In contrast to fights between relative equals where violence is used to settle conflicts, the perpetrators of partner assault or coercive control hope to suppress conflict or keep it from surfacing or to punish a partner for some perceived hurt or transgression, almost always by asserting the physical superiority of the person initiating the abuse. A marked lack of reciprocity characterizes both assault and coercive control. The difference is that in assault, dominance is accomplished through raw power alone, forcing a partner to apply a calculus of physical pain and suffering to reassess the benefits of past or future behavior, including resistance. Even when both parties use force and violence appears to be prompted by specific issues such as jealousy, partner assaults are always governed by the zero-sum assumption that only one party can "win." Sexual inequality plays some role in all three contexts. But whereas establishing or redressing inequalities may be a proximate aim in fights or assaults, the imposition of control in abusive relationships presupposes the unequal distribution of rights and resources even as the perpetrator takes the substance of inequality as the focus of his abuse, by imposing the victim's compliance with gender stereotypes, for instance. Asymmetry in sexual power gives men (but rarely women) the social facility to use coercive control to entrap and subordinate partners. Men and women are unequal in battering not because they are unequal in their capacities for violence but because sexual discrimination allows men privileged access to the material and social resources needed to gain advantage in power struggles.

Distinguishing fights from assaults is relatively straightforward. To most people, assaults are different because their targets *feel* assaulted and because their means, consequence, or frequency are so disproportionate to the grievances involved that they violate what the community regards as a legitimate way to address differences. Almost none of the men and only a tiny proportion of the women who report being hit to the NFVS, the NFHS, the Commonwealth Harris poll, and other general surveys seek or require outside assistance. This suggests that a good number of these assaults occur in the context of fights, a possibility that is supported by the extent to which couples report mutual violence. By contrast, the majority of those who report abuse to crime or safety surveys have sought outside assistance, suggesting they are primarily victims of assault or worse.

Distinguishing assaults from coercive control is much more difficult, in part because there is very little documentation of the extent to which control tactics are used in abusive relationships. An exception is the Quincy study of men arrested for domestic violence. Like these men, women arrested for domestic violence often have long histories of violence and substance use.[55] But the Quincy study also revealed that 6 in 10 of the men arrested had taken their partner's money as well as assaulted them and that more than half had restricted their partners in three or more additional ways.[56]

These data and additional evidence reviewed in chapters 7 and 8 suggest that at least 60% of the cases for which women seek help involve coercive control (estimates range from 45% to 79%). We can assume the remaining 40% involve partner assaults, although the actual proportion of abusive relationships limited to physical and emotional abuse is probably lower.[57]

Many of the puzzles created by the current definition are resolved when we omit fights from our consideration of abuse and subdivide the remaining cases into partner assaults and coercive control. Men's use of control tactics explains why even women who experience infrequent, minor, or even no assaults may nonetheless become entrapped in relationships where abuse is ongoing; why victimized women are many times more likely than victimized men to identify abuse as a crime or a safety concern, even when the similar levels of violence are involved; and why they are so much more likely to seek help. Because of its role in entrapment, control also makes women less able than men to effectively resist abuse or to escape physical abuse, increasing their vulnerability to violence, including fatal violence. The presence of control in a majority of abusive relationships, not men's greater physical strength or prowess, also explains why women's risk of abuse-related injury and death is so much greater than the comparable risks for men, why femicide has changed little despite the downward trend in severe partner violence against women, and why victims of battering present the unique profile of health, behavioral, and mental health problems described in chapter 4.

A clinician presented with chest pain in the ER would rule out the possibility of a heart attack before exploring less dramatic explanations such as heartburn. Confronted with incidents of minor violence, the professional's first responsibility is to determine if they are part of a larger regime of dominance. As a practical matter, applying a sheer calculus of means and harms to a history of force in relationships can usually distinguish fights from assaults. But because minor violence typifies both fights and coercive control, these patterns can only be distinguished in a historical context where the frequency of force over time is weighed alongside its interplay with tactics to intimidate, isolate, or control a partner. The prevailing emphasis on discrete incidents makes these distinctions impossible. Once violence is abstracted from its historical context, police, judges, and other providers are left with few options. They can do nothing about minor violence, thereby leaving both the least serious and most dangerous cases at bay, treat every case as serious, thereby loading the system with false positives about which little or nothing will be done in any case, or apply a straightforward calculus of harms, the strategy that led to tragedy in the DiMedici case.

The Relevance of a New Typology for Measurement

Nowhere is the sorry state created by the current definition more evident than in the failure to determine the incidence or prevalence of woman battering.

In the health sciences, *incidence* refers to new cases of a problem that arise in a given population in a specified time period, usually a year. If we know how often new cases of battering occur and whom they affect, we can calculate the risk that any given individual will be abused. Because prevention depends on stopping a problem before it emerges, we can only tell if prevention efforts are working if we already know how many new cases to expect. To determine incidence, we have to recognize a case and determine its onset. The onset of a problem can be identified subclinically, by the first appearance of "symptoms," such as an initial threat or assault; by meeting certain predetermined characteristics, as in a diagnosis for arthritis or AIDS; or when a problem is first reported. Decisions about how to define incidence have important implications for measurement and intervention. The child welfare caseload is disproportionately drawn from poor and minority women. So, when we rely only on CPS reports to define the incidence of child abuse, prevention efforts target disadvantaged communities.

Prevalence refers to the total number of active cases at a given time and is the key measure used to determine what resources are needed to manage a problem. Prevalence is the denominator when we want to know whether interventions are reducing the burden a problem places on the community.

In most crimes and illnesses with a very short duration, incidence and prevalence are interchangeable. A robbery ends when the thief leaves the premises. Most persons recover from the flu soon after its onset, making its incidence and prevalence virtually identical. Incidence and prevalence are also the same when problems resolve in a speedy fatality, such as in a homicide.

We only calculate prevalence separately from incidence when problems last for a nontrivial length of time while new cases continue to arise, increasing the total burden on the community in a given period. In these instances, prevalence (P) is calculated by multiplying the incidence (I) of a problem by how long it lasts on average, its duration (D), and is expressed by the formula $P = I \times D$. As long as there was no way to prevent the death of persons with AIDS, its incidence and prevalence were similar. Today, because of medical management, AIDS in the United States is a chronic health problem much like heart disease. Even if there are far fewer new cases of AIDS than of flu, the prevalence of AIDS and the resources it demands have increased dramatically because of its longer duration.

The confusion of incidence with prevalence in the domestic violence field began as soon as it adapted its case definition from criminology. Assuming that incidence and prevalence were interchangeable, researchers measured domestic violence as they would the flu—as an incident-specific problem that often recurred. The sum of violent incidents in a given year was alternately called the incidence or prevalence of domestic violence as it would be had we been measuring stranger assaults.[58] Between 17% and 25% of abusive incidents are isolated events. But "spontaneous remission" is atypical. In the Yale Trauma Studies, we found that if a woman had ever presented a domestic violence–related injury to the hospital, there was a 72% chance that her hospital visit during the study year was prompted by abuse and a 92% chance that she had presented at least one abusive injury at the hospital in the past 5 years.[59] Because the effects of abuse are cumulative, determining an appropriate response requires that we distinguish new cases from those that are ongoing. The NVAWS attempted to do this by asking about whether respondents had ever been raped, assaulted, or stalked, what is called lifetime prevalence. As we saw, this approach gives the prevailing confusion a historical dimension because it fails to distinguish persons whose abuse has ended from those who need help currently. This requires knowing when abuse started and how long it lasted.

An analogy to the measurement dilemma comes from early in the AIDS epidemic, when patients stricken with the disease presented a series of opportunistic infections. Until clinicians appreciated that a patient's susceptibility to these infections was a function of an underlying disease process and shifted to antiviral intervention, they were treated symptomatically and soon died. Because the current response to abuse treats each incident as discrete rather than as a manifestation of a chronic condition of entrapment, interventions have had little effect on women's long-term safety as we saw in chapter 2.

Estimating Abuse

If current research fails to address incidence and prevalence directly, it does allow us to approximate the "one number" that eluded the federal workshop.

In the Yale Trauma Studies, we identified 18.7% of the women who presented to our hospital with a complaint of injury as having been battered. Half of these women (54.5%) had presented at least one abusive injury during the year and just under 80% (14.6% of the total female population) had done so in the past 5 years, the figure we used to approximate the proportion of patients for whom battering was likely to be a current concern, the institutional prevalence. Among these women, the average time span between the first and most recent presentation of at risk injury—what we called their adult trauma history—was 7.3 years. This was a conservative approximation of the duration of their abuse because many of these women were undoubtedly abused for some time before coming to the hospital. Using the formula for prevalence, we estimated that the annual incidence of domestic violence in the hospital's female population was between 2% and 3%.[60] This meant that 14 to 21 of every 100 battered women who presented an abuse-related injury to the hospital were "new" cases. For the rest, between 79 and 86 women, abuse was ongoing.

Prevention requires a massive, community-wide effort. But these data tell us that effective early intervention by the health system could reduce the burden battering places on our health system by as much as 85%.

Thus, although prevention is certainly important, a sensible decision would be to target resources at early identification and effective case management.

Our estimates were based on a clinical sample and cannot be generalized to the population as a whole. Still, they come surprisingly close to approximations based on population-based studies. Studies with small, unrepresentative samples report the average duration of abusive relationships is 7.6, 7.78, and 7.86 years (compared to our estimate of 7.3 years), with the actual length of the relationships ranging from 6 months to 19 years.[61] A more conservative estimate comes from a longitudinal comparison of battered and nonbattered women by nursing professor Jacqueline Campbell. After interviewing battered women and following their relationships for just over 2 years, Campbell concluded that abusive relationships lasted 5.5 years on average. At the 2-year follow-up, 25% of the victims she interviewed were no longer being abused. But an identical percentage of the nonabused women she had used as controls were now being victimized.[62] Although the proportion of cases in Campbell's sample where abuse was ongoing was approximately the same as in our medical sample (75% to 72%), as was the rate of remission (25% vs. 21%), the incidence rate per year was more than 4 times higher than we estimated (approximately 12.5% vs. 2%–3%), almost certainly because we dated onset from the first incident recorded on the medical record.

To get at actual numbers, it is useful to recall that 25.4% of the women sampled by the NVAWS had been assaulted, raped, or stalked by a partner at least once as adults. Based on the hospital, community, and control studies, we can estimate that somewhere between 54% and 80% of these women remain at risk, yielding a very conservative prevalence of approximately 13.7% (137/1,000 women). Given an average duration of between 5.5 and 7 years, the most conservative estimate of incidence is between 2% and 3% per year (I=P/D), about what we found in the Yale studies. Extrapolating to the population indicates that battering may be a current problem for over 15.3 million women in the United States. This is considerably higher than the single-year estimate from the NVAWS, but considerably lower than the number of women they found had ever been victimized as adults. Somewhere between 2.2 and 3.3 million of these women are "new" cases, and around 500,000 of these women will escape further abuse after a short period. But for the vast majority, over 14.5 million women, battering is a continuing course of malevolent conduct that places them at great existential risk. Based on rough approximations of the ratio of assault to coercive control in the service population, we can estimate that 5.8 million of these cases (40%) involve partner assault and that the rest, 8.7 million women, are currently experiencing coercive control. These estimates are a first guess, are based on the lowest approximations provided by researchers, and are no substitute for solid research that applies an historical definition of abuse in a randomized population sample.

The Politics of Definitions

Definitions are the life-blood of social science. By declaring what sort of problem battering is, the violence definition determines whose knowledge is needed to understand and solve it, hence whose futures are tied to its fate. It determines to whom policy makers will listen, who will have access to external research funding and publication opportunities (hence to promotion or status), and who will benefit from the flow of clients and their fees. Change a root definition, and the political and funding landscape also changes.

But definitions do more than put food on our tables and resources in our hands. They also give a range of professionals the power to translate the jurisdictional authority the definition bestows into regulatory control over carriers of the problem. By privileging physical harms, the current definition ensures that only those persons who acknowledge violence in their lives will be deemed worthy of accessing opportunities for help and triaged accordingly, injured women here, perpetrators somewhere else, the process illustrated by the account of the California shelter in chapter 2. Because affected persons badly need assistance, they are constrained by this allocation process to present themselves, and even, as French sociologist Michel Foucault might say, to "know" themselves, in relation to the prevailing problem-related identity; fixing their attention on certain causes, consequences, or elements of their predicament and away from others; answering the questions put to them (but obviously not those that are not asked), and so producing "rates" and "cases" that validate the prevailing dogma. "Has your partner hurt you?" a medical resident asks her patient, and the question is echoed by police, judges, and researchers. In this way, women's experience is "storied," and the violence model is confirmed.

The process of shaping victims to fit images of their problems can be benign, as it was when drunks learned to assume the identity of alcoholics rather than criminals and recount a tragic history of downfall into addiction at Alcoholics Anonymous. But turning women's entrapment in personal life into the social problem of domestic violence has had the opposite effect, discounting the depth and breadth of their experience and excluding large numbers of victims by implicitly defining them as unworthy. Referring to the equation of abuse with violence, sociologist Walter DeKeseredy argues that "narrow definitions not only trivialize many abused women's subjective experiences, they also restrain them from seeking social support."[63] Without an "audience" for their victimization, the 8 to 10 million women experiencing coercive control in the United States remain in a twilight zone, disconnected and undocumented. This exclusion process reinforces the secrecy and isolation that are core tactics in coercive control.

In *Surviving Sexual Violence*, British social researcher Liz Kelly shows how difficult it is for women to develop a clear understanding of rape, incest, battering, and other sexual violations unless these problems are explicitly named. But she also emphasizes how the weight given to physical harm in most definitions of sexual violence confuses women who experience high levels of fear from seemingly normal (i.e., typical) acts of coercion or from sexual crimes that do not involve direct physical assault, such as exposure.[64] The same confusion currently afflicts victims of coercive control.

The violence definition of abuse has failed us. Women in my practice often conclude a lengthy history of coercion and control with the apology "I'm not really battered." What they mean is that the reality they are experiencing has no public audience and so that they have no way to give it voice. Until they do, the stories of battering they *do* tell must be interpreted dialectically, as a fragile synthesis of the dominant victimization narrative and the antithesis they are living.

4

THE ENTRAPMENT ENIGMA

In 1979, psychiatrist Alexandra Symonds, published an unusually candid article. When her profession dealt with families "where the main distur-bance was violence against the wife or sweetheart," she observed, they focused on how the women provoked their husbands, or how the women were getting satisfaction in some obscure way by being beaten. "The final proof of all this," she wrote, "was invariably a learned statement such as 'After all, why doesn't she leave him?'"[1] Symonds admitted that she, too, had been oblivious to the real situation of battered women earlier in her career. Although she had rejected the "myth of masochism" in favor of the woman-friendly ideas of Karen Horney and her school, she believed that the "dependent personality interacts with the aggressive, arrogant, vindic-tive personality in a mutually satisfying way." This theoretical explanation had served her as "a convenient way to push aside an unpleasant and painful condition."[2] Symonds believed her defensive response to victims of violence was widely shared.

A year before Symonds's article appeared, another psychiatrist, Elaine (Carmen) Hilberman, reported that 30 of 60 women referred to her for consultation at a rural clinic in North Carolina were being battered, often over many years. The referring clinicians had missed the abuse in all but four of these cases and focused instead on seemingly intractable behavioral or mental health problems.[3]

The psychiatric establishment in the 1970s believed women brought abuse on themselves because they were "masculine," "frigid," "overemo-tional" with "weakened ties to reality," or had "inappropriate sexual expression."[4] But by the late 1980s, the "myth of masochism" and other transparent accounts that blamed the "wife-beater's wife" for her abuse had been widely discredited, in no small part because of the work of feminist mental health professionals.[5] Empirical work by psychologists and social workers had demonstrated that battered women had a better sense of reality than their assailants and, compared to nonbattered women, were actually more "social," more "sympathetic," less "masculine" though not necessarily more feminine, exhibited greater ego strength, and employed a greater range of strategies to change their situation than nonbattered women in distressed relationships.[6]

And yet the same question, "Why doesn't she leave him?" or its obverse, "Why does she stay?" continues to gnaw at the moorings of the domestic violence revolution. The durability of abusive relationships remains their central paradox. Everyone knows or knows about women who have exited, then returned to abusive relationships, often multiple times. Approximately half of the women who utilize emergency shelter return at least once to their abusive partner.[7] For millions of women, violent partnerships, an oxymoron if there ever was one, is everyday reality.

"Honor killings" by fathers or brothers of women who have rejected their husbands remain common in Pakistan, Nigeria, and other fundamentalist societies.[8] During the current U.S. occupation of Iraq, even women who were kidnapped by insurgents have been killed by their families because of their "disgrace." Law, custom, and religion choke off the personal independence of millions of women in these societies from birth. But most women in liberal democratic societies are fully engaged in the market, enjoy full rights as citizens, and routinely end bad relationships for reasons much less substantial than life-threatening violence. This is illustrated by a remarkable statistic: between 1960 and 2000, the proportion of American women aged 20 to 24 who were married dropped from 70% to 23%.[9] Dramatic sexual inequalities remain deeply embedded in economic and personal life in the United States and other highly industrialized societies. But inequality should not be confused with subordination.

Because women have such ready access to rights and resources in liberal democratic societies, it is widely assumed that if abusive relationships endure, it is because women choose to stay, a decision that seems counterintuitive for a reasonable person. The logical explanation is that women who make this choice are deficient psychologically or in some other respect. Yet researchers have failed to discover any psychological or background traits that predispose any substantial group of women to enter or remain in abusive relationships. Battered women do suffer disproportionately from a range of psychological and behavioral problems, including some, like substance abuse and depression, that increase their dependence and vulnerability to abuse and control. As we will see momentarily, however, these problems only become disproportionate in the context of ongoing abuse and so cannot be its cause. This chapter deals with the entrapment enigma: why women who are no different from any of us to start, who are statistically normal become ensconced in relationships where ongoing violence is virtually inevitable, and are prone to develop a unique problem profile when they do so. Once again, the prevailing response confounds rather than illuminates women's experience.

Explaining the Duration of Abuse

There is no shortage of explanations for why women stay with abusive men. Because their family history or personality provide no answers, accounts focus on changes induced by the abuse itself, the relative status of the partners, and the dynamics in abusive relationships.

The most sophisticated explanation is that women's dependence on abusive men and the problems they develop in this context are byproducts of violence-induced trauma. Proponents of trauma theory hold that exposure to severe violence so overwhelms the ego's defense mechanisms that a person's capacity to act effectively on their own behalf is paralyzed, producing a post-traumatic reaction or a disorder such as post-traumatic stress disorder (PTSD) and a range of secondary psychosocial and behavioral problems. Trauma theory compliments earlier accounts of how violence-induced changes in a victim's personality make it difficult for her to exit an abusive relationship, particularly the theory of battered woman's syndrome (BWS), which ascribes women's entrapment to "learned helplessness," a form of cognitive distortion induced and reinforced by cycles of violence.[10] There are two alternatives to the psychological model: a feminist view emphasizing how the inculcation of sexist beliefs (such as the identification of marriage with feminine self-fulfillment) and persistent sexual inequalities foster women's dependence on abusive men, a variant on the inequality hypothesis discussed in chapter 2, and a sociological perspective that focuses on the intimate nature of abusive relationships and the extent to which the use of force to resolve disputes in these relationships is learned and supported by social norms.

These strands are woven together to form the dominant victimization narrative, a story that shows how women's beliefs and vulnerabilities make it virtually inevitable that they will stay in or return to abusive relationships. This story is given flesh and blood by the media. The TV producer consults a psychologist about an episode for the ABC police drama *NYPD Blue*. The result is state-of-the-art. The sister of a female detective appears at the station tearful and bruised, the result of a beating by her husband. The detective confronts her sister, then goes to the apartment and threatens to hurt the husband if he beats her again. The perp apologizes and promises to reform, seemingly confirming the sister's assurance that he is sorry. If this was an episode in *Law and Order: Special Victims Unit* or one of the new forensic shows such as *CSI*, a psychologist would explicitly identify the sister's gullibility with the honeymoon phase of the cycle of violence described by Lenore Walker. But even the older, more traditional audience for *NYPD Blue* senses that another explosion is inevitable. This faux knowledge, the fact that viewers imagine they know what the victim does not, makes us unwitting converts to the dominant narrative, fixing the enactment of learned helplessness in our minds as a frame for understanding other battered women we may encounter in real life. True to the narrative, the victim returns to her husband and is killed several episodes later. But is she a victim of her husband or of the dominant model? Even had the detective arrested the husband, because her sister would refuse to testify, the man would be quickly released, explode again, and probably take her life. Has our recruitment to the cognizante deepened our empathy for victims or further mystified the actual dynamics in abusive relationships? Is it the woman who is helpless or is it we, the audience, who feel impotent to protect this hapless victim? If the latter is true, what are the implications for the large segment of battered women and their partners in the audience? When a woman's confession that she is caught in the cycle is greeted with a sigh of recognition by her support group at the shelter, whose experience is being voiced? Is this her story or part of the meta-narrative we identified in the introduction?

Each of the explanations of why abuse continues applies to some battered women. Violence can disable coping responses and induce a range of problems, including paralyzing fear or a childlike dependence. Economic and related disadvantages often combine with traditional beliefs to inhibit women's desire to break off any relationship as well as their capacity to manage on their own.[11] Intimacy is a cherished value to millions of women, some of whom admit they will "take a beating" if they think things will eventually work out. But none of these explanations get at the heart of why abusive relationships endure.

Do Women Stay?

Underlying the question of why battered women stay are the beliefs that they have the opportunity to exit and that there is sufficient volitional space *between* abusive incidents to exercise decisional autonomy. As we saw in chapter 3, these beliefs are demonstrably false in the millions of cases where abuse is unrelenting, volitional space closed, or decisional autonomy is significantly compromised. An equally controversial presumption implicit in the question is that exercising the option to leave will reduce a victim's chance of being hurt or killed. In fact, around 80% of battered women in intact couples leave the abusive man at least once.[12] These separations appear to decrease the frequency of abuse, but not the probability that it will recur. Indeed, the risk of severe or fatal injury increases with separation. Almost half the males on death row for domestic homicide killed in retaliation for a wife or lover leaving them.[13] As we've also seen, a majority of partner assaults occur while partners are separated. So common is what legal scholar Martha Mahoney calls "separation assault" that women who are separated are 3 times more likely to be victimized than divorced women and 25 times more likely to be hurt than married women.[14]

The fact that separation is hazardous is not news to battered women. Many of my clients have told me they were never more frightened than in the days, weeks, or months after they moved out. Abused women are much less likely than the professionals whose help they seek to regard decisions about physical proximity as means to end abuse and much more likely to regard separation as a tactical maneuver that carries a calculated risk within the orbit circumscribed by assault or coercive control. The disjuncture between what victims and outsiders expect from separation remains a major obstacle to effective intervention and communication in the field.

Evidence that abuse victims call police, seek protection orders, turn to health providers, and enter shelters in huge numbers discounts the claim that they are reluctant to seek help. But their aggressive help seeking raises another troublesome question: why hasn't the proliferation of user-friendly services limited the duration of abuse in the same way antibiotics end strep infections? Again the answer has been sought by dissecting the victim's beliefs and behavior rather than the perpetrator's behavior or the inadequacy of the helping response. When the same victims call police repeatedly, repeatedly show up at the ER, or cycle in and out of shelter and the abusive relationship, it is hard to resist the conclusion that something is wrong with them. If advocates find this view politically untenable, it is continually reinforced by their experience. After receiving help, my clients have returned to live with and even married abusive men who raped them, stabbed them, burned them with cigarettes, tied them up and left them to die in a basement, killed their pets, or hurt their children. In a recent case, a senior at Hunter College beat her boyfriend with his own construction hammer during one of his dozens of assaults, leaving him partially paralyzed. Then, when she was out on bail, she married the man, apparently in response to pressure from his sister, because he promised not to testify if she did so, and because she felt guilt that he would no longer be able to earn a living. Even the most seasoned professionals are tormented by such cases. One common response is identified by Symonds and by Loseke's study of the California shelter, to manage frustration by applying pseudo-psychiatric labels such as "hypochondriac" or "woman with well-known complaints" to battered women, effectively isolating them from future help. In the Yale Trauma Studies, 80% of all such labels we found on women's medical records were applied to battered women.

Trauma theory offers a more helpful explanation: that women's failure to utilize services effectively is a byproduct of their abuse. By giving professionals a handle on why women have failed to extricate themselves from abusive relationships, trauma theory encourages them to provide supportive counseling and other resources to victims albeit with limited expectations about success. This approach has been particularly useful in countries (such as Finland and Denmark) or in service sectors (like mental health, child welfare, or substance abuse treatment) where "feminist" ideas remain suspect. But in shifting attention from the perpetrator's behavior to the victim's response, trauma theory can also discredit a woman's capacity for rational action while resurrecting the belief that her fate is in her hands.

Theories of Abuse

Explanations of why abusive relationships endure are inseparable from the three major accounts of battering: the sociological account that holds that violence against women is normalized in families, a feminist account closely identified with the battered women's movement, and the psychological perspective rooted in trauma theory. Each is constructed around a different dimension of the battering experience.

The Sociological Account

When the shelter movement began, there were only intriguing hints that battering was more prevalent than anyone suspected. Sociology had been largely silent about woman battering for a century when two of its number, Suzanne Steinmetz and Murray Straus, proclaimed the family was "a cradle of violence" at a 1970 meeting of the National Council on Family Relations.[15] The following year, Richard Gelles, a doctoral student at the University of New Hampshire, compared 40 couples labeled "violent" by a local agency to 40 neighboring couples. To his surprise, 37% of the comparison group had also experienced at least one violent episode and in five of the couples, violence was a "regular occurrence."[16] Based on this serendipitous discovery, Gelles speculated that assaultive behavior might be occurring in more than 7 million homes! Like his mentor, sociologist Murray Straus, he assumed that partner violence was rooted in family dynamics. "Not only does the family expose individuals to violence and techniques of violence," he wrote, "the family teaches approval of the violence."[17]

Over the next two decades, a range of scholars, many with ties to the research program at the University of New Hampshire, developed the body of work known as the family violence school. Sociologists had long distinguished the types of conflict endemic to and even supportive of primary relationships, such as families, from the violence that typified gangs and the criminal subcultures. The family violence school combined these two strands of research in a way that turned the notion of conflict on its head. Sarcastically dubbing the salutary view of aggression the catharsis approach, they insisted that even the mildest forms of force used in dispute settlement or to discipline children properly belonged on a continuum with child abuse, wife beating, and intimate homicide. To measure the occurrence of violence and abuse on this continuum, they developed the Conflict Resolution Techniques Scale (CRT), the first iteration of the widely used Conflict Tactics Scale (CTS). Families hosting the more dramatic forms of violence were called "violence-prone," a deviant subtype. But data indicating that at least some of these behaviors were virtually universal, with 80% of families admitting to spanking, for instance, suggested the family itself could be understood through its propensity for violence.

The family violence school offered an eclectic array of explanations for its findings, highlighting everything from the emphasis on individualism in the United States and the mass media's view that force was an acceptable salve for interpersonal problems to the sexual inequalities that persisted in marriage. If "the marriage license is a hitting license," they insisted, so too is the family the cradle in which violence on the street is born and raised, a claim that had particular salience for a country that was less than a decade removed from the urban rioting of the 1960s. The only causal postulate that could be tested was the assertion that violence witnessed or experienced by one generation leads to violence in the next, a belief that remains widespread despite the dearth of supporting evidence. The durability of violent relationships did not puzzle the family sociologists. However dysfunctional violent families might appear to outsiders, they stayed together because their members saw the use of force in response to conflicts as "normal, routine and generally acceptable." Their surveys validated this claim. The "violent family" was a stable and apparently self-enclosed, sociological type.

The Feminist Model

Ironically, the dissemination of results from the family violence surveys supported a rising consensus that women were the principal victims requiring help, not families or couples, and that men were the primary source of their problem. With a few marked exceptions, largely in response to the shelter movement, policy makers in the United States recognized abuse as a woman's issue and provided substantial funding to local services for women. By contrast, in Britain where the antifeminist views of Chiswick founder Erin Pizzey provided a counterweight to the National Women's Aid Federation (WAFE) and divided the refuge movement on critical policy issues, the government has emphasized state-initiated programs over direct funding for grassroots women's groups. Still elsewhere, in China and Finland for instance, local services, including most refuges, are administered by the traditional service sector rather than local women's groups.

The first feminist account of domestic violence since Cobbe's nineteenth-century tract on wife torture was Del Martin's *Battered Wives*.[18] Published in 1976 explicitly to support the nascent shelter movement in the United States, Martin drew a radical critique of patriarchy, identified the problem of its prevalence and duration with marriage primarily, emphasized its roots in women's status as male property, effectively critiqued the service response (particularly by police), and proposed far-reaching reforms, including enhanced employment opportunities for women. Following Del Martin's lead, several years later, Rebecca Emerson Dobash and Russell Dobash, American sociologists who had emigrated to Scotland, published *Violence Against Wives*.[19] Their account illustrated the myriad ways in which religion, law, and political institutions had supported violence against women, again highlighting the link between patriarchal power in society as a whole and unequal power relationships between men and women in marriage. Based on a large sample of police cases from Scotland, they showed that abuse was overwhelmingly directed by men against women and provided an incisive critique of how the service response actually contributed to abuse, a theme echoed by feminist advocate Susan Schecter, our work on the medical system, and in a range of articles on what sociologist Mildred Pagelow called "secondary battering."[20] Apart from Pizzey's insistence that women got entangled in abusive relationships because they had been made violence prone by their experiences in childhood, by the 1980s, the popular media were disseminating the feminist account of "battered wives" and advising women on how to "get free."[21]

The Psychological Account

Alongside criticism of the propensity for psychiatry to blame victims for their abuse, feminist clinicians targeted their profession's fear of strong, aggressive women and its corresponding tendency to project a male stereotype of how women should be (dependent, ambivalent, accepting) through an exaggerated emphasis on the professional role as helper. This approach put victims engaged in couples' treatment in the same double bind they were experiencing at home by communicating that they would get approval only if they were reliant, a role adaptation that could be catastrophic and even fatal. In an incisive critique of the family systems approach to battered women, psychologist Michele Bograd linked the projection of these female stereotypes to the use of quid pro quo behavioral contracts in which the husband promises to control his temper and the wife agrees to comply with some of his requests, usually by accepting limits on the independence he feels threatening.[22] The advocacy movement remains strongly opposed to the use of couples counseling, mediation, reconciliation, and other approaches that fail to recognize the imbalance in power that victims and perpetrators bring to the table.

Psychologist Lenore Walker's 1979 book, *The Battered Woman*, had a greater impact than any other work on how abuse victims are understood, represented by the media, and treated by the service system. In marked contrast to the academic tenor of most feminist writing on abuse, Walker combined dramatic case material with observations based on a study of women who had volunteered to be interviewed about their abuse.

Walker concluded that battered women could be differentiated from women living in marriages that were simply unhappy or unfulfilling by three factors: the "continuous occurrence of life-threatening incidents of violence"; psychosocial factors that bound battered women to their batterers "just as strongly as 'miracle glue' binds inanimate substances"; and a "cycle of violence" through which they passed at least twice, involving stages of tension, "explosion," crisis, and reconciliation.[23]

Reasoning by analogy to the demonstration of learned helplessness in animal experiments, Walker identified a similar pattern in the depressive sense of fatalism among her volunteer subjects. This was the miracle glue in her theory, created and reinforced by the two other facets of battering relationships she emphasized: continuous, life-threatening violence and a cyclical pattern of men's responses that left women confused about the real dangers they faced. She dubbed the resulting gestalt the battered woman's syndrome (BWS) and elaborated its various dynamics in several more books and numerous chapters and articles.[24] Walker identified herself as a feminist, acknowledged the importance of economic discrimination, described social isolation and other forms of coercion as "social battering," relied heavily on interviews with survivors, and positively assessed a range of interventions, including safe houses, arrest, and protection orders, that are central to the strategy advanced by advocates. But the single thread that unified her work and was widely publicized is that women stay with abusive men because they are rendered helpless and dependent by violence.

The diagnosis of PTSD offered a clinical account of women's psychological and behavioral reactions to violence that was more nuanced than the BWS model and more closely linked to traditional psychiatric theory. Like BWS, it was designed to explain why almost anyone might develop clinically significant symptoms when confronted with extreme violence or other events that fall "outside the realm of normal human experience." To paraphrase concentration camp survivor Viktor Frankl, "in an abnormal situation, it is normal for persons to respond in abnormal ways."[25]

Three Approaches, One Theme

These models seem worlds apart. Sociology pictures the family as a battleground from which alarming rates of pathology emanate, largely because all family members are socialized to accept force as a legitimate response to tension and conflict. Looking at the same familial arena, feminists trace the durability of abusive relationships to a hierarchical structure (sometimes identified with patriarchy) through which males translate their superior social power into authority over women and children and the sexist ideology that supports this hierarchy. In trauma theory, women stay because they develop a repressive syndrome of psychological dependence induced by repeated acts of severe violence.

The interventions these theories support also differ. The family violence approach favors counseling over arrest and supports cultural changes that challenge normative support for violence as a means of dispute settlement. Feminists favor broad-based challenges to sexual inequality as a long-term strategy and a combination of community-based, criminal justice, and governmental strategies to empower female victims and hold perpetrators accountable in the short run. The most common use of BWS is the battered woman's defense mounted to represent victims who are charged with crimes related to their abuse.

Despite these differences, what is most striking are the assumptions these accounts share about the origin, dynamics, and consequences of woman battering, what I have identified with the domestic violence model. In all three approaches:

- *Woman battering is equated with severe physical violence.* Differences center largely on what motivates violence and in what ways men and women participate.
- *Domestic violence is sited in the family and marriage.* Even feminist writers tend to equate victims with "wives."
- *Wives are identified as what the Dobashes call "appropriate victims" because of their special vulnerability as women.* This special vulnerability is alternately ascribed to men's greater strength, the status of married women as male property, sexual inequalities in power, or psychological deficits induced by the violence itself.
- *The harms caused by battering are associated with the physical and psychological consequences of severe violence.* Researchers differ in which secondary problems they emphasize, and family violence researchers rarely discuss psychological dynamics at all. But even those who reject Walker's model of BWS agree that these effects are elicited by "traumatic violence."

Each of these propositions is partially valid. Marriage and the family are critical contexts for abuse; some women do normalize abuse or suffer a depressive syndrome of dependence; and domestic violence is often the principal expression of battering and can be both traumatic and injurious. Still, whether they are considered separately or as part of a larger paradigm, these propositions provide neither an accurate description of woman battering and its effects nor a credible account of why abusive relationships endure.

The Yale Trauma Studies: The Health Consequences of Entrapment

The three models were already available in the late 1970s when Anne Flitcraft and I set out to identify the scope and health consequences of woman battering by reviewing the medical records of women who came to Yale's emergency service complaining of injury. We had met dozens of battered women here and abroad who were anything but the hapless victims of circumstance depicted by Walker. But we turned to the emergency room for our subjects because we shared the view that violence and injury were the defining moments of abuse. Our work is summarized at length elsewhere, and other researchers have used more direct methods to identify abuse in health settings.[26] I review our major findings here to illustrate that the outcomes uniquely associated with the durability of abuse have yet to be adequately explained.

Findings

Our most dramatic results seemed to confirm the identification of partner abuse with violence. Of the 3,676 female trauma patients in our random sample, 18.7% had come to the emergency room with at least one abuse-related injury and these women accounted for 40% of the more than 5,000 injuries ever presented by the total sample, making partner violence the single major source of injury for which women sought medical attention. The hallmarks of these injuries were their frequency, duration, and sexual location. Battered women averaged one ER visit a year (compared to an average of one in the lifetime for nonbattered women), and 14% had been to the emergency service more than 10 times with trauma.

The research also supported another tenet of trauma theory—that battered women suffered a distinct profile of medical, psychosocial, and behavioral problems. Compared to nonbattered women, battered women were 5 times more likely to attempt suicide, 15 times more likely to abuse alcohol, 9 times more likely to abuse drugs, 6 times more likely to report child abuse, and 3 times more likely to be diagnosed as depressed or psychotic.[27] Absolute numbers were as significant as relative frequencies. Nineteen percent of all battered women attempted suicide at least once, 38% were diagnosed as depressed or having another situational disorder, and 10% became psychotic. As trauma theory predicted, their problem profile only became distinctive after battered women presented an abuse-related injury and developed in tandem with the history of violence. The vast majority of women who had ever been abused still appeared to be in abusive relationships either at the current visit or in the recent past. And the length of their trauma history was directly correlated to the frequency of injury visits, and the emergence of the multiproblem profile. It seemed incontrovertible that violence and injury were the key markers of abuse, that secondary problems developed in tandem with escalating violence, and that it was the combination of violence and the secondary problems it elicited that explained women's entrapment.

From the vantage point of their medical records, women's multiproblem portraits unfolded with tragic predictability. Shortly after an abusive episode, a woman would typically reappear with a range of medical complaints, then with AOB (alcohol on breath) or drug use, then with another injury, a suicide attempt, as depressed or with a presentation of "nerves." This progression seemed so automatic, the rhythm with which self-destructive behaviors followed injury seemed so natural, and the cumulative impact of professional intervention so minimal that the domestic violence model appeared to be validated, though no particular explanation appeared more credible than others.

Anomalies

Despite lending some support to the view that violence could cause a range of psychosocial problems, our research contradicted key tenets of the dominant model. There was little or no evidence that battered women suffered from learned helplessness or that abuse occurred in the context of marriage or intimacy, for instance, and the connection of violence to trauma, women's secondary problems, and their entrapment with abusive men was tenuous at best.

To begin, the failure of health professionals to identify abuse accounted for the paucity of official cases, not women's reluctance to seek assistance, which they did in large numbers and more promptly than victims of stranger assault or car accidents. Clinicians made an occasional note that a woman had been "beat up by boyfriend." Because they were more concerned with the mechanism of injury (such as "hit with ashtray") than its source, however, domestic violence was mentioned in only one abusive episode in 40. Of 429 visits battered women made to the psychiatric emergency services, for example, abuse was identified at only 25 and never listed as a diagnosis, an even lower proportion of properly identified cases than in Hilberman's North Carolina sample. The clinical facts inscribed on medical records portrayed women whose souls were crushed by an inscrutable and hostile other. But their passivity and incomprehension as these facts accumulated in their presence made clinicians complicit in the construction of battering in the same way that the National Guard troops who disregarded pleas for emergency food and water were complicit in the suffering of those who had been displaced by the flooding in New Orleans following Hurricane Katrina.

Nor was marriage or the family the typical context for abuse. Instead, the vast majority (73%) of victims identified themselves as single, separated, or divorced. Married women were less likely to report abuse than any group except widows.

Nor was the violence women suffered the kind normally thought to elicit trauma. All of our subjects had come to the ER complaining of injury. But only 1 injury in 50 was serious enough to require hospitalization, and there was no evidence of injury at all in 10% of the cases. Their multiple sequelae suggest these cases were serious. But it was not severe violence that made them so.

The secondary problems victims developed in the context of being abused presented the strongest evidence they had been traumatized.

Alcohol or drug abuse and depression were among the problems that clearly contributed to women's entrapment. But the vast majority of women did not develop these problems. The more we learned about the extent and devastating impact of coercive control, the more remarkable it seemed that only 10% of abuse victims experienced a psychotic break, that 80% did *not* attempt suicide, and that 60% were *not* depressed. In fact, in multiproblem caseloads like the child welfare system, battered women look comparatively problem-free compared to other women. Among Child Protective Services (CPS) cases in New York City, 84.5% of the domestic violence victims had no mental health problems, and battered mothers were half as likely to be abusing drugs as nonbattered mothers (11.3% versus 19.4%) or both alcohol and drugs (1.4% versus 2.0%).[28] Despite long histories of abuse, the vast majority of women in shelters continue to function and parent normally.[29]

Nor was it clear that violence was the principal cause of the secondary problems battered women developed. Being hit repeatedly can be infuriating, frustrating, or depressing and may push women who are already using drugs into addiction by removing their capacity to control their use. But the relatively minor nature of the force to which our patients were subjected made it highly unlikely that coercion was the sole or even the major stressor in these cases.

Hundreds of hospital patients in our samples had been mugged, assaulted, and/or raped by strangers, and many had been beaten up on multiple occasions. We knew of numerous cases in which men had been assaulted, shot, or stabbed by their female partners and of women and men who had been assaulted by same-sex partners. But there was no clinical or research evidence that these victimized groups developed anything like the complex of problems we found among battered women, let alone did so in similar proportions. Some yet-to-be-identified process other than violence was clearly affecting these battered women. Identifying this process might explain their vulnerability to abuse, its duration, and the emergence of the distinctive problem profile.

The Economy of Trauma

Trauma theory had originally been designed to resolve precisely this puzzle, namely, why an otherwise normal population developed a range of problems in the absence of any underlying disease process. But both Walker's learned helplessness model of depression and the traditional model of PTSD were ignited by severe violence. The classic precondition for PTSD is exposure to an event that "involves actual or threatened death or serious injury" and that induces "intense fear, helplessness or horror."[30] The unique quality of traumatic experiences like natural disasters, wartime atrocities, or rape lies in their economic dimension. The sheer intensity of the unexpected and statistically rare event makes it impossible to assimilate, accommodate, or defend against using normal mental processes. No sooner are coping mechanisms mobilized (the fight or flight response) then they are overwhelmed, eliciting the sort of devastating sense of impotence so vivid among victims of Hurricane Katrina in 2005. The exposed individual fixates on the event in memory, effectively freezing it in time, and attempts to ward off its most disturbing features, particularly the feelings of fear and helplessness in its presence, through somatization or other symptom formation, anxiety (a warning sign) in the face of seemingly similar events, and active attempts to avoid the recurrence of the trauma through constant or *hyper*vigilance. In addition to hypervigilance and avoidance, the ego employs other defensive and adaptive maneuvers, such as repression or loss of affect (feeling), separating or splitting the traumatic memories and feelings from other emotions (dissociation), and even preemptive violence. Traumatic events periodically resurface despite these efforts, either as distinct memories (reliving the trauma) or as a wellspring of feelings (flooding) that disrupt an individual's composure at unexpected times (intrusion). Additional reactions included under a PTSD framework include anger, inability to concentrate, reenactment of the trauma in disguised form, sleep disturbances, a feeling of indifference, emotional detachment or attachment disorders, and profound passivity in which the person relinquishes all initiative and struggle, a state very much like learned helplessness.[31] When the PTSD model was extended from Vietnam veterans who had witnessed atrocities to victims of sexual assault, child sexual abuse, and battering in the 1980s, the economic emphasis was maintained. Dysfunctional outcomes were gauged to the severity of traumatic exposure and the frequency of severe violence, what were called their "traumagenic" dynamics.[32]

The noninjurious and disparate nature of most abuse-related violence made a straightforward application of this calculus difficult. The prevalence, frequency, and duration of abuse in relationships also makes it difficult to apply a classic understanding of trauma as a time-limited event outside the realm of normal experience. Recognizing that the traditional model failed to capture "the protean symptomatic manifestations of prolonged, repeated trauma," psychiatrist Judith Herman introduced a variation on the official formulation that she called "complex PTSD."[33] Complex PTSD recast the original symptom categories as hyperarousal (chronic alertness), intrusion (flashbacks, floods of emotion, hidden reenactments), and constriction, "a state of detached calm . . . when events continue to register in awareness but are disconnected from their ordinary meanings" and linked these symptoms to a protracted depression. Sufferers of complex PTSD oscillate emotionally between floods of intense, overwhelming feeling and states of no feeling at all, a pattern that is reflected in personal relationships that alternate between desperate dependency and complete withdrawal.[34] Over time, intrusive symptoms diminish and constrictive symptoms dominate, leading to a degree of restraint on inner and outer life that may mimic an enduring personality characteristic.

The fear elicited by the traumatic events also intensifies the need for protective attachments, leading some women to unwittingly move from one abusive relationship to the next. Some sufferers may cut themselves or provoke violent incidents, if only to induce the sense of detachment or disconnection that magically protects them from anxiety.

Lenore Walker and Judith Herman take an ethical as well as a therapeutic stance that clearly fixes ultimate responsibility for harm on the perpetrator, shifts attention from a victim's personality to what has been done to her, and hence to her safety, and makes clear that any normal person could exhibit an identical reaction to similar trauma. But does trauma theory resolve the dilemma faced by Symonds and her cohort of practitioners or merely cast it in a different guise?

Does Trauma Theory Explain Entrapment?

The most general claim of PTSD theory is incontrovertible—that extreme events, including exposure to life-threatening violence, can elicit clinically significant transient and/or long-term reactions in otherwise healthy persons. These reactions can extend from the terror and helplessness captured by diagnoses of BWS and PTSD to major depressive, sexual, and dissociative disorders; cognitive changes in how one views oneself and understands the world, including the occurrence of violence; and relational disturbances, most dramatically illustrated by the Stockholm syndrome and other forms of traumatic bonding found among hostages and sexually abused children, where escalating violence actually increases a person's attachment to the abuser. To accommodate this range of responses, trauma theory has been increasingly applied to a broad spectrum of events and resulting conditions, ranging from brief stress reactions where no intervention is required through a condition of dissociation and chronic psychic paralysis.

Herman's revision of trauma theory retains the direct causal link between the continuous occurrence of life-threatening incidents of violence or prolonged repeated trauma and the clinical outcomes identified as criteria for BWS or PTSD. Several studies confirm that many battered women suffer from the symptoms of complex PTSD (as described by Herman) or classic PTSD (as outlined in the *Diagnostic and Statistical Manual of Mental Disorders*, IV-R [DSM-IV]), particularly if they have been sexually as well as physically assaulted.[35] These victims reexperience trauma, avoid events that remind them of previous assaults, and exhibit numbing and increased arousal and anxiety. Other studies suggest a higher than normal prevalence of psychosexual dysfunction, major depression, generalized anxiety disorder, and obsessive compulsive disorders among battered women, all consistent with a PTSD framework.[36] But there is no evidence from population-based or controlled studies that full-fledged BWS and/or PTSD are widespread among battered women, that they are more common in abuse cases than other psychological problems, or even that they are more common among battered women than among other population groups.

Each of the women whose cases are summarized in part IV suffered repeated and severe violence, though only Donna saw a doctor for assault-related injury (a sprained finger) and only Bonnie was ever hospitalized (after being stabbed in the neck with a hair pick). Like many other defendants in my caseload, each exhibited symptoms of PTSD, though whether as the result of violence or other factors was not clear. Bonnie was diagnosed with PTSD, though the court found this unconvincing as I did. Laura's enactment of household rituals under Nick's command suggested she was suffering from Stockholm syndrome, an example of traumatic bonding. But evidence from the Yale Trauma Studies, research with veterans, and population studies indicate that the PTSD constellation is only one of many reactions to stress. As forensic psychologist Mary Ann Dutton notes, PTSD excludes such common but complex psychological sequelae of victimization as alterations in affect regulation, consciousness, self-perception, perceptions of perpetrators, relations with others, and systems of meaning, alterations provisionally referred to in DSM-IV as disorders of extreme stress not otherwise specified.[37] Using the Minnesota Multiphasic Personality Inventory (MMPI), Dutton and her colleagues identified five distinct profile types among battered women in counseling, indicating different patterns of psychological functioning, including a profile considered "normal."[38]

Judy Herman and Mary Ann Dutton write eloquently about the unequal dispersion of sexual trauma, and hence of its consequences, due to sexual inequality. But the economic emphasis in trauma theory and its individualized focus on a victim's reactions make it difficult for the model to incorporate this insight into assessment or treatment. The related emphasis on extreme violations leads to a parallel problem, a distortion of the battering experience that highlights severe violence at the expense of the more diffuse and more typical forms of abuse. It is hard to see how a conspicuous form of evil can be both "banal" in Hannah Arendt's classic label for Adolf Eichmann and "traumatic." Where feminist psychologists tend to view PTSD as a transient response to oppression, the PTSD I saw among Vietnam veterans during my clinical training was a chronic, largely untreatable condition almost always confounded by a history of substance abuse. To the feminist clinicians, a diagnosis of PTSD signals the need for enhanced advocacy efforts as well as supportive therapy. In practice, however, it is increasingly used as a substitute for broader interventions and as a justification for treating the victim rather than sanctioning the perpetrator, a situation social work professor Stephen Rose and his colleagues call "disguised betrayal."[39]

Even where clinical evidence points to a woman's entrapment due to trauma, a broader understanding of the abuse experience often suggests an alternative account. In Walker's schema, victims are entrapped by learned helplessness after at least two cycles of violence, largely because they accept their partners' promises to reform. But among the 14% of battered women who report experiencing the full cycle Walker describes are many who decide not to pursue outside options because they fear others will accept their partner's version of events, not because they do, a fear that is regularly reinforced in family and criminal courts where a range of professionals discount allegations of abuse.

Post- or "Intra"-Traumatic?

The classic applications of the PTSD model are to cases where the traumatic episode(s) and the post-traumatic reaction(s) can be clearly demarcated as in stranger rape or exposure to atrocities in war. Even in complex PTSD, the prolonged trauma is assumed to be over when symptoms appear. Because coercion and control often continue in the face of separation and other events normally thought to signal the end of an abusive relationship, however, a victim's reasonable reaction to ongoing coercion and control can easily be misinterpreted as post-traumatic rather than adaptive or *intra*traumatic. One of the earliest links of PTSD to violence against women was the classic account of rape trauma syndrome, where victims evidenced hypervigilance, "exaggerated" fears, depression, distrust of others, withdrawal from close relationships, and a sense of impending doom after a sexual assault.[40] As part of the Yale studies, medical researcher Martha Roper, MD, found that an abusive partner was the source of a third of all rapes in the hospital population and half of all rapes to women over 30.[41] For these victims, symptoms that could easily have been interpreted as post-traumatic reactions to rape were really adaptations to ongoing abuse. Bonnie's psychiatrist diagnosed her dramatic weight loss in the weeks after Lessup moved out as a post-traumatic reaction. What he did not appreciate was that Lessup continued to stalk and threaten her, even hiding in wait for her in a tree outside her home.

Beyond Trauma Theory

If traumatic violence is not the source of women's problem profile, what is? The Yale studies provided only a few clues.

The problems women presented in the hospital studies suggest a pattern of chronic and diffuse stress that has little in common with the more focused and intense trauma anticipated by BWS and PTSD. The vast majority of health visits by battered women were to nonemergent medical sites. Instead of injury, they involved headaches; chronic pain syndromes; gastrointestinal complaints; atypical chest pain; hyperventilation; sleep, mood, and appetite disorders; requests for tranquilizers or sleeping pills; anxiety disorders; agitation; or reports that they felt immobilized. These problems are consistent with the high levels of fear identified with mental torment in the Finnish national survey. The stressors in these cases are clearly ongoing, almost certainly involve nonphysical factors as well as coercion, and are sufficiently serious to drive a substantial subgroup of otherwise normal women to self-medicate with drugs or alcohol, attempt suicide, and develop a range of somatic problems.

Gender Entrapment

Trauma theory originated in an attempt to externalize the source of women's problems in abusive relationships. But it is increasingly being used to support mental health rather than justice intervention and as an alternative to more political, advocacy-oriented approaches, particularly in Scandinavian countries where women's high rates of labor market participation suggest structural inequalities are not a major issue. Although the prevalence of PTSD among abuse victims can be measured, there is no easy way to assess the relative contribution of trauma to women's entrapment, particularly compared to structural facets of the environment (such as sexual discrimination), the culture (such as sexism), or the abusive situation (such as control over necessities). The most convincing version of how violence and structural inequalities are interrelated at the individual level is provided in *Compelled to Crime*, sociologist Beth Richie's ethnographic comparison of three groups of abused women incarcerated at Rikers Island in New York, two black and one white.[42] Contrary to stereotype, the black women who remained in abusive relationships had been the "stars" in their families of origin, were raised to believe they could readily tackle any problems thrown at them, enjoyed high self-esteem, and exhibited identities as competent, resourceful, and potential-filled girls who aspired to success. When these stars bumped up against the limits set by gender and race discrimination at school or at work, their extraordinary capacities were displaced into their relationships with destructive effect: modifying their social expectations, they became absorbed in the private sphere where success meant "making things work" at home, even if this entailed supporting abusive partners financially and emotionally. Raised to believe they could change the world, when these women were refused entry as fully entitled adults, they determined to use their skills to change the men in their lives, often against incredible odds. By contrast, the white and African American women who had lower expectations about themselves and their relationships to start were more likely to leave or drift away from failed relationships when abuse occurred.

Obviously, millions of white and minority women become entrapped in abusive relationships who are not stars and who reject the sexist myth that they are responsible for fixing men. But the link Richie and other feminists provide between the enactment of gender and the microdynamics of entrapment in personal life is a crucial bridge from the conventional paradigm to a fully drawn model of coercive control. A broader view highlights the extent to which men can subordinate women in personal life because of the greater shares of relative income, education, and other resources they bring to bear in relationships and how this disadvantage is reproduced in ways that weaken their position in the market.[43] But the particularity of battering takes shape against women's newly won equality as well as continuing race and sex discrimination. Even women who are not individual stars share in the social possibility all women in liberal democratic societies bring to relationships today, that for the first time in history they can develop, express, and fulfill themselves as subjects without mediating their agency through personal dependence on significant men.

It's the Men, Dummy

When pressed, advocates will turn the question "Why do they stay?" on its head and remind us that, since abusive men create the problem, we should ask why *they* do it. This rephrasing makes sense. At best, equating the durability of abusive relationships with women's decision to stay is inexact; at worst, it is a victim-blaming formulation that masks the extent to which the dynamics in abusive relationships are shaped through continual negotiation about proximity and distance. A range of researchers have speculated about what makes abusive men tick, why they behave differently from the majority of men, or what factors set the general climate in which men and/or women feel they have permission to hurt the significant others in their lives. This literature variously roots male violence against women in biology or male nature; childhood exposure to parental violence, character disorders, or psychopathology; our culture's emphasis on violence as a solution to interpersonal problems; and the socialization process by which boys exposed to violence integrate this learning into their ideas of manhood.

Far more promising is an emerging descriptive literature drawn from ethnographic research or clinical experience with offenders and/ or their victims. The best work in this genre is Lundy Bancroft's popular account *Why Does He Do That?* Bancroft describes how some boys develop the attitudes, beliefs, and habits of abusive men. But his primary focus is on the behaviors themselves, including myriad control tactics, and the benefits he derives.[44] Identifying the concrete privileges men glean from battering shifts attention from deterministic or essentialist interpretations of manhood to an understanding of abuse as a rational, instrumental, and gendered "performance" or "enactment" of masculinity in modern societies.[45]

Much of the tactical repertoire men deploy in abusive relationships is only intelligible as a way for men to protect their investment in a partner in response to her attempts to separate or get help. To this extent, it is men who *stay*, not their partners. Regardless of whether their dependence on their partner is primarily material, sexual, or emotional, there is no greater challenge in the abuse field than getting men to exit from abusive relationships. It is common in my caseload for men to stalk their partners before or after separation; harass them at work; park outside their job; hold children hostage when a partner goes to the hospital; repeatedly call them at work or at home; leave threatening messages on their cell phones; show up at their new residence at odd hours; perform periodic "house checks" or "inspections"; break in and leave anonymous "calling cards"; demean them to business clients, co-workers, and family members; cancel or run up debt on their credit cards, forge their names on personal checks, and raid their bank accounts; show up unexpectedly at social or family gatherings; move in next door; take a job in the same workplace; appear spontaneously at the children's school or soccer game without notice; check their mail; hide outside their apartments; and hire or solicit friends to watch or follow them. In a recent murder case, the woman ended the relationship with her boyfriend because she learned he was having an affair. He broke into her brother's downstairs apartment and tapped into the upstairs line. When the brother—who was only pretending to be asleep—told his sister about the surveillance, the boyfriend killed him. As strange as it may sound to say this, abuse is hard and dangerous work, in no small part because women have far greater access to support and resources than they did in the past. To establish their regimes of dominance, Nick (chapter 9), Frank (chapter 10), and Lessup (chapter 11) expended thousands of hours in surveillance, rule making, and enforcement. That women are more likely to be killed by partners than men is small comfort to the perpetrators who *are* killed or seriously hurt by victimized partners. Men take up these challenges for three compelling reasons: because women's gains threaten the privileges they believe are their due simply because they are men, because women's gains increase the potential rewards if abuse is successful, and because they can think of no equally effective way to secure these privileges and benefits.

The public continues to ask "Why don't they just leave?" But the question almost all of my female clients press on me is "Why did *he* do it?" My answer highlights the proximate benefits men get from coercion and control. When Nick took Laura's money to support his gambling habit (chapter 10) or set up the embezzlement scheme in which she was charged, or Lessup refused to leave Bonnie's home unless she paid off a car loan and gave him the car, I made the parochial assumption that they were motivated by material gain. This explanation does not satisfy the women I work with. What they really want to know is why men go to such elaborate lengths to attain these benefits and why they choose these benefits over the more easily accessible and arguably far more satisfying rewards to be gleaned from intimacy and trust. On one occasion, Nick took Laura for a drive, told her he regretted past abuse, and asked her nicely to loan him money. When she refused, he became furious and beat her, clear evidence of the instrumental nature of his violence. But Nick's material interests do not explain why he devised an elaborate set of rules to govern her every move in the house or why Frank set up a logbook for Donna. It is tempting to speculate about what specific constellation of biology, personality, culture, and social constraints move some men to assume control over their partners as their personal project and others to embark on a different life course. If the focus on violence leads naturally to discussions of biology, aggression, and psychiatric problems, the link between these factors and the complex, highly instrumental patterns of isolation and control evident in coercive control is far more tenuous. I have worked with dozens of abusive men and spent countless hours listening to their partners describe their abusive behavior. Yet I am no less puzzled today than I was when I began this work about why specific men resort to abuse and others do not. What I am sure about is that before we can adequately answer this question, we need a much more detailed map of the behaviors we're talking about. Knowing where we are is critical, even if we can't be sure how we arrived at this place.

5

REPRESENTING BATTERED WOMEN

The pioneers in the battered women's movement saw shelter as a step toward social justice. Some of the women who called the hotline were fleeing for their lives. Their immediate safety was our first concern. But even for women in the midst of crisis, seeking shelter in the face of what political scientist Donald Downs calls "conspicuous subjugation" was a courageous act of survival that symbolized a desire to preserve autonomy and respect as well as escape harm.[1] Shelters hoped to politicize this desire by linking the mutual support provided within the facility to collective struggles to reform the structures that limited women's overall opportunities for independence, starting with the law and the helping system.

In formal support groups, during the ebb and flow of daily shelter life, and as women did the practical work needed to make the house run, they often heard their own voices unimpeded by regulation for the first time in months or years, got in touch with capacities and hopes that had lain dormant, and realized, in what could be an epiphany, that their hurt lay as much in the hopes and plans they had set aside as in their physical harms. The next step was to think of the men who had hurt them less as villains than as obstacles to their personal development, to reengage their life projects, and then to identify and act to remove the system barriers to development they shared with other women in the house and beyond. Relatively few residents became lifelong political activists. But even those who saw shelter merely as a respite carry the memory of securing safety and autonomy amidst a cooperative sisterhood.

Those who currently run or work at shelters are far better qualified than we were. But as they developed into full-service programs, there was a corresponding devolution in how shelters approached justice for battered women. Instead of trying to close the gender gap in opportunities and resources—a goal that was admittedly elusive even when confrontations with institutional providers and law makers were a daily occurrence—the shelter movement adapted the more pragmatic aim of securing safety and accountability by working with the justice system, particularly the courts and police.

Divisions among advocates about whether to partner with the state were already apparent at the 1978 hearings at the U.S. Civil Rights Commission. Shortly afterward, a number of local programs, including our New Haven shelter, rejected much-needed funding from the Law Enforcement Assistance Administration (LEAA), a federal agency established in the wake of urban rioting in the 1960s. Another early debate concerned how to relate to battered women who used violence themselves or were implicated in other types of criminal activity. Apart from a tendency to discount the significance of women's violence, advocates feared public sympathy for abuse victims would not extend to women who fought back and that openly supporting these women could cost us vital allies, particularly in the religious, law enforcement, and policy communities.

These attitudes evolved with the domestic violence revolution. Starting with a series of landmark court cases in the 1970s, a small coterie of "feminist lawmakers" who had been active in the civil rights, antiwar, and women's movements spearheaded reforms in civil and criminal law that reshaped how courts approach justice for battered women, including those charged with crimes against their partners or committed under the duress of abuse.[2] A second and much larger cohort of feminist lawyers is now engaged in representing the interests of battered women in the courts. The core of their approach is the battered woman defense, a legal strategy that applies the dominant victimization narrative to link the trauma women suffer because of abuse, their psychological state, and their justice claims in criminal, custody, or civil cases.

The battered woman's defense is a rallying cry for freeing women charged with killing their abusers. And justifiably so. Between 40% and 93% of the women in prison for murder or manslaughter killed partners who physically assaulted them, most in direct retaliation or to protect themselves and/or a child.[3] The defense has helped win acquittal for dozens of women charged with crimes committed in the context of abuse, mitigated the sentences of many others, and convinced governors in Ohio, Maryland, New York, California, Massachusetts, and a number of other states to pardon women imprisoned for killing men who abused them. On the civil side, all but two states have passed legislation recognizing the importance of domestic violence in custody disputes.[4]

These developments are inextricably tied to another: the legitimation of expert testimony on abuse. The domestic violence expert typically constructs a narrative around two parallel themes, a history of progressively more severe violence and other forms of oppression and the victim's deteriorating psychological state. Expert testimony on battering and its effects has been admitted, at least to some degree, in several thousand cases and in each of the 50 states plus the District of Columbia. Of the 19 federal courts that have considered the issue, all but 3 have admitted the testimony.[5] In criminal trials, expert testimony on battering has been used to support defense strategies in murder cases (based on temporary insanity, diminished capacity, justifiable homicide, and self-defense), as parts of habeas corpus proceedings, in sentencing, or to show that women committed assault, embezzled money, sold drugs, signed fraudulent tax returns, or failed to protect their children under the threat or duress of battering. Experts are also frequently called to help prosecute perpetrators when a victim refuses to testify or exhibits other behaviors that might compromise a claim that abuse occurred.[6] In civil and family courts, experts on battered woman's syndrome (BWS) regularly testify in proceedings that involve divorce, custody, or to support tort claims for injuries suffered as a consequence of abuse.[7]

This chapter explores the enigma at the heart of this popular justice strategy—that its utility for battered women is directly linked to its endorsement of the very sexist stereotypes that underlie the construction of woman abuse in the first place. Equally problematic is how little it serves the women who need it most: abuse victims whose history, class, or racial status places them beyond the reach of the dominant victimization narrative. The challenge is to advance the justice claims of battered women without demeaning their character or the purposes they carry into the world.

Activism and the Law

The claim that being battered justifies a violent response is relatively recent. Battered defendants traditionally concealed their abuse, fearing it would be identified as their motive for committing a crime against an abusive partner. Before 1900, only three self-defense cases involving women reached the appellate courts in the United States.[8] In the past, women faced a much higher standard in retaliation than men, largely because the common law allowed men considerable latitude in their use of force against wives, even to the point of considering husband-killing a form of treason.[9] So long as the use of force against female partners was widely accepted, women's retaliatory acts were rarely excused.

In the few instances when the law protected abuse victims, it applied only to women who were perceived as otherwise compliant, sexually disinterested, and innocent. At the dawn of the domestic violence revolution, it was still common for the media to contrast "good" women for whom aggression was alien (think of Grace Kelly in *High Noon* or Eva Marie Saint in *On the Waterfront*) to women who were predatory, cold-hearted, worldly wise, and/or sex-crazed, parts that were often played by members of stigmatized minorities like the marvelous Mexican actress Katy Jurado

(*High Noon*). However loyal or brave, audiences understood that "bad" women would be killed or abandoned by a story's end, presumably as just retribution for their independence or aggression.

In 1980, as part of a larger study of *Women Who Kill*, popular author Ann Jones provided the first sympathetic overview of the legal quandary faced by battered women who retaliated against abusive partners.[10] Despite growing attention to abuse, Jones pointed out that most battered defendants were still going to jail. But she also featured a number of widely publicized acquittals and warned of a male backlash against what some observers considered women's "license to kill." Shortly afterward, psychologist Angela Browne framed the life stories of 42 women who killed abusive partners. She found that these women were indistinguishable psychologically from a comparison group of battered women who had not used violence. Their extreme behavior, Browne concluded, reflected the level and frequency of physical and sexual violence to which they were subjected, the batterer's use of drugs and alcohol, the presence of weapons in the household, and the propensity for their partners to threaten or use violence against others, including their children.[11]

These pioneering works appeared against a background of dramatic improvements in women's overall economic and political status and concurrent changes in how the mass media portrayed strong men and independent women. In the 1970s and early 1980s, following an antigovernment backlash supported in some states by the organization of paramilitary groups, the bombing of the federal building in Oklahoma City, and attacks on abortion clinics, film and TV dramas supplemented the old-style (state-employed) Western marshal and government agent with a breed of "Rambo"-like superheroes who operated outside the law to enforce a higher code of morality (read: fundamentalist religion, traditional family values) that the bureaucrats in Washington (read: Democrats) had abandoned. As Sylvester Stallone, Charles Bronson, and other actors underwent the changes (painted faces, masks, and so on) that transformed Rambo, the Hulk, Batman, the Terminator, and Superman from "mild mannered" to violent enforcers of this higher justice (secular authority is uniformly ineffective, effeminate, and/or corrupt) in the name of paternalism and protectionism, they mimicked (and so helped normalize) the Jekyll to Hyde transformation of abusive partners. In this climate, women took their place alongside male defenders of community standards, appearing as FBI agents, prosecutors, political leaders, judges, corporate executives, detectives, and army officers. Films like *Sleeping with the Enemy* and *Thelma and Louise* went further, suggesting that it was reasonable for ordinary women or femme outlaws to take justice into their own hands if they were mistreated by men, in part because no one else could be expected to come to their aid. Portraying women as representatives of state authority also sent the message that they were legitimate targets of anti-authoritarian sentiment.

Women's legal options were also changing. By the late 1970s, it was standard practice for lawyers representing battered women to highlight rather than conceal their abuse, usually as a way to justify their use of violence, mitigate the seriousness of what they did, or excuse them from criminal acts because they had been coerced. No longer were women's claims to self-defense assessed solely by the traditional standard of how a "reasonable man" would respond. In 1977, a Washington State appellate court reversed the murder conviction of Coville Indian woman Yvonne Wanrow for killing an intruder she believed intended to rape her. Thereafter, battered women could use the Wanrow instruction to claim that a history of sex discrimination led them to resort to force more readily (i.e., with less provocation) than a man would have in an identical situation. The importance of the Wanrow instruction lies in its applicability to confrontational situations in which women use greater force than is used against them, a situation that comprises as many as 75% of the cases where women kill abusive partners.[12] The traditional battered woman's defense is also assumed to have special utility in these cases as well as where women respond proactively based on past abuse, someone other than the abusive partner is the woman's target, or the battered woman commits a crime because her partner has coerced her to do so.

The Abuse Excuse?

The battered woman's defense is loosely constructed around the trauma model of abuse described in chapter 4 and particularly around battered woman syndrome. It is the most successful example of a new type of psychological evidence that has been brought into the courtroom to frame a process of victimization. The argument traces a victim's perceptions and behaviors to the traumatic nature of the abuse they have suffered, showing how a series of events involving violence, sexual assault, sexual abuse, or equally noxious forms of oppression elicit psychological dynamics that culminate in the alleged crime.[13] There has been growing criticism of syndrome arguments in cases involving wartime trauma, rape, kidnapping, and child sexual or physical abuse. But according to criminal law scholar Stephen Schulhofer, the "Walker model has won extraordinarily rapid and widespread acceptance in the courts."[14]

In a typical case, the battered woman's defense is constructed by mental health clinicians who qualify as experts on BWS, which many states equate with abuse. It may seem strange that an expert is needed to explain why a woman might retaliate after a long history of being beaten. But few events elicit as much contention as when women attempt to justify their violence in court with what Harvard law professor and prominent defense attorney Alan Dershowitz dubs "the abuse excuse."[15]

The source of ambivalence toward these defendants is not hard to identify. Justice is supposed to attend to facts and remain blind to character. But in reality, courts weigh appeals for sympathy against the type of person the defendant is imagined to be, particularly if a serious crime is involved.

Battered women are especially vulnerable in this respect because their behavior, albeit exhibited under stress, often suggests character flaws that seem incompatible with their being worthy victims. Like Francine Hughes, they may endure dozens or even hundreds of similar assaults, return repeatedly to the abusive relationship, defend their partners against discovery or sanctions, misrepresent their situation in professional settings, and fail to report abuse. If they had real opportunities to leave, a court may wonder, why didn't they take them? Or jurors may ask: why did she retaliate now, after enduring abuse for so long? Past denials can make a victim's credibility an issue. Judge and jury may wonder: "Is this woman only talking about abuse now because it benefits her?" A claim of self-defense or other mitigation may seem far fetched if no assault was in progress when the woman acted violently, or the assault was relatively minor, or she could have escaped or called for help instead of retaliating, even if she is not required by law to retreat. If she has obviously been victimized, her status is lowered in the court's eyes if she also has comorbid psychiatric or substance use problems that might distort her perceptions or judgment. The battered woman's defense was devised to respond to these and related problems by correcting the misperceptions of lay jurors and portraying the victim's actions as the tragic but inevitable consequence of trauma-induced psychological malaise.

Legal Fictions and Expert Narratives

The evidence reviewed earlier shows that trauma theory captures the experience of only a small proportion of abuse victims. But its lack of correspondence with women's actual experience has had little effect on the application of the trauma model in the legal context. This is because the temporal and procedural constraints that shape courtroom drama necessitate a representational short-hand that is better assessed by whether it facilitates a process that is considered fair and conforms to dominant normative beliefs than by whether it corresponds to experiential, psychological, or sociological reality. In the court setting, BWS and post-traumatic stress disorder (PTSD) function as "legal fictions," forensic constructs of limited empirical validity that facilitate legal judgment, in large part by providing a narrative framework on which reasoning can build.[16] Because of the domestic violence revolution, popular sentiment in many countries now favors excusing women who use violence in reaction to a history of devastating abuse, and it is widely believed that a victimization narrative based on trauma theory is a good way to put this sentiment to work for particular defendants. A credible argument can be made that trauma theory supports a representational strategy that elicits greater empathy for the predicament in which battered women find themselves than portrayals that more accurately grasp the complexities of what has actually occurred.

The story line provided by trauma theory appeals to judges, lawyers, advocates, and prosecutors for the same reasons it appeals to the mass media—because it emphasizes thematic elements that are widely associated with the sorts of tragedies to which women are believed to succumb, external malevolence, descent into depression and dependence, and acts of desperation driven by fear. When supported by appropriate performative elements, these themes invite jurors to enter the narrative to rescue the pitiable naif who stands before them, completing the story with a fairy-tale end, even when the facts establishing guilt or innocence are murky.

Legal scholars have increasingly analyzed how the law takes shape through stories (as much as through rules or policies) and how, in turn, stories are structured in legal contexts so they can be accepted by jurors and other public audiences as more or less legitimate substitutes for real-life experiences. The actual turn of events that brings someone to trial can be extraordinarily confusing. To help the nonspecialists who comprise a jury reach a probative judgment, stories organize the complex fragments of experience to reveal temporal linearity, elicit an epiphany ("Ah, now I see how it was"), and delineate "motives," "harms," "guilt," and "innocence." If the story takes its substance from the facts of a case, its structure and moral themes are designed to bridge the divide that separates legal reality (procedures, rules of evidence, and so on) from the normative meanings jurors and other legal audiences bring to the courtroom. As political scientist and constitutional law scholar Donald Downs points out, "facts only speak for themselves (in a courtroom) . . . when there is social consensus about the normative meaning of the act. When social and legal norms are contested, what one makes of an erstwhile criminal act will depend on one's normative assumptions."[17] When battered women are put on trial, jurors are almost always called on to weigh the defendant's victimization against the harm the defendant has caused. The function of the victimization narrative is to help them decide what they think *should* have happened given the clash of moral forces involved.

Once the elements of a narrative are clear, judge, jurors, experts, lawyers, or witnesses are free to provide conflicting stories or even to substitute unspoken interpretations (what political scientist Jim Scott calls "hidden transcripts") that override the normative consensus, effectively nullifying the "official transcript."[18] When Los Angeles policeman Mark Fuhrman admitted he had used the *n* word in the Simpson trial, defense attorney Johnnie Cochran could bring a race narrative into play that allowed judge, jurors, and members of the public audience to interpret subsequent evidence in ways that neutralized much of the state's case, including Nicole Brown Simpson's desperate 911 call. The battered woman defense draws on comparable narrative power. Domestic violence was a nonstarter in the O. J. Simpson trial. But its value as a framework for structuring dissembled realities into recognizable narrative is that it follows a coherent storyline from which it is possible to draw conclusions about worthiness. In a traditional self-defense case, the defendant's act is weighed against an attack or a perceived threat. By helping the court imagine harms that transcend the existential circumstances surrounding the alleged crime, the battered woman defense becomes particularly important when clear evidence of self-defense is lacking, such as an eyewitness or physical injury, or if the retaliatory response for which the victim is charged is disproportionate to the attack that occurred. By embedding the defendant's act in a history of prior victimization and depicting the tragic persona before the court as the byproduct of this oppressive process, the narrative finesses the normal pathway to fact-finding, suggesting that a defendant's present claims of victimization are credible because she has been a "victim" of this offender in the past and is suffering accordingly. A defense attorney can use trauma theory to explain why she perceived the attack as more serious than its physical dynamics suggested, to prove that a woman is the type of victim depicted by BWS, that is, someone who has been subjected to severe violence, or to reframe a range of colateral behaviors and/or problems—such as why she lied about the abuse when she went to the hospital—that confound her claim to be innocent. Once the expert has shaped the experience of battering into a story of personal tragedy, the defendant recounts her history according to this form—as a downward spiral of increasing desperation, for instance—giving life to the narrative in the same way the TV drama about the detective's sister outlined in chapter 3 gave life to Walker's cycle of violence theory. If things go as planned, the expert also gives the imprimatur of science to the woman's account, facilitating ethical judgments about otherwise morally ambiguous situations.

The sort of determinism implicit in the battered woman defense lies somewhere between the moral incapacity implied by legal insanity and the justification involved in self-defense. Its function in legal proceedings is to allow jurors to accommodate changing mores within standard rules of legal procedure.

Typical of the confrontational situations in which battered women kill abusive partners is a recent case in which my 30-year-old client stabbed her live-in boyfriend after he had kneeled on her stomach and punched her, splitting her lip. Referring to the history of abuse, the woman told him, "I'm not going to let you hurt me. You're not going to hurt me. I'm sick of it." She picked up a small paring knife and when her boyfriend came at her again, fists clenched, she cut him fatally. Several decades ago, the evidence in this case would have been organized into a narrative of blame: she threatened him, picked up the knife with the intent of hurting him, then took revenge for his earlier attacks. Because a "reasonable man" could have retreated or met his attack with comparable force, a jury could conclude that her violence was disproportionate. But the current moral climate of sympathy for women who transgress normal ethical constraints under this sort of duress poses a dilemma to the law and by implication to judge and jury, how to excuse behavior that is deliberate yet clearly provoked and justified, even if not strictly defensive.

To avoid the possibility that jurors will simply nullify evidentiary standards in such cases and set free persons who win their sympathy, the law meets changing community beliefs halfway. With battered women, this initially involved reconstituting the "irresistible impulse" or "hot blood" defense classically used to excuse men who killed their wives in fits of jealousy as a version of temporary insanity, the defense used successfully by Francine Hughes in the burning bed case.[19] Hughes was acquitted although there was little evidence that she was technically insane when she removed her children to safety, then returned to set the fire that killed her sleeping husband. Similarly, when Lorena Bobbitt cut off her husband's penis, psychiatrist Susan Feister convinced a jury that this good, traditional Catholic whose hopes for a decent marriage were betrayed by her husband's philandering, was driven temporarily insane by remembering all the times he had physically abused and insulted her. Neither woman was responding to an imminent threat. By allowing them to construct their victim stories as if they had lost control of their impulses, the jury could effect an outcome widely believed to be just without the law's having to acknowledge that a history of past abuse allowed the victim to take a life or an important body part.

The Expert as Storyteller

In the United States, persons are qualified as experts if they can assist the court's deliberation by providing pertinent information not generally available to a layperson. The expert is introduced as a purveyor of disinterested information, often of a scientific nature, a conceit that both sides in the adversarial process sustain by a lengthy qualification process replete with a list of degrees, publications, and honors. But another side of expertise comes to the fore when we consider its role in narrative construction. In ambiguous cases like the Hughes trial, expertise functions less as a scientific deus ex machina than as a moral weathervane to help sensitize judge and jury to changing notions of harm that have not yet been formally incorporated into legal doctrine. At its best, in providing a framework for linking improbable events to clinical conditions, experts give the court the courage to do what it dare not do explicitly or on its own: stretch the understanding of the law within the law toward standards of popular judgment. The grounds for self-defense has yet to broadened to recognize that past abuse might prompt a reasonable adult to use force preemptively when threatened or when an assault is imminent. Experts help jurors square their normative beliefs about a woman's victimization with the conventional legal understanding of her crime. Once the law changes to reflect the realities of woman battering, prevailing domestic violence expertise will be modified or irrelevant.

A classic example of how science helps courts accommodate changing mores was the role played by psychologist Kenneth Clark's experiments with black and white dolls in the U.S. Supreme Court's landmark decision in *Brown v. Board of Education*. Despite the fact that Clark's research was flawed in every major respect—the sample was tiny, the control group inappropriate, black students in segregated and integrated schools showed similar preferences, and the effects of segregation could not be isolated—his poignant story of how segregation led black children to identify with white dolls (which was irrelevant to the constitutional issues involved) converged with the popular belief, which the Court shared, that the separate but equal doctrine was not merely wrong but harmful.[20]

Even more relevant is the transitional role of expertise in rape cases. During the 1920s, to conform to governing sex stereotypes, rules of criminal court testimony were revised in accord with recommendations by an American Bar Association committee headed by John Henry Wigmore that judges order a psychiatric examination of victims in any case that went to a jury because of the "well-known psychiatric finding that women and children often lie about rape."[21] In the 1970s, with women's liberation pressing for reform, popular sentiment shifted to favor rape victims. In this climate, experts were often called to support a victim's credibility by attributing any paradoxical behavior, such as an initial denial that a rape had occurred to rape trauma syndrome. The passage of rape shield laws and laws making rape in marriage a crime made such testimony largely redundant. At present, courts tend to restrict the admission of expert testimony on rape trauma syndrome to cases where the alleged rapist uses the victim's failure to promptly report as a defense.[22]

In linking the progress of violent acts to a decline in psychological functioning, the current defense strategy meets a number of critical challenges to legal narrative: it reflexively identifies a new class of psychological harms, documents that the woman is actually suffering these harms, traces these harms to abuse, and shows how the alleged criminal act(s) was elicited by the violence-induced psychological condition, and hence was not willful.

But is the current approach satisfactory? Does it overcome the obstacles to representing their experience battered women faced in the past? And how does relying on the battered woman's defense affect the status of actual and potential victims and offenders outside the courtroom?

Dilemmas and Contradictions in Historical Context

There are few more dramatic illustrations of women's limited recognition by the justice system than the contrast between the oppression of women in personal life and the legal status of this oppression.

So long as domestic violence was treated as "just life," woman battering was only visible to the law when it took the extreme form of wife torture or wife murder. Severe cases of wife beating were occasionally prosecuted, but the modal situation we call domestic violence today had no legal standing.

Battering was a common target of nineteenth-century reformers in England and the United States. The term *wife beating* was first used in the 1856 campaign for divorce reform in England.[23] As early as 1852, a London magistrate published statistics on assaults by men on women and children in London, indicating that one in six assaults occurred within the family.[24] An 1853 Act for the Better Prevention of Aggravated Assaults Upon Women and Children provided 6 months in prison, a fine, and an order to keep the peace for 6 months. Then in 1857, the first recorded lodging place for victims of assault was opened in London by the Society for the Protection of Women and Children. The lodge also provided legal advice to victims of battering and stationed observers in courtrooms to monitor cases involving women and children.[25] British feminists Harriet Taylor, John Stuart Mill, and Frances Power Cobbe spearheaded these reforms. In popular articles and widely circulated pamphlets, they compared cruelty to wives and to animals, insisted that "wife torture" would persist so long as men saw women as their property and demanded full economic and social justice for women.[26]

Violence against wives was first prohibited in the United States in 1641, two centuries before a husband's absolute right to chastisement was abolished in England and wife abuse outlawed.[27] But little was done about the problem until the 1850s, when agitation growing out the temperance movement linked wife beating, divorce, and suffrage. In the 1870s, Lucy Stone helped publicize abuse in a widely circulated newsletter but failed to convince lawmakers in Massachusetts to enact domestic violence reforms.[28] In 1885, a coalition of Chicago women's organizations agreed to provide legal aid and personal assistance to female and child victims of abuse and rape, monitored court proceedings, and sent women to a shelter run by the Women's Club of Chicago where they could stay for 4 weeks. These efforts failed to take hold, however, and in 1896, the Protective Agency for Women and Children in Chicago merged with the Chicago Bureau of Justice and eventually became the modern Legal Aid Society.[29]

Turn-of-the-century campaigns against wife beating in the United States relied heavily on Republican lawyers and judges, supporters of the "social purity movement" and its "vigilance societies," as well as on feminists such as Stone, Susan B. Anthony, and Amelia Bloomer, a mix that resembled the coalition that supported the Violence Against Women Act (VAWA) in the mid-1990s. Between 1870 and the 1920, many states rescinded or severely limited the legal right of men to beat their wives or made wife beating a crime.[30] These laws combined protectionist rhetoric with an elite moralism primarily directed at "immigrant brutes," blacks, and other groups thought to comprise the dangerous classes. Illustrative was the campaign led by American Bar Association president and Republican governor of Connecticut Simeon Baldwin to pass flogging bills and restore the whipping post for abusers, punishments that were used against black men almost exclusively.[31]

Feminist agitation was more central to legislative efforts in Britain than in the United States. But even so ardent a polemicist for women's rights as British journalist Cobbe emphasized the distinction between "the nagging harpy" or "virago" who got the worst of "mutual combat" and the "chaste, sober, faithful, honest and industrious" victim who suffered "wife-beating properly so-called."[32] The wife-beating laws Cobbe helped shepherd though Parliament between 1870 and 1895 covered only women whose husbands had been convicted of aggravated assault and who could demonstrate that their future safety was in danger. A wife found to be abused was granted custody and her husband ordered to pay child support. But excluded from protection, custody, or maintenance was any wife who had committed adultery, an accusation that is still the most common charge brought by abusive husbands. This approach effectively deprived typically working class "rough women" of the legal remedies afforded "respectable women," most of whom were middle-class. Moreover, legislation in Britain and the United States was only applied to the most heinous cases of wife abuse. As Cobbe pointed out, an unintended effect of this approach was to set normative boundaries around how female subordination was enforced but to leave its essential dynamic undisturbed, normalizing lower levels of abuse.

Turn-of-the-century child savers in the United States saw domestic violence, child abuse, and child sexual abuse as flowing from a single source of illegitimate male power in the home and routinely used police to remove perpetrators, a protectionist approach historian Linda Gordon links to "social feminism."[33] But by the 1920s, many of these same groups had come to view divorce, female employment, and extending the franchise to women as posing the major threat to domestic harmony and child rearing and shifted their strategy from sanctioning "immigrant brutes" to family maintenance through female correction, the approach that remains the core strategy in child welfare. Some cities hosted domestic violence police units staffed by female officers or social workers.[34] Even so, "family" or "domestic relations" courts typically seized "domestic trouble cases" as occasions to discipline battered mothers for "neglect"; help tenement wives master habits of cleanliness, nutrition, and child care; and reassert the importance of traditional feminine roles. In the social work classic *Social Diagnosis*, Mary Richmond offered the case of John Polson, "tenement dweller," who beat his wife regularly because of "the sameness of the menu, the wife serving only hash and stew." A Philadelphia judge captured the common judicial sentiment. "If the woman has not been living the right kind of life," he told a divorce attorney for a battered wife, "I will not make an order on the man to support her."[35]

In the 1930s, behind euphemisms like "marital discord," the classic texts that gave birth to marriage and family counseling urged therapists to deliberately avoid the subject of physical abuse so as not to alienate the husband.[36] Although women entered the job market in ever larger numbers after World War II, leaving the traditional farm economy far behind, it was not until the emergence of the rights-oriented movements in the 1960s that an effective challenge could be mounted to the paternalistic currents that discounted women's independence.

Dilemmas in Legal Representation

If battered women were offered slim protections from abuse until the 1970s, those who retaliated faced almost insurmountable barriers. An affirmative conception of female aggression was incompatible with the broad range of male prerogatives embodied in legal doctrine well into the twentieth century. Married women in nineteenth-century Europe and America were unable to sign contracts; they lacked title to the wages they earned and to property, even property inherited or owned prior to marriage; in the event of legal separation, they had no claim on their children. They could not vote, hold political office, sit on juries, or enter many of the professions or trades. It was only in 1970 that British men lost the right to sue their wife's lover after a divorce for the unpaid services they had provided. Adult single women were only slightly better off.[37]

Until the mid-1970s, there were only three options available to battered women who used violence against an abusive partner in a nontraditional self-defense situation. They could claim they were insane, were "helpless and innocent," or had been confronted with a level of brutality that went beyond what the reigning patriarchy should permit.[38] Although these representations could protect a given individual, they also provided an occasion to publicly critique, refine, and reinforce women's performance of traditional roles, thereby creating a number of dilemmas for battered women and their attorneys. To protect themselves and their children, women were forced to deny the reasonableness of their acts, abandon their social bonds with other women, and confirm both the governing stereotypes of female inferiority and, by implication, the rationality of male domination so long as it was enforced with acceptable means. Among the minority of defendants who adapted incapacity defenses, many succeeded, but only by representing themselves in ways that diminished women's status as a class.

The Insanity Dilemma

Behind the norm of domesticity, the most obvious explanation when an otherwise respectable ("normal") woman responded violently to abuse was that she was insane. In *Women Who Kill*, Jones argued that it was easier for courts to acquit on the grounds of insanity than to acknowledge that behavior widely viewed as part of the marriage contract could provoke a rational woman to violence. To the courts, the only acceptable murderess was an otherwise innocent woman driven mad by moral corruption, social misadventures, or female sickness.

Jones recounts the case of Fanny Hyde, brought to trial in Brooklyn in 1872 for murdering her employer and lover, George Watson. Fanny's attorney, Samuel Morris, described how her seduction at age 15 by Watson set off a chain of events that, in combination with her subsequent abuse at his hands and her "dysmenorrhea," led to "transitoria mania." Fortunately, transitoria mania came and went in a flash. So did such variants as ephemeral mania, temporary insanity, and morbid impulse. Medical experts were commonly called in these cases to show how women's nature might easily become distorted, particularly during their menstrual periods and if they were unmarried or worked outside the home, driving them insane from "moral causes," such as extreme violence, incest, or rape.[39]

The dilemma posed by the insanity defense was that women who wanted to claim its protection had to deny that their response was rationally motivated by the same logic that guided other human beings, thereby rendering their experience unintelligible to themselves and the wider (and largely female) audience for such trials. The underlying message was paradoxical. It was generally accepted that men could (and should) respond violently to life-threatening force. But women who used violence to protect their physical integrity were only excused if they had been propelled by irrational forces outside the bonds of civil discourse, a claim that compromised their political identity. As noxious as it might be to set the murderess free, it would be far worse to permit a courtroom drama in which such common family practices as marital rape, child molestation, and physical abuse were shown to lead logically to violent outrage in their female victims or witnesses.

The Respectable Woman Dilemma

An alternative to pleading insanity was to appeal to the court's paternalism by portraying the abused woman as frail and helpless. This stereotype reinforced the belief that women were men's property, objects who might be acted on but who could not act effectively on their own behalf. Women were expected to be grateful and quiet and view the chivalry men substituted for justice as setting them apart as "real men" who could be relied on to protect women from the "vile seducers" who deserved punishment. Women who lacked these character traits or stood up for themselves were fair game.[40]

In her book on child welfare, *Heroes of Their Own Lives,* Linda Gordon illustrates a related point. Because women's maternal instinct was considered part of their biological inheritance, they were far more likely to elicit sympathy when they called on authorities to protect their children from violence rather than themselves, or when they acted to protect their children from a violent male. Because norms supporting women's subordinate status were an important source of battering in the first place, a defense based on women's "natural" state of subordination, submissiveness, and maternity increased their vulnerability as a class to violence.

Both defense options were premised on the belief that aggression and violence were unnatural in women, and so were unavailable to women who openly flaunted social convention, whatever their social class, as well as to working women, immigrant women, or members of racial minorities or other groups thought to be aggressive by nature. In 1847, Mary Runkle of Whiteboro, New York, fought back with her fists in the middle of the night against her husband, who had been punching, kicking, and choking her since tea time, and then strangled him. Although Mary claimed "she did not intend to murder him, but did so in defending herself against assault," she was hanged. Still, to spare Mary the sight of the gallows, a hole was cut in the upstairs floor and the rope passed down to the office below where she sat waiting tied to a chair.[41] Women as well as men publicly defended the view that "ladies" could be shocked into insanity, but that "rough women" like Mary should be convicted, sent to jail, or worse. In denying an affirmative role for female aggression in domestic life, the gender stereotypes upheld through court decisions implicitly disparaged women's aggressive behavior in the economic and political spheres as well, an outcome which the social purists and child savers welcomed.

The "Violent Brute" Dilemma

The third alternative was for a woman to present various proofs to the court that the violence she had suffered was far in excess of what she or her kind deserved. Implicit in the focus on extreme violence (physical or sexual) as the catalyst for her own violence was the belief that women like her could be expected to remain passive ("pure") when faced with "normal" (less violent) forms of domination. This was a variation on the dilemma Cobbe identified, that punishing only extreme violence normalized lower levels of abuse. By extending protection only to women who had been severely injured, the courts excluded the vast majority of battering situations, where abuse was a routine occurrence and women's retaliation was motivated by a frank desire to get out from under. The violent brute defense posed an individual's need for court protection against women's collective need for social justice. As Jones tells us, "Women who blamed certain individuals rather than society for their grievances and who sought redress through personal revenge rather than political action did not threaten the social structure but, in affect, affirmed it."[42]

In sum, the nineteenth-century legal system in the United States acknowledged abuse only for female defendants who represented themselves as passive, helpless, and ladylike victims driven mad by the violent excesses of a moral deviate. These terms were acceptable because they supported women's oppression as a class; legitimated the status of women as male property (to be used, but not "abused"); denied women an affirmative capacity for aggression, rationality, and fear ascribed to men; sustained the distinction between "respectable" and "rough" at the basis of an elite and racialist paternalism; and fostered the belief that the normal pathologies induced by male domination were not a proper matter for public concern. Ironically, the emphasis on innocence and submissiveness as feminine characteristics contributed to a certain fatalism among working class viragos. Apparently less entitled to a public defense than their more conventional sisters, they could consider themselves lucky to have experienced only normal levels of abuse. Or they could strike out violently when attacked.

Contemporary Defense Strategies: The More Things Change . . .

The application of the vast edifice of research and helping services to relieve the personal suffering of abused persons is an important contribution to human progress. Despite this, the defense of abuse victims who kill or assault abusive partners continues to rely on the same basic legal fictions it did two centuries ago: sex-stereotyped notions of female weakness, insanity, self-defense of a victimized innocent against excessive brutality, and on the mixture of these views reflected in the battered woman's defense.

The Burning Bed Revisited

One hundred years after Fanny Hyde was acquitted, attorney Arron Greydanus claimed that when Francine Hughes set fire to the bed in which her husband was sleeping, she was temporarily insane.[43]

Mickey assaulted Francine Hughes almost immediately after they were married in 1963, when she was 16. Over the next 8 years, his physical abuse ran the gamut from slapping through kicking, burning, choking, and stalking, extended through four pregnancies, and occurred whether he was drinking or not. He had forced her to eat off the floor, kicked the baby, and locked the dog out of the house so that it froze to death. On the numerous occasions when Francine left, once for 6 months, he would alternately threaten to kill her and beg for forgiveness, promising to stop drinking and never hit her again. Each time they separated, Francine was urged to return by either his parents or hers. When she returned to nurse him after Mickey was in a suicidal car accident, he beat her with his cane and repeatedly warned that he would kill her if she ever tried to leave him again. Despite his intense jealousy, in preparation for a final break, Francine took a part-time job, enrolled in school, secretly began to save some money, and developed a close friendship (her first in many years) with a fellow student who was also a police officer.

In March 1977, Francine returned home from the business school she was attending and put a TV dinner in the oven for her husband. That night, apparently furious at the idea that school might be more important to her than serving him, Mickey threw the dinner on the floor, forced Francine to clean it up, and then slapped and kicked her. Next, he ordered her to put her textbook and school notes into a trash can and burn them, which she did. He told her she would quit school. She argued, and he beat her again.

We have already reviewed what happened next. Her daughter called the police, and Mickey threatened Francine in their presence. After they left, she told her four children to wait in the car, retrieved a gasoline can from their garage, returned to the house, entered the bedroom where Mickey was sleeping, poured the fluid on and around the bed, and set the fire that burned the house to the ground, killing Mickey. Then, she drove to the Ingham County sheriff's office and confessed.

For Michigan feminists, the years of abuse Francine endured epitomized the experiences of battered wives, and her dramatic response symbolized their justified right to defend themselves. Believing that a jury of her peers would readily accept Francine's response as rational, they urged her attorney to argue self-defense.[44] But Greydanus worried that a self-defense plea would fail, largely because Mickey was asleep when Francine set the fire and so did not pose the imminent danger required by self-defense law. Instead, he stood with legal tradition and pled temporary insanity. As in Hyde's defense, the technical rationale for pleading temporary insanity was to make evidence of long-standing abuse admissible in court to establish what was going on that night in Francine's mind. To a nineteenth-century jury, Hughes's alleged condition when she retrieved and meticulously poured gasoline around her husband's bed would have sounded suspiciously like "transitoria mania."[45]

The only evidence that Francine was insane was that the definitive step she had taken in resisting Mickey's abuse contrasted markedly with her earlier submissiveness. There was one significant difference between this defense and the arguments used to acquit the battered murderess in the nineteenth century. Greydanus argued that the battering itself caused Hughes to crack, not a predisposing frailty inherited with female gender.

Despite Francine's acquittal, her feminist supporters felt betrayed. The insanity label would stigmatize Francine, they argued, making it impossible to communicate why the country needed to act decisively to relieve the millions of women who faced a similar situation. Their concerns were unnecessary. In response to the verdict, *The Washington Post*, *Time*, *Newsweek*, and dozens of other publications complained that "the killing excuse" gave women a virtual license to retaliate and would most assuredly start a trend.

The Gendered Standard of Self-Defense

Editorial writers had reason to worry. Or so it appeared from the publicity given to the self-defense acquittals of Joan Little (1975), Inez Garcia (1977), and other women who killed men who sexually assaulted them shortly before or soon after Francine's act of defiance. These cases dramatized an important change in women's representation—the emergence of a feminist jurisprudence. Three months before Hughes set fire to her house, feminist legal scholars Elizabeth Schneider and Nancy Stearns from the Center for Constitutional Law won a precedent-setting appeal from the Washington State Supreme Court that would have allowed Greydanus to claim self-defense simply because at the time of the fire, Hughes believed that the sleeping man posed a threat to her life.

Application of the "reasonable man" (or, later, "the reasonable person") standard in self-defense penalizes women in two ways: they are judged by an inappropriate masculine yardstick and their subjective perceptions are held to be irrelevant to the question of whether a theoretical reasonable person would have acted as she did. In appealing the Washington case, Schneider and her colleagues set the problem of reasonableness in the broader context of women's inequality.

The Washington case involved Yvonne Wanrow, who had wounded one attacker and killed another whom she believed to be a child molester and rapist. In her 1974 trial, Wanrow pleaded impaired mental state and self-defense. Despite the fact that the 5'4" woman was in a leg cast and walked with a crutch when she shot the 6'2" intoxicated intruder, she was sentenced to two 20-year terms and one 5-year term. In presenting what is known as the Wanrow jury instruction, the Washington State Appeals Court overturned her conviction, holding that a woman's reasonable perception of danger may differ from a man's. The opinion emphasized both Wanrow's specific physical vulnerability due to her diminutive size and condition at the time of the attack and the special vulnerability that resulted because women as a class suffered the effects of sex discrimination. Wrote the court,

> The respondent was entitled to have the jury consider her actions in the light of her own perceptions of the situation, including those perceptions which were the product of our nation's long and unfortunate history of sex discrimination. . . . Until such time as the effects of that history are eradicated, care must be taken to assure that our self-defense instructions afford women the right to have their conduct judged in light of the individual physical handicaps which are the product of sex discrimination.[46]

The assumption that "reasonable" women have a lower threshold of fear than men reflected the sexist ideology of an earlier epoch. But the Wanrow standard derived from a sociohistorical analysis sympathetic to feminism and allowed a battered woman to claim self-defense even where her violence was preemptive or where she merely believed she would be attacked or killed if she failed to respond. The one prerequisite for using *Wanrow* was that the female defendant be identified with the historically victimized class.

State of Indiana v. Ruth Childers

Wanrow was followed by a number of cases in which gender differences were cited as the basis for modifying conventional standards of self-defense.

But it also laid the foundation for a new line of argument that linked the specific type of victimization associated with battering to a unique form of psychological vulnerability.

In 1978, in Benton, Indiana, Ruth Childers was charged with murdering her former husband, Clifford, who had battered her for 18 years. Clifford returned to their farm intoxicated and began throwing furniture and other things belonging to Ruth and her teenagers out of their rented moving van. After calling the sheriff, Ruth confronted Clifford with a shotgun and told him to leave ("You've interfered once too often," she reportedly said). He lunged at her, the gun went off, and Clifford was killed. Expert testimony established that the gun was defective and had probably gone off accidentally, reducing the crime to involuntary manslaughter. But for Childers to be acquitted of all charges, she also had to explain why she thought she needed the gun in the first place, even though Clifford had neither threatened nor assaulted her that day. To answer this question, the defense called Dr. Elisa Benedek, a psychiatric expert on the newly described pattern known as battered woman's syndrome (BWS). Benedek reviewed the history of violence, described the symptoms of learned helplessness, and explained why, based on the sense of futility and dependence imposed by the violence, battered women develop an exaggerated sense of their assailant's power and are convinced they are in greater danger than a third party might perceive. Despite Benedek's impressive credentials, the jury convicted Childers and she was sentenced to 5 years in prison, the maximum allowed in Indiana for involuntary manslaughter.

The Battered Woman's Defense

Notwithstanding the outcome of the Childers case, defense attorneys welcomed a psychological theory that promised to combine the best elements of previous approaches. Walker's model of BWS offered the psychological substance lacking in the temporary insanity plea and shaped it into a narrative of victimization that explained why women perceived danger where a "reasonable man" might not, thereby incorporating the advantages of *Wanrow* as well. The woman's predicament was still traced to the violent behavior of the batterer. But Walker responded to two questions left unanswered in the Hughes case: why women stay with violent men and why a battered woman might strike out violently even when not immediately threatened. According to Walker, after undergoing the cycle at least twice, the victim succumbs to learned helplessness, a form of depression that gives her an exaggerated sense of her partner's power and control. She concludes that escape is impossible and concentrates instead on survival, employing denial, numbing, or in extreme cases proactive violence to cope. Why women retaliate when they do is unclear in Walker's model, particularly given the passivity associated with their depressive condition, though their response may be prompted by their distorted perception of danger, their perception that alternatives are unavailable, or their sense that survival requires proactive violence.

Within a decade of its formulation, most states had upheld expert presentation of BWS as at least partially exculpatory in criminal cases. A number of courts have limited this presentation to claims of self-defense, though Georgia and Texas courts have held the opposite, that such testimony is only relevant in cases where there is no actual threat of harm, and California and some other states limit experts to a general description of BWS and its dynamics, such as why victims of domestic violence conceal, minimize, or lie about the violence.[47] In this circumstance, experts help the court appreciate an unusually oppressive circumstance that might compel persons to act in ways jurors would not expect. Alternately, defense experts may interview the defendant, validate her claims to be battered by identifying the situationally specific causes and elements of BWS, and link these elements to the action (or lack of action) in question.

Today, BWS is used more broadly than Walker intended and encompasses the spectrum of symptoms exhibited by victimized women. Experts testify about "battering and its consequences" rather than merely about the Walker model. Mary Ann Dutton, a leading forensic psychologist, includes a woman's futile efforts to resist abuse as part of a "revised" BWS, for instance, allowing experts to root retaliatory violence in past experience rather than delusion or depression.[48] The court may ask not merely whether a woman's claim to have been afraid is plausible given the history of abuse, but whether in fact she actually feared for her life at the time she acted and whether this was reasonable based on past abusive incidents.[49] The alternative account is that her fear, though not justified by the immediate facts, was the result of a mental dysfunction, perceptual distortion, or "greater sensitivity to danger" caused by BWS. In a landmark case in Kansas, the court concluded from expert testimony that "battered women are terror stricken people whose mental state is distorted and bears a marked resemblance to that of a hostage or prisoner of war."[50] Where the batterer is on trial or in civil proceedings involving both parties, the calculus of harms can be calibrated to fit a catalogue of penalties, monetary damages, or civil remedies.

Courts have also defined BWS as a special case of PTSD.[51] The expert narrative on PTSD is typically more technical than the story of BWS, is presented by a psychiatrist, and draws from a different theoretical tradition than the learning theory that undergirds BWS. Yet the basic claim is the same, that the trauma of severe or threatened violence has distorted the victim's perception, causing her to exaggerate the danger she confronts. In her revised conceptualization of complex PTSD, Herman adds a sense of helplessness, despair, or paralysis of initiative akin to Walker's model.[52]

As we saw in chapter 4, the most important feature of a victimization narrative based on trauma theory is that it shifts the onus from the victim (as "crazy") to the perpetrator and normalizes the woman's violence as a survival-oriented response induced by the psychological effects of being abused. This is particularly true where the trauma expert stresses the transient nature of the post-traumatic response, points to the cumulative effects of abusive violence over time, and highlights how the battered woman develops an acute sensitivity to danger based on her past experience, even when an outsider might interpret her partner's proximate behavior differently, what Blackman calls her "heightened reason."[53] Assessments for BWS or PTSD can help explain the effects of repeated severe violence where a woman has distorted her predicament, where the cycle of violence described by Walker has played a role in her decision making, where she is severely depressed or otherwise passive, or where learned helplessness offers a credible explanation for why she failed to seek help or report abuse. Diagnoses of BWS or PTSD can elicit enhanced advocacy, facilitate acquittal, support a plea of self-defense, diminish responsibility for criminal acts, or support a custody petition by stressing how removing the perpetrator or providing other safety measures can relieve the victim's symptoms. A diagnosis of full-fledged BWS or PTSD can also be used to empower victims by validating their claims, reducing their self-blame, and by encouraging counselors to focus clinical intervention on redressing imbalances in power.

Still, despite their utility in some circumstances, both the Wanrow instruction and the battered woman's defense rooted in trauma theory can significantly compromise the justice claims of battered women.

The Limits of *Wanrow*

The most serious limit of the Wanrow approach is that granting a privilege in violent retaliation to women who distinguish themselves from men by their greater weakness and vulnerability reifies their inequality by tying their rights to membership in a disadvantaged class. To access the benefits of *Wanrow*, women must represent their actions one-dimensionally through their "victim self," making a fetish of weakness, passivity, and subordination that further impugns their claims to full equality as a class.

An important principle of equal protection is that the law should compensate for negative differences in perception and experience that result from sexual inequality. But *Wanrow* approaches this principle using the ill-conceived liberal theory that all significant differences between the sexes reflect social deficits inherited from inequality. This formulation has two troublesome implications. The first is that meaningful differences in perception will only persist so long as inequality persists or, as *Wanrow* puts it, "until such time as the effects of that history are eradicated." At this point, *Wanrow* implies, the "reasonable woman" will resemble the "reasonable man" and so can be judged by the same (masculinist?) standard.

More immediate problems for battered women are raised by the second implication of *Wanrow*, that the law need not consider the positive aspects of female identity that differentiate women as sexual beings from men.

These positive differences extend to the range of subjective capacities women elaborate in their approaches to love, sex, dress, work, art, family life, child care, and play. Although these capacities are certainly linked to sexual inequality, women's widely touted capacity for nurture to their default roles as primary parent and caretaker, for instance, they are developed independently of these constraints. When she risked her life by returning to the house to protect her child from her husband, Terry Traficonda was both enacting the exaggerated protective responsibility women inherit from the unequal division of household labor and expressing a courageous impulse to self-sacrifice we would hardly want eradicated.

Many women "stay" with abusive men because love, loyalty to a partner, gratitude for past support, marriage, the integrity of their family and striving for a real partnership even in the face of domination mean more to them than personal safety or other self-interests served by leaving. Though some may consider these beliefs hopelessly naive or romantic, they have a positive valence in female subjectivity as well as an evolutionary function in the maintenance of the race. But in the current parlance of self-defense, battered women on trial are expected to provide a convincing account of why they failed to walk away from the relationship before the assault(s) that provoked the target incident. This *preretreat* duty has no counterpart in how the criminal law assesses men's responsibility in confrontational situations.[54] But it forces victimized female defendants to either conceal their actual motives for staying or portray them as weaknesses of character or personality, the alternative reinforced by *Wanrow* and the battered woman's defense.

Without an affirmative conception of femininity, neither the "particularity" that genders coercive control nor the proactive resistance women mount to its imposition is intelligible. Even women who assault or kill abusive partners primarily to preserve their physical integrity are also protecting their right to invest their unique capacities as individuals and as women in their life projects. A key facet of empowering battered women on trial involves representing their sense of difference as something to be constitutionally preserved, a point to which I return in subsequent chapters.

As categorical forms of discrimination become less pronounced, sexual differences may become more individualized and less bound to normative conceptions of appropriate gender role performance. Many differences between men and women may disappear altogether, as *Wanrow* contends. But the aim of real equality is not to eliminate difference but to maximize the role of personal choice in its elaboration. Indeed, it is because sexual differences are both enduring and historically specific that it is necessary to maintain equal treatment as a legal ideal and to continually articulate relevant standards to approximate this ideal in just outcomes.

Reframing the Role of Sex Discrimination

Wanrow equates discrimination with gender-specific disadvantages that alter how women perceive and respond to threats. In fact, what is "gendered"

are the predicaments faced by battered women, not merely their perceptions, physical development, or response. Their troubles happen *because*
they are women.

To illustrate, imagine we do not know the gender of the parties in the
burning bed case and are only told that one partner had been raped by the
other; forbidden to leave the house, go to school, or call their family; and
forced to clean up the dinner thrown onto the floor and to burn their
school books and notes. The fact that the obvious scenario involves a male
perpetrator and a female victim illustrates the extent to which these tactics
are gendered by women's default roles in personal life. The principal
expression of sex discrimination in battering is the construction of women's
entrapment around sex-specific expectations, experiences, and harms that
have no obvious counterpart among men.

To extend this point, now imagine reversing the roles in the burning bed
case so that Francine had somehow managed to rape Mickey or humiliate
him in these other ways and that the jury found this credible. Is there any
question that jurors would intuitively grasp the overwhelming shame a
man would feel in this situation and grant him the right to "lose it" and kill
her without his having to claim he was insane? Psychiatrist James Gilligan
argues that the cornerstone of male violence are offenses to their "respect."[55]
Persons with little to lose often place more emphasis on personal affronts
than others. But as the attention paid to corporate and political scandals
illustrates, the public tends to weigh disrespect by how far someone is taken
down from their initial status or position. Degradation is easier to recognize
in men than in women because men are assumed to occupy a higher position of status to start with, and hence to have further to fall. Conversely,
degradation is harder to appreciate when it involves persons who are
already devalued or activities that are already constrained by normative
consignment such as housework or cooking or child care. In Walker's original study, victims reported that to avoid abuse, they made extra efforts to
keep the children quiet (84%), made sure the house was clean (84%),
cooked something they knew he liked (87%), and avoided subjects he did
not like to discuss (91%).[56] The fact that not only Mickey, but also his family, her family, and probably some jurors as well expected Francine to cook
his dinner, clean up, provide sexual service, and stay home to care for her
husband, made the full impact of his coercion and control hard to appreciate and diminished the empathy jurors could feel for her outrage. This
made insanity the only plausible account for why she set the fire. Moreover,
it takes proportionally less coercion to enforce constraints that are already
normative (such as *how* the house is to be cleaned or how sexual service is
provided) than to impose these behaviors de novo, which is what would
be generally required to get men to perform in these ways. It is only under
the most severe constraints—in prison, POW camps, mental hospitals, and
in boot camp—that men experience humiliations analogous to those suffered by Francine in any substantial numbers Men's relatively advantaged
status explains why jurors regularly acquit men, but rarely women, who
employ a "hot blood" defense to excuse crimes of jealousy or other passions.

As we will see in chapter 8, anywhere from 50% to 80% of perpetrators use forms of tactical degradation—such as monitoring their partner's time, money, movement, dress, or conversations—comparable to those experienced by Francine Hughes and Terry Traficonda. Unless he was gay (and so implicitly shared women's devalued status) there would be little question about a man's right to a liberatory response if his autonomy was compromised in these ways. But instead of measuring the infringement of their liberties against the dignity we associate with fully entitled adults (the "reasonable man" standard) and assessing their response accordingly, abused women are expected to prove themselves worthy of justice by presenting proof they have been physically and psychologically harmed.

The Practical Limits of Traumatization Models

To what extent does the victimization narrative constructed from trauma theory overcome the limits of *Wanrow* or nineteenth-century legal fictions?

The battered woman's defense is successful largely with victims whose profiles fit or are perceived to fit the descriptive terms of the BWS. Because this frame emphasizes the disabling effects of violence rather than strengths or survival skills, it excludes rough women, those perceived to be independent, including women who have successful careers, and women who have either not experienced severe violence or whose oppression was constructed largely around nonviolent forms of coercion and control. These groups comprise the vast majority of battered women who seek our help.

The "Respectable Woman" Dilemma

Attempts to prove that a woman's extreme reaction to battering is a posttraumatic response to violence rather than strategic or an expression of her violent character invokes the "respectable woman" dilemma confronted by nineteenth-century defendants. In the eyes of the court, if a woman has responded violently to abuse in the past or has ostensibly gone about her life despite past abuse, the claim that current violence was traumatic is suspect.

Valoree Day

Valoree Day, a 25-year-old motel maid from Groveland, California, fought back during repeated assaults by her boyfriend, Steve Brown, throughout their 16-month relationship. On the night Brown died, he chased her with a knife, threatened to kill her, and repeatedly stabbed at the bedroom door behind which she was hiding. When he finally cornered her, still holding his knife, she stabbed him with a kitchen knife she had grabbed to protect herself. He bled to death. Day was convicted of involuntary manslaughter and sentenced to 6 years in prison after the prosecution successfully argued that her violent behavior throughout the relationship was incompatible with self-defense.

Day appealed her conviction, arguing that her first attorney had failed to introduce expert testimony on battered women's experiences. But the California attorney general's office countered that her behavior was inconsistent with that of a battered woman because she did not exhibit the "docile, submissive, humble, ingratiating, non-assertive, dependent, quiet, conforming and selfless" traits characteristic of battered women.[57]

A series of decisions in New Jersey illustrate the agonized efforts through which courts go to reconcile the actual experiences of battered women with the victimization narrative built around trauma theory. Gladys Kelly had been battered by her husband throughout their 7-year marriage, starting from the day after the wedding. On the day she killed him, Mr. Kelly had been drinking and beat her in public, biting and clubbing her. During the struggle, in what she claimed was self-defense, she wounded him fatally with a pair of scissors. When a defense expert on BWS was excluded and the appeals court upheld the exclusion, Elizabeth Schneider, one of the attorneys in the Wanrow appeal, argued the relevance of expert testimony before the New Jersey Supreme Court, emphasizing its importance for determining the reasonableness of Kelly's fear. In remanding the case for retrial, the New Jersey Court wrote a lengthy account of battering that relied on Walker's model. The opinion focused on why Kelly had not left her abusive husband rather than on the grounds for her fear and emphasized the personality traits Walker identified with battered women, including "low self-esteem, traditional beliefs about the home, the family, and the female sex role, tremendous feelings of guilt that their marriage is failing, and the tendency to accept responsibility for the batterer's actions."[58] It also emphasized that "in order to be a battered woman, the woman and her abuser must go through the 'battering cycle' at least twice."[59] This criteria alone disqualifies the 85% of victims who do not experience the cycle of violence.

According to the *Kelly* opinion, a domestic violence expert could clear up myths by emphasizing the victim's "inability to escape despite constant beatings, her 'learned helplessness,' her belief in the omnipotence of her battering husband; and sometimes her hope that her husband will change his ways."[60] This testimony could bolster Gladys Kelly's credibility in the eyes of the jury by demonstrating that her experiences "were common to women in abusive situations." But if Ms. Kelly was suffering what her expert described as "psychological paralysis" as a result of the beatings, how could she muster the psychological strength to stab him with the scissors? The court seemed to acknowledge that too great an emphasis on her helplessness might cloud the straightforward question of whether she, "because of the prior beatings, numerous beatings, as often as once a week, for seven years is particularly able to predict accurately the likely extent of violence in any attack on her."[61] It remained unclear how the same woman who suffered the personality changes induced by battering was suddenly able to accurately understand her past experience and predict danger.

The New Jersey Supreme Court decision in *Kelly* emphasized repeated, severe abuse in establishing BWS. In a civil case, *Cusseaux v. Pickett*, the New Jersey court added other conditions identified with the domestic violence model, "recurring physical or psychological injury," and "a past or present inability to take action to improve or alter the situation unilaterally."[62] These criteria were applied by another New Jersey court in July 1994, when Christina Giovine filed an 11-count divorce complaint against her husband, Peter, alleging habitual drunkenness (count one) and extreme cruelty (count two) and claiming compensatory and punitive damages based on a "continuous and unbroken wrong commencing on or about March 1972 (when he had first assaulted her) and lasting until May, 1993, resulting in severe emotional and physical damage."[63] On appeal, Ms. Giovine argued she had not filed her case within the 2-year statute of limitations of the 1972 assault because, as a result of BWS, she was unable to aggressively seek help or even claim abuse. The *Giovine* court waffled. It agreed that battering constituted a "continuous tort," a significant step forward that has now been codified in Illinois. Because it adapted *Kelly*'s view that the "medical condition of battered woman's syndrome does not occur until a woman is battered at least twice," it concluded, however, that the 1972 assault did not constitute battering but could be used to support a claim of BWS if linked to the next assault in 1978. Unfortunately for Ms. Giovine, she had listed these assaults in a counterclaim to a divorce action filed by Mr. Giovine in 1980 (they later reconciled). This showed, said the court, that she could "take . . . action . . . to improve or alter her situation," hence was not suffering the "psychological paralysis" commonly associated with BWS. This catch-22—that action to seek redress is prima facie evidence that a plaintiff is not really battered, and hence not entitled to damages for suffering ongoing abuse—is a recurrent theme in domestic violence cases. In a liability case in which I testified, Dr. Walker testified that the fact that my client was representing herself at trial meant she was not a battered woman and so was exaggerating the harms she had suffered.

The New Jersey cases proceeded *as if* a woman's psychological debility (BWS) is the primary factor that prevents her from leaving and that her failure in this regard is the problem to be explained, not continuing abuse by the partner. Staying in a relationship is still commonly taken as evidence that it could not have been truly abusive. But the failure to stay can also demonstrate a level of decisional autonomy that is incompatible with being a battered woman.

The Insanity Dilemma

BWS and PTSD are not classic psychiatric diseases, because they have external causes that would affect any normal person exposed to similar trauma in identical ways. Many advocates and some clinicians approach

PTSD as a transient disorder that much like the "transitoria mania" claimed by nineteenth-century defendants, is thought to abate in a relatively short time in response to supportive interventions that rebuild the victim's sense of trust and integrity while diffusing traumatic memories. The PTSD I saw among veterans was a chronic and often disabling psychiatric condition that was only minimally responsive to therapeutic or pharmaceutical management.[64] But the view one accepts makes little practical difference in legal settings where mental health descriptions of any kind are taken as diagnostic, with all the attendant stigma, creating the burden of insanity borne by battered women in the past. Even when a diagnosis of PTSD or BWS is introduced to win sympathy for victims and shift attention to perpetrators of violence, it often fosters sex stereotypes of female incapacity and emotional frailty that mask a woman's reasonable efforts to resist or seek assistance for abuse, discounts her credibility as a witness to her own experience, and undermines her position in custody or child welfare proceedings. As Finnish scholar Suvi Kestinen observed about the application of trauma theory in counseling agencies working with abuse victims, "The mother was regarded as so traumatized by violence that her capacity to ensure the safety and take of the children was severely weakened. Neither was she thought to be able to recognize the needs of the children. . . . the motherhood of an abused woman was seen to lack essential elements and create a risk for the child's normal development."[65] Along these same lines, one well-known feminist psychologist claims that "the psyches" of the battered women she studied "were fully products of the violence they endured. It is as if there was nothing left, no part of them had been shielded from the ravages of the violence."[66] Once the victim self is portrayed as a tabula rasa on which the batterer's will is writ large, a will to self-preservation, let alone self-defense, is hard to identify, let alone support.

The Normalizing Effect of Trauma Models

Traumatic life events, like other misfortunes, have more severe consequences for those who have been sexually abused as children or suffered other problems. But traumatization theories are premised on the belief that normal persons exposed to a similarly unbearable reality would seek to manage events in the same general way. Even if the specter of psychiatric disease can be managed, the level of behavioral determinism implied by this argument confounds the cultural insensitivity of trauma theory by frustrating the law's interest in free will or mens rea. As Downs emphasizes, "syndromes . . . are formulaic and politicized in ways that pay insufficient heed in their own rights to the subtleties of reality and individual cases, and unnecessarily compromise the presumption of individual responsibility upon which legal justice and equal citizenship rest."[67]

Current responses to the quandary created because only a few of those exposed to similar trauma employ retaliatory or fatal violence are no different from in the nineteenth century. One answer is that the violence that elicited the response for which a woman is being tried was greater than in the past—the violent brute dilemma. Another is that she was shocked by the nature of the violence, perhaps because he tried to have sex with her son or crosses some other invisible line— the "innocent" spouse dilemma. If evidence of severe violence is lacking, the defense can also claim that trauma caused her to exaggerate the danger she faced (the PTSD claim in chapter 11) or that she "cracked" under the cumulative weight of the abuse—versions of the insanity defense. All of these choices create a spiral of logical dilemmas that ultimately devolve into how the court views the defendant's character and whether, perhaps because of its sympathies, it simply wants to set her free. This was not the case in *Kelly*. Although Lenore Walker testified that the defendant was suffering from BWS at her retrial, the prosecution's expert testified she was not, and Gladys Kelly was convicted.

Even as exposure of courts to an ever broader range of cases has increased their sensitivity to the dynamics of abuse, it has also raised the bar on the level of violence and psychological harm they require before a trauma defense is accepted. Reliance on a harms calculus resurrects the dilemma Cobbe pointed to a century ago: lower levels of abuse are normalized, the cumulative effects of ongoing abuse are masked, and women who suffer the more typical pattern of routine, low-level assault are disqualified.

Is the battered woman's defense effective for the small proportion of victims to whom it applies?

Walker claims to have successfully employed the BWS in over 150 murder trials.[68] But an optimistic assessment of the battered woman's defense is not justified by other evidence. The mean prison sentence for women charged with killing abusers actually increased 250% from 1979 to 1983 (from 4.1 years to 10.2 years), shortly after the BWS model was adapted.[69] In a subsequent study of 114 female-perpetrated spousal homicides, over half of the offenders received prison sentences, with an average of 16 years to serve.[70] Reviewing 26 cases on which expert testimony on BWS was admitted, forensic psychiatrist Charles Ewing reports that in 17 (roughly 2 out of 3), the battered woman defendant was convicted of murder, manslaughter, or reckless homicide, a conviction rate that approximates the general conviction rate in such cases.[71] In Browne's 1987 study, charges were dropped against only 1 of the 42 battered women who killed abusers. Susan Osthoff directs the Philadelphia-based National Clearinghouse for the Defense of Battered Women, the nation's major depository of information on criminal cases involving battered women. In 1991, Osthoff estimated that 72% to 80% of women accused of killing abusive partners were still being convicted or accepting a plea, and many received long, harsh sentences.[72] Things may have gotten worse since then. A review of the literature on sentencing in 1997 noted persistent gender inequities in the indictment, prosecution, and sentence determination of women who kill their abusers.[73] Meanwhile, a study of persons incarcerated in Missouri for killing their partners found that the modal sentence for men was markedly less severe than the sentence for women, possibly because women are more likely than men to use a knife or a gun.[74]

Ewing illustrates the limits of the syndrome defense by citing the 1983 murder of Marshall Allison in his sleep by his common-law wife, Leslie Emick, in response to a long documented and brutal history of physical abuse. Emick's self-defense claim was bolstered by the testimony of a psychiatrist, who presented a rendition of BWS that was faithful to the Walker model. The expert testified:

> The abused wife undergoes a personality change as the abuse increases. She becomes frightened and unable to project her thinking into the future. She lives her life from one beating to the next and her thoughts relate solely to her efforts to avoid the next beating. The wife is usually hopeful that, if she pleases the husband, the abuse will stop. For his part, the husband usually expresses remorse after a beating and attempts to reconcile with gifts and/or promises to refrain from abuse in the future. The wife then sees the husband in a different light and is filled with false hope. Another aspect of the syndrome is that the wife eventually feels that she cannot escape her tormentor and that she will be tracked down if she attempts to flee the situation. Her self-esteem vanishes and her confidence is shattered. She feels that no one would believe her if she told them about the abuse and, thus, she keeps it to herself.[75]

New York's self-defense law excuses deadly force only if the defendant is "confronted by the appearance of danger . . . which aroused in her mind an honest and reasonable conviction that she was about to suffer death or serious physical injury."[76] As is quite common in such cases, the prosecutor argued that abuse motivated Emick's violence and that "the very ongoing nature of the abuse prove(ed) that Miss Emick was under no imminent danger, particularly from a sleeping man." This was a variant on the rationale that led police to leave the Hughes house after Mickey's threat to kill Francine—he hadn't killed her before, so he wouldn't do so now. It would be hard to find a better example of normalization.

In Emick, the expert answered the question "why now?" by arguing that the murderous response reflected a pattern of short-sighted thinking that was distorted by years of abuse. More often, the victim's response is prompted by her acute sensitivity to nuances in her partner's behavior honed over years of abuse, what psychologist Julie Blackman calls the "special reasonableness of battered women." Many women describe responding to a certain "look in the eye" that signals that violence was inevitable and imminent.[77]

Ewing argued that Emick was convicted because of the male-oriented criterion for self-defense, not because Walker's model failed her. An indication of bias is that as many as 40% of the convictions of abuse victims for murder are overturned on appeal.[78] But even had the *Emick* court accepted the expert's testimony at face value, the best that could be hoped for was a finding of diminished capacity, not an acquittal.

Courts have responded more positively to the battered woman's defense as judges and juries have become sensitized to the realities of domestic violence. But despite its popularity, there is limited evidence that the battered woman's defense is a substantial improvement over the defenses available to women who retaliated against abuse a century ago.

The case of Nathaline (Nate) Parkman, a client charged with the first-degree murder of her boyfriend, illustrates how current defense options fail to address the representational dilemmas faced by rough women, women who initiate violence, like Francine Hughes, or women who seek help aggressively.

State of Connecticut v. Nathaline Parkman

Nate Parkman was a 35-year-old African American substance abuser who lived with her two children in a second-floor apartment. During the course of her relationship with Larry W., she suffered assaults that included punches, kicks, an attempted drowning, an "ambush" with a club, rape, and multiple beatings. Nate had neither phone nor electricity and Larry had broken the window next to the back door and kicked in the front door so that it would not lock. On previous occasions, she had reported her injuries to the hospital, her social worker, and the police. Larry had been jailed twice for his assaults and had just been released pretrial under a protective order. The previous night, he had threatened to cut her when she slept, a threat she took seriously because this had happened previously. Here is Nate's description of what happened next.

> I heard Willie and Larry talking s—t under my front window . . . Larry was talking about what he was going to do to me. Larry said he was going to f—k me up. I was leaning out the front window of the apartment and I yelled back that he couldn't do anything more than what he did to me in the past. After that I decided to go outside. Larry is good for waiting and then coming to get me. I was afraid of what he was going to do to me. I was tired of his doing those things to me. I wanted to get him before he got me. I put my green long coat on and tucked the knife up my right sleeve. I walked out the back door. . . . I saw Larry coming out of the bar. Larry came up to me and I told him I was tired of his talking s—t to me and threatening me. I said "If you're going to do me, do me now." He told me he would come see me later, after dark. I slipped the knife down my sleeve into my right hand . . . and with the knife stabbed Larry once in the chest. I turned around and slid the knife back up my right sleeve and walked back to my apartment. . . . I thought of hurting myself but said no because he deserve everything.

Unlike Yvonne Wanrow, Nate was a large and powerful woman who shared none of the physical handicaps associated with her class. She had a history of arrests for assault, drug sales, and prostitution. Nor did she evidence learned helplessness. She had reported Larry's abuse to all the appropriate authorities and on multiple occasions. Her life decisions were undoubtedly shaped by sex and race discrimination. But no one involved in her case, least of all myself as her expert witness, believed that her unique vulnerability to physical abuse was the product of sex discrimination in the sense identified by *Wanrow*. But if neither *Wanrow* or BWS applied to Nate's defense, neither did the traditional reasonable man standard, because by putting the knife in her sleeve and approaching Larry in the street, she had taken preemptive action not encompassed even by the broadest standards of self-defense. Nor was she insane.

In her apartment, Nate felt like a hostage waiting to be attacked. Larry had ripped out her phone, broken the lights there and in the downstairs hall (where he had attacked her before), broken her windows (including the window next to the back door), and kicked in the front door so it would not lock. Based on his past assaults, his threat to "f—k" Nate up that night was entirely credible. As she told me, "he is good for waiting and then coming to get me." Nate could have left with her children. But they would have had to pass Larry in the street, putting the children at risk. She would have had to pass Larry to get to a phone and call police. Besides, when she had Larry arrested in the past, he had been quickly released and returned, even more determined to hurt her than before.

No currently available defense grasps the multiple and cumulative constraints that directly contributed to Nate's sense of entrapment or the feeling of existential terror that drove her to confront and kill Larry.

In addition to providing a faithful representation of women's experience that courts can understand, an adequate legal theory of battering should be applicable to women regardless of their race, class, sexual orientation, or personal history. Walker based her model of BWS on a sample of 400 women in the Denver area who had experienced at least two abusive assaults. Despite including a small group of women from prison, her sample was not merely highly selective, but overwhelmingly white (only 6% were black), college educated (63% had some college), and middle or upper class (51%).[79] There are no randomized or control studies that show that BWS is distinctively associated with abuse or even that women who exhibit the form of cognitive depression Walker labeled learned helplessness are less likely to leave abusive men and seek outside assistance than other women. In fact, 75% of the women who Walker interviewed to build her model had left their abusive partners, and many had been violence-free for a number of years.

Even if the BWS model encompassed their experience, jurors might still hesitate to see poor, minority, or aggressive women as victims worthy of a mental health defense. This may explain why the best-known acquittals of women who killed male assailants involved minority women like Inez Garcia, Joanne Little, and Karen Straw, who relied on traditional pleas of self-defense.[80] In contrast to these cases, the threat faced by Nate Parkman was more global than imminent. Nate's experience presented strategic as well as factual dilemmas. When I interviewed her in prison, she was being medicated for depression, had suicidal thoughts, was alternately flooded with rage and guilt, and reported nightmares about her own death, symptoms consistent with both BWS and PTSD. Other psychological indicators also pointed toward a post-traumatic disorder, including an ambiguous sexual identity, short-term memory loss, dull affect, and low self-esteem. But a violence-induced traumatic syndrome was contraindicated by Nate's history of aggressive help seeking, a clear understanding that Larry was responsible for the violence, and a self-consciously strategic attitude about her fate. Nate deliberately went into the street to "get him before he got me." Her physical appearance—she was thickly set, black, and muscular—added to the problem of convincing a jury that cognitive deficits resulting from trauma had rendered her helpless.

Traumatization theory also conflicted with Nate's personal needs. Her major role conflict centered around her feelings that although killing Larry made her appear like a bad mother, it had been necessary to protect herself and her children. She was disappointed that her own mother could not see this, particularly because her mother was caring for her girls while she was in jail. Emphasizing her diminished capacity would have undermined her sense that she had chosen the best path to protect and provide. In stabbing Larry, Nate was both refusing to be a victim and making a proactive decision about what she wanted for herself and her children. The challenge was to communicate this to the court.

Psychological Self-Defense

Cases like Nate's highlight the benefit of basing defense claims on an affirmative conception of womanhood that emphasize the subjective costs of entrapment for feminine identity. The theory of psychological self-defense (PSD) developed by forensic psychiatrist Charles Ewing illustrates this approach.

In conceptualizing the effects of battering, Ewing believes we need to expand the concept of the self, normally equated with only physical life and bodily integrity, to include "those psychological functions, attributes, processes and dimensions of experience that give meaning and value to physical existence."[81] His approach resolves the core dilemma posed by the BWS: "why now?" With the escalation of abuse, he argues, "most battered women experience a turning point when the violence or abuse done to them comes to be felt as a basic threat, whether to their physical or social self or both." Suddenly realizing she is in grave danger, the woman is left in a state of "pervasive fear that consumes all of her thoughts and energies."[82] It is out of this crisis—as the battered woman identifies with "the victimized self"—that she is forced to take "practical actions to see that the victimization stops or does not reoccur."

The notion of a turning point corresponds more closely to battered women's experience than an emphasis on a proximate epiphany associated with immediate risk. From the moment Donna (chapter 10) realized she "was living on the edge of a roof and any day he was just going to push me off," her existence was dominated by a pervasive fear that she would be killed, and she focused only on what she could do each day to ward off this fate. Using the concept of PSD, I could reframe what might otherwise have seemed a cold and calculated decision by Nate to "do him before he does me" as a reasonable response to an accumulated assault on every aspect of her being. Larry's assaults on her apartment (e.g., the fact that she was denied a safe domicile), his violation of the protection order, and his threats could be joined with the ineffectiveness of outside helpers, the history of assault, and fear for her children in an overall picture of the unacceptable paradox in which Nate was trapped: she could negotiate the time and place of her next beating, but not whether it would occur. The other actors in the process—police, hospital staff, the court, even her friends—operated from this same premise, responding only after she was hurt. Even in her decisive moment, the control she exercised over her fate was negative, challenging Larry to "do me now." Then she stabbed him, preserving her psychological self by relieving what had become, for her, an unacceptable state of dread.

Ewing's conception of human identity is interactive and highlights a class of harms to the self that can be expressed without resorting to potentially stigmatizing descriptions of a woman's deficits. The main damage Nate suffered had less to do with physical or psychological trauma—though both were present—than with her feeling that Larry had so circumscribed her capacity to freely act that she was dying as a distinct person, the same fear expressed by Lavonne, Donna, Lisa, and numerous other women in my caseload.

Ewing's conception of psychological self-defense lacks critical elements essential to a successful legal fiction, however. He avoids the reductionist implications of many trauma theories by depicting the self under siege as integral to personhood. Unlike PTSD or BWS, the damage he highlights does not constitute a syndrome—avoiding the generalist fallacy of syndrome defenses—or a psychiatric condition. But it is hard to see how the proofs he would offer could sidestep the tension between credibility and disability that plague other trauma defenses. At the very least, the justice system would have to grant psychological personhood the same standing as political personhood, something courts have been reluctant to do. Conversely, for juries to view the self as damaged by abuse, they must envision persons as legitimate vessels for psychological personhood. As we've seen, stories that focus on psychological harms evoke images of worthiness that are rarely applied to members of disadvantaged groups such as Nate Parkman.

Ewing's approach stops at the point where social justice for battered women must begin—at the juncture of subjectivity and citizenship. The seminal experience of battering is an infringement on liberty, equality, and autonomy. The intersubjective identity Ewing describes carries our purposes into the world through a process of representation and engagement that is the essence of political existence in liberal societies. The capacity to individuate through one's choices and influence the world accordingly underlies the operation of virtually every institution in civil society, including the family, workplace, market, and state. Locating the persona under attack within the discourse of rights and freedoms links it to justice claims that courts widely recognize in the public sphere and gives it a political standing that commands respect regardless of its social status or the psychological or physical harms it presents.

By restricting her life as he did, Larry jeopardized Nate's autonomy, her right to be the sort of mother she wanted to be, and her "liberty," including her right to go and come freely as she chose. In certain circles, the fact that Nate was poor, black, and a female would disqualify her claim to have her rights fully protected. But if Nate lacked a self, she would not have proactively defended it with such vigor. What drove her into the street that night was the existential threat to her standing as a free woman, the fact that Larry intended to subordinate her purposes to his as well as hurt her physically, to make her his thing. This, she could not allow.

The Burning Books

A similar realization led Francine to set the fire. In the months before the fateful evening, she had taken a part-time job, saved money to escape, returned to school, and enlisted a confederate to support her plan to leave. These experiences undermined the degree of subservience Mickey could command at home: after she started school, she substituted TV dinners for home-cooked meals on the nights she had classes, left him home with the children, and consented to sexual relations only when she wanted them. He assaulted these small affirmations of selfhood by attempting to degrade Francine back into her gender role. To remind her that she was "merely" a woman, Mickey forced her to eat off the floor, clean up "the mess," and burn her school books. The implication was that Francine could choose between voluntary or forced submission, forms of unfreedom that were different only in degree—the same nonchoice that confronted Nate Parkman. What was special about that night in Michigan was not the level of abuse Francine suffered, but that Mickey was assailing her return to school, the safety zone she had opened in their relationship to breathe the air of a free person, her moment of autonomy. The burning bed was a liberatory response to the burning books. Of course, had Greydanus adapted this argument to explain Francine's murderous rage, the jury would have been incredulous.

Neither Francine's nor Nate's actions were the desperate acts of persons who had lost all hope of survival, as the syndrome defense would have it. Both women made tragic choices, and both were flooded with guilt because of these choices. Both women were fully responsible for what they did, not driven to their acts by forces beyond their control. Their defense lies not in the frailty of their character, personality, sex, class, or culture, not even in the proximate harms they faced from abusive partners. Their defense stems from the irreducible core of autonomy, liberty, and justice on which a free society rests. To fully comprehend this, to appreciate what was taken from women like Francine, Ruth Childers, and Nate and grant them an unqualified right to resist, what I have called a liberatory response, we need to first imagine them as fully entitled citizens with the same standing as the men they killed.

Part III

From Domestic Violence to Coercive Control

6

UP TO INEQUALITY

This section reopens inquiry into the nature of women's oppression in personal life by broadening the current focus on violence to encompass a class of harms that bears directly on individual liberty, the chance for equal personhood, and the political bonds that join free and equal persons in a democratic community. Revisioning these harms changes everything about how we understand and respond to the abuse of women by male partners.

This chapter gives the perpetrators and victims of woman battering what Yiddish writer Isaac Beshevis Singer calls a "historical address." It tracks the evolution of abuse from wife beating in traditional patriarchal societies to wife torture during the transition from industrial to modern corporate societies, and then to coercive control, the emerging strategy of choice for men who seek to dominate female partners in liberal democratic societies

Male domination is no more immutable or inevitable than racial supremacy or other dominant-subordinate relationships based on biological or social inheritance. Instead, it forms and reforms to meet the progressively more potent challenges posed by women's liberation. My argument is straightforward: that men have devised coercive control to offset the erosion of sex-based privilege in the face of women's gains, filling the void created as institutional support for male domination is disassembled by installing patriarchal-like controls in personal life. As I have hinted already and show in detail in subsequent chapters, coercive control typically complements frequent, but often minor, assaults with tactics to intimidate, isolate, humiliate, exploit, regulate, and micromanage women's enactment of everyday life. If the threats posed by equality prompt men to initiate coercive control, its foundation is continued sexual discrimination and particularly women's default consignment to domesticity. To implement coercive control, men must personalize their dominance over women by piecing together the remnants of structural and cultural constraints on which male privilege depended in the past and tailoring the resulting strategy to their individual relationships. The result is makeshift and transparent, setting the stage to eliminate sexual dominance in everyday life once and for all. As always, the devil is in the details.

The Construction of Male Dominance

Violence against women has been a weapon in men's arsenal for centuries. But this truly is qualified by an equally compelling reality, that the where, when, why, and how of men's coercion in women's lives and its link to other oppressive strategies are contingent on the structure of sexual power in a given time and place and how it is contested. Aggression may be biologically based. But prevailing forms of violence are rooted in calculations of the relative benefits, risks, and costs entailed in using force in one situation but not in others. The constitution of women's agency is also historically specific and both motivates and constrains how abuse is delivered. Male domination is about what women *are* and *have*, not merely what men *are* or *want*.

Feminist texts highlight four components of male domination: institutional constraints on women's opportunities and behavior, patriarchal rule, or sex discrimination; "sexism," a cultural ideology that rationalizes these constraints by identifying them with female "nature"; marriage and the family as core sites for shaping gender stereotypes; and coercion, the proximate means by which institutions and/or individuals actualize male power over women at these sites.[1] The following sections track how the changing interplay between these elements and women's developing agency was expressed in three historical constellations of abuse.

Traditional Patriarchy: Personal Violence in the Context of Political Control

In traditional societies, patriarchy is the governing political principle that organizes economic, public, and family life—the single thread that runs through law, custom, and religion to join the personal power of the husband over his wife to ruling networks of older, wealthier, and more religiously qualified men. Female subordination is a social fact established in women's families of origin, transferred to their marriage, and enforced across a broad political spectrum by a network of male-dominated institutions, such as the monarchy, the feudal estate, and the Church. Regardless of whether male elders govern through a centralized sovereignty or communally based networks centered in tribes, clans, or religious brotherhoods, women in this world have few alternatives to dependence on the significant men in their lives. The main line of formal authority in patriarchal society runs from the elders downward through the hierarchy of males. Women are effectively the property of men, the way cattle are, and their behavior and obligations in everything from how they dress and whom they marry to how they address their husbands are prescribed by public rules and enforced by public sanctions that remain the same whether their husband is a prince or a peasant. This fact—that women are equal in their subordination to men—helps compensate men for the rigid hierarchies through which their own inequalities, exploitation, and oppression are organized.

Women experienced varied degrees of subordination in ancient civilizations.[2] But for our purposes, the relevant fact is that while all men shared equally in the right to beat their wives and beatings or even killings could be expected or even required in circumstances where an honor code or a rule of obedience had been violated, whether women were beaten had no appreciable effect on their social standing and offered only very limited advantages to men. Where women are already subordinate, wife beating is supported by the patriarchy. But its specific dimensions are a function of situational factors specific to individual or familial circumstances rather than an overriding social logic. Whether women are beaten bears on the quality of their lives, but not on their relative freedom, because they have none. This is why women in traditional societies attribute abuse by their husbands or other family member, including mother-in-laws and a man's senior wives, to fate and bad luck.

The relationship between politics, economics, and domestic life changed during the Middle Ages in Europe, but without appreciably altering women's confinement to the family or the degree of their subordination to men. As far as women's obedience to their husbands was concerned, the major questions that excited public notice—hence official interpolation by Church or state—involved the content, context, and extent of their obligations, the means of their punishment (illustrated by the debate about "the rule of thumb"), and how to subdivide their loyalty to satisfy competing claims from male heirs or other men in their network.

This complex political network of obligation and protection remained largely in tact until the beginnings of the industrial revolution in the sixteenth century. This is not to say that women were always passive to their fate or that wife abuse was uniformly endorsed. A review of court records for Essex County (Massachusetts) in the last years of the seventeenth century reveals that women were assailants in 21 of 108 cases involving some form of violent behavior and victims in 34, a rate that is virtually identical to those recorded among working-class women in London in the 1860s.[3] Wife abuse was illegal in colonial New England, and community-based practices like the Cheverie or "riding the stang" were occasionally used to punish wife beaters. But women rarely brought complaints before New

England courts because penalties were few and enforcement rarely extended to allowing a wife to leave or divorce an abusive husband. Moreover, as is illustrated by the "skimmington" in which Lucetta is murdered in Thomas Hardy's *The Mayor of Casterbridge*, women who cheated or disobeyed their husbands were the most common targets of these community rituals. So long as male dominance was secured by formal restraints on women's mobility, sociability, dress, and the like, disobedience afforded few benefits.

The Industrial Revolution: Wife Torture, Inequality, and the Culture of Sexism

Capitalism and the establishment of representative democracies in the West destroyed the institutional support for patriarchy and threatened its material base in women's domestic labor. Women's formal status as subordinates to men was replaced by a system of sexual inequality based in institutional discrimination and ideological separatism. The economic and political dimensions of this story can only be sketched.

Towns had maintained local markets for centuries. From the sixteenth century on, however, the development of long-distance trade elicited a far-reaching network of horizontal economic relationships that challenged the political regulation of local commerce by the guilds and corporations and bypassed the vertical relationships of dependence that rooted personal domination by husbands in an estate system and self-contained household economy.

The mercantilist system gradually gave way to manufacturing, transforming trade in raw materials and finished goods from a source of wealth to a secondary source of domestic employment and subordinating what remained of household production. One result of this process was the growing separation between each family's individual economy, albeit oriented toward a commodity market, and the old supra-individual system of political authority on which the personal power of men depended.

Moving production out of families eliminated an important economic rationale for domestic tyranny. It also opened a new space where personal life could flourish as voluntary and intimate that contrasted sharply with the coercive nature of the state and the depersonalized and competitive character of emerging markets in labor and other commodities. In the interstices between this new conjugal arena, private enterprise, and the state, a "public" formed, comprised of "private people come together" in the words of German sociologist Jürgen Habermas, to restrict state coercion and, in the name of individual rights, to allow the maximum amount of freedom for (and in) the private sphere of commodity production, exchange, and family life.[4] The newly emerging classes of wage workers, merchants, and entrepreneurs aligned to support broadly based representative institutions through which they could influence public policy without playing a direct role in its formulation.

In theory, the new political culture of individual rights and liberties should have offered women credible alternatives to domestic subservience. It did not, at least not immediately. Although large numbers of single women were employed, until the late nineteenth century and in many countries well into the twentieth, women could not own and control property, enter contractual agreements, enter the professions, or vote, sit on juries, or hold public office. Husbands even owned the earnings of the proportionately few married woman who worked outside the home. Because individual rights were closely tied to property ownership and men owned the property, women were excluded from the benefits of citizenship. Industrialization widened the space separating home from productive labor, made the receipt of wages the mark of "real" work (and so of manhood), and led to the declining visibility and status of women's contributions in the home. As the bourgeois family became the cellular module for organizing social life, women were burdened with satisfying needs for health, education, socialization, service, and support they had formerly met in conjunction with community networks.[5]

Sexism, "Wife Torture," and the Domestication of Violence

The cultural configuration modern feminists dubbed "sexism" appeared alongside industrialization and democratization, helping reconcile women to their exclusion from commodity production and full citizenship by identifying femininity with deference and women's confinement to the home, effectively making necessity a virtue. At the core of this ideology was what historian Nancy Cott called the "canon of domesticity."[6] If the laws of marriage made the social model of striving for wealth irrelevant for women in preindustrial societies, this canon went even further, prescribing self-renunciation and dependence as moral reference points for a wife's being, traits that were manifest in service to husbands and other family members. Domestic ideology reinforced the claim by liberal political philosophers that women's natural subordination made the family a nonviolent vessel for bonding, self-sacrifice, and the delicate psychic economy that undergirds civic virtue. This was contrasted with the self-interested and self-regarding autonomy that propelled men to seek their prospects in civil society and treat one another instrumentally, as means to personal ends. State regulation was essential to manage the potentially violent consequence of competition between equals in the market. But the stability of sexual hierarchies made violence improbable in personal life, placing it outside social concern.

Sexist ideology contributed to woman abuse in three critical areas. In depicting a range of traits that were presumably natural to femininity, it laid the groundwork for invidious comparisons between the ideal woman and real wives that inevitably found the latter wanting, particularly in the laboring classes where these traits were hardest to sustain, contributing to a barrage of criticism and "correction" by men and widespread feelings of inadequacy among women. Second, by representing women's economic and political marginality as a natural consequence of their biology and the atrophied persona developed within the domestic sphere as the essence of the truly feminine, the domestic canon obscured the social nature of their vulnerability to violence, isolation, and control in personal life. Most important, the canon helped "domesticate" the aggression borne in market competition and class exploitation by redirecting it toward women and children.

Throughout the nineteenth century, strikes, riots, and crime were synonymous with industrial and urban life, a fact trade unionists, socialists, and communists attributed to glaring inequities in wealth and opportunity occasioned by capitalism. The prevailing gender ideology offered an alternative reading that rooted violence and other forms of social deviance in male character and psychology. Sexist imagery identified the domestic arena as a safety valve, where women's responsibility to "civilize the brutes" could extend to passively absorbing their hostility. As a complement to state repression of working-class militancy, such views also helped men rationalize wife beating, sexual promiscuity, and substance abuse as so many ways to "blow off steam," a rationalization that remains widespread. Popular accounts portrayed violence as a natural, inevitable, and largely irremediable aspect of everyday life in working-class homes. In *Hard Times* (1854), Charles Dickens's satire of utilitarianism, industrialization, and trade unions, class violence is displaced into secret violence within the home and the abused working-class woman presented as being best suited to the passive role ascribed to her by Victorian gender ideology. In the 1880s, English novelists George Gissing and Rudyard Kipling also portrayed class violence as a family affair rather than a social phenomenon, alternately depicting brutish men and passive women or put-upon men and raging viragos. In encouraging men to domesticate their violence rather than direct it at public targets, gender ideology helped make women human buffers for the range of feelings excited by exploitation, the chronic failures of capitalism, and for personal as well as social frustrations.

"Wife Torture" as a Response to the Failure of Domesticity

Robbed of their economic function as junior partners in household production but excluded from direct access to industrial employment, women's status relative to men was initially weakened by the rise of business enterprise, and they were forced to define their needs within a framework of material dependence on husbands and their wages. Sent off to seek their livelihood by day in the "jungle filled with wilde beasties," men increasingly relied on their wives to provide an emotional "haven in a heartless world" by performing a level of domestic work sufficient to free up time for their own rest, leisure, and self-development. The conjugal ideal was premised on an ephemera, however, because working-class families could barely survive let alone thrive on the low and sharply fluctuating family wage given to men. As the nineteenth century wore on, the contradiction at the core of women's role became increasingly glaring. Ever greater levels of self-exploitation were required to support the illusion of home as a space cleared of hard work and exploitation, the reality that gave birth to domestic economy. Violence mediated this contradiction and its complement, women's attempt to resolve it by seeking paid work outside the home.

Sexism and the ideology of domesticity delayed women's quest for full personhood. But the material pressures for women to seek their future outside the realm of necessity and selflessness to which they were bound were too great, and the appeal of entering society as full persons too seductive to be countered by ideology alone. Violence was the next line of defense when sexist ideology failed to reconcile women to their marginal and subservient status in the face of expanding economic opportunities and political rights. Apart from the fact that violence made a mockery of the conjugal ideal, because wages frequently dropped below subsistence, and cycles of unemployment were continual from the eighteenth century onward, women could only keep their families afloat by taking an ever more active hand in domestic economy, policing their husband's drink, or confiscating his wage on pay day (as in the practice of "tipping up"), an aggressive stance that could make them appear more virago than lady-like.[7] As parodied in *Emma* (1815) and other Jane Austen novels, the alternatives were to delay marriage or childbirth, refuse sex, enter "service," or endure a father's autocratic demands instead of a husband's. But once they partnered, women were expected to make up for material insufficiencies through sweat equity or to "go without," an expectation that was illustrated by the common practice of male favoring (making sure all men and boys are fed before women eat) whose effects included high rates of female tuberculosis in agricultural districts where men enjoyed relatively long life expectancy. Or women could supplement family resources by bartering or selling domestic skills such as wet-nursing or laundering. The ultimate option was to enter the workforce directly.

By adapting one or more of these paths, nineteenth- and early twentieth-century women helped stave off impoverishment in millions of homes. But this also created myriad problems for the sexual hierarchy on which liberals pinned their hopes for family peace, stirring feelings of self-sufficiency, equality, and resentment in women and feelings of shame, jealousy, failure, anger, and dependence in men. Because these tensions were endemic to working-class family life in industrializing societies, when men responded to them with force, violence quickly escalated into a spiraling torrent of abuse, resistance, and recrimination. One result was the pattern of chronic and severe abuse in working-class families that Frances Power Cobbe identified as wife torture.

Writing in the 1860s about "Wife Torture in England," Cobbe argued that violence against wives was rooted in the mutually reinforcing systems of sexual inequality and gender stereotypes.[8] Few men who beat women were held accountable, regardless of circumstance. But she drew on court

cases and anecdotal information to show how differences in class circumstances elicited different types of abusive behavior. Men in "respectable"
drawing rooms could depend on broadly defined gender norms to regulate
a wife's behavior and so needed only an occasional "blow or two" to exact
obedience. In sharp contrast was the situation in the working classes, where
material circumstances made regulatory norms less effective. Here, a class
of viragos "gave as good as they got." In the "kicking" districts of Liverpool
and London, unprecedented levels of violence were illustrated by routine
beatings with "hob-nail boots." Cobbe offered a ready explanation for why
the "persistent torture of women" in the laboring classes was so widely
tolerated even by "good men" endowed with "higher sensibilities." Both
groups shared the notion

> that a man's wife is his PROPERTY, in the sense in which a horse is his prop-
> erty (descended to us rather through the Roman law than through the cus-
> toms of our Teuton ancestors). Every brutalminded man, and many a man
> who in other relations of life is not brutal, entertains more or less vaguely the
> notion that his wife is his thing, and is ready to ask with indignation (as we
> read again and again in the police reports), of any one who interferes with his
> treatment of her, "May I not do what I will with my own?"[9]

Brutality in the lower classes, Cobbe believed, provided the backdrop of
fear that allowed regulation to proceed unchallenged in middle-class
homes.

In addition to being pushed into the social world by the paltry wages
men brought home, women were drawn to labor, commerce, education,
and civic life by the possibilities for personhood that these activities represented. The ideas of sovereignty, autonomy, and choice—of being regarded
as if they were free and equal—of gaining a political voice through association that was unencumbered by the weight of natural virtue, were all
preferable, whatever the reality, to the all too real experience of domestic
isolation and servitude, whatever the ideal.

The Fight for Equality

Men found ready support in the law for their use of violence to sustain
domestic servitude amid women's attempts to support themselves and
their families. Nineteenth-century laws allowed (even encouraged) them
to exploit women who took gainful employment in what amounted to
conjugal theft, whereas women were denied a similar right to support
from men. In a widely circulated pamphlet, Cobbe observed, "The legal
act by which a man puts his hand in his wife's pocket, or draws her
money out of the saving's bank, is perfectly clear, easy, inexpensive . . . the
corresponding process by which the wife can obtain food or clothing from
her husband when he neglects to provide it, where may it be? Where is it
described?"[10]

Along with John Stuart Mill and Harriet Taylor, Cobbe was convinced that political inequality was the source of sexual exploitation in the home because it allowed men to make laws that reflected their limited experience and enhanced their personal power. Against this narrow self-interest, this generation of feminist reformers appealed to sex-neutral principles of citizenship, individual freedom, and equality before the law, hoping to expand the reach of public rights to encompass women. To ease Tory fears that women would use equality to enter the job market and undermine the values of home and hearth, Mill reassured them that domestic life would be more peaceful if women could choose it freely, which they surely would.[11] Cobbe led the fight to criminalize wife torture and provide its victims with financial relief. But she agreed with Mill and Taylor that the problem of domestic violence would resolve only when the structural barriers were removed that kept women from enjoying the same political rights as their husbands, fathers, and brothers. Only when women were the legal equals of men (and no longer property de jure) would men cease to treat them as property de facto in the home.

The nineteenth-century women's movement addressed wives' status as male property and demanded a right not to be beaten alongside prohibition, which afforded greater access to male wages, the abolition of slavery, the right to divorce and own property, to work for wages, to child custody, birth control, independent citizenship, access to schooling and co-education, and the franchise. Because most white men already had these rights, reformers pitched their appeal in the language of universal egalitarianism. As Mill put it in his classic tract on *The Subjection of Women*,

> The equality of married persons before the law . . . is the only means of rendering the daily strife of mankind in any high sense a school of moral cultivation. . . . Already in modern life and more and more as it progressively improves, command and obedience became exceptional facts in life, equal association its general rule. . . . We have had the morality of submission and the morality of chivalry and generosity; the time is now come for the morality of justice.[12]

These principles were realized piecemeal, as women's political power was enhanced by the expanding material base provided by female employment, social welfare legislation, and the heightened status women enjoyed on the home front during the world wars. An important marker of women's growing autonomy in determining the habits of their lives was that by the 1920s, women's historical disadvantage in life expectancy relative to men had been reversed in the United States and Europe.

The liberal faith that economic and political rights would free women from oppression ignored the independent influence of sexist ideology on the organization of personal life. But if the combination of capitalism and democracy has not eliminated women's second-class status in relationships or families, it has gone a long way toward ending their subordination to men, particularly in those areas where religious or community opposition to the spread of the market ethos into everyday life was swept aside by the separation of Church from state, neutralized by injecting a spiritual element into economic activity (the Protestant ethic) or was minimal to start. In the United States, Great Britain, Canada, and much of Western Europe, even the staunchest opponents of liberal reform now couch their arguments in terms of the Lockean values of individual freedom, social mobility, egalitarianism, and property rights rather than communal traditionalism. The women's movement successfully exploited this sentiment, forming critical alliances with religious and moral conservatives in its fights for greater personal freedoms for women on issues such as birth control or the regulation of domestic violence. As important was the support U.S. women gleaned from business elites who appreciated their potential contribution to commerce and industry. After World War I, much of business regarded women's traditional service in domestic life in the same way most women did—as an obstacle to their transformation into the sophisticated purveyors of consumption, public service, and wage work required by a rapidly expanding economy. Those historian Stuart Ewen called the "captains of consciousness" in business and advertising urged the "new woman" to abandon frugality in favor of spending; substitute product loyalty for loyalty to home, hearth, or husband; replace homemade with store-bought goods; and seek self-expression through employment and purchasing.[13]

Whether the relationship between women's liberation and U.S. business constituted a "marriage," as Ewen contends, or merely a convenient flirtation, the alliance helped normalize women's emergence as worker-citizen-consumers and remove the stigma inherited from images of militant suffragists and ax-wielding Prohibitionists. Business support for female independence was not unqualified. Deference, self-sacrifice, and other values implicit in women's default role as homemakers keep the social costs of reproducing the workforce down, apply downward pressure on all wages, and allow women to be treated as second earners who can be paid less than men for comparable work. Business shared the fantasy of many modern husbands, that women could simultaneously satisfy two masters, providing a ready source of inexpensive, qualified labor for expanding service, support, and production sectors by day while devoting the rest of their time to producing, raising, and civilizing families and sexually servicing men. Maintaining this balance proved difficult, however, because the market values of choice, independence, and self-interest critical to women's success as producer/consumers undermined the conjugal ideal of female deference and the identification of marriage and family life as the primary sites for self-expression. In Cobbe's world as today, a significant subgroup of men have tried using coercion to mediate the tensions created by the clash of women's social commitments. But there is a critical difference. The female agency men confront today is constituted from a wealth of rights and resources that make violence alone increasingly ineffective as a sole means to secure control.

The Great Sexual Transformation

In the years since World War II, and particularly since the 1960s, the status of women in the Western democracies and in many other parts of the world has undergone a transformation that is historically unprecedented. The dramatic expansion of basic industry in the United States after the wars is unthinkable apart from the huge mass of labor that immigrated to the United States after 1880 and the Great Migration of Negro sharecroppers to Northern cities. But the parallel expansion of the commercial sector during this period, the rapid recovery of European industry after World War II, and the global dominance of U.S. corporations after 1950 are equally unintelligible apart from women's move from marginally or temporarily employed, disenfranchised housewives to the epicenter of economic, political, and cultural life.

Employment

In supporting women's emancipation from traditional roles, liberal elites were doing no more than hitching their stars to the massive collective transformation women had already begun.

Women's drive for equality began with property rights and the demand for political participation, concerns that primarily aided more affluent women. "Married Women's Property Acts" were passed in Great Britain and the United States in the 1850s, alongside legislation protecting women from the harshest forms of brutality by their husbands. By the end of World War I, all but 4 states had changed their laws to give wives full property rights, and women had won the vote in 12 states, in the major British colonies (New Zealand, 1893; Australia, 1902; and Canada in 1917) and had limited suffrage in England. By the end of World War II, women had won virtually all of the legal, political, and economic rights for which the first wave of feminists campaigned, including the rights to divorce and gain custody of their children.[14]

Women's participation in the workforce increased at a steady pace throughout the twentieth century in tandem with their political and legal rights. In 1900, one woman in five in the United States was employed outside the home. In 1948, when the U.S. Bureau of Labor Statistics started to track participation, the rate had grown to 32%. But only after 1960 did women's participation rates climb dramatically, reaching 59.3% in 1996. Among younger women age 25 to 34, labor force participation rates more than doubled in this period, from 36.0% in 1960 to 75.2% in 1996. By the century's end, women's overall labor market participation had peaked at 60.2%, and by 2002, women represented just less than half of the employed workforce (46.6% versus 53.5% for men) and comprised a majority among some groups of younger workers.[15]

The changing sites of female employment are as important as their labor market entry. At mid-century, women's employment options were still limited to the female services (school teaching, nursing, clerical work, for example) and lower paying jobs in retail, service, and manufacturing. Today, women comprise 28.8% percent of lawyers, 26.6% of physicians, 42.3% of college and university teachers, and 53% of accountants and are heavily represented in many other nontraditional job sectors historically dominated by men. Women are still concentrated at the bottom of the occupational ladder, in fields like health, education, social work, clerical work, and sales where sex segregation remains a major issue, and they comprise only a tiny proportion of the top corporate and government positions in the United States. Still, by 1994, women had surpassed men numerically as well as proportionally among those classified as executives, managers, and in the professional specialties.[16]

During the early Industrial Revolution, when they were generally excluded from basic industry, women played an important role as fillers when male employment slacked or was insufficient, in seasonal jobs, or in towns where the surrounding male labor force was needed in farming, as in the early New England textile plants. Because women's work for wages was an extension of their domestic role, a form of service to their husbands or families designed to produce supplementary income, it could be treated as a secondary form of employment rather than as competition for men's jobs. Similar assumptions run through the history of women's work, from the "mothers' line" created by British industry during World War II through the "mommy track" urged on U.S. business in the 1980s. In each instance, the understanding was that women's work was voluntary and hence their time commitments flexible, that their domestic role allowed business to pay them less than other employees, and that they would leave the workforce permanently when they married or had children.

An important marker of women's changing status and the corresponding weakening of pronatalist ideology is the extent to which they remain in the workforce throughout their married and childbearing years. Labor market participation rates have been increasing even more rapidly for married women and mothers in these groups than for single women. During the twentieth century, labor market participation for married women jumped from 5% to 60%, and the increase for mothers is almost as great.[17] In 1999, 55% of women with children under age 1 were in the labor force, compared to just 31% in 1976. By 2000, four out of five mothers with children aged 6 to 17 years (79%) were in the workforce.[18]

Education

The great transformation in women's status reflects both the pull of increasing opportunities, particularly in expanding service and governmental sectors, and the push provided by the desire for independence and the need for income to support families. Women's increasing access to education was critical to both dynamics. Education is an investment in social capital that is wasted if not fully exploited.

Coeducation in elementary and secondary schools in the United States developed rapidly after 1850, driven as much by economic considerations as a concern for equity. By 1940, just over one woman in four in the population had completed high school (26.3%), though this proportion was already higher than among men. High school graduation rates for both sexes increased most dramatically in the 1970s. By 2003, when more than four out of five in the U.S. population had completed high school, women and men had similar completion rates (85% and 84.1%, respectively) and women were as likely as men to have had at least some college (51.9% versus 53.2%). Women's greatest relative gains were in their rates of college graduation, the key to income opportunities today. After losing ground to men between 1950 and 1960, women's graduation rates have increased by almost 500% (from 5.8% to 25.7%), with the largest proportional gains again occurring in the 1970s. By 2003, women in the U.S. population who were 25 years or older were 89% as likely as men to have completed college.[19]

Civic Participation

Civic life was the third arena from which women were historically excluded, both directly, because they lacked the vote and other rights of citizenship, and indirectly, because they were discouraged from participating in the public forums that were the foundation for the civil polity and set the terms for how scarce public resources were allocated. Women's exclusion from these realms reinforced their literal dependence on men and the extent to which their sense of themselves was derived reflexively from the limited contacts within the sphere of the family.

Until well into the 1920s, civic life in the United States, Great Britain, the rest of Europe, and Scandinavia was dominated by the old middle-class trinity of doctors, lawyers, and clergy, the world satirized in Sinclair Lewis's *Babbitt*. Still, by the 1870s and in the decades until women got the franchise, the politically diverse group of middle-class reformers historians have dubbed social feminists or social mothers fought to extend the values of family and motherhood to the public arena. Women's civic involvement in the United States today is still directly related to income. But women from all social classes are more likely to be involved in civic life than men.[20] The proportion of women registered to vote varies markedly from Hawaii, the state with the lowest female voter registration rates at 51%, to North Dakota, where the rate is 91%. But women are more likely than men to be registered in every state but Pennsylvania. In all but seven states, women are also more likely to actually vote.[21]

Political scientist Jean Bethke Elshtain is one of a number of scholars who believe that the revitalization of political life in the United States demands that the women's movement restore the emphasis turn-of-the-century social feminists placed on the importance of marriage and families as source of community solidarity and the defense of privacy against outside intrusion.[22] Although married women are more likely than unmarried, never married, or widowed women to participate in a variety of community development and civic activities, women who are employed full-time are actually more likely than any other group to be active in local political or civic institutions, suggesting that women's political interest is sparked by their broadening participation in the social world, not by family life or marriage, as Elshtain believes. Women are also more likely than men to build friendship and support networks through their civic involvement than are men.[23]

Interestingly, the only factor that consistently differentiates women's willingness to be involved in volunteer associations, civil causes, and local politics from men's is their greater concern for their personal safety, particularly in public spaces.[24] This suggests that some form of "outside intrusion" (which Elshtain opposes) that preserves women's capacity to move freely through a broad spectrum of public spaces may be a prerequisite for the revitalization "communitarians" support.

Culture: Interpreting Work to Families

Cultural images have recorded the transformation in women's status since the 1960s and storied it through moral narratives that shape how women understand what is happening in their lives.

Until the development of the movies, magazines were the principal source of these stories. The Gibson girls sketched at the turn of the century by popular illustrator Charles Dana Gibson have been compared to Victorian Barbie dolls.[25] Gibson's women are tall and slim-waisted with flowing skirts and long hair usually piled high on their heads into a chignon. Their look is alternately soft and imperious, calm, with a somewhat mischievous smile, while exuding a studied inattention that suggests calculation rather than indifference. Their attitude toward men, sexuality, and marriage is reflected in a drawing (1903) in which three members of "the weaker sex" watch closely as a fourth examines a tiny man doll through a magnifying glass, using a long hair-pin in her other hand as a probe. Readers would have recognized the reference to the surgical theater paintings by Hinckley or Eakins. Like the surgeons, these women are patrician rather than working class and adapt a WASP superiority to their object that is antithetical to rural, immigrant, or racial taxonomies. But the implied comparison with the surgeons parodies as well as comments on women's enterprise, suggesting through its frivolity that their attention is wasted on the man doll, as is the pent-up aggression symbolized by the probe. The fact that these "girls" are joined in a single exercise rather than posed in an isolated romantic setting would also have signified something new to the audience of female readers, a capacity for collective feminine resourcefulness that would become a key trope in the 1920s. These women are capable of professional work (like the surgeons). But they have nowhere to go.

The flapper hitched the self-interested calculation of Gibson's women to the bold adventurousness they had repressed. Named by the British after young birds about to leave the nest and popularized by the drawings of John Held, actress Clara Bow, and comic strip character Betty Boop, flappers were aggressively androgynous rather than traditionally feminine: their breasts are hidden (and were often bound by cloth wraps), their waist invisible, their corset removed, their knees bare, their hair cut short, and their arms and legs in continual motion like a boy's (hence the French appellation *garçon*). But this imagery is neither asexual nor transgendered. When we couple their "male look" with the flapper's propensity for makeup—which earlier audiences would have identified with prostitution—these Jazz Age youth seem like machines stripped for economy and efficiency, transgressively feminine, and ready to do whatever it takes with themselves or others to get what they want, save cook, clean, or mother. This generation formed the centerpiece of the consumer revolution in the 1920s and the newly emerging service, sales, and office workforce.[26]

As Vachel Lindsay had predicted in 1915, by the late 1920s, movie directors (and behind them the producers and studios) were exercising a level of control over what their audiences experienced that was unavailable to department store moguls like Edward Filene, illustrators, or even to the new public relations men like Ivy Lee and Edward Bernays.[27] Unlike magazine images, movies are received collectively, leave little time for critical appraisal, and play off subliminal levels of awareness that can subvert as well as confirm the explicit story on the screen.

Early Depression-era cinema offers an interesting mix of escapist fantasy, realistic drama, and screwball comedies that satirized nationalism (*Duck Soup*), families and children (W. C. Fields), sexual propriety (Mae West), and other pillars of middle-class conformity. But by the mid-1930s, responding to pressure from guardians of public morality and the largely female audiences for film, Hollywood replaced its portrayal of women as sex objects with independent career women who struggled to integrate work and family roles. An important transitional film in this genre is *Craig's Wife* (1936), a remake of the 1920s Pulitzer Prize play by George Kelly. The original is an antifeminist morality tract centered on a middle-class housewife who loses everything, including her sanity, husband, and family, because she is obsessed with possessions and her husband's career. With upward mobility at a halt, many Depression-era films stressed the greater importance of love than economic success for women. But Dorothy Arzner, one of the few established female directors under the studio system, had a more radical idea. Instead of depicting Harriet Craig as cold and manipulative, she shaped Rosalind Russell's performance into a multilayered character who describes her marriage as a bargain needed to secure a permanent home. This "practical arrangement," which her niece Ethel sees as "dishonest," contrasts with the more traditional (presumably honest) marriages depicted in the film, that of her own mother who died of a "broken heart" after being abandoned by her father and of the neighboring couple, the Passmores, in which the husband kills his wife after discovering she has had an affair, then kills himself. As in the play, Harriet is abandoned by her husband, daughter, and friends. But in the film, Harriet's isolation stems not from her ambition but from her attempt to realize this ambition vicariously through the traditional route of heterosexual love, marriage, and family. In *Working Girls* (1931), Arzner suggested women should express their ambitions directly through a job and in *Christopher Strong* (1933), she discounted love as an alternative, ending Katharine Hepburn's career as an independent aviatrix in a suicidal plane crash precipitated by her love affair with the title character. But *Craig's Wife* set the stage for the larger message hinted at by Gibson, that the social bonds women form with one another around work or in the community provide a viable alternative to heterosexual dependency and marital isolation.

Popular lore has Rosie replace her rivet gun with a vacuum to make room for her returning husband after World War II. In fact, women's labor market participation slowed during the 1940s and 1950s, but did not decline; instead, it increased sharply in service and administrative support jobs that were critical to the fastest expanding sectors of the economy, and then took off in the 1960s, as we've seen. Insofar as women's work is visible at all in the popular culture of the period, it is portrayed as harmful to women's chances to have a satisfying family life. In the film version of the Rona Jaffe novel *The Best of Everything* (1959), Joan Crawford plays a successful editor with a publishing house and Hope Lange, her college-educated secretary with ambitions to be like her boss. Crawford is so miserable at her career that she quits to marry a widower, only to return to work shortly afterward, having discovered "it's too late" (to have a family), a lesson not lost on her younger colleague. As the credits roll, we see Hope, who has risen in the ranks to become a lonely editor like her idol, leave the office in a business suit and hat. She sees the male co-worker with whom she has previously spent a night (one of the "hot" sex scenes that explain why the novel is often reissued) and removes her hat as they kiss, presumably the prequel to her trading in her job (and any male-like ambition) for marriage.[28] This echoed what sociologist Philip Slater called "Spockism," the belief that well-educated, professionally prepared women could fulfill themselves by staying home to interpolate their infant's every utterance.[29]

The audience of working women would have seen something more than soap opera moralism in *The Best of Everything*. By the late 1950s, women's participation in the workforce was so indispensable to economic growth and family survival that reversing this trend would have meant economic disaster. In the film, Hope meets her life partner at work, a signal that the office was becoming an important social site. The representation of work as intrinsically unrewarding also helped ground female ambition rather than curb it, particularly as women were most likely to enter the settings sociologist C. Wright Mills called "Brains Inc." (the education, information, and publishing bureaucracies), "The Great Salesroom," and "The Enormous File." Film might offer women a romantic escape from domestic drudgery; work would not. Because women lacked a "wife," paid employment was likely to enhance tension during women's "second shift" at home. To accommodate the real demands of work and career, the film suggested, women should lower their expectations about marriage and accept levels of disappointment and frustration that had heretofore been thought incompatible with the family ideal, a message that dominated family therapy well into the 1960s. If they insisted on "the best of everything," they could make do with executive jobs and hot sex on the side but no husbands or children, the route widely followed by female executives in the 1950s.[30] Female employment as well as housework were conspicuously missing from the popular media of the 1950s and 1960s, an illustration of the low regard with which both were held. In *The Feminine Mystique*, Betty Friedan called housewives "parasites"; in *Pursuit of Loneliness*, Philip Slater called them "nobody."

All this had changed by the 1990s. With barely a nod to traditional family life or the importance of marriage and children to fulfill women's ambitions, TV dramas featured strong women as physicians, lawyers, forensic scientists, FBI agents, judges, prosecutors, police officers, and politicians, all formerly male roles Conflicts between career, marriage, and childbirth were portrayed as involving complex trade-offs, and career-favoring choices were no longer linked to tragic outcomes in personal life. In recent episodes of *ER*, the popular NBC drama about medical interns and residents in a public hospital, a female Asian resident decides to put her child born out of wedlock up for adoption and continue her career; a female surgeon becomes a mother while barely missing a day's work; a partially disabled lesbian internist gains custody of the child born by her deceased Latina lover; and an African American male surgeon, a single dad, takes a less demanding position to gain custody of his son. *Grey's Anatomy* goes further, offering the workplace (a hospital) as a site of sexual liaison and fulfillment as well as a place to socialize and train. Reruns of *I Love Lucy*, *The Cosby Show*, or shows like *Seventh Heaven*, *The Sopranos*, *Coronation Street*, *Desperate Housewives* (or the British version, *Footballers' Wives*) are still sufficient to sustain women who choose not to work outside the home (and can afford to do so), wax nostalgic for a time when home or pub life was where the drama was, and consider affairs "extra-marital" rather than business as usual. But even these shows depict women with traditional views as either the butt of humor or, as is the case for the Edie Falco role as Tony Soprano's wife in the HBO dramatic series, *The Sopranos*, as in far more turmoil about their roles than their professional counterparts.[31] The core family medium is no longer hiding the fact that most women work (as it did in the 1960s) or representing marriage as the aim of social life at work, as in the *Mary Tyler Moore Show*. Today's TV women are hip to a lesson still only implicit when *The Best Years of Our Lives* was made—that the alternative communities established at work provide today's family drama for women as they did historically for men and do so across divides by age, race, ethnicity, country of origin, or sexual orientation. The lesson from women's great transformation is clear: whereas personality and capacity are born and nurtured in families, they can only be fully realized in a wider social arena that includes work, education, politics, civic engagement, and a diverse social life. Coercive control is meant to respond to this lesson.

Up to Inequality

Booker T. Washington ended his autobiography *Up From Slavery* by describing his reception in Richmond, Virginia, the former capital of the Confederacy. Twenty-five years earlier, he had slept on the street in Richmond because of poverty. Now, he had delivered a message of "hope and cheer" to an integrated audience at the Academy of Music, a hall that "colored people" had not been allowed to enter until the night he spoke.[32] With hindsight, given the continued de facto segregation of American blacks, some readers might think Washington's title was ironic.

The revolution in women's status might be similarly titled "Up to Inequality." As a result of their quantitative gains, women in democratic market societies are no longer bound to men or family life the way they were less than a century ago. But the picture of female equality presented in popular media is no more realistic than the earlier portrayal of women as domestic slaves. What is true is that women have become so much less *unequal* that a *qualitative* change in their status has occurred sufficient to prompt a corresponding shift in how men oppress them in personal life.

Even this limited claim may seem suspect when we examine women's economic progress more closely or ask whether improvements in women's general position have carried over into their personal relationships with men. The relative shares of income, education, rights, and other sources of power men and women bring to the relationship have been altered. But differences are still substantial. For example, at least some of the reduction in women's relative disadvantage reflect the deterioration of men's position, not women's gains. In 25 of the states where the ratio of women's to men's earnings increased between 1995 and 1999, it did so in part because men's earnings fell (in constant dollars).[33]

The vast majority of women workers fall into three of the six categories into which employment is usually divided: technical, sales, and administrative support (40%), managers and professionals (32.2%), and service occupations (17.4%). Very small proportions of women work in skilled or unskilled blue-collar jobs or in agriculture, where men are heavily represented. Women slightly outnumber men in the higher paid occupations, including managerial positions, and enjoy relatively high status in areas of the United States, where these jobs are overrepresented. But they make substantially less than men in these roles. So, whereas 10% of male managers are in the top decile of all earners, women occupy only 1% of these top positions and only 6% are in the top two deciles.[34] According to Catalyst, a foundation that tracks women's progress in the corporate world, just 93 (4.1%) of the top-earning executives in *Fortune* 500 companies were women in 2000, a proportion that has only improved slightly since then.[35]

The most dramatic inequalities persist in an area where women's gains have been widely publicized: the gap between male and female earnings. According to official figures, since 1960, women went from earning just 59 cents for every $1 a man earned to 76.5 cents in 2002. In 2004, median annual earnings for women working full-time year-round were $31,223. Men with similar work effort earned $40,798. Comparing weekly earnings, data that exclude the self-employed and does not reflect pay differences such as annual bonuses, the gender gap ratio has improved by more than 9 percentage points since 1990 and in 2005 stood at 81.0, an all-time high.[36] Remaining gaps in Great Britain or other members of the European Union are even smaller. But what is less widely appreciated is that these ratios are derived by comparing the annual earnings of women and men who work full-time for a full year prior to the survey. These comparisons are misleading because they fail to consider the actual differences in male and female earnings over time that result because women are far more likely to work part-time than men and so to have many fewer hours where they earn income and more likely to have years of zero earnings due to their disproportionate responsibility for family care. To get a more realistic picture of the resources they actually bring to the table, economists Stephen Rose and Heidi Hartmann compared men and women's earnings in their peak earning years (ages 26 to 59) using a 15-year time-frame (1983–1998) and irrespective of whether they worked full- or part-time or left the workforce for a period to raise children or care for sick family members. Over the 15 years, women earned an average total of only $273,592, while the average working man earned $722,693 (in 1999 dollars). Thus, the gap in real, disposable income between men and women is 62%, almost three times as large as the gap commonly cited for the United States.[37] Had Rose and Hartmann's study included the added value of benefits, the resulting sex differences in earnings would have been even greater, because women continue to have much less access than men to high-paying, unionized jobs and so are less likely to have a variety of benefits than men, including health insurance and Social Security.

Despite these gaps, millions of women reject "bad bargains" and set up independent households each year. But the inequalities in income and employment highlight the enormous obstacles women continue to face in doing so and the possibility that they remain vulnerable to a reverse tipping point, when declines in average earnings or the increased costs of housing or other necessities reduce their political leverage, including their capacity to set up on their own or exercise other social rights that a younger generation of women take for granted. Nor is such a reversal improbable. Between 1996 and 2002 in the United States, as women's poverty actually increased in a number of states, their political representation dropped in a third of the states, the number of states with waiting periods for women seeking abortions increased from 14 to 22, and an additional 9 states implemented family caps, denying benefits to children conceived or born while a mother is receiving welfare, all direct blows to women's capacity to live independently.[38] Experience in India, China, the former Soviet Union, and much of Europe as well as in the United States make it clear that a combination of culture, sexist ideology, and religious fundamentalism continue to constrain women's capacity to translate their economic and political gains into increased bargaining power in relationships or families. But any weakening of these gains raises the specter that traditional sex hierarchies will be restored. In the United States, even where both partners work, the man can expect to average approximately $50,000 a year during his prime years of employment, whereas the woman can expect only $18,000. This gap is more than sufficient to support the differences in status that are exploited in coercive control. Any shift in the relative share of power in personal life that favors men exacerbates the imbalanced distribution of work in the home, further weakens women's autonomy, and makes them more vulnerable to sex segregation, other forms of job and wage discrimination, and to a further deterioration of the social rights that allow them to work full-time and/or set up independent households in the first place.

Shifts in Housework

Economic discrimination increases women's vulnerability to abuse. But far and away the most important vestige of their subordinate status is women's default consignment to domestic service.

As women's participation in the labor market increased, so did men's share of domestic work, rising from 20% to 30%. This change reflects a number of factors, including pressure from female partners and a growing sensitivity among men to women's burden. But more pragmatic motives are also at work. As one "new man" told sociologist Arlie Hochschild, "when my wife began earning more than me, I thought I'd struck gold."[39] Men's increased contribution is still largely limited to work around the margins, doing some combination of dishes, taking out the garbage, cooking "special" meals, mowing the grass, driving children to daycare and school, and changing the oil and light bulbs, with women doing everything else. Hochschild argues that the old gender division has simply been replaced by the extension of female exploitation to encompass paid employment as well as domestic service, what she calls women's "double shift."[40] Neither business nor government compensates for this reality. Though employed women are twice as likely as working men to provide 30 hours or more care giving for parents or parents-in-law, far fewer employed women than men have sick leave, vacation leave, or flexibility in their hours.[41]

Understanding Changes in Women's Status

The persistence of significant sexual inequalities does not obviate the larger point. Survey data, interview studies, and behavioral evidence based on help seeking consistently indicate that the vast majority of women, victimized or not, view themselves as men's equals, support equality in intimate relationships, and reject abuse in virtually any form.[42] By the late 1970s, a majority of American men also voiced their support for sexual equality in family affairs.[43] Resurgent fundamentalism in the United States and state and federal passage of DOMAs (Defense of Marriage Acts) have not reversed the trend for fewer women (or men) to identify domesticity or family life as the center of their personhood.

Women's activities in and around the home—housework, sex, consumption, child care, and other forms of personal service—comprise the only arena of female inequality that is susceptible to negotiation in personal life. As such, next to the money entering (or not entering) the home, it is the major source of interpersonal conflict as well as the major object of male control. For couples who are living together, the division of domestic work determines how space and time are allocated and utilized in personal life, including leisure, with important implications for social networking and job advancement. Much attention has been given to Harvard Professor Robert Putnam's plaint that more men are "bowling alone."[44] But the fact that they are bowling at all or spending hours at the gym, on the golf course, at the local bar or pub, or watching football games is largely the result of women's vastly disproportionate assumption of home maintenance and child care. Apart from the value added to other activities by time "off the clock," there is mounting evidence linking both free time and the social networking it facilitates to health, mental health, and satisfaction with life.

Domesticity adds little to women's social status. During the Reagan administration, Carolyn Graglia, David Gelernter, and other ultra-conservatives dubbed low-income, stay-at-home moms "welfare queens" and pressed for welfare reforms that moved them into wage markets. These same critics now rail against Betty Friedan and other feminists for denigrating women's traditional role in the home.[45] Discounting housework undoubtedly affects the self-esteem of full-time homemakers. But the more salient issue is how their continued consignment to housework impacts working women, who now constitute the majority. Employed women who must also work the "second shift" report far higher levels of anxiety than nonemployed women, more health problems, and much greater resentment of their husband's relative privilege than women in the past.[46]

Although domestic roles remain a key site of female exploitation and stress, they are no longer the focal point of female identity. Nor does women's enactment of domestic roles isolate them from civic engagement as it did in the past or automatically bestow unfettered control over the most significant family assets or decisions on husbands or other partners. So long as women had few alternatives to heterosexual coupling, their only hope of staving off a tyrannical partner was to cling ever more tightly to the domestic canon by increasing their self-exploitation or sexual service or using their wiles, the "dishonesty" for which Dorothy Craig is vilified by her daughter. Today, at least in the United States and large parts of Europe, millions of women package economic and social resources to support autonomy within or apart from dependent relationships to men, remaining single, forming same-sex relationships, divorcing, delaying marriage and/or childbirth, "supplementing" the relationship, pursuing a career, returning to school, taking two paying jobs, opening a business, or heading a family without husbands. In this context, homemaking is understood as a necessary burden rather than a trap or as something they trade for male protection and support. If things go badly in a relationship, women can always do for themselves or with other women what they did with or for him. It is the lost connection between women's status, domesticity, and dependence on men that coercive control is designed to reinstate.

The Changing Face of Domination: From Domestic Violence to Coercive Control

Political scientist Iris Young defines domination as a relationship of mastery in which the subordinate experiences herself as the subject of the unreciprocated authority of the other and life opportunities and resources are disproportionately allocated accordingly.[47] Sentient beings become persons only because they are recognized as such. When personhood is set in a matrix of unreciprocated authority, subjectivity atrophies.

Young's definition applies most directly to traditional and preindustrial societies where power is parsed out across a pecking order of men, much in the way other forms of property are distributed. In these communities, whether women "know" the significant men in their lives can make all the difference in their fate. But there is no compulsion for anyone to know them, one reason they can be hit at will. The industrial and political revolutions of the seventeenth and eighteenth centuries freed men to exchange their labor for a wage, an unequal but reciprocal relationship in which they were known only in their role as producers. Liberal democracy extended the principle of reciprocity to governance, fashioning a people's voice out of the franchise and supporting political parties, newspapers, and a range of complementary institutions that comprised the sphere of public activity and opinion.

Reciprocity was extended gradually to women as they demanded social recognition, and it became increasingly apparent that economic development and the maintenance of working- and middle-class families required that their untapped labor power be exploited. There was no need to police relations in private life so long as traditional sex hierarchies were stable. But by the late nineteenth century, these traditional hierarchies were in disarray, largely due to the progress of capitalism, democracy, and the organized women's movement, and there was an increasing social investment in women as workers, consumers, and citizens. Women were being moved out of the sphere of unquestioned male control in personal life, but they were afforded little protection against the inevitable backlash. One result was that family life looked increasingly like the state of nature to which men only had originally been consigned, replete with stepped-up competition and physical and sexual abuse. Wife torture emerged in the gap between provocation and protection, as society competed with individual men for women's loyalty and labor but remained ambivalent about granting them full substantive equality.

The domestic violence revolution began in the 1970s amid the broadest renegotiation of the sexual contract since the emergence of modern industry. Spawned by the civil rights, peace, and student movements of the 1960s, the influence of the modern women's liberation movement extended far beyond its activist base. The movement's importance lies less its specific programmatic focus than in the extent to which it articulated the values women from all social backgrounds who used their new access to jobs, education, and politics to initiate divorce, demand contraception, abort unwanted pregnancies, delay marriage and childbirth, reduce the number of children they bore, form single-parent and same-sex families, enter the professions, and participate in civic life in unprecedented numbers. Violence had provided men with an alternative to reciprocity, a way to prevent women from bringing equality home. But after 1960, women's access to resources reached a tipping point at which violence was no longer sufficient to enforce their dependence on individual men. The irony here is that the domestic violence revolution targeted an oppressive strategy—the physical abuse of women—that was already being supplanted across a broad front by coercive control.

In the 1990s, we find even the staunchest defenders of free market ideals echoing the fears voiced by traditionalists a century earlier—that if women are allowed to embrace the individualism at the center of the democratic and capitalist credos on a par with men, family life will implode. What they mean is that sexual hierarchy will collapse. These fears are justified.

The Specificity of Coercive Control

Coercive control was born in the microdynamics of everyday life. So there is no sure way to document exactly when men began to complement their use of force with a range of direct controls or when it became the oppressive strategy of choice. Around the time the first shelters opened in the early 1970s, a handful of feminist psychologists identified the condition in which their abused clients were living as hostage-like and called it "coercive control." Many in the first cohort of shelter residents talked freely about the importance of control in their lives on the rare occasions when they were encouraged to do so, suggesting that coercive control was already widely disseminated. Although there is nothing written about coercive control prior to the 1970s, every researcher since then who has asked about control tactics in personal life has found their deployment to be widespread. Cobbe, Mill, Taylor, and other nineteenth-century reformers may have missed a similar despotic regime, much in the way domestic violence was often missed, though this seems unlikely. Even in those periods when wife beating received no official attention or little popular support, there is an unbroken record of its occurrence in popular lore, legend, art, theater, legal records, and histories of marriage and families. But none of these sources mentions a regime of isolation, intimidation, or regulation that approaches coercive control in intensity or scope. This is almost certainly because men had no need for coercive control as long as women's daily regimen of obedience was fully regulated by religion, and custom or sexism was codified in the law.

Whether or not coercive control is new, its deployment today is designed to stifle and co-opt women's gains; foreclose negotiation over the organization, extent, and substance of women's activities in and around the home; obstruct their access to support; close the spaces in which they can reflect critically on their lives; and reimpose obsolete forms of dependence and personal service by micromanaging the enactment of stereotypic gender roles through "sexism with a vengeance."

The Male Dilemma

As women break free from their consignment to the Other to imagine and construct their sexual identities across the entire spectrum of social possibilities, male sexual identity also becomes unhinged from its fixed position in heterosexual life, making it possible for men to flexibly define their sexual persona as receptive and deliberative as well as authoritative. The transformation of women from men's personal servants to social labor is a critical moment in human progress, not least because it injects a huge mass of creative capacity into the development process, substantially reducing the overall burden of necessary labor for us all. The socialization of women's labor, in turn, enhances female autonomy in personal life and so the potential to create truly reciprocal partnerships capable of supporting traditional domestic functions far more effectively and efficiently than is possible in partnerships where capacity is drained in a zero-sum game of power and control. From an evolutionary standpoint, this potential seals the fate of coercive control, much in the way that the expansive nature of industry sealed the fate of the traditional patriarchy or that the emergence of wage labor sealed the fate of chattel slavery.

In the name of sustaining traditional male privileges, coercive control suppresses the revolutionary potential of sexual reciprocity for *both* sexes: by downsizing the subjective capacities women inherit from their new social agency, men suspend their own capacity for reciprocity, trying to reconstruct from within relationships, de novo, the rigidities of power and control they once inherited with their biology. Each household governed by coercive control, each relationship, becomes a patriarchy in miniature, complete with its own web of rules or codes, rituals of deference, modes of enforcement, sanctions, and forbidden places, all devised with a particularity that is completely foreign to traditions of male dominance.

Its very invisibility on the public stage suggests that coercive control depends on at least tacit support from law, discriminatory structures, and normative consent. To this extent, male power in personal life continues to be "delegated." But its major features reflect the absence of such delegation. In coercive control, male dominance is constructed person-to-person through a series of particular constraints that are created, deployed, produced, represented, improvised, organized, found, contested, stolen, borrowed, usurped, or manipulated in unique relational contexts and for myriad proximate ends and effects. This process takes place through the simultaneous application of multiple technologies, drawing on force to exact obedience in one moment and on control tactics that are more spatially or temporally diffuse in the next.

In a world where even relative isolates are embedded in complex networks of work, consumption, service, and communication, abuse can only be kept secret on any substantial scale with the collusion of a range of actors, most of whom can be encouraged to *see* what is already in front of them with minimal prodding. Despite the belief that abuse happened "behind closed doors" in the past, it was almost always widely known to outsiders, neighbors, and family members, just as harms to children were well known, though intervention was infrequent. Present attempts to keep abuse hidden are a function of the changing normative status of violence in the home as well as of the extent to which egalitarian values of personhood have been extended to women and children. But even if coercive control is successfully hidden, its individualized nature has the paradoxical effect of depriving men of the consultation, role models, and social support on which their learning depends in other areas of activity, such as work or sports. Our culture is permeated with models of how to use violence to hurt or control others. But there are relatively few opportunities for men to learn how to encompass the increasing breadth and complexity of women's agency with control tactics in personal life. Without social support, men intent on deploying coercive control must rely on their wits, inventing and personalizing their tactical oppression as they go along, a process that is fraught with the potential for error, retaliation, and harm. As many abuse victims are quick to tell me, the "wits" available to men in these relationships are a limited resource.

To an outsider, the state of subordination produced by coercive control resembles the subjugation experienced by women in traditional societies. A victim's options appear fixed, subjectivity atrophied, her behavior dictated, her fate certain. But subordination feels very different when it is enforced on a personal level in a society that officially celebrates female equality and independence than in a society where women's dependence on men goes with the landscape. When a group of people that is formally free and equal is constrained, personal feelings of rage, shame, and failure are much greater than when members of an already subordinated class are abused, an important reason why the anger suffered by victims of coercive control often seems disproportionate to the proximate harms they have suffered.

Many of the same facets of coercive control that make it so insidious also increase the risk to perpetrators. Women have been greatly emboldened by formal equality, dramatically increasing their capacity and willingness to initiate violence or to retaliate violently against oppression in personal life. Men may use coercive control to snuff out women's autonomy. But no amount of control mounted from personal life can eliminate the potential for retaliation in a world where women's agency has diffuse social roots.

The tactical regime men employ to oppress women in personal life is chosen with the expectation that women will resist. This is why it often seems grossly disproportionate to what is needed to subdue a particular will. Like male violence, women's tactical resistance to dominance has also changed over time as their agency has developed. Women's absolute access to rights and resources as well as the differential access created by race, class, or cultural divisions determine whether women interpret their condition as a tragic but inevitable extension of how things are, as bad luck, as shameful, or as provocative in the extreme. Just as a victim's imago of her partner reflects a combination of his proximate power with the power added by sexual inequality, so does the exaggerated level of coercion and control men deploy, their "hypercontrol," reflect an image of women that combines their personal capacity for resistance or independence with their social agency ("women's lib").

Despite a certain tactical continuity in the use of force against women over time or across cultures, battered women confront historically specific constellations of sexual dominance and liberation, not male authority or opportunities for freedom in the abstract. The appearance of coercive control in the modern context has less to do with the immutability of male dominance than with the choice made by a large subset of men to defend their traditional prerogatives against the perceived threats posed by women's increasing economic independence, cultural autonomy, and political/legal equality. This choice is not an immanent feature of masculinity and certainly not the by-product of psychiatric disease. Most men decide to compromise their privileges in the face of female equality and accept a certain reciprocity, as unfamiliar as this may feel. Indeed, it is this fact that makes the behavior of the minority who deploy coercive control more outrageous.

The sheer cacophony of images promoting individuality, self-help, decisional autonomy, opportunity, and equity among women in the United States has had two simultaneous and contradictory effects.

As law professor Martha Fineman points out, "as adherence to the historic family form has begun to wither away, the complementary power relationships embedded in the traditional family have had to be made explicit in order to be preserved."[48] This is another way of putting the argument here: that once the material and political basis for the patriarchy was displaced and the illogic of privilege based solely on sex exposed, the preservation of male power required ever more deliberate and transparent strategic intervention in women's lives. But the diffusion of egalitarian and individualist imagery also leads us to expect that peoples lives will be self-directed, blinding us to the types of microregulation that characterize coercive control. However shocked we may be by the harsh treatment of women by the Taliban, it is inconceivable to most Americans that millions of modern women in our midst could be suffering under regimes of intolerance that are no less totalitarian than those imposed by fundamentalist cultures. Even less conceivable is that the cause of this backwardness is inextricably bound to the nature of the equality we believe separates us from these cultures.

To make contemporary women their personal property, the modern man must effectively stand against the tide of history, degrading women into a position of subservience that the progress of civilization has made obsolete. But he must do even more. Because women in the liberal democracies enjoy rights and resources that extend over a broad terrain, the technology of control men devise must be equally expansive in time and social space, reaching into the economic, political, and social realms to which women's freedoms have given them access, into their educational lives, their workplace, and their involvement with the public sector And men must do this without attracting public attention.

The appearance of coercive control against a background of formal equality is one of the more tragic ironies in sexual politics. But it would be a mistake to interpret this seeming contradiction as implying that either sexual equality is a sham or that the form of dominance described is merely ephemeral. Had women's sovereignty not threatened male hegemony, it would not have taken centuries to achieve. But this new tyranny is only possible because the same societies that now promise women full sovereignty continue to disadvantage them as a sex.

7

THE THEORY OF COERCIVE CONTROL

A woman wears the same outfit every day, rarely goes out, and continually paces back and forth in a small space. Imagine how hard it would be to explain her behavior if you were unable to reveal that the woman is confined in a jail cell. The domestic violence field faces a similar predicament when it tries to account for how battered women behave without identifying their "cage." The literature documents violent acts and the harms they cause in agonizing detail. But this work suffers the fallacy of misplaced concreteness: no matter how many punches or injuries or instances of depression are cataloged, the cage remains invisible as long as we omit the strategic intelligence that complements these acts with structural constraints and organizes them into the pattern of oppression that gives them political meaning. We see the effects of dominance, anger, depression, dependence, fear, substance use, multiple medical problems or suicide attempts, calls to the police or visits to the ER or shelter, but not domination itself. Given the abstraction of these effects from their context, it is unsurprising that more attention is paid to the personality and behavior of victims than to what perpetrators do.

Start with the cage, and everything changes. Suddenly, seemingly discrete, unrelated behaviors and effects fall into place. The iron rods—a barrage of assaults, a locked door, missing money or a distributor cap, rules for cleaning, a mysterious text message, a timer set at the telephone—are now recognized as "bars."

Laura broke into a cold sweat when the number of a local department store came up on her beeper. Within minutes of the phone ringing at the Connecticut mansion an Emmy-award winning filmmaker shared with her husband, hives covered Sarah's arms and face.

Laura retrieved the number from the trove she had stored in memory. Nick's birthday was approaching. A few nights earlier, she had failed to guess the significance of his sending the number of the local gym or what would happen if she continued to go there with her co-workers. The penalty was being punched. Now, her safety depended on guessing what he wanted from the department store. Sarah knew the house rule: she had to answer the phone by the third ring. Take these reactions out of their contexts, the prior assaults, the power relationships, the consequence of losing the "beeper game," and the "or else" warning behind the telephone rule and the acts appear trivial, even affectionate. The terror they incite is unintelligible, even crazy.

The analogy only goes so far. It is one thing to appreciate how persons can experience personal life as a cage—something many of us feel at some point—and quite another to understand why a huge population of otherwise normal women can feel like prisoners as they go about the rounds of daily existence. Institutions of confinement are formidable structures. But the vectors of inequality that set the stage for coercive control are much more ephemeral. As Frantz Fanon demonstrated in his studies of colonized peoples, where power is structured through privileged or coerced access to resources required for personhood or full membership in the political community, its explicit expressions in distinct forms of subjectivity are largely reflexive and can be properly interpreted only in the context of dominant-subordinate relationships.[1] Absent sexual inequality, the same acts have different meanings. A woman keeps track of her partner's other relationships, even scans the web sites he has visited or scans his e-mails. She uses various wiles to control his purchasing choices or flies into a jealous rage at the slightest pretext, withholds herself sexually and emotionally to feel more powerful, embarrasses him in front of his friends or hers, and perhaps even slaps him when he spends the rent money to buy drugs. Men use controlling tactics much more often than women do, just as they use the severest forms of violence more frequently, and are somewhat more likely than women to be motivated by a desire to control a partner.[2] But it is the social endowment men inherit from sexual inequality, not the motives or frequency of these acts, that allows them (but rarely women) to shape discrete acts into patterns of dominance that entrap partners and make them subordinate.

The female victims of coercive control differ from the colonized people in Fanon's account. They are the formal equals of the men who oppress them, not their subjects. Their subjugation occurs against a background of entitlement as well as inequality, the paradox of equality addressed previously. France exploited the Malagasy, about whom Fanon writes as a class, and took little interest in their personal life as long as the flow of natural resources and labor was undisturbed. But male dominance is no longer a social fact in liberal democratic societies. So if men insist on subordinating female partners they must do so directly and personally in each relationship. These qualities mark coercive control as deliberate and malevolent, setting the stage for them to be defined as criminal.

Precursors to the Coercive Control Model

Narrowing the focus to violence was not inevitable. An alternative framework was already available when the first shelters opened. The understanding of woman battering as coercive control has its roots in the 1950s and 1960s with the applications of learning theory to the experiences of persons undergoing severe restraint in nonfamilial settings, particularly hostages, prisoners of war, inmates, mental patients, and members of religious cults. The parallels between these experiences and abuse extended from the tactics deployed to the proximate and long-term harms inflicted.

In their efforts at thought reform with American prisoners during the Korean War, the Chinese used coerced persuasion, a technique by which a person's self-concept and resistance was broken down ("unfreezing"), the controller's altered picture of reality was substituted ("changing"), and the new view of reality was installed ("refreezing), typically through "random, noncontingent reinforcement by unpredictable rewards and punishments."[3] In the late 1970s, two feminist psychologists, Camella Serum and Margaret Singer, noticed that perpetrators of abuse employed these same or similar techniques, placing their partners in a coercive control situation of child-like dependency on the controllers.[4] The next iteration of the theory was in a treatment model for abuse developed by psychologist Steven Morgan who labeled wife abuse "conjugal terrorism" and noted the "remarkable" resemblance between the attitudes and behavior of the violent husband and the political terrorist.[5]

Building on this work, another clinician, Lewis Okun, wrote what remains the definitive chapter on the coercive control theory of woman battering. Okun drew an extended analogy between coerced persuasion, the experience of women being conditioned to prostitution by their pimps, and the experiences recounted to him in his counseling work with abusive men and battered women.[6]

As in earlier work, Okun emphasized the breakdown of the victim's personality in the face of severe external threats and highlighted the extreme emotional and behavioral adaptations to this process, ranging from guilt, loss of self-esteem, identification with the controller's aggressiveness, and fear of escape to difficulty planning for the future, detachment from violent incidents, and overreaction to trivial incidents. Although he echoed trauma theory in stressing that any normal person would respond to coercive control tactics in a similar way, his major focus was on the structural and systemic components of the abusive relationship rather than on severe violence, which he saw as simply mediating the power dynamics involved. In *The Battered Woman*, Lenore Walker had categorized the victim's social isolation as one foundation of learned helplessness. Okun linked isolation to "torture" (conjugal terrorism), threats, and the larger pattern of control by which batterers constricted the victim's decision-making powers (and, in some cases, prohibited all independent decisions). Extending the analogy to brainwashing and prostitution, he described how batterers controlled women's access to information (including censorship of mail and phone calls), exhausted them physically (e.g., by keeping them awake at night), and limited their movement, often to the point of forcibly confining them. He recounted torture-like experiences reported by his clients ranging from being burned with cigarettes and having their heads forced under water to the forms of control over bodily functions encountered in the Traficonda case that opens this book.

The next important contribution to the theory was by Ann Jones, a feminist author and journalist whose popular 1980 treatise on *Women Who Kill* is discussed in chapter 5. In *Next Time, She'll be Dead*, Jones drew on the human rights literature rather than on learning theory to extend the analogy made by Okun and others between the control skills men deployed in battering and similar techniques used with hostages, inmates in concentration camps, and American POWs. In a dramatic table, she juxtaposed the Amnesty International "chart of coercion" and comments by shelter residents to illustrate such methods as "isolation," "monopolization of perception," "induced debility and exhaustion," "threats," "occasional indulgences," "demonstrating omnipotence," "degradation," and "enforcing trivial demands." Jones also highlighted the psychological effects—"total destruction of the will"—and the fact that thoroughgoing control could be accomplished without physical violence.[7]

The nascent movement to counsel batterers produced a parallel strand of control theory. Feminist pioneers in the battered women's movement Del Martin, Susan Schechter, and Ann Jones embraced a definition of woman abuse as controlling behavior that created and maintained an imbalance of power between the batterer and the battered woman. When he founded Emerge in Boston, one of the nation's first counseling programs for violent men, David Adams expanded on a similar definition, broadly construing battering as "controlling behavior" and defined any act as violent "that causes the victim to do something she does not want to do, prevents her from doing something she wants to do, or causes her to be afraid "regardless of whether assault was involved."[8] Adams recognized how abuse prevents women from advancing their purposes in the world, moving women's agency center stage as the target of control, and highlighted the propensity for abusive men to replace their violent patterns with more subtle forms of intimidation and control after arrest. Emerge directly confronted men's control skills as well as their excuses for violence, asked their clients to keep control logs (built around a checklist of violent and controlling behaviors), and assessed their intent by the intimidating and controlling effects of their behavior on women's autonomy rather by stated motives. In recognizing control as an array of skills, Emerge replaced the essentialist view of violence as intrinsic to masculinity with an analysis of abuse as work. Under the leadership of Ellen Pence, the Domestic Abuse Intervention Project (DAIP) in Duluth, Minnesota, used video portrayals to sensitize men to their control patterns. The reasoning by the DAIP was refreshingly straightforward: because men "learned" the tactics they deployed to subordinate their partners, they could unlearn them when appropriate sanctions were combined with reeducation. This interpretation minimized the systemic sources of domination Okun had stressed and the privileges derived from control. But it clearly identified battering as rational, instrumental, and intentional behavior rather than impulse driven or the byproduct of a dysfunctional personality or upbringing.

Yet another counselor, Lundy Bancroft, spelled out the rationality of coercive control implied in the analyses by Adams and Pence. In *Why Does He Do That?* Bancroft detailed the rewards men gleaned from controlling behavior. The "ballooning collection of comforts and privileges" included the "heady rush of power" that provided intrinsic satisfaction; "getting his way," especially when it matters the most; the availability of someone to take his problems out on; free labor from her and leisure and freedom for him; being the center of attention, with priority given to his needs; financial control; ensuring that his career, education, or other goals are prioritized; the public status of partner and/or father without the sacrifices; and the enjoyment of a double standard where he was exempt from rules that apply to her.[9] In *When Loves Goes Wrong*, Jones joined with Susan Schechter, perhaps the best-known domestic violence advocate in the United States, to adapt the categories of coercive control theory for a popular audience. They restored the focus on dominance, referred to perpetrators as "controlling partners," and defined abuse as "a pattern of coercive control that one person exercises over another in order to dominate and get his way."[10] The book included a lengthy checklist to help victims identify commonly employed control tactics, grouping those that resembled the forms of psychological abuse described by Okun, Adams, Walker, and others under such headings as "criticism," "moodiness," "anger and threats," "overprotection and caring," "denying your perception," "ignoring your needs and opinions," and "shifting responsibility."

Jones and Schechter emphasized women's emotional investment in the abusive relationship, presumably to encourage victims to "disinvest." This minimized the structural dimensions of control that constrain freedom of choice, action, and movement regardless of emotional attachment. To help clarify this dimension of abuse for judges, erstwhile prosecutor Sarah Buell has them remove their wallets, car keys, and other personal items. Then she asks them to reconsider their belief that victims should "just leave." A perpetrator's moods may determine whether a victim will be allowed to sleep through the night, take her medicine, go to work in the morning, or purchase milk for the children. But the fact that a victim's survival requires her to develop an acute sensitivity to these moods does not mean she is emotionally invested in maintaining the relationship, let alone ambivalent about breaking things off. Similarly, if victims hesitate to challenge a partner's deceits or walk away from his insults, this is less often because they are manipulated than because of the structural controls in place and the feared consequences of resistance. Again, it is the added constraint imposed by its context that gives so-called psychological abuse an entirely different valence when used by men than by women.

The most vivid representation of the structural dimensions of battering is the wheel developed by the DAIP in Duluth and adapted for use in hundreds of service settings. With "power and control" as its hub and surrounded by a rim of physical and sexual violence, the spokes of the wheel are subdivided into economic abuse; coercion and threats; intimidation; emotional abuse; isolation; minimizing, denying, and blaming; using children; and abusing male privilege. Jones and Schechter incorporate many of these categories, adding control through decision making. Importantly, physical and sexual violence are last on their list.

Sandwiched among the better known control tactics on the Jones and Schechter checklist are "picking out your clothes," "telling you what to wear," or "forbidding you to shop." These tactics share the coercive and objective character of material constraints, such as control over money or other necessities. Because they target aspects of women's already devalued role in relationships, however, they also give coercive control a gendered dimension that distinguishes it from all other crimes that involve power and control. Telling a woman what to wear or forbidding her to shop may seem trivial compared to burning her with cigarettes or taking her money. But by including these tactics, Jones and Schechter opened a new window onto entrapment in personal life.

The Generality of Coercive Control

At the core of coercive control theory is the analogy to other capture crimes like hostage taking or kidnapping, a comparison that illustrates what Elizabeth Schneider calls its "generality."[11] The singular advantage of the analogy is that it links women's predicament in personal life to the larger discourse of rights and liberties we apply to citizen-victims, including the human rights discourse, implicitly undermining a major rationale that limits justice intervention in what are deemed just family matters. By using the gender-neutral language of power and control to frame abuse, the hostage analogy also supports an approach women have repeatedly used to gain legal rights men already possess, such as the right to vote or sit on juries. Called "formal equality," courts or legislators are asked to imagine the wrong involved if men were denied these rights solely because of their sex, to attribute the observed lack of parity to discrimination, and then to level the playing field so that women are treated identically to men. From this vantage point, the right of abuse victims to "equal protection" reflects the resemblance of abuse to assault and other harms from which men and strangers are already protected. The analogy also supports the belief that battered women are "hostages at home," suggesting abuse is a political crime like terrorism.

Emphasizing its generality has enormous heuristic value because it exposes dimensions of partner abuse that have gone largely unnoticed and that are not normally associated with assault, such as the monopolization of perception or "ways to make me crazy" as well on tactics used to isolate victims, monitor their behavior, or break their will. Interviews with victims of battering reveal the prevalence of rituals of degradation like those to which POWs, prisoners, hostages, kidnap victims, or residents of "total institutions" are subjected. These include humiliating sexual examinations, unannounced room searches, bathroom inspections, interrogations, forced confessions, lockdowns (where a victim is not permitted to leave her room or the house or use the phone for a period of time), periods of forced silence, and being denied access to rites of personal hygiene, eating, sleeping, and toileting. Talking about persons in the third person or acting as if they are invisible is often used to humiliate prisoners or mental patients. Japanese prisoners during World War II describe their humiliation when the wives of British officers undressed in their presence. In a murder case that has yet to come to trial, the husband regularly told the children in front of my client, "If your mother isn't here when you come home from school, look under the ground in the back yard, right where the dog is buried."

Thinking of women as victims of capture crimes also helps reframe their reactions. Reflecting the high value we place on individual liberty is an almost unqualified right for POWs, kidnap victims, and hostages to act proactively to free themselves, even if this means killing their captors when they are most vulnerable. Reframing abused women as hostages suggests they be accorded a similar right, thereby bypassing narrow standards of self-defense. Rarely do we apply demeaning stereotypes to persons who commit violence in the defense of their freedom or autonomy.

Confession, compliance, even supplication are role syntonic for victims of forced imprisonment or torture. So even if we reserve the highest regard for persons who fail to crack under these conditions, like Admiral James Stockdale, the highest ranking naval officer taken prisoner in Vietnam, we have enormous respect even for POWs who merely endured, like Arizona Senator John McCain. By contrast, as law professor Isabel Marcus points out, rather than sympathize with the female targets of domestic terrorism, their compliance, dependence, and other responses to episodes of assault are critically evaluated according to culturally endorsed images of individuals as autonomous, mobile, and able to take charge of their lives. I have worked with former POWs and torture victims who were ashamed at things they did or said under pain of death or worse. But an even more profound shame infects women who have experienced coercive control because of the familiarity of the setting where their abuse occurs, the widespread assumption they have freely chosen their lot, and because there is much less clarity than in other capture crimes about the duress under which they enact humiliating rituals, have sex with strangers, commit crimes contrary to their nature, or hurt or allow others to hurt their children in ways they know are inappropriate. Reframing their predicament as hostage-like and calling it coercive control dispels much of this ambiguity.

The hostage analogy also illuminates the structural dimensions of battering that allow controllers to regulate a woman's behavior, including isolating them from sources of support; taking their money; depriving them of such necessities as food or medicine; suppressing conflict and resistance; closing off opportunities for escape, communication, or transportation; and laying down and enforcing rules for everyday conduct. These parallels further underline the weakness of psychological accounts of why women stay. What hostages and POWs lack is the opportunity to escape or otherwise act effectively on their own behalf, not the will to do so.

The Particularity of Coercive Control

Emphasizing the generality of power and control takes us only so far.

Despite the fact that controllers use many of the techniques deployed in other capture crimes and with similar effect, the main elements of coercive control set it apart from all other forms of oppression. Its particularity lies in its aim—to usurp and master a partner's subjectivity—in its scope of its deployment, its individualized and personal dimensions, and its focus on imposing sex stereotypes in everyday life. The result is a condition of unfreedom (what is experienced as *entrapment*) that is "gendered" in its construction, delivery, and consequence.

The Frequency and Routine Nature of Violence

The violence used in coercive control resembles the violence used in capture crimes in three ways primarily: it is designed to punish, hurt, or control a victim; its effects are cumulative rather than incident-specific; and it frequently results in severe injury or death. A hostage's size, strength, or physical prowess is irrelevant to his or her vulnerability. Similarly, in coercive control, the victim's susceptibility to injury is a function of the degree to which her capabilities for defense, resistance, escape, or to garner support have been disabled by a combination of exploitation, structural constraints, and isolation. This is what historian Linda Gordon has in mind when she writes that "what makes a battered woman is her socially constructed inability to escape."[12]

From this point, the two scenarios diverge dramatically. To start, in no other capture crime does the incidence of assault approach the frequency or duration in partner abuse, with women in shelters averaging 69 assaults in the preceding year and many women sustaining hundreds, even thousands of assaults in abusive relationships over many years.[13] Even if victims of torture, POWs, or hostages are repeatedly assaulted, these attacks are usually concentrated in time and place and designed to inflict fear or pain primarily. By contrast, abusive violence is temporally diffuse, often occurs at multiple sites, and is typically minor but routine.

The Personal Nature of Coercive Control

Kidnapping for profit is common. But in most cases of torture, terror, or hostage taking, the motives are political (even if state sponsorship is indirect), and the captors and victims are strangers, a fact that made the photos and life sketches of missing loved ones posted on billboards after the terrorist attacks of September 11, 2001, so powerful. The lack of personal knowledge forces the torturer or prison guard to rely on crude, generic means of inflicting pain, techniques to which the prisoner is vulnerable because they have been removed from familiar social settings. The victim's persona interests the oppressor only as a source of resistance to attain his primary end—to extract obedience, a confession, or information.

Whatever their technical resemblance to the techniques used in torture, everything about the experience of coercive control reflects its personal and individualized nature, from its proximate motives and relationship-specific organization through the tactics deployed. The victim's agency is its principal target, and its familiar setting is critical to instilling fear. The personal nature of coercive control begins with the controller, whose individual needs are the focus of everything he does, and extends to the means deployed. Only in coercive control do perpetrators hone their tactics to their special knowledge of everything from a victim's earnings and phone conversations to her medical problems, personal fears, sexual desires, and illicit activities. One husband in my practice would jump out of a closet where he was hiding to "surprise" his wife when she returned home. Although he claimed this was only a joke, he knew his action terrorized her because she had shared a childhood experience when an uncle had lain in wait in a closet, then raped her. The sudden destruction or unexplained disappearance of familiar objects that have a special meaning to the victim is a related tactic. A week before she fatally stabbed her abusive husband, he destroyed the last direct connection Girlene Soares had to her family in Brazil, a baseball hat that had belonged to a brother who drowned.

The Experimental Nature of Coercive Control

Their male partners have burned the women in my practice with cigarettes, held their heads under water in the toilet, and denied them sleep—common techniques used in torture. But in most cases, the technology is experimental and interactive, rather than generic and evolves through a process of trial and error based on how a victim responds. The regulatory regimes in coercive control run the gamut from primitive, transparently self-serving prohibitions or commands to seemingly objective performance standards that the perpetrator appears merely to adjudicate. In a "letter of instruction" sent to me by a police officer, the perpetrator commanded, "If I decide that we sleep together, you will humbly comply without a fight"; "Do not physically resist me"; and "Don't allow me to ask you three times. If you do not answer within 30 seconds after I ask you a question the second time, be prepare [*sic*] to pay for it." At the other extreme is the Kafkaesque impersonality conveyed by Nick's rules that Laura's bedspread be exactly one and three-eighths inches off the floor and that she vacuum daily "so you can always see the lines." The log book described in chapter 9 falls between these examples. Donna was to record everything she did during the day, seemingly an objective standard of performance. But Frank would interrogate her nightly, find fault, and beat her regardless of what she had done or written down. The point here is that whether the rules that comprise the infrastructure of coercive control are clearly drawn to satisfy the personal needs of their author, as in the letter of instruction, or are designed to conceal these needs beneath a seemingly objective set of dictates, as in Nick's list, they are always improvised, idiosyncratic in the extreme, and designed to enforce personal obedience rather than the sort of generic conformity to authority demanded of hostages, POWS, or residents of total institutions like prisons or mental hospitals.

Privileged Access and Property Rights

In contrast to the forced access involved in capture crimes, the privileged access partners maintain to their victims is the most important explanation for why abuse is ongoing, even when partners are separated. Privileged access reflects five interrelated factors: the presumption of intimacy, the personal knowledge intimacy affords, claims to exclusive possession or "property rights," the material benefits associated with possession, and the failure of outsiders to effectively intervene. When hostages, kidnap victims, and POWs are sexually assaulted, this is usually secondary to extracting information or compliance. By contrast, as Lundy Bancroft illustrates at length, coercive control is unintelligible apart from the immediate material, sexual, and other benefits perpetrators garner from exploiting victims. If the benefits derived from abuse help explain why perpetrators persist, the presumption of intimacy and property rights cast a veil over a relationship that inhibits outside intervention and allow offenders—often with the collusion of friends, family members, and helping professionals—to garner unique knowledge about a partner's movements, habits, resources, and vulnerabilities. This pattern of personalizing property rights is often complemented by more or less explicit "ownership" contracts. These may consist of verbal agreements, as when a woman agrees not to make her partner jealous; be signed symbolically, as when Miguel burned his tattoo on Lavonne's arm to let other men know she belonged to him; or be affirmed by training victims to react in predetermined ways to cues such as finger snapping, a set number of telephone rings, a nod, or, in one case, two taps of the foot. Property rights are also expressed more generically by a controller's insistence that he set the terms for every encounter. If a woman tries to walk away from an argument or refuses to get out of bed in the middle of the night to review her faults or tries to separate, she is reminded that the lecture, interrogation, sex, her job, or the relationship "ends, when I say it ends." The ultimate expression of property rights is the right of disposal illustrated by the statement that frequently precedes femicide, "If I can't have you, no one will."

The Spatial and Temporal Extension of Control

The spatial and temporal dimensions of coercive control are far broader than in comparable instances of power and control. To prevent escape, hostages, torture victims, or POWS are confined. A good deal of the suffering for these victims, as well as pressure to break, comes from the felt contrast between their existential loss of liberty and their normal condition of freedom in the familiar world "outside." Literal confinement is common enough in coercive control. Women in my practice have been locked in closets, rooms, or apartments; barred from leaving the house; made to sit in their cars for hours; forced to sit without moving on a coach or on the floor; or forbidden to drive or to go out by themselves. In a highly publicized case where a child was killed, the husband told his wife she could leave their room at the homeless shelter with the baby but could not take a key. Because the door to the room locked automatically when it closed, she was effectively confined to the room when he left for work or to buy drugs. Another man took his partner's shoe to keep her from leaving his apartment to go to work. As frequently, however, men deploying coercive control prevent escape and exposure through a spatially diffuse pattern of rules, stalking, cyber-stalking, beepers, cell phones, and other means that effectively erase the difference between confinement and freedom by extending surveillance and behavioral regulation to all those settings where victims might restore their identity or garner support, including work, school, church, service, family, and shopping sites. In *The Manchurian Candidate*, Hugh Condon's 1959 novel, and in the film versions with Frank Sinatra (1962) and Denzel Washington (2004), the assassin has been brainwashed by an alien government into following orders in a robot-like fashion when a cue was given.[14] Analogous forms of behavioral regulation through social space are a common facet of coercive control and are often set off by electronic or telephonic signals, as in Nick's beeper game or the phone rule in Sarah's home. Diffuse regulation of this sort leaves the impression "there is no outside, outside," significantly reducing the efficacy of protection

The extensiveness of coercive control is complemented by its intensiveness. As regulation is diffused to sites where victims normally feel safe and independent, they make ever more desperate attempts to forge moments of autonomy within the sphere of oppression where they can reflect on their situation, contemplate their options, and retain a sense of self—what I term their "safety zones." In response, controllers devise tactics to penetrate these zones, using microregulation to quash the last vestiges of free time or space. They commonly go through a partner's closets, drawers, mail, e-mail, Web favorites, diaries, phone bills, pocket books, or checkbooks, to identify slips or let the victim know "there are no secrets." In one case, the boyfriend, a police officer, not only had his spies monitor whom my client met or talked to at the mall but also went through her purchases, ripping up a blouse and see-through bra because they were too "sexy." Sarah's husband reviewed all phone messages on the answering machine when he came home, calling any number he didn't recognize and insulting the party. So extensive and penetrating are control tactics that many victims conclude their partner is omnipresent, a feeling that is a major source of their depression, substance use, and suicide attempts and helps explain the failure of many abused women to promptly report critical incidents, such as harms to their children, even when they seemingly had opportunities to do so.

The spatial extension of coercive control and the use of tactics to penetrate everyday life mean that the typical condition of victims is to be free and subjugated at once. Subjugation in these instances is more dynamic than in the typical capture crime and evolves to match each attempt by victims to create a safety zone. As the dilemmas faced by Francine Hughes illustrated, any decision—to return to school, take a job, seek legal assistance, start a diary, buy a new bra, even to cook something new—may be interpreted as a sign of disloyalty, independence, resistance, and worse, and so is permeated with a sense of dread of a corresponding constriction of freedom. Women's fear that their stolen moments of autonomy will be detected, invaded, and evoke physical or other reprisals can be so intense that they precensor "dangerous thoughts" that might lead to independent action and harm. After many years of abuse, Kathy went to a legal services attorney to start divorce proceedings. The next day, when the lawyer foolishly telephoned the house, her husband secretly listened on an upstairs line. That night, he confronted her with his knowledge that she was trying to leave him and beat her severely. He told her he knew what she was up to because he could read her mind, a claim she believed because she could think of no other way he had discovered her plan. At this point, she felt escape was no longer an option. A month later, she employed a man she met through a casual encounter to kill her husband, which he did.

The invasion and constriction of psychic as well as social space can paralyze independent judgment or thought. One client with a graduate degree in economics from Yale had lost the ability to tell time or do simple sums. After another client's husband went to jail in a widely publicized drug case involving the Mafia, the government seized the couple's Long Island home and charged the wife under the theory that she must have known about the illegal business taking place there. The government's evidence included bags of money being left at the front door after the man's incarceration and a tax return, which she had signed, listing their annual income at only $25,000, despite their ownership of a boat, and her furs, luxurious home, and several Mercedes-Benzes. Suffice it to say that after hours of interviewing the Dominican wife—who had been coercively controlled throughout their 18-year marriage, literally confined to the house for months at a time, and beaten senseless on numerous occasions early in the marriage—I was convinced that she was too frightened to even ask herself where the money came from or how they could enjoy the luxuries they did on so little income.

The Prevalence and Social Structure of Coercive Control

Terrorism and political kidnapping are effective as threats because their unpredictability and apparent randomness increase the potential risk felt by every citizen within the potential target area. But nothing in these crimes begins to approach the importance of coercive control as a social fact either empirically, because it is so widespread, or sociologically, because its perpetrators and victims belong to identifiable social classes whose relationship of domination/subordination has far-reaching ramifications for citizenship, economic development, and social progress. Kidnappers and terrorists typically target the affluent, though not always, of course. Coercive control is predicated on the devalued status of women. The terrorist and hostage taker are known publicly through their acts. Because the structural dimensions of coercive control are typically hidden from view, their effects are only known indirectly, through how the victim behaves, and it is she who is widely thought to "have the problem." After Nick's death, Laura attempted suicide and was briefly hospitalized. When she described the household rituals he had imposed on her through his lists, her psychiatrist diagnosed her with an obsessive-compulsive disorder.

The Normalcy of Coercive Control

Torture, kidnapping, and brainwashing are rare events that leave no doubt in a victim's mind about their risk. But the core tactics in coercive control build on practices that are governed by gender norms in relationships, such as ceding major financial decisions to men or quitting work to "make a home," or target devalued activities to which women are already consigned, like cooking, cleaning, and child care. When men extend these prerogatives in an abusive regimen by monitoring a partner's every expenditure, appropriating her credit card, or requiring detailed menus as Frank did, there is enormous ambiguity about where appropriate expectations end and risk begins, even if the woman feels unsafe. Outside observers share this confusion. The injection of high levels of fear into the ordinary round of daily life and the difficulty in fixing its source are among the most remarkable features of coercive control.

Gender Entrapment

The most dramatic facet of control strategies is their focus on responsibilities linked to women's default and devalued roles as homemaker, caretaker, and sexual partner, the dimension of sexual inequality that has been least affected by women's gains in public arenas. Women are still judged as more or less competent by how they perform their second shift. Nowhere is this more evident than in family court, where women's failures as homemakers are highlighted while men's neglect of domestic work is rarely considered a relevant factor in determining their fitness to parent. And although men may be singled out for praise if they cook meals or take primary responsibility for children, those who take on these roles in any more sustained way are alternately portrayed as comic, as in the films *Mr. Mom* or *Mrs. Doubtfire*, or pathetic, like the "wives" or "bitches" of male prisoners, who clean their cells and provide sexual service. By contrast, women playing men are considered uppity and become the brunt of violence, as was illustrated by Hilary Swank's powerful portrayal in the 1999 film *Boys Don't Cry* or Charlize Theron's portrayal of a battered mother who becomes a mineworker in the 2005 film *North Country*.

The micromanagement of how women enact gender is a major theme of the next chapter. Suffice it to say here that tactics to regulate the most obvious facets of female gender—how women look (such as picking out their clothes or destroying clothes that are sexy) clean, cook, care for or discipline their children, whether they work, how they make love and to whom, and so on—are routinely complemented by less transparent forms of gender debasement, such as regulating which shows they are allowed to watch on TV or forcing them to watch pornography to "see how it *should* be done."

The Dialectics of Domesticity

Ironically, the fact that only a minority of women in the liberal democracies identify their femininity with marriage or domesticity may make them more vulnerable to the micromanagement of their household routines than in the past.

Relatively affluent women may still leave the workforce during their childbearing years and return only part-time or identify as full-time homemakers. According to a 2000 survey of Yale alumni between 1979 and 2005, among graduates in their twenties, only slightly more men than women said that work was their primary activity. But among alumni in their forties, the proportion of males who said work was their primary activity (90%) was almost twice as high as the proportion of females who made this claim.[15] The authors conclude that women become less identified with work as they age. It is more plausible that the importance of paid employment has increased with each successive cohort of women graduating from Yale, as it has nationwide. The evidence summarized in chapter 6 shows that the vast majority of today's women enter and remain in the job market even when they have young children Of course, this is as much a function of economics as individual choice, since female-headed households are a growing proportion of all households and family survival and mobility increasingly require women's financial contribution.

The low regard in which working women hold domesticity is reflected in the oft-heard joke that what they really need is "a wife." But the very fact that most women now regard the economy, polity, civic, and social life as the principle arenas for their self-expression makes them far less able than their forebears to rationalize their default consignment to domesticity or to protect themselves against the demeaning effects of the fact that domestic work is physically and emotionally demanding, sex-segregated, unwaged, socially isolated, technically underdeveloped, anonymous, and intellectually deadening. In a recent TV season, this reality was parodied in the hit show *Desperate Housewives* and in a less unsuccessful "reality" show where housewives changed places for a week. The central conceit in the reality show was that replacing an officious organizer with a live-and-let live hippie would wreak havoc on each family's dynamics, countering the sexist message that all women are interchangeable. Unfortunately for the show's producers, what was remarkable was how little difference these changes made. Husbands and children simply shifted the focus of their demands, but not their substance. Nothing so clearly symbolizes the constricted world imposed through coercive control than the selection of the daily round of household responsibilities that are already devalued in a woman's own eyes as well as in the eyes of others as the critical battlefield on which she must defend her dignity and autonomy.

The Salience of Domesticity

This is not the whole story, however. Women's economic progress may have reduced the role of domestic life as compensation for their exclusion from mainstream social life. But it is impossible to appreciate the particularity of the harms caused by coercive control unless we also recognize that sustaining households, civilizing men, caring for family members, and raising and sending out children into the world are necessary social functions that can instill pride of purpose and accomplishment, much like their public sector counterparts. They also serve more pragmatic functions within sexual power dynamics. Being a competent homemaker and a "beautiful" woman support claims on partners for money, goods, services, and an active social life. Domesticity and sex stereotypes situate women's second-class status, just as wage work sites the exploited status of laborers or picking cotton sited the status of slaves. But gender roles are also a means through which women imaginatively express their individual and collective personhood and, by confronting the limited possibility for doing this within the existing structures of personal and family life, within the limits of their status as "just women," set out to develop and expand this role, making femininity the realm of the possible. Nothing so clearly reveals women's propensity to retrieve vestiges of autonomy and self-expression from even the most odious aspects of their daily round of activity than the effort expended by controlling men to root out their individuality from the nooks and crannies of these routines. Ironically, it is often here, where women's agency is least noticed, that many battered women make their stand, as Francine's reaction to her degradation illustrates.[16]

When controlling partners regulate women's performance of their role, whatever secondary gains they derive from enacting domesticity evaporate. They can no longer claim recognition for their gift of love or service, and the connection of these activities to their sense of mastery and self-worth is severed. Degrading women back into the stereotypic portrayals of wife, mom, and lover, not only makes domestic work but feminine identity itself feel like fixed externalities, alien forces that trap them rather than release their creativity, the process sociologist Beth Richie calls gender entrapment and Anne Flitcraft and I describe as "patriarchal mothering."[17]

Masculinity and Feminine Stereotypes

An outstanding question is why men bother. Although the benefits in time, service, and enjoyment men garner from women's service are real enough, in most of these cases, the direct regulation of how women enact domesticity adds only marginal benefit to chores women would perform on their own and whose performance could be modified with more benign means, if not as dramatically. For example, there would seem to be only a minimal difference between the TV dinner Francine left for Mickey that fateful evening and the usual fare she produced under compulsion. In fact, the immediate object of micromanagement is less important than its larger role in solidifying a woman's generic obedience to male authority: her "doing femininity" in ways that accord with his stereotype of her gender role allows him to "do masculinity" as he imagines it should or *must* be done. Many of the men in my practice regulated women's housework, appearance, and performance to confirm their sexual identity by negative example, proving they were *not* women (often to defend against homoerotic impulses they found intolerable) by constructing the women in their lives as reflections of the sexual difference they both craved and feared. To the extent that their identity was reflexively tied to the ritual performances they commanded, any change in routine or even a minor "failure" in their physical world—a dish breaking, the discovery that there was no beer in the fridge, that the bedspread was "messed," or that the required four packs of cigarettes had not yet been hand-rolled—elicited feelings of panic and, in one case, a homicidal rage.

Arlene and John

Arlene D.'s physically abusive husband, John, was a successful contractor in Iowa. John's lavishly decorated home office contrasted markedly with the family's living room, where stuffing was visibly coming out of the couch and easy chairs. Arlene home schooled their five children, one of whom was learning disabled. When John felt she had neglected her household obligations, he went from room to room gathering up "unnecessary" toys, books, and furniture (including the family TV), threw them into the yard, and burned them. One of his punishments was to make the family dog "disappear." Despite a hefty income, he insisted that household help was not needed. At one point when he had $70,000 in his account, Arlene was forced to sell math curricula to buy milk. The woman drew enormous support from her leadership in the state's home schooling movement and from the evangelical religious community of which the schooling was a part. As soon as the oldest boy went on to college, John declared the children would now go to public school so Arlene could attend properly to his needs. He also made his family leave their church after a visitation in which Jesus revealed to him that the minister and the other congregants were homosexuals. In response to Arlene's pleas, John agreed she could continue the home schooling, but only if she left her leadership position, stopped attending home schooling meetings, and completed all household chores (laundry, shopping, cooking, and the like) before 5 P.M., so she could devote herself fully to him in the evening. Trying to keep her agreement while attending properly to schooling led to frequent fights with the children, whom she tried to enlist in the housework, a point the evaluating psychologist emphasized, along with Arlene's growing depression, when he recommended the father get custody.

John's victimization of Arlene was designed to enter and deconstruct the agency she had carefully built to resist his coercive control. She thought of her housework as a service she performed for the family so the children could get the best education possible; both were a continuation of her calling. Her connections to the church and school network allowed her to retain a feeling of competence despite John's physical assaults, his disdain for her work, continued ridicule, and his denying her money. The coerced agreement changed all this. It transformed housework into her payment to John for the right to teach the children and turned home schooling into a problem of time management. By simultaneously cutting Arlene off from the two external sources of support and recognition, the church and the home schooling network, John left her feeling frozen and alone, the source of her depression.

By contrast with Arlene, John's world was sharply divided into work and home, a separation symbolized by the contrast between his well furnished office and a home in disrepair, and his periodic purges of toys and other household goods were designed to reconcile his rigid view of women's work—to cook, clean, and be able to devote herself to him in the evening—with the chaos created by his insistence that Arlene raise and school the five children with no allowance and no help. His best efforts went to naught, however. The fundamentalist congregation provided the only social setting in which John's patriarchal worldview got any support. Because Arlene also drew sustenance from the congregation, however, continued membership threatened to undermine his control. In revealing that the church was filled with homosexuals, Jesus gave John a means to tighten his hold on Arlene that was consistent with his hypermasculine fantasies.

Agency and Victimization in the Lives of Battered Women

John's meticulous deconstruction of Arlene's autonomy takes us full circle back to the cage analogy with which we began the theoretical discussion of coercive control. Taking this analogy too literally masks the dynamic interplay of agency, coercive control, victimization, and resistance in the lives of battered women. Their sense of efficacy offers women like Arlene an important defense against depression and submission. Abused women *are* victims, but this reality is effaced and may even be exacerbated if they are seen only through their victimization, particularly in disadvantaged communities. As bell hooks argues, women who face exploitation daily cannot afford to "relinquish the belief that they exercise some level of control, however relative, over their lives."[18] Finding no way to reconcile the need to feel strong with the reality of being oppressed, many victims retain their sense of integrity by minimizing or denying their state of oppression, refusing to identify themselves as a battered woman or by deciding to tough it out and projecting a sense of bravado that can increase isolation, invite retaliation, and greatly increase risk. An unrealistic sense of control that can be easily shattered is common to many victims of oppression.

Coercive control theory replaces the portrait of psychological deterioration at the center of the current victimization narrative with a picture of an affirmative femininity that victims vigorously defend against illegitimate authority. By framing the controller's oppression as an attempt to co-opt and deconstruct a woman's personhood, it reaffirms what many victims themselves feel, that they are living in a conscious and self-determining relation to domination, albeit a relation that is severely constrained by objective limits on their choice and action, the idea expressed by the notion that they exercise "control in the context of no control." This seeming paradox is actualized in both the literal assertion of subjectivity in abusive relationships through open resistance, refusal, and the adaptation of safety and survival plans and when women nest their subjectivity in behaviors, physical symptoms, or other manifestations that sabotage the effect of control strategies on personhood while conveying seeming compliance to the perpetrator. Agency and victimization live one within the other in abuse and the presence of one is evoked by the other, some time long after the literal battering has ended. When Nick presented Laura with the list, she thought of Charlton Heston in *The Ten Commandments* and laughed, risking a beating. But long after he was killed, she continued to enact the rituals he had designed for her. She did this as a kind of mockery, as a caution against his return to hurt her, and because, by representing him through the rituals, she could satisfy his demands and gain a sense of competence and esteem she could never get from him directly. Hope and fear, courage and cowardice, pride and paralyzing fear alternating moments on a continuum of oppression in the lives of women entrapped by coercive control.

Safety Zones

Nowhere is the struggle between agency and victimization more apparent than in the process by which women forge safety zones to secure moments of autonomy, rehearse survival or escape strategies, plan resistance, regain a momentary sense of control or self-worth, and recover pieces of their lost voice or subjectivity. These zones can consist of literal physical spaces at home, work, church, school, or elsewhere where they can garner support or resources to escape; relationships the perpetrator cannot control with friends, family members, co-workers, service providers, neighbors or lovers; or they can be more ephemeral. As control becomes ever more comprehensive, the refuge in which women seek safety becomes more abstract, more secret, personal, or even internal. A day book may serve this purpose, or a diary or objects that have a special meaning only to the victim—a photo, an object, like the dead brother's hat described earlier, a dress that reminds her of a safer place or happier time, or a behavior that the perpetrator is unaware of, such as taking pills, staying awake when the partner thinks they are asleep, and even, as in Donna's case, not eating to save money. Indeed, as I suggested was the case with Laura, rituals imposed by the abusive partner can be enacted in ways that give women a sense of self-ownership without tipping him off. When she made her bed according to Nick's strictures, Laura would maintain a modicum of esteem by "guessing" at the height of the bedspread from the floor rather than measuring it or by leaving specks of dust underneath the chair to see if he would notice. These specks were her safety zone. Zones can involve literal time apart from the perpetrator, or a place in consciousness to which a victim retreats during an assault or a similarly degrading ritual when they split off from what they are doing or others are doing to them and fix on a point, a crack in the wallpaper, a memory of another time, or some trivial facet of their lives far removed from the present.

Some abused women overcompensate for extreme emotional deprivation by inappropriately meeting their needs for recognition, support, and love through their children, a process of enmeshment that may deny youngsters the autonomy they need to flourish. Enmeshment has classically been treated as a personality or behavioral deficit in mothering. But it may also signal a woman's desperate attempt to sustain her personhood in the safest way she knows. In this case, the best approach is to identify and remove the structural constraints that keep her from meeting her needs more appropriately. Experiencing the emotional reciprocity in parenting allows many mothers who are being coercively controlled to reflect critically on the lack of empathy or reciprocity in their adult relationship.

Search and Destroy Missions

Because safety zones offer women an alternative to subordination, they rarely go unchallenged. If abusive relationships were filmed in slow motion, they would resemble a grotesque dance whereby victims create moments of autonomy and perpetrators "search and destroy" them. Donna got her little brother to sleep over, and Frank forbade it; she fixed on the icons, which he summarily destroyed; she secretly ate, and he put her on the scale and beat her for gaining weight; she opened a post office box to which the bills were sent, which he discovered and closed. As the home schooling case illustrates, negotiation and trade-offs around safety zones are continual. John burned Arlene's high school diploma and photos of her parents. Although he allowed her to retain her role as teacher, as it became clear that her connections through the home schooling network were steeling her courage, he constructed the agreement that set her up to fail with the children. Donna liked going to Weight Watchers, because it got her out of the house. But she gorged herself and so failed to lose, even though it meant further beatings. These behaviors, which she described as "stupid," gave her a secret sense of power and control over her fate, even as they ensured her trips to Weight Watchers would not end. The beatings would have happened under any circumstance. Now, they were a response to something Donna had actually done.

Even when women nest their resistance in somatic symptoms, controllers may pursue them, controlling their medication or their access to drugs or alcohol, or forcing them to see a psychiatrist. Women do not yield up their safety zones easily. Men attack women's autonomy at their peril. Indeed, as Francine's case illustrates, battered women are as likely to make critical decisions about their futures, including the decision to run from or kill a partner, following the closing of a safety zone as they are after an assault. We will recall that Kathy hired the man to kill her husband only after he "read her mind" and beat her senseless for going to legal services for a divorce.

Toward a New Theory of Harms

An important challenge to coercive control theory is identifying the harms it causes with universally recognized principles of justice.

A basic tenet of liberal political theory since Locke is that the positive features of personal or family life are best preserved if they are insulated from state interference as well as from the self-direction, self-regard, and liberty claims required in the market. Susan Okin opposes this view, echoing a growing feeling that justice principles be extended to private and family life.[19] But exactly which principles should be extended? As we've seen, the application of equal protection to abuse reflects the antidifferentiation principle according to which all differences are interpreted as invidious and a rule that excludes men or whites is as evil as a rule that excludes women or blacks.[20] This principle makes sense with assault, which affects both sexes in similar ways. But an equity interest in state protection is harder to identify with coercive control because its unique dynamic is shaped around the disadvantaged status women inherit with their gender. An added challenge is to specify a justice interest in acts that target behavior that is already devalued by social convention, widely considered burdensome, and assumed to be women's work on men's watch. Feminist legal theorist Catharine MacKinnon makes a persuasive case that sexual harassment and pornography are extreme forms of gender bias because they help reproduce women as objects for men's use and pleasure.[21] This is also the effect of coercive control. But MacKinnon is addressing constraints imposed in civil society, where there is a well-defined social interest in unencumbered self-direction and so in protecting associated rights and enforcing obligations. Talking about the freedom to do housework is something akin to defending the freedom to pick cotton without challenging slavery. A growing consensus favors intervention in relationships where there is extreme violence, stalking, or an injury to a child. But by the time abuse reaches this point, coercive control is likely to have severely eroded a woman's personhood from the inside out, the way carpenter ants devour a house.

Sameness is not the only basis for an equal protection argument. Another important impetus for equal protection was the recognition of the subordination of blacks and women through slavery, disenfranchisement, segregation, and a general denial of full citizenship. This approach is hostile to differences because they perpetuate the subordination of minorities, not because difference itself is thought to be invidious. The application of the antisubordination principle of discrimination in statutory cases is both more group based than the antidifferentiation principle and more interested in impact than intent. Another advantage is that victim voices are critical to interpreting the harms it causes.[22]

Still lacking is a broader picture of the harms caused by coercive control sufficient to muster public reasons for their abolition.

The Limits of Safety

The domestic violence revolution was unequivocal in its emphasis on safety, garnering public support by highlighting the physical injuries caused by abuse. In the activist shelters that formed the vanguard of the advocacy movement, the right to physical integrity was linked to restoring women's self-direction within a collective practice that targeted changing the system that imposed and reproduced sexual inequality. Safety remains at the core of shelter practice and policy reform. But a growing body of literature emphasizes how control, manipulation, isolation, and the other tactics that comprise coercive control inhibit women's self-direction, compromise their liberty, and cause a range of harms that are not easily subsumed under safety concerns. In her pioneering history of the shelter movement, Susan Schechter emphasized how "violence restricts women's ability to move freely and confidently into the world and therefore hinders their full development. The fear of violence robs women of possibilities, self-confidence and self-esteem. In this sense, violence is . . . an attack on women's dignity and freedom."[23] This understanding echoes the argument that violence against women is "a political problem requiring a political solution."

Freedom from Control as a Human Rights Issue

The argument that battering violates women civil liberties has been developed most fully in the international context where successive United Nations conferences and numerous nongovernmental organizations (NGOs) have framed gender violence as a violation of human rights.

Women's social position presented unique challenges to a traditional human rights framework. Following Western political theory, the concept of human rights initially developed to protect individual rights to autonomy and freedom, expanded to protect these individual rights from state intrusion in the international context, and subsequently was enlarged to include state responsibility where its agents committed rape or other instances of gender violence or failed to prosecute such instances where this failure could be traced to discrimination.[24] In its most recent iteration, human rights theory adapts a broad notion of gender violence that includes isolation, limitations on autonomy, and other prominent features I have identified here with coercive control; highlights the causal role of battering in perpetuating sexual inequality and discrimination; posits an affirmative responsibility for states to intervene; and identifies community-level activism as a critical tool in pressuring states to act and, in lieu of state action, in directly preserving women's autonomy.[25]

Starting with the Universal Declaration of Human Rights (1948) which Eleanor Roosevelt helped draft, various treaties passed by the UN General Assembly included the right to liberty and security; the right to live free of torture or cruel, inhuman, or degrading treatment or punishment; freedom of thought, conscience, and religion; and freedom of association. But both official and nongovernmental agencies initially treated these as "negative rights" designed to counter state interference and only slowly extended them to violence against women by state agents. Only in March 1991 did Amnesty International (AI) begin to report on the rape of women prisoners as a form of torture.[26]

In 1989, in a review of monographs titled *Violence Against Women in the Family*, the UN Commission on the Status of Women in Vienna linked abuse to the harms that are prominent in coercive control. The report concluded: "Not only are women denied equality with the balance of the world's population, men, but also they are often denied liberty and dignity, and in many situations suffer direct violations of their physical and mental autonomy."[27] Another major step occurred in 1993, when the UN General Assembly adopted the Declaration on the Elimination of Violence Against Women that explicitly rooted abuse in unequal power, highlighted its role in reproducing male domination and female subordination, included "psychological violence" and intimidation in community settings such as work or school alongside the traditional forms of physical violence against women, and emphasized "arbitrary restrictions on liberty."[28] It also cited government inaction to protect women from these forms of violence as a human rights abuse. In a parallel development, the Committee on the Elimination of Discrimination Against Women (CEDAW) identified gender-based violence as a form of discrimination that "seriously inhibits women's ability to enjoy rights and freedoms on a basis of equality with men."[29] CEDAW argued that rape and domestic violence are causes of women's subordination rather than simply its consequence. Also in 1993, the World Conference on Human Rights in Vienna took the next logical step, declaring gender-based violence a human rights abuse.[30] CEDAW had taken a similar position a decade earlier, but it lacked the standing of the World Congress. A similarly broad understanding of violence against women appears in the Inter-American Convention on the Prevention, Punishment and Eradication of Violence Against Women, which came into effect in March 1995, a treaty signed by 28 nations.

Among international agencies, the World Organization Against Torture, an international coalition of NGOs, has come closest to grappling with the nonviolent dimensions of battering. Like so much of the literature on coercive control, it draws an analogy between public and private forms of torture: "Just as torture by a state official typically takes place when the victim is in incommunicado detention, at the unsupervised mercy of his interrogators or captors and without access to the outside world, battered women, because of their domestic situation, live isolated from family and friends and others."[31]

In 2004, AI launched an international campaign to combat violence against women with the publication of *Stop Violence Against Women: It's in Your Hands*. The report provides examples from dozens of countries of state sponsored gender violence, violence in the family, and violence against women in the community. Most important for our purposes, its conception of abuse lends itself to a broad concern with economic and social justice and emphasizes the links between community-level activism and the state reforms in law and policy with which human rights activists have been traditionally concerned. The diversity of its cultural audience prevents AI from supporting abortion rights and other traditional feminist concerns. But the human rights literature on which it draws is unapologetic in its feminism. Even as the advocacy movement has become increasingly atomistic in its concern and focus, international women's and human rights organizations have embraced a broad definition of liberty harms and returned to the emphasis on collective empowerment as the principal context for ending abuse with which the domestic violence revolution began.

Lessons Learned

By linking gender violence, intimidation, economic oppression, and limitations of speech, movement, and social connection, the human rights literature provides an excellent segue to a fully developed theory of coercive control. In the schema I adopt, "control" subsumes this broad range of limitations on speech, movement, and social connection, objective constraints such as control over money, information, and decision making, and the gender-specific regulations identified by Jones and Schechter. I use the overarching term *intimidation* to encompass a range of tactics that supplement violence and are also employed to induce fear and humiliation. These extend from threats, stalking, and the destruction of personal property through the myriad forms of manipulation and psychological abuse others have spelled out.

The human rights discussion makes it possible to identify each of the broad tactical categories implicated in coercive control with a corresponding rights violation. Any element of coercive control can abrogate any or all of these rights. Within a broad justice discourse, it is nonetheless useful as a practical matter to link each component offense to the right it offends most immediately—violence to the right to security, intimidation to the right to dignity and to live without fear, isolation to the right to autonomy, and control to liberty rights. Security, dignity, autonomy, and liberty are rights that are universally recognized as worthy of state protection.

The human rights literature roots women's justice claims for protection from gender violence in an affirmative concept of freedom. The preexistence of autonomous individuals capable of rationally calculating their self-interest and acting without coercion is the basic conceit in democratic and market societies. Whatever the limits of this conceit, its centrality in both human rights and democratic discourse makes it useful to frame liberty as the natural endowment to be self-directing, rights as the formal entitlements to enact these liberties, and freedom as what we would or could do with liberty and rights if our access to them was unobstructed. In *The Imaginary Domain*, legal philosopher Drucilla Cornell adds yet another dimension to this conception, identifying the minimal conditions for freedom as an unencumbered will—the right to choose; a deliberative capacity, the ability to weigh alternatives according to their relative costs and benefits; and a domain of free movement—the possibility of taking our purposes into the world, of acting without constraint.[32] Persons who lack these prerequisites cannot transform themselves into individuated beings who can participate in public and political life as equal citizens. In jeopardizing these prerequisites, in stifling their liberty and obstructing access to rights, coercive control prevents women from practicing freedom. This is the essential wrong that demands correction.

The principle of egalitarianism—that the opportunity for true personhood should be open to all on an equal basis—is another core tenet of liberal democracy. In liberal equity theory, the state's role as guardian of equal opportunity is based on the view that invidious distinctions in the market such as discrimination in housing or employment comprise the major obstacles to equal opportunity. This assumption underlies the "colorblind" test currently preferred to affirmative action as a means to achieve racial equality in employment. Level the playing field so that blacks and whites and men and women are treated in the same way, and outcomes should redistribute themselves according to merit or skill. It is also assumed that any unequal outcomes by caste or class that remain result largely from fortuitous personal or cultural factors for which the state bears little responsibility. This view fails to encompass the substantive differences persons inherit from their sociological placement in disadvantaged or oppressed groups as well as from their consignment to cultural roles, such as homemaking, that constrain their access to equality.

The insensitivity of the egalitarian principle to historical or sociological differences is remedied by a final contribution of the human rights discussion to an understanding of coercive control, the recognition that gender violence in personal life is an important *cause* of inequality because, in denying women the social and economic prerequisites for independence and individuation, it puts them on an unequal footing with men. Applying this analysis to societies where women enjoy formal parity with men makes it clear that constraint in personal life remains a major source of sexual inequality that affects overall social progress.

Framing Rights in Personal Life

What philosopher Mary Ann Glendon calls "rights talk" is an important way that liberal societies address the disadvantages that accrue when social outcomes are predetermined for particular groups by obstacles to their individual liberty in the market.[33] Rights are won by groups, and their denial is assumed to have a negative social effect. But in liberal political and legal theory, they are the property of individuals. Although debate continues about whether an "intent" to discriminate must be established to demonstrate that rights have been violated rather than merely a discriminatory effect, it is universally assumed that persons suffer harm if fundamental rights are violated such as the right to physical security, speech, thought, or movement. Rights frame our access to the prerequisites for liberty, what law professor Duncan Kennedy calls "the affirmation of free human subjectivity against the constraints of group life."[34] A legal rights approach to justice has been criticized because we risk cutting ourselves off from the collective action that actualizes rights in everyday life when we represent them as individual endowments provided by the state and rely on state adjudication to address social injury (such as sexual harassment), unfair outcomes (such as sexual inequality in employment), or to mediate competing rights claims (between personal security and the right to privacy, for example). Still, in delivering rights, the state assumes responsibility for supporting freedom and projects an ideal of justice and equality among persons to which it can be held accountable. Rights talk need not obscure the importance of political action so long as we distinguish access to equal rights—formal equality—from the fact that people need rights in large part because substantive inequalities persist that the state has either brought about, helped perpetuate, or tolerated.

Despite their clear relevance, applying the rights to liberty and equality to coercive control presents special problems. Coercive control operates in the context of an interpersonal or family ethos of need, interdependence, and other-regarding intimacy that has traditionally been hostile to liberty, equality, and legal rights. Although the individuality, self-regard, and capacity to pursue one's self-interest required by civil society are bred in personal and family life, they are not expected to be practiced there, least of all by women. An important question is whether, in referring to partner violence as "domestic," "intimate," or "conjugal," we aggravate this dilemma by removing abuse from the civil rights agenda or help extend this agenda to personal life, an aim of the advocacy movement. We have identified the second problem already, that it is difficult to apply rights claims to aspects of personal life that are either widely viewed as unrelated to basic liberties (such as the right to dress or spend money as one wishes) or are already devalued.

Feminist political philosopher Wendy Brown identifies the two classic solutions to the apparent incompatibility of the family ethos and the self-interest implied in rights rhetoric—to assign the family ethos to women and the market ethos to men, or to split the subject into diametrically opposed psychic orientations, with men and women assuming different postures relative to rights and ethics depending on their social location.[35] The second solution, where women have different rights in their roles as employees and citizens (spheres traditionally identified as male) than in families, is illustrated by an ad for American Express in which a female executive is parachuting from a plane with a briefcase in one hand and a teddy bear in the other. Only her credit card allows her to "have it all." These approaches converge in millions of families where women are expected to split their psychic orientation (the double shift described by Hochschild), while men's rights to privacy and dignity are carried over from the market to the family.

The Concept of Personal, Informal, or "Soft" Rights

There is a third solution to this tension: to identify informal rights in community settings that protect women against abuse and afford them redress. As the recent AI report on gender violence makes clear, most persons in the world direct their personal lives according to entitlements rooted in the normative fabric of everyday life rather than in legal codes. Like legal rights, informal rights are asserted amid competing claims, involve ongoing negotiation, and elicit sanctions that range from peer disapproval to physical punishment or even death. But they possess a situational particularity that contrasts markedly with the comparatively individualistic, abstract, and universalistic focus of legal rights. Because informal rights are rooted in tradition and custom, they tend to be more conservative than formal entitlements, may provide the grounds for subverting legal rights, and can legitimate male oppression even when official policy favors equality, as is illustrated by the persistence of honor killings in countries where women are the constitutional equals of men, such as India, Pakistan, or Bangladesh. At the same time, the existence of informal rights helps persons avoid the dilemmas that arise when the fictional liberties associated with formal equality come up against the practical limits imposed by longstanding community practices. To ward off the resulting social inconsistencies, disadvantaged communities improvise norms and values that are appropriate to real life, devising what sociologist Leon Chestang called a "situational ethic."[36] Recognizing that Lessup's search for employment was hindered by a combination of racial bias and prejudice against "Rastas," Bonnie Foreshaw accepted his "right" to live off her income when he was out of work. But he had no comparable right to take her money or to use predatory violence or control.

Widely shared informal principles govern how we assess the behavior of men and women in families and relationships. If the normative status of women's consignment to housework or child care is generally uncontested, standards of fairness, appreciation, respect, and autonomy are applied to their enactment of this roles, affording women the encumbered right to shop, clean, or maintain unobstructed access to their children or members of their extended family. These "soft rights" operate largely without notice and are only articulated as entitlements when they are challenged or abrogated in some way. Moreover, men claim informal rights in relationships and families that parallel or may conflict with women's informal rights.

In contrast to the rational, abstract individual who is the imagined beneficiary of legal rights, informal rights are rooted in an idea of personhood as a function of interdependence, express the values shared by a community with which their bearer identifies, represent a moral claim for recognition or place in the world, and have an emotive connection to liberty and equality that can be both rich and immediate. Political struggle is no less important in establishing informal than formal rights. It took decades of protest against the squandering of family income on drink before the wives of Welsh miners won the "right" to take their husband's wages on pay days through "tipping up." The wives or mothers waited outside the front door for their men to tip up their wages so that the transfer would be public and peaceful, minimizing the possible use of violence to withhold the funds. Informal rights specific to local cultures or communities are particularly important as a defense against abuse in contexts where it is widely recognized that more harm than good for the group as a whole will result from an appeal to the state for protections. The AI report cites an example from Senegal, where a participatory model that involved the entire community in a discussion of human rights, reproductive health, and problem solving identified female genital mutilation as a problem and garnered widespread support to end the practice. A parallel example is the preference for dealing with abuse through "peace keeping" rituals rather than formal policing in some Native American communities, lesbian communities, and among religious minorities.[37]

Informal rights help compensate vulnerable minorities for the lack of formal equality. At the same time, the sense of entitlement women bring to personal life is a function of their overall social standing as well as of the relative shares of income and other resources they bring to a relationship. This process becomes much more complicated when it comes to the rights embedded in the daily round of domestic chores. Because activities cannot be free and consigned simultaneously, what is at stake here is not liberty or equality in an absolute sense but the freedom to distinguish conditions that are more or less functions of necessity (such as whether to feed the children, shop, or clean the house) from moments where it is possible to feel autonomous, deliberative, or self-directed (such as what to prepare for dinner or whether to clean and shop after work, in the evening, or on weekends). In this context, in the process of negotiating what kind of freedom is possible in personal life under conditions of gender inequality, soft rights take on enormous importance.

Privacy Rights

The concept of privacy rights provides a final perspective on the liberties infringed by coercive control. As elaborated by the U.S. Supreme Court in cases involving birth control and abortion, this understanding addresses the tension in personal life between formal and informal rights as well as between self-interest and a needs-based and other-regarding intimacy.

The Bill of Rights in the U.S. Constitution does not mention privacy. But privacy has consistently been recognized as fundamental to the rights the constitutional amendments are designed to protect. The right to privacy has traditionally been equated with noninterference in personal life, an interpretation that left abuse victims with few options. Following the doctrine of interspousal immunity in tort law, for instance, courts consistently refused to allow recoveries for injuries that would be compensable but for the fact that they were inflicted in the private sphere. The Supreme Court extended what Justice Brandeis called "the right to be left alone" by protecting women from state intrusion in private affairs in *Griswold v. Connecticut* and in its landmark decisions on abortion, *Roe v. Wade* and *Doe v. Bolton*.[38] These decisions went further than Brandeis, establishing an affirmative right to government protection for what the Court called "zones of privacy" that encompass many of the material and social conditions of equality and self-determination that are jeopardized by coercive control. In his concurring opinion in *Roe v. Wade*, Justice Douglas drew on the Ninth, First, Fourth, Fourteenth, and Fifth Amendments to identify the realms of autonomy he believed were pertinent to freedom in these zones. The significance of the Ninth Amendment is the implied protection it offers to the range of customary, traditional, and informal rights embedded in the fabric of everyday life, but not specifically identified by the constitution. Among these rights, I include self-respect and the other conditions of personhood emphasized by Drucilla Cornell and the "liberty" referred to in the Fourteenth Amendment and covered by "the Blessings of Liberty" clause in the Preamble to the U.S. Constitution. Although these amendments refer largely to negative liberties, the rights protected by the First and Fifth Amendments extend to "autonomous control over the development and expression of one's intellect, interest, tastes and personality" and so bear on personal relationships.[39] Because *Roe* deals with the right to abortion, Douglas emphasized the decisional dimension, what he refers to as "freedom of choice in the basic decisions of one's life respecting marriage, divorce, procreation (and) contraception, and the education and upbringing of children."[40] But his interpretation of the rights that merit state protection extends from the freedom from bodily compulsion to such "amenities of life" as the "freedom to care for one's health and person" and the "freedom to walk, stroll, or loaf."[41] Summarized as the affirmative rights to bodily integrity, autonomy, self-determination, and self-direction, these are precisely the freedoms that are abrogated by violence, intimidation, isolation, and control over women's daily routine.

For Justice Douglas, privacy rights are part of a larger right to liberty protected by the Fourteenth Amendment to the constitution that itself takes its meaning from an overarching conception of equality. This approach to privacy encompasses a positive right to a space where self-development, consciousness, and decisional autonomy can thrive. It is their right to privacy in this broad sense that we seek to restore by guaranteeing victims of coercive control the material and social conditions of equality and self-determination.

8

THE TECHNOLOGY OF
COERCIVE CONTROL

The preceding two chapters sketched the evolution of coercive control from earlier forms of violence against women and identified its primary harm with the suppression of personal liberty. This chapter describes how perpetrators use coercive control, its technology. I distinguish the strategic aims, dynamics, and effects of coercive control from partner assault as well as from fights; group the tactics deployed into four dynamics (violence, intimidation, isolation, and control); and document the prevalence of these tactics. The interplay between the selection of coercive and controlling tactics and persistent sociocultural constraints is illustrated by the special vulnerability of immigrant women. I draw on case material to capture the dynamics and experiential effects when men deploy this technology. The low-income, minority, and immigrant women who are disproportionately represented in the shelter population and my criminal caseload typically suffer higher levels of violence than the middle-class, native born, and white women and men who make up the majority of my counseling and family court clients. But the broad contours of abuse in these groups are identical.

Defining Terms

Coercion entails the use of force or threats to compel or dispel a particular response. In addition to causing immediate pain, injury, fear, or death, coercion can have long-term physical, behavioral, or psychological consequences. With the marked exception of mind games and other forms of intimidation where the threat of force is implied rather than explicit, the mechanisms, effects, and authorship of coercive acts are transparent. By using coercion, controllers compromise scope of effect for immediacy.

Control is comprised of structural forms of deprivation, exploitation, and command that compel obedience indirectly by monopolizing vital resources, dictating preferred choices, microregulating a partner's behavior, limiting her options, and depriving her of supports needed to exercise independent judgment. Control makes up in scope of effect what it lacks in immediacy and is rarely confined to a specific time or space. Control may be implemented through specific acts of prohibition or coercion, as when a victim is kept home from work, denied access to a car or phone, or forced to turn over her paycheck. But its link to dependence and/or obedience is usually more distal than coercion and so harder to detect, making assigning responsibility a matter of working back from its effects through a complex chain of prior events. The result when coercion and control are combined is the condition of unreciprocated authority Young identifies as domination and victims experience as *entrapment*.

The sweatshirt case illustrates the complex ways in which distal effects coercion and control are linked in a chain of dominance.

The Sweatshirt Case

Cheryl was the star pitcher for her factory softball team. After several innings when she pitched well, her boyfriend, Jason, would come onto the field and offer Cheryl her sweatshirt, saying, "Darling, you're cold. Why don't you put this on?" To the dismay of her teammates, Cheryl would "fall apart."

Cheryl's teammates interpreted Jason's gesture as caring. But to Cheryl, the message was that she had violated an agreement not to make him jealous. The sweatshirt was his warning that, because of her infraction, she would have to cover up her arms after he beat her. Cheryl's "mistake" was to draw attention to herself by striking out the opposing batters. She quickly corrected this fault by falling apart. She was also too frightened to pitch well.

Cheryl recognized that her panic was induced by Jason's offer. But when Donna curtailed her eating to placate her husband's obsession with her spending and her weight (chapter 9), she truly believed this was a "good way to economize." When she shared this at a family dinner, Frank (correctly) interpreted this as a plea for help and beat her for being "so stupid." These control tactics centered on gendered enactments. But they also targeted mundane areas of everyday life that are not normally thought of as norm- or rule-governed.

In most crimes, we work backward from the outcome to those responsible. Money is missing from the till, and we look for the thief. Control often is literally hidden "behind closed doors." In addition, as I've emphasized, it can also be difficult to detect because its means and effects merge with behaviors widely associated with women's devalued status in personal life—being deferential, thrifty, thin, and unnoticed. The tactics involved are easily confused with the range of sacrifices women are expected to make in their role as homemakers, parents, and sexual partners. Anthropologists have been particularly sensitive to what Nia Parson calls "the banality of sexism" because their training prepares them to look critically at how our usual practices of casting experiences as "natural" or "normal" obscure the greatly consequential workings of power in social life.[1] The hyper-regulation of everyday routines typical of coercive control *works* because the normative constraints already embedded in women's performance of everyday chores merge with their fear of not doing what is demanded. Because similar performative constraints are also linked to how men and women enact love, regulatory strategies are often disguised as expressions of affection, as in the sweatshirt example. Abusive partners have bought my clients clothes, asked them to quit waitressing at a strip club, begged them to leave the phone off the hook when they're apart so "I know you're there for me," asked that their daughter adopt their grandmother's name, or shown up unexpectedly at their job. The only clue that something is wrong in these cases may be the victim's inchoate sense that it is dangerous to refuse the request or that this is about him, not her. A woman described negotiating custodial issues with her ex-husband. "After talking for an hour about what I wanted and needed," she reported, "he announced 'Now, let's talk about me.'" If those who bear its brunt or witness these events are unclear about whether they are loving or controlling, imagine how difficult it can be for researchers, police, health providers, or advocates to identify the infrastructure of control.

How should we respond to the sweatshirt incident, or to sexual inspections, or when men monitor the time their partner spends on the phone or regulate how long she and her children can spend in the bathroom? What makes this sort of regulation more than merely an idiosyncratic variant of the expectation that women will be loyal, obedient, and deferential? What if the rules appear consensual, like Cheryl's agreement not to make Jason jealous? Why should a court take Cheryl's perception of threat as more credible than Jason's insistence he was just being caring? The answers lie in the interrelationships between these acts, not in the acts themselves, and in their oppressive context and effects.

Regulatory strategies are also commonly confused with the imbalance in decision making typical of heterosexual relationships or are masked by the fact that the supposed victim earns more money than her partner, pays the bills, hires outside help, or makes crucial decisions about household purchases, the children's future (such as which schools they attend), or other aspects of daily living. What marks control is not who decides, but who decides who decides; who decides what, whether, and how delegated decisions are monitored; and the consequences of making "mistakes."

Gender Strategy

Coercive control is a gender strategy. By *strategy*, I mean a patterned and self-interested way in which socially identifiable groups mobilize scarce resources to pursue major life goals in an important arena of their existence, such as work, marriage, or schooling. Strategic analysis assumes that our behavioral repertoires in these and other nontrivial facets of everyday life are relatively consistent, have identifiable temporal and spatial dimensions, and are unintelligible apart from the matrix of power in which they arise, the norms to which they respond, the relative benefits and sanctions they elicit in specific social and historical contexts, and the general consequences they effect. Although strategies only remain viable if they succeed in effecting their aims and consequences to some extent, I am referring here to collective behaviors that are rarely programmatic or conceived or implemented by persons with broad social goals in mind. To the contrary, the proximate means and motives by which these strategies are implemented are a function of individual personalities, preferences, and situational variables as well as of their perceived efficacy, and the tactics selected tend to be spatially diffuse and highly individualized. Moreover, the pattern that makes these behaviors strategic is recognizable largely in retrospect. What marks behaviors as strategic is their collective reality, aggregate consequence, and the extent to which the link that joins this reality to its consequence is mediated by structural dimensions of the economy, polity, and civil life. Couples divorced in the 1960s and 1970s for the same myriad reasons that have always led couples to separate. The fact remains: Women in these decades left marriages, initiated separation or divorce, delayed marriage or childbirth, reduced the number of children they bore, and set up families without husbands on a scale that compelled public recognition and response. Starting with the notorious Moynihan Report in 1965 and extending at least through the 1996 U.S. Welfare Reform Act and the passage of Defense of Marriage Acts (DOMAs) by Congress and a number of states under Presidents Clinton and George W. Bush, policy makers recognized the strategic nature of this behavior and attempted to influence it by changing financial and other incentives for marriage and family formation.

Divorce trends are examples of gender strategies, the subset of collective behaviors that encompasses how men and women constitute themselves as such, how they "do" masculinity and femininity in a particular epoch at the range of sites where gender takes on its social meaning, including school, work, family, and intimate relationships. The substantive benefits/losses persons derive or experience from enacting these strategies constitute their "materiality." The materiality of coercive control refers to the tangible and symbolic advantages men accrue from dominating and exploiting female partners and the substantive deprivations women suffer.

Strategic thinking allows us to identify, categorize, and target the various tactics men use to establish mastery over their partners without losing sight of either the bigger picture or the individualized nature of these tactics.

Men set out to realize their individual purposes in the world, not to become controllers. Establishing mastery over another independent adult in personal life is complex and difficult work for which there are no guide books, not even for "dummies." If it is recognized at all, the fact of domination in personal life is usually perceived only indirectly through signs of assertion, command, dependence, and subordination in a relationship. We see a controlling or a demanding husband or a servile or timid wife, but not the lines of power that join control to command. Even the victims of coercive control only recognize their predicament gradually, as they come to know themselves reflexively through what Drucilla Cornell dubs the "masculine imaginary." So numerous and varied are the tactics men use in coercive control that any attempts to categorize them are bound to seem arbitrary. Lists of such tactics are many pages long. Yet once we posit coercive control as a strategic form of power, its parts fall into place. As long-term researcher and advocate Lee H. Bowker observes, "I often allude to the idea that batterers use such similar techniques and strategies, they must all have gone to the same school to learn them."[2]

The gender strategy of coercive control has three dimensions: a basic set of beliefs and values about what it means to be a man and woman in today's world, a "gender ideology"; a package of resources, tools, techniques, and tactics to implement these beliefs, a "gender technology"; and an "action plan" that applies this technology in particular relationships in accord with the beliefs and preferences. The values and beliefs that lead certain men to equate their manhood with sexual mastery are beyond the scope of this book. My concern here is with the emerging gender technology, the *what* and *how* of partner dominance. The cases in part IV illustrate what happens when these tactics are implemented.

The Dance of Resistance and Control

The technology of coercive control is designed to respond to women's agency and resistance. This does not mean that women's behavior causes coercive control any more than buying a car causes car theft or devising security codes to protect financial transactions on line causes hacking. If women did not have the power, resources, relative equality, and creative capacity that comprise their agency, men would not work so hard to capture and redirect it for their personal benefit.

Women's reactions to the introduction of overarching material and structural controls run the gamut from outrage and bewilderment to shame. Abusive partners appreciate what the loss of autonomy means to women and shape their tactics accordingly. In anticipation that their target will attempt to break free or seek support, they may extend their efforts to isolate and control them in ways that can appear vastly disproportionate to the immediate resistance they confront. One client's husband went so far as to follow her to an evening sewing class with his headlights off. He drove off the road into a ditch and was almost killed. His paranoid fantasy was that the sewing class was merely a pretext for his wife to meet other men. But his action was also propelled by his insight that getting out of the house and spending time with others nourished her autonomy, making his efforts to control her that much harder. Doreen's case illustrates how control is shaped to match a woman's agency.

Doreen

Doreen was swept off her feet by Jack, a prominent physician at an Ivy League medical school, and married him just weeks after they met. He insisted that she give up her prominent position in the world of finance, sell the numerous properties she owned, and invest the proceeds in his medical research. When she announced her intention to redecorate their new home, Jack said he would "help." He picked up a sledge and began knocking down walls. Doreen's gourmet cooking was a point of pride. Jack would phone to tell her what he wanted for dinner and at what time he would be home. He would arrive several hours late and "go wild" because the food was not "fresh." With their son at the table, he would insult Doreen's cooking, claim she was poisoning him and the boy, and throw the plates at her. When friends came to the house, he would create scenes, scream insults at callers on the phone, and order her about on social occasions in ways that were humiliating. When Doreen discovered a tumor, he told her it was nothing. When a doctor friend recommended she be seen and the tumor proved cancerous, Jack held her against a wall and sprayed her with Raid, telling her this was his "cure." He insisted she use a hospital where he was not known by the residents, believing they would think she was "dirty" and lose respect for him. Disregarding the advice of her doctors whom he called "button pushers," he threatened to make a scene unless she came home against medical advice 24 hours after the surgery. She developed sepsis and might have died had an older daughter by a previous marriage not intervened and called an ambulance.

The cancer and the hospital stay threatened not just to expose the physician's abuse but to give Doreen's life a focus other than Jack's needs. His fears were justified. Realizing how close she had come to dying, Doreen sued for divorce because, she told me, "I couldn't continue to fight both the cancer and my husband." But this did not end his attempts to control her life. No sooner had Jack moved out than he reported a number of zoning and health violations, including the fact that Doreen was conducting a business on the property. Her home was put under virtual siege by a range of inspectors.

Doreen's capabilities as an independent woman were well developed and widely recognized. But many of the men in my practice target the smallest signs of their partner's autonomy.

Kenny

Kenny owned a motorcycle shop, drove a Harley, dressed in black, and was so imposing in a group that included a serial rapist and a man on trial for killing his wife that when I took his usual seat one evening when he was absent, several men gasped as if I'd be struck by lightning. He described his wife as a "feminist bitch," an image with which the other men identified. To our eyes, Sylvia was a petite, soberly dressed, reticent, and religious young woman who repeatedly defended her role as a traditional wife. Still, she admitted, often when their twin infants were crying, she would ask Kenny to carry the dishes to the sink, a request that threw him into the rages that led his assaults.

Kenny's borderline reaction was based on an insight his wife shared— that she had chosen deference among the many possibilities made available by women's new opportunities, a posture she appeared to be abandoning when she asked for his help. When he called her a feminist bitch, he was responding to this display of "power," albeit with a small *p*, to what he read as her signal that she could always choose differently, though her upbringing made this unlikely.

Without considering what women's agency looks like from the perpetrator's standpoint, his actions can appear crazy. They are usually not.

The Typology of Abuse

Couple Fights

In chapter 3, I suggest that the majority of incidents population surveys identify as domestic violence are properly understood as fights in which one or both partners use force to address situationally specific conflicts, neither is sufficiently fearful to seek outside assistance, both partners view the use of force as a legitimate (if not necessarily desirable) form of conflict resolution, and injury is very rare. Even among men identified by the National Family Violence Survey (NFVS) as having been "severely" assaulted by their wives, only 1 in 100 required medical attention, many times fewer that the proportion who report seeking help for abuse to crime or safety surveys.[3] Ninety percent of younger men and even 87% of the presumably more vulnerable population of older men who have been hit by female partners say they are *not* frightened by their partner's violence.[4] A growing source of trouble in these relationships is whether rights assigned by fiat or by sex-linked double standards will be readjusted to accommodate women's new social standing, making every fight about larger equality concerns as well as immediate issues. As psychologist Jean Baker-Miller writes, "Inequality generates hidden conflict around elements that the inequality itself has set in motion."[5] The distinguishing feature of common couple fights is that these struggles around inequality occur in a normative context where both partners regard getting physical as a legitimate way to express feelings, assert independence or address differences in power.

Unlike assaults, fights can have positive outcomes for couples. In a study of 272 newly married couples who came to their clinic at SUNY-Stonybrook, psychologist Daniel O'Leary and colleagues reported the counterintuitive finding that those who used force to settle their differences were significantly more likely to be "satisfied" with their relationships than couples who did not. Force and conflict declined over time in these relationships, the opposite of the pattern reported by assault victims.[6] In the Finnish national population study, 40% of the women who reported violence said their partner had used force at least 7 years earlier, but not since then. These relationships were more stable, long-lasting, and egalitarian than other relationships where assaultive violence was used. Only 6% of the women whose relationships had been characterized by fights felt their decision making was being restricted in any way. Meanwhile, where "name calling" and other forms of humiliation were virtually universal in situations characterized by assault or coercive control, only 12% of the women involved in fights reported even name calling. Half of these women had felt "hatred" for their partner at one time. But few had called police or suffered injuries and now reported many fewer emotional or behavioral problems (such as fear, depression, low self-esteem, sleeping difficulties, or loss of sleep) than women who experienced assault or coercive control.[7] The vast majority of women in the Finnish subgroup was employed and middle class. But among a sample of inner-city women who reported using violence with a male partner, a significant subgroup felt it had "worked," even when they got the worst of an exchange.[8]

Many of these women had undoubtedly learned to fight in schools or neighborhoods where choosing not to respond when you are disrespected can cause violence to escalate with more serious consequences than if you fight and lose.

There may be compelling reasons for communities to address the use of force to resolve differences, particularly where children are exposed, violence overflows into public settings, or fights escalate. Fights are not always easy to distinguish from assaults or coercive control, and there is a real risk that judges, police, or other providers will apply this distinction to dismiss a range of genuinely abusive situations as just fights or as instances of high conflict where no protection is needed. The critical issue here is respecting whether the offended party seeks help or protection, an obvious sign that an abuse investigation is warranted, even if the evaluator suspects that the claim of violence is being used to gain leverage in a court case. In any case, intervention efforts are confounded if authorities cannot distinguish fights from genuine abuse.

Partner Assault

Partner assaults are what most people recognize as domestic violence, where violence and threats are used to hurt, subjugate, and exert power over a partner, to satisfy a grievance, express anger, monopolize scarce resources, establish privilege, and to keep differences from surfacing by making independent action and conflict too costly to pursue. Partner assaults are typically repeated, escalate in severity over time, and usually continue after a couple separates. Though a significant proportion of men and women endorse assault as a legitimate means to get their way and some victims see "taking a beating" as an unfortunate but inevitable component of getting involved with men, the vast majority of its victims view assault as illegitimate and seek outside assistance. Assaultive violence is more likely to be unilateral, severe, frequent, and accompanied by threats than the force used in fights, where the modal dynamic is mutual. Women respond violently to partner and stranger assaults in similar proportions, though estimates of how often they do so range from 8% to 25%.[9] But even when the levels of violence are comparable, assault victims are more likely to seek outside assistance than participants in fights because of what they perceive as the motive, meaning, and context of the violence. Police, court, and shelter studies indicate that between 19% and 40% of male perpetrators limit themselves to physical and emotional abuse.[10]

The Contexts of Assault

Assault is primarily deployed in two contexts: to hurt or subjugate a partner who is formally independent and equal—the most common situation in liberal democratic societies—and to reinforce cultural mores that dictate female subordination to their husbands.

Assault is the oppressive strategy of choice for men and women who suffer from medical, behavioral, or psychiatric problems; are part of a gang or criminal subculture; or who subsist in circumstances such as homelessness that make any sort of ongoing, stable partnerships difficult to maintain. We need not be detained here with the small proportion of cases where violence is caused by mental illness, post-traumatic stress disorder (PTSD), seizure disorders, intermittent explosive disorder (IED), or similar psychophysiological processes. Assault is also common in same-sex relationships, an issue to which I give independent treatment in the conclusion. Female as well as male perpetrators of partner assault are often reenacting scripts implanted through sexual abuse or other childhood trauma or, like participants in fights, are trying to put themselves on a more equal footing with partners by "giving as good as they get." These women can be as brutal, mean, and unforgiving as any man.

Christine

Christine entered an after-hours club where her sometime boyfriend, Charles, was drinking. On a dare, Charles slapped Chris's face. This felt "like a fly landing," she told me. In response, she knocked Charles down and kneeled on his chest while onlookers laughed. As she was leaving the club, Charles jumped on her back. She threw him aside, pinned him against the wall, and stabbed him fatally with a pen knife. Christine had been sexually abused as a girl and had a history of being abused by previous boyfriends. One beat her repeatedly with a board until her brothers had him killed. When the men dared Charles to hit her, they were exploiting her reputation for violent outbursts against other women and men.

Many men arrested for domestic violence already have substantial records of nonviolent as well as violent crime.[11] Assaults committed in the criminal subculture appear to be less frequent but more injurious than the assaults committed as part of coercive control; victims as well as perpetrators are often using alcohol and/or drugs; jealousy or possessiveness are common motives; and the couple's relationship often forms, dissolves, and re-forms over many years as counterpoint to other violent and nonviolent relationships in which both partners are involved. Importantly, though, victims of assault often retain their autonomy.

Jamilah

Jamilah's partner, Tyrone, was an obsessively jealous man with a long history of arrests for drug dealing and burglary. Early in the relationship, she retaliated when Tyrone attacked her. During one assault, she cut his eye open with a punch. In another, she knocked him to the pavement. Jamilah cared for a mother who had been partially paralyzed by a stroke, worked an evening and a day job (in part to support a drug-addicted brother), and parented their two girls. Many of Tyrone's assaults occurred at parties, bars, or on the street when he believed Jamilah was paying too much attention to other men. After Jamilah developed a debilitating thyroid condition, his assaults escalated, and she broke off the relationship. When he got out of jail and found she was living with a woman she met in the shelter, he tried to run her down in a car. A week later, he broke into their apartment and assaulted her. When the court denied her request for child support because Tyrone's drug earnings were off the books and he refused to help with their children, she threw a gasoline fire bomb into the hotel room where he stashed his drug money.

Jamilah suffered significant injury as a result of Tyrone's assaults. Because he did not control her work, money, or interfere in her family life, however, she developed none of the secondary problems associated with abuse. She retained her autonomy throughout the relationship and continued to work two jobs, support her brother, and care for her mother and children. Women bear the overwhelming burden of partner assaults even when they retaliate effectively, as Jamilah did early in the relationship. In a study involving 91 hospitals that compared male and female victims of partner assaults, women comprised 84% of the patients treated for injuries.[12] In any given case, partner assault can compromise a person's autonomy, undermine their capacity to work or parent, and afford ready access to a victim's resources. Against the background of female equality, however, assault alone is rarely sufficient to elicit these consequences. This is illustrated in Finland, where 70% of the women are in the labor market, all citizens are guaranteed a minimal livelihood by virtue of statutory social security support, and families with children and single parents are supported by special family policy measures. According to the national survey, abuse is an ongoing problem primarily in relationships where violence is complemented or replaced by a range of other dominating and intimidating behaviors.[13]

Partner Assault in Immigrant and Fundamentalist Communities

As a means of establishing dominance, partner assault is most effective when it can play off the convergent restrictions on women's autonomy, marriage choices, education, career options, and comportment at home or in public that continue to characterize many traditional and fundamentalist communities. Whatever formal rights women in these societies may enjoy, their functional status resembles the status of women centuries ago.

Ana

Ana shares her house in war-torn Serbia with members of her husband's family who fled the war in Bosnia. They are all men, and none of them work. They wait for her to prepare their food, wash and iron their clothes (even though there is no washing machine or running water), and clean the house. Ana has a little garden to grow vegetables, but the men will not help with that either because "gardening is not men's work." The men give her no money. So besides all the work in her home, she cleans neighbors' houses for money. She must keep this work secret so the men do not take what little money she earns or beat her for causing them shame by showing that they are not capable of providing for the family.[14]

Ana's husband hits her. But his abuse merely complements the super-exploitation she inherits with her cultural role. When similar patriarchal beliefs are transplanted to market societies where they lack the legal or institutional support they got at home, two important changes occur: the husband becomes much more central in enforcing and monitoring female obedience and across a far broader plane and women are removed from their families, neighbors, and community elders or other authorities on whom they might have depended to check their husband's violence. These changes increase the probability that husbands will rely on severe violence as well as the possibility that women will respond violently. In juxtaposing egalitarian to traditional values and pressuring immigrant families to accommodate new economic realities, migration poses a series of challenges for which patriarchal cultures are often unprepared. One way to meet these challenges is for immigrant men to extend their oppression from assault to control, an adaptation that can make their authority transparent and increase their own risk.

Nahima

Nahima, a Palestinian woman, was charged with attempted murder after she beat her husband with a club while he slept off an alcoholic stupor. The marriage had been arranged by their families, who had met in a Palestinian refugee camp. Her husband's "disrespect" began on their marriage night, when her failure to shed virginal blood convinced him that she was "dirty." With this as his excuse, he beat and sexually assaulted her repeatedly and forced her to sexually service three of his nine brothers, his uncle, and several men unrelated to him by blood, including a man he brought home from the video store. Nahima viewed this as bad luck within a broad range of patriarchal prerogatives set off by her loss of virginity in the camp. Because of his place near the bottom of the male pecking order, the husband had also been forced to have anal intercourse with his older brothers. But he crossed an invisible cultural line when he threatened to have sex with their son. No longer able to appeal to her father or brother to help her, she felt she had no recourse other than to act on her own.

If women's enactment of their traditional roles in the adopted country increases the importance of voluntary compliance and direct enforcement, both are undermined as they reflect on their situation from the vantage of new economic realities (such as the necessity for them to work outside the home) and opportunities.

Shamita

Shamita was obliged to cook, clean, and service her husband's brother and several nephews who stayed in their home in Schenectady, New York, for extended periods. Despite the frigid weather, her husband limited Shamita's dress to the thin cotton saris she had brought from India, effectively confining her to the house from September to early May. When Shamita protested, he locked her and their son outside in the cold. When she was uncooperative in other respects—attempting to join a Christian church choir or to take classes at a local college—he wrote to her father for assistance with her discipline. Later he threatened her with "bride burning." He also beat her. Despite his objections and a stern reprimand from her father, Shamita took her son to the evangelical church, joined the choir, took classes in psychology, and initiated a divorce.

The expectations that wives will be virginal, adhere to traditional rituals, or serve members of their husband's extended family seriously limit their access to economic opportunity and personal autonomy. In the name of relativism, it is easy to forget that the rules governing traditional cultures are as much a function of male control in these societies as they are its supports. There is no counterpart among men to the belief that the bride be virginal in Palestinian culture, for instance, and women may be beaten or even killed by their own families if they leave abusive husbands.

Some wives become even more devout after they emigrate because adherence to traditional rituals gives them a feeling of place and a claim on their husband's respect in a world where the women he encounters are likely to be employed or independent. Shamita's husband saw her attending the evangelical church as a sign of disobedience, a view her father reluctantly supported. But to Shamita, its fundamentalist credo allowed her to express her independence while still embracing the belief that women were men's subordinates. This compromise backfired during the divorce, when members of her new congregation testified on the husband's behalf, although they barely knew him.

The immigrant community is nested within a world of secular institutions where traditional expectations and constraints must be conveyed through family, church, and extended social networks. Ironically, formal and informal supports for male dominance may be even stronger among American-born women living in fundamentalist religious communities.

A Jehovah's Witness

A devoted Jehovah's Witness was repeatedly assaulted and emotionally abused by her husband, also a Witness. The woman reported her abuse to the church elders, an all-male body of lay ministers responsible for counseling parishioners on religious and family matters. In response, the elders advised their "sister" to try harder to please her husband and God. One consequence of following their advice—becoming more devout and accepting responsibility for her problems—was that she began to cut and starve herself, losing so much weight that she was admitted to the hospital. When she again brought her complaints of abuse to the elders, this time showing them the marks from her husband's belt, she was "disfellowshipped," a form of ostracism that prevented other Witnesses from communicating with her, cutting her off from her entire social network. As isolated and miserable as these experiences made her, she only took the elders to court when they made her abusive husband an elder in clear violation of the church doctrine in which she still believed.[15]

Partner assault in immigrant or fundamentalist communities often evolves into coercive control when the already weakened "law of the fathers" is further jeopardized by the range of cultural influences to which women are exposed. Because the Witness had been trained as a paralegal, she could sue the church. Although the suit was dismissed, she took enormous satisfaction from being able to confront the elders about their hypocrisy in depositions.

Leaders in these communities are more tolerant of men who deviate from cultural precepts than of women who do so because men's options are more varied and less strictly defined to start, they earn most of the money on which community institutions depend, and it is accepted that they will have regular dealings with and so be tempted by the outside world. But women's relations with the outside world are strictly monitored. In a Texas case, a rabbi was initially sympathetic with an abused congregant whose husband was also having an affair. But when the woman had her husband arrested, the rabbi publicly condemned the woman for going outside.

Men do not have unqualified discretion in traditional communities, however. In the Jehovah's Witness case, the abusive husband was eventually ostracized for adultery. After he assaulted his mother and sister, Donna's husband, Frank, was cut off by the Albanian community in which they lived.

When secular market influences destabilize traditional controls over women's options, immigrant or fundamentalist men often initiate abuse or reach outside their culture for the means to sustain their authority. Traditional societies have few mechanisms to realistically accommodate these influences. As a result, when a woman like Shamita or the Witness deviate from their prescribed roles, the first explanations are that the husband has failed as a "man" (to keep his wife in line, for example) or that she is morally deficient, because she lacks appropriate "respect," for instance, or is simply crazy. These accounts more readily support an escalation of abuse than negotiation or compromise, even when this undermines the male's immediate self-interest. Donna's employment was crucial to the family's survival. But her working made it impossible for her to prepare traditional Albanian meals every night for Frank and his family. To Frank, this symbolized her disrespect and meant she was "lazy" and "stupid," traits for which he beat her. Nothing in Albanian lore prepared Frank or Donna for the impact of their new economic situation on their role expectations or their respective capacity to meet these expectations. Nor did the traditional expectations help Frank cope with Donna's social relations at the bank, an issue that would never have arisen in a culture where paid employment was proscribed for women and their behavior outside the home was policed. All that Frank understood was that dependence on his wife's income meant dishonor, an implication he could not confront because Donna's contribution was essential to their survival. Frank's response was to escalate his abuse and try to micromanage Donna's behavior outside and inside their home through a log book. But these steps further isolated the family and caused Donna to lose her job, alternately undermining the cultural foundation and the material support for his authority, leading to the escalating coercion and control to which Donna responded by killing him.

Coercive Control

The categorical division of coercive control into violence, intimidation, isolation, and control is designed to highlight a reality to which victim experience gives eloquent testimony, that male domination in personal life is organized through a "technology" that is situationally specific and yet articulated at key points with larger discriminatory structures. This technology is developed through trial and error to contain the subjectivity of a particular woman yet patterned in ways that give it a predictable shape and dynamic. The categories are derived from women's accounts of their abuse and its observable dynamics and consequences. Thus "isolation" should be understood as something men do, something women experience, and as an objective effect of identifiable tactics. But the primary purpose of the categories is heuristic: to help us organize its tactical elements into a coherent picture that can provide a foundation for the analysis and management of coercive control. Relationships where isolation is the dominant element look and feel different from situations in which violence, control, or intimidation predominate and the ways in which they are combined differ from relationship to relationship. If its overall pattern marks coercive control as a recognizable strategy, its particularity reveals its malevolent intent.

The Structure and Dynamics of Coercive Control:
Partner Violence

Violence is used in coercive control with the same aims as in assault, though the concurrent use of other means to establish dominance, prevent escape, repress conflict, appropriate resources, and establish privilege lessens its importance in achieving these aims. But if the presence of structural controls lessens the utility of severe violence in imposing subordination, by reducing women's options, it also makes them more vulnerable to violence, increasing the probability they will be injured.

Assaults and threats violate the universally recognized right of free adults to bodily integrity. Sexual identity, subjectivity, and citizenship are all predicated on physical constancy. Physical security roots the process of experimentation and risk taking through which the self unfolds, allowing persons to imagine, develop, rehearse, and implement different ways of being in the world. Violence restricts risk taking both in an economic sense—by mobilizing and exhausting our limited energies for self-protection—and psychologically, by subordinating issues of happiness, moral purpose, and experimentation to the singular aim of remaining safe.

Partner assaults frequently involve extreme violence, "beatings," choking, burning, rape, torture, and the use of weapons or other objects that cause severe injury, permanent disfigurement, even death. In a recent British survey of 500 women who sought help from Refuge UK, 70% had been choked or strangled at least once, 60% had been beaten in their sleep, 24% had been cut or stabbed at least once, almost 60% had been forced to have sex against their will, 26.5% had been "beaten unconscious," and 10% had been "tied up." As a result of these assaults, 38% of the women reported suffering "permanent damage."[16] When Bonnie Foreshaw learned her second husband was sleeping with a woman from his work, she told him to leave. In response, he stabbed her in the throat with a hair-pick, sending her to intensive care. Joan M. suffered brain damage as the result of her husband's assault and was hospitalized for almost a month. Then, he enlisted two psychiatrists to convince a court in Huntsville, Alabama, that she had been rendered unfit to parent by her consequent reduction in IQ.

When opportunities to avoid or escape assaults are foreclosed by structural barriers, such as the denial of a car or access to a phone, fear of pain can freeze the self in time and produce a cognitive paralysis expressed in the self-censorship of dangerous thoughts. Unbearable anxiety can be elicited even by such trivial choices as what to wear, what to make for dinner, or whether to talk to a family member after church. Some victims defend against this anxiety by shutting it away, exhibiting a stunning lack of affect in the face of danger, or by repressing the memory of assault, a process that takes extreme form in dissociative processes such as splitting. Lavonne still bears scars on her arm from cigarette burns inflicted by Miguel, her live-in boyfriend. "I felt dead inside when he burned me," she told me and was unable (or refused) to cry or beg. Laura described enacting the domestic rituals Frank outlined for her "like a ghost." This is the feeling women seek to escape by carving safety zones out of the fabric of everyday life.

Sexual Coercion

In the English study of women who had sought refuge, 27% of the victims reported they were forced to have sex against their will often or all the time.[17] Dorothy's account of being raped by the boyfriend she eventually killed illustrates how sexual assault is part of the broader pattern of humiliation and dominance it punctuates.

> Jim became obsessive over me. I could not go out with my girlfriends. My clothes were under scrutiny. On several occasions I was told to change my clothing. He would make derogatory remarks about my appearance and made me change. It was a power struggle. He wanted to rule my life. I on the other hand had experienced this before and did not like what was happening. Sometime last summer after a heavy night of drinking we were having an argument and he became physically abusive to me. I locked myself in the bedroom and he broke down the door. I was raped. This is one of the worst memories of my life. Jim had a gun and he hit me with it. He ripped my clothes off and he attacked me. I tried to leave several times that night, but I had no clothes and he was standing guard over me. The next morning he went and bought me some new clothes so he could take me home without anyone noticing.

To Dorothy, rape was one component of Jim's strategy to rule her life rather than a distinct form of victimization. If literal rapes fall on a continuum with digital inspections and other forms of explicitly sexual humiliation, the implied threat of sexual force allows an abusive partner to dictate the when, how, where, and even the with whom of sex. This was illustrated by Donna's admission that "I never said 'no' to him again," after Frank bound her hands with a belt and "had his way" shortly after they married. The fear hanging in the air also explains why, in the context of abuse, passive forms of coercion such as the silent treatment or even withholding sex or affection constitute pressured sex. When she hesitated to provide sex on demand, one client told me, her abusive husband sulked, brooded, and made snide comments and threats under his breath. She quickly complied with his demands because the memory of his past violence made her feel like she was living with a "time bomb." Another common pressure tactic is for abusive men to threaten to "get it on the street" if a partner refuses sex or insists he use a condom, raising the specter of AIDS. Dorothy also linked Jim's sexual assault to other aspects of his sexual demands, such as how she dressed or her friendships.

Violence as Routine Behavior

Despite the occurrence of severe assault, it is the frequency, relatively low-level, and cumulative effects of minor violence that distinguishes coercive control. Women suffering intimate partner terrorism are assaulted six times more often on average than women in couples characterized by domestic assaults. Some idea of the level of these assaults is conveyed by the English sample, wherein 58% of the women reported they were "shook or roughly handled" often or all the time. Moreover; 65.5% were pushed, grabbed, shoved, or held "too hard"; 55.2% were slapped, smacked, or had their arm twisted; and 46.6% were kicked, bit, or punched with this frequency. These incidents are often combined in a typical pattern and enacted with little affect, leading many victims to experience physical abuse as routine behavior that resembles other routine events, such as eating, sleeping, or going to the toilet. The routine nature of violence in coercive control is illustrated by the finding that the heart rate of batterers who use control—whom one research team call "cobras"—actually declines when they assault their partners.[18]

Sarah

Sarah, the Emmy award–winning TV journalist, reported few incidents of severe violence. But her day book was filled with scribbles indicating "Dave goes crazy." These notes referred to a ritual enacted almost nightly: Dave would arrive home, have a drink, listen to the answering machine, call back any men whom he didn't recognize, interrogate Sarah about her day, begin to rant and rave, throw or break objects, and scream insults at her. Then, he would push or shove her into their bedroom and close the door, effectively locking her in for the night, far from the numerous lovers he imagined she entertained.

The cumulative effect of this assaultive routine can be a hostage-like state of physical paralysis, subjugation, and chronic fear that has no counterpart in any other crime in private or public life.

Angela

Angela Bowman, a slight 25-year-old African American woman, was charged with stabbing her boyfriend, Roger Harris, with whom she lived at his mother's house. This high-spirited young woman suffered from such severe sickle cell disease that she had been forced to leave school in the 9th grade and was unable to earn an independent livelihood. She reported only three assaults, when Harris punched her with a closed fist, when he knocked her down after she had accused him of stealing her jewelry, and a third episode on the night of the stabbing. When she told him she was leaving his house, he had thrown her against a door, then threatened to cut her eyes out with a screwdriver. No amount of probing elicited more detail, even though the three incidents failed to explain why she felt "trapped." As she was literally going out the door of my office, I asked, "Did he ever put his hands on you when you didn't want him to?" Angela turned, gave me a look that told me "why didn't you say so?" and delivered a lengthy monologue about the dozens of times Roger had pushed, shoved, slapped, or grabbed her; held her wrist; pulled her hair; broken things of hers; twisted her arm; stepped on her hands or feet; and held her down. These incidents occurred "daily" or "all the time." The cumulative effect of low-level violence by the 192-pound Harris was to make this 105-pound young woman a virtual hostage in his mother's house. Angela felt like nobody because nothing she wanted, felt, or said made any difference. This sense of total subjugation combined with the proximate attack to prompt the stabbing.

Typical episodes of violence end with typical responses. Victims admit their guilt, cry, beg for forgiveness, agree to sexual intercourse, or pass out, often mirroring the same disembodied and ritual quality as the abuse. To survive, they become astutely sensitive to the details of abuse rituals and can pick up nuances that signal escalating danger. Girlene called home before she left her cleaning job and could tell by the tone in her husband's voice what to expect. Lavonne realized Miguel meant to seriously hurt her 9-year-old daughter when his eyes got "dark" and began snapping his belt in the girl's presence, something he had done only with her in the past. In other cases, enhanced risk is indicated by a violation of a safety zone that was previously off-limits or their partner's disregard for a reaction that previously ended the abuse, such as the victim's crying or the arrival of police. Jim usually stopped when Dorothy begged and cried. On the night she stabbed him, Jim was completely unresponsive to her pleas, possibly because he was high on drugs.

The Contradictory Pretexts for Violence

If the enactment of violent episodes is predictable, its pretexts are constantly changing to reflect the perpetrator's mood shifts and his contradictory demands. Donna was beaten for spending too much money and for not making purchases Frank believed to be crucial, for talking to him when he was in a bad mood and for not recognizing when he was upset. Abusive men who are violent when they feel betrayed or abandoned are often violent when women are tender as well. The contradictory and changing occasions for abuse leave many victims feeling that anything they say can lead to violence, but nothing they say is heard. They may alternately get "hysterical" or feel they've lost their "voice," both literally and metaphorically. "I felt I had to scream simply to be heard," Lavonne told me. In response to these feelings, women may try to cope with their state of chronic risk by seeking alternative ways to feel in control, by talking to themselves, for instance, becoming symptomatic, medicating their anxiety with drugs or alcohol, or hurting themselves, like the Jehovah's Witness, examples of "control in the context of no control."

Is Violence Cyclical?

The only popular description of how abusive violence unfolds is Lenore Walker's account of a cycle that includes successive phases of tension buildup, an explosion, and the so-called honeymoon phase. The cycle model perpetuates several myths about abusive violence. One is that assaults are neatly circumscribed. In fact, abusive assaults are typically comprised of numerous acts of coercion and control of varying degrees of severity and may extend over an hour, all night, or be separated by periods of R&R, when the offender sleeps, goes out to buy beer or drugs, or he or the victim goes to work. Shorthand phrases like "beaten up" or even "battered" fail to convey the dense texture of these incidents. As Jim's rape of Dorothy illustrated, for their victims (though often not for male perpetrators) these assaults are experienced in relation to their nonviolent predicates and seque-lae rather than as distinctive or purely physical. The abstraction of dis-crete violent acts from the larger context of abuse reflects a male-oriented perspective on events.

The notion that tensions build before exploding in violence is only par-tially accurate. For one thing, many victims experience tension as chronic rather than episodic, feeling they are always "walking on eggshells." In these cases, the good times can generate as much anxiety as his brooding because the subsequent rage is proportional to how far he has "come down" (due to something she has done or not done in his eyes). For another thing, many men move from hurt to rage without passing through the intermediary emotions reflected in a buildup. According to Doris, age 67, her husband's assaults occurred without warning. "I said, 'Gee, isn't the sky beautiful tonight?' and he turned around and knocked out my teeth."

Dave yelled and cursed. But like a typical "cobra," Frank rarely raised his voice during his attacks on Donna. Images of hapless women killing enraged attackers in self-defense are inapplicable to these cases. Some men seethe with rage beneath their calm surface or are excited to violence to assuage their fear of being abandoned by the women they are beating. Others get a rush from violence, which they seek to recapture through abuse just as addicts seek excuses to get high. Once men come to rely on violence, its absence can evoke the same somatic reactions women develop in the presence of violence, including depression, substance abuse, and suicidal thoughts. During a separation, many men convince themselves that their former partner is the source of their distress, obsess about her, deprive themselves of basic necessities like food or sleep, and may stalk or kill them.

Even in the relatively few cases where men apologize, their motives can run the gamut from genuine contrition because of guilt or shame through manipulation designed to solicit forgiveness or win postabuse favors, such as sex. Batterers lie to themselves or others about the abuse, admit the abuse but minimize its seriousness by insisting "it was nothing," or shift responsibility to their partner. Thus, 82% in the English sample blamed their partners for the violence all of the time (58.7%) or often (23.4%) Many men combine these reactions or move from one to the other when confronted with evidence of their actions. The O. J. Simpson "suicide" note illustrates how many controlling partners perceive events through a veil of primary narcissism that suggests that they are the real victims, not their partners, and may persist in claiming to be battered themselves even after being confronted with evidence of the harms they've caused.

Ms. Davis

In *Davis v. Davis*, the woman sought to end her third marriage, the man's second. The couple had been married for only three years and had no children in common. The husband was a prominent scientist and appeared calm and rational on the stand. Ms. Davis, a self-employed artist with a small income to support her daughter from a previous marriage, was emotional, angry, and overwrought. The woman's claims to be impoverished were seemingly contradicted by three Mercedes cars in her name and weekly taxi bills to the train station from their house of almost $200. In a separate suit, the husband claimed to be his wife's "love slave" and sought to recover $600,000 in gifts, including several diamond rings and a fur coat costing $50,000. The only witnessed assault had occurred prior to the marriage. Medical records documented several injuries, one sustained when Ms. Davis claimed her husband threw her from a moving car. The only evidence that he had caused these injuries was a diary the woman had kept, but hesitated to turn over because it also contained her sexual fantasies. I described various acts of control to the court, including an incident where Dr. Davis lay on top of his wife for 10 hours to keep her from skiing. But the judge viewed these as more eccentric than brutal. To show his good intentions, the husband put the bills for his "gifts" into evidence in their original envelopes. This convinced Ms. Davis to turn over her diary. A comparison revealed that the gifts were purchased immediately after an assault, presumably as an apology. What clinched the award of significant damages to the wife, however, was that the diary also recorded another round of assaults that coincided with the dates on which the bills arrived. On these occasions, no gifts followed.

Narcissism makes many perpetrators masters at impression management. Knowing this, some victims fear his version of events will be believed rather than hers. Many victims also accept a man's apologies because they feel compromised by circumstances surrounding an assault. Jim made numerous attempts to reconcile with Dorothy after he raped her. Although she kept him away for a time by threatening to report the rape, she never called the police because she had stayed the night and returned home in the new clothes he bought her. Courts frequently interpret delayed reporting as ambivalence on a victim's part, or worse, as an act of opportunism designed to redress some grievance.

The Stolen Bra

A police officer exercised complete control over his partner's going and coming, had her followed, harassed her male friends, blocked her car in at the state mental health facility where she worked, and assaulted a co-worker who intervened. He had forced her to steal small things from the job, including Ace bandages and several sheets. Her work included caring for a patient who compulsively ripped her bras shortly after she put them on. In the process of purchasing large quantities of brassieres for the woman, my client used her patient's voucher to buy a French bra for herself, which she hid in the back of her underwear drawer, a small rebellion against a boyfriend who meticulously went through her clothes, tearing up those that were too sexy, and reviewed her checks and credit card receipts. When the woman broke things off, the officer kidnapped her from work and held her hostage for a week. But she escaped and called the state police. Tipped off that the police were about to arrest him, the man took the bra, which he had found, ripped and hung on her door to show what he would do to her, and presented it along with a package of other goods she had "stolen" for him to the woman's boss and she was fired, though she had worked at the facility for 15 years. At his criminal trial, the man's defense lawyer convinced the jury that because the woman had stolen from her workplace and refused to discuss the theft with her supervisor, she was also lying about the kidnapping. Despite the fact that a previous girlfriend testified that the man had beaten her as well, he was acquitted.

Violence and Jealousy

Despite their partners' claims, most battered women are not feminists in any programmatic sense. Nor are they completely innocent of the infractions abusers imagine. When a batterer brings a litany of complaints about a woman's failures to the table, he is expressing something of which she is also painfully aware—that conventional role behavior does not meet her needs and that her behavior contradicts his expressed sense—a sense she may share—of how women *should* behave. However fantastic the man's accusations, many of the women with whom I work are deeply ambivalent about the default roles they have inherited and many perform them unevenly. Even those who are the most committed to traditional gender roles are often forced by the realities of sexual inequality to negotiate for their needs in devious ways that make them vulnerable to criticism, much like Craig's wife. Acknowledging this reality helps us understand the internal dynamics of coercive control.

Infidelity is the most frequent violation used to justify violence, in part because it is one of the few rationales for partner abuse that is still widely endorsed, even in the legal system. Sixty percent of the men in the English sample accused their wives of affairs often or all the time.

Male jealousy is as often the context for intimidation, isolation, and control as it is for physical abuse. Male controllers in my practice have smelled or otherwise inspected their partner's underwear; listened to answering machines; searched the house for lovers; locked their partners in the house or in the bedroom; recorded their conversations (or had their children do so); tapped their phone lines; read their diaries; torn their clothes so they can't go out or thrown them out the window; ripped out phones; measured the breakfast cereal to see if others had eaten it; forced them to report in and out; hid under beds, in closets, or in trees outside the house; monitored the house with surveillance cameras; lain on them for hours to prevent their going out; stalked them; insisted they be accompanied at all times; and forced women to adopt a compromising pose (such as bending backward over a chair or table) while the man probes for "evidence." Some of the more dramatic expressions of jealousy reflect repressed homoeroticism, where the man projects onto a female partner the attractions to other men he cannot acknowledge in himself, holding a gun to her head while she has sex with another man, for instance, or in a case summarized earlier, randomly bringing a man home to have sex with his wife. Women's assaults on men are also motivated by jealousy. However, the property interest men have in women gives their jealousy the uniquely morbid or sadistic quality first detailed by British psychiatrist Michael Shepherd.[19] In these situations, women describe being assaulted like soon-to-be-discarded personal property, kicked like a broken TV, suggesting that perceived betrayal is as much the consequence of a prior process of reification, of turning the woman into a possession or thing, as the cause of her depersonalization, a process illustrated in the discussion of "marking."

Victims accommodate a partner's jealousy by cutting off old friendships and curtailing their social activity. To placate their partner and prove their loyalty, they quit school or church, stop seeing friends or family, and come straight home after work, choices that increase their felt isolation and so may actually heighten their interest in supplementing the relationship. At the same time, battered women often use affairs or secret friendships as part of their safety zone, as Francine's relationship with the police officer at school illustrated. Thus, jealous fantasies and accusations may often have a basis in fact or be self-fulfilling.

Intimidation

Intimidation, the second major technology used in coercive control, instills fear, secrecy, dependence, compliance, loyalty, and shame. Offenders induce these effects in three ways primarily—through threats, surveillance, and degradation. Intimidation relies heavily on what a woman's past experience tells her a partner is likely to do and what she imagines he might do or is capable of doing. But intimidation is also rooted in a pervasive sense that women are vulnerable to male violence in any public setting, what Riger and Gordon call "the female fear."[20] This fear leads many women to look to heterosexual relationships for protection and to exaggerate the dangers of living on their own. If violence undermines the capacity for physical resistance, intimidation deflates psychological power relative to the offender, a process that contributes to the bigger-than-life imago victims maintain. In Gelles's research, not one abusive woman used threats as a major tactic.[21] Threats and insults are effective in coercive control because women cannot walk away or laugh them off without incurring punishment.

Threats

Threats violate the person's right to physical and psychic security and tranquility. In the English study, 79.5% of the women reported that their partner threatened to kill them at least once, and 43.8% did so often or all the time. In addition, 60% of the men threatened to have the children taken away at least once, 36% threatened to hurt the children, 32% threatened to have the victim committed, 63% threatened their friends or family, and 82% threatened to destroy things they cared about. Credible threats are criminal offenses. But few are reported to police and almost none result in an arrest, even when the threatening partner is widely known as dangerous or has harmed the victim in the past. In a recent case, the offender had served 8 years in prison for stabbing a previous girlfriend, the current victim had reported her boyfriend's threats to kill her to the police, there was a warrant for his arrest, and the police themselves warned her that he had a gun (in violation of his parole) and was likely to kill her, which he eventually did. During the investigation, the police admitted the warning was designed to scare the woman into giving information about her boyfriend's drug activity, not to protect her. As we saw in the sweatshirt case, threats have an immediate effect on a victim's autonomy regardless of whether or not they are carried out.

Threats run the gamut. Nick threatened to kill Laura almost daily and carried a "silver bullet" with which to do so. Among the most frightening are threats with no specific reference or that are so ambiguous ("You made me jealous") that victims feel they will be carried out no matter what they do. In the case in which the husband told the children they could find their mother buried near the dog, he never directly assaulted her. "I watch CSI and Forensic Files," he told her, "and know not to leave marks." On the morning she shot him, she found the gun case open and the guns missing—apparently as a result of a theft—when she returned home to awaken him for work. When she told him, he said, "If you're telling the truth, I would have to kill you." He had told her repeatedly that the only three things that meant anything to him were his guns, his recliner, and the children, as a distant third. He ordered her to bring him a gun he had hidden away, which she did. Then he told her to put it in the case and to let him sleep for another half hour. Overwhelmed with anxiety about what he would do when he awoke and learned the truth about the guns, she shot him.

The sweatshirt example illustrates another terrifying scenario, where the victim feels isolated in her fear and even crazy because her terror contrasts with the positive reaction of others. In settings like the hospital where the risk that openly aggressive behavior will expose abuse, offenders often rely on these invisible threats, giving signs of disapproval such as a raised eyebrow or clenched fist only seen by the victim or signaling control in ways providers interpret as solicitous, such as volunteering to see that his partner doesn't smoke or drink during a pregnancy.

Violence against strangers, friends, or property is often used to communicate what a man is capable of doing if she falls out of favor or tries to get help, as when the physician helped his wife "redecorate" by taking a sledgehammer to the walls or screamed and cursed at his ex-wife on the phone. When a friend implicitly criticized Miguel for abusing Lavonne by telling him, "She treats you like a prince," Miguel beat the man so badly, "there was blood everywhere."

Intimidation can establish a regime of control even when the victim has not been assaulted. Dorothy offered this account of the first incident of Jim's violence: "Once, when he was angry about my buying a dress for myself, he just turned and put his fist through the car windshield. All I could think was 'I'm glad that isn't me.'" In the second incident, he punched a hole in the wall near her head. Although the rape constituted Jim's first direct assault, his intimidation had already caused Dorothy to curtail talking on the phone, seeing friends, and driving herself to work. In *M*, Fritz Lang's masterpiece about a serial murderer of children, he demonstrated that the horror we imagine can be worse than the act itself. Peter Lorre (the killer) enters the alley after the little girl. Then, several minutes later, the ball rolls out, slowly, back down the alley into the street. In coercive control, the idea of physical harm planted in the victim's mind can have more devastating effects than actual violence.

Child Abuse as Tangential Spouse Abuse

Thirty-six percent of the women in the English study and 44% of 207 battered women in the United States questioned by professor of social work Richard Tolman reported that their partners threatened to hurt the children or to report them for abuse, a pattern I call "child abuse as tangential spouse abuse."[22] Here, the offender treats the child as an extension of the mother and as a way to hurt or control her, often when she is less accessible, during a separation or divorce for instance, or has stopped responding to direct threats or violence.

The unemployed bank executive got his wife to comply by threatening or actually hitting the children, knowing that assaulting her would jeopardize her lucrative professional career on which his lavish lifestyle depended. Related tactics include threats to involve the child welfare system or, in more middle-class homes, lengthy legal battles in which men who have shown little prior interest in their children's welfare demand custody or liberal visitation to continue their control or force their wives to compromise on financial issues. Child abuse as tangential spouse abuse is a particularly effective intimidation tactic during separation and divorce, when the offender's access to his partner, but not to the children, may be limited. In one divorce case, an abusive husband, a prominent cardiac surgeon, threatened to stop tuition payments and the children's medical insurance unless his wife continued providing secretarial services gratis and allowed him to stay in her apartment (and share her bed) for two years after their divorce.

Because it is common for children to be removed to foster care solely because the mother is being abused, the threat that a husband will call child welfare is quite credible.[23]

Maria

Battista met Maria in Italy, where she lived on her family's horse farm. Even when the children were small, he would insist she leave them in a small room above his restaurant while she set up the pizza ovens, cleaned, and waitressed. Battista beat her with the metal lining of a rug, among other objects, forced her into the snow without shoes, made her sleep in her car on several occasions, and made her cook Sunday dinner for himself and his girlfriend. He also beat the children. Neighbors testified they heard screams from the house and that, when they asked the younger boy about the abuse, he had replied "Daddy has big hands." Maria provided detailed accounts of how the boys reacted to seeing her hurt. After their separation, the mother worked as a maid at the Marriott and was given temporary custody by the court, in part because the man's own sister testified about his abuse. Battista told the older boy to record his mother's phone calls and threatened suicide if he didn't comply. When she found the tapes in the boy's drawer, Maria was furious, and threw a shoe at the teenager, hitting him in the foot. A school nurse reported the boy's injury to Child Protective Services (CPS) and temporary custody was shifted to the father because of Maria's "child abuse." At trial, despite extensive testimony about Battista's violence, both teens testified they had seen nothing, a report the court-appointed evaluator accepted uncritically. The husband got full custody, fulfilling his threat that he would send Maria back to Italy "without your cherry, without money, and without your children."

Miguel also used the children to extend his control. "Whenever I went out," Lavonne reported, "he made sure one of the girls stayed home with him. Even if I went to the bus stop. He was real sweet about it, like he was trying to help. But I knew what would happen if I tried to take them all out of the house at once." Lavonne took two of her children to Head Start. "The Head Start teacher knew something was wrong," she told me. "But when she asked me, I was afraid to say anything. He told me if anyone found out, they would take my girls. And I believed him." Although Miguel had raped, burned, choked, and beaten Lavonne dozens of times, the CPS worker who came to the house reported she was "overwhelmed" and unable to properly care for her five children while he was a "supportive boyfriend who helps her with childcare." Children often pick up fear of their father by observing their mother's reaction to his abuse. Direct evidence of violence is often lacking in these cases either because abuse has not been reported or, more often, because actions taken in criminal court, such as the issuance of protection orders, fail to surface in the divorce proceeding due to failures in intrasystem communication. Confronted with the combination of a hostile child and unsupported allegations of abuse, it is increasingly common for the father's attorney to raise the specter of parental alienation syndrome

(PAS), a pseudo-scientific diagnosis which many evaluating psychologists are all too willing to support. By contrast, although it is commonplace for offending fathers to turn children against their mothers, as in Maria's case, this behavior is rarely linked to abuse or described as alienation. After telling their mother that the children were away for the weekend, one father would dress the children and have them wait for their mother to arrive on the front stoop.

The Battered Mother's Dilemma

The battered mother's dilemma is a form of intimidation in which the perpetrator forces the victim to choose between her own safety and the safety of their children. A particular incident may bring this dilemma into sharp focus, as when Terry Traficonda realized she might be hurt or killed if she attempted to protect her child from her husband's abuse. Typically, however, the battered mother's dilemma describes an ongoing facet of abusive relationships where the offending partner repeatedly forces a victimized caretaker to chose between taking some action she believes is wrong (such as physically disciplining her child in inappropriate ways), being hurt herself, or standing by while he hurts the child. Confronted with these dilemmas, victims attempt to preserve their rationality and humanity by selecting the least dangerous option—another instance of control in the context of no control. Ignorance of the constraints under which a caretaker is responding often leads agencies to mistakenly hold her culpable and respond punitively, thereby aggravating rather than relieving the dilemma.

Active and Passive Threats

Offenders intimidate victims through many of the same tactics used to extract information or compliance from POWs or hostages, withholding or rationing food, money, clothes, medicine, or other things on which a woman depends. Thirty-eight percent of the men in the English sample stopped their partner from getting medicine or treatment they needed, and 29% of the U.S. men did so. Threats that involve the silent treatment, physical or emotional withdrawal, or other passive-aggressive means, can be equally devastating. Fully 87% of the battered women in Tolman's sample reported that their partners used the silent treatment to frighten them, and half of the men in the English sample did so. Men in my practice have disappeared without notice for days on end, stopped taking their antidepressants, stopped talking to their wives (in one case for two years), quit alcohol or drug treatment, "forgot" to pick up or feed the children, and threatened or attempted suicide if their partner didn't comply with their wishes. In the English sample, more than half of the men threatened to hurt or kill themselves if the woman left, and 35% used the same threat to get her to obey. Withdrawal, threatening to leave, or withholding affection or sex (60% in the English sample) is particularly devastating when a partner is already isolated from other sources of adult social interaction, is financially dependent, relies on her partner for child care or other vital services, draws her sense of safety/danger from his verbal cues, or relies on making him "happy" to be safe. After a disagreement at the dinner table about how a word was spelled, the heart surgeon stopped talking to his teenage son for 3 months. The private building contractor who worked out of his home "disappeared" periodically for 3 or 4 days, leaving Arlene with no money for the children or access to the bank account (he had taken away her card because of a "stupid purchase"). When he returned, he would berate her for not knowing where he was and yell at the children for worrying that he might have left them or been killed.

Controllers use many threats considered role syntonic for males, such as driving too fast or smashing things when a sacred object of theirs (such as a favorite baseball hat or a recliner) is mishandled. Fully a third of the men in the English sample used "driving dangerously" to intimidate their partners. When heavyweight boxer Mike Tyson smashed the furniture in the New Jersey home he shared with Robin Givens and her mother, Givens feared for her life and called the police. But the state's attorney refused to prosecute Tyson for what he regarded as a "temper tantrum." In any case, he explained, "It's his furniture. He can do what he wants."

The view that certain forms of intimidation are normative in male culture was illustrated in a bizarre custody case in which a 26-year-old stockbroker drank himself into oblivion nightly. In the living room of their large but sparsely furnished estate, alongside the TV and couch, there were two cages inhabited by large "simians." The man would enter a cage several evenings a month to have a "head butting" contest with one of the apes to see "who was tougher." To Ginny, on whom he also used his head, both the ritual and the presence of the apes was terrifying. But when I described the ritual to the children's attorney in the case, he assured me this was not unusual, because he and other young lawyers sometimes had head-butting contests in a local singles' bar.

Anonymous Threats and "Gaslight" Games

Another class of threats, illustrated by the meticulously organized cabinets in the movie *Sleeping With the Enemy*, involves anonymous acts whose authorship is never in doubt. To frighten their partners, men in my caseload have left anonymous threats on answering machines, removed pieces of clothing or other memorabilia from the house, cut the telephone wires, slashed a woman's tires, torn up newspapers and left them on the doorstep, stolen their partner's money or their mail, determined their address by stealing mail from family members, removed vital parts from their cars, or left subtle signs that they have entered a home from which they are excluded by court order. At the other extreme, they exploit secret fears to which they alone are privy, like the man who played peek-a-boo with his wife to remind her of the uncle who had waited for her in the closet, than raped her.

In the 1944 film *Gaslight*, Charles Boyer created various visual and auditory illusions to convince his wife, played by Ingrid Berman, that she was insane. Gaslight games are designed with a similar end and are illustrated in my practice by stealing things from a woman's pocketbook that mysteriously reappear after a desperate search, turning the gas on after she thinks it is off, and reparking her car during the night. Some games are less subtle. Miguel would put his hand over Lavonne's mouth while she slept so she couldn't breathe and then pretend to be asleep when she woke up gasping for air. To cope, she would simply lie awake until he went to work, then be too exhausted to care for the babies. One husband—the owner of a steel company—removed his wife's expensive camera from their New York apartment, insulted her for losing his gift, and then secretly returned it to its place when the police arrived to investigate. Forty-seven percent of the English men tried to convince their partners' friends, families, and children that she was crazy (almost 30% did so all the time), and almost a third threatened to have her committed to a mental hospital.

Perpetrators will also threaten their partners by telling transparent or outrageous lies, having affairs they make sure she knows about (30% of the English men), or saying or doing things in a public setting that insult or embarrass them. In one case, the German husband put pornographic shots of him having sex with another woman on the Web where his American wife was sure to see them, then told her, "You're driving me away with your insane accusations." The intent is to remind the victim how dangerous confrontation can be and how dependent she is for her well-being on accepting his version of events, regardless of how ridiculous.

Surveillance

Surveillance deprives persons of privacy by monitoring their behavior, usually to gather information without their knowledge. In coercive control, surveillance falls on a continuum with a range of monitoring tactics and has the additional aims of conveying that the perpetrator is omnipotent and omnipresent and of enforcing behavioral constraints either directly, by letting the victim know she is being watched or overheard, or indirectly, by garnering behavioral information that can be used to regulate or embarrass her later. One of my clients was returning from the flea market, eating a bun, and driving, when she saw her husband behind her, honking. "You know we've been watching you," he told her. Persons subjected to constant or visible surveillance become isolated from outside support or isolate themselves and severely curtail their coming or going; where, how, or whether they work or attend school; what they say to neighbors, friends, family members, or strangers; whom they see; and what they do when they are alone. The extraordinary range of tactics batterers deploy to monitor a partner's behavior and intrude on their social or private lives goes far beyond anything currently anticipated by criminal statutes. In a case sketched earlier, after the woman broke things off because her boyfriend was having an affair, he broke into the downstairs apartment rented by the woman's brother, plugged a phone into the wall, and listened to her phone calls while the brother slept. Having overheard her talking to a male friend, he proposed they resume their relationship since "we're now even." When she refused and revealed she knew what he'd done, he killed her brother.

Stalking

Stalking is the most dramatic form of tracking and the most common behavioral component of coercive control next to assault. Of the estimated 10.2 million U.S. citizens who were identified as ever having been stalked by the National Violence Against Women Survey (NVAWS), 4 out of every 5 (79%) are females and, because men stalk same-sex partners at the same rate as they do women, almost 9 of 10 stalkers (87%) are males. Fifty-nine percent of the female victims (4.8 of 8.2 million) are stalked by a man with whom they have been intimate, accounting for 4.8% of all women in the United States and 5% percent of women (n = 503,485) reported being stalked by an intimate partner in the 12 months preceding the survey.[24] Most of these cases (57%) occurred either during the relationship only (23%) or during the relationship *and* after the separation (36%) as opposed to only after separation. Women are almost nine times more likely to be victims of stalking by a partner than men.[25]

After California passed the first antistalking law in the United States in 1990, every other state followed suit. Stalking is reported more often than domestic violence, and a much higher proportion of offenders are prosecuted and go to jail, though the numbers are still relatively small. For every 100 female stalking victims identified by the NVAWS, 52 reported the crimes to the police, 13 men were prosecuted, 7 were convicted, and 4 went to jail.[26] But the response in domestic violence cases is probably even less aggressive. A study of how a model Domestic Violence Enhanced Response Team (DVERT) in Colorado Springs responded to 1,765 cases over a 6-month period found that 16.5% of the cases involved stalking or stalking-like behavior. But only one suspect was formally charged with stalking.[27] Stalking in abusive relationships rarely begins or is limited to the period after couples separate. But almost none of the stalking police identified occurred while couples were together.

As a means of intimidation, partner stalking is distinguished by its duration—lasting 2.2 years on average, twice the typical length of stalking by strangers—its link to domestic violence, and its combination with complementary forms of intimidation and control. Of the 4.8 million women stalked by present or former partners, 82% were followed, spied on, or "staked out"; 81% were assaulted; and 31% had been sexually assaulted by the stalking partner. In 9% of the cases, almost 450,000 relationships, the stalker either killed the family pet or threatened to do so. Sixty-one percent of the female stalking victims received unsolicited phone calls,

45% were also threatened verbally or in writing, and roughly 30% had their property vandalized or received unwanted letters or other items. "These men," the researchers observed, "tended . . . to restrict their wives' activities and friends, withhold money, isolate their wives, demean and frighten their wives and insist on knowing their whereabouts constantly."[28] In other words, stalking in these cases was merely one facet of coercive control.

The link to violence, harassment, and other forms of control has not gone unnoticed. When they are arrested and prosecuted for stalking in domestic violence cases, men are frequently charged with a broad array of co-occurring crimes, including harassment, menacing or threatening, vandalism, trespassing, disorderly conduct, intimidation, breaking and entering, and assault. Although this "packaging" approach is designed to enhance sanctions, it fails to capture the range of bad acts exhibited by controlling partners, discounts the cumulative effects when these acts occur as part of a single pattern and are directed at a single victim, and completely misses the elements of subordination and entrapment, the most dramatic consequence when these acts are combined. Because most of the crimes charged are relatively minor and incident specific offenses, packaging can fragment the course-of-conduct dimension of stalking or harassment and so reduce the seriousness with which they are taken.

Microsurveillance

Controlling partners view intimate relationships as a zero-sum game in which each sign of a partner's separateness is interpreted as something taken from them. To detect disobedience or disloyalty, they may survey the minute facets of a woman's everyday conduct in ways that are inseparable from the microregulation unique to coercive control, targeting not merely where they go, but how fast they drive (for instance), or how much money they spend, entering everyday routines in ways that obliterate autonomy. This type of surveillance injects fear even into such perfunctory choices as whom they ask for directions or which route they take home as well as when they arrive, until choice itself becomes frightening. In my caseload, intimate surveillance extends from going through drawers, pocketbooks, diaries, or closets to monitoring time, phone calls, bank accounts, checkbooks, and stealing identity, using global positioning devices (cyber-stalking), or installing video cameras to track or monitor a partner's movements. Surveillance is almost universal in abusive relationships. Eight-five percent of the women in the Tolman study and over 90% of the English women reported that their abusive partner monitored their time, for instance. Particularly in combination with microregulation, microsurveillance gives coercive control an intensiveness found in no other form of oppression.

Surveillance also makes intimidation portable. Most controllers use "check-ins" of one sort or another to monitor their partner's behavior during the day, calling them, having them call in repeatedly, or checking in with co-workers. Theresa was expected to beep out when she left the house and beep in when she returned. Frank drove by the house several times during the day. If the lights were on, he assaulted Donna for "wasting money." He also called home from work several times an hour. Nick called Laura 15 or 20 times a day at work, monitored her whereabouts when she left with "the beeper game," and called her at night from the bar, having her leave the phone off the hook when he went to sleep. The "third ring" rule was an example of surveillance. Terry's husband took a job in an adjoining office so he could watch her during the day. When Jamilah took a smoking break at Burger King, she would often find that Thomas sitting in his car in the lot outside.

The direct consequences of microsurveillance can be dramatic. A client was expected to answer her cell phone promptly whenever and wherever her husband called, or he would subject her to an evening of cursing and screaming. To test her loyalty, he would call her while she was riding to work on her bike, causing several accidents, one in which she broke her arm. Donna was forced to quit a job because she talked to "the wrong person" (an old girlfriend) at work, and Jamilah lost her job at a fast-food restaurant when her boyfriend confronted the manager. When Arlene took longer than the 20 minutes she was allocated to go to the store to buy cigarettes, she was forbidden to shop alone. Laura was denied driving privileges for a week because the new hub caps she bought would attract attention. On another occasion, she was physically punished when a used-car salesman said he had seen her driving fast. This tight scrutiny turns some abused women into recluses. Others devise an elaborate web of surreptitious activities, calling home from pay phones, having bills delivered to anonymous post office boxes, engaging in afternoon affairs, and sneaking food, clothes, or sex.

Degradation

Controlling men establish their moral superiority by degrading and denying self-respect to their partners, a violation of what Drucilla Cornell calls "the degradation prohibition."[29] According to philosopher John Rawls, self-respect is a "primary good" without which "nothing may seem worth doing, or if some things have value for us, we lack the will to strive for them. All desire and activity becomes empty and vain, and we sink into apathy and cynicism."[30] When Donna described herself as dead inside, she was illustrating how important self-respect is to personhood.

Emotional abuse is particularly harmful in the context of a primary dependence, as when a parent degrades a child, when survival depends on approval, alternative sources of support are unavailable, and when the object of degradation is deeply invested in how the other feels about them (as well as in their judgment) and is unable to muster positive self-talk or other forms of resiliency to counter negative messages. The adult victim of coercive control is in no sense childlike. But the tactics used in coercive control can so disable a woman's capacity to affirm her femininity that she mimics a childlike dependence on approval that significantly amplifies the effect of insults.

Virtually all of the women in the English survey reported that their partners called them names (96%), swore at them (94%), brought up things from their past to hurt them (95%), "said something to spite me" (97%), and "ordered me around" (93%) and in more than 70% of these cases, this happened often or all the time. Regardless of class or culture, variations on epithets such as "bitch," "ho," "pig," are universal in abusive relationships in the United States. Despite being severely abused physically and sexually in her family of origin as well as by her first husband, Hazel Collins completed her GED and graduated from a cosmetology college in South Carolina, where she was voted "best dressed." To humiliate her, Donald Rogers would repeatedly call her "dirty," criticize her for not bathing, and tell her "you aren't shit" and "all bitches are the same." Treating a partner like an animal is a common degradation tactic: women in my practice have been forced to eat off the floor, wear a leash, bark when they wanted supper, or beg for favors on their knees. On several occasions, Mickey Hughes rubbed food all over Francine's face and hair after dumping it on the floor. Again, insults and put-downs are effective in coercive control because they play off complementary forms of deprivation, intimidation, and control that disable a victim's capacity to respond and target areas of gender identity where the partner's self-esteem may already be poor (such as her looks or her weight) as a result of other forms of abuse, which she identifies with her autonomy and are being compromised by violence.

If isolation increases the effects of degradation, batterers also use degradation as an isolation tactic, embarrassing their partners in public or among friends, family, or workmates. The man who beat his wife when bills for his gifts arrived also called her corporate clients and told them she was a "slut" and "thief." The companies withdrew their commissions, largely because they didn't want to get involved in a personal dispute. A psychiatrist would allow his artist wife to attend lectures, then show up unexpectedly and berate the speaker in ways that made it impossible for her to stay. Shortly after she had major surgery for cancer, the physician husband ordered Doreen to run to the kitchen and retrieve his drink during a cocktail party with business associates. He was well aware that the medical device she was wearing would burst with the sudden activity (as it had with similar exertion the previous week) and spatter fluid over her clothes.

The interplay of degradation, other forms of emotional abuse, and complementary forms of oppression are illustrated in the Dillon case.

Alvin and Amanda Dillon

Alvin Dillon first assaulted Amanda in 1990, shortly after they married, while he was in the military. Over the next 10 years, if things didn't go exactly as he wished, he would fly into a rage, push or slap her, break her things, and threaten to walk out. Their finances were in complete disarray, in part due to his alcoholism. But any questions from Amanda made Alvin feel "abandoned," and he would hit her or withdraw for days, leaving her to make do with the little money she had. She returned to school, but he demanded she drop out. Then he took a job requiring a good deal of travel, leaving her "trapped" in the house with two young girls. He also bought a condominium where he kept a mistress. After two explosive incidents in which he punched her and threatened her with a frying pan, Amanda had Alvin arrested and removed. When he returned, the assaults and intimidation resumed. With the support of battered women's group, Amanda filed for divorce and was granted custody and alimony. Alvin began coming to the house daily, begging her to take him back for the sake of the children, appealing to her strict Catholic upbringing, and promising her a new life. He would stop drinking, sell the condo, and give up the girlfriend. Amanda withdrew the divorce action and allowed him to return, causing several friends to desert her as well as her support group. The day he returned home, Alvin told her, "I have you where I want you." He took her car keys and ridiculed her in front of the girls. Later that day, he followed her around the house with a video camera to show "how crazy you are." When she tried to stop him, he grabbed her wrists. She called the police, but there was nothing they could do. Feeling completely desolate, she told Alvin "you have won," and took a nearly fatal overdose of pills with the children present. He changed the locks, refused to let the children visit their mother in the hospital, and was granted temporary custody.

To Amanda, the video incident symbolized that she had lost even minimal control over events in her household or in the lives of her girls. In her suicide attempt, Amanda attempted to restore her self-respect by taking control over the harm done to her. If she could not control whether she was hurt, taking the pills allowed her to control *when* she was hurt and *how*. Recognizing this, the social work staff at the hospital helped her regain custody of the children.

Shaming

In shaming, perpetrators of coercive control demonstrate a victim's subservience through marking or the enforcement of a behavior or ritual that is either intrinsically humiliating or is contrary to her nature, morality, or best judgment. In a perverse inversion of the 1950s high school practice in which girls proudly wore rings or letter jackets to signify their "trophy boyfriends," abusive men have forced women in my caseload to bear tattoos, bites, burns, and similar marks of ownership visible to others. Marking signifies that a man has a personal interest in this woman that he will defend. But it also signifies she is vulnerable to exploitation or further abuse by others. Because of its link to ownership, marking often becomes a source of self-loathing and can prompt suicide attempts. Although there is no study evidence on this practice, it is so common that the National Coalition Against Domestic Violence (NCADV) and the American

Academy of Facial, Plastic, and Reconstructive Surgery have developed a jointly run free program for removing tattoos and other scars inflicted on battered women and their children by abusers.[31] Shaming also involves ritual enactments associated with sex or basic bodily functions, such as eating, showering, dressing, sleeping, or using the toilet. Clients in my practice have been made to sleep standing up, wear their "bad" clothes for days without changing, eat without utensils, shower repeatedly or in cold water, denied toilet paper, and forced to use the bathroom with the door open, locks removed, or with a timer. Shaming involves forcing a partner to obey rules that would be used to discipline a child, such as staying at the table until they've eaten all their food, compelling them to eat food that has been intolerably hot with spices, or completing routine activities within specified time periods.

Forcing women to engage in anal sex against their will is a common form of shaming used on my clients, another possible displacement of repressed homoerotic feelings. In the English sample, 24% of the women reported being forced to engage in anal intercourse at least once. In one case where the couple frequently engaged in anal sex, the woman was punished by being forced to receive her husband without lubrication, a "rape" for which he was prosecuted by a courageous state's attorney.

Shaming rituals often extend to the children, where the batterer uses or insists on forms of inappropriate discipline that the mother is too fearful to stop. In my caseload, perpetrators have hung a teenage daughter out the window by her legs, broken a child's arm (which had eventually to be amputated), made children stand for hours in the cold or sit at the table all night because they misbehaved or didn't finish their dinner, and sexually abused them and presented the most transparent denials. Usually because they believed the alternative discipline by the male partner would be worse, mothers in my caseload have put their children in an ice-cold shower, beat them with a belt, burned their hand on a stove, kept them in a basement with no access to the house, and delayed reporting (or used useless home remedies to treat) serious injury. Once a victim has done things of which she is ashamed, she is even more vulnerable to degrading insults and threats that she will be reported for child neglect or abuse.

In a related form of shaming, victims are forced to commit crimes that compromise their position with their employers or as credible witnesses to their abuse. In an immigration case, the abusive husband gave his wife—a middle-aged Dominican woman with no history of criminal activity—a list of clothes he wanted her to steal, drove her to the department stores, and waited outside. On the several occasions when she was caught, he would simply disappear, knowing she would be too fearful to tell the police the truth. When Mark's socks were not perfectly clean or Joanne did something else wrong, he moved into his "war room" in the basement. While there, meals were to be delivered by the children and his wife was to make no attempt to contact him until her crime was undone.

Isolation

Controllers isolate their partners to prevent disclosure, instill dependence, express exclusive possession, monopolize their skills and resources, and keep them from getting help or support. The degree of isolation abuse victims suffer was illustrated in the statistic cited earlier, that in one study of shelter residents, 36% had not had a single supportive or recreational experience during the previous month.[32] Isolation undermines the moorings of social authority and identity, eviscerating a woman's selfhood and constraining her subjectivity.

Most women enter intimate partnerships in the throes of synthesizing a consistent identity out of the multiple roles forged in what sociologists call the institutions of primary and secondary socialization: the family of origin, school, and peer group. In the next stage of development, the formation of agency, they project their identity into the wider world through specific life projects, experiments in forging and meeting their aims in three arenas primarily—intimate relationships and the families formed as their consequence; the broader universe of extended family, friendships, community life, and public service; and at and through work. In these spheres women "imagine" themselves (to paraphrase Cornell) in relation to various audiences of significant others, actively differentiate their sense of inner being from those around them, and act in and on the world.

Isolation affects each of these arenas. It curtails women's access to and choices about institutional roles, prevents them from garnering social support or recognition, severely constrains the audiences which they can access, and forecloses choices about life projects and opportunities for self-expression. By cutting women off from alternative sources of information and support and inserting themselves between victims and the world, controllers become their primary source of interpretation and validation. In extreme cases, the perpetrator's reality becomes embedded between a victim's "I" and her "me," shaping not merely how she behaves with others but also how she knows and experiences her self when she is alone. Her "me" may be confounded with his, making identity feel like an alien force, as in Laura's case. The victim of coercive control is isolated from the moorings of her identity and, because identity is first and foremost a social construction, from her own unique personhood.

Isolation evolves through a cat and mouse game in which victims attempt to establish and perpetrators to locate and destroy safety zones where autonomy can be preserved and practiced. The controlling partner causes his partner to lose or quit her job, and she finds another or returns to school; he prohibits contact with old friends, and she develops supplementary relationships; he steals her letters, and she starts a diary or sets up a secret Web address. His hope is to make who and what she is who and what she is *for him*. Even if he is hurting her physically, because she is isolated, she may believe that he alone can protect her. She may go to work, see friends, attend family gatherings, or receive counseling. But she moves through these realms like a corpse on furlough for whom the very idea of spontaneous action, let alone freedom, can evoke an existential panic.

Isolation From Family

Controllers make women's relationships to their family of origin a primary target of isolation. Victims in my caseload have been defended by children, stepchildren, grandparents, ex-husbands, and in-laws. Family members have beaten or threatened the abusive partner, hired others to hurt or kill him, called police, devised devious escapes, secretly given the victim money, kept her children or her pets while she was in hiding, testified against the abuser (even when the victim was too fearful to do so), and financed years of legal struggle. In a New Jersey case, the boyfriend forbade any contact with the victim's politically powerful mother or father, but allowed her to go ice skating. Desperate to help, the mother convinced police to use an officer disguised as an ice skating instructor. The boyfriend followed the woman to her lessons, suspected something was awry, and beat her so badly she spent a week in intensive care.

The perpetrator's family may also conspire in a woman's isolation, a major issue in the burning bed case.

Girlene

Girlene and her children were staying with her mother-in-law in Brazil when her abusive husband, Tony, immigrated to Danbury, Connecticut, to join his brothers. Concerned that her son was using drugs, the mother-in-law pressured the girl to join her husband and helped arrange the $10,000 loan needed to get her into the United States illegally. The husband quickly resumed his abuse, beating the woman on a daily basis, and she left him. The brothers were initially supportive because they recognized her husband's abusive behavior. But they pressured her to return because they feared they would lose their loan if she returned to Brazil. The second time she left him, the mother-in-law told her she would never see her children again unless she returned, which she did.

Their special relationship may give family members privileged knowledge about the relationship as well as special access to the victim. This was why the adult daughter from a previous marriage was able to rescue her mother when her physician husband forced her to return home immediately after cancer surgery. In another case, a victim's six sisters arrived at her New York apartment en masse from Georgia and liberated her from a hostage-like situation of control. Conversely, women often use family visits to protect themselves from abuse. Frank would not beat Donna when she had her little brother sleep over. Finally, Frank simply forbade the boy's visits.

In response to this potential support, abusive men in my caseload have forbidden calls or visits to families or limited visiting time, assaulted or threatened family members, forced victims to chose between "them" and "me," listened in during family calls, denied the money needed to travel to visit family members, moved their family to another town or state, stolen money from family members, showed up drunk or otherwise embarrassed their partner at family gatherings, waited outside with the car running during family visits, raped a victim's sister, put warning notes on a victim's car when she attended church with her family, engineered situations guaranteed to alienate women from their families, and destroyed family mementos, photos, gifts, letters, and the like. Just over 60% of the women in the British sample said their partners threatened their family or friends. And 60% of the women in the U.S. sample and 48% in the British sample reported that partners kept them from seeing their families.

Lavonne

Victims often decide to end relationships with family members to placate their partners. Miguel told Lavonne it would "look better" if she stayed home and made cooked meals instead of eating at the diner where her mother and sister worked. Believing she had her best interest at heart, she agreed, and then the physical abuse began. Maintaining family ties can involve intense struggle.

Lavonne was determined to go to her mother's for Christmas dinner. Miguel returned home from work drunk, found Lavonne in the car, and a tugging match with her mother ensued, which the mother won. Miguel followed in his car but was in an accident. He phoned and told Lavonne he was going to kill himself unless she returned immediately. Lavonne called the police, who were at her house when she returned. Miguel was arrested, but for leaving the scene of the accident rather than his abuse, and Lavonne was brought along as a translator, denying her a rare opportunity to escape. When they returned home, Miguel beat her senseless. She agreed her mother was "the devil."

I am frequently contacted by parents or siblings desperate to stop a family member from being abused. Few situations elicit similar feelings of impotence. Isolation is even more successful when family relationships are strained to start, the parents align with the perpetrator, or the victim has also been abused by a family member, a particular problem for adolescents. In one case, my client had limited her children's contacts with her parents because they were alcoholics. As a result, the parents testified for the abusive husband during the custody dispute. Victims in these cases often find a surrogate family for support, though this can also be problematic. Wanting to finish high school, Lavonne moved in with her boyfriend's family when her own parents separated in her last year. During the stay, the boyfriend raped her. But she graduated and never told his parents, with whom she remains close. In another instance, when the wife described her son's abuse to her mother-in-law, the woman told her, "Do what you have to girl, I'll be here." But when the woman stabbed the man while he was choking her, his mother told the court the victim had only been interested in her son's money.

Family members also reside in a woman's interior psychological space, where they can help buffer humiliation. In response, controllers try to root out feelings, values, communications, memories, or images of family members that prevent his monopolizing her attention or defining her personhood. Isolating a woman from her children is a complementary tactic. The home-schooling case sketched earlier, in which the husband had a visitation from Jesus, involved a long sequence of isolation tactics, primarily constructed around divided loyalties.

Arlene D.

When John was thrown out of his parents' Ohio home, he insisted Arlene run away with him to Iowa without telling her own parents. As another test of her loyalty, he demanded she steal her father's gun. Arlene later mended the breach with her parents, but John refused to let them visit, burned their pictures, and destroyed their letters along with her high school picture and diploma. He would yell, "You're driving me crazy the way your mother drove your father crazy." When her father got cancer, he told her, "Your mother is killing him, the way you're killing me." By the time her father died, the couple had separated, so Arlene could go to the funeral. But John refused to let the children attend because "they barely knew him." As we saw earlier, John cut the children off from their friends after he won temporary custody and replaced their home schooling, which involved a complex network of supports, with "cyber-schooling" that required no human contact. He told the children he would kill himself if their mother got custody.

Isolation often provides the setting in which abuse begins or escalates. Moving out of a parent's apartment or changing residence is common occasion for this process, largely because it makes the consequences of abuse or control less visible. When Lavonne met Miguel, she and her children were living with her mother. During this time, he hit her once and she threw him out. But Miguel returned, blaming his behavior on his drinking and promised to reform. This would be easier if they had their own place and if she stayed home, like a real "señorita." As soon as they moved into their own apartment, abuse escalated sharply. Although Lavonne prided herself in her housekeeping, the household was in complete disarray and she was forced to steal water from their neighbors. With Donna as well, assaults became a daily occurrence only after Frank's mother and sister moved out. Friends and family may often isolate a victim whose partner is widely known to be abusive. After Girlene stabbed her husband during an assault, he commanded her to "come here." Afraid he would kill her, she ran from the apartment into the street, pounding on neighbor's doors to call the police. No one would give her entry because they feared Tony's retribution and didn't want to "get involved." He bled to death.

Immigrant Women

Immigrant and fundamentalist women are particularly vulnerable to isolation because traditional cultures are typically patrifocal (i.e., built around the husband's family), reject divorce or separation, assign custody in a marital dispute to the father, discourage women's working, and ostracize women who abandon tradition or reject their obligations as wives. Some women prefer "any male companion" to the deadening isolation females experience in many orthodox or traditional communities and view immigration as an opportunity to escape the watchful eyes of extended family members. But émigré women also leave their support systems behind, while their husbands join or are quickly followed by friends or relatives, as in Girlene's case. Isolation presents special problems for women who migrate from rural communities where they had an important social function to metropolitan areas where they do not, significantly increasing vulnerability to abuse. Abusive husbands can also exploit the ethic of traditional service as a pretext to isolate their wives, as Shamita's husband did when he forbade her to drive or shop and insisted she wear a sari whenever she went out. When a nephew temporarily moved in, she cooperated in his support. But when her brother-in-law arrived, he moved into the second bedroom, the bedroom doors were locked, and her husband shopped and cooked for himself and his brother, leaving Shamita to make do with the remains. Although Donna was acquitted of murder because of the sordid history of abuse, her parents cut her off because she had killed her husband. Immigrant women who are abused are entitled to special protections in the United States, Canada, and other countries. But many are nonetheless reluctant to use criminal justice, particularly if they lack the language skills to understand or participate in the legal system, are in the United States illegally, are working off the books, or because they fear their husband's family will take revenge against them or their families (or in Girlene's case, her children), or that he will be deported.

Isolation From Friends

Because they provide immediate support in a community of peers to which the abusive partner may also belong, a woman's friends can threaten a controller even more than family members. Girlene stayed with a co-worker when she left her husband. On one occasion, he followed them home, cut them off, and pounded on the car window for his wife to get out. Her friend told him she was not going with him and then, when Girlene became frightened of what he might do, arranged to meet him to "talk" at the police station, where Girlene would be safe.

Perpetrators may conceal their abuse from a woman's friends; openly threaten, attack or even shoot them; or flaunt abuse to frighten them away. Victims end friendships because they are ordered to do so, as illustrated in Laura's and Donna's cases, or because, after their friends are degraded as whores or bad influences, they see the "me or them" choice as a test of loyalty. After she lost her job, Donna reports: "I had to call him at work to get his permission when I went out and when I got back. At night, I had to give a full report of what I'd done. If I talked to anyone—anyone, even his cousin—I got in trouble. All my friends were 'sluts' and he was sure they were trying to fix me up." Friendships are also regulated when women are denied access to phones or cars, as they are in more than half of abusive relationships in the United States and England, when the controlling partner insists on "coming along," employs spies, locks them up, provides explicit rules for behavior with friends, or interrogates them about each social contact. Women in my practice have also been denied the right to carry pictures of friends, write about friendships in their diaries, record the names of friends in their date books, read or write letters to friends, or speak to friends even if they meet them accidentally on the street. "Love" is a common excuse for isolation. Aurelio Camina was continually jealous, no matter how often he and his wife had sex. Although Tatiana had no relationships of any kind outside the house, he would repeat, "I love you so much. No one can have you but me. Otherwise I will kill someone."

Perspecticide

One of the most devastating psychological effects of isolation is the abuse-related incapacity to "know what you know," called "perspecticide."[33] I described two examples earlier.

Tatiana

In one case, the FBI brought charges against a wife who claimed to have had no knowledge of her husband's using the house to sell drugs or of how family could maintain a boat and their fancy home on an official income of just $24,000. I was convinced Tatiana had censored "dangerous thoughts" about how her husband made a living after years of isolation, abuse, and control. Although there had been sporadic physical violence in the 18-year marriage, the main component of her abuse was isolation. She had stopped seeing her family early in the marriage. Aurelio refused to drive her to her parents, and she had no license. On the one occasion when she took the bus there and a cab home, she was beaten for wasting money. She had no friends, and Aurelio would object whenever she tried to make her own friends. "He was my 'best friend,'" she said sarcastically, imitating his voice, "he knew what was best for me." Aurelio would frequently come home with a group of people, but she was never included in the group and mocked in front of them if she attempted to join in, then sent from the room crying. He agreed to let Tatiana return to school and said he would care for their son. But when she came home, the boy had had an "accident" and broken a tooth. She understood this veiled threat and quit school. When the boy was grown, she signed up for a ceramics class. After the second meeting, she went to a bar with other women from the class. When she returned, Aurelio told her never to do that again. She quit this class as well. Aurelio would stay away for 3 or more days at a time, allegedly on business. He also insisted Tatiana carry a cell phone whenever she went out. While he was away from the house, even when he was out of town, he would telephone her periodically to "check in" and she was to record—and report—the details of her coming and going. She could never question him about where he was going, for how long, or why.

Vivian

The second case involved a woman charged with signing a fraudulent tax return. Physical abuse was constant and she was threatened with harm if she refused to sign the returns, an instance of duress. Although Vivian had never been seriously injured, she had been a virtual prisoner on their Greenwich estate, where she was forbidden to work, confined during most of the day to a bedroom suite, and denied any help or contact with family or friends. She was not even allowed to shop. Before the marriage, Vivian had done graduate work in economics at Yale. But when we met she could neither add simple numbers nor tell time.

A chilling personal experience illustrates how fear of what can happen if the "secret" gets out forced women to remain isolated even among friends.

Mrs. Anderson and Her Girls

My wife and I made friends with Rebecca Anderson at Yale, where our children were taking swimming lessons together, hers as part of home schooling. We talked about our work and hers and when the classes ended, we invited the family to dinner. The woman demurred, explaining they were moving to Florida. Several months later, while training in another city, I was asked to demonstrate interview techniques with a family of abuse victims I'd never met. The anonymous family that entered the room turned out to be Rebecca and the girls. They had been virtual prisoners in their home, allowed out only for the lessons, and had contacted the agency after being on the run since shortly after the lessons ended. Unable to conceal my surprise, I explained what was going on to the group, then asked Rebecca why she hadn't shared her situation with us, particularly since she knew domestic violence was our specialty. "I was afraid that if I told you," she confessed, "You would make me do something or I would feel I had to do something—to change the situation. The thought of that terrified me."

Separation can make a woman who has already been isolated feel more vulnerable, not less, particularly if she depends on proximate cues from her partner to detect danger. A man in my practice used members of a motorcycle gang headquartered at a tattoo parlor to watch his partner when he was on the road. After he was arrested and served with an order of protection, the woman took an apartment down the street from where he lived, frustrating advocates at the shelter. But the woman felt more secure in a setting where she could observe his movements than in a new neighborhood where he could appear unexpectedly. When a woman is isolated, the perpetrator may parse opportunities to socialize as means of control. For her birthday, Nick gave Laura permission to go out, ordered a limo, and told her to invite three girlfriends. The car arrived with a card instructing her to "ask the driver for the rules." The rules concerned where they could go, what they could do, and when they were to be home. Written on the window was "I love you. Happy birthday."

Work

Psychologist Hans Hartmann emphasizes the importance for ego development and individuation of having access to a sphere that is free of psychic conflicts. The construction of safety zones where women can imagine themselves as something other than victims serves a similar function and is often the critical demarcation between submission and resistance. Work was a refuge from family life for many of the men in my clinical practice. Today, work is also a common safety zone for women.

Coercive control significantly impacts women's employability as well as their performance at work. In a randomized sample of low-income women, Susan Lloyd from the Joint Center for Poverty Research in Chicago found that those who had been physically abused, threatened, or harassed by a male partner in the 12 months prior to the study had lower employment rates, lower income, and were more likely than nonabused women in the sample to exhibit depression, anxiety, anger, and other problems that affect their labor market experience over time.[34] Many perpetrators depend on women's earnings. Donald bought crack with the money Hazel made cutting hair and gave him for rent and car payments. She was forced to rely on her mother's food stamps for food. Nick relied on Laura's income to support his gambling. Lessup relied on Bonnie's work as a machinist for all household expenses, support, and his car. But work also gives women access to support, income to escape, and a sense of pride in accomplishment, even if their job is menial. Coming to work with bruises can elicit support as well as cause shame. Because Hazel appeared at the beauty salon with her hands bandaged, her face swollen, and with lumps of hair noticeably missing, Donald became so notorious in the South Carolina town that he was unable to find employment. Bonnie's role as shop steward in the machine shop gave her the fortitude to stand up to Lessup even at the height of his abuse. Simply having a job signifies that life will go on when the abusive relationship ends.

More than a third of women in the U.S. and English samples were prohibited from working by their abusive partners and over half were required to "stay home with the kids." Many of the women in my practice have been forced to quit their jobs or been fired because of the actions of an abusive partner. Perpetrators also isolate or regulate their partners at work or compromise their status there in other ways, by making them chronically late or absent, for instance. Men in my practice block in their partner's cars, take their keys or items of clothing, demand sex just before they go to work, or refuse to perform such crucial chores as transporting a child to day care. Where a woman's income is critical to sustain a man's lifestyle, controllers tread a thin line, trying to maximize the income their partners bring home, by getting them to take a second job for instance, while regulating their social relations at and around these jobs. Men in my practice drive their partners to work and/or pick them up, show up unexpectedly during the day, call to check in at numerous times, call other employees to verify their partner's whereabouts, or take positions at the same or a nearby place of business. Fearing Laura would meet men at work or discuss her domestic situation, Nick called her office repeatedly during the day and prohibited her from going out to lunch with co-workers. When several clients who worked at our local telephone company told me their boyfriends kept them from socializing with co-workers by picking them up at lunch time, the line of cars outside the building at noon took on new meaning. So she wouldn't inadvertently attract male co-workers, Laura was to cut her hair and was forbidden to wear makeup or hair spray to work. Several times a week, she met co-workers at a local gym, "the only place I went besides work that was mine. I had friends there. And he knew it." Then, one day, she told me, "He simply said, 'no more gym.'"

To finance her divorce, the portfolio manager depended on the bonus from the sale of the brokerage where she worked to a larger firm. A week before the deal was completed, the potential buyer received an anonymous note detailing the weaknesses in the wife's group and critical of everyone's performance but hers. Concluding she had sent the note, her partners bought her out. This forced her to use the divorce money to go into business for herself. A writing expert confirmed what the woman suspected: that her husband had monitored her calls and authored the report.

Racial Dynamics in Isolation

White women are already more isolated from family and friendship networks than black women when they enter abusive relationships and are also less likely to be employed and more likely to depend on their partner financially.[35] Conversely, abusive white men are more likely than black men to be employed and less accepting of women's economic independence. Whereas abusive white men foster material dependence by forbidding partners to work or denying them money, their black counterparts are more likely to exploit the woman's economic role as provider or police her behavior at work. The complicated history of racial discrimination in employment has also made black male perpetrators more willing than whites to assume domestic chores like cooking and housework and less prone to enforce traditional gender roles.[36] White women often see their extended family as a trap from which they seek escape. By contrast, the greater importance of multigenerational, extended family, and friendship networks for black women make family boundary issues a continual source of struggle in their abusive relationships and attempts to isolate them the fulcrum of their humiliation. Because of the importance they attach to family and kin, black women are more likely than white women to attempt suicide when they are isolated as well as to kill their partners in this context, as we've seen.

But they are also less likely than white women to jeopardize children, family ties, or employment by medicating their stress with substances.[37] Employed, middle-class black women in particular often exhaust their psychic resources trying to keep their families from discovering the chaos in their personal lives.

Isolation From Help

Perpetrators keep their partners from getting professional help or try to manipulate these visits to their advantage. Dozens of my clients have been kept from calling police, going to the hospital, taking an abused child for care, or seeing a mental health professional. Partners of the women in my practice have ripped phones out of the wall, hit them with the phone when they tried to call, canceled appointments, accompanied them to the hospital and made sure they were never interviewed alone, refused to drive them to the hospital or give them money for cab fare, called police first, answered all questions on their behalf, made threatening signals to stop potentially harmful answers, and kept children at home as a warning of what could happen if they talked about the abuse. A state police officer charged with domestic assault broke into the office of his wife's psychiatrist and demanded she change her diagnosis so he could convince the court her allegations were crazy. Another husband, a psychiatrist himself, had his partner write prescriptions for his wife without having seen her and kept her from seeing anyone else. When Lavonne went to the hospital to have Miguel's child, he accompanied her even when she went to the bathroom. Though she was covered with bruises, medical staff never questioned her about abuse. During another hospital stay, when Lavonne wanted to leave the children with her mother, Miguel insisted they stay with him, letting her know what would happen if she "talked."

Control

At the center of coercive control is an array of tactics that directly install women's subordination to an abusive partner. These tactics affect dominance by three means primarily: exploiting a partner's capacities and resources for personal gain and gratification, depriving her of the means needed for autonomy or escape, and regulating her behavior to conform with stereotypic gender roles. Control is effective because it provides the material basis for differences in personal power, actualizes sexual inequality in concrete behaviors, and constrains the sphere where independent action is possible, depriving women of the objective basis for resistance or escape.

Access to Necessities

What I call the materiality of abuse begins with a partner's control over the basic necessities of daily living, including money, food, sex, sleep, housing, transportation, routine bodily functions (such as using the toilet or showering), communication with the outside world, or access to needed care. In this, coercive control resembles the most serious capture crimes and differs markedly from other forms of domestic abuse.

As we saw earlier, perpetrators deprive partners of money and other vital resources in more than half of all abusive relationships. This involves taking their money, denying them access to money on which they have a legitimate claim, as the contractor did in the home-schooling case, or appropriating their personal property.

Money may be taken directly through theft, violence, or intimidation. Nick took Laura's money out of her pocketbook; the unemployed bank executive coerced his wife into building an English mansion for his private pleasure; the Ivy League medical doctor pressured his wife to sell her homes and invest the proceeds in his research institute; and Roger forced Angela to use her earnings for all household expenses. In another case, a woman agreed to turn her paycheck over to her partner to buy drugs when he threatened to reveal her whereabouts to the drug gang against whom she had testified. Money to which a woman is entitled may be explicitly exchanged for services, as when the heart surgeon threatened to cut off the children's college tuition if she refused to work as his secretary without pay, or taken through deceit and fraud, as when a steel executive forged his wife's name to his support checks and then deposited them in his account. Deprivation may be routine or used as punishment. Women in my practice have been kept from carrying checks or opening their own accounts, forced to deposit their pay in accounts to which their husband alone had access, and forbidden to use their credit cards or forced to turn them over for safe-keeping. In the English sample, 79.1% of the women reported that their partners limited their access to money.

Controllers often get a partner's money by restricting their access to other resources. Because she refused to turn over her money and fled with her son on weekends, Bonnie was forbidden to drive to work. When Laura loaned her Christmas bonus to her aunt instead of saving it for Nick, he enlisted her in a theft to test her loyalty. For punishment, he blocked in her car or took her distributor cap.

Regardless of the family income, the distribution of money within abusive relationships is sharply skewed in the man's favor, a condition that puts millions of women in affluent homes at enormous disadvantage in divorce cases or custody disputes. Illustrative was the woman whose husband gave her expensive gifts after he abused her. Although there were three Mercedes cars in her name, they had standard transmissions, which she could not drive. After they separated, her husband was able to keep the credit cards and telephone in his name, monitored her calls and expenses, and used the threat of canceling these services to order her about.

The three cases in the next section illustrate another common scenario, where controllers require detailed records or oral accounts or all expenditures, conduct daily or weekly interrogations focused on expenses, accompany partners when they shop, or insist that all expenses be preapproved, including the purchase of clothes.

Donna chose to deprive herself of meals to meet Frank's demands for economy, Terry Traficonda was limited to cold pizza during the final week of her life, and the husband in another case left his wife tied up in the basement for several days without food or water. These are the only instances in my practice where an absolute lack of food was a major issue. Nevertheless, the women in my practice have been strictly limited in their food purchases, forced to eat off the floor, to eat food that was unbearably hot, to stay at the dinner table until they ate something that made them sick, to prepare food to order for the man's family, and to submit weekly menus for approval. In a current murder case, the woman's nickname was "dinner on the table." She was forced to stand beside the table until the husband finished seconds before eating herself.

Similar controls extend to other basic necessities, including sex. Though 30.6% of the women in the English sample reported that their abusive partners "deliberately withheld affection or sex" often or all the time, Nick was one of the few controlling partners in my practice who used *not* having sex as a weapon. He had raped Laura on the pool table, regularly had sex with other women, and was riding on his motorcycle with another woman the night he was killed. But Laura was "too pure" to have intercourse until they married, he decided. This did not prevent him from taking her money, restricting her movement, and attacking—even shooting at—men she saw, even as friends. The far more common scenario is where men demand regular sexual intercourse even after the couple separate or divorce. All manner of punishment is used to control the when, where, how, and with whom of a woman's sexual activity.

Control over sex is often explicitly linked to other forms of gendered obedience. In an Iowa case that received international coverage, Travis Frey, age 33, was arrested after he kidnapped his wife in response to her filing for divorce, tied her to a bed, and raped her several times. During the trial, Ms. Frey gave the prosecution the "marriage contract" her husband had drawn up. Titled "Contract of Wifely Expectations," it listed Frey's explicit sexual demands, offered "good behavior days" (GBDs) if his wife complied (7 GBDs for anal sex; 3 for fellatio, for example), and outlined how she was to prepare for sex with such bizarre rules as "You will shave every third day" and "be naked within 20 minutes of the kids being in bed."[38] At trial, Mr. Frey claimed that the couple had drawn up the contract together when they were in college and that it represented their sexual fantasies, not his demands. As we've seen, contracts forged in the context of unequal power relationships are often drawn with the woman's consent, though here, as in most such instances, the application of rules only to her behavior signals the constraint involved. For present purposes, the most intriguing aspect of this contract is the microscopic detail with which the demands were laid out (extending to the width of the blade with which she was to shave, for example) and the extension of these demands to the wife's day to day conduct. A year after the 2004 remake of *The Stepford Wives*, Ms. Frey was commanded "not to argue (about anything with me or to me)," complain, cry, sob, whine, pout, show displeasure, raise her voice, be "condescending," ask for anything, or "be distracted from me by other things."[39] I only have three contracts in my possession that are this explicit. But dozens of women have described identical patterns of regulation in their personal lives.

Micromanagement of Everyday Life

If exploitation provides its material foundation, the infrastructure of coercive control is the extension of regulation to minute facets of everyday life, particularly those associated with women's devalued domestic and sexual status. The regulation imposed by controllers in my practice covers everything from when and what their partners eat and how they drive, wear their hair, or dress to how they toilet or clean themselves or their children and what they watch on TV. Constraints often progress from the general to the particular. In the home schooling case, Arlene was to "have dinner on the table at 5 and have completed all laundry, household chores, paper grading, and class preparation before then, so you will be fully available to me in the evenings." But as Mrsevic and Hughes put it, "As men's control over women increases, the infractions against men's wishes get smaller, until women feel as if they are being beaten for "nothing."[40]

The centrality of microregulation is a major focus of the cases described in part III. Suffice it to say here that such regulation crushes the spirit even more fundamentally than the deprivation of basic necessities because it leaves little space for personhood to breathe. The irony, to reiterate, is that the liberties denied by this process are so much a part of the taken-for-granted fabric of everyday affairs that their violation usually passes without notice. In the Iowa case, the media called the contract "the smoking gun." In fact, however, Mr. Frey was convicted of assault in the third degree, and no connection was made either by the media or at trial between the violence and the pattern of subjugation for which the contract was plain evidence.

Empirical Support

Empirical support for the coercive control model comes primarily from reports of nonphysical tactics used against abused women who seek assistance. This chapter relies heavily on two such sources, a test by Richard Tolman of a Psychological Maltreatment of Women Inventory (PMWI) with 207 battered women and 407 abusive men and an assessment of an expanded version of Tolman's instrument, a 98-item Experience of Abuse questionnaire (EAQ), with 500 abuse victims by British psychologist Roxanne Agnew-Davies and her colleagues. Tolman was able to distinguish a dimension of verbal/emotional abuse from a dimension of dominance/isolation typified by monitoring women's time or keeping them from seeing their family or leaving the house. Constraints related to physical appearance, housework, and other facets identified with female gender roles were not only common but linked to the domination/isolation dimension rather than to the types of emotional or psychological abuse that are common in all abuse cases. In other words, the micromanagement of women's everyday enactment of gender roles was a critical piece of men's dominance strategy.

Between 75% and 95% of the women in the United States and English samples reported they had experienced 10 of the tactics at least once, indicating that they typically are used as part of a larger pattern of constraint. The English sample was limited to female victims. But half of the offending men in the Tolman study admitted using at least six of the behaviors with their partners, including "monitoring time" (59%), "treating like an inferior" (62%), and "ordering around" (58%), with between 20% and 40% acknowledging they kept their partners from seeing friends (37%) and/or their family (20%), prevented them from leaving the house (26%), and restricted their use of the car (21%).[41] The English study also tapped the intensity of coercive control by assessing how frequently these tactics were used often or all the time.

Men also reported being emotionally abused by female partners in the Tolman study. Not only did women report being subjected to these tactics much more often than men, however. In addition, this disproportion grew dramatically as questioning shifted from forms of verbal abuse (such as "being treated like an inferior") to structural forms of isolation, intimidation, and control. Males comprised 82% of the perpetrators who kept their partners from getting "self-help," for instance, 76% who forbade a partner to work, and 70% who prevented a partner from leaving the house.[42]

These studies provide compelling evidence that a majority of abusive relationships for which women seek help are characterized by the range of nonviolent harms identified with coercive control. There is no reason to think the women and men in these studies differ from the victims and perpetrators who seek help with abuse generally. Still, because these studies were based on clinical populations (shelter residents and persons in counseling) and lacked control groups, there is no way to know whether similar constraints are common in relationships that partners consider not abusive or in abusive relationships for which women do not seek assistance. The English researchers link a range of domination/isolation behaviors to psychological harms. But they cannot say to what extent or even whether these behaviors prompt women's help seeking or how their salience for victims compares to the importance of physical or sexual harms. Some of the same constraints were identified in the Finnish national sample. Among the women who reported partner violence to the Finnish study, one woman in three was restricted from seeing friends and family (30%–34%), for instance, one in four (16%–26%) were prevented from making financial decisions or shopping, and almost half (41%–49%) were "continually humiliated."[43] An estimated 30% of the Finnish sample reported variants of coercive control classified as "partnership terrorism" or "mental torment," where violence had been replaced by control and intimidation. Since the Finnish study was population based rather than drawn from helping sites, it includes many women who may not define their abuse as emergent. This is why the reported frequency of intimidation and control tactics is lower than the rates reported by U.S. and English women. But the rates are still impressive.

Despite their broad range, these studies only touch on some of the most common and devastating control tactics. The subjects were asked if a partner was "stingy" with money, for instance, but not whether he took their money or restricted their sleep or access to food or medicine. They were asked whether they were kept from working, but not whether control tactics extended to the workplace or to other social arenas such as school or church. In Quincy, 38.1% of the men arrested for domestic violence admitted preventing their partners from freely coming and going in their daily routine, 58.5% said they denied their partners access to money and other resources, and almost half reported restricting their partners in three or more additional ways.[44] The prevalence of these tactics is particularly significant when we recall that fewer than half of these men were cohabiting with the victims whom they abused. Abused women in a representative sample of 734 welfare recipients in Massachusetts were eight times more likely than nonabused women (16% to 2%) to report that a current or former boyfriend would not let them go to school or work.[45] On the basis of a reanalysis of court and shelter interviews, sociologist Michael Johnson concluded that 68% of women who seek court assistance and 79% of women who seek shelter have been subjected to "intimate terrorism," where control tactics accompanied physical abuse.[46]

Table 8.1 compares the extent to which male perpetrators in the U.S. and English studies employed 18 tactics linked to coercive control. Tolman merely asked respondents whether they used a particular tactic or it was used against them. But the English study identified the frequency as well as the prevalence of these tactics by allowing subjects to choose between "Never," "Once/twice," "Sometimes," "Often," or "All the Time." The first two columns in the table present the prevalence of these tactics in the U.S. and English samples. The third column presents the proportion of abuse victims in the English sample who reported that the tactic was used often or all the time.

Link to Fatality

Not only is coercive control the most common context in which women are abused, it is also the most dangerous. In a large, methodologically sophisticated, multicity study, nursing researcher Nancy Glass and colleagues drew on a range of information sources to compare 224 abuse

TABLE 8.1   Proportions of Victimized Women Reporting Isolation and Control

| | Tolman (N = 207) | Agnew-Davies (N = 509) | |
	"At Least Once"	"Once"/ "Sometimes"	"Often"/ "All the Time"
Criticized way took care of house	.82	.77	.49
Treated like an inferior	.92	.94	.78
Gave silent treatment	.87	.80	.50
Upset when chores not done	.79	.79	.5I
Acted like partner was servant	.84	.86	.63
Ordered around	.89	.93	.66
Monitored time	.85	.82	.75
Acted stingy with money	.20	.79	.56
Kept partner from medical care	.29	.42	.22
Did not allow going to school	.62	.67	.52
Did not allow socializing	.79	.89	.71
Demanded she stay home with kids	.54	.78	.61
Kept from seeing family	.60	.73	.50
Restricted car use	.54	.42	.3I
Did not allow to leave house	.62	.81	.47
Did not allow to work	.35	.58	.40
Tried to make feel crazy	.89	.93	.75
Threatened to take children	.44	.64	.40

Sources: Richard Tolman, "The Development of a Measure of Psychological Maltreatment of Women by Their Male Partners," *Violence and Victims* 4, no. 3 (1989): 159–177; Roxanne Agnew-Davies, Personal communication of raw data tables shared via e-mail June 2, 2006; Anne Rees, Roxanne Agnew-Davies, and Michael Barkham, "Outcomes for Women Escaping Domestic Violence at Refuge." Paper presented at Society for Psychotherapy Research Annual Conference (Edinburgh, June 2006).

cases where women were killed to similar cases where no death occurred. They found that the presence of firearms was the most important risk factor for femicide, particularly if the man had threatened to kill the victim in the past. But two factors unique to abusive relationships also predicted fatality: whether the couple had separated after living together, and whether an abuser was highly controlling in addition to being violent. When both factors were present, the chance that a woman would be killed by her partner was 900% greater than when they were not.[47] Significantly, the factors thought to be key in the domestic violence model, such as the severity and frequency of violence, the co-occurrence of sexual abuse, or the perpetrator's use of alcohol, did *not* predict whether a victim would be killed.

Separating the Effects of Control

So long as research in the field equated abuse victims with persons who had been assaulted, it was impossible to tease out the independent role of violence and control tactics in women's entrapment or whether entrapment and other outcomes thought to result from violence could occur even in the absence of assault. By using the Women's Experience With Battering (WEB) Scale developed by psychologist Paige Hall-Smith and her colleagues to identify subjects as "battered," psychologist Cynthia Lischick turned the conventional approach on its head. Starting with women who were *entrapped* rather than physically abused, she uncovered a significant subgroup of battered women who had never been assaulted and who exhibited the signs and symptoms of abuse as the result of intimidation, isolation, and control. A conventional screen based on the Conflict Tactics Scale correctly identified about half of the battered women. By contrast, a screen based on coercive control was all inclusive.[48]

The Finnish survey also identified a subgroup of women who were suffering "mental torment" though they had not been physically abused for at least 7 years. These women were much older than Lischick's sample of young women, averaging 54–64 years. Despite the absence of violence in their lives, as we've seen, they reported higher rates of abuse-related problems than any other group, including younger women in currently violent relationships or younger victims of partnership terrorism. Compared to women who had only been physically assaulted by their partners, these women were three times as likely to report "fear," (91% versus 39%), four times as likely to feel psychic "numbness" (78% versus 18%), and more than six times as likely to have difficulties sleeping (72% versus 14%) and concentrating (62% versus 10%).[49] These findings illustrate the cumulative effect of entrapment via coercive control.

In sum, coercive control is not merely the most prevalent context for women's entrapment in personal life; it is also the most devastating. This is true both in the short term, as its link of control to fatality indicates, and over time, as the Finnish study shows. Partner violence remains a critical piece of this process and is often sufficient to effect subjugation. But physical abuse and the associated risks of injury or death are as likely to be the consequence of entrapment as its cause. Indeed, in relationships characterized by coercive control, women's prospects may not be substantially better if violence ends, is minimal, or has never occurred.

What Kind of Power Is Control?

Behind the litany of torments I have described, it would be easy to forget that coercive control takes shape on terrain that is contested by women's assertions of agency and the challenge their hard-won equality poses to traditional male privilege. To appreciate this dynamic, it is important to distinguish the power all men and women display in personal life and that some men view as threatening their privileges from two other forms of power—the male power expressed through tactical control and the sort of power kings exercise over their subjects or bosses deploy at work. The power we normally put into play in personal life is "a capacity to produce intended effects," the definition introduced by John Locke in his *Essay on Human Understanding*, and "liberty" the opportunity "to perform, or not to perform, voluntary actions according to the determinations of the mind."[50] This sort of power is somewhat contingent on social position, because persons with money or political influence are better situated to produce effects congruent with their intentions than persons without these advantages. But Locke's point was that all free persons have this capacity to a greater or lesser degree and can exercise it, under normal circumstances of liberty, without depleting the capacity or liberty of others to do the same. Power here is an immanent dimension of subjectivity and so not reducible to a fixed quantity that can be neatly subdivided or even permanently alienated. If it is bounded on one side by what is historically possible for someone in your social position, the social source of power, it is bounded on the other by how a lived personhood transforms these possibilities into life projects through individual volition and action. This allows for gradients of intention and effect that capture what political scientist Jim Scott calls "the power of the weak" as well as of the strong and helps us understand how men can command a disproportionate share of resources and so *have* power sociologically speaking, while nonetheless feeling threatened by women's power and compelled to usurp it through control.

A core conceit in democratic theory is that we choose how to apply the affirmative power Locke describes even when we devote our creative capacity to realizing effects determined by others—in love, service, or wage work—and that the flow of power in personal life is governed by the same contract that defines exchange relationships between buyers and sellers in the market. Critical to this conception are the beliefs that the least fortunate among us maintain control over the disposition of their power, whether when they work, vote, or marry; that the freedom to exercise this disposition as well as the proper love of liberty and equality needed to sustain this disposition are bred in the institutions of primary and secondary socialization (e.g., family, school, and community); that privacy rights are first and foremost intended so that individuals can develop and express the "determinations of their mind" without external constraint, particularly by government; and that the liberty rights needed to develop and express this individuality form the natural core of citizenship, which the state is obligated to protect. Complementing this affirmative notion of power is the credo accepted by every classical economist from Adam Smith through Karl Marx: that the sum of intended effects, organized through the division of labor, is synergistic and provides the engine of our collective ingenuity as a people.

Coercive control nips this process in the bud. By foreclosing women's liberty, their opportunity to imagine and freely choose to perform certain activities and not others, it disables a vast store of life energy that would otherwise contribute to social progress.

These grand designs for a free people point to the larger significance of coercive control. But to grasp its essence, we must also appreciate that liberty resides in precisely those mundane expressions of everyday life that are constrained through coercive control. The car keys are misplaced, a tire has gone flat, a dress is not hung in its place, a lamp has broken, she has forgotten to buy beer, the boy has spent too much time in the bathroom, the trip home took longer than permitted, the wrong hub caps have been put on the car, the guns in the cabinet are missing—controllers take any deviation from routine or expectations, any mistake or accident, as a sign of disloyalty. As missteps accumulate, some victims lose their sense of efficacy entirely, the feeling that what they do makes a difference or could do so, until, like Lavonne, they have to scream just to be heard.

The Universal Masculine: The Irrational Foundation of Control

Addressing control is far more difficult than stopping men from being violent. Masculinity in our society is identified even more closely with being "in control" than it is with the use or capacity to use force. Many men confuse the need to preserve this feeling of control with dominating women. They also demand constant proofs that the equation of control, manhood, and dominance is operational, even when the same proximate benefits can be attained in less convoluted ways. From the perpetrator's perspective, the problem here is that women's innate liberty makes the experience of controlling them quite different from controlling the speed of a car, say, or using the remote to change the TV channel, where the authority lines established from command to effect seem clear. The Iowa marriage contract illustrates the absurdity of confusing the control of people on whom you also depend for feelings of worth with controlling things. The dilemmas this confusion poses touch an emotive dimension of manhood that transcends literal signs of female deference or dependence.

We will recall Bill, the motorcycle salesman in our men's group, who became enraged by his wife's slightest request for help, to carry a dish to the sink when she was holding their twin babies, for instance. To him, these requests made her a "feminist bitch," even though, as we learned in our support group, she placed him on a pedestal and served him in every conceivable way. Had he simply refused to help, she would have found some other way to cope. But this possibility, that she could make do on her own, was threatening because it suggested, as her deference did as well, that she had a will and choice, that they interacted in a field in which she would request and he respond, ending the nonreciprocal nature of the authority he put at the center of his manhood. Like many other men in my practice, being in control sustained an extreme process of sexual differentiation for Bill that could only be realized by diminishing or denying any positive or creative valence to femininity, including the will to submit. To Bill, his wife's obedience and submission were less important than his belief that these effects were byproducts of his command.

The concrete advantages men accrue through control provide its rational basis. But we cannot avoid the startling reality that the instrumental dimensions of coercive control are often subordinated to a contradictory dynamic where control is sought through irrational, arbitrary, and impossible demands that give it the feel of terrorism and yield no proximate benefit other than the feeling of dominance itself.

The irrational nature of control tactics illustrates what can be called "control for its own sake," a pattern illustrated again and again by the cases in the next three chapters and that, I believe, reflects the larger reality emphasized in chapter 6—that there is no longer any rational social foundation for male dominance. Whatever men may say in chat rooms, bars, or fundamentalist retreats, in the mundane world in which most of us live, there is no credible basis for allocating resources and/or authority based on presumed sexual differences in intelligence, strength, rationality, wisdom, technical know-how, calm under stress, sexual versatility, endurance of pain, problem solving ability, and any of the other traits that were once considered immanent features of masculinity. Of course, racism, anti-Semitism, and other beliefs that justify invidious distinctions based on presumed innate differences have survived for centuries without a rational foundation. The problem today is that women not only recognize the frailty of men's claim to immanent authority—have they ever not?—but also occupy a social position in which their success requires them to live *as if* their claims are equal to men's. Given the enhanced reach of the Internet, it may still be possible to find women who are deferential by nature or willing to apply their supposed relational skills to support what a member of one of our men's groups called his "science gene." But as a general rule, men who insist on differentiating themselves through these stereotypes have no other choice than to superimpose them in their personal lives by directly devaluing and constraining women's development. If men in the liberal market societies want a world where male dominance over women in personal life makes sense, they have to create it.

The Three Rs: Rationality, Reasonableness, and Righteousness

Despite its complex construction, beneath the surface of coercive control is the transparent equation of masculinity with humanity, the unreflective assumption that "the universal masculine" is the legitimate standard for what is rational, reasonable, and right in relationships, habits of mind that I call the three Rs, and that the feminine represents what is irrational, emotional, and immoral. Men who enjoy these habits of mind think they are entitled to continually assess what their partners think and feel, how they behave, and how they use their personal time and resources. By contrasting their own propensity for reasoned and rational argument to their partners' "crazy" views and behaviors, controllers build an elaborate pseudo-logic out of sarcasm, disdain, and insult that they then bring to bear on judgments about women's everyday behavior.

The irrational foundation for these postures is exposed by their transparent link to dominance and cruelty. "Reasonable" batterers in my practice become sadistic if their partners are made vulnerable by an injury, sickness, pregnancy, or some misfortune, for instance. When the female financial executive lost her wallet, her unemployed husband, the former bank executive, insisted she return at night and on foot to the streets of New York, retrace her route from work, and not come home until she found it. When the woman insisted on visiting the Westchester English manor she was paying to have built for him, she fell into a hole in the flooring. As she lay injured, her husband stood by, cursing and berating her for being stupid, the same accusation Frank used when he beat Donna for gaining weight or forgetting to buy him cigarettes. To display their skill at reasoning, batterers subject their partners to endless monologues and "lessons," often keeping them awake or making them stand through an entire night, as the heart surgeon did with his wife. The physician who tried to "cure" his wife by spraying her with bug poison interpreted her cancer as a deliberate strategy to call attention to herself and away from him. Ironically, his interpretation of pain in others as a threat to the attention he craved had been one motive for his becoming a doctor. His wife's vulnerability also elicited feelings of fear and tenderness in him that he found intolerable.

Righteous men take the moral or religious rather than the intellectual high ground, projecting a Manichaean world where good and evil are sharply demarcated and always knowable, usually by them and after the fact. These men barricade themselves and their families against the outside world, sometimes literally, and continually test their partners' moral purity and loyalty against the polluting effects of "bad influences." They ascribe any hurt, failure, or disappointment to their partner's malevolence (rather than her stupidity), and she is punished for being bad or evil. During the custody dispute in the home-schooling case, the two oldest boys whom the husband had brainwashed testified that their father was "the Truth" and that they literally felt the spirit of "Jezebel" coming out of their mother's house and entering them when they came to home on visits. This was the same man who had a personal visitation from Jesus and presented himself as his disciple to his children, his wife, and the court. Righteous batterers often enter a woman's life as her protector or savior, sometimes from other abusive men or troubled families of origin, and project their need for purity onto their partners, as Nick did with Laura. The "new" woman is often contrasted with the "evil bitch" he has left. Shortly after they married, the physician screamed and cursed at his ex-wife on the phone with his new wife in the room, then assured his new wife that he would never yell at her in this way because she was different. Rituals of punishment are introduced as cleansing or purifying exercises, sometimes literally. By the time they were arrested for risk of injury to their five children, Miguel was insisting Lavonne shower the children five or six times daily. But the aura of purity is quickly dispelled and the woman's "true nature" of defiance revealed when she shows signs of independent judgment, as the bike salesman's wife did when she asked for help with the dishes. As the protective fantasy wanes, modes of correction are introduced, and idealization gives way to the realization that "All bitches are the same." The leveling effect of such assurances fuses anger a particular woman with anger at the sex.

What I am describing are not distinct types or rationales for abuse, but variations on a single theme—the universal masculine. Over time, the three Rs are reduced to one-liners. Roger would come home "bored" from work and start accusing Angela. "Why did you do what I told you not to do?" he would ask her repeatedly, appealing to an unwritten set of rules hidden deep in his mind. Angela had no idea what he was talking about. Suddenly he punched her with a closed fist on the side of her face. She tried to leave the room, going into the kitchen. But he yelled for her not to walk away from him, followed, and punched her again, causing her face to swell. The fact that assaults punctuate ostensibly rational behavior makes any verbal give and take or confrontation with an abusive partner highly risky, a lesson often lost on therapists or family court judges.

When we met, Donna still saw herself through the prism of the three Rs, describing herself as stupid. Months after Nick's death, Laura was still too fearful to give up the cleaning rituals or disobey other rules on Nick's lists. Once victims understand their partners can no longer control them, virtually all admit they found the three Rs transparent, the moralism hypocritical, and the erstwhile rules governing their behavior arbitrary or ridiculous. But so long as women are caught up in the orbit of domination, so long as disobedience carries grave risks of punishment or deprivation, their very transparency adds to the power of the three Rs.

The Economy of Rules

The implicit or explicit expectations at the heart of regulation extend micromanagement through time and space. The rules may be general ("you cannot make me jealous") or specific ("answer the phone by the third ring"), written down (as in Laura's case), implied (as in Donna's and Bonnie's cases), negotiated (as in the case of the softball pitcher), or only discovered after they are broken. Rules link control to violence by laying down a structural foundation in contracts, agreements, or commitments that women are punished for violating when they act crazy, stupid, or just bad.[51]

The functional appeal of rules is their economy and the illusion of order and rationality they simulate. Alongside their complaints that their wives and children disrespected them, the men in our groups waxed nostalgic about fathers who allegedly garnered obedience from their wives and children with an occasional slap (on their face or their mom's), a belt, or, in the case of a policeman's father, a simple rap on the table. Confounded by their failure to secure deference with similar means, perpetrators blame their partner's willfulness. They are also embarrassed, exhausted, and emotionally drained by the levels of violence, surveillance, and control required to keep their women in line, guarantee that when they return in the evening dinner will be ready or the house cleaned or the children bedded or their wives ready for sex. Real men, they think, should command deference without demanding it. In *Worlds of Pain*, psychologist Lillian Rubin describes a similar dynamic, where men from abusive homes forswear violence in their own families.[52] But when they feel things getting "out of control," they fall back on the model of authority they experienced as total and effective when they were children. Instead of giving them the feeling of being in control, using violence makes them feel like failures, both because they have adapted the tactics they forswore and because their inner world feels chaotic rather than like the totally controlled world they experienced as children when their fathers were abusive. Violence also fails them in another crucial way. Without much prompting, these men acknowledge that the cost of their abusive efforts exceeds their benefits, particularly when they try to extend their control to their wife's behavior at distal settings such as work. They may continue their abuse. But they despair of ever earning the respect or compliance they crave. No matter what they do, problems signaling their lack of control continue to surface.

The formulation of rules is an economical response to this dilemma that promises to deliver obedience while reducing the expenditure of physical and emotional energy. When the prominent media personality married, he convinced the anchorwoman to end her career and devote herself to his Connecticut estate and mothering his two grown children by a former marriage. To ease his obsessive jealousy during his workdays in New York City, he introduced the phone rule, that she answer calls by the third ring. Two centuries earlier, women involved in household production typically spun, wove, brewed beer, or completed other domestic tasks under their husband's surveillance. The phone rule provided this modern husband with an economical alternative to personal surveillance. Indeed, uncertainty about when her husband would call created even greater fear than if he had remained home. The fact that she broke out in hives when the phone rang suggested the stakes involved in not doing as she was told. Fear that her cell phone might malfunction limited the extent to which she was willing to leave the house during the day, significantly increasing her isolation and vulnerability to control.

Rules can be economical for whichever partner is mobile, particularly with modern communications technology. Frank enforced his rule about saving electricity by making spot checks during the day to see if Donna had left lights on. In two other cases, drug dealer boyfriends required that their partners check in and out by beeping them, a technology rendered largely obsolete by cell phones. In another case, where the man sold drugs outside the backdoor of the apartment, his partner was only to take 23 minutes to shop, a rule he enforced by having her set the stove timer before she left the house. If the alarm went off, he locked the front door, so she could enter only around the back where he was waiting. But regulation of a partner through social space can be problematic. Despite Nick's rules, Laura maintained a range of relationships with co-workers, friends from high school and college, and her numerous cousins. To keep her from socializing with her co-workers, Nick issued the direct prohibition "no more gym." Laura's other relationships were too diffuse and unpredictable to regulate this easily, however. So, Nick devised the beeper game, where he sent a number to Laura's beeper while she was with friends and she had to guess its significance "or else."

The Experimental Nature of Control

Unless the only intention is to maim or kill, as in terrorism, the application of violent means is calibrated to the ends sought and requires adjustments in dosage, target, or type depending on how victims respond. Creating fear, isolation, obedience, or subjugation through nonviolent means is even more complicated and requires an acute sensitivity to personal and situational nuances for which there is no ready template. As a result, coercive control is far more idiosyncratic than assault and evolves through a far more complicated process of trial and error. Violent episodes are often similar regardless of circumstance. But in no two cases of coercive control is the mix of violence, intimidation, isolation, and control identical.

Control skills are perfected slowly as behaviors and excuses that have been standardized within cultures are adapted to the unique circumstances in millions of relationships, often over months or years. If rules elicit consequences the offender interprets as positive, they are reinforced or extended. If not, men may fall back on more direct forms of intimidation and violence, or they may innovate, introducing new forms of surveillance like the beeper game, more detailed rules, or by denying access to the means of communication or transportation used to bypass the original regulation.

The experimental character of coercive control belies the impression that abuse is fully formed at its inception. To victims, the regime of rules and constraints often feels fixed and immutable. But it is no more perfect a proxy for actual stability in personal life than governmental regulations are in public life. For one thing, given the saliency of liberty referred to earlier, resistance and "rule failure" are constant, forcing offenders to continually abandon or revise their tactics and devise new controls. Even when controls take resistance into account, where, when, and how intensely it occurs are unpredictable. This prompts controllers to try and anticipate contingencies by making rules, surveillance, and punishment more detailed. Or, they may take the opposite tack, by issuing comprehensive dictates like "you won't make me jealous." The first tactic defeats one of the major purposes of rules—to affect general regulation that does not require microsurveillance. The opposite problem is created by making rules all-encompassing. When applied to the variety of real-life situations, general rules lend themselves to multiple interpretations, setting off an open-ended process of negotiation, adjustment, and modification. The rule "you won't make me jealous" was continually put on the table for debate and reform. While negotiations between the softball pitcher and her boyfriend often ended with Jason's assaulting Cheryl, her providing sexual favors, or both, the very existence of debate reinforced the sense of female agency the husband was trying to quash. Another problem with rules as a management tool is that their object controls much of the information on which sanctions are based, leading to a condition of what public administrators call contract failure. Victims have an obvious self-interest in violating a partner's strictures, have numerous opportunities to do so, and can keep critical information secret by lying or withholding details. The result is that policing relationships or domestic behavior comes to resemble policing in the community, picking up only a tiny fraction of transgressions. To avoid her partner's jealous rages about her having changed her underwear, after she showered, the nurse put on the same underwear she had been wearing during the day. Because Frank "freaked out" when the bills came, Donna had them sent to a post office box. Offenders may respond to contract failure with unannounced spot checks. Nick repeatedly called Laura at work to make sure she stayed at her desk and was not flirting with other men. Lessup hid in the tree outside Bonnie's house to make sure she didn't violate his rule to not go out. Detective work may involve reading mail, interrogating friends, or listening to calls. Or a controller may simply guess that a violation occurred, constructing elaborate sexual fantasies in which their partners are involved with other men, or badger their partners until they confess.

Thus, close examination reveals deep fissures in the system of regulation that compromise its efficacy and nullify its legitimacy. Spot checks disrupt the offender's day as well as his victim's, while stepped up surveillance recreates the inefficiencies regulation was designed to overcome. Rules can become so complex that they yield indifference rather than obedience or make the victim so anxious about mistakes and being hurt as a consequence that she freezes, invents violations to get it over with, or strikes out with fatal consequence. The housewife (played masterfully by Gena Rowlands) in the 1974 John Cassavetes film *A Woman Under the Influence* gradually loses touch with reality as her working-class husband (played by Peter Falk) demands she provide meals for the entire company of firemen he brings home unannounced, then beats her when the spaghetti she throws together is not up to his standards of how to entertain. For the Rowlands character, as for Laura, and the woman (Carrie Snodgrass) who is tortured by her upwardly mobile husband (Richard Benjamin) in the prefeminist 1970 film *Diary of a Mad Housewife*, the expectation of obedience and conformity is crazy-making because it clashes with the culture of autonomy in which these women are immersed. Here, too, the batterer acts like a state, resorting to force as the sine qua non of behavioral control when law fails. Early in their relationship, the former newscaster stayed home during the day, as her husband requested. But he supplemented his demands for isolation with detailed orders for how she should shop, maintain the estate (without outside help), keep up social appearances, and manage the lives of his grown children. Because it was impossible for her to fulfill these demands to the letter, she honored their spirit by carrying a phone wherever she went and spending hours completing tasks by phone or via computer that could have been done far more efficiently in person. Unable to recognize that his mounting demands were undermining his control over his wife's behavior, each night when he returned home, the husband reviewed e-mail and phone messages, returned calls to anyone whose voice or address he didn't recognize, and pored over phone messages and deleted logs to ensure that he had covered the turf. So was the emotional economy he had salvaged during the day through the telephone rule undone by a regimen that exhausted him emotionally each night. Even these efforts proved futile as we saw from the wife's frequent notations that he "went crazy." What appears as a stable regime of routine subjugation evolves through a complex interplay of experimentation and resolve that devolves into chaos.

Its experimental nature makes coercive control lonely and dangerous work. To effect their ends, offenders must accommodate the unique challenges posed by dominating a particular woman. Certain aspects of coercive control are socially mediated, such as the gender stereotypes men enforce, or are learned from the media, family history, and informal talks with buddies or in counseling. But where coercive tactics are relatively standardized in our culture, control tactics such as cyber-stalking, making rules for housework, or regulating dress by buying a woman's clothes, require sophistication in areas where men are rarely expert. Their innovative and individualized character distinguishes attempts to regulate women's lives through coercive control from the regulatory regimes in traditional cultures. The more insidious means of oppression I have encountered—such as the rule about the sari, the log book invented by Frank, the telephone rule, the list devised by Nick, the sweatshirt strategy, the physician's ploys around his wife's cooking, or the beeper game—were so devastating because they were original, context-specific, and captured the unique creative capacities of the women targeted. Transported to another relationship, another context, the same devices would have evoked a dismissive chuckle rather than terror. These tactics also took extensive time to create, impose, and enforce.

Robbery, theft, embezzlement, and other crimes have adapted their means to changing opportunities and new forms of detection. So, too, has the technology of women's oppression in personal life been reorganized to respond to the changing opportunities and challenges posed by their gradual liberation. To protect banks or certain privileged forms of communication from attack, security personnel have introduced sophisticated monitoring, alarms, and means of encryption. Short of full sexual equality, there is no comparable way to "harden the target" of coercive control. Nor can its social consequences be written off as an expense of doing business.

Part IV

Living With Coercive Control

9

WHEN BATTERED WOMEN KILL

Everyone in court was transfixed by the 911 tape, particularly Donna's relatives. "I just killed my husband," a voice reported to the emergency dispatcher. "I can't take it anymore . . . with a gun . . . I'm dying. . . . I have my little son here." Twenty-two-year-old Donna Balis did not look up. Sitting in handcuffs and leg shackles, she cut a pitiable figure and was audibly sobbing.

On that early February morning in 2000, the responding police officer found Donna in a nightgown on the front porch of her multifamily home in South Orange, New Jersey. She was "somewhat in a hysterical state and said she'd been involved in a beating," Officer Munson reported. "She said she was tired of being beaten." Donna was "cooperative" and showed him a .38-caliber revolver on top of the refrigerator. The gun contained five shell casings, but no live bullets. A medical examiner's report identified a gunshot as the cause of her husband's death. Gunpowder around the wound indicated that the weapon had been fired at close range. Donna was charged with the murder of her husband, Frank, and her bond was set at $250,000.

In the darkness, Munson testified, he couldn't tell if Balis had been beaten. The prosecutor was more candid. He acknowledged that "Photographs of Balis's body taken at the hospital after the murder do show bruises . . . Do I know where they came from? Only from what she said." The dead man had no criminal record of abuse. An uncle of the dead husband told reporters, "The poor guy was working 16 hours a day since he came over here [from Yugoslavia] about 5 years ago." Quoted in the newspaper, a neighbor described the couple as "quiet and . . . considerate" and were "shocked" by the shooting. The news also surprised Donna's defense attorney, who had been the family lawyer. This was his first criminal case. "I had no idea any of this [the abuse] was going on," he apologized sadly. "They always seemed like a happy couple."

The few documents I received from the lawyer were little help. There were several medical visits that could have involved abuse. A hospital record of a bad sprain to Donna's left wrist in April 1996 noted a "heavy object fell on left hand." Several months later, a fracture of her right hand was attributed to her slamming the car door on her right third finger. Violence could have caused a presentation for "neck and back pain." But so could the "auto accident" to which it was attributed. A note following an abortion in 1998 hinted at an element of control. She underwent the procedure, the doctor wrote, "at her husband's insistence and against her wishes and religious scruples." Still, abuse was only mentioned explicitly in Donna's medical exam after her arrest and in the three-page statement she gave police. And this statement emphasized Frank's general dissatisfaction with her behavior rather than violence. According to Officer McCarthy:

> Mrs. Balis described her husband as "a very complex person." She stated that he had always demanded from her an exact "outline" of how she spent her day. She said that she would have to prepare a summary of meals planned for the month for his approval. She said "he was never happy with macaroni or steak and potatoes"' but instead demanded meals such as veal marsala. Even with such menus planned she said she could never please him, she never did anything good enough for his demands. She relayed one incident which prompted a beating. Explaining that they had bought their house about one year ago, he once asked her to tell him what they needed for the house. She said she began to name some things (nothing specific named) and he asked her if she thought shades were important. She replied, yes, they were also something that they needed. He then demanded to know why she hadn't thought of them herself, why she wasn't caring enough. He then began to beat her."

Donna's statement was not deemed sufficiently relevant to introduce at her probable cause hearing. The only specific reference to the night's events appeared in a hospital report that her husband had been drinking "and that he assaulted her last night with it ending around 1:30 in the morning." The couple then went to bed as they had on numerous occasions after similar assaults. But a change occurred whose significance I only appreciated later. Instead of "having his way" with her as he usually did, Frank went directly to sleep. Donna's statements sounded like the grievances of a malcontent, not the "excited utterances" of the traumatized housewife the defense attorney wanted me to present.

At my request, Donna prepared a personal history of roughly 70 handwritten pages. This, as well as our interviews and various medical and psychiatric reports are the basis for the following summary. Her injuries when she was arrested, the medical record of past "accidents," and her detailed history convinced me Donna was battered throughout the course of her 4-year marriage. In isolation, this information merely provided a motive for the shooting. The manner of the shooting made a traditional plea of self-defense out of the question. Still, Donna insisted her life was in immediate danger that night and that successful retreat was impossible. The challenge was to make her perceived predicament credible in a court of law.

Donna's Story

Donna was the first in her family of Albanian immigrants to be born in the United States. Her marriage to Frank, a Yugoslav citizen and ethnic Albanian, was prearranged by their parents. Frank and Donna met twice prior to the wedding, once before an Albanian priest and once at their blood tests, when they shook hands. Because of their marriage, Frank received his green card.

The preamble to the Albanian wedding ceremony had three parts, each symbolizing the woman's transitional status from daughter to dependent wife and mother, the roles she was expected to adopt. Donna emerged with her father and traveled in a procession of more than 40 ushers from her parents' home to the new apartment. There she waited alone, watched by a single bridesmaid, while the others had lunch. After lunch, they built a small fire (in a pan in this case) and she walked around it three times for good luck. Then, they put a little boy onto her lap so she would produce plenty of baby boys.

Apart from the cultural trappings, the couple looked like other working-class Americans. Donna had just graduated from Columbia High School in Maplewood and worked at Marshall's Department Store, 9 A.M. to 6 P.M., with overtime. Frank, who had two years of college in Yugoslavia, was working at a painting job during the day and then at Mr. Doughnut until 10 P.M., where he cleaned.

Domestic Violence Begins

The first episode of physical abuse occurred just 2 weeks after the wedding, in October 1995. Donna was on the phone with Frank's uncle and laughed at something he said. Frank walked over, slapped Donna in the face "for laughing on the phone," and told her never to do so again. Concluding he was the jealous type, she dismissed the incident and vowed to obey his wishes.

The next assault occurred 3 months later, in January. Donna would pick Frank up in their old Ford at his new job at a pizza restaurant. One night, when the car ran out of gas, Donna called and Frank came to help with a friend. He was silent on the way home. When they got back, he took her into the bedroom and "beat me up." Frank's mother was visiting at the time, and Donna was several weeks pregnant. Shortly afterward, he beat her again and then wanted to make love. When she told him she was too sick to make love, he raped her. She described it this way: "He wanted to fool around and I told him no. He kept persisting and taking off my clothes and I kept fighting him off. He took his belt and tied my hands behind my back and he had fun. I never wanted him to do that again like that so I never said 'no.'"

Frank's assaults became more frequent, excited by any slight to his demands or feelings. In August 1996, toward the end of their first year together, they were driving in downtown Irvington late at night when Donna admitted she had forgotten to tell her father something for Frank. He slapped her and forced her out of the car, telling her to walk home. She was terrified. When she finally arrived at their house hours later, he questioned her about why she had gone so slowly, then beat her severely. Then he apologized, and they had sex.

Beatings diminished during the end of Donna's pregnancy, when Frank's uncle Martin was living with them, but they did not cease: she was hit for getting a flat tire, though "only around the legs," and then, in the last month, "punched in the head" for missing a right turn. Donna used her pregnancy to avoid sex and went to bed early. In response, Frank introduced the log book.

The Log Book

In September 1996, Frank gave Donna a book in which she was to record how she spent each day, whom she saw or talked with on the phone for example, any and all expenditures, and meal plans for the month. At night, Frank would return home from work, have a few beers, call Donna downstairs, and interrogate her about the entries. At first, the interrogations were followed primarily by verbal abuse. Frank would go into a rage about how "stupid" or "forgetful" she was. But in June, Donna was hit for "forgetting to record she had bought cigarettes." Soon afterward, the interrogations became the major context for assaults. "If I said something he didn't like, he would hit me. If I couldn't account for exactly where I was, he would hit me. If I forgot I saw someone, just a friend, no big deal, it would be like why didn't you tell me you saw him?"

Shortly after the log book was introduced, their son, Frank Jr., was born. Frank told Donna that the pain of the delivery was nothing compared to how hard it was to make her pregnant. This became an ongoing theme of his verbal abuse. Another theme was money. During Thanksgiving dinner in 1996 with her family, Donna attempted to explain to her brother Alex how easy it was to save money. "I don't eat dinner anymore," she told him, "except for the baby food Frankie eats." When they got home, Frank beat her for "telling her personal things."

In January 1997, Frank's mother and sister moved in. By this time, Donna was working as a bank teller. She hoped that having his immediate family around would be good for Frank. While she was rearranging the furniture for his family, Donna left the living room lights on. Seeing the lights from the restaurant, Frank returned home, and yelled at her because, even though they didn't pay for electricity separately (it was included in the rent), "she didn't need to go crazy."

The day her brother-in-law was to arrive, Donna cashed her paycheck. Frank questioned her, and she could not account for $20. Frank started to beat her. When his mother intervened, he threw her out of the room and intensified the assault. From then on, Frank took Donna's paycheck. The expectation that Donna was to cook, clean, transport, and service Frank's mother and sister occasioned numerous fights. In June, Frank sent Donna and his brother Zef to a family wedding in Detroit. He told her, "I hope you never come back." In July, while the Balises were getting dressed for a wedding, Frankie came into the bedroom and put his finger into the fan, sustaining a small cut. With the baby in his hand, Frank beat Donna "all over my head." She was still crying when they reached the hospital, but the nurses thought it was because Frankie was hurt.

In January 1998, Donna learned she was pregnant again. She begged Frank to be allowed to have the baby, but he told her she was "too stupid" and forced her to abort the pregnancy, occasioning the sympathetic hospital note.

As the result of increasing conflict between Frank and his family—including one fight in which Frank broke his sister's nose—in March 1998, Donna was sent to search for a new apartment. Frank beat Donna because she didn't bargain, because she asked his permission about each apartment, and because one apartment she found was too small. When they finally took a place in nearby Bloomington, Frank forced Donna to leave behind the personal shelf ornaments that had been given to her by her family.

At this point, Donna realized Frank was "always in a temper" and was capable of killing her.

Increasing Isolation

When word of Frank's assault on his mother got out, the couple became "outcasts" from the Albanian community. Combined with the move to a new apartment, this isolation was the background against which physical abuse escalated. Of this period, Donna says, "there were so many beatings, they jumble in my mind." Records from our interviews suggest it was not unusual for Frank to assault Donna three or four evenings a week. Frank focused on Donna's "loyalty." He beat her when she refused to tell callers that her husband's violence against his family was their fault. Frank often punished Donna for talking to people she saw. So she stopped talking to friends and relatives, even those she met accidentally on the street, limiting her social life to her immediate family.

In June 1998, Donna bought Frank a chain and cross he had wanted for Father's Day. On this occasion, he assaulted her because she could always remember stupid things but never important ones. He hit her, she told me, "whenever we talked about anything and everything." In July, Donna was beaten because the TV antenna came out of the wall. In August, during a religious festival celebrated by Frank's family, Donna served her family dinner at the normal time but contrary to tradition. Because her little brother slept over, she was "saved from a beating," though Frank beat her the next night. In September, Donna failed to respond to an alarm clock and was pushed off the bed onto the floor. In October, Donna was beaten because, in rejecting their loan application, the bank cited the reason Frank told her to put down. She should have "thought for herself." She was beaten for not thinking about the immediate future. Frank also beat her for thinking only about "tomorrow, not today." Donna was beaten because in November, a year earlier, she had paid her Macy's credit card late and it came up on their credit history when they applied for a mortgage. By fall 1998, Donna was hardly buying any clothes because she feared Frank's anger.

Violence as Routine

Three years into the marriage, assault was routine. "It had become a regular thing where I would expect a beating every time we were together," she told me. Frank's assaults centered on the log book. By this time, Donna had to provide a description of her activities for every hour. She was beaten if any of her time was spent not "making us prosper." There was to be no time for her to just relax. She was beaten for writing things down that she didn't get to or for things she intended to do tomorrow. She thought, "he can tell I don't care about the marriage because I never give ideas." But when she had suggestions, he got mad and beat her because she was "unrealistic."

In November 1998, Donna asked Frank to remove the guns from a drawer where Frank Jr. had been touching them. Frank pointed the gun at her, she stepped to the side, and he followed her with the gun, telling her not to move, wearing a funny smile. After that, she realized he wanted to kill her, but she "put it in the back of my mind."

By early 1999, the interrogations became more frequent. Now, in addition to the evening sessions, Donna was required to call Frank at work each day and answer his questions about her activities.

Donna tried to minimize Frank's abuse. Having her brother sleep over was protective, particularly when Frank told her in advance she was going to be hit. When her older sister was visiting her parents, she went to their house to sleep. Even so, Frank beat her when she wanted to visit her parents because she had "nothing more important to do." She was beaten "constantly" for forgetting something or not doing something. If he felt she was lying, he beat her "senseless." When Frank worked late on Christmas, Donna asked what kind of food he wanted for New Year's. He beat her because she didn't know what would please him. During this period, beatings were so frequent, Donna more clearly recalls nights when she was not assaulted.

In February 1999, Donna's brother-in-law offered to fix their furnace at cost. The reminder that they had little money made Frank ashamed, so he beat Donna. In April, Donna talked about possibly being able to open their own restaurant some day and was again beaten for not thinking about the immediate future. In April, Donna offered to help Frank load a dumpster. This suggested he was incapable of doing the work himself. He followed her into the house and beat her. She sustained a sprained wrist, resulting in her second medical visit.

Typically, because Frank beat Donna around the head, she used her hands to protect herself. By May, her fingers were so swollen and mis-shapen she could no longer wear the rings she received on her wedding day. In June, Donna was in an accident with her sister in the car. Frank told her if Frank Jr. had been in the car, he would have killed her.

In spring 1999, Frank also put Donna on various diets. At one point, he told her to join Weight Watchers, which she did. Each night thereafter, he put her on the scale. If she hadn't lost weight, he beat her.

In August, for the Assumption Feast, Donna's parents went to Frank's brother's house. After her brother and sister left, Frank beat her up for dropping a glass. During a beating, Frank fractured Donna's finger, the injury attributed to the car door. While shopping for a sofa set, Frank asked Donna what she thought and she said, "nice." At home, he beat her for being so useless. Frank told Donna all his problems would be over if she was dead and that he and the baby could live fine without her.

In October 1999, Donna was rear-ended by another car, this time with Frankie in the vehicle. She sustained whiplash, which caused persistent headaches and pain and numbness in the back of her neck. Frank beat her on the head because Frankie could have been hurt. In the months that followed, he beat her "every time the subject of accidents came up, telling me how stupid I was." Donna bought a toaster for $14 and was beaten for not asking him. She was also beaten for not buying a microwave oven.

By late 1999, Donna rarely left the house, except to go to work. She describes herself as too frightened even to go to the store unless told to do so. One afternoon, she was in the basement doing a wash and failed to hear his call. The resulting beating was so bad, she finally admitted he was right, that she had gone to the store without his permission. He beat her again. Donna was beaten for taking his cigarettes and for leaving some old newspapers in the car.

When Donna's girlfriend from work called the house, Frank questioned her about what they said, told her not to trust anyone, then hit her. Afterward he calmed down and told her, "relax, why are you so nervous?" She asked her friends not to call.

At first, the abusive incidents followed a set pattern. He would question her, then assault her, then stop. They would go to bed and have sex.

Sometimes, now, after beatings, questioning about her activities resumed and Donna was beaten again if she didn't have "solutions."

In November 1999, Frank pointed his gun at her and told her that it would be easy just to pull the trigger and she would be dead and all his problems would be over. Even if he went to jail, he said, he would have food, clothes, and a roof over his head.

Realizing that Donna's brother would tell her parents about the abuse, Frank forbade Donna to have him over on his day off or when he was home. One result was that Donna kept Frankie awake so that she could sleep with him instead of being beaten.

When Donna told her mother not to let a woman friend take advantage of her, Frank beat her because she was no one to give advice. "Instead of loving you," Frank told her, "every day I hate you more and more."

Donna was beaten for charging $25 for a skirt on their credit card. As a result, Frank told her she was too irresponsible to have charge cards and canceled them.

Because so many of the assaults seemed to be occasioned by Frank's anxiety about money, in December 1999, Donna got a postal hold order and began regulating the flow of bills coming into the house. On Christmas day, Donna's brother Marky got lost after church, and Donna kept Frank waiting in the car while she helped her family find him. He started to pull away from the curb. When they got home he beat her senseless for having her priorities wrong. On New Year's Eve, Frank asked Donna if they should open the champagne. Donna said no because they were drinking wine. He poured two glasses of champagne, then hit her in the head with the bottle.

In January 2000, Donna was fired from her job at the bank because she had missed so many days due to the abuse. Too frightened to tell Frank what happened, she told him that she had quit and was beaten. Besides her immediate family, the bank had been Donna's only source of social support. On January 29, less than a week before she shot him, Donna made the decision to leave. She secretly packed a suitcase and loaded her car. Her plan was to go after she picked Frankie up at her mother's. She had some money hidden away. She agonized about the decision for 2 days. If she left her husband, she knew, she would be ostracized by the Albanian community, including her family. Cultural mores also dictated that Frank would get their son. The idea of having to survive on her own was overwhelming. Afraid of what would happen if Frank found the suitcase, she unpacked the car and put her things away.

On February 1, 2000, Donna's car wouldn't start, and she took Frank to work in his car. That night, after an interrogation about the car, he beat her severely. He beat her again the next day when the keys got locked in the car while it was running. That night, to avoid a beating, she took Frankie into her bed. Frank came upstairs, put Frankie in his own bed, and ordered Donna downstairs. After lecturing her about dinner being late and the car episode, he began to beat her, punching her in the head and kicking her side as she crawled from the family room to the living room, hitting her head against the bathroom wall. Then he stopped, but she was aware that this was only a hiatus. She considered various ways to escape, but concluded they wouldn't work. Then he started again, finally knocking her flat. She realized something terrible was going to happen to her. Almost as suddenly as it started, the beating ended and they went to bed. But Frank went right to sleep. At 5:30 A.M., Donna awakened, took a gun from above the dresser mirror, and shot at Frank five times, hitting him at least twice. She took Frankie downstairs and returned to retrieve the gun because "I was afraid he would come after me." Then, she called the police.

Donna ended Frank's abuse by killing him, a relatively rare outcome in domestic violence cases. Unlike Donna, most women who kill abusive men do so during an assault. Much of the dynamic that led up to the death was shaped by its cultural context. Like so many immigrant and fundamentalist women in my caseload and the women who suffered "wife torture" during the transition to liberal democratic society, Donna lived in two worlds, striving to configure her identity as a woman at the point where traditional beliefs in female subordination confronted the more egalitarian values instilled at her high school, at Marshall's and the bank, and on TV. Had they lived in Albania, where members of extended families can still enforce the cultural obligations women inherit with marriage, it is likely that Frank's violence would have been sufficient to secure his dominance. But in suburban New Jersey, it was not.

Violence

Their sheer frequency was the most impressive feature of Frank's assaults. His violence increased in frequency and intensity over the 4 years of the marriage, occurring several times a month during the first year, at least once a week (usually during his day off) between 1997 and March 1998, and "constantly," "every day," and "whenever I saw him" after that. Although I was only able to delineate 50 separate violent episodes, the actual count was probably 10 times this number.

By winter 1996, the assaults followed a typical pattern. Frank returned from work between 9 and 10 P.M., drank beer for an hour or so, called Donna down from bed, went over the log book, and questioned her at length about what "she had done for us" or with some unstated idea in his mind. Questions were quickly followed by accusations and name calling. Then, as punishment for something she had or had not done, he would slap and punch Donna in the head, pull her hair if she tried moving away, then knock her down. She would then crouch, turn her 5'9" frame into a ball with her arms covering her head, and he would kick and punch her in the back, arms, hands, and side. Toward the end of the relationship, he would drag her by the hair or kick her hard enough to move her into the wall. By 1998, he regularly beat her senseless if he thought she was lying about her time. Assaults began with criticism, though these were not arguments because Donna played no role. Nor were they punishments, because the offenses were largely imagined or invented on the spot. Nor was Frank trying to get her to do something differently. With the marked exception of the sexual assault, the beatings were simply part of the presex evening ritual, like washing up or eating, and added little to Donna's deference, which was already complete. When he stopped beating her, Frank would go up to bed, expecting her to follow so he could have "his way."

The cumulative effect of these assaults was that Donna suffered a "slow death" to which she believed she would succumb if the abuse was not stopped. It may seem insensitive to say so, but on a continuum of assaultive behavior, Frank's attacks were relatively mild, at least until the last months. He never choked Donna and never shot, stabbed, or burned her. He punched her in the face only once, raped her on only one occasion, and hit her with an object (the champagne bottle) only once. Frank never broke any of her bones or injured her seriously enough to require hospitalization. Had they been reported, the vast majority of the assaults would have been charged as misdemeanors. None of the assaults caused permanent disfigurement; none caused pain that matched the whiplash from her car accident. It was the cumulative intensity rather than the severity of his assaults that elicited Donna's feeling that she was being smothered alive. Like so many of the battered women I see, assault became an expected part of her everyday life until, as she put it, "I woke up and went to sleep with the same feeling. I was living on the edge of a roof and at any moment 'whoosh,' I would just fall off." She also realized that how she behaved had little effect on whether she would be hurt. Frank threatened to shoot Donna with the gun several times. But it was only on the night of the fatal shooting that she believed he intended to kill her.

Frank's Personality

Frank drank more than a case of beer weekly, was probably an alcoholic, and beat Donna when he was drunk. But he was sober during most of his assaults. We could speculate endlessly about the roots of Frank's volatile personality evident in this violent outbursts against his mother and sister. To those who knew him best, his workmates, members of his extended family, and his lawyer, he seemed quiet, hard-working, and friendly. His uncle's comments suggested that Frank's work life was much more stressful than he let on. Violence may have helped ease this stress. But there was little evidence of psychopathology in Frank's history and the marked absence of anger during the assaults suggests they were more instrumental than expressive. "Relax, why are you so nervous?" he asked Donna one evening after he hit her. If anything, both the construction of the log book ritual and the routine, almost sadistic application of beatings in conjunction with a detailed examination of entries, pointed toward an

obsession with control that I have found in a wide range of male populations, including business executives. A Nigerian man, interviewed about
abuse of his wife that included more than 60 assaults, admitted he was
wrong to beat her. But he became increasingly agitated as he recalled how
she challenged his authority. "You can't imagine yourself beating your
wife?" he asked the interviewer. "You can't imagine yourself being pushed
to that level? But some people just push you over the edge, and you do
things that you are not supposed to do. For God's sake. You are the head
of the home as the man. You must have a home that is submissive to
you."[1] Frank beat Donna because he could, particularly when the risk of
exposure or outside intervention was nil, and because he saw his beatings
as a way to enact his identity as a man.

Isolation

Assaults became routine and control total after the couple moved in
March 1998, and this pattern was solidified in 1999 after Donna lost her
job at the bank and Frank had more time off from work. Donna also felt
more vulnerable after the move because Frank forced her to leave behind
the traditional objects that linked her to her family and culture and that
had served as an important safety zone. Being isolated also helped keep
the violence hidden. The only assault witnessed by someone other than
Frank's mother and sister occurred impulsively, when Donna told another
uncle on the phone that her brother was visiting and Frank walked over,
punched her in the nose and then, when she dropped the phone, dragged
her to the bedroom and beat her. If isolation led to increased violence,
escalating physical abuse also heightened the risk that Frank would be
exposed as a wife beater, leading him to step up his attempts to isolate
Donna, increasing her vulnerability. Despite his efforts to avoid leaving
marks, Frank's family and Donna's friends at work frequently saw her
with bruises, a black eye, eyes red and swollen from crying, and swollen
hands. Fear, cultural proscriptions, and an increasing sense of fatalism
kept Donna from frankly discussing her situation with any but one co-
worker, however, and no one else questioned her.

The episode shortly after the marriage when Frank punched Donna for
laughing on the phone initiated his systematic attempts to prevent her
from having supportive relationships with his or her family, Frankie, or
other members of the Albanian community. After losing her job, Donna
abandoned her friendship with a woman at the bank. Her social isolation
contrasted with Frank's continual "presence." When his family was visiting, she became their virtual slave. His mother and sister reported her
behavior to Frank, and she was beaten if she hesitated to serve them or
when she tried to go on errands by herself. Particularly after he assaulted
his sister and mother, Frank tightly regulated Donna's relationships with
other Albanians, even those she met on the street. Fearing she would say
the wrong thing, she avoided even casual contacts. In 1999, Frank told

Donna her brother or other siblings could no longer sleep at their house or she at her family's. When she was at home during the day after losing her job, Frank checked up on her constantly, driving by, watching her from the nearby restaurant where he worked, and dropping in unexpectedly to make spot checks.

The shame caused by Frank's attack on his mother caused even Donna's parents to stop visiting, complementing the ostracism by other Albanians and making them virtual exiles. Symptomatic of how isolated she became from her family's protection was the beating she received in 1998 when she kept Frank waiting in the car after church while she helped her family look for her missing little brother.

Sexism With a Vengeance

Frank's violence was framed by gender-specific expectations mediated by his cultural background. There is no record of his using violence against male family members such as his uncles, or against unrelated males. He was consumed with fear that if word of his abuse got out, other Albanian men would confront him, particularly those from Donna's family. Frank's violence targeted the stereotypes and entitlements he believed distinguished himself as a man from Donna as a woman: she was "stupid," "fat," "ugly like a whore," frivolous (laughing on the phone), alternately "independent" and "not able to think for herself"; forgetful and scatterbrained ("thinking of the future"); had no sense of money; and was disloyal. He punished her for unapproved expenditures, not doing enough for their family, meals that failed to meet his expectations, weight gain, and her numerous acts of stupidity. To Frank, "doing masculinity" required continually reaffirming the three R's (reason, rationality, and righteousness) by using her as negative example. Two beliefs were key to his violence: that real men could solve any problem put to them (but Donna could solve none) and that manhood was incompatible with shame (but not femininity, which was shameful by definition). Because problems he couldn't solve surfaced repeatedly, as they do in most of our lives, abusing Donna helped defend him against the embarrassment caused by any event that fell outside his comfort zone, such as financial difficulties, a car accident, a broken furnace, failure to get a loan, an alarm going off unexpectedly, the TV antenna coming loose, a woman failing to be home for an appointment, or when several bills arrived at once, until he became fixed on the idea that she was the reason there were so many mistakes and embarrassments in his life. Because his abuse effectively paralyzed Donna, it ensured an escalating spiral of failure, projection, blame, and punishment. When problems and embarrassments persisted despite his abuse, Frank expanded his tactics horizontally: by micromanaging Donna's every activity or contact, he hoped to close the spaces from which problems arose or, at least, to neutralize the one witness to his degradation he could not avoid.

Given Frank's extensive violence, it might seem that Donna had a credible case for self-defense. She did not. Apart from what she told police, there was no documented history of physical abuse or any other event meriting legal notice prior to the homicide. The state's attorney claimed the bruises could have come from anywhere and that the only evidence of domestic violence was "what she told me." Frank employed a multifaceted course of coercive conduct to subjugate Donna throughout their 4-year relationship. But the prosecutor emphasized that he had never seriously injured her, he had never been arrested, and there were no witnesses to his assaults—indeed, neighbors described them as "quiet" and "considerate," and his alleged threats to kill her were undocumented. My expert testimony could certainly add weight to Donna's story, particularly if I speculated that her medical records indicated abuse, an argument supported by co-workers who saw Donna at the bank with her eyes blackened on several occasions, and explained why abuse can be serious even in the absence of injury or police involvement. But this was unlikely to be enough.

It would have made little difference if Frank had been arrested or Donna had been forthright with medical providers. And this could have made things worse. As in the O. J. Simpson case, the low level of injury involved suggested domestic violence was far too minor to justify taking a life. An arrest would have increased Frank's fury, not assuaged it, while allowing the prosecutor to argue that Donna did, in fact, have options and had used them in the past. Even her statement that "I can't take it anymore" on the 911 tape could be interpreted to support premeditation rather than as evidence Donna was entrapped, particularly given her litany of complaints about Frank to police. This woman seemed more dissatisfied than wronged.

A Battered Woman's Defense?

My job as an expert witness was to provide insight unavailable to a layperson into how Frank's abuse contributed to his death. One option was to use a battered woman's defense to show that the accumulated violence she suffered rendered Donna incapable of thinking clearly or acting effectively on her own behalf; caused her to exaggerate the danger she faced, even from a sleeping man; and blinded her to the option of escape or calling police before the murder. Her failure to call police in the past or to frankly discuss her problems with her doctor or lawyer as well as the indecision about leaving illustrated by her loading and then unpacking the car all suggested learned helplessness. The shooting could be interpreted as the desperate act of a trauma victim who sees no other way out.

In certain respects, Donna was a good candidate for this defense. Frank showed remorse only once—one night when he wanted sex—and never promised to change. But if there had been no cycle of violence, the other critical elements of battered woman's syndrome (BWS) were conspicuous: repeated, possibly severe assault; threats to kill; and a victim who had never sought outside assistance though she acknowledged Frank had threatened to kill her and that she believed he would do so. In not reaching out, Donna was exceptional. As we saw in chapter 5, battered women are aggressive help seekers, typically seek medical care for their injuries even more promptly than auto accident victims, are generally forthright about their situation when asked, and report assaults to police where they are injured as readily as persons assaulted by strangers and more readily than victims of stranger assault when they are not injured.[2] I attributed Donna's reluctance to seek help to her cultural inheritance and her fear of the consequences of exposure. But it might also have reflected her psychological disability.

I could have relied on post-traumatic stress disorder (PTSD). Donna minimized or repressed Frank's threats, both consistent with trauma. The fact that she had returned to retrieve the gun after she killed him because she thought he would pursue her suggested she attributed god-like powers to Frank, a clear sign of distortion. She also blocked significant details of the shooting, reported crying at odd times during the day, had flashbacks to abusive episodes, exhibited the classic "startle" response, and was hypervigilant, though much of this reaction had been displaced into an obsessive desire to protect Frankie from discovering how his father died. When we met a month after the shooting, she was still so overwhelmed with guilt, anxiety, and self-loathing that a brief hospitalization was needed as a caution against suicide—another symptom consistent with BWS or PTSD.

A claim that Donna was suffering BWS or PTSD when she shot her husband might have mitigated her guilt, leading to a lesser charge of manslaughter or a reduced sentence. But the prosecutor could weave the same facts into an equally plausible story of a premeditated killing and find support for this account from Frank's family and workmates. In this narrative, Donna resented Frank's tireless efforts to put the family on solid economic ground, not least because it led to him being sexually inattentive. Unsure about whether to leave him or to stay, and fearful she would lose custody if she left, she unpacked her bags and began secretly to save money because she had decided to take her husband's life when the opportunity presented itself. The final straw was his refusal to have sex on the night of the fatality. Yes, he occasionally lost his temper and maybe even have hit or beat her, possibly the source of the bruises she presented. But this hardly justified her sneaking into their bedroom, taking his gun and firing it into his head. Abused women often "stay" because they fear even more dire consequences if they leave. But Frank had repeatedly expressed the hope that Donna would leave or die.

This case would probably have never come to trial had Donna shot and killed a stranger who threatened, beat, and raped her; took her money; cut her off from her family; and then forced her to subordinate herself in every way imaginable under threat of death. But there was nothing in the court's experience that helped it understand how a husband could so constrain his wife's life and liberty as to cause the "slow death" Donna described. This was why the defense lawyer contemplated arguing that Donna's perception of danger had been so distorted by trauma that she mistakenly believed "I am dying" (as she said on the tape) even though her husband was asleep.

From Domestic Violence to Coercive Control

Despite prominent signs of distress, Donna was not suffering full-blown PTSD or the depression associated with BWS. Instead, I sensed a dual, even contradictory persona behind her presentations, a lived tension mirroring her cultural marginality between the profuse negative self-assessments with which she projected her "victim" self and the "survivor" self that allowed her to document years of mistreatment with intelligence and energy. Donna admitted she was "depressed," experienced appetite and sleep problems, and had suicidal thoughts. She also offered poignant descriptions of being "fat," "stupid" and "forgetful," suggesting her self-esteem was low. When Frank ordered her to go to the store to buy him cigarettes and beer, she recounted that she would return with one, but not the other, showing how "forgetful" she was. She illustrated her "stupidity" by pointing to her inability to accurately record information in the log book or to lose weight. Because being forgetful and stupid caused beatings, these were serious character flaws in her view. But Donna exhibited none of the hopelessness, withdrawal, inattentiveness, or flat affect of my seriously depressed clients. Instead, until she was fired because of her repeated absences, Donna worked as a bank clerk and had multifaceted friendships with co-workers. In recounting her history before, in, and after her relationship with Frank, she exhibited an acute sensitivity to detail (but not hyperacuity) rather than distraction or memory problems. She got appropriately angry when describing Frank's irrational control over her life and was positively animated when presenting her suicidal symptoms. The sadness that seemed to overwhelm her at times was multidimensional and situation-specific, not flat or diffuse. During our interviews, she sometimes sobbed inconsolably. Even then, she emanated a strong presence. She was in a state of profound mourning and had little of the absence or emptiness that accompanies helplessness or despair. Donna looked and acted depressed. But she lacked the feel of a depressed person.

It became gradually apparent that Donna's current depressive symptoms masked the guilt she felt about her own violent behavior and her anxiety at how her son would react when he learned the truth. In the relationship with Frank, depression had helped Donna contain a mounting homicidal rage, part of which she directed, protectively, at herself and part at him. Now she feared the unspent rage might resurface and drown her in self-loathing. Her violence had been cathartic, even satisfying— another source of guilt, particularly in a culture where women are expected to bear their burdens stoically. Donna had significant problems. But given the circumstances, she was remarkably intact psychologically.

At Donna's request, I have changed the names, dates, and places in this case. I met the real Donna early in my forensic career, when I was just learning to decipher elements of coercive control. However hard I tried to keep her focused on Frank's violence, she persistently returned to the structural dimensions of the predicament she had described to police on the night of the shooting. She had begun her description of the homicide to the police by recounting a dispute over food. "He was never happy with macaroni or steak or potatoes but demanded meals such as veal marsala," she told officer Munson.[3] My first thought was that she had displaced the unbearable anxiety associated with Frank's assaults and her own act to mundane facets of their lives as a way to normalize (and so withstand) the trauma. Only slowly did I recognize that she was articulating the most profound harm she had suffered.

The Survivor Self

I followed Donna's lead because of the sheer personal magnetism she exuded, because she adamantly insisted the nonphysical degradation she suffered was more salient and consequential than Frank's violence, and because I was grasping for straws. The violence she recounted was arbitrary, even sadistic. Yet the log book was far more emblematic of the entrapment she felt on the night of the shooting. When I raised the subject of violence, she looked and acted like the victim she had been in the face of Frank's physical brutality. Her shoulders drooped and she seemed suddenly much older than her 26 years. But she came to life when she talked about how she had hidden the bills, squirreled money away, "forgotten" to carry out his orders, told him she would no longer serve his mother and sister, even when she discussed how she had gotten fat. Through the worst of it, she wanted me to know, her agency had survived.

Gradually, the core injustice Donna had suffered became clear to us both. At the time of the shooting, she felt like a virtual prisoner in her own home, lacking basic material and social supports. She had lost her job, had no access to money, and was cut off from her family and friends. Her power to choose her clothes or what to eat or when to have sex or to sleep had been taken from her. Frank, not Donna, controlled the most basic acts that comprised her identity, including her movement and the speech act, what she said, whom she spoke to, even on the phone. Whatever she said, whatever she felt, whatever she meant—all were wrong or stupid. This was the terrain on which she chose to make her stand, drawing a circle around the core of her survivor self, mobilizing whatever internal resources she had to make her line of defense. When discussing the violence, she was alternately passive and agitated, perfunctory and depressed. But when she discussed the constraints on her liberty, she became calm: delineating the objective parameters of her situation made it possible for her to locate herself in relation to justice claims in ways discussing the violence did not. She was able to see, and then help me see, that in the climate of intimidation, isolation, and control, her anger, rage, and resistance—even her denial—had been completely rational. Far from contradicting her nature, the shooting was the culmination of this resistance. This was not the last gasp of someone who wanted to survive no matter what, but an affirmative statement driven by the impulse to be free. For Donna, killing Frank was a logical extension of her mounting rage at being dominated.

Had Donna physically resisted Frank's violence, he most likely would have shot her, as he threatened. Like soldiers who are prepared for combat by learning to fire their weapons at the enemy automatically, thus avoiding the paralyzing fear evoked by thinking "its him or me," Donna's denial of her physical danger was survival-oriented. But even at her most desperate, she continued to resist Frank's domination, though her resistance was hidden in a psychological and behavioral underground where it could be safely displaced. Her "forgetting" to buy bear and her "stupid" inability to lose weight could be interpreted as cognitive impairments or as self-destructive. She took responsibility for numerous problems she had not caused, telling him she had gone to the store when she had not, for instance, instead of admitting she had missed his phone call because she was doing the laundry. To Donna, these behaviors were part of a struggle to sustain her identity as an autonomous person while being denied the space to do so—control in the context of no control. Until she was safe, it was too dangerous for her to do anything but somatize her resistance in forgetting, weight gain, and other seeming mistakes and failings. This process allowed her to tolerate the beatings or, more exactly, to control them internally by constructing a negative self that was "responsible" for provoking them and then managing this self. Blaming herself for what went wrong created the space in which she could strategize about how to do things differently and so, ironically, to retain an element of the choice Frank was trying to snuff out.

Isolation also played a complex role in Donna's survivor self. Frank beat her for using her nephew's sleepovers to protect her, for "saying the wrong things" when she met members of the Albanian community, and for explaining to her family how missing meals was evidence of frugality. The Albanian lore that Donna respected prescribes that a woman be rejected if she leaves her husband and that the husband retain custody of the child. A rational fear of these outcomes and her deep religious and cultural beliefs in the obligations associated with marriage helped trap Donna in her relationship with Frank, paralleling the process of gender entrapment Beth Richie has identified among battered African American women. Even when virtually every facet of her daily existence was scrutinized by Frank, however, Donna experienced staying with him less as an act of submission than as an affirmation of her ties to her culture, her immediate family, her friends (apart from work), and to a range of possessions and beliefs that gave her life personal meaning.

In the end, we determined to focus the court's attention—and Donna's—on the objective restraints Frank imposed on her liberty, his coercive control, and the tactics by which she attempted to retain and assert her autonomy. The futility of openly resisting violence was clear: when she refused sex, Donna was raped; when she spoke up against the beating on the advice of a friend at work, she was even more severely abused. But within the familial and cultural context she shared with Frank, Donna did everything she could to avoid beatings. She tried to fulfill his wishes by compromising her desires in every imaginable way, served his family almost as a slave, put mail on hold to regulate the receipt of bills to his satisfaction, went to bed early with their son so she would not be awake when he came home, complied with his sexual demands, slept at her family's house whenever possible, and confirmed his accusations, even lying on more than one occasion to do so. Compliance weakened her objective situation. But it gave her the pride she needed to endure; the same culture that trapped her in a subordinate role also instilled a sense of identity at sharing an inheritance of indigenous prowess with a broad community of women she could not see or talk with on the phone.

Because Frank "was a different person when anybody was around," Donna tried to surround herself with family members whenever possible, bringing her younger brother Nicky over, "and falling asleep" with Frank Jr. Only in the last week did she plan to escape, a strategy she quickly abandoned because she feared ostracism, losing her son, and Frank's retaliation, all reasonable fears. She also contemplated seeking help and escape on the night of the shooting. But she realized Frank had the car keys, he would stop her from using the phone, would catch her if she ran downstairs, and that none of the local stores were open.

The Significance of Control: The Log Book Redux

Donna kept returning to the log book and the nightly ritual of interrogation. The book itself was not a sufficient prop to establish a defense against the murder charge. But it became emblematic of how her every movement had been scrutinized, entered, and regulated, reproducing for the court the sense of suffocation she felt throughout the marriage and the continuing and complete control that made her feel trapped even by the sleeping man.

The log book was the immediate expression of Frank's control over her access to money and other basic necessities. Frank made no entries. Although Donna worked, she had to turn her paycheck over and was beaten when she failed to do so promptly or spent any money on herself or the house. Their charge cards were in both names. But when she used one for a small, unauthorized purchase, she was beaten and made to cancel her account because "she was too stupid." Frank's use of money as a fulcrum of control was mediated by his sense of identification with family finance. He even beat Donna when two or three bills came at the same time. Throughout the marriage, any expenditure of money, failure to get a loan, embarrassment because Donna's brother-in-law offered to save them money, even Donna's failure to buy beer as ordered (though there was beer in the house) led to assaults.

Donna was also to include a complete monthly menu of meals for Frank's approval in the log book. Despite her full-time job and caring for their son and members of his family, she was expected to cook a complete Albanian meal each night. She was beaten if the food was not to his liking or meals were late or not served in the proper manner. These are the sort of gendered expectations we find in patriarchal cultures like those that dominate sub-Saharan Africa, where, because women tend to be less educated than men, they already work longer hours and transport three times as much weight as men, hauling firewood, water, and sacks of corn on their heads.[4] As a result of Frank's anger at how expensive food was, by November 1996, she was skipping dinner. Because she was chronically hungry, she took every opportunity she could to get "free food," continually snacking at work or while doing her chores, the immediate cause of her failure to lose weight.

Frank tried to control what and how much Donna ate. Her weight was an important focus of struggle. She now recognizes that her being heavy was one of the few expressions of control she had over her body, a point of resistance in the face of Frank's numerous plans to make her diet. Going to Weight Watchers (which she could only do if she failed to keep her weight off) was a rare chance to get out of the house. That Frank put her on the scale and beat her for not losing weight was secondary to the autonomy she felt.

Frank completely controlled their sex lives, apparently feeling comfortable with sex mainly in conjunction with violence. After the rape, she simply gave into him whenever he wanted sex.

Frank's possessions were untouchable, Donna's of no value. When she took a cigarette from his pack—he had 10 cartons in the house—she was beaten. But when they moved, he forced her to leave all of her trinkets and memorabilia behind.

Marked exceptions to his control were her car—which she needed for work—and her relations with Frank Jr., although some of the most serious beatings involved the car and Frank would frequently beat Donna with Frank Jr. in the room, explaining that mommy was "a bad girl."

Nothing threatened Donna's sense of capacity as much as Frank's control over her daily routine. By controlling her appearance (her clothes, weight), when she went to sleep, whom she talked to on the phone and in the street and how, what she bought, when and if she went out and how she drove, Frank made it clear that Donna was no more than a child who could not act responsibly or control her own life or destiny.

His control extended to minute facets of her everyday behavior, even when she was alone. When he noticed a light on in the house during the day from the restaurant where he worked nearby, he returned home and beat her for stupidity, even though electricity was included in the rent. He checked up on her constantly, beating her if she failed to hear the phone or telephoning with instructions to buy beer or cigarettes.

Donna came to believe she was incapable of making the most basic decisions for herself, which led her to think Frank was justified when he complained she had done nothing today "for us."

Donna was beaten "whenever I started to talk . . . expressed a feeling, anything, everything." Even her thoughts were monitored. Blamed for what went wrong, she would promise to make things better in the future. But she eventually gave up the hope that the beatings would stop if only she pleased Frank. She got hit no matter how she conducted herself day to day.

Donna came to care little about her physical appearance. Her hands were so misshapen, she couldn't wear her rings and they had to be removed with pliers.

Freedom and the Unraveling of Coercive Control

Donna's case illustrates how coercion and control become intertwined over time: hurting her made it difficult for her to resist offenses to her liberty; by reducing her liberty, her discretion with money, food preparation, going and coming, and talking on the phone, Frank made any and all of her acts of autonomy and personhood unsafe. But its very totality ultimately proved the undoing of his coercive control.

Even on the cultural island where Donna spent much of her time, violence could not affect the control Frank sought over her life. In traditional patriarchal cultures, many women appear to accept the fact that failures in domestic responsibilities will result in abuse. About half of the women interviewed in Zambia in 2001 and 2002 by the World Health Organization said that husbands had a right to beat wives who argued with them, burned the dinner, went out without their husband's permission, neglected the children, or refused sex.[5] Although the Albanian culture with which Donna and Frank identified retained many of these beliefs, Donna had alternative roots in a cultural world that valued independence and autonomy and rejected abuse. Interestingly, her marginality did not lead her to reject Albanian culture or even question whether being her husband's servant was a proper role. But in marked contrast to other women in the community for whom Albanian lore was second nature, Donna understood that she had chosen this lifestyle as her mooring voluntarily and so could also reject its values in certain areas. This realization—the fact that she had chosen to serve—gave Donna a certain pride in her suffering, the sense of connectedness that infuriated Frank.

Donna was working outside the home when they met and continued to do so out of necessity. When she lost her job, the family went on a downward spiral. Thus, Frank was confronted by a contradiction he could not resolve: to keep Donna home as his personal servant, to obliterate her access to egalitarian values, meant to lose the chance to "make it" in a world with which he also increasingly identified. Beating Donna suppressed this contradiction but did not resolve it.

The fact that Frank had to work two jobs left Donna unguarded during the day and much of the evening, a condition that would have been remedied in traditional societies by scrutiny by family members (such as Frank's mother and sister) or others in the community. The purity of her cultural deference was further tarnished by her access to money, friendships with co-workers, and a vision of social possibility that continually pushed options other than tolerating fate to the surface. Ironically, because Donna was required to record "everything," the log book provided a record of the life outside the Albanian community Frank wanted her to do without, forcing her to attend even more closely to this life than she normally would have—her experience with co-workers, landlords, auto mechanics, merchants of all stripes, and all the other potentially volatile transactions in which she touched equality and independence. In this way, the very center of her oppression, the log book, became a safety zone as well as a symbol of her shame. The experiences recorded therein were critical to the family's survival. So they could not be quashed with violence. Instead, Frank tried to monitor Donna's interactions with the outside world without internalizing its values. But this proved impossible: though he might beat her for "thinking too much," he also required her to "think of the family" when negotiating about rent, buying food, or caring for the car. Determined to live like a traditional patriarch with his mother, sister, and brother while working at a doughnut shop, Frank was forced to constrain Donna's transactions through coercive control. His first impulse was to exact double duty, allowing her to use her liberty to bring money into the home while enforcing tradition in their personal life, hoping to make up through violence, vigilance, and her sweat equity what the material and social limits of their lives would not allow, the same fantasies that drove nineteenth-century men to wife torture. But when the means Frank deployed cost Donna her job, their personal finances hit bottom. Try as he might, calling from work to check if the lights were on, making spot checks whenever he could get away, beating her to stop the bills, he simply could not quash the residue of liberty and dignity she brought to the marriage. He turned on those he identified with the traditional images of his manhood, his family, the seeming source of the demands he was trying to live out, assaulting his mother, sister and cousins, banishing her brother and family from his home. The result was that he and Donna were exiled from the community of peers whose social recognition he craved. In the end, he came to recognize his standing only through Donna's progressive degradation, trying to beat out of her the shame he felt at being a king with no kingdom or court. As an object, she was useless even to his exaggerated pridefulness. But in making her an object, he also eliminated whatever subjective ground remained for her loyalty.

On February 1, 2000, Frank beat Donna because her car wouldn't start. The next day, the car was towed to a service station. On the evening of February 3, Donna picked up Frank at work and they got her car from the garage. When they arrived home, he told her to leave the car running, which she did, locking the doors for safety, thinking he had another set of keys. But Frank had left his keys in the car. Her suggestion that they ask the police for help made him angry. He finally unlocked the car with a knife.

Frank was seething because of the car episode. Wearing her housecoat over her pajamas for protection, Donna fell asleep with Frankie in her bed because she knew an assault was coming. Frank took their son back to his bed after midnight, then woke Donna and told her to come downstairs. After a brief argument centered around the fact that dinner had been late, he returned to the car episode and began to beat her on the head, kicking her repeatedly in the side as she crawled on all fours to get out of the living room, begging him to stop. Then he banged her head into the wall in the bathroom. Donna began to panic and felt she couldn't breathe. Suddenly, Frank withdrew. In the past, this would have been the end, he would be calm, and she would have been allowed to go to bed, he would have followed and had his way with her. But this time it was different. He wasn't calm. She knew something worse was going to happen. It flashed through her mind that she might run for the phone, but he was standing there. She remembers thinking they had a rotary phone and she would never be able to dial for help before he stopped her. She considered running down the stairs, but she had no car keys and the nearest stores were closed. Then he started beating her again without restraint, knocking her flat. Not only was the beating particularly severe, but that night, unlike other nights after a beating, he didn't have sex with her when they went to bed. Instead, he was strangely silent. She felt he had crossed an invisible barrier of resolve and thought "something terrible is going to happen."

When Donna awoke, it was the middle of the night. She took his gun from the chest near the bed and fired at him, then got Frankie and went downstairs. Not realizing the full significance of what had happened, she thought he would come after her unless she went up and got the gun. So she returned to the bedroom one last time.

Although the violence had ended earlier that night, removing Frank's gun and taking it down with her was an act of ownership. However small, it was the first act of independence in her new life.

The log book proved to be the turning point in the trial. I described how Frank had her record every detail of her day, including all expenditures. He would come home, have a few beers, call her downstairs, question her about each item, and then beat her for some error in judgment or recording. When I finished my account, the prosecutor confronted me directly. "Dr. Stark," he said with pointed sarcasm, "What if I told you that I have my wife keep all her expenditures on the computer and question her about them at the end of each week. Would you consider me a 'batterer?'" So caught up had he become in his recitation of his own ritual that he was unaware that the judge and jury were staring in disbelief. When he had returned to his seat, I simply sat still and waited, not replying. It took only a moment for him to hear the stunned silence in the courtroom and realize that his own incomprehension of what had occurred symbolized the state's. His case was lost.

To satisfy Frank's relatives, Donna accepted a short stay in a program run by the state for battered women. Her confidence restored, she returned to school to complete a college degree and briefly became an outspoken advocate for the rights of battered women. This rapid change was possible because her defense emphasized the strengths she exhibited against the brutal deprivation of her basic rights. She was liberated, though she still felt responsible for Frank's death.

10

FOR LOVE OR MONEY

The scam was simple. Laura Ferrucci was the bookkeeper for Bryant Air. Knowing the company frequently did business with the Davis Remodeling Company of West Haven, Laura's boyfriend, Nick Monsanto, opened a checking account for Davis Remodeling Company at his home address. Each month, when Laura paid the bills, she printed a check to the dummy company but excluded it from the bank statement. At first, either the president of Bryant or his wife signed the checks, mistaking the dummy company without the West Haven address for the legitimate business. Later Laura brought the checks home, Nick forged the president's name, and then deposited them in his account.

Three years after the scam began, a routine audit revealed an estimated $350,000 in missing funds. Laura admitted her role in the theft, but she claimed it was Nick's idea and that she had not personally benefited from the scheme. She had no prior criminal record and an exemplary history of steady employment, personal responsibility, and family care-giving. Still, her excuse seemed self-serving because Nick had been killed in a motorcycle accident several months before the theft was discovered. Even after his death, small amounts of money had been missing. Laura promised to sell her car and make good-faith efforts to repay the rest according to a schedule. But pressure from the company led to her being charged with larceny in the first degree. According to Dominic Lacotta, the company president, Laura's actions had destroyed the sense of family at his business. They had treated her like a "daughter" and she had "betrayed" them.

When we met, Laura was working as a secretary but had made little restitution. A few months before, in a suicidal gesture, she had taken what the psychiatrist at a local hospital called a "histrionic" (i.e., attention-seeking) overdose. She was diagnosed with major depression and a borderline personality disorder with histrionic and antisocial features. The psychiatric report also listed the death of her boyfriend, her legal troubles, and having been raped by her cousin on two occasions 4 years previously as major stressors and noted she was anorexic, having admitted to bulimic behavior for some years. Despite a tendency to "confound" or "conceal" her history, her psychiatrist also attributed the unusual detail she provided about other events and her adherence to certain peculiar housework rituals to an obsessive-compulsive personality disorder.

Laura's attorney asked me to assess whether she was a battered woman and so could adapt a duress defense. This defense is available in Connecticut if someone has engaged in proscribed conduct "because s(he) was coerced by the use or threatened imminent use of physical force . . . which force or threatened force of reasonable firmness in his situation would have been unable to resist."[1] Excluded from the defense are persons who "intentionally or recklessly" place themselves in situations in which it is probable that they will be subjected to duress.

There was no mention of domestic violence in Laura's records or police files, and Nick had no criminal record. She nonetheless provided an impressive history of physical abuse and intimidation throughout their 6-year relationship. She risked being beaten, even killed, if she refused to do as Nick instructed, she told me. Among other techniques, I use criteria-based content analysis to assess the internal validity of a client's account, looking for signs of rehearsal or repeated word or phrase patterns, for instance, noting whether she recalls extraneous details, a common response to trauma, or tries to conceal difficult material or minimize her own role in events.[2] I assess external credibility by comparing what I am told with what is known about woman battering as well as with eye-witness accounts or any documents in a case. By these standards, Laura's account was credible.

Laura understood I needed evidence for a duress defense. And she repeatedly admitted being terrified by Nick's violence. Even so, she insisted that she stole the money because she loved Nick and was afraid he would abandon her if she did not cooperate in his scheme. This was also the state's argument. We might lessen Laura's sentence by portraying her as an abuse victim. But "love" did not constitute "duress," however painful it might have been, because it meant she had willingly put herself in harm's way. Our only hope was to show that her "love," fear of abandonment, and dependence on Nick's approval were as much the consequences of his abuse as her fear of being hurt or killed.

Given Laura's history, a central issue in assessment was whether her actions were primarily the consequence of the abuse or of her psychiatric problems. I could counter the prosecutor's claim that she had fabricated the history of violence, in part because Nick assaulted Laura in public places. But the state's psychiatric expert posed a more formidable challenge. He would argue that borderline personality disorder (DSM-IV 301.83) included "a pervasive pattern of instability in interpersonal relationships" and "angry disruptions in close relationships" consistent with fights. Impulsivity is another prominent feature of persons with borderline personality. To avoid abandonment, they will take severe actions that go against deeply held moral scruples. Also common in borderline patients is a Manichaean view of the world in which some persons are idealized, others scorned. Given her idealization of Nick and her fears of his leaving, the psychiatrist would hold, it was not only possible that Laura had embezzled the funds, but probable that she did so voluntarily. Even more troubling was the most pronounced feature of a borderline disorder—a sense that the self is incomplete without the presence of another. This could explain both Laura's extreme dependence on Nick and why, to prevent abandonment, she had acted in ways that were contrary to her previous history and best judgment. Some borderline persons exhibit psychotic features. But the illness is rarely sufficient to support an insanity defense.

I was impressed (but not convinced) by the psychiatrist's assessment. One of our more dramatic findings from the Yale Trauma Studies was how often clinicians attributed the transient fears, recurrent suicide attempts, feelings of emptiness, and intense anger presented by battered women to a borderline personality disorder instead. These women were also thought to be attention seeking, histrionic, manipulative, or excessively emotional.

Laura's ritual behavior also complicated her defense. Persons with obsessive or compulsive traits are usually overly concerned with rules and morality and respectful to a fault of authority. But the state psychiatrist would point out that the same meticulous attention to detail reflected in the housework rituals characterized her embezzlement. Two other facts also made a claim of coercion problematic—that Nick and Laura lived apart during a significant portion of their relationship, including the period when most of the thefts occurred, and that she continued to embezzle small amounts of money after his death. A psychiatrist I consulted suggested the continued thefts were her "memorial" to Nick. When I shared this explanation with the public defender who had been Laura's original attorney, she admitted seeing a memorial-like construction in Laura's bedroom built from several of Nick's personal possessions, decorated with his photographs and surrounded by candles. Numerous clients profess love for the men who abuse them, write to them in jail, carry or sleep with mementoes, or enact rituals that symbolize their devotion even after they have killed them. But I suspected Laura's memorial represented something more.

The challenge posed by this case was a variation on the question left unanswered by our studies at Yale. Why would a strong-willed, intelligent, economically independent young women become so enmeshed with a man who hurt her that she put everything she valued at risk, including her life? The answer proved that the log book was no anomaly.

The Lists

In our first interview, Laura recounted the history of Nick's physical violence and intimidation. For our next session, she prepared what she called an "unfinished" narrative of more than 50 single-spaced pages about the relationship. Though the account was lively, the level of detail piqued my concern. I asked Laura whether she considered herself obsessive or compulsive. Without a pause, she answered, "Definitely." I asked what she did that fit these categories. Her CDs and cassettes were kept in alphabetical order, she admitted; her clothes were color coordinated and sorted by length in the closet; she vacuumed daily so "you can see the lines"; and "everything in the refrigerator is organized by size." She even alphabetized the food in the cupboards. I was impressed, particularly given the constant struggle against entropy in my own household. I had learned in my social work training that this sort of ritualistic pattern often becomes manifest in late adolescence. So I asked Laura if she had been this way in high school or at Smith College, where she graduated magna cum laude.

"Oh no," she smiled. "I was a complete slob."

Next, I asked her when this behavior started, a question the psychiatrists had apparently not put to her. This touched a nerve. She continued to look at me. But her eyes told me she was somewhere else. Then she was back, having retrieved whatever she was searching for. Without comment, she reached into the overstuffed briefcase she brought to our meetings and retrieved a sheath of pages from a yellow legal pad on which someone had written with magic marker in flowery script. With pages in hand, she stood up. Before this, her perkiness had seemed strained. Now, she put her all into the drama she enacted, shifting from Nick's voice to hers—sarcastic, bitter, and very funny.

"Shortly after we met," she began, "Nicky had started 'mentioning' little things around my house that could be done differently. 'Things just aren't in their right places!' he would say." Laura became Nick, shoulders back, chin down on her neck, standing on her toes, simulating his 6-foot frame and barrel chest.

> I laughed at the funny expressions he made. But he didn't think it was funny—it really bothered him. So much that he would have to stop whatever he was doing and move things to their "right spot." "Now leave it there! That's its home and it likes it!"
>
> This included everything from decorations to perfume bottles to items in the refrigerator. Mostly, I left things the way he wanted—it wasn't hurting anyone. The refrigerator was impossible to keep the same way all the time. Whatever I used last went into the closest available space—who in their right mind would stop and think "Did I put the milk in its right home?" (Then, again, who in their right mind would be telling you about this either?) I should have known better. Nick got furious and put everything back in "its home" and threw away anything that didn't fit. "Don't buy anything until

you run out of it—there's no room for anything else in there. It's just perfect the way it is, now that I'm done with it. Leave it this way!"

Now that he was on a roll, he decided to fix my whole house and correct my "misguided ways." He thought it would be good practice for me since "our" house would be run his way. Nick went into my bedroom with a legal pad, a marker, and a glass of water. I was not allowed to even stand near the door while he worked on the lists.

Four hours later, Nicky came bounding out of the bedroom holding up sheets of paper in each hand. I had always thought that he had a striking resemblance to Charlton Heston, but at that moment it was uncanny. He was Moses carrying down the Ten Commandments. I had to pull my feet up on the couch in case the rug started to divide. There was no way to contain my laughter, I was hysterical. Nicky even laughed with me for a little while. Then it was time to discuss the new rules. The pages were full of what Nick promised would be more than enough to keep me busy at home. As usual, he was right.

Laura stopped. The narrative was done. She handed me the lists. They were subdivided by room and by tasks:

Living Room
- vacuum daily "so you can always see the lines"
- remove cocky picture of naked lady
- potpourri with floral scent—1 liquid on each end table and 1 dry on top of TV
- NO Bozworth [Laura's dog] on the couch
- CDs and cassettes in alphabetical order
- everything kept clean, neat, and in its place

Dining Room
- vacuum daily "so you can always see the lines"
- table always set with ONLY two settings
- fresh flowers daily so scent will mix with living room
- always eat at table, even when alone
- everything kept clean, neat, and in its place

Kitchen
- cupboards kept in alphabetical order and faced
- refrigerator sorted by size and faced—as instructed!
- fully stocked shelf just for Nicky (lots of Hostess surprises!)
- no dishes left on counters or in sink . . . wash and put away immediately
- small plastic bag under sink for wet, messy garbage . . . to be emptied daily!
- plastic garbage bags can be used outside in cans to combine everything
- throw out anything that doesn't match . . . better to do without than look like a pauper!
- everything kept clean, neat, and in its place

Bedroom
- vacuum daily "so you can see the lines"
- closets color-coordinated and sorted by length
- dressers symmetrical with only perfume, 2 pictures (Nick plus Poppy), and nail polish
- drawers in order of the way things are put on
- telephone, answering machine, notepad, pencil, 1 book, and 1 picture of Nick on nightstand
- bed made first thing every morning
- sheets changed every Sunday morning
- 2 upright cushions, 2 throw pillows, 2 ruffled throw pillows, and 1 stuffed animal from Nick on bed
- shoes on closet floor . . . matched, clean, and color-coordinated
- belts hung from closet door . . . color-coordinated
- everything kept clean, neat, and in its place

Bathroom
- towels matching and hung evenly
- apple-cinnamon potpourri over toilet
- toilet seat always left down
- shower curtain always closed
- all personal items kept in closet or under sink . . . out of sight!
- Johnson's baby powder . . . only!
- everything kept clean, neat, and in its place

Spare Room
- vacuum daily "so you can always see the lines"
- closet with dresses or work clothes . . . color-coordinated and by length
- dress shoes on floor . . . matched, clean, and color-coordinated
- wall organizer for gym accessories
- bed should have same sheets on it . . . or else!
- everything kept clean, neat, and in its place

House Rules
- NO MEN IN THE HOUSE!
- NO MEN ON THE TELEPHONE!
- NO PICTURES OF MEN (except Nick, God, or Poppy)
- BE A GOOD GIRL AT ALL TIMES

The lists were an epiphany, a unique piece of archeological evidence that honed in on the microdynamics of gender. Donna's log book was self-administered, with few explicit instructions on what to enter. Although she rarely avoided punishment altogether, she could fabricate entries. The last instruction on the lists, to be a good girl at all times, was similarly open-ended and pointed toward an all-encompassing level of evaluation and punishment. But the other rules were inflexible. Suddenly, the endless petty complaints about their wives from men in my groups took on ominous significance. Here, in Nick's writing, were all of the behaviors the psychiatrists had interpreted as evidence of Laura's obsessive compulsion. He had not only managed to transfer his "rules" to her, but had her make them her own. But how?

In themselves, the lists explained very little. If Laura thought the rules were ridiculous, a jury would wonder why she obeyed them. The lists could be used to symbolize Nick's influence over her, and so be linked to the embezzlement, particularly if we could show that she obeyed his instructions because she feared his violence. Because the psychiatrists never asked about Nick's threats or violence, they assumed the rituals were rooted in Laura's personality, inadvertently reinforcing the mantra Nick had repeated ad nauseum—that she was crazy, not him. Threats and violence were certainly important pieces of the puzzle. But coercion alone did not adequately explain why Laura internalized the rules as her own and continued to enact them—and derive a certain satisfaction from their enactment—after Nick's death, just as she continued to steal small sums. By making rules part of her self-system, Laura gave them a life of their own. But the prosecution psychiatrist would interpret this as yet another tribute to Nick rooted in her love.

I was to learn that Laura's rituals, like her participation in the embezzlement scheme, were defensive adaptations to three aspects of Nick's coercive control: isolation from potential sources of support, the extension of his control through social space, and control over the microdynamics of her everyday life. The lists were rooted in his morbid jealousy. Nick supported his rules for the bedroom by marking the bed frame so he could tell if the bed was used. Laura had to discard any pictures of other men, rewrite her address book (which he would check weekly for men's phone numbers), and if "he ever heard a man's voice on the phone, he would turn around and leave without a word—just a glare of hatred on his face (Another week of punishment!)." By the time Laura implemented the embezzlement scheme, little in her life was her own. Everything she had, did, or thought was evaluated by Nick's rules. Even her pocketbook would be searched regularly for "evidence" so Nick would "know if I was doing something different in my routine." He kept a record of her long-distance calls. Like the husband of the Emmy winner described earlier, he would call any number he didn't recognize.

"What do you have to hide from me?" he would ask. "If you loved me there would be no secrets."

Because of his control, Laura conducted her daily life even when she was alone according to Nick's sense of how it should be; because of isolation, she could not access alternative ways of being. I would also learn that by making his reality hers, she not only capitulated to his coercive control; she also sustained herself. Taking in Nick's persona degraded Laura. But it also proved vital to her survival in the face of coercive control.

Family Background

From a clinical standpoint, Laura's family history of significant loss, isolation, abandonment, and traumatic violence would be sufficient to explain her dependence, fear of abandonment, idealization of Nick as a parental substitute, and affection for someone who was hurting her.

Laura's biological father was a drug addict and mental patient. When she was still a baby, he was found hung in prison, though his "suicide" was in suspicious proximity to a beating by police. The trauma this caused the family was still apparent. After Laura was sentenced unexpectedly to a short prison term, the court clerk brought her watch, necklace, and other personal items to her mother who was waiting in the hallway. Flashing back to her husband's imprisonment, the mother collapsed in shock. After her father's death, Laura and her mother moved in with her grandparents and cousins, and she assumed responsibility for her mother's care and happiness while she herself was "looked after" by her cousins, particularly her cousin Stanley, whom she considered her brother.

Her mother remarried, and Laura initially idealized John, her new stepfather. But when they started another family while she was in high school, she felt pushed aside, developed a serious asthma condition, and exhibited anorexia, almost certainly as a somatic manifestation of her feelings of rejection and her need for attention. After high school, she moved briefly to Louisiana to live with an aunt, but she returned to nurse her grandfather during a terminal illness, feeling at his death that she had again lost a father. By this time, relationships with her mother and stepfather had deteriorated so significantly that when she briefly moved back home after a failed engagement, John assaulted her, breaking her wrist, injuring her ribs, and leaving a permanent scar on her throat where he choked her. Laura had John arrested and got a restraining order to keep him out of the house. But charges were dismissed, he and Laura's mother resumed their relationship, and Laura moved out permanently.

It would be difficult to imagine three more dramatic acts of parental rejection than her father's suicide, her stepfather's assault, and her mother's choice to take John back. Because she had prematurely had to care for the two people to whom she felt closest, her mother and her grandfather, she had learned to keep her own feelings locked up, to remain detached to a certain degree, expecting very little in the way of caring from others, a problem that was linked to the attention-getting (histrionic) facets of the eating disorder and her difficulty reading the early signs of danger in her relationship with Nick. Many of the feelings she described suggested early onset depression, a diagnosis that appeared periodically in her psychiatric history alongside the anorexia. Laura had repeatedly been betrayed by her real family. It was possible she was unconsciously using the embezzlement to enact a revenge fantasy against or to guard against a repeat betrayal by the family that formed around her at work.

But this negative assessment omits the critical fact that Laura countered the abandonment by her primary family by developing a powerful attachment to her extended family—"the Ferruccis stand united"—which gave her the resiliency she needed to finish high school against extraordinary odds, find a job, establish an independent household as a teen, move to an aunt's in Louisiana, stand alone in pressing charges against her stepfather, and graduate from Smith with honors. Moreover, although Laura became somewhat disassociated in times of emotional pain, she coped well when relationships with other significant men in her life had gone sour. Her strength and independence were evident when, just 2 weeks after rejection by a fiancé in October 1995, she moved into her own apartment—the first home that was hers alone. Then, she encountered Nick Monsanto.

The Relationship

The Beginnings

Laura met Nick on Halloween night in 1995 at a singles bar. Without warning, a tall, "stunning" man grabbed her from behind, pulled her under his Halloween costume and held her there, despite her hitting him with her fists and screaming. He pursued her outside the bar, kissed her roughly when she refused to give him her number, and had to be pulled off by two bouncers. Nick took a second coincidental meeting as an omen that she belonged to him, talked of marriage, and told her he would never let her go. Laura was moved by his good looks and interpreted his persistence romantically. He called her that night at 3 a.m. and insisted she talk him to sleep, which she did. From then on, if he could not get to sleep, it was her fault. His calling followed a ritual: after he returned home from a bar, he would ask whether she was alone then conclude, "Don't hang up until I start snoring or I'll kill you." Or, also in the middle of the night, he demanded she come to his house for sex, making up incredible stories if she demurred. His calls increased in frequency, sometimes to one an hour. The fact that she would do "anything" for him was a sign of her love.

The fact that Laura had confused attention with caring early in her life may have led her to confuse Nick's need for proof of loyalty and his jealous rages (which ended with a backhanded slap followed by roses) with love. Once, she got furious when she found him with another woman. In response, he screamed that he would kill her if he caught her with another man. Nick or his friends assaulted other men Laura dated. When they argued, Nick would beg Laura to apologize. If she didn't recant, his tone would change and he'd tell her he would kill her if she didn't. But Laura liked the security his attention afforded. Unlike the other men she had known, here was a man who would stick around.

Their sexual relationship was also volatile. Nick refused to use condoms. One time he grabbed her, threw her on the table and had sex, breaking the table. They broke off on several occasions, though he would still call regularly. Then, one night, Laura's "best friend" and "brother" since childhood, her cousin Stanley, sexually assaulted her, sending her into a psychological tailspin. She moved out of her apartment, distanced herself from Nick, and found a male roommate, though not a lover.

Despite its sharp fluctuations and Nick's occasional resort to violence when he was jealous, up to this point, their relationship resembled many others in which the struggle for power and autonomy are dominant themes. Although the violence was only initiated by Nick and designed to hurt or punish rather than merely resolve differences, it was usually precipitated by disputes in which Laura was an active player. She demanded Nick meet the same standards of loyalty he imposed on her, used anger and breaking things off periodically to negotiate for change, and dated other men. This level of independence was unbearable to Nick. As a result, during the following 8 months, he established the regime of coercive control.

Laura cautiously reconstructed her social life after being raped by her cousin. She worked briefly at a local health club. Then, she took the job as a bookkeeper for Bryant Air. She was working out at the gym and made a host of friends among her new co-workers.

Nick got her number at the new job and began calling her regularly. When he discovered she had a male roommate, he flew into a jealous rage and abused and insulted her. Instead of backing down, she told him to leave if he didn't trust her. He apologized, cried, and they reconciled. Laura agreed to move. She moved into her boss's brother's house, one basis for the claim her co-workers were her new "family."

When Laura complained about "rough sex," Nick announced a rule of abstinence because their love was "sacred." For the first time, they were able to share as "friends," though Nick still called her every hour at work or at home until late at night when he was usually drunk.

During this period—and immediately following a minor assault—Nick introduced the lists. He had already established rules to test Laura's loyalty. She had to dress according to his standards; wear her hair a certain way; go to work, the gym, and home, nothing more; and was forbidden to talk about her day if it involved contact with another man. He began calling the gym, then demanded she call before leaving for the gym and when she got home or she would be forbidden to go there. If any rule was violated, there was a fight, he would hit her, then give her the silent treatment for several days. She had to memorize and abide by the rules. If she did what he told her, she was a "good girl," particularly if she remained home, answered his calls, and accepted his chronic put-downs without protest. If there was the slightest variation—for instance, if she cursed at all—she was a "bad girl" and got the beating and the isolation she "deserved."

The beatings were rarely severe—usually involving a slap or a single punch—but they were humiliating. Laura felt even more devastated when Nick cut her off. But this reflected the anxiety of not knowing when he would reappear, not her personality problems. She was beginning to feel extremely insecure about whether she was meeting his expectations when he wasn't around. She was still seeing some friends and her co-workers. But even when she was alone with them, she felt she was "on" with Nick. Now these limited contacts were also restricted, and he became her major source of personal contact with the outside world, her leader, as he put it. When he was absent or cut off contact, she felt directionless and empty, feelings that meshed with her anorexia. Her personal security required that he be pleased with her, as if she were a POW or a hostage. In a classic conditioned response, she imagined the consequences if she did something bad when she was alone and was frightened, identifying his approval with safety. But pleasing Nick was nearly impossible. Because his rules and judgments were driven by his chronic insecurity, his alcoholism, and his unpredictable mood swings, they were no more predictable, internally consistent, or clear than the rules governing Donna's entries in the log book. Increasingly his addiction to gambling shaped his demands, particularly with respect to money. He might "explode" at any time and without warning, going from clam or an apology to rage in an instant.

Material Control

Laura's proof of loyalty only made Nick more distrustful. He checked her address book weekly for men's phone numbers, and listened for men's voices on her answering machine. The jealousy—which she now realized extended way beyond love—provided a context for Nick assuming control over her material resources. He went through her checkbook, questioning each withdrawal or expenditure. He approved all her bills (or she couldn't pay them) and reviewed all her long-distance calls, calling numbers he didn't recognize. When she challenged him, he would tell her, "What do you have to hide from me?" "I'm doing it for your own good . . . someone needs to take care of you. You make me crazy like this."

He insisted she pay full attention while he was talking. If he felt she did not, he would grab her, pull her hair, and drag her across the room or bounce her across the room using his chest. Or he would reach out when she was walking by and grab her by the hair.

At Christmas, after Nick failed to get credit for a car stereo, he demanded she apply. When Laura was also denied, he insisted she use her expected Christmas bonus for the radio. Her being turned down for credit was a signal: he took her checkbook and made a list of how to budget. Trying to ward off humiliation, Laura made up a counterlist of ways to economize that highlighted the absurdity of Nick's rules, including getting a roommate, and staying late at the office to get overtime pay, things she knew Nick opposed. Instead of being amused, this time he beat her severely. Then he refused to see or talk to her for days, calling when she wasn't home and leaving long abusive messages on the machine, until she removed the machine. Several nights later, she found her car blocked in by his. Then he called to tell her she would stay in until the "answering machine was fixed." The next day she found a rose in her front seat. Laura found these apologies even more terrifying than Nick's threats.

Whenever she planned to do something with family or friends, he described them as sluts or whores and told her he didn't want her near them. In his view, "everyone was trying to break us up."

The Embezzlement Scheme

Work was a safety zone for Laura. She took pride in doing a job well and maintaining relations with co-workers Nick didn't "own." Work became a major arena of struggle. Nick was jealous of her male co-workers and enraged by her working overtime, a sign of her independence. Although Nick needed money to support his gambling, the embezzlement scheme was designed initially to sabotage Laura's support at work and the moments of autonomy she experienced at the gym and with her co-workers. Nick wanted to be her "boss" at Bryant Air as well as her leader away from work. Obedience to any other boss was out of the question.

Nick was now slapping Laura almost every day they were together. Based on the frequent marks and bruises she carried, even his friends told her he didn't care for her. Oddly, despite the signs and hourly calls at work, her boss and co-workers said nothing.

When Nick introduced her budget, she broke things off again. During this lull, she agreed to loan her aunt the Christmas bonus. Instead of getting furious, Nick had an alternative plan to see "how much you really love me." He "tested" Laura's willingness to break the law with a fraudulent scheme to get a stereo. He stole the stereo, then enlisted Laura to return it for a refund, which she did, even without the receipt. When she passed this test, he carefully instructed her on how to print a check to the fabricated company that was in his name at the bank. He was now gambling as well as drinking regularly. Although she made excuses to prevent committing another crime, she ultimately printed additional checks to which he signed the name of her boss's mother. Laura intercepted the checks so they weren't included with the bank statement. With her friendships and sense of security undermined, she felt as scared (and constantly on guard) at work as she did at home.

From Control to Domination

If Laura's isolation set the context for the embezzlement scheme, its initiation was followed by an escalation of physical abuse and the extension of Nick's control to every area of her life. Her resistance was now circumscribed by her complete material and psychological entrapment.

Laura argued with Nick repeatedly about the checks. In response, he blackened her eyes, slammed her against walls, punched her in the kidneys and ribs—always "for your own good." She made him do it, Nick claimed, because her thoughts of disloyalty, of being a bad girl, made him "crazy." Laura's anger mounted. But so did her desire to win his approval or at least not to displease him. Now, the silent treatment made Laura panic, feelings she mistook for love and fear of abandonment. Even so, her courage returned during a hiatus in their relationship and her protests escalated. One night, after his falling asleep delayed their going out, she told him "I hate this . . . I want this to end." He acknowledged her pain but wanted to make things work. Then he said he needed a check to fix his house. She refused and he "flipped," backhanded her, knocked her against the car, and punched her. She gave him a check, which he forged several days later.

In 1998, to feed his compulsive gambling, he took more than $10,000 from her account in addition to the fraudulent checks. On other occasions, he simply took her wallet or chased her around the room and took her pocketbook. His license plate read "MoMoney."

When knee surgery made it impossible for Laura to use a standard transmission, she bought a Ford Probe using stolen money for the down payment, the first time she had benefited from the thefts. She secretly considered this a "loan" for the money he had taken from her. Now, a new set of rules covered such minute details as having to clean her car wheels every night, use strawberry fragrance twice a day in the car, and clean hard to reach spots with cotton swabs. Then, Nick made her exchange the Probe for an Altima.

Nick called Laura before work, every hour throughout the day, when she got home from work, and before he went to bed. She had to call for permission before going anywhere. He filled the answering machine tape so no one could leave messages. Then, he forced her to change her telephone number so other men wouldn't call.

He had occasionally blocked her car in as punishment; now he did this nightly, moving the car in the morning so she could go to work. Before doing this, he checked the house, the car, and the clothes she wore for work (making sure she was wearing a slip, for instance). By the end of 1997, she had to dress exactly as he wanted. Once when she was wearing a T-shirt through which he could see her bra, he ripped it off. On another occasion, he tore off her bathing suit because he didn't want her to wear a bikini. If she failed any test, he would backhand her. When she wore her favorite shorts to a house warming, he cursed her, beat her, then put her head through the garage window.

The Beeper Game: Control Extends Through Social Space

The penultimate symbol of Laura's entrapment was "the beeper game," a variant on a form of control commonly used by drug dealers with their girl-friends in inner-city neighborhoods. Laura was to wear Nick's beeper, particularly when she was with friends. He would page her as often as every 5 minutes to check up on her. For the game, Nick would leave callback numbers on her beeper and she would have to guess their significance. For instance, he would leave "911" or the police number and she would have to guess what would happen to her if she called for help. Or he would beep in the number of a local department store and she would have to guess what new shirt he wanted. He reviewed the numbers on her beeper. Once she refused to turn over the beeper to him, and he slammed her against the car.

Nick was particularly jealous of Laura's dog, Boz. Boz was not allowed on the couch or in the car, and she was forbidden to pet him while Nick was over. When Nick found a *Playgirl* calendar in Laura's house, he punched her in the kidneys and knocked her down. She was beaten again for renting the video *9 1/2 Weeks*, which Nick believed was "inappropriate" because of its explicit sex. When his mother was away on trips to Florida or Italy, Nick demanded Laura cook for him, his father, and his brother. He would specify what he wanted, say, baked ziti, and tell her exactly how much space it should occupy in the refrigerator. If it didn't fit exactly or he didn't want it, he threw it on the ground.

Laura mounted what resistance she could, trying repeatedly to break things off. At the end of April 1998, while she was still on crutches from the first knee surgery, she told him she was no longer attracted to him and things should end. He was supposed to drive her to her mother's for a 1-hour visit. He arrived late and so drunk that one eye was still closed, like Popeye, she recalls. He pinned her in the corner of the kitchen, pushed her up against the wall, put his face in hers, then told her, "I knew you were still attracted to me, think about that all day, bitch," and walked out. In the summer of 1998, he gave her a pre-engagement diamond ring to scare other men away. He told her it would be buried with her.

Nick would lock her in the basement when she was tanning. Then he would come down, pull down her pants, and check the tan line to make sure she was truthful. He checked the page numbers in her book nightly to make sure she was home in bed reading.

In August 1998, Laura got her second knee surgery. When she returned home, he carried her to the bathroom, then checked the answering machine in the bedroom. Because her friend Michael had called from Australia, he smashed the machine, then left.

In September, Laura was still on crutches. When she appeared at a local bar with his cousin's sweatshirt around her waist, he jumped her on the dance floor, requiring five bouncers to pull him off. Later that night he attacked another friend for talking to her, throwing a beer bottle at him, and she left, furious, for her car. The bartender sent Nick's friend Jason to help her to the car, but Nick threw him against the wall. Laura was terrified and began screaming and swinging her crutches at him. He threw her crutches across the street and told her, "this is no game." Then he slammed her against the wall and punched her, leaving her screaming as he walked away. At 3 A.M. the next morning, he broke into her house and pinned new rules to her bed, including "no drinking ever again." He took her phones and her car so she would "have time to think about your behavior."

Total Isolation

So completely did Nick regulate Laura's social contacts that her birthday gift in January 1999 was permission for her to go out. He ordered a limo and told her to invite three of her girlfriends. He had the car come to his house first. When they got in the car there was a package with a card and instructions to "ask the driver for the rules." The rules concerned where they could go, what they could do, and when they were to be home. Written on the window was "I love you. Happy birthday." A few weeks later, a Chrysler salesman they met told them he recognized her car and that she had been going "fast." Nick punched her in the leg and then drove recklessly to teach her a lesson. When she begged him to stop, he backhanded her. Then he told her he had a silver bullet to kill her with if he caught her cheating. She tried to make a joke out of the threat, telling him a silver bullet was for werewolves and he should use a hollow bullet. He beat her for being a "wise ass," then told her he would kill her before getting a "divorce." Any infringement of his rules resulted in a beating. When he caught her wearing a stick-on tattoo, he ripped her shirt off, dragged her by the hair to the bathroom, then rubbed the alcohol on her arm so hard it bled. "No tattoo ever" was the new rule.

Her going to the gym was already limited to one evening a week. In early 1999, he forbade her to go altogether. In March, fearing she would meet men or discuss her situation with co-workers, she was forbidden to go out for lunch during work. He would have lunch and dinner with her, then go drinking with his friends. She was to cut her hair and forbidden to wear makeup or hair spray. Restrictions for going out now shifted from one night per week to one night per month, and he specified the places she could go. When she saw an old boyfriend, Nick arranged a drive-by shooting by his friend.

By spring 1999, Laura was desperately trying to break things off. In response, on one occasion, he said he would leave. "See ya," he said. She started to watch TV. Nick threw rocks at the screen. Then she saw him, like a kid, curled up on the porch. She walked into another room. Suddenly, he broke down the door, came after her throat, threw her against the wall, backhanded her, and kicked her. She was screaming for him to stop. "Now you know you're mine," he told her. She could barely walk and had bruises all over her face and was forced to take time off from work.

She was not allowed to buy anything without his permission and had to save all receipts from purchases for him to review. Nick decided Laura was not to repair her car because it was "man's work." He had lied to her about ordering tint, so she ordered it herself. This infuriated him. He came looking for her, broke her screen door, then, finding no one home, searched the parking lots until he found her with a girlfriend, grabbed her by the hair, pulled her to his truck, and took her home. After he chased her around the house, she pushed the couch into his groin and yelled that he had lied about the tint. In response, he put his fist through her car windshield.

Intimidation

When she ordered a car phone and went to have it installed, the installer told her "Nick said to blow up your car." Nick forbade Laura to spend Easter 1999 with her family. As a compromise, they agreed she would cook food for her family and he would drop it off. Because he got drunk and wasn't home, he failed to pick her up. She sat at home in the dark, crying and embarrassed to tell her family what happened, until he called from New York City and told her to wait. At two or three in the afternoon, she went over to give his mother a cake. Nick was practically unconscious, told her to get him a glass of water, "don't make too much noise," and to put the water to his lips, yelling at her when she stopped. When he jumped up suddenly to stop the phone ringing, he knocked over a shoe box containing notes on all his other girlfriends. When she told him how hurt she was, he knocked her off the bed and kicked her in the back, and she went flying.

Nick owned two guns and was taking shooting lessons. "I imagine your face on the target," he told her. Each hole was something that she had done to make him mad. On one occasion, they were arguing in his room. Suddenly, he pushed her down, off the bed, kneeled on top of her chest, put the gun against her head, and told her she could never leave him or he would kill her. Then, he announced, "It's over with."

The Monday before Nick died, she saw a senile couple on *The Dating Game* and decided she didn't want to end like this. They drove to the beach, and she told him it was over. He cried and told her she couldn't leave. She agreed to give him another chance. Later, she discovered a tape recorder under the seat.

The night he died, they had a fight, and she again told him it was over. He threatened to kill her. Then he went out and began drinking. After each shot, he called her, until he could barely speak. He was killed in a motorcycle accident, driving with a woman in back.

Postmortem

It took several months for Laura to believe Nick was gone. Apart from guilt at causing his death—Nick's friend left a note on her beeper blaming her—her entire life was conducted according to his rules. She was still color coordinating her skirts when we met, keeping her CDs in alphabetical order, even vacuuming (if less often) "until you can see the lines." She continued to steal small amounts of money.

Nick assaulted Laura several hundred times, at some points slapping her or pulling her hair every day. He also raped, kicked, choked, and punched her and threw her into walls, dragged her across the floor, and knocked her senseless. Yet she never required medical care and never called the police. Had she done so, Nick would have been arrested, because these events occurred in a city with an aggressive police response. Even so, unless the theft had been uncovered, he would not have spent more than 24 hours in jail and, like Philip Traficonda, would undoubtedly have assaulted Laura more seriously when he got out. Given her psychiatric history, it is unlikely that clinicians would have taken her reports of abuse seriously. Nick frequently warned that he would kill Laura if she did not obey him. The presence of gun, his target practice, the announcement that he had silver bullets reserved for her, his detailed accounts of how he would kill her, and his putting the gun to her head made his threats credible. Even today, it is highly unlikely that police or the courts would package these acts as a serious crime. Apart from the several attempts to protect Laura by Jason, none of the numerous friends or co-workers who witnessed the abuse or its consequences called police or intervened to prevent it. At the trial, I emphasized the irony presented by the lack of support Laura received from her "family" at work, asking rhetorically whether such neglect typified how they treated a "daughter."

The Psychological Profile

Laura reported a number of symptoms of PTSD, including flashbacks, startle sensations in response to sudden movement or noises, low self-esteem, distrust of men, a fragile sense of boundaries, continued insecurity about personal safety, hypervigilance, and chronic anxiety. She was fearful of going out at night and of driving, had poor concentration, jumped when people approached her from behind or suddenly, suffered from sleeplessness and nightmares, and continued to enact many of the rules on the lists. She regularly conversed with Nick's ghost. As surprising as this may sound, however, her day-to-day functioning was remarkably unimpaired. She was performing well at a new job, had reestablished close relationships with her mother and stepfather, was appropriately oriented toward her current reality, and could discuss her history objectively, with humor, and showed anger and sadness when appropriate. Her capacity to soothe herself with self-talk was remarkable, and she continually reminded herself that Nick was dead and that his ghost was her own creation, though she had difficulty adjusting her behavior at home to these insights.

Laura adapted to the combination of coercion and control she faced by reestablishing a familiar childhood script, distancing herself from her physical self, stepping outside her body, and functioning through significant phases of her relationship—particularly after the thefts began—as if none of this was truly happening to her. She was periodically anxious and depressed during the relationship and had suffered chronic fatigue, an almost infantile desire to please Nick, feelings of helplessness, an obsessive concern with following his rules, and low self-esteem. When her defenses failed to protect her or numb her fears, she minimized her danger. Sometimes her fear of Nick was paralyzing; at other times, she was overwhelmed by fear he would abandon her. Periodically, her defensive depression gave way to rage. Although Nick's drunken binges made him vulnerable, Laura never bought a weapon or contemplated using one. Still, had he lived, it is likely that, if he hadn't killed her, she might have killed him or herself. Laura's suicidal gesture was rooted in a range of feelings occasioned by Nick's death, including unspent rage, emptiness, feelings of abandonment, and guilt both at causing his death and at the relief it occasioned.

With the exception of the lists and the beeper game, Laura's predicament resembled the subjugation of dozens of the battered women in my practice. Far from being "predisposed" to abuse by her previous history, Laura had never been abused by other boyfriends and stood up to her stepfather's abuse despite the family crisis it precipitated. At the same time, Nick's coercive control played off psychological currents in her past. Psychotherapy and medication have helped her resolve or manage her most prominent symptoms, though she clings tenaciously to her eating disorder.

By contrast with Laura, Nick presented a classic composite of borderline, histrionic, narcissistic, obsessive, and compulsive traits. Given his history of alcohol and gambling, the fantasies evident in his pathological jealousy, frequent bar fights, and his pronounced paranoia, he may have been actively delusional. But however dysfunctional, Nick's intense passions and good looks gave him sufficient charisma to command intense loyalty, even from male friends like Jason whom he had consistently mistreated. His friends described Nick as "nuts." But they meant this as a sign of respect, even of affection, and they blamed Laura for his death. After he died, friends left death threats and other messages on Laura's phone that suggested they shared her feelings of extreme dependence and abandonment. As a local businessman, Nick's father was able to help him get a number of part-time jobs, and he had many girlfriends. Unless they commit a dramatic crime, men like Nick rarely encounter the mental health or justice system. Within the Italian working-class world he inhabited, his eccentricities, even his outbursts of violence, fell well within the range of acceptable male behavior.

Nick's Coercive Control

If Laura's background contributed at least as much to her resilience as to her dependence on Nick, how can we explain the most intriguing facet of this case, her complete incorporation of the rules he laid down in her enactment of gender? I have already referred to sociologist Beth Richie's analysis of gender entrapment, where black women, frustrated by racism in the labor market, displace their skills to make things work in abusive relationships. Like these women, Laura initially believed she could apply the same survival skills to Nick she had used successfully to survive a family history of abuse and abandonment and to care for her mother and grandfather. Although she recognized the risks involved in a relationship with him from their first fortuitous meeting at the bar when he pulled her under his cape, she also found his all-consuming attention appealing, at least initially, and believed his abuse derived from the extreme vulnerability to rejection reflected in his frequent bouts of crying and pleas for acceptance. But these dynamics had far less influence on Laura's reactions than the structural dependence Nick imposed by appropriating her money, monitoring her time and behavior, isolating her from critical supports, and using threats and violence to neutralize the possibility of resistance to his control. With coercive control in place, Nick could parcel out resources or opportunities for social contact in exchange for Laura's obedience, the process driven home by the lists. Nick's threats and violence terrified her at times. Still, in the face of threats to kill her, she was strong enough to tell him it was over just before he died. Laura consented to the embezzlement scheme, as she claimed, because her fear that Nick would abandon her was greater than her fear of his violence if he remained or of what might happen if she was caught. As symbolized by the beeper game, this fear was a by-product of Nick's success in extending his control to the most distal facets of Laura's life, including her relations at work, at the gym, and with her extended family. In doing this, he cut her off so completely from alternative sources of information and support that his reality became hers and pleasing him, winning his approval, became the source of her self-assessment as well as the sole guarantor of her safety. With the social moorings of an autonomous identity pulled from under her, Laura felt empty, a feeling to which she responded by making enactment of the domestic rituals the center of her being, seemingly replacing her self with a degraded persona built from Nick's erratic needs. In Nick's abandonment, she faced a psychological death that she dreaded more than physical death.

The Generality and Particularity of Nick's Control

Like the coerced persuasion used with hostages or to brainwash POWs, the abrogation of Laura's most basic liberties was the backdrop for securing her compliance. Prominent among Nick's tactics were those on Amnesty International's chart of coercion, including isolation, monopolization of perception, "induced debility and exhaustion," threats, occasional indulgences, demonstrating omnipotence, degradation, and enforcing trivial demands. Two common torture tactics were particularly effective against Laura's resistance—frequent "tests" that pitted her desire to be proved "loyal" against her moral scruples and the selective use of punishment and rewards. Even if she failed these tests, as she occasionally did, taking risks to win his approval conditioned her to put his demands before her own safety.

But Laura was not Nick's hostage. Critical to the control exercised in classic capture crimes is the process called "role stripping." Prisoners, mental patients, POWs are removed from their familiar setting, their personal possessions are confiscated, and their movements are tightly circumscribed through literal confinement and formally administered rules. Along with other means of social debasement, the social distance between captor and captive is maintained in these instances by using a uniform, number, or other stigmatic designation such as a psychiatric diagnosis to replace the victim's established identity.[3] Compliance is helped in this situation by continued promises of freedom, even if this only means special rations, privileges, or a temporary respite from pain. Nick's control was constructed in Laura's home, at her work, and at other social settings (such as the gym or the bar where she went with her cousins) that were not merely familiar but where she could reasonably expect support if threatened. Although Nick used various nicknames for Laura, it was her own name that felt increasingly alien. The rules applied to hostages depersonalize them; Laura's entrapment was intensely personal, driving her ever more deeply into the microcosms of her normal routine rather than removing her from it. The issue of social distance between controller and victim is much more complicated in situations involving coercive control than it is in where captor and captive are from different worlds. Nick refused to allow her to establish any significant social distance from him, disregarding her efforts to break things off, maintaining telephone contact throughout the night, stalking her, assaulting or arranging for an assault on her friends, and finally ensuring that any relationships at work would be mediated through him. Laura needed his permission to have other relationships, he dictated their form (as in the case of her birthday gift), and continually intruded in her social life through the beeper game. Once the embezzlement began, the danger of being exposed was a continual barrier to closeness, at least with her co-workers, the only other persons she saw regularly apart from her cousins.

Laura continually contested the social distance Nick sought to impose at a level that would be impossible in an institutional setting or POW camp. If she initially interpreted his disrespect for her boundaries as love, when she recognized that his persistent intrusions on her time threatened her autonomy, even when they were separated, she demanded equal rights, including the right to see other persons, a gambit that enraged Nick. He ended their sexual relationship, in part so he could pursue other women. But social distance posed serious problems to his maintaining control. He could keep her from going to the gym and under surveillance at the mall and other public places. But Laura continued to earn a living, a fact on which he depended to support his addictions, and to live independently, a reality about which he could do little if he hoped to continue gambling, drinking, and partying. These realities destabilized his coercive control and allowed Laura to periodically break things off, resist him physically on occasion, argue, laugh at him, refuse him money, join the gym, move in with a male roommate, recruit someone (her cousin, Jason, or Nick's other friends) to protect her, and establish other relationships, particularly at work. Resistance often led to beatings. But on several occasions, Nick backed down in his requests or renegotiated the terms of compliance, as when he substituted the stereo test for the bonus check Laura loaned to her aunt. In Donna's case, this tension was largely resolved when she lost her job at the bank, causing her relationship with Frank to implode. But in this case, instability forced Nick to innovate by raising the intensity and extensiveness of his tactical control, sharply distinguishing the dynamic here from the comparatively static, predictable nature of other capture crimes. Because Nick could not completely isolate Laura without hurting himself, he had to enter and reconstitute her relations in the spaces where she enjoyed relative autonomy, and he did so by using loyalty tests, hourly phone calls, the beeper game, and by expanding the lists to behaviors outside the home. The embezzlement scheme synthesized these contradictory themes, forcing Laura to exercise her relative liberties at work by making choices that jeopardized her autonomy and freedom.

Spatial Dimensions of Control

Chapter 4 emphasizes that the persistence of the controlling partner better explains the durability of abusive relationships than a victim's inclination to stay or her ambivalence. This case illustrates how the extension of control through social space makes it possible to maintain dominance without physical proximity. On several occasions before she feared his abandonment, Laura capitulated to Nick's demands to resume their relationship. But it was Nick who clung to the relationship through thick and thin. His dependence on Laura had complex emotional and psychosexual overtones. Like many men in my practice, even as he feared closeness, Nick craved attachment, loyalty, devotion, and approval as well as behavioral compliance. When she pulled away, he panicked, tightening his control and increasing his abuse, a strategy guaranteed to heighten her alienation. Still, the psychological complexities should not overshadow the substantial material benefits that provided the principal motive for Nick to subvert any attempt to break things off.

The Controller's Dilemma

Prisoners often accommodate captivity by adapting the captors' perspective as their own, as was famously illustrated by Jews who became surrogates ("capos") for Nazi guards in the concentration and death camps. More complicated parallels are the "Uncle Tom" or "Uncle Tomahawk" role by which members of minorities seek favors by adapting an almost childlike subservience to their oppressors and the feminine counterpart, the naif who feigns innocence and dumbs down to elicit favors. But however his subjects rationalize or adapt to their captivity, the captor/oppressor in these situations is only interested in behavioral compliance. By contrast, a core dilemma for the perpetrator of coercive control is how to separate his role as subjugator from the persona he wants the victim to respect, even love. What Walker calls the cycle of violence and battered women identify as the Jekyll and Hyde quality of the abuser, what Laura experienced as Nick's erratic conversion from crying and begging to violence, is nothing more than a subjective reflection of the tension created when illegitimate authority and the need for genuine fealty are housed in the same body. To get a handle on this dilemma, controllers alternately distance themselves from the means of their domination and then own these means if only because even forced submission feels more personal and tolerable than betrayal and abandonment. To sustain the illusion that Laura's punishment was the by-product of her misbehavior (being "bad") rather than his malevolence, Nick externalized his control in rules that were as comprehensive as they were impossible to obey. As the arbiter of the rules, he was merely an enforcer, a position he believed compatible with having her best interests at heart, the rationale parents give for corporal punishment. When he introduced the lists, Nick shared a laugh with Laura, as if the rules had been delivered to them both from on high, the origin of Laura's allusion to Moses. But Nick could not sustain this distance, because it was obedience to *him* he craved, not behavioral conformity in the abstract, and it was her resources on which he depended, not her compliance with his rules. So he quickly reinterpreted Laura's laughter as demeaning him. The same mechanical compliance that satisfies prison guards leaves controllers feeling empty and neglected. Nick's response to this feeling was to make the rules increasingly complex and erratic, increasingly personal. But this made it increasingly difficult and ultimately impossible for Laura to comply, just as Donna ultimately found it impossible to meet Frank's contradictory demands for entries in the log book. Laura's ritual enactment of household tasks threw into negative relief the turmoil in Nick's inner world, the sense of being out of control that he tried to manage through the rules in the first place, as well as with alcohol, gambling, self-loathing and, in the end, what was in all probability a suicidal act.

The Stockholm Syndrome and the Dialectics of Compliance

The effect of this extreme control on victims deserves a separate monograph. Suffice it to say that as the erratic spiral of the oppressor's expectations comes to reflect the incoherent inner world from which they emerge, the victim faces a terrible choice. She must either abandon hope of meeting her partner's expectations—an option that leaves her undefended against the existential risk of being killed—or substitute the rules and all they imply for her fear and trembling, not merely viewing herself from the standpoint of the malevolent other but integrating his standpoint into her self-system so that self-respect and self-soothing come from her internalized version of the standards set by the person who is hurting her. This dynamic is described clinically as the Stockholm syndrome, a name derived from a 1973 robbery in which bank employees defended their captors after they were freed from a 6-day ordeal. The third option, to simply not comply with Nick's rules, was unbearable because of the danger it posed.

Their complex and contradictory nature made it impossible for Laura to win Nick's approval by complying with his rules. His inner calculus of pain and pleasure determined whether she would be deemed "bad" and punished, not her behavior. By internalizing the rules, by "owning" them, Laura found a way to master their unpredictability and the chronic anxiety they elicited. If the rules were hers and not merely Nick's, she could draw a certain satisfaction from meeting them even when he was violent, constructing an imago of him within herself that was orderly, reasonable, and approving and which could contain her mounting rage in the obsessive enactment of domesticity. The Nick within was protective, not merely delusional. It allowed Laura to hide her survival self in an internal image of her victimizer and so counter the emptiness that made her victim self so vulnerable to self-loathing. Laura's inner conversation with her "Nicky" protected her against annihilation even as her behavioral conformity made her appear lost in the rules. When Nick was killed, the imago's function began to atrophy, the rage surfaced in a suicidal gesture, and she ever so slowly began to exorcise her demon, first in the memorial in her bedroom, then in the apparition that appeared to her with decreasing frequency. By offering her an alternative to subordination to Nick, obedience to his rules served Laura as a form of control, albeit in the context of no control.

Laura's material and physical subjugation unquestionably distorted her sense of reality, damaged her self-esteem, and caused her to regress to a time when the approval or disapproval of significant adults was the primary basis for self-worth. As a result, she rationalized levels of violence against herself as well as other acts that violated her basic sense of reason and responsibility, let alone her notions of right and wrong. The point remains. However useful a psychiatric or psychological account might be in explaining the affective content of Laura's response, the primary components of her dependence were constructed according to a strategic logic of domination that directly constrains autonomy and liberty and operates independently of psychological dynamics even when it is nested within them. The rewards and incentives for dominance are similarly objective and material. With only a minimal investment on the controller's part, money is appropriated or stolen, food cooked and served ("lots of Hostess surprises . . . for Nicky"), sex provided on demand or not, emotional support delivered, children cared for, cars washed, the house cleaned, and respect shown if not felt.

From Victim to Survivor

By the time Laura stole the money, she had come to associate love with the absence of punishment, so that being a good girl no longer meant caring for others—as it had when she was growing up—but complying with a set of rules and routines from which she hoped to gain approval. Nick took her power of self-protection. But he also took her power of self-definition, an equally critical component of personhood and citizenship. Laura internalized not merely the lists but a good deal of the world as it was presented to her by Nick, a world in which it was her own faults as housekeeper, money manager, cook, and sexual partner that made him "crazy" and provoked his criticism and the assaults. If she was to blame for his discontent, as well as for his violence, alcoholism, addiction to gambling, and jealousy, then she might prevent it by altering her behavior. When this didn't work, she turned his rules into a fetish she used to replace him, drawing a certain satisfaction from her obsessive completion of the household rituals. Oddly, her obsession allowed her to complete the rituals without identifying too closely with them. What Nick (or her psychiatrists) could not see was that like many prisoners who survived the concentration camps, when control over the larger parameters of her life was taken from her, Laura maintained her sense of identity by creating moments of autonomy and choice in the interstices of the rituals she was commanded to perform, forgetting to turn a corner of the bedspread back, not vacuuming under the coach, just as Donna bought Frank's cigarettes but "forgot" his beer. As Nick pursued Laura through the interstices of her personal life, going room to room, activity by activity and, finally, moment by moment, she hid her passion for personal liberty in the place Nick was least likely to look—in the household rituals he commanded, the behavioral representation of his authority.

After Nick's death, to cope with her guilt as well as her fear of losing the positive reinforcement she derived from the rituals, Laura continued to cook and clean as she had when he was alive and continued to embezzle small amounts of money. These behaviors had multiple meanings. As long as she was driven by obsession, Laura could ward off the shame her behavior occasioned. Moreover, her behavior would reassure him, were he to return, that nothing had changed. At the same time, these behaviors, like the bedroom monument the legal aide attorney had witnessed, were replacements as well as representations of Nick, ways to know where he wasn't as well as to know where he was. If it was safe to love the memorial, it might be safe to love and eventually, to love without it.

At her trial, the prosecutor presented the personal items Laura had bought with money stolen after Nick's death and played up her failure to repay what was stolen. Apart from establishing a continuity with the past, these behaviors also reflected Laura's anger at the idea that someone in her situation should be held legally accountable for what they say or do,

her anger that the state was carrying out the work Nick began by appropriating her resources, and her rage, which she was finally able to articulate, at the "family" of co-workers who had remained silent in the face of
her ordeal. It took several years for Laura to retire her vacuum, substitute
candles to her dead father for the candles she lit for Nick, stop color
coordinating her clothes, and transition back into the world where it was
possible to make mistakes without being raped, beaten, or otherwise
punished and where there was a reasonable chance that her brains, inner
beauty, loyalty, humor, and enthusiasm for life might be rewarded with
the love and respect that is our birthright.

11

THE SPECIAL REASONABLENESS OF
BATTERED WOMEN

Bonnie Foreshaw lived with her son in Bloomfield, Connecticut, a middle-class suburb of Hartford. After 3 years of an abusive marriage, she had finally convinced her husband, Lessup, to move out, though she had to put a car in his name and pay off the loan to get him to do so. He continued to watch the house, called to threaten her, and often followed and harassed her when she went out. For protection, Bonnie bought a .38-caliber handgun on the street, though she had never fired a weapon. She took the gun with her late one evening in March 1986, when she drove a female friend home to the notorious East End of Hartford. She dropped her friend at around 12:30 A.M., then stopped for a nonalcoholic beer at the Progressive League, a Jamaican social club. She put the small weapon in her blouse. A stranger named Freeman asked to buy her a drink. Bonnie demurred, not meaning to offend. "You think you're too good?" the man retorted.

Not wanting trouble, Bonnie set her unfinished drink on the bar and walked out of the club without a word. Her car was parked across the broad avenue. Freeman followed her out the door, just three steps or so behind. At the gate in front of the club, Bonnie saw Joyce Amos, part of the small group who had been drinking with Freeman. Amos was visibly pregnant. "What did you do?" she asked. Bonnie shrugged, suggesting she had no idea, asked Amos to tell Freeman to leave her alone, and continued walking. Amos said something to Freeman, apparently repeating Bonnie's request, and they argued briefly. By this time, Bonnie had started to cross the street, cutting through a gas station on the corner. Freeman followed, with Amos close behind, taunting Bonnie. He called her "a blood clotter." As she reached the passenger side of the vehicle, Freeman and Amos crossed around the back of the car and stopped on the driver's side. "I'm going to f—k you up," he threatened, then put his hand in his pocket. "In that neighborhood, that meant a knife or a gun," Bonnie explained. "Why did he cut me off if he didn't intend to hurt me?" Drawing the gun out of her blouse, Bonnie fired, into the air she thought. A split second before, Freeman pulled Amos in front of him as a shield. The bullet entered the woman's shoulder and turned downward, into her heart, killing her. Bonnie saw Amos and Freeman fall, assumed they were responding to her warning shot, got in her car, and drove away. A few blocks away, she threw the gun out the window.

Early that morning, Bonnie was arrested and charged with the murder of Joyce Amos and illegal possession of a weapon. She told police what happened and took them to the spot where she had thrown the gun. But it was never found.

Following Bonnie's arrest, right to life groups in Connecticut demonstrated at the office of the chief state's attorney, demanding she be charged with murdering the unborn fetus as well as Amos. Joined by local police, federal authorities raided Bonnie's home, allegedly in response to reports it was a drug den, and seized her home under the federal forfeiture provision. No drugs were found. But the $80,000 or so expended on the forfeiture proceeding and repurchasing the house exhausted the assets Bonnie needed for bail and to hire a private attorney. The court appointed an attorney who had never tried a murder case and had little criminal trial experience. In jail, she was given medications for depression that made her so drowsy she had trouble staying awake during the trial, let alone actively participating in her defense.

Bonnie insisted she had fired the gun to protect herself and scare Freeman, not to hurt him. Although she had never met him or Joyce Amos, Freeman had a long history of violence that included a conviction for assaulting a police officer. Her inexperienced attorney concluded that self-defense didn't apply because Freeman had not actually assaulted Bonnie and she had admitted purchasing and owning the illegal weapon. Instead, he argued that her responsibility was diminished because, at the time of the shooting, Bonnie was suffering a post-traumatic stress disorder (PTSD) caused by her history of domestic violence. One consequence of this legal strategy was that several witnesses who might have confirmed Bonnie's version of events were neither interviewed nor called to testify.

A court-appointed psychiatrist, Dr. Grayson, found Bonnie's account of both her abusive history and her current predicament credible, but reported no evidence of psychiatric disease. Grayson wrote, in part:

> Bonnie Foreshaw admittedly fired her gun at a man who allegedly had been swearing at and verbally threatening her. She reportedly believed that he was about to harm her physically and sought to protect herself. . . . It seems probable that if Bonnie Foreshaw was verbally threatened by the man outside

the bar, that after all the physical abuse she seemingly has endured at the hands of men in the past, she would act to defend herself and would probably be prone to react quicker to perceived danger than most others would. In other words, she seemingly has been predisposed to look for danger and respond quickly to possible harm from men who appear to represent a threat to her.

Grayson pointed to medical evidence that Bonnie was under considerable stress prior to the shooting and had experienced a dramatic weight loss as a result. In his opinion, however, she was mentally competent. Grayson recognized Bonnie's perception of danger and her quick response as the logical by-products of her abusive history. But her defense attorney interpreted his report as very damaging. Hoping to salvage an insanity defense, a week before the case went to trial, he asked Dr. Price, another psychiatrist, to assess Bonnie. Price concluded she was suffering from PTSD at the time of the shooting as the result of previous domestic violence. In her testimony, she recounted Bonnie's abusive history and summarized medical evidence recorded by a physician, Dr. Stone, that she had lost 60 pounds in the months before she fired at Freeman, going from 170 to 110 pounds, reported chest pains (with no evidence of cardiac problems), and had been diagnosed as depressed—all symptoms consistent with stress. Because of her PTSD, argued Price, Bonnie exaggerated the danger posed by the man who was pursuing her. In effect, she said, Bonnie mistook Freeman for Lessup, her abusive husband. When she shot the gun, she was trying to hurt Lessup, not Freeman or Amos. The major difference between the two psychiatric assessments was that Grayson had treated Bonnie's perception as reasonable rather than as distorted.

Price was easily discredited. She knew little about the facts of the case and, according to Bonnie, had interviewed her for less than 15 minutes. Nor was there any clinical evidence of Bonnie's distorted sense of reality. Freeman largely confirmed Bonnie's version of events. But his thick patois made his testimony difficult for jurors to follow. Several other witnesses claimed that Bonnie had cursed at Freeman and Amos, left the scene and then returned with the gun, and had fired with the intent to harm them. She was convicted of murder and on the weapons charge and sentenced to 45 years in prison, at the time, the longest prison sentence received by a woman in Connecticut. Two weeks after the trial ended, all drug charges against her were dropped. We met in preparation for a habeas corpus petition, after Bonnie had served 9 years in the Women's Correctional Facility in Niantic.

Background

As a little girl, Bonnie moved from Jamaica to Miami with her parents amidst a huge family migration. "Now, my mother was one of 14 children," she writes. "By the time I arrived in Miami, over 200 family members were there, from Chicago, New York, New Jersey, Virginia, Georgia, Alabama, and Jamaica."[2] Her father, a construction worker, was "a weekend drunk" who mainly beat her mother on the weekends. To protect herself and her daughter, her mother would go to a relative's on Friday evenings or rent a room Bonnie refers to as their "safe house." The couple divorced when Bonnie was 4, and her mother went to work as a maid, wanting no part of welfare, leaving her for 6 days with various sisters, cousins, friends, and sitters. Bonnie was sexually abused (but not penetrated) by two of her cousins. By age 6, she was wearing a key and taking herself to the sitter's. Her mother remarried shortly afterward and had two children with "Mr. Fred," one when Bonnie was 8 and another when she was 12. Mr. Fred hit her mother and continually degraded Bonnie, calling her a "whore" and "black bitch," insults that taught her how to "disappear in plain sight," a skill she put to good use later in life. Although he never hit her, after Mr. Fred touched her sexually, her mother sent her to stay with relatives. She would return to the house during the day to care for the children, a job she continued after bearing a daughter at age 13 and dropping out of school.

Bonnie's first husband, Howard, whom she married as a teen, had a good job when they met and appeared to share her desire for stability. But a drug habit turned into addiction and he became extremely abusive. He gave her black eyes, broke two of her vertebrae after hanging her off a balcony, kicked out two of her front teeth, and attempted to kill her for refusing to give him money to buy drugs. After Bonnie helped Howard through drug rehabilitation in New Jersey, they moved back to Florida. But his drug habit returned. After almost dying of an overdose, he was killed when a drug deal went bad.

After Howard's death, Bonnie moved to Hartford and was trained at a machinist. When she married Perry at age 32, her earlier wildness had subsided. Perry was even more abusive than Howard. He stole money from Bonnie and her son, Mark, beat her with a baseball bat, and stabbed her in the throat with a pick, resulting in a week's hospitalization.

Despite this dramatic history, in 1983, when Bonnie met Lessup Foreshaw at a training for union stewards at the University of Connecticut, she had turned her life around, a fact that she attributes to her becoming a dedicated Rastafarian. She was suffering no major psychological or medical problems and was happier than she had ever been. Fulfilling a dream, she owned her own home in suburban Bloomfield, had a stable job as a skilled machinist, had been elected shop steward by her co-workers, and was widely respected for her defense of employee rights. Her daughter was married and lived nearby, and her son was doing well in school. All of these factors, but particularly her income, appealed to Lessup. For her part, Bonnie decided to marry again mainly because she believed her salary might be insufficient to support her home and her son. Lessup was also a shop steward and a Rastafarian.

For 6 months, things went relatively well. Then an old issue resurfaced. When Bonnie refused to give Lessup full access to her paycheck and savings, he tore up their marriage license and beat her, kicking her sides and back, head, and ears, fracturing several bones. She was hospitalized. Physical abuse escalated in the ensuing months. He put a gun to her head, choked her, and threatened her with a knife. When they went to Jamaica on a holiday, he beat her on the plane; when they returned, because she was too slow at customs, he punched her and her mouth filled with blood. Lessup demanded sex after most assaults. In the meantime, he had lost his job.

Previous husbands had beaten Bonnie to take her money or when she accused him of infidelity. But Howard and Perry had taken little interest in controlling other aspects of her life. By contrast, Lessup aimed to subordinate her to his will. As she tried to escape the physical abuse, he expanded the scope of his authority with threats, isolated Bonnie from friends, and extended his attempts to control her to her work. He forbade her to see anyone, talk on the phone, or answer the door. He scrutinized everything she did and beat her for any act he associated with disloyalty or disobedience. Once, he broke Bonnie's fingers for writing Christmas cards—"who told you you could write Christmas cards?" he demanded. He also beat her for watching TV.

Like many hard-working members of the Jamaican community in Hartford, Lessup could not read or write. So Bonnie had to manage the checking account and pay the bills. But he repeatedly demanded she put the house in his name ("if you love me") and beat her when she refused. Work and her family had been Bonnie's anchors regardless of other events in her life. These now became Lessup's target. He would keep her up at night until she became so tired she had to miss work.

During the week, Bonnie could not avoid Lessup and still go to her job or keep Mark in school. But she escaped on weekends, just as her mother had. She met Mark at her older daughter's after work on Fridays, left town, dropped him at school on Monday, and went directly to work. Lessup's response was to forbid her to drive: he would take her to work, check up on her repeatedly during the day, show up at her work, then pick her up in the evening. When he injured her, Lessup took her to the doctor and told him it was job-related. Bonnie had been a leader at work. Now, work began to feel like a trap. Embarrassed by Lessup's control, she stopped socializing with co-workers. She wore long sleeves to conceal her injuries. Moreover, her home life now felt like "work for Lessup." As she reported, "So many days, my work had no end. I was a prisoner. My life was his."

When Bonnie had Lessup served with legal papers to initiate a separation, he beat her for "going to the white man." Just weeks before the shooting, Lessup told Bonnie he would only leave if she agreed to pay off the $500 owed on a red Datsun and sign it over to him. She agreed, and he moved out. But little changed. He told her she could not go out except to work and frequently drove by to check on her. He would call regularly to remind her that "anything I want to do to you, I can do." One day, when Bonnie left the house, Lessup jumped down in front of her from a tree where he had been hiding, frightening her so badly she wet her pants. Shortly after this incident, in February 1986, Bonnie visited Dr. Stone for stomach problems. In a letter referring Bonnie to a psychiatrist, Stone noted that she was suffering "extreme anxiety" due to "home situation." He prescribed some minor tranquilizers and recommended that the psychiatrist help her with stress management. Instead of seeing the psychiatrist, Bonnie bought a gun.

Traumatization or Self-Defense?

The drug raid on Bonnie's house was designed to undermine her defense and confounded the problems already faced by her inexperienced lawyer. Drug charges were still pending when she went to trial and the state's attorney portrayed her as "a known drug seller," though he knew no drugs had been found and that she had neither a history of drug use or any drug-related arrests. Apart from the image problems the drug connection presented, before going to trial, the defense had to decide whether to claim that abuse-related PTSD caused Bonnie to exaggerate the danger she faced or rely on a traditional self-defense plea predicated on the reasonableness of her actions. Because Bonnie had been abused throughout her life but had no previous history of violence, the defense also had to explain why this exemplary mother and worker had seemingly cracked now.

Dr. Price argued that Bonnie's history of severe abuse caused her to confuse Freeman's behavior outside the club with the menacing acts of her husbands and respond to the threat she imagined he posed. Strictly speaking, this was not the insanity defense employed by Francine Hughes, though the two had much in common. As we've seen, the trauma model normalizes the distortions caused by abuse by highlighting the fact that exposure to similar insults could elicit a similar adaptation in anyone. In other words, the defense claimed that Bonnie's responsibility for the violence was diminished not by an internal malfunction but by her victimization, an external source of stress.

As a trauma defense required, Price attempted to frame the trigger event by retrospectively constructing a narrative of progressively more serious assaults culminating in the victim "cracking" in the defining moment. Applying this story line to Bonnie's case was difficult because Lessup's violence had decreased significantly after they separated, though he continued to stalk, threaten, and harass her, issues that were precluded by her exclusive focus on severe assaults. Just as important, although she had never fired a gun before and was frightened by her confrontation with Freeman, Bonnie had coherent explanations for each of her actions on the night of the killing. If she confused Freeman for Lessup, this appeared to have been her only lapse in reasoned judgment.

Dr. Grayson offered an alternative interpretation of Bonnie's actions that captured her experience as she understood it: that she had reacted to the threat posed when Freeman cursed her, moved toward her in a menacing way, and put his hand in his pocket. With slight modification, Grayson's observation could have supported the argument that Bonnie was endowed with a more astute sense of danger than someone without her history of abuse, what psychologist Julie Blackman calls a "heightened reasonableness."[3] I will return to this point momentarily. Price echoed the state's contention that Bonnie had overreacted to Freeman, though she insisted this was the product of her background rather than of a malevolent will. There was no independent evidence either from Grayson or Dr. Stone that Bonnie was experiencing flashbacks, delusions, hypervigilance, a diffuse sense of personal boundaries, dependence, inappropriate affect, or any of the other well-known symptoms of PTSD.

Bonnie suffered a range of stress-related health problems, including the dramatic weight loss, chest pain, and depression. Although Stone linked her extreme anxiety to her home situation, his notes made it clear that he was stumped about why these problems had emerged after Lessup's assaults had stopped and he had moved out. His prescription of tranquilizers and referral to a psychiatrist for stress management expressed his frustration. By contrast, Price insisted that Bonnie's medical problems were the early signs of the violence-induced PTSD that only became fully manifest during the shooting.

None of the clinicians who interviewed Bonnie recognized that her current symptoms, as well as her decision to purchase the gun, were adaptations to the ongoing danger Lessup posed after they separated and he had replaced his violence and micromanagement with stalking and intimidation. Unlike the tangible fear induced by physical assault, his threats to her liberty were intangible, diffuse, and difficult to counter, eliciting a free-floating anxiety that bordered on panic. Against Lessup's "demonstrations of omnipotence," her well-honed strategy of disappearing in plain sight was ineffective, as it often was against physical abuse. Bonnie's sense of isolation was exacerbated because Lessup's campaign of terror was invisible to everyone else, including the helping professionals to whom she turned. Because her problems were intratraumatic rather than a post-traumatic reaction, without removing the source of the threat, antidepressants and stress management would have provided little relief. He could have been arrested for stalking, harassing, and threatening her. But she feared this would make things worse, because he would have almost certainly been charged with a minor crime (as Perry had been when he stabbed her) and reassault her. Her decision to buy a gun was arguably the most rational of the limited alternatives Bonnie had, and her decision to defend herself against Freeman was an extension of the same logic of self-protection. Missing the context for her actions, her attorney and Price could not see this and so misinterpreted Bonnie's purchase and use of the gun as symptoms of past abuse rather than as responses to the deprivation of her liberty and autonomy. It was her misfortune, and of course Amos's as well, that Freeman unknowingly stepped into the long line of men who contributed to this deprivation.

An Affirmative Defense

Without credible evidence that Bonnie's perceptions were distorted, the defense argument crumbled. In the habeas corpus presentation a decade after her conviction, we reshaped Bonnie's experience into an affirmative narrative that explained how the violations of liberty she was suffering led her to purchase the illegal gun, take it with her that night, make a reasonable judgment of Freeman's intentions, and resist his attempt to humiliate and oppress her. Had this been her original defense, she would have been acquitted on the murder charge, though she might have convicted of the lesser charge of manslaughter. Although Bonnie had never met Freeman and so was unacquainted with his propensity for violence, her unique history enabled her to see what the average person might not, as the state's psychiatrist suggested, that a man who follows you, attempts to limit your mobility, curses you, threatens to "f—k" you up, and then reaches into his pocket means to harm you, possibly fatally. Self-defense law requires only that your belief that serious harm is about to occur be reasonable when you respond, not that the harm have been actually inflicted or in progress. Even where the objective danger in a given episode does not support the degree of imminence required for self-defense, the victim's overall circumstance can evoke in her an honest belief that such danger is present and without the accompanying stigma of illness.

On one level, Dr. Price was right. Freeman's acts recalled Lessup's attempts to deprive Bonnie of basic liberties, and she was stirred to act by anger at her ongoing entrapment as well as by a reasonable fear of what Freeman would do. Lessup had not merely regulated Bonnie's access to vital resources such as money, food, clothing, car, and the phone. By coopting the rights and resources to which adult citizens are entitled, he had also impugned her capacity to participate as a full and independent (i.e., self-directed) adult in the web of relationships that were vital to her identity as a woman, mother, family member, homeowner, friend, worker, and union leader. To the extent that coercive control jeopardizes political identity as well as the integrity of our personhood, it can be expected to elicit a level of outrage and resistance among otherwise free persons that is comparable to the response we would expect, and even praise, from a POW or hostage who possess the means to free themselves. Given its connection to liberty, even when such a response is violent, we distinguish it qualitatively from a visceral response to physical attack and rarely require that it be proportional to the harm used or threatened. The deprivation of rights and liberties may be harder to identify when it occurs in personal life than in other capture crimes. But the injustice involved is no less and the liberatory reaction no less justified.

Lessup taught Bonnie a lesson she had not gleaned from her previous husbands—that the experience of being dominated is qualitatively different from the experience of physical subjugation and is not exhausted by a catalog of physical and psychological harms. Freeman was obviously not Lessup. Yet to Bonnie, the threat he posed to her freedom and autonomy was identical. It should have been the state's burden to show that this interpretation was incorrect. On its part, the defense could have focused on the incredible perseverance, courage, and resilience she mustered in the face of her history to establish her vocation, raise her children, discipline herself as a Rastafarian, set up an independent household, and be selected for a leadership position in her union. These were not the achievements of someone driven by impulse or passion. The world Bonnie had created for herself and her family against adversity framed her character and motives on the night of the shooting and provided compelling evidence of the substantive rationality she carried with her to the street. Only by grasping the scope of Bonnie's agency and the lengths to which she had already gone to protect it can we grasp her decision to defend it with a gun.

In prison, Bonnie drew on her profound and deeply personal sense of moral accountability to sustain an essential subjectivity, as she had in the brutal relationships with her husbands. When we met, after years of incarceration, she still felt responsible for the death of Joyce Amos, though not guilty of killing her intentionally. Her sense of responsibility was deepened because Amos had tried to protect her.

Reframing Bonnie's Quest for Autonomy

At trial, Bonnie was denuded of the purposes she carried into the world and appeared to be little more than the punching bag the men in her life tried to make her, a pathetic figure whose actions were a tragic but inevitable by-product of circumstances. Her medicine-induced weight gain reinforced this representation. Her psychiatrist and defense counsel used the image of a woman without choice sympathetically. If she was acted on but could not act under the power of her creative reason, she should not be held fully accountable for her violence.

The heart of Bonnie's defense was a stereotypic dichotomy between men as powerful and women as powerless. By contrast, the coercive control model draws on a more dialectical and historically specific image of struggle. In this narrative, women strive to personally actualize and deploy the formal equalities and liberties to which their new status entitles them, to express their desire, reason, and imagination through their life projects against restraints on their liberty and other obstacles put in their path. The outcome of these struggles in any given relationship may be negatively determined by some combination of sexual inequality, sexist acculturation, and personal oppression. But their subaltern status does not change the moral calculus that led Francine, Bonnie, Donna, and many other women in my caseload to conclude that freedom and autonomy are worth defending, even if the costs are high. On a daily basis, women's resistance to coercive control may be subdued, understated, and even hidden rather than fierce. Even so, it is rooted less in the instinct for physical survival or a desire for safety in a narrow sense than in a political aim—to sustain an autonomous existence and a reasonable chance of influencing fate. These goals form the basis of a defense strategy in cases of coercive control.

Howard, Perry, and Lessup were attracted to Bonnie by the same strengths in survival, caretaking, and initiative that first became apparent when, as a child herself, she left school to care for her mother's new child, her aunt's girl, and her own daughter. With the exception of one grandmother (whose husband had died young), every woman in Bonnie's extended family was abused by their male partners. From this, she concluded that domestic violence is a continuing risk in all heterosexual relationships. This did not diminish the power of women in her eyes. She sees her female relatives as strong-willed and independent, not as victims, and looks to their strategic prowess as a model of what can be accomplished in the face of hardship. One such model is her cousin Bertha who, despite several abusive relationships, finished night school, became a beautician, and today owns four salons. Bertha and the network formed among her other female relatives also taught Bonnie that it was necessary to insulate your major spheres of independence from the men in your life. With regard to sex, she understood, "if you don't give it up, they will rape you." But this principle—that men could get what they wanted from you with force—did not extend to her children, her work, her money, or the essentials her family required. If she understood that "sometimes you had to take a beating," she stood up strongly when Howard, Perry, and Lessup went after the material basis for her independence and her family's survival. Although she supported Howard during his drug treatment and contributed significantly to Perry's upkeep as well, Howard was killed and she was able to break things off with Perry before they took control over her life. Bonnie believes "men end abusive relationships, not women," a basic tenet in this book. However, she also understood that this outcome can be helped along if you provide proper incentives. Perry left when Bonnie paid him off. So did Lessup. But Lessup was not content to live off Bonnie's money and support; he wanted to control her directly, and to do so, he insisted on breaking her spirit as well as her bones. He saw the relationship as a zero-sum game in which even such minor expressions of autonomy as writing a Christmas card without permission symbolized power taken from him. This was Bonnie's first exposure to coercive control. It was the ways in which Lessup's treatment of her differed from the abuse suffered from Howard and Perry that framed her very different response.

Framing Bonnie's Actions: The Moral Imperatives of Street Talk

A jury might have excused Bonnie if she had shot and killed Lessup. As they did with Donna Balis and Francine Hughes, juries frequently stretch the conditions required for self-defense if they believe an abusive partner got what they deserved. But like Nate Parkman, the woman who confronted and then stabbed her abusive boyfriend in the street, Bonnie acted in a public arena where this sentimental discourse afforded little protection. She had no prior history of violence. Nor was she easily provoked, as the state claimed. Like other members of her family, she was willing to take an occasional beating, in part because the consequences of fighting back or calling police were often worse. Her religious convictions, close family life, and stable history of successful employment also gave her an aura of middle-class respectability that undermined the state's desire to portray her a streetwise drug dealer and cold-blooded killer. The fact that her character and social situation bolstered her version of events presented a serious problem for the state.

To overcome the fact that Bonnie's actual life contradicted its case, the prosecution constructed an alternative persona for her, largely by playing the race card and appealing to the widely held stereotypes of blacks and Rastas. The trumped up drug charges and the pretrial raid on her home were the first steps in this process. But what proved critical was the racial imagery constructed during the trial. Because Bonnie's suburban home life, religious faith, and stellar record as a mother, machinist, and union steward made it more likely that she was Freeman's victim than the aggressor, her social situation was kept out of court. By the time Price took the stand to present Bonnie as a hapless victim of circumstances, the prosecution had already convinced jurors she was a vengeance-seeking Rasta ("jobless, reefer-smoking bums") of the sort one would expect to find habituating a Jamaican bar.

To impugn Bonnie's motive, the prosecution scripted testimony by Freeman and his friends that relocated her in an urban street drama as a character who was Freeman's equal and co-conspirator in the death of Joyce Amos.

Freeman's history of assaultive behavior was not admitted. But his dress and his heavy Jamaican patois placed him squarely in a world where people can be moved to violence as readily by insults as by physical threats. The rules governing when and how disrespect leads to violence on the street are complicated. Although words can provoke a fight, street culture also recognizes exchanging insults as a status game where no violence is implied or threatened. To determine which function words or gestures serve in a particular verbal encounter, both actors and their audience must decipher the motives and meanings of key participants. Though the appearance of a weapon raises the stakes and stylistic complexity of public display, it need not signal an intent to cause harm. Low-income and minority women enjoy an equality on the street that is absent in more conventional or middle-class settings, though misogynist banter is also given considerable scope. Disrespect can be far more salient in public than it is in private. A common "linguistic community" can be elusive even where both parties share a common social identity. But consensus on meaning is completely confounded if persons bring different interpretive frameworks to their exchange, as was the case when Bonnie rejected Freeman's offer to buy her a drink or when he called her a "blood clotter." Their class differences were critical to Freeman's perception that Bonnie's rejection was condescending as well as to her view that his pickup attempt and cursing were inappropriate.

To reconstruct Bonnie as the type of person prone to commit preemptive violence, witnesses assigned her words and gestures of the urban cognizante. By giving her "street talk," witnesses established two key illusions that made the violent scene recognizable to the jury—that Bonnie shared an interpretive framework with Freeman, including his values, and so, to borrow a term from literary criticism, "deliberately misread" his motives to advance her aggressive intent.

Street morality normally applies an honor code based on principles of equity and justice to distinguish legitimate from illegitimate violence. Little stigma attaches to violence where an insult is recognized as real, for instance, if a stranger boasts about "taking" someone's wife, providing it is roughly equivalent to the offense. But a person who responds violently to an identical comment made as a status-seeking gesture among friends during a put down contest is considered a "hot head," "troublemaker," or unstable. Because weapons are readily available in U.S. cities, misreadings, deliberate or not, threaten the precarious cultural balance on which social relationships on the street depend. As a result, their purveyors are condemned or ostracized, regardless of whether or how the law is involved.

The legal system cannot be expected to follow the nuances of street morality, let alone renegotiate them, though the ever-present possibility of jury nullification makes it impossible for courts to disregard street values altogether. This gap between law and lore is bridged by inviting witnesses from street culture into the courtroom to testify, including police or other professionals who work there, and then allowing them to freely script scenes that express their moral reading of a given encounter and maximize the chance that the legal outcomes will correspond to this reading. This practice is rationalized by highlighting opportunities for cross-examination, the right to present alternative scripts through defense witnesses, and by pointing to perceptual difficulties that lead to natural differences among eye-witnesses. Charges of perjury are rarely leveled at even the most transparent falsehoods during trials. No witnesses referred to Freeman's encounter with Bonnie inside the club, reflected on why he followed her to the car, why Amos and he argued, why she accompanied him, or what he meant by calling Bonnie a blood clotter or by his other threatening words or gestures. Instead, Freeman's witnesses began where they believed the confrontation should have ended, with Bonnie turning on him and Amos and threatening them both. They described how Bonnie then left the scene, retrieved the gun from her car, and returned to continue the fight, waving the gun while she threatened and cursed them, then firing. Lest this leave ambiguity about responsibility, Bonnie was given speaking lines that made her motives clear. According to Mrs. Wrubel, a companion of Freeman's, Bonnie called Amos a bitch and announced (about Freeman) "he disrespected me" before she shot. In Freeman's account, Amos told Bonnie not to curse and she replied "get out the way so I can kill the motherfucker." The contrast between Bonnie's crude language and aggressive action and her victim's hapless attempts at mediation illustrated her culpability from the perspective of street morality. She was the hot head whom the others, well versed in the ups and downs of street fights, had tried to calm.

The voice witnesses gave to Bonnie situated her linguistically for the jury as someone with a ghetto identity who would carry out the malevolent intent to "kill the motherfucker." Portraying Bonnie as impulsive and filled with irrational rage made it unnecessary to identify a more exacting cause of her action. Racial stereotypes did the rest. The sociological reality was that Amos was Freeman's compatriot and Bonnie the outsider. But Bonnie and Amos were given speaking lines that reversed this relationship, linking Bonnie to Freeman and placing Amos apart from and above the fray. Witness accounts of what happened were hopelessly contradictory, both internally and with one another. What stuck with the jury was the verisimilitude of the language. Importantly, apart from his self-justifying attribution of blame, Freeman confirmed that he had followed Bonnie from the bar, kept fighting with her, that there was only a short distance between them when she fired, and that he used Amos as a shield. But his thick Jamaican accent also played to the pragmatics of racism in the courtroom, discrediting him as a witness to events even as it made him largely unintelligible to anyone but Bonnie. The result was that Bonnie and Freeman became joined in the jurors' minds as equally culpable. Given this frame, even Bonnie's work as a machinist reinforced the stereotype: she worked at a "masculine" job, hence could be expected to act (and to be treated) like a man on the street. Two bad Jamaicans had sought one another out for a reckoning. And Joyce Amos—who had, after all, asked Bonnie not to curse and Freeman to leave her alone—was the "innocent" victim whose fate was tragically sealed by trying to intervene. The prosecutor played to this story by producing a gun for the jury that was about twice the size of the weapon Bonnie claimed she had stored in her bra but had thrown away. The judge allowed the substitute weapon despite its obvious prejudicial effect.

Reframing Victimization

The only way to offset this portrayal would have been to represent Bonnie's actual identity outside the world occupied by Freeman, Amos, and their friends—to counter race talk with talk of class and family. This required an alternative moral discourse with a grammar of motives rooted in the working-class world of black family life where complex events are carefully evaluated and persons take cautious but effective steps to protect themselves and their families from predatory aggression, as Bonnie had throughout her life. Every element of her behavior could be narratively framed as a logical progression with an unpredictable and tragic outcome—purchasing the gun to protect herself against Lessup, carrying it that night to a dangerous section of Hartford, stopping at the bar, refusing Freeman's offer, hastily retreating, asking Amos to intervene, and firing a single warning shot—and grounded in her history. Having given interpretive significance to what she had learned from this history, Bonnie would emerge as a rational subject fully entitled to defend her perceived self-interest as aggressively as was necessary. The only risk in this gambit was that examples of her assertiveness could reinforce the prosecutor's case.

The victimization narrative offered an alternative to this affirmative approach that was consistent with Bonnie's depressive state during the trial, removed her from the scene, at least psychologically, and explained why she behaved in a way that was inconsistent with her character. But Bonnie herself vehemently rejected this account. In meetings with her defense attorney, she insisted she had accurately understood Freeman's intentions, that her fear and anger were reality based, and that she had used what she believed was the minimal force needed to preempt an attack. When she came to trial, Bonnie had been taking antidepressants three times a day for many months, and it had made her withdrawn, suicidal, and obese. When she entered prison, she had dropped from her normal weight to 110 pounds. Now, 9 months later, she weighed 240 pounds. Apart from the medication that kept her drowsy during the trial, her persuasive powers were undermined by the fact that she saw herself as a survivor rather than as the victim she was asked to portray on the stand and dis-believed what was said about her by the psychiatrist and her lawyer. The other major problem with the psychological argument was that it robbed her of an opportunity to interpolate her behavior on the street as the log-ical outcome of a reflective life. Price and the defense attorney saw PTSD as the best way to neutralize the prosecution's witnesses. But for the jury, the claim that Bonnie was crazy reinforced the version of events offered by Freeman's friends and discredited her own description. In the end, on the balance scale of courtroom drama, the victimization story lacked the moral authority and emotional salience of the story constructed by the state's witnesses. Victimization offered Bonnie a voice with which to throw herself on the court's mercy. But it was no more her voice than were the ghetto speeches delivered for her by the prosecution. For street Rastas, mercy is in short supply.

The Appeal

The habeas corpus appeal was brought by John Williams and Elizabeth Pollan, Connecticut attorneys with distinguished histories of trial work on behalf of civil liberties. The defendant must prove that the counsel provided failed to meet the minimum standard of competence required. Supported by myself and Brooklyn Law School professor Elizabeth Schneider, the formal legal argument was that Bonnie's lawyer had seriously erred in not pursuing self-defense, as Bonnie wanted. Had he done so, he could have called domestic violence experts like myself who might have made a convincing argument on her behalf.

The victimization narrative woven by Price dropped a plumb line from Bonnie's current depressive state to her childhood history of abuse. The alternative story emphasized how her voice of reason developed through her progressively more sophisticated survival strategies. Responding to her growing capacity to cope with abuse, the men in Bonnie's life stepped up their oppression, culminating in the full-blown regime of coercive control introduced by Lessup. Price highlighted the facts that Bonnie was sexually abused by her stepfather, bore a child as a teen, and dropped out of high school. Equally important, we argued, was that she left home to escape her stepfather's abuse and left school as a teen to successfully care for two children in addition to her own. Here, as in the rest of her life, difficult choices made at great personal risk were motivated by a profound sense of self-protection and responsibility to others. An example illustrates the continuity of these lessons. To help Bonnie cook for the children in her care at age 13, her mother would call, tell her when to put the chicken up to boil and then divide the required cooking time at each step according to the minutes between TV commercials, two commercials standing for 22 minutes, and so forth. Many years later, this was how Bonnie taught her son Mark to prepare dinner while she worked the swing shift at a machine shop. "Cook slowly and patiently for the best results," Bonnie urged, "and let the beat of the music be the pulse of your soul."[4]

The same caring she had provided for Howard during his drug ordeal was evident in Bonnie's commitment to the Rastafarian faith, her charity work, her refusal to drink (the beer she got at the club was nonalcoholic) or curse, and in her numerous attempts to use police, counselors, physicians, and others to mediate or end the abuse with Perry and Lessup. This work continued at the York prison in Niantic, the facility where she is being held. Not only was she providing formal and informal counseling for other inmates, but was active in York prison's chapter of Literacy Volunteers (a junior high school drop-out, she now reads voraciously and teaches reading to others) and support groups such as Alternatives to Violence.

An Alternative Voice: The Special Reasonableness of Battered Women

The history of Bonnie's resilience and resistance to abuse established an alternative moral context for her behavior on the night she shot Joyce Amos. There were two issues here: the beliefs or lessons Bonnie drew from her history of battering and how she applied these beliefs or lessons to assess the danger she faced that night.

Psychologist Julie Blackman argues that the special knowledge battered women possess of what can happen in interpersonal relationships serves as an alternative framework for their choices in difficult situations.[5] As illustrated in the sweatshirt case and by the obsessively ordered cupboard in the film *Sleeping With the Enemy*, women's experience of coercive control is filled with gestures and other behavioral cues that their astute sensitivity tells them are threatening but appear benign or unintelligible to outsiders. Because many of the risks incurred in these situations are unavoidable, women may refocus downstream, choosing to modify the harms inflicted rather than to try to stop themselves from being harmed altogether. Over time, as victims are forced to ever more closely monitor their partner's behavior to detect signs of impending harm, they devise a repertoire of preemptive defenses, ways of simulating affection, loyalty, obedience, and contrition, for example, or of insulating their bodies both literally and symbolically, that can become as complex as the strategy of coercive control itself. This is illustrated by Bonnie's skill at disappearing psychologically while remaining in plain view. She had initially learned this skill from her stepfather, who beat and touched her sexually. Mr. Fred would yell obscenities at her. "I can't hear him because I'm not here. I'd tell myself, stand there, blank faced. He's so stupid, he doesn't even know I'm gone."[6] Later Bonnie tried this tactic with her abusive husbands. The "reasonableness" to which Blackman refers is the cognitive expression of this system of accommodation—the set of thoughts, ideas, plans, interpretations, tactics, and the like—through which victims of coercive control learn to classify threats and adapt the appropriate response. This special reasonableness differs from the legal standard commonly applied in self-defense cases.

The cognitive system devised by battered women develops on two levels simultaneously: they learn to assign specific risks to specific behaviors, a "particular" reasonableness that helps them survive in a given relationship; and they develop a "general" reasonableness that applies the knowledge gleaned in abusive relationship to assess the potential danger inherent in exchanges in the wider world. Because this knowledge originates in the singular challenges to self-preservation presented by abuse, the assessments it generates can be extremely conservative and exaggerate the need for avoidance or protection from danger or betrayal in encounters with "normals" in ways that can mimic hypervigilance and other symptoms of PTSD.[7] The difference between the empirical inaccuracy of these perceptions and the exaggeration, avoidance, withdrawal, and numbing symptoms typical in PTSD is that where the latter are constructed to defend the ego against internal demons, their credo allows women to "see through" situations that persons without their experience miss at their peril. Applied to interpersonal dilemmas where safety, autonomy, or liberty are put at risk, this reason allows victims to transcend the existential and potentially self-destructive imperatives prescribed by impulse or instinct and deploy rational choice in the service of life goals and self preservation in somewhat the same manner as a well-trained police officer or soldier might in the heat of battle. It was Bonnie's special reasonableness that Dr. Grayson recognized.

Bonnie is a soft-spoken, deeply religious, and extraordinarily articulate woman who commands a level of respect bordering on reverence at York prison, even from her guards and the prison administrators. She has merely to enter the prison courtyard for all eyes to fix on her imposing physical presence as she walks, head erect, serenely smiling, her long grey hair held together in a net that gives her the appearance of a holy woman. As a result of a several-year struggle during which she was placed in segregation because of her refusal to wear the new uniform pants for religious reasons, she is the only prisoner in a skirt.[8] Spending any significant time with Bonnie makes it apparent that only its racialist blinders kept the court from seeing the absurdity of her placement in the violent street culture occupied by Freeman and his friends. Had she not been made stuporous by medication or had her character been accurately depicted, the prosecution would have been forced to answer the question that never surfaced at her trial: why would a deeply religious woman in the throes of separating from her abusive husband, with no history of violence, a good job, and a happy family life, good home, and excellent future prospects, risk all by shooting at a man she had never met or, as the prosecution contended, at a woman whom she had neither met nor had any reason to hurt?

Bonnie's Credo

To explain why Bonnie fired the gun, it is helpful to reconstruct her credo, the general principles she gleaned from her experience of abuse and applied to her encounter with Freeman. This credo evolves as victims reconcile lessons learned from the dilemmas posed by abuse with their underlying values and life goals. Bonnie formulated her basic values as a teen: to minimize harm to herself, care for others in trouble even if this means personal sacrifice, and provide and maintain a safe and supportive environment for her family. These values were never easy to implement and occasionally appeared contradictory. Over the years, she had made tough choices—to stay with Howard and try to end his drug use and preserve her family by marrying Perry and Lessup despite the danger these men posed to her safety. These decisions had turned out badly. When she discovered Howard was stealing to pay for his drug habit, she could have left him. But she stuck with him through imprisonment, drug treatment, and relocation to Florida. Howard returned to drugs, almost killed her in an assault, and was eventually murdered by a drug dealer.

Bonnie experienced systematic injustice at the hands of men and, later, in the legal and prison systems. Despite this, she sustained both a respectable working-class existence and a strong belief that the world was just and fair, which she brought to relationships. To buffer the inconsistencies between this belief and the brutality, racism, and injustice in the world that surrounded her, Bonnie devised a "situational ethics" that allowed her to make practical judgments about how to read and respond to signs of trouble in particular situations without abandoning her general optimism or the infectious faith in people she took with her to work, religion, friendship, and family relationships. The disconnection between her general values and practical judgments left her vulnerable to bad choices. But it also supported a sense of her intrinsic worthiness in the face of extrinsically imposed devaluation.

At the other pole of Bonnie's credo were the postulates that comprised the special knowledge she derived from her experience of abuse. Its most relevant tenets are these:

- When a man has been drinking, he becomes violent.
- If a man wants to hurt you, he will do it. There's no use trying to please him.
- There is no way to predict which men are abusive and which men are not.
- When a man follows you, he means to hurt you.
- When a man restricts your freedom of movement, you are extremely vulnerable to assault and control.
- When a man beats you, he can hurt you really badly.
- Violence, either proactive or retaliatory, solves nothing. If you fight back against a violent man, this almost always makes things worse.
- You cannot expect people around to help you.

It would be mistaken to take each and every facet of this credo too literally. Clearly, not every man who follows someone means to hurt them. And fighting back against a violent man can often deter further violence. As a whole, however, these tenets afforded a conservative guide that helped Bonnie negotiate reality on behalf of her primary goals and values.

"If a man has been drinking, he becomes violent."

All of the men who beat the women in Bonnie's extended family also drank heavily. Alcohol also played a major role in the violence she experienced from her three husbands.

Bonnie herself had used alcohol when she was younger and lived on "the wild side." Some years earlier, she had been arrested for DWI, her lone encounter with police before the shooting. Since then, she had not consumed hard liquor. If she stopped at the bar where liquor was served, it was largely for the company, because she had been socially isolated by Lessup for some time. Freeman and his friends had been drinking at the club for nearly 4 hours prior to Bonnie's arrival. Even before he spoke to her, she noticed that he was intoxicated and judged the danger of violence to be high.

"If a man wants to hurt you, he'll do it."

There's no use to trying to please men determined to hurt you. Where many women believe that a partner's abuse is their fault, Bonnie is very clear that she did nothing to provoke violence by the men in her life. She also felt powerless to control the level of violence to which she was subjected. With Perry, she said, "There was no stopping him if he wanted to do something to me." With Lessup, it was the same. "I knew I couldn't win trying to please. I still got beat up. I've been hurt so many times." Linked to the understanding that she had little control over whether a man initiated violence was her fear of being hurt. When Freeman became aggressive at the club, Bonnie's impulse was to retreat rather than to placate him. "I didn't want no beatin'," she told me.

"There is no way to predict which men are abusive
and which men are not."

Vogue, Mademoiselle, Redbook, and *Better Homes and Gardens* periodically present lists of warning signs to help women stay out of abusive relationships. But only one fact predicts the likelihood of current violence far better than all other risk factors combined—whether the person has been abusive to this woman or others in the past. This criterion is hard to apply because past behavior is often hidden. Men who initially treated Bonnie decently soon become abusive. When she first met Howard in New Jersey, he had a good job and put her on a pedestal. Only slowly did it become apparent that he was stealing at work to support his drug habit. Howard's father had killed his mother. "He came from a turbulent childhood," explains Bonnie, "and soothed his pain with drugs." She became his caretaker, but when his drug use resumed, his violence escalated dramatically.

Bonnie met Perry through a mutual friend in 1979. She was employed as a machinist at Wagner Electronics. Like Howard, Perry also had a good job. During the courtship and while they lived together prior to the marriage there were no fights, he helped out at home, and he was good to her children, all signs she interpreted to mean he was different from Howard. He drank, but only on weekends. Shortly after they married, however, she found him at home with another woman and concluded the marriage was over. Next, she learned that he had lied about virtually every detail of his background, apparently because he was ashamed of being poor. When she asked him why he had lied he beat her for the first time.

Bonnie met Lessup at a shop steward training at the University of Connecticut, hardly a place you would expect to find trouble. Like Perry, he held a good job, was a family man, and cooked and did other chores around the house. By this time, Bonnie was a devoted Rastafarian. Her commitment of Jah (the Rasta deity) affects every aspect of her being, from how she dresses, talks, and what she eats to the ways she thinks about herself and those she is close to. Lessup's mother told Bonnie that he had beaten his father as well as a previous wife. But Lessup, too, had become a devoted Rasta and Bonnie believed this had changed him in the same ways it had changed her. Six months later, she was hospitalized because of his physical abuse.

Regardless of whether she misread signs of abuse, these experiences taught Bonnie that it is almost impossible to decipher men's personality from what they say, to identify their motives, or to predict how they will behave in the future based on their current behavior. One corollary of this tenet is that any man can be violent if he has the opportunity, an observation seemingly borne out by the universality of abuse in Bonnie's extended family.

Despite her basic trustfulness, the value she places on minimizing harm to herself and her family led her to interpret words and actions in terms of their short-term potential to generate a worst-case scenario. She recognizes this has made her somewhat cynical about relationships with men and more cautious than is probably necessary or healthy. Even her son's "cutting" contests with his friends frighten her, in part because she has difficulty distinguishing when the boundaries that make it fun have been crossed. She also points out that women who have not been battered consistently underestimate the danger men pose, overestimate the predictability of their partner's behavior, and delude themselves into thinking they can control what he does. She has seen violence erupt from when people were supposedly having fun too frequently to be sanguine about the games men play with women or with one another. She also met numerous women in prison who profess to shock when their husbands had affairs, went off with other women, or became abusive.

When Freeman asked if she thought she was too good for him, she assumed he was angry and might make trouble. So she left the unfinished drink and walked out of the club. Had they been asked, the waitress in the club as well as other patrons could have established Freeman's intent. As he was following her across the street, Freeman called Bonnie a blood clotter, one of the most humiliating Jamaican curses. From this, she concluded he posed a real threat.

"When a man follows you, he means to hurt you."

Just a week before the shooting, Lessup had jumped from the tree, causing Bonnie to wet her pants. He told her on the phone that he was watching her, which she had no choice but to believe. He also drove by periodically to check on her whereabouts. From this as well as earlier experiences, Bonnie concluded that Freeman intent was malevolent when he followed her out of the club, even before he cursed or stuck his hand in his pocket. What might have appeared to an outsider as an exaggerated interpretation was no more than a literal reading of Freeman's actions based on experience. "'I'm going to f—k you up' . . . means trouble . . . they will do it," she told me. If this was "just talk" as Freeman's friends insisted, why was he following her?

"When a man beats you, he can hurt you really badly."

Bonnie had been hospitalized on several occasions because of abuse. So she understood that the consequences of assault could be extremely serious. Unlike someone who was never abused, her fear of Freeman was reality-based. "I was very scared. I had been beaten before. I did not want to be on that end of the stick anymore." This image contrasts markedly with the impetuous, gun-waving moll painted by the prosecution.

Bonnie had little trouble deciding to retreat from the club or return to the car when the intoxicated Freeman approached her in the bar, responded sarcastically when she told him he couldn't buy her a drink, followed her, and cursed her. However, when she pondered what actions to take when Freeman cut her off and put his hands in his pocket, two key elements of Bonnie's credo clashed—her fear of being hurt and her conviction that retaliatory violence was both wrong and useless.

"Violence, either proactive or retaliatory, solves nothing. If you fight back against a violent man, this almost always makes things worse."

Based on these elements of her credo, Bonnie had chosen not to retaliate in previous confrontations with abusive men. She holds these positions largely on pragmatic grounds, drawing on a wealth of examples from her life. She had seen her aunt shoot the father of her children, and another aunt had cut her husband in response to abuse. In each case, the results for the woman were tragic. "What good did it do?" she wonders. In her own relationships with Perry and Lessup, any attempt to strike back led to an escalation of violence. Bonnie fought back on only one occasion, during a beating by Perry. "I had the fork," she reported, "when he fell after beating me, I was stabbing him in the calf with the fork. I saw fear on his face. 'Oh my God,' I thought, 'what is he going to do to me now?' After he beat the hell out of me, he made me go to the bathroom and bandage him up." As Bonnie's daughter put it, "if she fought back, she could get it worse."

Thus, although Bonnie was terrified of being hurt or worse, she adamantly opposed the use of force, largely because she knew the consequences might be disastrous.

"People around won't help you."

Bonnie might have called for help, perhaps even called the police, although no serious crime had occurred. Once she was outside the club, she had no access to a phone. In the past, when she had relied on the police, they had been little help. They never arrested Lessup. Meanwhile, on the single occasions when Howard and Perry were arrested for abusing her, they were given probation, evidence, Bonnie thought, that the police won't help. Appealing to onlookers was a more realistic option. Bonnie did ask Joyce Amos to keep Freeman from pursuing her and according to several witnesses, Amos and Freeman did talk (and perhaps even argued) about his behavior. But Freeman persisted. Witnesses put at least half a dozen persons, including three of Freeman's companions, in the immediate area. Except for Amos, no one said or did anything to mediate the dispute or keep Freeman from pursuing or threatening Bonnie. Bonnie's partners had assaulted her in public in the past. Perry had even come to her workplace and threatened to kill her. None of her co-workers had gotten involved. These experiences are the basis for her conviction that it is futile to ask for help.

Someone else might have interpreted and responded to events that night in a different way, leading to a different outcome. Another woman might have left the gun in the car, accepted Freeman's offer to buy her a drink, or jokingly explained why she had refused. Another woman might even have flirted with Freeman or been more strategic about avoiding a pickup. Bonnie's capacity for nuance was limited because Lessup took virtually any suggestion of playfulness as a pretext for abuse, leading Bonnie to speak flatly, without affect, even before she was loaded with medication. Freeman testified that he left the bar not to follow Bonnie but because he had arranged for friends to drive him home. Another woman might have simply waited him out at the club or responded differently to a man who was behind them. The assumption that Freeman was following her was conjecture, though not entirely. She also guessed that he had a gun or a knife in his pocket, an assumption that was never proved or disproved. Freeman had a history of serious assault, including assault of a police officer. It is still possible that he meant his remarks, curses, and pursuit to be harmless, that they were the idle expressions of a drunk, part of a male status game as his friends claimed. Another woman might have gotten into her car and driven away without incident, though Freeman was on the driver's side. Another woman might have threatened him with the gun but not fired.

The issue is not whether Bonnie's interpretations of Freeman's actions were accurate or whether there were other, more reasonable responses she could have made. The point is simply that her understanding of the danger she faced and her response were drawn from an astute and experience-tested understanding of situations in which men use violence and control to hurt or dominate women. Her response was neither impulsive nor the result of a perception distorted by trauma. Though Bonnie was afraid of what Freeman might do, her response was not driven by fear. Her responses, at the club or at her car, were based on judgments calculated to accomplish long-standing ends—to minimize harm to herself and those she loves. Nor were her responses those of a "reasonable man." The probability that a man would draw on a long history of coercion and control to determine how to react to potential danger is virtually nil. Nor was Bonnie's response identical to how someone with a different history of abuse would respond. The voice of reason to which she listened in her confrontation with Freeman was distinctly and uniquely hers, though it was no less rational because of this. Lessup was one of the most feared "dreds" in Hartford. So, while persons in East Hartford commonly carry illegal weapons, to protect herself Bonnie purchased and carried the gun in suburban Bloomfield, where buying a gun on the street is uncommon. She had it with her to keep herself and her friend from being hurt, not because she had an aggressive intent. Nothing illustrates this more clearly than the dilemma that almost paralyzed Bonnie when Freeman cut her off and put his hand in his pocket. Although she saw that he meant to hurt her and could do so seriously, she was equally convinced that trying to hurt him would only make things worse for her. As he moved to the driver's side of the car, her fear of physical harm gave way to another perception, that her freedom of movement was being jeopardized, that her escape route was blocked, just as it had been when Lessup jumped out of the tree in front of her. Only then, when she saw the liberty that meant so much to her in jeopardy, did she reconcile her conflict about whether to defend herself. Even so, she drew and fired the gun once in the air, as a warning, successfully opening up the retreat she wanted. She saw Freeman and Amos fall, to avoid being shot she thought, and made her escape. Had she sought to hurt either of them or both, she clearly could have taken advantage of their sudden vulnerability. Horrified that she had fired a weapon, she threw the gun out the car window.

During her trial, Bonnie was asked how she felt about the long litany of crimes Lessup had committed against her. "I felt embarrassed," she replied, a response her attorney thought minimized her physical abuse in the minds of the court. After all, he had broken her fingers and seriously injured her in other ways. How could this be reduced to "embarrassment?" So he never asked Bonnie what she meant. During the habeas corpus appeal hearing, we offered Bonnie a chance to explain. No longer medicated, she paused for only a moment. "Embarrassed" meant to be hurt, she replied. Then, she corrected herself. "No," she added, "it means to be taken advantage of, to be 'degraded,' something akin to humiliation." She leaned over on the stand and faced the judge and in a quiet, almost apologetic voice told him, "A woman should not have to be 'embarrassed.'"

When Lessup introduced Bonnie to coercive control, he added a final postulate to her evolving credo. In response to this new lesson, what we might call "the credo of liberty," she fired the gun.

CONCLUSION: FREEDOM IS NOT FREE

For the first time in history, a majority of women in market societies have sufficient social power to choose a course of personal development that is not determined a priori or directed primarily toward the enhancement of the significant others in their lives. Despite persistent sexual inequities in earnings, benefits, and opportunities, millions of women are choosing to define their dignity, capacity, and creative expression outside the boundary of heterosexual dependence. In just a generation, the proportion of U.S. women raising children who have never been married has gone from 6.8% to 43.3%, an increase of more than 600%; similar increases have occurred in the United Kingdom.[1] Women are not rejecting either men or family life. The proportion of women with children and/or partners has not changed appreciably in decades. What women are rejecting in huge numbers is the functional identification of femininity with early and permanent domestic partnerships based on unrewarded self-sacrifice, where their dependence on a man is basis for a stable relationship or is directly exploited rather than freely chosen.

Still, as the Pulitzer Prize–winning playwright Suzan-Lori Parks puts it, "freedom is never free." At the heart of this book is a paradox—that the same opportunities that permit women to live independently also provide a major incentive for coercive control. Because women are more equal than ever before, men intent on subordinating them have expanded their tactical repertoire beyond coercion, relying heavily on the huge gap that still separates women's formal status as men's equals from their reality. Millions of women are entrapped in personal life because interventions to stem woman abuse are largely ineffective and because the movement to end it has failed to address the inequalities at its core.

Constraining women's liberties in personal life makes them more susceptible to inequalities in the workforce and solidifies heterosexist hierarchies in other public arenas. Inequities based on sex are so tightly woven into the fabric of everyday life that they can surface anywhere, even in ostensibly egalitarian settings. Their condition of existential vulnerability makes women acutely sensitive to being devalued while at the same time limiting their capacity to respond aggressively. One result is that millions of women experience a chronic tension between needing to "act up" for equality at work, school, or at informal social or family gatherings and not appearing to do so lest they be marked as unfeminine or their vulnerability exposed. This predicament gives the taken-for-granted liberties violated by coercive control (such as speech, movement, or access to money) a saliency in women's lives typically lacking among men.

In the romantic vernacular, love and intimacy compensate women for their devaluation in the wider world. Personal life does something more. It provides the stage where women practice their basic rights, garner the support needed to resist devaluation, experiment with sexual identities, and imagine themselves through various life projects. Coercive control subverts this process, bringing discrimination home by reducing the discretion in everyday routines to near zero, freezing feeling and identity in time and space, the process victims experience as entrapment. Extended across the range of activities that define women as persons, this foreshortening of subjective development compounds the particular liberty harms caused by coercive control. To quell coercive control means responding to women's immediate predicament; to prevent it requires addressing the substantive inequalities that make it possible for female subordination in personal life to remain a social fact.

This concluding chapter considers the challenges posed to law, policy, the service system, and the advocacy movement by reframing woman battering as the liberty crime of coercive control. I outline a three-pronged strategy: to craft a statutory response; to refocus justice, service, and grassroots advocacy on women's freedom and autonomy as well as their safety; and to reengage the advocacy movement in "the dance of justice."

The Dilemmas of Reform

In deciding how best to help victims of coercive control, we face a dilemma. Governments alone possess the power needed to counter coercive control and ensure that women can reject abusive partners without further interference. But state involvement in personal life must be approached cautiously, particularly when, as is now the case in the United States, there is a growing willingness to regulate women's choices about pregnancy termination, sexual orientation, and decisions about marriage. As the compromises we made to pass the Violence Against Women Act (VAWA) suggest, state institutions will try to accommodate women's needs in ways that frustrate their larger interest in full equality and independence.

The domestic violence revolution challenges behavior many men believe is their prerogative. But calling on the state to remove the structural sources of personal entrapment goes further, challenging the normative foundation of male privilege itself, threatening a major source of the state's legitimacy and opening a political Pandora's box that could make controversies about abortion or gay rights look like parlor disagreements. A backlash by self-proclaimed "men's rights," "fathers' rights," and "conservative feminist" groups is already under way.

A related dilemma is that public engagement with state institutions has changed the advocacy movement almost as much as it did the service response. Shelters were conceived as a political service that could protect and support women while mobilizing their resourcefulness to challenge institutional discrimination. But partnership with traditional services and the legal establishment eroded the incentive to activism that brought droves of volunteers to the autonomous shelter movement, dulled its political edge, eliminated even the embryonic struggle to end discrimination against women in economic and political life, and reduced advocacy in hundreds of communities to missionary casework. Many shelters are now players in the social service game they originally hoped to change.

In *Bearing Right: How Conservatives Won the Abortion War*, Slate correspondent William Saletan argues persuasively that the movement for reproductive rights turned away from its political roots in feminism in the late 1980s when, following the advice of pollster Harrison Hickman, NARAL Pro-Choice America shifted the emphasis of its campaign from the rights of women to opposition to government intrusion, exemplified by its popular slogan "Who decides? You or them?" The base supporting abortion broadened considerably. But by the early 1990s, a majority of those who supported reproductive rights also favored state laws requiring minors to inform their parents if they sought an abortion and opposed federal funding for poor women's abortions, what Saletan calls "pro-choice conservatism."[2] The parallels to developments in the domestic violence movement are chilling.

These developments—stagnation of the movement and the failure of intervention—are part of a piece. The early initiatives in the domestic violence revolution rested on an insufficiently articulated principle: that political pressure rooted in collaboration with survivors of abuse was the key to ensuring that formal rights embodied in law—in this case, the rights to safety and equal protection—served to liberate rather than entrap women. This same approach also guaranteed the vitality of the movement. If the movement's political moorings are shaky, this underlying principle remains sound.

Outcomes for battered women can be dramatically improved by shifting the focus of research, policy, and intervention to coercive control. But this will not happen unless the advocacy movement is revitalized at its base. There should be no illusions about the seismic sociocultural and structural changes this entails. Indeed, at least in the short run, challenging men's use of control strategies to protect their already fragile privileges will increase opposition to our efforts to protect women from harm in personal life. This fact alone may convince some that the current course should be maintained, however imperfect.

Because the same structural inequities that shape coercive control also limit the movement's capacity to end it, a more global question than whether interventions work is whether the politics that surround their formulation improve the prospects for women's liberation generally, whether the issues and reforms we introduce unsettle the disciplinary mainstream on which sexual inequality depends or open new spaces where an autonomous women's movement can thrive. Regardless of whether interventions improved their long-term prospects, until the mid-1990s, everyone who came to shelter or worked in any way with abused women understood that their charge was being set by emancipatory dynamic outside their proximate administrative settings. When perpetrators were handcuffed, health or child welfare professionals asked women about abuse, and judges issue protection orders from the bench, all parties understood that something new was happening because women had demanded it. This understanding needs to be restored.

I have no interest in writing a political obituary. The point of describing how the domestic violence revolution is stalled is to stimulate debate about how to put it back on course. If the play of power begun in the 1970s has lost momentum, where we go next will determine whether the reforms that define the domestic violence revolution are a temporary salve or merely one step toward ending sexual injustice, our ultimate end.

Challenges to Intervention

That a new strategy is needed to address coercive control is obvious. Less clear are its components, how to implement them successfully, or the wisdom of tackling the problem now. I propose to criminalize coercive control. But this would bring us precariously close to defining male domination in personal life itself as a crime, directly threatening a core tenet of liberal jurisprudence, that it is possible to protect or compensate individuals without becoming entangled in the structural sources of their vulnerability. Respect for the distinction between an existential response to violence and a programmatic response to sexual inequality has been critical to the success of the domestic violence revolution, particularly in the legal system.

An incremental approach may be preferable to the more comprehensive strategy I propose. In Scotland, England, and other nations as well as in the United States, a definition that captures elements of coercive control has been put into play at a number of levels, and dozens of shelters, hospitals, child protection agencies, and other services now screen their clientele for fear and control as well as violence. Psychological abuse is being increasingly recognized by researchers as a core element of domestic violence and is being included in surveys and interview protocols. It should be relatively easy to disseminate this approach more widely.

But what then? By all accounts, there appears to be little difference between how researchers and helping professionals are approaching coercive control and how they approached domestic violence—documenting individual acts without identifying their political context or consequence, once again depicting the bars without grasping that they are part of a cage or that the resulting harms infect the very core of what makes us a free people. Not only does law enforcement continue to target incident-specific physical harm. Even where screens are augmented to include elements of coercive control, almost no one has devised intervention strategies to tackle the new forms of oppression being identified. Moreover, even if service professionals should agree to confront coercive control, unless they are armed with a far more comprehensive understanding of oppression in personal life and driven to act by a community-based movement at their back, can we really expect law, medicine, or social work to tackle the regulation of housework or of everyday activities such as dressing, driving, or using the phone; the isolation of women from friends or family members; prohibitions on education or employment; or even the financial exploitation of otherwise normal adults? A ready target of education would be courts that issue protection orders, because it is possible to prohibit a range of harmful behaviors other than violence even if they are not technically illegal. But how would these orders by monitored, who would enforce them, and how?

Where coercive control has been explicitly acknowledged, its dynamic has been interpreted one-dimensionally, undermining rather than enhancing women's empowerment. Instead of recognizing the dialectic of agency and oppression around which it is constructed, observers conclude that women entrapped by coercive control are even less able to act on their own behalf than victims of partner assaults. In commenting on a case that involved a regime of coercive control, New York's criminal court observed, "The destructive impact of violence in . . . an intimate relationship may be so complete that the victim is rendered incapable of independent judgment even to save one's own life."[3] To "break the control of the abuser" where a regime of control is in place, law professor Ruth Jones urges courts to assume guardianship over the woman's affairs, much as they now do with children or the frail elderly, a paternalistic approach that shifts the source of a woman's dependence but does nothing to free her.[4]

Coercive control has no easy fix. Addressing a problem of this magnitude requires new laws, defense and police strategies, additional funds, a revision of the research agenda in the field, new assessment tools, and substantial changes in how we service, protect, and empower battered women and their children. To muster the political will for these changes, to put coercive control on public agendas, requires that the considerable skills of the advocacy movement be mobilized. Even if this process could be short-circuited with a shopping list of new programs or policies, this would be unwise. As Yale political scientist Jim Scott makes clear in *Seeing Like a State,* the best intentioned reforms are unlikely to make things better—and often will make things worse—unless they evolve organically from the real possibilities taking shape in everyday lives of men and women. Broadening the discussion of how men oppress women is a first step. The sort of commitment needed to counter the entrapment of women in personal life can only emerge from a far-reaching public dialogue that brings those who have survived coercive control together with the multiple constituencies determined to end it.

The following discussion of the challenges posed by reframing domestic violence as coercive control is meant to be tentative rather than prescriptive, less an agenda for action than a stimulus to debate.

Equal Protection Versus the Anti-Subordination Principle

The need to radically recast intervention starts with a core demand raised by feminist lawmakers: that the law treat battered women in the same way as it does persons assaulted by strangers.

Applying the equal protection principle makes sense only if partner assault or coercive control are comparable to stranger assault, which they are not. Except for the use of violence, coercive control bears almost no resemblance to assault: its aim is dominance rather than physical harm; it targets autonomy, liberty, and personhood; and the tactics deployed are far broader and more insidious. Even when abuse is limited to assault, the fact that it entails the repeated use of violence against a single person gives it a cumulative significance that justifies treating it more seriously than anonymous assaults.

Applying the equal protection principle within an incident-specific framework has been disastrous for intervention. Because the typical abuse incident involves minor violence, approaching battering as analogous to stranger assault has reduced it to a second-class misdemeanor that floods the courts without producing the justice outcomes citizens have a right to expect, creating the dilemma of ineffective demand examined in chapter 2. By 1998, domestic violence comprised one-third of the misdemeanor caseload in urban Brooklyn and rural Delaware alike, and the proportion has increased since.[5] Because of the narrow violence equation, many of these cases involve fights or dual arrests that have no place in criminal court. Because the odds that a genuine incident will result in jail are miniscule, reassault is virtually inevitable. In Charlotte, North Carolina, repeat assaults in a six-month period were uncovered in 59% of the cases where arrests were made, and the real figure is probably closer to 80%.[6]

The only way to afford genuine protection to abused women is to provide an enhanced response predicated on the course of malevolent conduct to which they are being subjected and their special vulnerability due to sexual inequality.

Coercive control brings the same political principle into play that we apply in hate crimes—that acts used to subordinate a class of victims who are already unequal are unjust in a different way than acts designed to hurt persons physically and so merit different interventions.[7] Application of the anti-subordination principle is strengthened by the fact that the oppressive tactics used in coercive control specifically target facets of sexual inequality, such as women's default consignment to housework, care-taking, or sexual service. The equal protection argument confounds and depoliticizes these distinctions.

The law must continue to approach partner assaults as gender-neutral. Shelters or other interventions designed to support women primarily are justified on the pragmatic ground that women comprise the vast majority of those who seek protection from partner assault and that sexually integrated facilities place female victims at risk. With coercive control, the rationale for gender-specific intervention lies in its construction and typical victims as well as its substantive focus on stereotypic female roles that have no counterpart in the experiences of men, children, or other groups. This does not mean women are incapable of coercive control or that men are never its victims. What it means is that, like rape, everything about coercive control takes shape around conceptions of male dominance and the structures that situate men as dominant relative to women, irregardless of whether the person being degraded and subjugated is biologically male or the perpetrator is female. Even the general dimensions coercive control shares with other capture or power and control crimes (such as forced isolation or material deprivation) take on a gendered cast from the *particularity* of the liberty harms women suffer. Francine was made to eat her dinner off the floor like a dog and to burn her books *because* she was a woman, not merely because she was the object of her husband's control. The assertion that affronts to women's worth and dignity merit a public response assumes an equity interest in women's rights and capacities. But this interest cannot be realized merely by restoring the prior condition of vulnerability or by giving women special rights as victims as in *Wanrow*. Rather, our equity interest takes shape around public pressure to advance substantive equality for women even as we respond to individual victims as if gender mattered.

The Moral Justification for Intervening in Coercive Control

Opposition to coercive control is grounded in the same reasoning that leads us to oppose subjugation of any kind: that persons should be treated as ends in themselves, as autonomous centers of freedom whose dignity and worth deserve the fullest possible support. Violations of liberty are the central moral wrong in coercive control, regardless of whether violence is their means. From this perspective, it is right and just to use force to resist or liberate oneself from coercive control, as did Donna, Francine Hughes, Nate Parkman, and Bonnie Foreshaw, even if self-defense in the narrow legal sense is not involved.

Taking individual sovereignty as a moral principle discounts the importance of collective identity as a framework for social development and minimizes the fact that millions of women identify with cultures in which they live out their lives as appendages to the desires, needs, or plans of their fathers, sons, or male partners.[8] In *The Subjection of Women*, John Stuart Mill argued that women must rely on their sexuality for power, striving to please those on whose sufferance they depend, so long as their self-expression is confined to providing men with a support system of caring and household labor. Even so, uneven development compels us to distinguish societies where economic development permits women to exercise a level of choice in their life course unavailable in societies where objective circumstances dictate a life of self-negation for *all* persons and the best that can be hoped for is equal bondage to necessity. In the latter context, where markets may not be sufficiently robust to accommodate all persons as workers or consumers, women may choose to sacrifice personal autonomy so that their family or community can thrive. But in modern, highly industrial societies, overall progress is stunted when women are forced to withdraw from or minimize their commitment to economic, political, or social life in substantial numbers. As I emphasize in chapter 6, women's importance as producers, consumers, and citizens in modern economies seals the long-term fate of coercive control in much the same way that women's attainment of formal equality has rendered domestic violence ineffective. Without a supporting political struggle, however, the long run could be very long indeed.

Naming the Problem

Naming is a political act. By fixing attention on specific behaviors, consequences, or dynamics that have not been previously linked, it moves them from the shadow to the center of consciousness, influences how we think of those we associate with a problem, and shapes the allocation of resources. Defining alcoholism as a disease transformed the understanding and treatment of a previously stigmatized population of drunks. Calling abuse victims battered women helped make them rights bearing. Without a name, the victims of coercive control remain invisible even to themselves. They lack an "address."

Names also help market social problems. Relabeling is needed because the current terms for abuse subsume large numbers of men and women whose behaviors do not merit public sanction, imply that physical harm is the single focus of intervention (rather than personal liberty or domination), stress the psychological or emotional dimensions of control (rather than its structural dynamic), and effectively exclude whole classes of victims whose survival depends on public recognition. "Coercive control" has limited caché, even in discussions about abuse, and lacks the political resonance of "violence against women" as well as its applicability to parallel forms of oppression in other cultures. The distinction between violence and control is not always sharp, because violence has controlling effects and can suppress liberties even without complementary tactical maneuvers. I consider coercive control a form of abuse or battering, though the former suggests that a perpetrator has overstepped authority that is otherwise legitimate, which male authority over women is decidedly not, and the latter typically refers to violence only. "Men who commit" and "women who experience" coercive control may be the best choices because they avoid the all-encompassing implications of designating persons by one aspect of their behavior or experience. I use *entrapment* to capture the unique experiential effect when structural exploitation, regulation, and other controls are personalized. But in the criminal justice world, someone is entrapped when they are seduced or manipulated into committing a crime by someone working with law enforcement, a meaning I want to deemphasize.

Perhaps the most controversial issue is whether to portray the intent and consequence of coercive control as domination or to stick with less politically charged words such as "abuse" or even "control." Alongside the cliché-ridden rhetoric that has characterized discussions of domination in left or feminist circles is the practical reality that reintroducing domination as the focus of concern will cost us allies with no particular sympathy for feminist issues, including those opponents of "violence against women" who accept traditional gender hierarchies and view women paternalistically. This viewpoint was illustrated when Connecticut Senator Joe Lieberman told a New Hampshire audience during his vice presidential campaign in 2004 that "strong men don't hit women, they protect them." The inclusiveness of our movement is a real achievement, even if it has left us straddling a troubling law-and-order agenda. Bringing nonviolent subjugation to the table will damage our base of support and funding, perhaps significantly, much in the way acknowledging abuse among lesbians caused a rift in the advocacy movement. In the current climate of reaction, the media may counter talk of domination by putting our battered sisters and their supporters back into jumpsuits; picturing them as crocks, cranks, harpies, or worse; and contrasting them to women who wait stoically for direction at their husband's side, no matter that their souls are dead.

Still, ledgers have two sides. Reassigning attention to domination could constitute a new audience, attract a cohort of activists energized by a desire to be free rather than merely safe, and lay the foundation for new alliances to replace those we lose. Specifying a class of rights hidden in the interstices of personal life, reintroducing domination and naming coercive control broadens the demand for justice beyond the relatively narrow emphasis on violence-free relationships, puts the attainment of substantive equality back on the table, and suggests an agenda of rights and redistribution that would attract constituencies from civil rights and labor that have kept their distance because of our emphasis on policing. Grounding the concept of abuse in an affirmative concept of feminine difference would also re-engage thousands of women and men who have been turned off by the current victimization narrative, including many victims, and the generation of younger women who have come of age thinking of sexual equality as their birthright. It might also attract true conservatives, persons who may think women are naturally different from men, but whose sense of right and fair play is deeply offended by the thought of women being treated as anything other than fully entitled persons.

The most compelling rationale for adding coercive control to our lexicon is the existence of a huge mass of women who must now struggle alone and unrecognized. When Private Jessica Lynch was identified as a prisoner of war in Iraq, the outpouring of public sentiment transformed the tragic series of military blunders that led to her capture into a parable of heroism. With no comparable name for the continuum of strategies that imprison women in personal life, there can be no community of support or outrage, hence no comparable story of heroism.

Forging a Story Through Talking and Listening

Naming challenges us to *story* coercive control. Before a problem gains public acceptance, it must be fit into a narrative that evokes public interest in intervention. Victim stories take shape through myriad conversations with receptive audiences in specific social settings that provide a fertile ground for mutual recognition.

The victim story associated with domestic violence emerged gradually as victims encountered one another, advocates, researchers, and various audiences of service professionals. Questions about domestic violence were not asked sui generis but were sited in a self-conscious social practice that generated the experiential knowledge that rooted intervention. Chapter 1 sketches an important step in this process: the evolution of hospital-based rape teams into a specialized, institutionally based response that took root at hospitals, police departments, and other facilities. Over the next few decades, we trained clinicians to identify "the battered women in your practice" by asking patients from whom they instinctively withdrew, "Is someone in your life hurting you?" Replicated in various settings this process of soliciting information by posing simple, direct questions produced the sort of clinical epiphany that inspired institutional reforms. We now realize that the resulting mode of talk and listening concealed as much as it revealed about the true nature of oppression in women's personal lives. But the production of knowledge through a self-conscious, institutionally based practice was a critical step in translating a range of diverse experiences into the core narrative that propelled the movement forward for two decades.

Asking clients, patients, or friends, "Is there someone in your life making you afraid?" or "controlling what you do or say?" or "making you do something of which you are ashamed?" promises an even more profound awakening than asking women about violence. Control is less visible than physical abuse was in the 1970s, constitutes the heart of how men dominate women in personal life, and touches one of the more profound shaming rituals in relationships with men. Once coercive control is identified, subsequent talk can be attuned to the inchoate sense of individual promise repressed or denied, life projects that remain attenuated regardless of whether violence is dramatic. "What has changed since last year?" we may want to know, and "Why?" Whatever the response, simply asking these questions communicates that the downward trajectory reflected in entrapment can be reversed by identifying its source in an external and deliberate strategy. Coercive control lacks the fungibility of violence. We can't see or touch its consequences the way we can injury. And literal deprivations and objective constraints pose even more formidable obstacles to disclosure than violence or fear. But even to notice that autonomy, self-determination, and the practice of liberty are matters of concern for justice or health and invite talk about how and with what consequences her life is being thrown off course helps install privacy rights in a woman's consciousness.

To ground these questions requires a semi-formal practice that resembles how we approached partner violence 20 years ago and that allows providers to continually revise their own expectations and response as new information is garnered from victims and their practice concerns are shared with colleagues. Asking women about partner violence in their lives helped us identify appropriate resources even as it provided the documentation needed to demand new resources. But asking was itself a form of intervention both because it shaped women's self-definition and because it set the terms of our interactions. The new intervention process would combine the best aspects of case management with consciousness raising, our own as well as that of our patients or clients, drawing on the multidisciplinary approach needed to counter the many facets of coercive control while relying on cosupervision, client feedback, and other devices for an ongoing critique of practice. Even if victims of coercive control are initially triaged to services designed for domestic violence, bringing isolation and regulation to the forefront will stimulate a creative tension which existing services will be forced to accommodate.

Rethinking the Politics of Shelter Work

The politics of how traditional institutions listen to, learn from, and respond to victims of coercive control will be set by the example provided in shelter work. An important first step in restoring the activist face of the shelter movement is to rethink the idea of sanctuary as a front-line response to women's oppression in personal life as well as the organizational politics of the advocacy movement as a whole.

Political philosopher Wendy Brown argues that the initial demands a social movement raises for freedom are often "reactionary," in that the injuries and constraints it resists are couched in terms that are already familiar to the institutional regime and in a form it already opposes.[9] To salve their fiscal and political insecurity, shelters adopted a freedom-numbing rhetoric dominated by what Brown calls the "economy of perpetrator and victim": subordination was reduced to "injury," emancipation to "healing" or individual "empowerment," and system change to individual "accountability" and punishment. Sheltering does not change the fact that millions of victims return to communities where abuse is endemic and where the major alternatives to retaliation or submission is to run, seek safety in a traditional relationship with a "good" man, or turn to police and the courts with all the attendant contradictions. The predicament faced by the battered women's movement in the United States is reflected, with important variations, in other countries as well.

Shelters remove women to a semi-secret site where they coexist mainly with strangers in a similar predicament, a process that resembles the use of quarantine to combat infectious disease. In the name of creature comfort, "refuge" in England and in several other countries now consists largely of removal to contained units rather than congregate living, eliminating the collective recognition that gave so much vitality to early shelter life. Most shelters enforce rules that constrain any but essential outside contact, despite the fact that this situation strictly limits resident activism. Residents leave shelter with a safety plan that may include a protection order and arrangements for independent or congregate living. But this approach cannot counter the controller's capacity to reach them across social space or insulate them from liberty harms that involve interference with their work, money, or friendships.

Revisioning shelter practice to accommodate coercive control entails balancing safety with women's needs to regain control over resources that are rightfully theirs, greater emphasis on reconnection with indigenous support networks, and proactive steps to help women reengage forestalled life projects. An immediate step would be to return control over daily activity at shelters to residents and enhance the role of victim "voices" in forums where anti-violence strategies are conceived.[10] But it is unlikely that entrapment can be effectively countered unless women's decision making is restored where it has been denied—at their workplace, school, or the informal settings where they live out their family and social lives— by advocates directly entering these arenas to help rebuild the support networks picked clean by controlling partners. A network of safe homes, modified refuges, or other forms of community-based sanctuary could play a vital role in this process, so long as women's safety is protected by numbers, public visibility, and an internal security system, as it was at Chiswick, rather than by seclusion or secrecy.

Shelter from coercive control might not take the form of a separate house or place at all, but rather consist of a proactive, fluid, and public process rooted in the reconstruction of women's indigenous support networks across the broad spectrum of their activities. In this process, advocates would operate more like community organizers than counselors, providing links to services only insofar as this was needed to build the network. Building a protective shield at their workplaces could have steeled Bonnie's and Laura's courage just as enlisting Donna's family could have resolved the cultural predicament she faced when she decided to leave Frank. If advocates left the closed world of the shelter to "go down among the women" in families, peer groups, workplaces, supermarkets, schools, churches, and daycare centers, they would quickly find natural allies among the victim's acquaintances as well as women and men who share her experience of being isolated or constrained in their personal development and so have a powerful self-interest in helping her recover her voice through collective support. Traditional shelters might still provide emergency refuge for victims whose safety cannot be assured in any way. But the main source of "shelter" would be the extension of the safety zones women have already built in their everyday lives. In addition to organizing support for individual victims, advocates would give political direction to individual concerns by facilitating the larger reforms in housing, employment, child care, and the like that *all* persons in the community require to feel secure, helping mobilize organizations as well as individuals. Its numerous links to sexual inequalities make it critical that actions to end coercive control be part of a larger social agenda, much in the way that local efforts to integrate lunch counters or work sites in the 1960s were linked to the national campaign for civil rights. As they were engaged in this process, women subjected to coercive control would appear less as victims to be nurtured or pitied (because their victimhood would be recognized as symptomatic of widely shared forms of oppression) than as persons who have stood up to domination and given it a name and a face, women who talked truth to power much as Rosa Parks did when she refused to move to the back of the Montgomery bus.

Advocacy movements do many things well. But they are not structured to provide a uniform programmatic response to developments in the field. In the United States, apart from several federally funded centers that offer technical assistance to local programs in health, law, and other specialized areas, two umbrella federations give the movement national visibility: the National Coalition Against Domestic Violence (NCADV), formed in 1978, and the National Network to End Domestic Violence (NNEDV), established around the Pennsylvania Coalition Against Domestic Violence in 1990. Shortly after the NCADV was founded, Congress appropriated $65 million to be spent over 3 years, primarily for shelter services. Since then, lobbying efforts by these and sister organizations helped shape federal legislation that increased U.S. government funding for state coalitions and local programs to almost $90 million annually by 2000.[11] With average budgets of approximately $1.5 million, most of which is passed through to shelters in individual states, the state battered women's coalitions provide the movement's operational infrastructure rather than a tightly knit national organization. If this structure allows shelters to accommodate the political realities in the states, it also inhibits the development of national leadership that can counter the forces of reaction and conservatism that currently influence policy making or provide the central coordination needed to radically change the form or content of intervention. State coalition leaders are often significant players in statewide policy making in areas affecting abuse and prominent in the "old girls' networks" that help set broader policy agendas in a number of states. Even so, these networks operate within the narrow confines of traditional party politics, attending to career ladders, patronage, turf building and the like, and have few if any links to broad progressive movements outside the capital. Women's Aid in Great Britain suffers from the opposite problem, with a solid national leadership that participates regularly in government policy making but little government funding, leaving refuge organizations to raise almost all their funds locally against a background of demands for them to provide an ever broader range of support for women and children.

Advocates are unlikely to shift course on their own. Constructing a political practice that is emotionally complex, activist oriented, and broadly focused on structural inequalities demands new organizational forms that express the movement's vision and provide a "home" to many levels of involvement as the movement grows.

Adapting a Typology of Abuse

The domestic violence model has the virtue of moral consistency, but it subsumes too broad a range of experiences to be practically useful. To properly address abuse in women's lives means to treat it as multifaceted phenomena, determine which of its contexts or expressions merit public concern, and differentiate our response accordingly. The typology rests on a distinction between partner assault and coercive control. The major differences between these types of abuse can be summarized along the following dimensions.

The Frequency and Cumulative Effects of Violence

The violence deployed in both assault and coercive control can be distinguished from mugging or other stranger assaults by its frequency, often involving hundreds or even several thousand incidents, by its use to suppress rather than resolve conflict, and by its cumulative effects on a victim's autonomy and physical integrity over time. In all abuse, a victim's vulnerability is a function of her capacity to escape and/or resist and can be measured by concurrent levels of fear, injury, and entrapment. In assault, where violence is used as a direct means of harm or control, the extent and level of coercion holds the key to assessment. But in coercive control, where violence is used to reinforce complementary forms of oppression, its frequency and effects, including injury or death, are as often the by-product of a woman's prior subordination as its cause. While the loss of autonomy can be a secondary consequence in partner assault, a victim's personhood is the main target in coercive control.

Privileged Access and the Presumption of Intimacy

As we saw in chapters 4 and 8, the fact that men enjoy privileged access to female partners is critical to the durability of abuse—why men *stay*—even after separation. In all forms of partner abuse, the presumption of intimacy inhibits outside intervention and allows offenders to garner unique knowledge about a partner's movements and vulnerabilities. But whereas this special knowledge serves mainly to facilitate a perpetrator's access to a partner in assault cases, in coercive control, information gathering can extend to a woman's phone conversations, diaries, deepest fears, toileting habits, and other facets of their lives. This allows men to personalize abuse in ways that distinguish it from other oppressive patterns of conduct.

Structural Constraint

The key difference between assault and coercive control is the presence in the latter strategy of structural constraints that allow men to exploit and redirect women's resources to satisfy their needs, regulate their behavior, suppress conflict and resistance, and close off opportunities for escape By violating such basic liberties as decisional autonomy, freedom of speech, and the privacy rights identified by Justice Douglas in *Roe v. Wade*, these constraints create an objective condition of subordination that resembles hostage taking and is independent of a victim's personality or perception Constraints are designed to anticipate resistance. As Laura's case illustrated, however, they may also become more expansive over time to accommodate the changing cost-benefit ratios created as the relationship evolves. The idiosyncratic and improvised substance of specific constraints contrasts with the generality of their form, indicating that the liberty harms involved remain the same regardless of the unique dynamics in a given case. The regulatory regimes in coercive control run the gamut from unstated rules or expectations ("you won't make me jealous") through primitive, transparently self-serving prohibitions or commands ("If I decide that we sleep together, you will humbly comply") to explicit designs for living that appear to have been delivered from on high like Nick's list. Women's social vulnerability due to persistent discrimination explains *why* men can introduce these constraints with relative impunity,

But differences in power in abusive relationships are continually being reshaped around women's attempts to carve out safety zones where they can experience moments of autonomy. In domestic assault, power flows directly from "the barrel of a gun" without the mediating influence of structural deprivation or objective rules. In coercive control, power appears in its postmodern guise, as diffuse, decentered, fragmented, and unified only in its consequence.

The Spatial and Temporal Extension of Abuse

Separation can be an effective antidote in cases where abuse is limited to assault by reducing the frequency of violence, for instance, though the risk of severe or fatal violence may actually increase. But physical proximity is largely irrelevant to ongoing victim risk in coercive control, where tactical regulation—and the feeling of entrapment—often extends along the entire continuum of a woman's activities. Cyberstalking, beepers, cell phones, and various tracking devices are commonly used to supplement traditional forms of surveillance, giving coercive control a unique extensiveness. This complements its intensity, the tactical penetration of everyday routines. One result is that victims experience the perpetrator as "always on."

Entrapment

The consequence of assault is a condition of subjugation based on fear of physical harm. Donna's feeling that she was living "on the edge of a roof" that she could fall off at any time captures the primary subjective outcome of coercive control: an existential condition of unfreedom or *entrapment* that is reflected in the distinctive problem profile that many battered women exhibit after the onset of abuse. Even when entrapment takes the extreme form of traumatic bonding, it is rooted in identifiable structural deprivations and liberty harms that can persist even in the absence of violence.

The Gendered Nature of Coercive Control

Women and men assault their partners in similar ways and with similar motives. Recently, I worked with a husband who was hospitalized three times after his wife's jealous assaults, a wife who cut her husband several times because she believed he was sexually assaulting her daughter (although she later admitted this was a projection from her childhood), and an immigrant wife who was 15 years younger and much taller than the husband she regularly assaulted when she wanted money or when he questioned her about leaving their child unattended. But I have never had a case that involved a female perpetrator of coercive control, and no such cases are documented in the literature. The asymmetry in coercive control reflects the asymmetric nature of sexual inequality, not the fact that women are less aggressive, controlling, or domineering than men. All assaults on women by their male partners have a sexual component, a fact reflected in the clustering of abuse-related injuries to the face, breast, abdomen, and other body parts identified with female sexuality. But coercive control is also *about* gender. To solidify their privileges, men undo their partner's unique femininity piece by piece, trying to degrade them into the stereotype against which they can "do" their manhood, albeit as a homunculus.

Putting the Typology of Abuse to Work in Public Law

In the past, the law treated most domestics as if they involved marital disputes, and so almost no victims were protected or perpetrators sanctioned. Mandatory arrest policies are predicated on the equally untenable assumption that all acts of force among partners that might cause injury constitute assaults. This approach protects a significant subgroup of victims and appears to have leveled the playing field somewhat by giving black women greater access to legal protections than in the past. But its costs include the trivialization of domestic assault and coercive control and the arrest of thousands of women who have committed no crime. Most abused persons are still unprotected. These problems, as well as the gross inefficiencies in other services for abused women, stem from the mistaken belief that domestic violence is a unitary and incident-specific phenomenon whose severity can be measured by injury.

The first challenge in implementing the typology is to exclude fights from our purview. In addition to sharply reducing dual arrests, excluding fights would allow us to garner incidence and prevalence data with real relevance to service planning and evaluation, improve the ratio of cases brought to justice outcomes in the legal system, and free up resources needed to upgrade the response to partner assault and coercive control. Although some fights may justify mandated counseling, mediation, or even sanctions, victims must be central to this determination process and doing nothing should remain a viable option.

A crude first step toward excluding fights is to focus only on acts that raise safety concerns for their victims, making special provision for immigrants and victimized members of other marginalized groups who hesitate to identify their risk because they fear the consequences of public exposure. The focus on safety issues excludes the large number of persons currently identified as victims or perpetrators of domestic violence who are involved in fights where neither party views violence as illegitimate or desires outside assistance. Many women charged in dual arrest cases fall into this group. As we saw, no safety concerns were raised by the vast majority of persons who reported the use of force in their relationship to the NFVS surveys.

The downside of relying on expressed safety concerns is that we could easily miss most cases of coercive control and cases of assault where violence is routine, but too low-level to elicit a sense of emergent risk.

Critics propose two alternatives to the current policy of mandatory arrest—to base arrest on victim discretion and to gauge sanctions to the degree of harm inflicted or threatened—standards that commonly guide how police respond to stranger assaults. But too close an analogy between partner and stranger assault would be unwise, as we've seen. Their frequency, cumulative effects, and link to witness intimidation suggest that partner assaults be treated as a course-of-conduct crime and so as closer in form to stalking or harassment than to assault. Moreover, because no effective means currently exists to prevent a perpetrator's continued access to the victim, her expressed wishes are often an unreliable gauge of actual risks. Still, in cases where partner assaults are noninjurious and both partners share a legitimate desire to work things out, it may be appropriate to rely on community-based options in lieu of jail, including batterer intervention programs and models of restorative justice in which norms favoring gender equality as well as violence cessation are key.[12]

Statutory revisions that exclude fights from interdiction or lower the level of sanctions applied to minor assaults only make sense after we can confidently differentiate them from the low-level, routine violence typical of coercive control, the most dangerous form of abuse. This cannot be accomplished by relying solely on victim discretion, because victim decision making is a major target of coercive control, or on a calculus of harms, because the violence used in coercive control is typically noninjurious. Taking constraints on victim volition into account can dramatically improve intervention decisions. In a recent case, the perpetrator pursued his partner to her family home, held her mother at bay with a screwdriver, insisted the girl leave with him, which she did, and then took her to his apartment where he assaulted her repeatedly. When the police arrived in response to the woman's call, she denied her partner was present. Despite the fact that the woman had no visible injuries, police considered the possibility that her will was being constrained, searched the apartment, and made an arrest. The man was convicted of kidnapping and assault in part because I could explain to the jury why, despite the minor nature of the violence involved, the woman's compliance with the boyfriend and her denial of danger were adaptations to his coercive control.

Implementing a typology of abuse would solve a number of practical problems. In addition to the justice and measurement gains already mentioned, it would increase victim cooperation with prosecution, elevate the status of domestics as a general justice issue, and improve the morale of associated personnel accordingly. Targeting resources to the type of harms inflicted would greatly improve the cost-effectiveness of intervention and help determine how resources should be allocated to violence prevention, crisis intervention, and broader systems' issues. These benefits would more than compensate for the increased cost of using stiffer sanctions and broadening women's options.

To support a revised legal focus on coercive control, local domestic violence collaborations should extend their policy agendas to highlight economic supports for women and children as well as reforms in housing, employment, and health care. These reforms would benefit low-income families whose capacity to cope with poverty is compromised by coercive control and those who are made poor by coercive control, like the fundamentalist woman from the Iowa home schooling case. Programs that have built postshelter housing, incorporated job counseling into safety planning, or have partnered with local business groups to provide employment for victims have had dramatic success in ending abusive relationships.

Which of women's many voices are we hearing when victims ask for help? Are we hearing what Carol Gilligan, Jean Baker Miller, and other "relational" psychologists consider "the different voice" of women rooted in feminine instincts for care-taking, self-sacrifice, and interdependence? Or, to paraphrase Catharine MacKinnon, is the voice we are hearing evoked by the man who is standing on the woman's neck? Until we can answer this question with confidence, the wisest approach is the most conservative—to treat every case involving partner violence as if we are dealing with coercive control unless a careful assessment of the perpetrator's history and the victim's experience proves us wrong.

Reframing Battering as a Liberty Crime

Winning public support to protect women from liberty harms in personal life poses another major challenge.

The coercion used in coercive control deprives women of the same rights to health, safety, bodily integrity, peace of mind, and physical mobility denied in a range of comparable violent crimes. But the rationale for intervention to stop coercive control shifts from physical integrity to our broader interest in personal freedom as a foundation for moral, political, and economic life. Subjectivity atrophies when women's exercise of liberty and equality is obstructed. The most deeply felt are the harms coercive control inflicts on women's sexual identity and in realms of everyday life where they imagine, devise, and express this identity in a distinct personhood. The new model of intervention would replace the paternalistic stereotypes that currently dominate the justice response by emphasizing what women have been kept from doing for themselves and so for economy and society. The new theory of harms is rooted in the minimal conditions for individuation identified by Cornell, including the right to self-respect emphasized by John Rawls, and in Justice Douglas's understanding of privacy as extending from the right to be left alone by the government to an affirmative right to liberty, a right to autonomy over the development and expression of one's "intellect, interest, tastes and personality," and the freedom to care for and express oneself.

A theory of liberty harms links broad social inequities to individual acts of victimization; explains why obstructing, monitoring, regulating, and exploiting women's personal activities constitute discrimination; and shows how these acts compromise women's personhood and their rights as citizens. Applying this theory suggests not only why interventions must target a broad range of harms in addition to injury but that victims be compensated for these harms, for instance, by extending existing victim compensation/disability programs or broadening tort law to cover the added medical expenses, lost wages, and the costs incurred because of deferred educational or career opportunities or of suffering degradation and dependence due to isolation, intimidation, and control. Even if victims are compensated for the degradation of femininity suffered in personal life the same way they are for sexual harassment at work, there is no easy way to compensate society for the most profound cost of coercive control—the aggregate loss to the polity of the contribution victims could and would make if their capacities were freely utilized instead of redirected to bolster the position of individual men.

If women's right to full autonomy in personal life was widely accepted or realized through their substantive equality, coercive control would not be effective in the first place and the gendered micro-regulation described here would already be visible and widely condemned. Some tactics used to isolate, intimidate, and control women are subtle. But the most common, like taking women's money, regulating their time, dress, mobility, or right to communicate freely, are not. As we've seen, the regulation of these activities is invisible in plain sight for two contradictory reasons. Decisional autonomy in using the phone, disposing of one's wages, picking one's clothes, or in how one drives, cooks, or cleans is taken so much for granted by men and most women that its abrogation goes unnoticed, and no one thinks of these activities as containing rights that can be violated. At the same time, because of their default consignment to homemaking, care taking, and the like, women are expected to accept the burdens associated with many of the activities that are regulated without complaint, making the status of choice in these areas ambiguous to start with. By contrast, men are praised when they perform these tasks because it is assumed they chose to do so. Popular writer Laura Shapiro captures this distinction when she quips, "we will know full sexual equality has arrived when men cook dinner even when they don't want to."[13] At one level, even the hyper-regulation reflected in Nick's lists merely personalize the disciplinary valence contained in normative expectations for how women will enact femininity. Like victims of coercive control, the advocacy movement is challenged to articulate a right to self-direction in arenas of life where gendered constraints are widely accepted.

Bringing liberty harms into play is particularly important in the justice setting, where traditional theories of victimization fail to capture the experience of entrapment. Because the FBI missed the extent to which Danielle DiMedici was entrapped by James Parker, its agents thought she was ambivalent about prosecution when she claimed her held her hostage without using force. Francine Hughes, Nate Parkman, Donna Balis, and the Palestinian woman who paralyzed her husband with a club responded with levels of force that were vastly disproportionate to the proximate levels of assault or intimidation they faced, making it difficult for them to claim self-defense. Their response was justified only because they were being deprived of freedom and autonomy, rights that we normally treat as inalienable. Of course, the fact that a right is unconditional does not mean victims have an unqualified license to use violence to restore it. Even had her jurors concluded that making Francine burn her school books or eat the TV dinner off the floor were degrading, without highlighting the overarching liberty harm constituted by the totality of her oppression, they would have been extremely reluctant to afford her a right to respond by taking a life. But the proportionality here, as in hostage taking or kidnapping, is between the act and the liberty harms involved, not the proximate threat of bodily harm a victim confronted.

Crafting a New Legal Response

A new body of criminal and civil law is needed to identify coercive control as a public wrong. At a minimum, the new statutes would define coercive control as a course-of-conduct crime much like harassment, stalking, or kidnapping, rather than as a discrete act, and highlight its effects on liberty and autonomy. Like harassment, the acts identified with coercive control would be recognized by their intent, consequence, and their functional role in the overall pattern of criminal conduct regardless of where they occur or the proximity of the perpetrator and victim when they occur. The log book, the beeper game, the telephone rule, and the sweatshirt offer could be identified as facets of a criminal pattern because of their regulatory intent, the implied consequences of noncompliance, and because they were linked to a history of violence and intimidation.

The personal and idiosyncratic nature of its tactics make it possible to capture the range of bad acts involved in coercive control only in a categorical way, by delineating violence, intimidation, exploitation, humiliation, isolation, and control as distinct dynamics of harm for instance, and by identifying a broad liberty right in personal life. An important initiative is Missouri legislation that defines domestic violence assault to include "controlling behavior" and purposefully isolating intimate partners, where *isolation* is defined as "unreasonably and substantially restricting or limiting access to other persons, telecommunication devices or transportation for the purpose of isolation."[14] A broad outline of its dynamics should make it clear that coercive control contains the major elements required for behavior to be deemed criminal: it is voluntary (as opposed to compelled by external circumstances), intentional, causes recognizable social harm, is distinctive in its harms and dynamics—and so can be differentiated from other bad acts—and is directed at a class of victims already made vulnerable by sexual inequality and discrimination. Those responsible for and victimized by coercive control are readily identified.

A victim must prove malevolence in domestic assault because injury can be caused accidentally or in self-defense, be self-inflicted, or result from psychological or biological malfunctions. None of these issues arises in coercive control, which unfolds over time and where the level of rational planning and particularity points directly to the actus rea (or guilty act) and the presence of the mens rea (or guilty mind) needed to hold persons morally responsible. Assaults, threats, stalking, harassment, and many other facets of coercive control are already crimes. But these crimes take on new significance when woven into the larger pattern of entrapment. Lessup's jumping out of a tree was a specific threat that would have frightened anyone. But the effect of his act on Bonnie was greatly magnified by his earlier abuse and control. By contrast, acts that are not normally thought of as criminal, such as the telephone rule or the sweatshirt offer, take their malevolent meaning only when they are joined with convergent acts in coercive control.

The magnified effects when otherwise criminal acts are combined or occur against a background of prior abuse and the important harms inflicted by acts of isolation and regulation that are not now criminal highlight why attempts by prosecutors to up the ante in domestic violence cases by packaging assaults with separate charges for threatening, harassment, stalking, and the like are inadequate. Packaging also loses the dramatic effect of imagining a single coordinated strategy and reduces what would constitute a Class A felony if charged as a single crime to a potpourri of second-class misdemeanors. The particularity of coercive control also makes another alternative to criminalization less desirable: to subsume coercive control under existing course of conduct crimes, such as hostage taking or harassment.

Far less dramatic changes are needed in civil than in criminal law. Earlier, we sketched the agonized efforts of New Jersey courts to grasp the ongoing nature of abuse. A more sensible approach was taken by the Illinois Supreme Court. In *Feltmeier v. Feltmeier*, it used an intentional infliction of emotional distress theory to hold that domestic abuse could qualify as a continuing tort.[15] The tort involved separate actions begun during the marriage but extending after the divorce and including assaults, throwing things at Ms. Feltmeier, preventing her from leaving her house, yelling insults, breaking into her locked drug cabinet, and stalking her. The court did not say that "the cumulative, continuous acts" were required to constitute the tort, hesitated to pinpoint "the moment when enough conduct had transpired to make it [abuse] actionable," and agreed such cases should be approached with "extreme caution" when allegations involve marital incidents. But it rejected the argument that Mr. Feltmeier's acts were separate offenses, acknowledged the law's difficulties in finding an effective way to hold perpetrators of domestic violence criminally or financially accountable, and dated the statute of limitations from the end of the conduct rather than the discovery of the injury, the dissolution of the marriage, or the occurrence of the second cycle of violence as in New Jersey.

Existing assault laws technically covered domestic violence. The rationale for crafting distinct domestic violence statutes was to fix attention on a class of victims and perpetrators that had received an inappropriate response from law enforcement. By contrast, crafting a legal response to coercive control would identify an entirely new complex of behaviors as wrong and raise the profile of liberty rights in personal life whose violation is not currently illegal. Violence by a partner has become a litmus test of the integrity of relationships. The normative force of defining coercive control as a crime would be even greater, opening up new arenas of expectation, promise, and struggle around substantive equality, autonomy, and freedom in personal life, and moving us toward the universalism and inalienability implicit when we affirm rights and capacities as human rather than particular.

The Boundary Challenge

In criminalizing coercive control, we mark as unacceptable in modern, democratic societies a particularly noxious means of exploiting the discriminatory effects of sexual inequality in personal life. Our aim is not to outlaw sexual inequality, let alone male domination, any more than laws against lynching were intended to outlaw racism. The success of reforms depends on distinguishing coercive control from the constraints implicit in the normative enactment of gender roles.

Because violence is a tangible means with observable consequences, the only major issue to resolve with partner assaults is which types of force merit sanctions or a service response. Because the tactics deployed in coercive control fall on a continuum with a broader range of normative behaviors, it is much more difficult to define where the normal expressions of inequality end and "the crime" begins. For instance, when does the belief that "a woman's place is in the home" become isolation? It would be a cruel irony if we decided not to punish coercive control because women's autonomy is already compromised by gender stereotypes. A practical solution to this dilemma is to focus on the perpetrator's behavior rather than on its translation into compliance, on the imposition of rules for socializing or performing household tasks, for instance, rather than the fact that a woman ends friendships or goes about cleaning ritualistically like Laura did. Investigation would still be required to determine whether the disproportionate assignment of responsibilities or resources is voluntary or the result of illegitimate controls, as in the case of the softball pitcher. To the degree that constraints are patterned, ongoing, nonvoluntary, and personalized, we can assume they comprise a planned and malevolent course of criminal conduct rather than normative behavior. My experience suggests this investigatory process is not as difficult as it sounds, because controls are typically explicit, transparent rather than subtle, and recognized by both parties as constraints.

The level of scrutiny required to decipher a pattern of bad acts in particular relationships creates another boundary dilemma—that the invasion of privacy needed to garner accurate information may outweigh the benefits of intervention or make police and other providers uncomfortable. Controllers rarely leave the sort of paper trail I had in Donna's and Laura's cases and frequently construct barriers to detection and access that can only be penetrated if service providers persist. Intrusiveness is as inevitable in cases of coercive control as it is in rape inquiries. Eliciting information from victims about fears, forms of degradation, and subjugation requires an even higher level of trust than asking about violence and assumes an openness and willingness to partner with abused women rather than patronize them that is rare among helping professionals. If the worst response would be to abandon the field of public law in the face of the boundary dilemma, it is nonetheless critical that intervention be justified by the probability that devastating harms of liberty and autonomy are involved.

Is Coercive Control Indentured Servitude?

Another facet of the boundary challenge is raised by a provocative proposal that has special applicability to coercive control, that sanctions against woman battering be based on the Thirteenth Amendment to the U.S. Constitution prohibiting indentured servitude rather than the equal protection clause of the Fourteenth Amendment. In a path-breaking article arguing this point, law professor Joyce McConnell traces the interpretive history of the Thirteenth Amendment, showing that its congressional framers in the 1860s were well aware of the parallels between slavery and women's status in private life as well as of the extent to which marriage as a form of service to husbands and families paralleled the role of wage labor.[16] Although she was apparently unaware of the coercive control model of abuse, McConnell draws a parallel between "extreme cases" of wife battering and the creation of slave-like conditions through the private use of force outlawed in the amendment and argues that the elimination of the marital rape exemption suggests that U.S. courts are willing to treat crimes similarly whether they occur in the public or private sphere.

A related proposal, illustrated by the civil rights relief to victims of domestic violence originally included in VAWA, is that we apply existing discrimination law to coercive control by extending the sex discrimination provisions in Title VII of the 1964 Civil Rights Act to personal life, treating isolation or regulation as civil rights violations, or apply laws prohibiting "sexual harassment" in the workplace.[17] Where criminal or tort remedies frame violence as a form of individual wrong doing or a cause of personal injury, enacting a federal civil rights provision identifies abuse as a group-based harm rooted in inequality, thereby giving victims a common point of reference to counter the claim it is a private concern or the result of their complicity.[18]

The belief that women are naturally suited to the private sphere of family life justified excluding them from public, law-regulated activities (such as the franchise) for centuries and insulated the home and family from the intrusion of law, denying women a shield against physical and sexual abuse. To this extent, the right to privacy is a right of men "to be let alone" and "to oppress women one at a time."[19]

Applying laws devised to regulate public behavior to personal relationships challenges the public/private dichotomy as well as the assumptions that have governed constitutional law, that "discrimination" (a federal concern) and relationship problems (matters for state courts) are mutually exclusive phenomenon and that the constitution is designed to protect individuals from intrusion by the state, not from one another. The premise behind this approach is that the spheres of intimacy, privacy, and family life are analogous, either through homology or convergence, with the public and economic spheres to which existing constitutional, civil rights, and human rights doctrine are normally applied. McConnell points to the historical convergence of the market and private life to support her point and reminds us that slavery was a social (private/family/cultural) as well as an economic system. She also reiterates an argument first made by Charlotte Perkins Gilman and reiterated in the 1920s by Eleanor Roosevelt and other women activists, that a clear social interest in whether women's unpaid labor in the home and in relationships is performed freely or under duress derives from its central contribution to the maintenance of market society. So long as the family is "open" to the market, inequality flows both ways: if sexual harassment imports women's availability to men from the home to the workforce, coercive control exploits women's social inequality to undermine their privacy rights. From this vantage point, pursuing controllers into private life merely extends law's function in the public sphere.

Personal life, economic life, and political life are interwoven in so many ways in modern, industrialized societies that it seems eminently reasonable to treat them as part of a single dynamic rather than as separate spheres. Even in the absence of coercive control, the relative shares of income, political power, and other resources women command disadvantage them in relationships even as their dependence on men in personal life is reproduced through sex segregation in employment and earnings.[20] Classic liberalism would use public law to protect individual bearers of private rights from encroachment by the state. But this takes for granted precisely what coercive control places at risk for women—the existence of a vital personal sphere that would flourish on its own but for illegitimate external intrusion. To respond appropriately to coercive control, we must abandon the belief that public law should only be concerned with public harms. However, this does not mean that the public and personal spheres should be conflated.

In attempting to encase women's subjectivity in their roles as homemakers, care takers, sex objects, and dependents, coercive control is nothing more than a projection of the male imaginary from the public to the personal sphere. The feminist critique demystifies this process by showing that "the private" is anything but a realm of comfort and safety for women. Taken to an extreme, however, this approach results in an overso-cialized view of personal life that misses its critical importance to women. Nothing emerges more clearly from my work with abused women than the importance they attach to moments of autonomy in personal life where they can discover, preserve, and experiment with the sense of what is uniquely theirs. Even if the "private" is defined reflexively, as the sphere where law is *not*, the "personal" represents an affirmation of differ-ence within this sphere, a way of individualizing social possibility against the normative regime that joins public inequalities to men's right to do with women as they please. Women struggle to sustain this sense of the personal not only against their reduction to stereotype but against any public identity that is fixed or static. When this struggle fails or is coopted, an existential crisis ensues, as Laura's case illustrated.

Drawing on Douglas's concept of privacy rights, the human rights literature, Locke's understanding of power, and Cornell's notion of the imaginary domain, I have suggested that the specific liberty harm imposed by coercive control is the threat it poses to an affirmative femi-ninity born largely in personal life and taken into the world through life projects. Although coercive control extends into the public sphere, it is designed to deny women a personal life. From this perspective, interven-tion aims to cultivate as well as defend as a matter of right the precondi-tions needed if women are to become individuated beings who can participate in public and political life as equal citizens. In contrast to the classic liberal view that sees individuality as given rather than made in relationships, I understand the possibilities for personhood as historically specific, relational, and as expressed through a continuous process of experimentation and subjective development, an interplay between the personal and the public. Any systemic attempt to degrade these possibilities or foreclose this interplay is a matter of the gravest public concern.

To the women in my practice, the sphere of liberty rights in personal life is an ideal worth fighting and even dying for and is the only solid foundation for real intimacy, even where they are constrained to spend a greater portion of their lives than men performing unrewarded domestic labor. Coercive control becomes a proper object for public rights and management because it adds yet another disciplinary component to the already distorted assignment of social roles. But at bottom it is experi-enced as violating a right to personhood that has no obvious counterpart in the market or public sector. Regardless of how unfairly sexual inequal-ities play themselves out in relationships, the major activities through which personal lives are created, the formation of personality and concep-tualization and development of life projects, devising one's sexual identity, the early socialization of children, the "romantic dialectic," are "a labor of love" and never reducible to economic principles or questions of power. I worry that applying discrimination law or laws against slavery directly to private life will diminish the particularity for which battered women struggle rather than reinforce it, albeit with the aim of leveling the playing field. What women want from personal life is to be recognized as different, private, and equal.

With the notable exception of federal judge Jack Weinstein's use of the Thirteenth Amendment to limit the right of Child Protective Services to remove children solely because their mother was a victim of domestic violence, courts have applied indentured servitude narrowly to "coerced labor" in the market where threats of and/or actual physical or legal coercion have been used rather than to situations involving psychological coercion, intimidation, or control.[21] Writing for the majority in *United States v. Kozminski*, Justice Sandra Day O'Connor explicitly warned that utilizing a standard of coercion that included the subjective experience of victims could criminalize "a broad range of day to day activity," presumably including forms of abuse.[22] In a separate opinion, Justice Brennan interpreted the amendment more broadly: to prohibit any means of coercion that actually succeeds in reducing the victim to a condition of servitude resembling that in which antebellum slaves were held, a view that could theoretically be applied to coercive control.[23]

McConnell counters O'Connor's objections by arguing that battering is, in fact, an issue of compelled work. Coercive control is unquestionably an economic crime, but only in part because women's unpaid domestic service is commanded rather than offered. Its larger economic importance is that by obstructing the full development and application of a significant portion of women's social labor, it sets irrational (personal, arbitrary) limits on exploitation and so on overall social progress.

McConnell cites the law's response to marital rape to illustrate the advantages to women when the law collapses the distinction between public and private acts. But the marital rape exemption actually supports the opposite point. Courts in many states continue to set higher standards of proof in sexual assault cases involving husbands or partners than when strangers are charged.[24] Meanwhile, because marital rape takes its special cast from the access, personal knowledge, and privileges associated with its commission by a partner, it *should* be treated differently and *more severely* than similar crimes committed by strangers. As a result of its unique relation to personal life, sexual assault is far more likely to be repeated when it is committed by partners and almost always occurs amid other forms of violence, intimidation, and control. The level of unfreedom, subordination, dependence, and betrayal associated with marital rape has no counterpart in public life. Arguments that equate public and private crimes have unquestionably helped win formal equality for women, particularly given the reluctance of federal courts to take up family concerns. But to achieve real or substantive equality requires fighting for women's right to assert difference and for a corresponding elevation of those sites in personal and public life where difference is made and given imaginative expression.

Reframing the Battered Woman's Defense

If we reject the general applicability of trauma theories to abused women, what should we put in their place? Battered women often complain that they do not recognize themselves in their representation as pathetic victims of another's will in the courtroom. What they mean is that the portrait of their victimization fails to capture the feverish and moment-to-moment calculation by which they have attempted to retain their integrity while keeping themselves safe. A woman who had mounted a traditional battered woman's defense told me that she felt like her ex-partner was talking during a closing argument in which her lawyer stressed her abuse-induced incapacities. The challenge is to provide a defense that encompasses the range of harms victims have experienced without compromising their liberty interest in equal personhood.

A defense based on coercive control builds its narrative around two complementary themes: the unfolding of a woman's life projects and their denial through the deployment of illegitimate authority. In this story, physical and psychological injury take a secondary role to the struggle to preserve freedom against oppression, connection against isolation, self-respect against humiliation, and intimidation, autonomy, and independence against agency denied. Guided by the moral presumption that personhood is an essential and irreducible ingredient of humanity and citizenship, the story presents the woman's defense of the privacy and liberty rights I have identified as its preconditions. Direct and expert testimony illustrate the four (or more) dimensions of coercive control and contrast who this woman is (her "survivor" self) with her "victim" self, the reflexive persona imposed through coercive control. Instances of deprivation are contrasted to corresponding expressions of agency: the taking of her money or restrictions of her work to her work record or earning potential; the burning of her books to the meaning of continuing education in her life; the limits or regulation of her time to the many ways in which she has self-directed her time to benefit herself and others; and the restraints on her movement to her quest for safety zones. The stage is set to reframe the overall victimization process through the prism of a woman's unfolding subjectivity. By treating her like his object, like she is nothing or nobody, her partner has degraded her sexual identity (as a woman), her political subjectivity (as a citizen), and her personal agency. The court takes the measure of her response by contrasting this victim self to the survivor who is strong, resourceful, reasonable, insightful, and aggressive.

Through no fault of trauma theory, juries are increasingly prone to resent what Marcia Clark, the lead prosecutor in the O. J. Simpson case, called "the culture of victimization," where victims claim they were psychologically compelled to respond by a history of insults.[25] The representation of coercive control makes no psychological assumptions about the motives that prompt abuse, its familial or personality precursors, its consequences, or what prompts women to respond. To the contrary, reactions that might appear to signal personality weakness, dependence, assertiveness, or aggression to an outsider are represented as tactical adaptations to an objective process of deprivation, exploitation, and control. A detailed account of its tactical infrastructure establishes that the pattern of abuse qualifies as coercive control by virtue of its dynamics and its spatial and temporal dimensions. As in hostage taking or kidnapping, the victim's right to respond and the particulars of her response are weighed against the overall strategy of entrapment, the temporal and spatial extension of her unfreedom, and the cumulative weight of oppression, not primarily against specific incidents of harm. This approach resolves many of the dilemmas that plague the current battered woman's defense, such as why victims may take advantage of the perpetrator's vulnerability by attacking when he is drunk or asleep, why they fail to escape when they are alone or physically able to do so, why their response seems disproportionate to the violence they face, and why they have responded now, even though they may not have in the past. The cumulative weight of oppression supports the conclusion that the response is a justifiable function of opportunity, not a response to existential harm.

Context is everything. The recitation of tactics establishes the broad pattern. But unless these tactics are shown to take their meaning from the larger strategy of coercive control, seasoned professionals are no more likely to grasp their meaning than the laypersons who comprise a jury. This is particularly true with events that occur in spaces (such as the home or street) where persons are thought to be self-directed or involve routine activities (such as shopping or meal preparation) in which a malevolent interest is hard to conceive. It would never have occurred to the psychiatrists treating Laura or Bonnie that the ritual cleaning and weight loss these women reported were instigated by external constraints. The possibility that a behavior reflects a trauma-induced delusion should be considered only after the lines of power that define the ostensibly free spaces through which battered women move are drawn and their special reasonableness has been explicated. With "hostages at home," there is rarely a single, primal event of violence or capture that sets the stage for all future reactions, as there is in kidnapping. Nevertheless, it is critical that the meaning of small or invisible treasons be set on the continuum of basic liberty violations. The court gained greater insight into how Donna and Laura had been degraded by the presentation of the log book and Nick's list of rules than it did from a straightforward description of the rapes and assaults they had suffered.

While retaining the Hobbesian concern with physical security critical to self-defense, the coercive control model opens a political space in which women can claim common justice resources as fully entitled citizens, irrespective of the degree to which they have been psychologically or physically damaged. In a conventional defense, a woman's acts of assertion are concealed or minimized to support her portrayal as a victim. The coercive control defense presents a lengthy catalog of a woman's direct and informal efforts to counter or free herself from abuse, assessing their relative success as part of her strategy of resistance. Seemingly self-destructive behaviors that compromise a woman's moral standing in the conventional approach are reframed in this context as efforts to preserve autonomy in situations where agency is disallowed. Thus, we were able to show that the woman who ingested the nearly fatal dose of pills in front of her children was striving to control how and when she was harmed in a context where the option of avoiding harm was unavailable—control in the context of no control. If she has taken a life, this is the culmination of a long, complicated history of agency asserted and denied, a reasoned act of liberation against a tyranny that she had failed to effectively void in other ways. The woman's presence in the courtroom as a compelling witness to her own experience makes it patently obvious that the life she preserved was worth saving.

Battering in Same-Sex Relationships

The VAWA contained a civil rights provision that allowed all victims of violence, including persons assaulted by same-sex partners, to bring a civil action in state and federal court to recover compensatory and punitive damages "and other relief a court may deem appropriate," so long as the crime was motivated, at least in part, "by an animus based on the victim's gender." Perpetrators of gender-motivated violence were subject to suit regardless of whether they had acted under color of state law or had been criminally charged or convicted. The Supreme Court struck down this provision of VAWA in 2000, in *United States v. Morrison*, largely because it found it inimical to federalism.[26] In an argument put before the Court, self-identified "conservative feminists" claimed that rape and battering are gender-neutral and so do not constitute discrimination because they are driven by "power and control" and because men, too, can be victimized.[27] Despite its feminist bent, much of the literature on lesbian battering makes a similar point: that the prevalence of violence in same-sex couples means that sexism is not the prime cause of abuse. Some writers even dub the feminist emphasis on *male* violence "heterosexism" because it discounts alternative sexual identities and arrangements as well as violence against same-sex or transgendered partners.[28] To legal scholar Sally Goldfarb, the conceptual dilemma is "how to reconcile the analysis of male battering as sexism with the reality that issues of power and control exist in many types of relationships."[29]

Current debates about same-sex violence proceed as if power and control, sexual inequality, and "an animus based on the victim's gender" are mutually exclusive explanations. A similarly simplistic view drives discrimination law, where plaintiffs must identify with one protected class only, making it difficult to proceed against institutions that discriminate against black women, say, but not black men or white women. In the real world, discrimination often targets persons with multiple stigmatized identities and for varying combinations of causes and motives, the pattern law professor Kimberly Crenshaw calls "intersectionality."[30] Battered women of color, battered lesbians, and many other marginalized groups experience animus as a multilayered phenomena rather than as bias directed against a single trait. Attempting to subdivide these oppressions creates competing rights claims that lack political coherence. The challenge is to determine the relative contribution of sexual inequality, power and control, homophobia, and other factors to heterosexual and same-sex abuse and then decide whether and how to proceed strategically from this analysis. Should we look at violence by men and same-sex or transgendered partners as a single phenomenon, replacing the emphasis on sexism with power and control, or mount parallel but separate campaigns to target heterosexual and same-sex partner violence?

Another problem arises because, despite the fact that the foundation, target, and effects of coercive control point to gender discrimination, the intent to discriminate required by law is often hard to identify, particularly when the regulation of everyday activities is the vehicle for control. The relational context in which coercive control occurs, the personalized tactical regime, and the fact that its perpetrators value at least some aspect of their target's femininity, and may even imprison her on a pedestal of purity as Nick did Laura, suggest that the dominance involved cannot be equated with the unequivocal prejudice typical in hate crimes against blacks, gays, or victims of stranger or acquaintance rape.

To perpetrators of coercive control, gender stereotypes provide a pretext for asserting male prerogatives, an ideological frame to guide regulation, and the ground of inequality on which sexual dominance proceeds. Direct expressions of sex hatred, such as "whore," "bitch," "fat pig," or "cunt," are common enough. But the most insidious forms of misogyny are hidden behind the sadistic insensitivity of rules, marking rituals like tattooing, methodical disregard for a victim's personal needs or interests, or the extreme form taken by normative gender expectations, what I've called "sexism with a vengeance," like forcing Bonnie to ask permission to write Christmas cards. Almost every victim of coercive control I've worked with felt their femininity was under siege, and every perpetrator understood he was defending the entitlements of manhood, even when the most obvious professions of hatred were directed at a victim's race, age, or disability. Again, however, it was often hard for me, as an outsider, to distinguish where the animus carried by normative sex hierarchies ended and personal hatred of women began. Less clear is how these dynamics play out in relationships where partners share sex-linked capacities, roles, and/or disadvantages.

To garner recognition of lesbian battering, advocates have emphasized its similarities to heterosexual abuse.[31] The consensus is that the rates and types of violence are comparable; that both share the use of sexual coercion, property destruction, and other forms of intimidation; that lesbian victims exhibit the same pattern of denial, minimization, or self-blame as hetero-sexual victims and that lesbian batterers have the same personality profile as male batterers.[32] This reliance on the domestic violence model masks the unique dynamics of same-sex abuse and exposes the same weak-nesses we have identified in the analysis of the domestic violence approach generally: with important exceptions, the literature on same-sex violence is silent about domination or control; equates abuse with a range of situations where force is used with very different meaning to partici-pants; emphasizes childhood precursors such as incest or sexual abuse and psychological or psychosocial variables such as "dependence" or a "need to control," while ignoring structural factors and forms of abuse other than violence; and relies on a one-dimensional view of victimization that discounts resiliency and agency.

Treating same-sex and heterosexual abuse as two facets of a single phe-nomenon makes it difficult to devise or target services appropriately. For example, the assumption that women who assume male roles are the typ-ical batterers in lesbian relationships leads the "battered butch" to be treated like a pariah by the shelter and gay communities, much like a male abuse victim might be treated. In fact, lesbians and transsexuals who are male identified accrue few of the social advantages associated with bio-logical masculinity and are as likely to be victimized as lesbians who play female roles. The equation of heterosexual and same-sex partner violence also leads service providers to conclude that lesbian and transsexual vic-tims require the same service mix as heterosexual women and only dis-crimination keeps them from accessing these services.[33] Although the battered women's movement has confronted homophobia among its provider shelters and partners, it has done little to identify or respond to the special needs of lesbian and transsexual victims. When sociologist Claire Renzetti did her path-breaking research on same-sex violence in 1995, fewer than 1 in 10 (9.3%) domestic violence agencies offered services targeted to battered lesbians, and the rest had no plans to do so.[34] Because relatively few lesbian victims have been identified at traditional service sites, we have little or no solid point-of-service information on their uti-lization patterns, though underutilization is a certainty. Although many lesbian victims seek counseling, only 1 in 50 calls police (a far lower pro-portion than among heterosexual victims), few use hotlines or shelters, and those who do rarely find them helpful.[35] Victim fears of bias, homo-phobia, and provider ignorance contribute to these patterns; they also reflect the fact that the unique service needs of lesbians, gay men, and transsexual victims have yet to be identified.

The National Violence Against Women Survey (NVAWS) was the first population-based study that attempted to separate victims who identified as lesbians. Its findings are fascinating because they directly challenge the conventional wisdom about victimization in this population. Of the women who identified themselves as lesbians to the NVAWS, 11.4% reported abuse by female partners over their lifetime, a little more than half the proportion of abused heterosexual women (20.3%) who did so.[36] This did not mean that lesbians were less likely to be victimized than heterosexual women, however. In fact, lesbians actually reported higher rates of abuse than any other group. This seeming paradox—that lesbians reported the highest overall rates of victimization and yet were only half as likely to be abused by a same-sex partner as heterosexual women were by a man—is resolved by one of the least publicized findings from the NVAWS, that women who currently identify themselves as lesbians were *three times more likely* to have been abused by a male than a female partner (30.4% versus 11.4%). Indeed, lesbians were actually half again more likely than heterosexual women to have suffered abuse from a man (30.4% versus 20.3%). Conversely, many women who abused partners in same-sex relationships also reported they had assaulted male partners.[37] The contexts in which lesbian women were abused by men were not fully spelled out in the NVAWS, making it impossible to say whether they were assaulted during a period when they self-identified as heterosexual or as lesbians. Some women were undoubtedly abused by men *because* they identified as lesbians. It is also possible that some women chose to identify as lesbians because of their history of abuse by men.

If heterosexual and same-sex abuse should not be equated, these data suggest it is also futile to sharply dichotomize either a victim's experience or the behavior of perpetrators as "same sex" or heterosexual. The key point is that experience of lesbian or transsexual victims is not exhausted by considering same-sex abuse.

Unraveling lesbian victimization entails conceptualizing the complex interrelationships and distinctions between battering in the gay and straight worlds and tracking the experience of victims and perpetrators both within and between these communities. In fact, lesbians are battered at the conjuncture of sexual inequality, heterosexism, and homophobia, intersecting dynamics that are exploited in different ways by male and female partners. But whether a lesbian is abused by a biological male or a female or whether the victim identifies as a male or a female or both, the abuser exploits the disadvantages women experience because of their sex, the expectations associated with their gender, and discrimination based on their sexual orientation. Heterosexual women are also constrained by these processes, but in very different ways than homosexuals, transsexuals, or lesbians.

Heterosexism refers to the normative regime that ascribes social value to heterosexuality relative to alternative sexual identities and disproportionately allocates opportunities, rights, and benefits accordingly, particularly those associated with marriage or family life. As a core ideology in Western culture, heterosexism couples an idealized picture of male/female partnerships and of marriage in particular as the basic unit of social reproduction with the depiction of nonheterosexual, homosexual, or transsexual relationships and sexual activity as outside the pale of normalcy, as deviant, immoral, or "sick," and of nonheterosexuals as "the other" in need of "correction" or "tolerance."

Heterosexism contributes to abuse as both a cultural ideology and a systemic form of discrimination. Among gays and transsexuals, heterosexist beliefs encourage role imitations of hypermasculine or feminine stereotypes that can lead to self-conscious desensitization to "empathy" or "feelings" and even to an "imaginary domain" of sexual identity expressed in physical distortions such as exaggerated breasts, makeup, or musculature. Although the motives for sexual surgery are complex and may include a genetic predisposition, the actual cosmetics of what is done to the body are sometimes guided by these stereotypes. The extent to which same-sex relationships mimic traditional sex roles is often exaggerated. Nevertheless, sexual desire and commitment in these situations are often structured around conquest, possession, and dominance, a by-product of both male stereotypes and the very real privileges exacted from male or female partners who are treated "like a woman." If heterosexism is internalized, it can evoke self-loathing in gays and the belief that abusive behavior is both justified and deserved. Same-sex partners may also defend against the hostile heterosexist world by withdrawing from an active social life and becoming so embedded in their relationships that any attempts at autonomy are interpreted as disloyalty, a pattern known as fusion, where partner violence is used to manage dependence and emotional distance.[38] Heterosexist beliefs also isolate same-sex partners from family, peer, and professional support systems in ways that can contribute to fusion as well as to dependence and entrapment. Conversely, lesbian abuse victims fear that reporting will lead to ostracism by peers or elicit violence from authorities against themselves or their partners. Alternately, lesbian couples or communities may compensate for the pervasiveness of heterosexist ideology by idealizing gay life in ways that mask its oppressive features, including women's use of violence to hurt or control other women.

Heterosexism also plays an important role in male battering. By defining same-sex partnerships as off-limits, heterosexism constrains women's relational choices in mates as well as friends, inhibiting the rejection of "bad bargains." This process is complemented when the ideology of heterosexual romance obscures the homosocial bonds of privilege that unify men as a group and the hierarchical basis for male/female relationships. As we saw earlier, heterosexism may cause men to project their homoerotic feelings onto their partners, weave elaborate sexual fantasies about sex with other men, and then beat their partners for harboring these fantasies.

Whatever cultural authority heterosexism exerts as ideology, it is able to constrain behavior only because of discriminatory laws and practices that materially disadvantage nonheterosexuals in everything from marriage, social security, health benefits, tax relief, and inheritance through parenting rights, housing, employment, and educational opportunity. This pattern of discrimination exploits homophobia, a widely accepted means of managing the boundaries of heterosexism by projecting personal or group fears of transgression onto homosexuals and transsexuals through an active program of hatred, violence, discrimination, and segregation. Like heterosexism, homophobia constrains women from exiting abusive relationships with men or women, rationalizes abuse in same-sex relationships, and isolates couples in ways that often lead them to become enmeshed. By focusing on the horrors of being a "fag," "sissy," "fruit," "dyke bitch," or "lesbo," homophobia mobilizes a defense of heterosexuality in the face of its failings and contradictions and encourages the sort of hyperheterosexuality enacted in coercive control. Nothing more clearly reveals the boundary functions of heterosexism and homophobia than the federal and state DOMA (Defense of Marriage Act) legislation. Although these laws purport to support marriage, they do so only negatively, by excluding gays from its privileges while providing nothing affirmative to enhance marriage, close relationships, or family life.

Sexual inequality contributes to same-sex abuse because its discriminatory effects with respect to income, employment, education, and household responsibilities provide the core issues around which fights occur. Because both parties share an identical sexual status, however, sexual inequality cannot be said to cause same-sex abuse. One result is that power and control in same-sex relationships are often constructed around racial, age, or class differences instead of sex and/or characteristics specific to a given relationship such as physical strength, personality, health, or wealth.

In my practice, I have encountered same-sex couples where perpetrators combined physical abuse with rituals of dominance, exploitation, isolation, and humiliation that resembled the patterns evident in coercive control; relationships in which there are rules for behavior in public, where one partner is forbidden to work or visit his or her family, or where child care and/or homemaking are regulated. Stalking and other forms of intimidation used in coercive control are also common in same-sex abusive relationships. Advocates who work with same-sex couples have told me that such patterns may even be typical.[39] But there is no evidence in the literature on same-sex violence that this is so or that can help illuminate whether, if coercive control does occur among lesbians or homosexuals, it has the same dynamics, consequences, or spatial dimensions as in heterosexual relationships or whether and how abusive dynamics are affected when race, class, or age differences form its core rather than differences in gender identity. The fact that the perpetrator of abuse cannot align her sexual persona with a privileged social role sets objective limits to domination in lesbian couples and suggests that physical abuse, threats, and indirect forms of control such as psychological manipulation will be more prominent than direct or structural constraints on everyday routines or material necessities. Though the combined effects of heterosexism and homophobia obstruct help seeking by same-sex victims, they also undermine the capacity for same-sex perpetrators to extend their control through social space, to seek public validation for abusive behavior, or to exploit race or class bias, thereby affording a safety zone for same-sex victims that is often unavailable in heterosexual relationships.

In an early article, longtime advocate Barbara Hart made an important distinction between domestic violence and lesbian battering that has been frequently quoted but rarely used as a basis for intervention. "Lesbian battering," she wrote, "is a pattern of violent or coercive behaviors whereby a lesbian seeks to control the thoughts, beliefs or conduct of her intimate partner or to punish the intimate for resisting the perpetrator's control. Individual acts of physical violence, by this definition, do not constitute lesbian battering. Physical violence is not battering unless it results in the enhanced control of the batterer over the recipient."[40]

Apart from anticipating the distinction made here between fights and other forms of abuse, Hart reminds us that the aim of lesbian battering is control even when only coercion is deployed. Even though a woman is the immediate beneficiary of this abuse, regardless of how or by whom a woman's autonomy or liberty is constrained, the overall power of women relative to men is diminished. To this extent, even when it is used as an instrument of control by another woman, lesbian battering is a facet of male dominance that affects the freedom of women everywhere as well as of the community as a whole.

Far more knowledge about the particularity of same-sex battering is needed before we can confidently design appropriate interventions. We do not know, for instance, whether the apparent preference of lesbian victims for counseling reflects the unique dynamics of lesbian abuse or continued institutional insensitivity to same-sex victims.

The same political and economic forces that favor the full release of women's capacities for social development are arrayed against the continued marginalization of gays by heterosexism and homophobia. Continued opposition to gay marriage influenced the 2004 presidential elections. Moreover, gays suffer widespread discrimination in arenas where heterosexual women enjoy near parity with men. Despite the current cultural backlash, however, gays continue to make significant strides in privacy rights, public benefits, and cultural visibility, a fact reflected in the repeated failure of President George W. Bush to muster congressional support for a constitutional amendment restricting marriage to heterosexuals. The challenge to the women's movement is to incorporate the pursuit of "gay rights" within the larger framework of sexual justice.

The Dance of Justice: Law, Services, and Political Change

The domestic violence revolution is stalled and the interventions it has spawned are largely ineffective because it has failed to come to grips with coercive control, a pattern of liberty harms that is several orders of magnitude more devastating than the traditional forms of domestic violence current laws, policies, and programs are designed to manage. Because coercive control is social, personal, and political at once, the response needed to put the revolution back on course must combine public law, services attuned to the variety of experiences in abusive relationships, and political action to address the roots of women's oppression in sexual and related inequalities. This approach has three prongs: formal adjudication to remove the immediate threat of coercion and control, the development of services that address a victim's immediate problems, and a revitalized political movement that tackles the roots of women's vulnerability by advancing sexual equity and political justice for women.

The claims of abused women to a higher standard of justice than the courts apply to domestic violence derive from the ongoing nature of partner assault and coercive control; their cumulative effects; the fact that coercive control targets dignity, autonomy, and material security alongside physical integrity; and from the social importance of freeing the class of citizens entrapped in personal life to fully employ their capacities on behalf of themselves, their families, and the larger community. As a way to achieve these ends, physical safety is insufficient, because even persons who are "safe" from violence cannot thrive if they are unfree, their capacities for self-creation are choked off, or they are constrained to subsume their needs, purposes, or pleasures to the needs, aims, or pleasures of another. A vigorous legal response to this oppression is consistent with the state's obligation to provide all adult citizens with equal access to the conditions under which personal capacities can flourish and they can feel worthy. As laws barring sexual harassment in the workplace illustrate, the principle that women's subjective and physical autonomy should be protected in the public sphere is widely recognized, in part because it is essential to fulfilling the labor contract and enacting citizenship. The challenge is to extend this defense to personal life, to affirm a right to personhood and the minimal conditions required for individuation. It is hard to imagine liberties more basic to personal development or citizenship than those suppressed by coercive control. Whatever their failings, only the state's legal and criminal justice systems have the scope of authority sufficient to counter these violations.

In the world I favor, police, prosecutors, and courts would employ their considerable power of coercion to remove those who assault or entrap women from their society. Appropriate adjudication of domestic assault and coercive control cases requires a level of bureaucratic formalism that applies the same criteria to all battered women and perpetrators albeit while considering variations in circumstance, motive, means, meaning, and consequence. Standardization of procedures makes the legal response predictable, so that victims and perpetrators know what to expect when they "enter" the law, and that justice staff can be held accountable for implementing these standards. When the procedures adapted by justice agencies are too narrow, as they are presently, those who fall outside their purview suffer the consequences and lose faith in the law.

But crafting a new legal response to woman battering is not enough.

Even as an ideal, law enforcement can only provide categorical protection and basic compensation for damages; it cannot restore the overall integrity of battered women. This requires constructing a response outside the legal bureaucracy based on the therapeutic conceit that each individual's or couple's situation is unique. The major obstacle to effective service is the lack of a conceptual framework to guide decision making, not a deficit in professional skill. Still, like the child who tries to stem the incoming tide by carrying water from the ocean in a pail, services are unlikely to improve women's lot on any substantial scale until the normative tide is turned against the structural dimensions and foundation of coercive control.

This brings us full circle, back to the commitment with which the advocacy movement began, a determination to enter the law as it is currently constituted, transform it, and deploy it on behalf of women in need. Law here includes the normative regime of sexual hierarchy that the statutory law reproduces and on which it relies for legitimacy as well as the formal institutions of policy making, adjudication, and law enforcement. These two realms of law, law as a culture that guides judgments and decision making in everyday life and as a system of rules that define the boundaries of permissible behavior, are inextricably joined in the foundation of coercive control; so they must also be joined in its undoing.

The domestic violence revolution in the 1970s and 1980s elicited an unprecedented level of institutional and cultural change in how women were regarded and serviced. This had less to do with our political savvy or skill than with a political fact—that we entered the legal, service, and policy arenas with the real and implied power of the women's liberation movement at our back. Inside the shelters, women who sought temporary respite from social oppression and deprivation found its antidote, at least embryonically, in forms of collective self-help that countered isolation with connectedness to other women, fear and intimidation with a renewed sense of possibility, and dependence on the malevolent other with material and personal interdependence. Counseling "worked" to disabuse women in this context because it occurred in a space from which not only violence but domination had been momentarily cleared, simulating the larger vision of what it would be like to live in a society where personal life was not prescribed or regulated from above or without but from within. Shelter residents changed because they could change and because once the constraints on creative self-development are removed, change comes naturally to persons who are unequal or have been oppressed.

The question with which I end is not whether to enter the law; there is no way to avoid the effects of legal and normative structures. The question is *how* to enter the law, whether to remain passive to the constraints it poses to our mission or to engage these obstacles strategically, hoping to once again release the law's capacity for transformation to support equal personhood for women. Many advocates have become so disillusioned with the state's response that they urge that domestic violence be returned to the sphere of private life for solution.[41] But victims of coercive control do not have the luxury of viewing the law's protection as an empty promise and withdrawing back into communities that view their problems as private business.

It may seem naive to expect that governments so deeply invested in the inequities at the root of coercive control will use their legislative and coercive powers to redress the injuries these inequities cause, particularly so long as their significance is masked by their fusion with women's default status in personal life. Moreover, we are asking the state to correct harms that men do not experience (as a rule) and that result in benefits whose protection gives the state legitimacy. As the critics of domestic violence laws remind us, the courts and police may reproduce prevailing dependencies even when they behave as they should. This is the essence of the process of normalization that worried Frances Power Cobbe more than a century ago. Punish only the most egregious physical harms, and other types of harms will flourish, as they have.

The fact that the domestic violence revolution happened at all should dispel the view that the state's response can be predicted solely by its vested interest in the status quo. What is remarkable about the decades since the great public reforms of the New Deal and the end of de jure segregation is not that the forces of reaction and conservatism have periodically seized the reigns of political power. What is remarkable is that the scope of civil and human rights has continued to expand in the face of these forces and on a worldwide scale.

Only in the Old Testament is law writ in stone. In reality, justice is less a fixed or formal property of a normative regime of rights or laws than an ever-present institutional capacity that can be actualized in special historical moments when political pressure forces legal institutions to act *as if* they favored personal autonomy and in opposition to the negative likeness established through dominant patterns of discrimination. I share the Hegelian faith that Right is a capacity inherent in all legal regimes. But unlike Hegel, I expect this capacity to be formed, hidden, re-formed, and released in specific sociohistorical spaces and in response to specific challenges posed by groups the law must accommodate to retain its legitimacy. Law can move the world toward greater equality and freedom because it is "practiced." Its narrative(s), its voice(s), is not given to us fully made but appears as a point in an ongoing dialogue with historically specific subjects. If we are compelled to enter the law by the predicaments women continue to face in personal life, so are the institutions of law compelled to meet us coming through their gates. Even in theocracy, but most certainly in democracy, the law must embrace those who most require its assistance in whatever form we can negotiate. It must engage us where we live, or become irrelevant, because it is through our respect, our compliance, and our love for its righteousness that the law lives. Law teaches obedience; but it also depends on it, as the United States learned during its experiment with Prohibition. The fact that the engagement with law is rarely one of equals or that it responds more readily to the pillars of wealth and official power than to the oppressed or victimized, to men more readily than to women, defines the challenge we face, not the limits of change. To survive, the law must ultimately appropriate the lore of everyday life into itself and reflect it back as a boundary for living. Even at its most certain, the law must actively interrogate those who engage it to determine whether law enforcement will prevail or disregard for particular laws will be generalized into resistance to law itself and to the state whose capacity for force stands behind the law. In this engagement, the defense of liberty is a deal breaker. This, then, is the dance of justice to which we bring our understanding of women's entrapment in everyday life through coercive control. For the millions of women who are assaulted or coercively controlled by their partners, the law is just when it becomes part of their safety zone; when they experience a synchronicity between their struggle to be free of their partner and their larger struggle to realize their capacity as women; when being *in* the law, calling the police, or appearing before a judge, or turning to child welfare, or entering a health center or a shelter becomes for them a "moment of autonomy" in which their voice is not only heard but magnified; and when their personal power, which they have been made to feel is a liability for too long, is suddenly recognized as a political asset. It is when women's affirmations of liberty are acknowledged and treated no differently than the affirmations of others who do not share their negative likeness, when their differences are equally valued, that those who suffer abuse will feel justice is done.

NOTES

Introduction

1. Another reason the prosecution decided not to call its expert was that a review of the domestic violence history would have revealed that the L.A. police on whose testimony they depended had not merely failed to enforce the domestic violence laws where Mr. Simpson was concerned but had regularly accepted his offer of entertainment and played tennis and swam at his house. How could a jury be expected to take the abuse seriously if the agency charged with protecting abuse victims had not? In addition, the defense never called its domestic violence expert, Dr. Lenore Walker, who had interviewed O. J. Simpson in prison and administered the Minnesota Multiphasic Personality Inventory (MMPI). Walker told the media that Simpson was not the "type" of batterer who kills, a moot point in this instance, because once a battered woman is killed, the probability that the abusive partner is responsible is extremely high.

2. The best summaries of these achievements are Susan Schechter, *Women and Male Violence: The Visions and Struggles of the Battered Women's Movement* (Boston: Sound End Press, 1982); R. Emerson Dobash and Russell Dobash, *Women, Violence and Social Change* (London: Routledge, 1992); Claire Renzetti, Jeffrey L. Edleson, and Raquel K. Bergen, eds., *Sourcebook on Violence against Women* (Thousand Oaks, CA: Sage, 2001); Albert Roberts, ed., *Handbook of Domestic Violence Intervention Strategies: Policies, Programs, and Legal Remedies* (New York: Oxford University Press, 2002); and Eve Buzawa and Carl Buzawa, *Domestic Violence: The Criminal Justice Response*, 3rd ed. (Newbury Park, CA: Sage, 2003).

3. On this point, see Marianne Hester, "Future Trends and Developments: Violence Against Women in Europe and East Asia," *Violence against Women* 10, no. 12 (2004): 1431–1448.

4. National Research Council, *Understanding Violence against Women*, eds. Nancy A. Crowell and Ann W. Burgess (Washington, DC: National Academy Press, 1996), p. 144.

5. Isabel Marcus, "Reframing 'Domestic Violence': Terrorism in the Home," in *The Public Nature of Private Violence: The Discovery of Domestic Abuse*, eds. Martha Fineman and Roxanne Mykitiuk (London: Routledge, 1994), pp. 11–35 (referred to subsequently as Fineman and Mykitiuk, *Public Nature*).

6. Christina Hoff Somers, "The Myth of Spouse Abuse," *USA Today*, October 26, 1994; Christina Hoff Somers, *Who Stole Feminism: How Women Have Betrayed Women* (New York: Simon & Schuster, 1994); Linda Mills, *Intimate Abuse* (Princeton, NJ: Princeton University Press, 2003); Kate Rophie, *The Morning After: Sex, Fear and Feminism on Campus* (New York: Little, Brown, 1993); Camille Paglia, *Vamps and Tramps: New Essays* (London: Penguin, 1995).

7. Jane Maslow Cohen, "Private Violence and Public Obligation: The Fulcrum of Reason," in Fineman and Mykitiuk, *Public Nature*, p. 357.

8. Alan Dershowitz, The Abuse Excuse: Cop Outs, Sob Stories and Other Major Evasions of Responsibility (New York: Little, Brown, 2002).

9. Thomas S. Kuhn, *Structure of Scientific Revolutions* (Chicago: University of Chicago Press, 1965).

10. In addition to Schechter, *Women and Male Violence*, and Dobash and Dobash, *Women, Violence, and Social Change*, other key early works in this genre are Russell P. Dobash and Rebecca E. Dobash, *Violence Against Wives: A Case Against the Patriarchy* (New York: Free Press, 1979); Del Martin, *Battered Wives* (New York: Pocket Books, 1977); Mildred Daley Pagelow, *Woman-Battering: Victims and Their Experiences* (Beverly Hills, CA: Sage, 1981); and Evan Stark, Anne H. Flitcraft, and William Frazier, "Medicine and Patriarchal Violence: The Social Construction of a 'Private' Event," *International Journal of Health Services* 9, no. 3 (1979): 461–493.

11. Cynthia R. Daniels, *Feminists Negotiate the State: The Politics of Domestic Violence* (Lanham, MD: University Press of America, 1997).

12. American Medical Association, "Diagnostic and Treatment Guidelines on Domestic Violence," *Archives of Family Medicine* 1 (1992): 39–47.

13. Richard M. Tolman, "The Development of a Measure of Psychological Maltreatment of Women by Their Male Partners," *Violence and Victims* 4, no. 3 (1989): 159–177; Cynthia W. Lischick, "Coping and Related Characteristics Delineating Battered Women's Experiences in Self-Defined, Difficult/Hurtful Dating Relationships: A Multicultural Study" (PhD diss., Rutgers Unversity, 1999).

14. Martha Fineman, "Implementing Equality: Ideology, Contradiction and Social Change: A Study of Rhetoric and Results in the Regulation of the Consequences of Divorce," *Wisconsin Law Review* (1983); Martha Fineman, *The Illusion of Equality: The Rhetoric and Reality of Divorce Reform* (Chicago: University of Chicago Press, 1991).

15. Druscilla Cornell, *The Imaginary Domain: Abortion, Pornography and Sexual Harassment* (London: Routledge, 1995), p. l8.

16. Linda Gordon, *Heroes of Their Own Lives: The Politics and History of Family Violence: Boston, 1880–1960* (Urbana: University of Illinois Press, 1988, 2002).

Chapter 1

1. Beth E. Richie, *Compelled to Crime: Gender Entrapment of Battered Black Women* (New York: Routledge, 1996), p. 51.

2. Elizabeth Pleck, *Domestic Tyranny: The Making of American Social Policy Against Family Violence From Colonial Times to the Present* (New York: Oxford University Press, 1987), p. 96.

3. Summaries of these trials can be found in Ann Jones, *Women Who Kill* (New York: Holt, Rinehart & Winston, 1980); Ann Jones, *Next Time She'll Be Dead: Battering and How to Stop It* (Boston: Beacon Press, 1994). Also see James Reston Jr., "The Joan Little Case," *New York Times Magazine*, April 6, 1975.

4. Susan Brownmiller, *Against Our Will: Men, Women and Rape* (New York: Bantam Books, 1978).

5. Margaret Gordon and Stephanie Riger, *The Female Fear* (Chicago: University of Illinois Press, 1991), pp. 15–18. In Brownmiller's account, installing fear is the conscious goal of rapists. She writes, "Man's discovery that his genitalia could serve as a weapon to generate fear must rank as one of the most important discoveries of prehistoric times. . . . From prehistoric times to the present . . . rape has played a critical function. It is nothing more or less than a conscious process of intimidation by which all men keep all women (emphasis in original) in a state of fear" (*Against Our Will*, pp. 14–15). This argument illustrates the shift from viewing violence as one among many means used to solidify male domination to its equivalent.

6. U.S. Commission on Civil Rights, *Battered Women: Issues of Public Policy* (Washington, DC: U.S. Commission on Civil Rights, 1978)

7. Susan Brownmiller, *In Our Time: Memoir of a Revolution* (New York: Dell, 1999), pp. 248–249, provides an account of these criticisms. She also cites a pamphlet by A. Edwards, a white lawyer with the National Lawyer's Guild, "Rape, Racism and the White Women's Movement: An Answer to Susan Brownmiller."

8. Murray A. Straus, "Wife-Beating: How Common, and Why?" *Victimology* 2 (November 1977): 443–458; Murray A. Straus, "Normative and Behavioral Aspects of Violence between Spouses: Preliminary Data on a Nationally Representative USA Sample," Symposium on Violence in Canadian Society, Simon Fraser University, 1977; Murray A. Straus, "A National Survey of Domestic Violence: Some Preliminary Findings and Implications for Future Research," Paper presented at Hearings on "Research Into Domestic Violence," U.S. House of Representatives, Committee on Science and Technology, 1978; Richard J. Gelles, *Family Violence*, 2nd ed. (Newbury Park, CA: Sage, 1987).

9. The seminal work on the early shelters remains Albert R. Roberts, *Sheltering Battered Women: A National Survey and Service Guide* (New York: Springer, 1981). See also Albert A. Roberts, *Battered Women and Their Families: Intervention Strategies and Treatment Programs* (New York: Springer, 1998). In addition to this work, the account of shelter development draws on Schechter, *Women and Male Violence*; Dobash and Dobash, *Women, Violence and Social Change*; and Sharon Vaughan, "Social Change Implications of Battered Women's Stories: A Narrative Approach" (PhD diss., University. of Manchester, 2003).

10. K. McCann, "Battered Women and the Law: The Limits of the Legislation," cited in Dobash and Dobash, *Women, Violence and Social Change*, p. 64.

11. Dobash and Dobash, *Women, Violence and Social Change*, p. 35

12. "Battered Women Need Refuges," pamphlet published by National Women's Aid Federation (London: Rye Press, 1976), 46 pp.

13. Jo Sutton, "The Growth of the British Movement for Battered Women," *Victimology* 2, nos. 3–4 (1977–78): 576–584.

14. Quoted in *National Women's Aid Newsletter*, n.d., p. 3. In author's possession.

15. Midge Costanza and Jan Peterson, *White House Meetings on Violence in the Family* (Washington, DC: Office of Public Liaison, 1977).

16. Cited by Dobash and Dobash, *Women, Violence and Social Change*, p. 35. When the NWAF developed its constitutional objectives, this aim, originally formulated in 1974, was dropped.

17. Anne H. Flitcraft, "Testimony," U.S. Commission on Civil Rights, *Battered Women: Issues of Public Policy* (Washington, DC: U.S. Commission on Civil Rights, 1978).

18. Glasgow Women's Aid, 1974–1975, pamphlet in author's possession.

19. Schechter, *Women and Male Violence*, pp. 63–64.

20. Roberts, *Sheltering Battered Women*.

21. Roberts, *Sheltering Battered Women*; Roberts, *Battered Women and Their Families*.

22. Roberts, *Sheltering Battered Women*; Roberts, *Battered Women and Their Families*.

23. Summaries of this criticism include Buzawa and Buzawa, *Domestic Violence*; Morton Bard, "Training Police as Specialists in Family Crisis Intervention: A Community Psychology Action Program," *Community Mental Health Journal* 3 (1969): 325–327; Morton Bard and Joseph Zacker, "The Prevention of Family Violence: Dilemmas of Community Interaction," *Journal of Marriage and the Family* 33 (1971): 677–682; Joanne Belknap, "Law Eforcement Officers' Attitudes About the Appropriate Responses to Woman Battering," *International Review of Victimology* 4 (1995): 47–62; Kathleen J. Ferraro, "Policing Woman Battering," *Social Problems* 36, no. 1 (1989): 61–74; Kathleen J. Ferraro, "The Legal Response to Woman Battering in the United States," in *Women, Policing and Male Violence*, eds. Jalna Hanmer, Jill Radford, and Elizabeth A. Stanko (London: Routledge, 1989); J. W. E. Sheptycki, *Innovations in the Policing of Domestic Violence* (Aldershot: Avebury, 1993).

24. Raymond J. Parnas, "The Police Response to the Domestic Disturbance," *Wisconsin Law Review* (Fall 1967): 914–960.

25. Darnell Hawkins, "Devalued Lives and Racial Stereotypes: Ideological Barriers to the Prevention of Domestic Violence among Blacks," in *Violence in the Black Family*, ed. Robert L. Hampton (Lexington, KY: Lexington Books, 1987).

26. Buzawa and Buzawa, *Domestic Violence*; Peter Finn and Sarah Colson, *Civil Protection Orders: Legislation, Current Court Practice, and Enforcement* (Washington, DC: U.S. Department of Justice, National Institute of Justice, 2000).

27. Donald J. Rebovich, "Prosecution Response to Domestic Violence: Results of a Survey of Large Jurisdictions," in *Do Arrests and Restraining Orders Work?*, eds. Eve S. Buzawa and Carl Buzawa (Thousand Oaks, CA: Sage, 1996); Elizabeth A. Stanko, "Would You Believe This Woman? Prosecutorial Screening for 'Credible' Witnesses and a Problem of Justice," in *Judge, Lawyer, Victim, Thief: Women, Gender Roles, and Criminal Justice*, eds. Nicole H. Rafter and Elizabeth A. Stanko (Boston: Northeastern University Press, 1982); Joel Garner and Elizabeth Clemmer, "Danger to Police in Domestic Disturbances: A New Look," in *National Institute of Justice: Research in Brief* (Washington, DC: Department of Justice, 1986); Ronet Bachman and Ann Coker, "Police Involvement in Domestic Violence: The Interactive Effects of Victim Injury, Offender's History of Violence and Race," *Violence and Victims* 10 (1984): 91–106.

28. Roger Langley and Richard Levy, *Wife Beating: The Silent Crisis* (New York: Dutton, 1977); Roger Langley and Richard Levy, "Wife Abuse and the Police Response," *FBI Law Enforcement Bulletin* 47 (1978): 4–9; F. Lawrenz, J. F. Lembo, and T. S. Schade, "Time Series Analysis of the Effect of a Domestic Violence

Directive on the Number of Arrests per Day," *Journal of Criminal Justice* 16 (1988): 493–498; David H. Bayley, "The Tactical Choices of Police Patrol Officers," *Journal of Criminal Justice* 14 (1986): 329–348.

29. Bard, "Training Police"; Bard and Zacker, "The Prevention of Family Violence."

30. Research on the police response is summarized in Buzawa and Buzawa, *Domestic Violence*; Bachman and Coker, "Police Involvement,"; Sara Berk and Donileen R. Loseke, "'Handling' Family Violence: Situational Determinants of Police Arrests in Domestic Disturbances," *Law and Society Review* 15 (1980–81): 317–346; Donald Black, "The Social Organization of Arrest," *Stanford Law Review* 23 (June 1971): 1087–1111.

31. David Garland, *The Culture of Control: Crime and Social Order in Contemporary Society* (Chicago: University of Chicago Press, 2001).

32. U.S. Attorney General's Task Force on Family Violence, *Final Report* (Washington, DC: U.S. Government Printing Office, 1984).

33. *Bruno v. Codd*, Supreme Court of New York, Special Term, New York County, 90 Misc. 2d 1047; 396 N.Y.S.2d 974; 1977 N.Y. Misc., July 5, 1977; *Scott v. Hurt*, 1976; *Thomas v. Los Angeles*, 1979.

34. *Thurman v. Torrington*, Civil No. H-84-120, United States District Court for the District of Connecticut, 595 F. Supp. 1521; 1984 U.S. Dist. October 23, 1984.

35. Buzawa and Buzawa, *Domestic Violence*, 109–124; Dobash and Dobash, *Women, Violence and Social Change*, pp. 174–213. An early analysis of the laws in each of the 50 states is contained in Barbara Hart, *State Codes on Domestic Violence: Analysis, Commentary and Recommendations* (Reno, NV: National Council of Juvenile and Family Judges, 1992).

36. As many as two-thirds of the prosecutors in major metropolitan areas have adopted "no drop" or evidence-based prosecution. Rebovich, "Prosecution Response." Other reforms are summarized in Buzawa and Buzawa, *Domestic Violence*, 190–212.

37. Ignorance may still be widespread, however. Even in the late 1980s, after many states had passed laws mandating arrest and police training in domestic violence assaults, a survey revealed that over 50% of the officers did not even know probable cause requirements for domestic violence–related assault. David A. Ford, "The Impact of Police Officers' Attitudes Towards Victims on the Disinclination to Arrest Wife Batterers," Paper presented at the Third International Conference for Family Violence Researchers (Durham, NH, July 1987).

38. Lesley L. Orloff and Catherine Klein, "Protecting Battered Women: Latest Trends in Civil Legal Relief," in *Women and Domestic Violence: An Interdisciplinary Approach*, ed. Lynette Feder (New York: Hawthorn Press, 1999). Compare, for instance, Del. Code Ann. tit. 10, § 945 (1992); Conn. Gen. Stat. Ann.§46b-14(1993); Ga. Code Ann §19-13-1 (1998).

39. Kimberle Crenshaw, "Mapping the Margins: Intersectionaliry, Identity Politics and Violence against Women of Color," in Fineman and Mykitiuk, *The Public Nature*, 93–118; Angela Browne, *When Battered Women Kill* (New York: Free Press, 1987); Peter D. Chimbos, *Marital Violence: A Study of Interspouse Homicide* (San Francisco, CA: R & E Associates, 1978); Franklin Zimring, Satyamshu K. Mukherjee, and Barrick Van Winkle, "Intimate Violence: A Study of Intersexual Homicide in Chicago," *University of Chicago Law Review* 50, no. 2 (1983): 910–930.

40. Jane Parrish, *Trend Analysis: Expert Testimony on Battering and Its Effects in Criminal Cases* (Philadelphia: National Clearing House for the Defense of Battered Women, 1995). Also appears in *Wisconsin Law Journal* 75 (1996): 102–127.

41. Evan Stark, "Preparing for Expert Testimony in Domestic Violence Cases," in Roberts, *Handbook*, pp. 216–254.

42. Center for Women's Policy Studies Newsletter, "The NCADV: A Grass-Roots Movement," 1981, p. 4.

43. Kerry Healey, Christine Smith, and Chris O'Sullivan, *Batterer Intervention: Program Approaches and Criminal Justice Strategies* (Washington, DC: National Institute of Justice, February 1998).

44. Kevin L. Hamberger, Dan G. Saunders, and Mary Harvey. "Prevalence of Domestic Violence in Community Practice and Rate of Physician Inquiry," *Family Medicine* 24, no. 4 (1992): 283–287; Evan Stark, "Health Intervention with Battered Women," in Renzetti et al., *Sourcebook*, pp. 345–369

45. American Medical Association Council on Ethical and Judicial Affairs, "Physicians and Domestic Violence: Ethical Considerations," *Journal of the American Medical Association* 267 (1992): 3190–3193.

46. U.S. Department of Justice, *Crime in the U.S. 1991* (Washington, DC: Government Printing Office, 1992).

47. National Center for Injury Prevention and Control, *Costs of Intimate Partner Violence against Women in the United States* (Atlanta, GA: Centers for Disease Control and Prevention, 2003).

48. Lee Bowker and Lorie Maurer, "Medical Treatment of Battered Wives," *Women and Health* 12, no. 1 (1987): 25–45.

49. Committee on Trauma Research, *Injury in America: A Continuing Health Problem* (Washington, DC: National Academy of Medicine, 1985).

50. For example, see American Academy of Pediatrics Committee on Child Abuse and Neglect, "The Role of the Pediatrician in Recognizing and Intervening on Behalf of Abused Women," *Pediatrics* 101, no. 6 (1998): 1091–1092; American College of Obstetricians and Gynecologists (ACOG), "Domestic Violence," ACOG Technical Bulletin (Washington, DC: ACOG, 1995); American Medical Association Council on Scientific Affairs, "Violence Against Women: Relevance for Medical Practitioners," *Journal of the American Medical Association* 267 (1992): 3184–3189.

51. American Medical Association Council on Ethical and Judicial Affairs, "Physicians and Domestic Violence: Ethical Considerations," *Journal of the American Medical Association* 267 (1992): 3190–3193.

52. American Medical Association, "Diagnostic and Treatment Guidelines on Domestic Violence," *Archives of Family Medicine* 1 (1992): 39–47; Stark, "Health Intervention"; Sherry L. Schornstein, *Domestic Violence and Health Care: What Every Professional Needs to Know* (Thousand Oaks, CA: Sage ,1997).

53. Elaine J. Alpert, A. E. Tonkin, A. M. Seeherman, and Howard A. Holtz, "Family Violence Curricula in U.S. Medical Schools," *American Journal of Preventive Medicine* 14, no. 4 (1998): 273–282.

54. A. E. Appel and G. W. Holden, "The Co-occurrence of Spouse and Physical Child Abuse: A Review and Appraisal," *Journal of Family Psychology* 12 (1998): 578–599. The estimate of 6.5% is from R. Emerson Dobash, "The Relationship Between Violence Directed at Women and Violence Directed at Children Within the Family Setting," Appendix 38, *Parliamentary Select Committee on Violence in the Family* (London: HMSO, 1976–1977). The estimate of 82% is from Alan Rosenbaum. and Daniel O'Leary, "Children: The Unintended Victims of Marital Violence," *American Journal of Orthopsychiatry* 51, no. 4 (1981): 692–699. The estimate of 3.3 million and 10 million come from Maura O'Keefe and Shirley Lebovics, "Intervention and Treatment Strategies with Adolescents From Martially Violent

Homes," in Roberts, *Battered Women and Their Families*. The estimate of 10 million is from Murray A. Straus and Richard Gelles, *Physical Violence in American Families: Risk Factors and Adaptations to Violence in 8,145 Families* (New Brunswick, NJ: Transaction Press, 1990), pp. 106–107.

55. When CPS caseworkers in Massachusetts included a stated goal of protecting adult victims, the proportion of cases in which domestic violence was revealed increased from 32% to 48.2%. E. Hangen, D.S.S., *Interagency Team Pilot Project: Program Data Evaluation, Office of Management, Planning and Analysis* (Massachusetts Department of Social Services, 1994). For summaries of these data, see Jeffrey L. Edleson, "The Overlap Between Child Maltreatment and Woman buse," available online at http://www.caw.umn.edu/finaldocuments/Vawnet/ overlap.htm (June 24, 2001); and Evan Stark, "The Battered Mother in the Child Protective Service Caseload: Developing an Appropriate Response," *Women's Rights Law Reporter* 23, no. 2 (Spring 2002): 107–131. Rosenbaum O'Leary. "Children: The Unintended Victims of Marital Violence."

56. Evan Stark and Anne H. Flitcraft, "Women and Children at Risk: A Feminist Perspective on Child Abuse," in Evan Stark and Anne H. Flitcraft, *Women at Risk: Domestic Violence and Women's Health* (Thousand Oaks, CA: Sage, 1996), pp. 73–98.

57. This story is told by Gordon, *Heroes*.

58. Jill M. Zuccardy, "*Nicholson v. Williams*: The Case," *Denver University Law Review* 82, no. 4 (2005): 655–670; Justine A. Dunlap, "Judging Nicholson: An Assessment of *Nicholson v. Scoppetta*," *Denver University Law Review* 82, no. 4 (2005): 671–690.

59. A search of relevant health and social science databases revealed that 12,000 research monographs on domestic violence have appeared through 2005. Harriet MacMillan and C. Nadine Wathen, "Family Violence Research: Lessons Learned and Where From Here?" *Journal of the American Medical Association* 294, no. 5 (August 3, 2005): 618. Because the sources reviewed excluded popular literature on the problem, most books, and many specialized law review articles, a conservative estimate of the real total would be between 15,000 and 20,000. By contrast, a similar search of databases related to child maltreatment in the same period yielded about 47,000 citations.

60. For a sampling of these views compare Barbara J. Hart, "Battered Women and the Criminal Justice System," in Buzawa and Buzawa, *Arrests and Restraining Orders*, pp. 98–114; Richard J. Gelles, "Constraints Against Family Violence: How Well Do They Work?" in Buzawa and Buzawa, *Arrests and Restraining Orders*, pp. 30–42; and Linda Mills, "Killing Her Softly: Intimate Abuse and the Violence of State Intervention," *Harvard Law Review*, 113, no. 2 (1999): 551–613.

61. Maria Eriksson, Marianne Hester, Suvi Keskinen, and Keith Pringle, eds., *Tackling Men's Violence in Families—Nordic Issues and Dilemmas* (Bristol: Policy Press, 2006).

62. U.S. Department of Justice, *Crime in the United States, 1996* (Washington, DC: Government Printing Office, 1997).

63. Lawrence W. Sherman and Richard A. Berk. "The Specific Deterrent Effects of Arrest for Domestic Assault," *American Sociological Review* 49, no. 2 (1984): 261–272.

64. Charles E. Lindblom, *The Policy Making Process* (Englewood Cliffs, NJ: Prentice Hall, 1980).

Chapter 2

1. Faith McNulty, *The Burning Bed: The Story of an Abused Wife* (New York: Harcourt, Brace, Jovanovich, 1980).

2. *New Haven Register*, "Farrah Fawcett's Ex-Boyfriend Is Convicted of Beating Her," August 19, 1998, A2.

3. Matthew Durose, Caroline Wolf Harlow, and Patrick A. Langan, *Family Violence Statistics: Including Statistics on Strangers and Acquaintances*, Bureau of Justice Statistics (Washington DC: U.S. Department of Justice, Office of Justice Programs, June 2005).

4. Overall trends as well as homicide data for specific years are taken from James Allan Fox and Marianne W. Zawitz, *Homicide Trends in the United States* (Washington, DC: Department of Justice, 2004 [cited 2005 September 15]). Available online at http://www.ojp.usdoj.gov/bjs/homicide/hmtrnd.htm.

5. For a sample of these claims, Juley Fulcher and Victoria Sadler, "Testimony to the United States Senate Judiciary Committee on the Reauthorization of the Violence Against Women Act," July 19, 2005. See www.ncdsv.org/ publications_vawa.html.

6. Durose et al., Family Violence Statistics, p. 17. On the accuracy of the UCR see Lawrence Greenfeld, Michael R. Rand, Diane Craven, et al., Violence by Intimates: Analysis of Data on Crimes by Current or Former Spouses, Boyfriends and Girlfriends (Washington, DC: U.S. Department of Justice, Bureau of Justice Statistics, 1998).

7. Buzawa and Buzawa, *Domestic Violence*, p. 38. The limits of the NCVS as a measure of domestic violence are discussed in Jacquelyn Campbell, Sandra Martin, Kathryn E. Moracco, Jennifer Manganello, and Rebecca J. Macy, "Survey Data Sets Pertinent to the Study of Intimate Partner Violence and Health," *Trauma, Violence and Abuse* 7, no. 3 (2006): 7–18; Jacquelyn Campbell, "Promise and Perils of Surveillance in Addressing Violence against Women," *Violence Against Women* 6, no. 7 (2000): 705–727.

8. A third source of official data on which the government relies for estimates of family violence trends is the National Incident-Based Reporting System (NIBRS), also an FBI database. Justice Department statistics on family violence that come to police attention and on family violence arrests come from this source. Although the NIBRS affords a high level of detail on specific incidents, including the age, race, gender, type of injury inflicted, type of weapon used, location, and the relationship of the victim to the offender, its conclusions are suggestive at best because it draws data from only 18 states covering less than 16% of the total U.S. population, may rely on as few as one police agency in these areas, and does not include any areas with a population of 1 million or more. Durose et al., *Family Violence Statistics*, p. 5.

9. Murray A. Straus and Richard J. Gelles, "Societal Change and Change in Family Violence from 1975–1986 as Revealed by Two National Surveys," *Journal of Marriage and the Family* 48 (1986): 465–479; Straus and Gelles, *Physical Violence in American Families*; Murray A. Straus, "Trends in Cultural Norms and Rates of Partner Violence: An Update to 1992," in *Understanding Causes, Consequences and Solutions*, eds. Murray A. Straus and Sandra M. Stith (Minneapolis: National Council on Family Relations, 1995); Richard J. Gelles, *Intimate Violence in Families*, 3rd ed. (Thousand Oaks, CA: Sage, 1997).

10. Murray A. Straus, "Measuring Intrafamily Conflict and Violence: The Conflict Tactics (CTS) Scales," *Journal of Marriage and the Family* 41, no. 1 (1979):

75–88. Also see revised version, "The Conflict Tactics Scale and Its Critics: An Evaluation and New Data on Validity and Reliability," in Straus and Gelles, *Physical Violence;* Murray A. Straus, Sherry L. Hamby, Sue Boney-McCoy, and David Sugarman, "The Revised Conflict Tactics Scales (CTS2): Development and Preliminary Psychometric Data," *Journal of Family Issues* 17, no. 3 (1996): 283–316.

11. Murray A. Straus and Glenda Kaufman-Kantor, "Change in Spouse Assault Rates from 1975 to 1992: A Comparison of Three National Surveys in the United States," Paper presented at the 13th World Congress of Sociology, Bielefeld, Germany (July 1994); Straus and Gelles, "Societal Change."

12. Callie Marie Rennison and Sarah Welchans, *Intimate Partner Violence* (Washington, DC: U.S. Department of Justice, Bureau of Justice Statistics, 2000).

13. This trend was first reported by Angela Browne and Kirk Williams, "Gender, Intimacy and Lethal Violence," *Gender and Society* 7, no. 1 (1993): 78–79; Laura Dugan, Daniel S. Nagin, and Richard Rosenfeld, *Exposure Reduction or Backlash? The Effects of Domestic Violence Resources on Intimate Partner Homicide. Final Report* (Washington, DC: U.S. Department of Justice, 2001).

14. Fox and Zavitz, *Homicide Trends.* Interestingly, in Canada, partner femicide has declined more than homicide by female partners. A comparison of U.S. and Canadian trends is in *Family Violence in Canada: A Statistical Profile 2002* (Ottawa: Canadian Centre for Justice Statistics, Statistics Canada). Also see Orest Fedorowycz, *Homicide in Canada—1999* (Ottawa: Justice Canada, Canadian Centre for Justice Statistics, 2000).

15. Durose et al., *Family Violence Statistics;* Zawitz, *Homicide Trends.*

16. Rennison and Welchans, "Intimate Partner Violence."

17. Rennison and Welchans, "Intimate Partner Violence."

18. Straus and Gelles, "Societal Change"; Straus and Gelles, "How Violent Are American Families?"; Gelles, *Intimate Violence;* Straus and Kaufman-Kantor, "Change in Spouse Assault Rates." The fact that telephone interviews replaced personal interviews in the third NFVS could explain some portion of the reported drop in severe violence because there was no assurance that the respondent was free to answer honestly.

19. Richard J. Gelles and Murray A. Straus, *Intimate Violence: The Definitive Study of the Causes and Consequences of Abuse in the American Family* (New York: Simon & Schuster, 1988); Gelles, Intimate Violence.

20. Rosemary Gartner, Katerine Baker, and Fred C. Pampel, "Gender Stratification and the Gender Gap in Homicide Victimization," *Social Problems* 37 (1990): 593–612; Robert Silverman and Leslie Kennedy, *Deadly Deeds: Murder in Canada.* (Scarborough: Nelson, 1993); Fedorowycz, *Homicide in Canada.*

21. Margo Wilson and Martin Daly, "Spousal Homicide, Risk and Estrangement," *Violence and Victims* 8, no. 1 (1993): 1–15; Margo Wilson and Martin Daly, "Till Death Us Do Part," in *Femicide,* eds. Jill Radford and Diana Russell (New York: Twayne, 1992); Margo Wilson and Martin Daley, "Who Kills Whom in Spouse Killings? On the Exceptional Sex Ratio of Spousal Homicides in the United States," *Criminology* 30 (1992): 189–215; Angela Browne, Kirk Williams, and Donald Dutton, "Homicide Between Intimate Partners," in *Homicide: A Sourcebook for Social Research,* eds. M. Dwayne Smith and Margaret Zahn (Thousand Oaks, CA: Sage, 1998).

22. Darnell Hawkins,"Devalued Lives and Racial Stereotypes: Ideological Barriers to the Prevention of Domestic Violence Among Blacks," in *Violence in the Black Family,* ed. Robert L. Hampton (Lexington, KY: Lexington Books, 1987).

23. S. M. Coley and J. O. Beckett. "Black Battered Women: Practice Issues," *Social Casework* 69, no. 8 (October 1988): 483–490; Evan Stark, "Race, Gender and Woman Battering," in *Violent Crime: Assessing Race and Ethnic Differences*, ed. Darnell Hawkins (Cambridge: Cambridge University Press, 2003), pp. 171–197.

24. Joan Zorza, "Must We Stop Arresting Batterers? Analysis and Policy Implications of New Police Domestic Violence Studies," *New England Law Review* 28 (1994): 929–990.

25. Richard R. Peterson, *Comparing the Processing of Domestic Violence Cases With Non-Domestic Violence Cases in N.Y. City Criminal Court: Final Report* (New York: New York City Criminal Justice Agency, 2001).

26. Rennison and Welchans, "Intimate Partner Violence."

27. William DeLeon-Granados, William Wells, and Ruddyard Binshbacher, "Arresting Developments: Trends in Female Arrests for Domestic Violence and Proposed Explanations," *Violence against Women*12, no. 4 (2006): 355–371.

28. Margaret E. Martin, "Double Your Trouble: Dual Arrest in Family Violence," *Journal of Family Violence* 12, no. 2 (1997): 139–157.

29. Lynne Vieraitis and Marian R. Williams, "Assessing the Impact of Gender Inequality on Female Homicide Victimization Across U.S. Cities: A Racially Disaggregated Analysis," *Violence Against Women* 8, no. 1 (January 2002): 35–63; Myrna Dawson and Rosemary Gartner, "Differences in the Characteristics of Intimate Femicide: The Role of Relationship State and Relationship Status," *Homicide Studies* 2 (1998): 378–399; Gartner, Baker, and Pampel, "Gender Stratification."

30. Rachel B. Whaley and Steve F. Messner, "Gender Equality and Gendered Homicides," *Homicide Studies* 6 (August 2002): 188–210.

31. James W. Messerschmidt, *Masculinities and Crime: Critique and Reconceptualization of Theory* (Lanham, MD: Rowan & Littlefield, 1993).

32. Murray A. Straus, "State-to-State Differences in Social Inequality and Social Bonds in Relation to Assault on Wives in the United States," *Journal of Comparative Family Studies* 25 (1994): 7–24; Dean K. Gauthier and Fred C. Pampel, "Gender Equality and the Sex Ratio of Intimate Killing," *Criminology* 35 (1990): 577–600.

33. Institute for Women's Policy Research (IWPR), *The Status of Women in the States*, (Washington, DC: Institute for Women's Policy Research, 2004).

34. Stephen J. Rose and Heidi I. Hartmann, *Still a Man's Labor Market: The Long-Term Earnings Gap* (Washington, DC: Institute for Women's Policy Research, 2004).

35. IWPR, *Status of Women*, p. 23.

36. Tameka L. Gillum, "Exploring the Link Between Stereotypic Images and Intimate Partner Violence in the African American Community," *Violence Against Women* 8, no. 1 (2002): 64–86.

37. An excellent discussion of how equality may have contradictory dimensions and effects on violence against women is provided by Kimberly Martin, Lynne Vieraitis, and Sarah Britto, "Gender Equality and Women's Absolute Status: A Test of the Feminist Models of Rape," *Violence Against Women* 12, no. 4 (2006): 321–339.

38. Carole K. Chaney and Grace H. Saltzstein, "Democratic Control and Bureaucratic Responsiveness: The Police and Domestic Violence," *American Journal of Political Science* 42 (1998): 745–768.

39. Janell D. Schmidt and Lawrence Sherman, "Does Arrest Deter Domestic Violence?" *American Behavioral Scientist* 36 (1993).

40. After the largely Democratic New York City Council charged in 1995 that a new "must arrest" policy was not being implemented, Republican Mayor Rudy Giuliani produced statistics showing that felony arrests had increased by 37.5% in domestic violence cases and misdemeanor arrests by 75.5%. The council remained skeptical. The prepolicy baseline on which Giuliani based his figures was only 7% of all 911 domestic violence calls. Arrests had only increased to 10%, a large proportional gain, but only a third or less of what other cities were reporting. D. Firestone, "Giuliani and Council Clash on Domestic Violence Effort," *New York Times*, April 5, 1995, p. 83.

41. Andrew R. Klein, "Re-Abuse in a Population of Court-Restrained Male Batterers: Why Restraining Orders Don't Work," in Buzawa and Buzawa, *Arrests and Restraining Orders*, pp. 192–213.

42. Marianne Hester, "Making It Through the Criminal Justice System: Attrition and Domestic Violence," *Social Policy and Society* 5, no. 1 (2006): 79–90.

43. Eve Buzawa, Gerald Hotaling, Andrew Klein, and Jim Byrne, *Final Report* (Washington, DC: National Institute of Justice, July 1999).

44. Richard Berk, "What the Scientific Evidence Shows: On the Average We Can Do No Better Than Arrest," in *Current Controversies on Family Violence*, eds. Richard J. Gelles and Donileen R. Loseke (Newbury Park, CA: Sage, 1993).

45. Molly Chaudhuri and Kathleen Daly, "Do Restraining Orders Help? Battered Women's Experience with Male Violence and Legal Process," in *Domestic Violence: The Changing Criminal Justice Response*, eds. Eve S. Buzawa and Carl G. Buzawa (Westport, CT: Auburn House, 1992) (referred to as Buzawa and Buzawa, *Changing Response*)

46. Ronet Bachman and Linda E. Saltzman, *Violence Against Women: Estimates from the Redesigned Survey* (Washington, DC: U.S. Department of Justice, Bureau of Justice Statistics, 1995).

47. Dobash and Dobash, *Violence Against Wives*; Jan E. Stets and Murray A. Straus, "Gender Differences in Reporting Marital Violence and Its Medical and Psychological Consequences," in Straus and Gelles, *Physical Violence in American Families*; Glenda Kaufman Kantor and Murray A. Straus, "The 'Drunken Bum' Theory of Wife Beating," *Social Problems* 34, no. 3 (1987): 213–230.

48. Daniel Brookoff, Kimberly O'Brian, Charles S. Cook, Terry D. Thompson, and Charles Williams, "Characteristics of Participants in Domestic Violence: Assessment at the Scene of Domestic Assault," *Journal of the American Medical Association* 277, no. 17 (1997): 1369–1373.

49. The 3% figure comes from Langley and Levy, *Wife Beating*. Other estimates are from Lawrence Sherman, *Policing Domestic Violence: Experiments and Dilemmas* (New York: Free Press, 1993); William Holmes and Daniel Bibel, *Police Response to Domestic Violence—Final Report for Bureau of Justice Statistics* (Massachusetts: Committee on Criminal Justice, December 1988). David H. Bayley, "The Tactical Choices of Police Patrol Officers," *Journal of Criminal Justice* 14 (1986): 329–348 estimates the proportion arrested at just over 13%. The highest figure comes from a study of assault cases over 6 years in two communities in western Massachusetts where police responded more aggressively to domestic than to nondomestic assault, even when only a threat but no force was used. Eve Buzawa and Gerald Hotaling, *An Examination of Assaults Within the Jurisdiction of Orange District Court*, Final Report (Washington DC: National Institute of Justice, June 2001).

50. Joan Zorza, "The Criminal Law of Misdemeanor Domestic Violence, 1970–1990," *Journal of Criminal Law and Criminology* 83 (1992): 46–72.

51. Hester, "Making It Through the Criminal Justice System."

52. J. David Hirschel and Ira W. Hutchison, "Realities and Implications of the Charlotte Spouse Abuse Experiment," in Buzawa and Buzawa, *Arrests and Restraining Orders*.

53. Connecticut State Police, *Annual Report on Family Violence Intervention Unit* (November 1991), p. 4.

54. Buzawa and Buzawa, *Domestic Violence*, pp. 143–162. See also Lynette Feder, "Police Handling of Domestic Violence," in *Domestic Violence: An Interdisciplinary Approach*, ed. Lynette Feder (New York: Haworth Press, 1998); Peter K. Manning, "Screening Calls," in Buzawa and Buzawa, *Changing Response*; Kathleen Ferraro and Tascha Boychuk, "The Courts Response to Interpersonal Violence: A Comparison of Intimate and Nonintimate Assault," in Buzawa and Buzawa, *The Changing Response*.

55. Stephen Brown, "Police Response to Wife-Beating: Neglect of a Crime of Violence," *Journal of Criminal Justice* 12 (1984): 277–288; Edna Erez, "Intimacy, Violence, and the Police," *Human Relations* 39, no. 3 (1986): 265–281; Donald G. Dutton, "The Criminal Justice Response to Wife Assault," *Law and Human Behavior* 11, no. 3 (1987): 189–206.

56. Carole A. Burris and Peter Jaffe, "Wife Abuse as a Crime: The Impact of Police Laying Charges," *Canadian Journal of Criminology* 25 (1983): 309–318; Dutton, *The Criminal Justice Response*.

57. J. David Hirschel and Eve Buzawa, "Understanding the Context for Dual Arrest With Directions for Future Research," *Violence against Women* 8 (2002): 1449–1473; DeLeon-Granados, Wells, and Binshbacher, "Arresting Developments," pp. 357, 359.

58. Donald Black's widely cited view that enforcement is inversely related to the social distance between offender and victim is detailed in *The Behavior of Law* (New York: Academic Press, 1976) and *The Manners and Customs of the Police* (New York: Academic Press, 1980)

59. Ferraro and Boychuk, "The Courts' Response to Interpersonal Violence."

60. Hirschel and Hutchinson, "Realities and Implications."

61. Donald S. Dutton, Stephen D. Hart, Lester W. Kennedy, and Kirk Williams, "Arrest and the Reduction of Repeat Wife Assault," in Buzawa and Buzawa, *The Changing Response*.

62. Robert C. Davis, Barbara E. Smith, and Laura Nickles, "Prosecuting Domestic Violence Cases with Reluctant Victims: Assessing Two Novel Approaches in Milwaukee," in *Legal Interventions in Family Violence: Research Findings and Policy Implications* (Washington, DC: National Institute of Justice and the American Bar Association, 1998).

63. Andrew R. Klein, "Re-Abuse."

64. Rebovich, "Prosecution Response."

65. Janice Grau, Jeff Fagan, and Sandra Wexler, "Restraining Orders for Battered Women: Issues of Access and Efficacy," *Women and Politics* 4 (1984): 13–18.

66. Klein, "Re-Abuse."

67. Adele Harrell and Barbara Smith, "Effects of Restraining Orders on Domestic Violence Victims," in Buzawa and Buzawa, *Arrests and Restraining Orders*, pp. 214–242.

68. Healey, Smith, and O'Sullivan, *Batterer Intervention*.

69. Jeffrey L. Edleson and Richard M. Tolman, *Intervention for Men Who Batter: An Ecological Approach* (Newbury Park, CA: Sage, 1992).

70. Jeffrey L. Edleson, "Do Batterers' Programs Work?" Domestic Abuse Project, *Research Update* 7 (1995): 1–3; Richard M. Tolman and Jeffrey Edleson, "Intervention for Men Who Batter: A Review of the Research," in *Understanding Partner Violence: Prevalences, Causes, Consequences and Solutions*, eds. Sandra Stith and Murray A. Straus (Minneapolis, MN: National Council on Family Relations; American Bar Association Commission on Domestic Violence, 1995); Barbara J. Hart, *Evaluation of Court Ordered Treatment for Domestic Violence Offenders, Final Report* (Washington, DC: Urban Institute, 1991); Edward W. Gondolf, "Evaluating Programs for Men Who Batter: Problems and Prospects," *Journal of Family Violence* 2, no. 1 (1987): 95–108.

71. Edleson, "Do Batterers Programs Work?" p. 3.

72. Donald G. Dutton, "Behavioral and Affective Personality Correlates of Borderline Personality Organization in Wife Assaulters," *International Journal of Law and Psychiatry* 17, no. 3 (1994): 265–277; Donald G. Dutton, *The Domestic Assault of Women: Psychological and Criminal Justice Perspectives* (Boston: Allyn & Bacon, 1988, 1995). Kevin L. Hamberger and J. E. Hastings,"Court-Mandated Treatment of Men Who Assault Their Partner: Issues, Controversies, and Outcomes," in *Legal Responses to Wife Assault, ed*. N. Zoe Hilton (Newbury Park, CA: Sage, 1993), pp. 188–229; Michael S. McLoskey, Mitchell Berman, Kurtis L. Noblett, and Emil Coccaro, "Intermittent Explosive Disorder—Integrated Research Diagnostic Criteria: Convergent and Discriminant Validity," *Journal of Psychiatric Research*, 40 (2005): 231–242.

73. Edward W. Gondolf, *Final Report: An Extended Follow-Up of Batterers and Their Partners* (Atlanta, GA: Centers for Disease Control and Prevention, November 19, 2001), p. 13.

74. Daniel K. O'Leary, "Controversies Regarding Psychological Explanations of Family Violence," in *Current Controversies on Family Violence, eds*. Richard J. Gelles and Donileen Loseke (Newbury Park, CA: Sage, 1993), pp. 7–30.

75. Alex Heckert and Ed Gondolf, *Predicting Levels of Abuse and Reassault Among Batterer Program Participants*, Final Report (Washington, DC:National Institute of Justice, 2001).

76. Dutton, *The Domestic Assault of Women*; Donald Dutton, "Patriarchy and Wife Assault: The Ecological Fallacy," *Violence and Victims* 9, no. 2 (1994): 125–140; R. L. Weiss and R. E. Heyman, "A Clinical-Research Overview of Couples Interactions," in *Clinical Handbook of Marriage and Couple Interventions*, eds. W. Kim Halford and Howard J. Markman (New York: Wiley, 1997).

77. Donald G. Dutton and Catherine E. Strachan, "Motivational Needs for Power and Spouse Specific Assertiveness in Assaultive and Non-Assaultive Men," *Violence and Victims 2, no*. 3 (1987): 145–156.

78. Donald G. Dutton, "The Outcome of Court-Mandated Treatment for Wife-Assault: A Quasi-Experimental Evauation," *Violence and Victims* 1, no. 3 (1986): 163–175.

79. Jeffrey Edleson and Martha Syers, "The Effects of Group Treatment for Men Who Batter: An 18-Month Follow-up Study," *Research on Social Work Practice* 1, no. 3 (1991): 227–243.

80. Edleson and Syers, "The Effects"; Maureen Pirog-Good and Jan E. Stets, "Program for Abusers: Who Drops Out and What Can Be Done," *Response* 9 (1986): 17–19.

81. John Goldkamp, Doris Weiland, Mark Collins, and Michael D. White, *The Role of Drug and Alcohol Abuse in Domestic Violence and its Treatment: Dade County's*

Domestic Violence Court Experiment, Final Report (Philadelphia, PA: Crime and Justice Research Institute, 1999).

82. Lynette Feder and Laura Dugan, "A Test of the Efficacy of Court-Mandated Counseling for Domestic Violence Offenders: The Broward Experiment," *Justice Quarterly* 19, no. 2 (2002): 343–375.

83. Robert C. Davis and Bruce G. Taylor, "A Proactive Response to Family Violence: The Results of a Randomized Experiment," *Criminology* 35, no. 2 (1997): 307–333; Robert C. Davis and Bruce G. Taylor, "Does Batterer Treatment Reduce Violence? A Synthesis of the Literature," *Women and Criminal Justice* 10, no. 2 (1999): 69–93.

84. Gondolf, *Final Report*; Edward W. Gondolf, *Batterer Intervention Systems: Issues, Outcomes, and Recommendations* (Thousand Oaks,CA : Sage , 2001, 2002); Edward W. Gondolf, "Re-Assault at 30 Months After Batterer Program Intake," *International Journal of Offender Therapy and Comparative Criminology* 44 (2000): 111–128.

85. Melissa Labriola, Michael Rempel, and Robert C. Davis, *Judicial Monitoring: Results From a Randomized Control Trial at the Bronx Misdemeanor Domestic Violence Court* (Washington, DC: National Institute of Justice, November 2005).

86. Adell Harrell, *Evaluation of Court Ordered Treatment for Domestic Violence Offenders*, Final Report (Washington, DC: Urban Institute, 1991).

87. Daniel Okun, "Termination or Resumption of Cohabitation in Women Battering Relationships: A Statistical Study," in *Coping With Family Violence: Research and Policy Perspectives*, eds. Gerald Hotaling, David Finkelhor, John T. Kirkpatrick, and Murray A. Straus (Newbury Park, CA: Sage, 1988).

88. Mina Piispa, "Complexity of Patterns of Violence Against Women in Heterosexual Partnerships," *Violence Against Women* 8, no. 7 (2002): 873–900.

89. Val Binney, G. Harkell, and Jo Nixon, *Leaving Violent Men* (Bristol: Women's Aid Federation England, 1988).

90. Chris M. Sullivan and Maureen H. Rumptz, "Adjustment and Needs of African-American Women Who Utilized a Domestic Violence Shelter," *Violence and Victims* 9, no. 3 (1994): 275–286.

91. This story is told by Kathleen Ferraro, "Negotiating Trouble in a Battered Women's Shelter," *Urban Life* 12, no. 3 (1983): 287–306. See also Kathleen Ferraro, "Processing Battered Women," *Journal of Family Issues* 2, no. 4 (1981): 415–438.

92. Rhea Almeida and Jacqueline Hudak, "The Cultural Context Model," in *Programs for Men Who Batter: Interventions and Prevention Strategies in a Diverse Society*, eds. Etiony Aldarondo and Fernando Mederos (Kingston, NJ: Civic Research Institute, 2002).

93. Jeffrey L. Edleson, "Advocacy Services for Battered Women," *Violence Update* 4, no. 4 (1993): 1–10.

94. Donileen R. Loseke, *The Battered Woman and Shelters: The Social Construction of Wife Abuse* (Albany: State University of New York Press, 1992).

95. Candace Clark, "Sympathy Biography and Sympathy Margins," *American Journal of Sociology* 93, no. 2 (1987): 290–321.

96. Loseke, *The Battered Woman*, p. 193.

97. Loseke, *The Battered Woman*, p. 194.

98. Jillian Riddington, "The Transition Process: A Feminist Environment as Reconstitutive Milieu," *Victimology* 2, no. 3/4 (1977/78): 563–575.

99. Mary Romero, "A Comparison Between Strategies Used on Prisoners of War and Battered Wives," *Sex Roles* 13 (1985): 537–547.

100. Almeida and Hudak, "The Cultural Context Model."

Chapter 3

1. Deboarah Sontag, "Bad Love: Fierce Entanglements—Domestic Violence Revisited," *NY Times Sunday Magazine*, November 17, 2002.

2. Gelles, *Intimate Violence*, p. 14.

3. Richard J. Gelles and Murray A. Straus, "Compassion or Control: Legal, Social and Medical Services," in Gelles and Straus, *Intimate Violence, p.* 54.

4. Gelles, *Intimate Violence*, p. 14.

5. Linda E. Saltzman, "Introduction." Special Issue, *Building Data Systems for Monitoring and Responding to Violence against Women, Part I,Violence Against Women* 6, no. 7 (2000).

6. Gelles, *Intimate Violence*, p.16. Broad working definitions may be appropriate in health or other settings where the primary intent is to rule out a serious problem and the consequences of being excluded from the risk pool as a "false negative" are much more serious that the consequences of being included as a "false positive."

7. Elizabeth Stanko, *Everyday Violence: How Women and Men Experience Sexual and Physical Danger* (Pandora: London, 1990).

8. Christina Hoff Somers, "The Myth of Spouse Abuse," *USA Today*, October 26, 1994, p. 13; John Leo, "Things That Go Bump in the Home," *US News and World Report*, "On Society" May 13, 1996.

9. Ronet Bachman, *Violence Against Women: Synthesis of Research for Criminal Justice Policymakers*, Final Report, Grant no. NIJ 98–WT–VX–K011, submitted to the U.S. Department of Justice, National Institute of Justice (2000); Ronet Bachman, "A Comparison of Annual Incidence Rates and Contextual Characteristics of Intimate Partner Violence Against Women From the National Crime Victimization Survey (NCVS) and the National Violence Against Women Survey (VAWS)," *Violence Against Women* 6, no. 8 (August 2000): 859; Glenda Kaufman-Kantor and Murray A. Straus, "Response of Victims and the Police to Assaults on Wives," in Straus and Gelles, *Physical Violence*; Stark, "Health Intervention."

10. Jeffrey L. Edleson, "The Overlap Between Child Maltreatment and Woman Abuse," available online at http://www.vaw.umn.edu/finaldocuments /Vawnet/overlap.htm (citing Eric Hangen, DSS Interagency Team Pilot Project: Program Data Evaluation, Office of Management, Planning and Analysis, Massachusetts Department of Social Services, 1994).

11. Patricia Tjaden and Nancy Thoennes, "Prevalence and Consequences of Male-to-Female and Female-to-Male Intimate Partner Violence as Measured by the National Violence Against Women Survey," *Violence Against Women* 6, no. 2(2000): 142–167; Patricia Tjaden and Nancy Thoennes, *Prevalence, Incidence and Consequences of Violence Against Women: Findings From the National Violence Against Women Survey* (Washington, DC: National Institute of Justice Centers for Disease Control and Prevention, 1998).

12. Among the aspects of the NFVS that contribute to overreporting are its reliance on self-reports by perpetrators rather than by victims alone (women tend to overreport their own violence), its introductory emphasis on the pervasiveness of marital/partner conflict (the NVAWS makes no such normalizing reference), and its direction to respondents to describe "how often the following acts occurred" in the previous 12 months. The NVAWS simply asked whether anything happened that made the respondent feel "unsafe."

13. John Schafer, Raul Caetano, and Catherine L. Clark, "Rates of Intimate Partner Violence in the United States," *American Journal of Public Health* 88, no. 11 (1998): 1702–1704; Murray A. Straus and Richard Gelles, "Societal Change and Change in Family Violence From 1975 to 1985 as Revealed by Two National Surveys," *Journal of Marriage and the Family* 48 (1986): 465–479; Murray A. Straus, "Trends in Cultural Norms and Rates of Partner Violence: An Update to 1992," in Straus and Stith, *Understanding Causes*, pp. 30–33.

14. Bachman, "A Comparison of Incidence Rates"; Bachman and Saltzman, "Violence Against Women: Estimates."

15. Bachman (in "A Comparison of Incidence Rates") readjusted NCVS data using the same counting rules as the NVAWS and found that the reported rates statistically similar, a conclusion challenged by Michael Rand and Callie Rennison, "Bigger Is Not Necessarily Better: An Analysis of Violence Against Women Estimates From the National Crime Victimization Survey and the National Violence Against Women Survey," *Journal of Quantitative Criminology* 21, no. 3 (2005): 267–291.

16. Commonwealth Fund, *Health Concerns Across a Woman's Lifespan: 1998 Survey of Women's Health* (New York: May 1999).

17. Evan Stark, "The Battering Syndrome: Social Knowledge, Social Therapy and the Abuse of Women" (PhD diss., State University of New York, Binghamton, 1984), p. 510.

18. Buzawa and Hotaling, *An Examination of Assault*. Figures from the Scottish Executive's "Statistical Bulletin," 2005 show that, of 43,678 domestic abuse incidents record by police for 2004, fewer than half (19,243) involved spouses (8,525) or cohabitees (10,718).

19. Tjaden and Thoennes, *Prevalence, Incidence and Consequence*. The risk of partner assault by women is also 50% for men who are living separately than for married or cohabitating men (.9 versus .6), though the absolute numbers are relatively small.

20. *New Haven Register*, "Farrah Fawcett's Ex-Boyfriend Is Convicted of Beating Her," August 19, 1998, p. A2; Connecticut Deptartment of Public Saftey, *Crime in Connecticut 1995*.

21. Bachmann, "A Comparison of Annual Incidence Rates"; Buzawa and Buzawa, *Domestic Violence*, p. 13.

22. Dobash and Dobash, *Violence Against Wives*.

23. The 1992 National Alcohol and Family Violence Survey, which included parts of the NFVS, found that approximately 1.9% of married/cohabiting women were severely assaulted by a male partner annually and approximately 4.5% of married/cohabiting men were severely assaulted by wives annually. The 1995 National Alcohol Survey also included parts of the NFVS. It found that 5.2% to 13.6% of couples experience male-to-female violence annually and 6.2% to 18.2% experienced female-to-male partner violence.

24. Tjaden and Thoennes, *Prevalence, Incidence, and Consequences*.

25. See Lisa Brush, "Violent Acts and Injurious Outcomes in Married Couples: Methodological Issues in the National Survey of Families and Households," in *Violence Against Women: The Bloody Footprints*, eds. Pauline Bart and Eileen Moran (Thousand Oaks, CA: Sage, 1993), pp. 240–251; Maureen Pirog-Good and Jan Stets, eds. *Violence in Dating Relationships: Emerging Social Issues* (New York: Praeger, 1989); John Scanzoni, *Sex Roles, Women's Work and Marital Conflict* (Lexington, MA: Lexington, 1978); Susan B. Sorenson, and Cynthia A. Telles,

"Self-Reports of Spousal Violence in a Mexican-American and Non-Hispanic White Population," *Violence and Victims* 6 (1991): 3–15; Jan Stets and Murray A. Straus, "The Marriage License as a Hitting License: A Comparison of Asaults in Dating, Cohabiting, and Married Couples," *Journal of Family Violence* 4, no. 2 (1989): 161–180; M. L. Bernard and J. L. Bernard, "Violence Intimacy: The Family as a Model for Love Relationships," *Family Relations* 32 (1983): 283–286; Margaret Plass and J. C. Gessner, "Violence in Courtship Relations: A Southern Sample," *Free Inquiry in Creative Sociology* 11 (1983): 198–202; June Henton, Rodney Cate, James Koval, Sally Lloyd, and Scott Christopher, "Romance and Violence in Dating Relationships," *Journal of Family Issues* 4 (1983): 467–482; J. M. Makepeace, "Gender Differences in Courtship Violence Victimization," *Family Relations* 33 (1986): 383–388.

26. Barbara Morse, "Beyond the Conflict Tactics Scale: Assessing Gender Differences in Partner Violence," *Violence and Victims* 10, no. 4 (1995): 251–272.

27. G. Marie Wiltand and James Bannon, *Domestic Violence and the Police: Studies in Detroit and Kansas City* (Washington, DC: Police Foundation, 1977).

28. Brookoff et al., "Characteristics of Participants in Domestic Violence."

29. Peter Jaffe and Carol Burris, *An Integrated Response to Wife Assault: A Community Model* (Ottawa: Research Report of the Solicitor General of Canada, 1982).

30. Andrew Klein, *Spousal Partner Assault: A Protocol for the Sentencing and Supervision of Offenders* (Quincy, MA: Quincy Court, 1993); Hester, "Making it Through the Criminal Justice System."

31. R. H. C. Teske and M. L. Parker, *Spouse Abuse in Texas: A Study of Women's Attitudes and Experiences* (Huntsville, TX: Sam Houston State University, Criminal Justice Center, 1983); Patsy Klaus and Michael Rand, *Family Violence. Special Report.* (Washington, DC: Bureau of Justice Statistics, 1984).

32. Jayne Mooney, *Domestic Violence in North London* (Middlesex: Middlesex University, Centre for Criminology, 1993).

33. Neil Jacobson and John Gottman, *When Men Batter Women: New Insights Into Ending Abusive Relationships* (New York: Simon & Schuster, 1998); Edward Gondolf, "Who Are Those Guys? Toward a Behavioral Typology of Batterers," *Violence and Victims* 3 (1988): 187–203; Gondolf, *Batterer Intervention Systems.*

34. Liz Kelly, *Surviving Sexual Violence* (Cambridge: Polity Press, 1987).

35. Stark and Flitcraft, *Women at Risk*; Stark, "The Battering Syndrome"; G. D. Rath, L. G. Jarratt, and G. Leonardson, "Rates of Domestic Violence Against Adult Women by Male Partners," *Journal of the American Board of Family Practice* 2 (1989): 227–233; Jean Abbott, Robin Johnson, Jane Kozial-McLain, and Steven Lowenstein, "Domestic Violence Against Women: Incidence and Prevalence in an Emergency Department Population," *Journal of the American Medical Association* 273, no. 22 (1995): 1763–1767; Kevin Hamberger, Dan Saunders, and Mary Harvey, "Prevalence of Domestic Violence in Community Practice and Rate of Physician Inquiry," *Family Medicine* 24, no. 4 (1992): 283–287; U.S. Department of Justice, *Violence Related Injuries Treated in Hospital Emergency Departments* (Washington, DC: U.S. Department of Justice, August 1997.)

36. Louis Harris, *The First Comprehensive National Health Survey of American Women* (New York: Commonwealth Fund, 1993).

37. Stark, "The Battering Syndrome," pp. 461–479. But according to the U.S. Department of Justice Special Report, *Violence Related Injuries Treated in Emergency Departments*, 28% of abuse victims required admission and another 13% required major medical treatment.

38. Connecticut Department of Public Safety, *Family Violence Arrests Annual Report*, 1999.

39. Caliber Associates, *Symposium on DV Prevention Research* (Washington, DC: Department of Defense, 2002).

40. This conclusion is reached by Linda G. Mills, *Insult to Injury: Rethinking Our Responses to Intimate Abuse* (Princeton, NJ: Princeton University Press, 2003); John Leo, "Things That Go Bump"; Somers, "The Myth of Spouse Abuse," p. 13.

41. Francis Power Cobbe, "Wife-Torture in England," *Contemporary Review* 32 (April 1878): 55–87.

42. Murray A. Straus, "Physical Assaults by Wives: A Major Social Problem," in *Current Controversies on Family Violence*, eds. Richard J. Gelles and Donileen Loseke (Newbury Park, CA: Sage, 1993), pp. 67–87.

43. Brush, "Violent Acts."

44. Debra Umberson, Kristin Anderson, Jennifer Glick, and Adam Shapiro. "Domestic Violence, Personal Control, and Gender," *Journal of Marriage and the Family* 60 (1998): 442–452.

45. Tjaden and Thoennes, *Extent, Nature, and Consequences*, exhibit 11, p. 28.

46. Straus, "Physical Assault by Wives," p. 74.

47. Demi Kurz, "Physical Assaults by Husbands: A Major Social Problem," in *Current Controversies on Family Violence*, eds. Richard J. Gelles and Donileen Loseke (Newbury Park, CA: Sage, 1993), pp. 88–102; Russell Dobash, R. Emerson Dobash, Margo Wilson, and Martin Daly, "The Myth of Sexual Symmetry in Marital Violence," *Social Problems* 39 (1992): 71–91; Shamita Das Gupta, "A Framework for Understanding Women's Use of Non-Lethal Violence in Intimate Heterosexual Relationships," *Violence Against Women* 8 (2002): 1364–1389; Suzanne Swann and David Snow, "The Development of a Theory of Women's Use of Violence in Intimate Relationships," *Violence Against Women* 12, no. 11 (2006): 1026–1045.

48. Straus, "Physical Assaults by Wives," p. 74.

49. Suzanne Swan and David Snow, "A Typology of Women's Use of Violence in Intimate Relationships," *Violence Against Women* 8 (2002): 286–319. Das Gupta, "A Framework."

50. Diane R. Follingstad, Shannon Wright, and Jeri Sebastian, "Sex Differences in Motivations and Effects in Dating Violence," *Family Relations* 40 (1991): 51–57.

51. Paige Hall-Smith, Irene Tessaro, and Joanne Earp, "Women's Experiences With Battering: A Conceptualization From Qualitative Research," *Women's Health Issues* 5 (1990): 173–182; Paige Hall-Smith, Jo Anne Earp, and Robert DeVellis. "Measuring Battering: Development of the Women's Experience With Battering (WEB) Scale," *Women's Health: Research on Gender, Behavior and Policy* 1, no. 4 (1995): 273–288.

52. Lischick, "Coping and Related Characteristics."

53. Michael P. Johnson, "Patriarchal Terrorism and Common Couple Violence: Two Forms of Violence Against Women," *Journal of Marriage and the Family* 57 (1995): 283–294.

54. Michael P. Johnson, "Conflict and Control: Symmetry and Asymmetry in Domestic Violence," in *Couples In Conflict*, eds. Alan. Booth, Ann Crouter, and Mari Clements (Mahwah, NJ: Erlbaum, 2001).

55. Lynne Dowd, Penny Leisring, and Alan Rosenbaum, "Partner Aggressive Women: Characteristics and Treatment Attrition," *Violence and Victims* 20, no. 2 (2005): 219–239.

56. Eve Buzawa, Gerald Hotaling, Andrew Klein, and James Byrne, *Response to Domestic Violence in a Proactive Court Setting: Final Report* (Washington, DC: National Institute of Justice, July 1999).

57. Buzawa et al., *Response to Domestic Violence*; Johnson, "Patriarcal Terrorism"; Johnson, "Conflict and Control"; Linda Marshall, "Psychological Abuse of Women: Six Distinct Clusters," *Journal of Family Violence* 11 (1996): 379–409; Mary Ann Allard, Randy Albelda, Mary Ellen Colten, and Carol Cosenza, "In Harm's Way? Domestic Violence, AFDC Receipts, and Welfare Reform in Massachusetts," Executive Summary (Boston, MA: McCormack Institute and Center for Survey Research at the University Of Massachusetts, February 1997); Diane Follingstad, Anne F. Brennan, Elizabeth S. Hause, Darlene S. Polek and Larry L. Rutledge, "Factors Moderating Physical and Psychological Symptoms of Battered Women," *Journal of Family Violence* 6 (1991): 81–95.

58. Richard J. Gelles, "Estimating the Incidence and Prevalence of Violence Against Women. National Data Systems and Sources," *Violence Against Women* 6 (2000): 784–804.

59. Stark and Flitcraft, *Women at Risk*, p. 11.

60. These data are presented in Stark, "The Battering Syndrome," pp. 435–466.

61. Michael Frisch and C. J. MacKenzie, "A Comparison of Formerly and Chronically Battered Women on Cognitive and Situational Dimensions," *Psychotherapy* 28 (1991): 339–344; Karen Landenburger, "A Process of Entrapment in and Recovery From an Abusive Relationship," *Issues in Mental Health Nursing* 10 (1989): 209–227.

62. Jacqueline Campbell, Linda Rose, Joan Kub, and Daphne Nedd, "Voices of Strength and Resistance: A Contextual and Longitudinal Analysis of Women's Responses to Battering," *Journal of Interpersonal Violence* 14 (1998): 743–762.

63. Walter DeKeseredy, "Current Controversies on Defining Nonlethal Violence Against Women in Intimate Heterosexual Relationships: Empirical Implications," *Violence Against Women*, 6 (2000): 728–746.

64. Kelly, Surviving Sexual Violence.

Chapter 4

1. Alexandra Symonds, "Violence Against Women: The Myth of Masochism," *Journal of American Psychotherapy* 33 (1979): 161.

2. Symonds, "Violence Against Women," 162.

3. Elaine Hilberman and Kit Munson, "Sixty Battered Women," *Victimology: An International Journal* 2 (1977–78): 3–4, 460–470.

4. Lucile Cantoni, "Clinical Issues in Domestic Violence," *Social Casework* 62, no. 1 (January 1981): 3–12; P. D. Scott, "Battered Wives," *British Journal of Psychiatry* 125 (1974): 443–441; John E. Snell, Richard Rosenwald, and Ames Roby, "The Wifebeater's Wife: A Study of Family Interaction," *Archives of General Psychiatry* 11 (1964): 107–113.

5. Alan M. Stone, "Presidential Address: Conceptual Ambiguity and Morality in Modern Psychiatry," in *The Gender Gap in Psychotherapy*, eds. Patricia Reiker and Elaine (Hilberman) Carmen (New York: Plenum, 1984), pp. 5–14; Elaine Hilberman, "Overview: The 'Wife-Beater's Wife' Reconsidered," *American Journal of Psychiatry* 137 (1980): 1336–1347; Judith Herman, "Histories of Violence in an Outpatient Population: An Exploratory Study," *American Journal of Orthopsychiatry* 56, no. 1 (January 1986): 137–141; Bruce Rounsaville and Myrna Weissman,

"Battered Women: A Medical Problem Requiring Detection," *International Journal of Psychiatry in Medicine* 8, no. 2 (1977–78): 191–202; Michele Bograd, "A Feminist Examination of Family Systems Models of Violence in the Family," in *Women and Family Therapy*, eds. C. Hanson and M. Ault-Riche (Rockville, MD: Aspen, 1986), pp. 84–107.

6. Jerry Finn, "The Stresses and Coping Behavior of Battered Women," *Social Casework* 66 (1985): 341–349; Barbara Star, "Comparing Battered and Nonbattered Women," *Victimology* 3 (1978): 32–44; Barbara Star, Carol Clark, Karen Goetz, and Linda O'Malia, "Psycho-Social Aspects of Wife Battering," *Social Casework* (October 1979): 479–487; T. T. Graff, "Personality Characteristics of Battered Women," *Dissertation Abstracts International* 40, no. 7-B (1980): 33–95.

7. Michael Strube, "The Decision to Leave an Abusive Relationship Empirical Evidence and Theoretical Issues," *Psychology Bulletin* 104 (1988): 236–250; Ida M. Johnson, "Economic, Situational, and Psychological Correlates of the Decision-Making Process of Battered Women," *Families in Society: The Journal of Contemporary Human Services* 73 (1992): 168–176; W. C. Compton, J. R. Michael, E. M. Krasavage-Hopkins, L. S. Schneiderman, and L. Bickman, "Intentions for Post-Shelter Lliving in Battered Women," *Journal of Community Psychology* 17 (1989): 126–128.

8. Amnesty International, *Its in Your Hands: Stop Violence Against Women* (London: Peter Benenson House, 2004).

9. Eric Hobsbawm, "Retreat of the Male," *London Review of Books* 27, no. 15 (August 4, 2005), available online at http://www.lrb.co.uk/v27/n15/print/hobs01_.html (April 14, 2006). Statistic cited from Goren Therborn, *Between Sex and Power: Family in the World 1900–2000* (London: Routledge, 2005).

10. Lenore Walker, "Battered Women and Learned Helplessness," *Victimology: An International Journal* 2, no. 3–4 (1977–78): 525–534; Lenore Walker, "The Battered Woman Syndrome Study," in *The Dark Side of Families*, eds. David Finkelhor, Richard J. Gelles, Gerald Hotaling, and Murray A. Straus (Beverly Hills, CA: Sage, 1983); Lenore Walker, *Terrifying Love: Why Battered Women Kill and How Society Responds* (New York: Harper & Row, 1989); Lenore E. Walker, *The Battered Woman Syndrome* (New York: Springer, 1984).

11. Irene Frieze, *Hurting the One You Love: Violence in Relationships* (Belmont, CA: Thomson Wadsworth, 2005).

12. Mildred Daley Pagelow, "Adult Victims of Domestic Violence," *Journal of Interpersonal Violence* 7 (March 1992): 87–120.

13. Elizabeth Rapaport, "The Death Penalty and the Domestic Discount," in *The Public Nature of Private Violence*, eds. Martha Fineman and Roxanne Mykitiuk (New York: Routledge, 1994), pp. 224–254.

14. Renat Bachman and L. E. Saltzman, *Violence Against Women: Estimates*; Martha Mahoney, "Legal Images of Battered Women: Redefining the Issue of Separation," *Michigan Law Review* 90, no. 1 (1991): 24–30.

15. Suzanne Steinmetz and Murray A. Straus, "The Family as a Cradle of Violence," *Society* 10, no. 6 (1973): 50–58; Suzanne Steinmetz and Murray A. Straus, eds., *Violence in the Family* (New York: Dodd, Mead, 1974).

16. Richard J. Gelles, *The Violent Home* (Newbury Park, CA: Sage, 1974), p. 50.

17. Gelles, *The Violent Home*, p. 171.

18. Del Martin, *Battered Wives* (New York: Pocket Books, 1977).

19. Dobash and Dobash, *Violence Against Wives*.

20. Susan Schechter, "Psychic Battering: The Institutional Response to Battered Women," Paper presented at Midwest Conference on Abuse of Women, St. Louis,

(October 1978). Schechter, *Women and Male Violence*; Stark, Flitcraft, and Frazier, "Medicine and Patriarchal Violence"; Pagelow, *Woman-Battering*. A critical summary of early feminist work on abuse is Winnie Breines and Linda Gordon, "The New Scholarship on Family Violence," *Signs: Journal of Women and Culture in Society* 8, no. 3 (1983): 490–531.

21. "Battered Wives: Now They're Fighting Back," *U.S. News and World Report* 81 (September 20, 1976): 47–48; V. S. Bedard, "Wife Beating," *Glamour* 76 (August 1978): 85–86; J. Bell, "New Hope for the Battered Wife," *Good Housekeeping* 183 (August 1976): 94+.

22. Bograd, "A Feminist Examination."

23. Walker, *The Battered Woman*, pp. xvi, 55–70.

24. Walker, *The Battered Woman*; Walker, *The Battered Woman Syndrome*; Walker, "Battered Women and Learned Helplessness"; Walker, "The Battered Woman Syndrome Study"; Walker, *Terrifying Love.*

25. Viktor Frankl, *Man's Search for Meaning* (New York: Simon & Schuster, 1997), p. 38.

26. The full findings from the Yale Trauma Studies are reported in Stark, "The Battering Syndrome."More recent work includes Abbott, Johnson, Kozial-McLain, and Lowenstein, "Domestic Violence Against Women"; Rath et al., "Rates of Domestic Violence"; Hamburger, Saunders, and Harvey, "Prevalence of Domestic Violence." Also see Susan McLeer and Rebecca Anwar, "A Study of Battered Women Presenting in an Emergency Department," *American Journal of Public Health* 79, no. 1 (January 1989): 65–66.

27. These findings are summarized in Stark and Flitcraft, *Women at Risk*, chaps. 1, 3, 4, and 6.

28. Susan Mitchell-Herzfeld, *The Adoption and Safe Families Act (AFSA) Study*, The Evaluation and Research Unit of NY State's Office of Children and Family Studies (Unpublished Report dated December 14, 2000).

29. Chris Sullivan, "Beyond Searching for Deficits: Evidence That Physically and Emotionally Abused Women Are Nurturing Parents," *Journal of Emotional Abuse* 2 (2000): 61–62.

30. *DSM*-IV (Diagnostic and Statistical Manual of Mental Disorders), 4th ed. (American Psychiatric Association, 1994), p. 428.

31. Judith Lewis Herman, Christopher Perry, and Bessel van der Kolk, "Childhood Trauma in Borderline Personality Disorder," *American Journal of Psychiatry* 146 (1989): 490–495; Charles Figley, "Posttraumatic Stress Disorder," Parts I and II, *Violence Update* (March and May 1992): 1 and 8–11; Alan Kemp, Edna I. Rawlings, and B. L. Green, "PTSD in Battered Women: A Shelter Sample," *Journal of Traumatic Stress*, 4, no. 1) (1991): 137–148.

32. David Finkelhor and Angela Browne, "The Traumatic Impact of Child Sexual Abuse," *American Journal of Orthopsychiatry* 55, no. 4 (October 1985): 530–541.

33. Judith L. Herman, *Trauma and Recovery: From Domestic Abuse to Political Terror* (London: Pandora, 1992).

34. Herman, *Trauma and Recovery*, pp. 43–47.

35. David Finkelhor and Kersti Yllo, *License to Rape: Sexual Abuse of Wives* (New York: Holt, Rinehart, & Winston, 1985); Hilberman, "Overview"; Star, Clark, and Goetz, "Psycho-Social Aspects of Wife Battering."

36. Mary Ann Dutton, "Critique of the Battered Woman Syndrome Model," *Applied   Research   Forum*   (1996),   available   online   at   www.vawnet.org/

DomesticViolence/Research/VAWnetDocs/AR_bws.pdf (accessed January 16, 2000).

37. Dutton, "Critique of the Battered Woman Syndrome."

38. Mary Ann Dutton, Sean Perrin, and Kelly Chrestman, "Differences Among Battered Women's MMPI Profiles: The Role of Context," Paper presented at the 4th International Family Violence Conference (Durham, NH, 1995).

39. Stephen Rose, Carolyn Peabody, and Barbara Stratigeas, "Responding to Hidden Abuse: A Role for Social Work in Reforming Mental Health Systems," *Social Work* 36, no. 6 (1991): 408–413.

40. Ann Burgess and Linda Holmstrom,"Rape Trauma Syndrome," *American Journal of Psychiatry* 131 (1974): 981–986.

41. Marty Roper, Anne H. Flitcraft, and William Frazier, "Rape and Battering: An Assessment of 100 Cases," Unpublished paper, Department of Surgery, Yale Medical School (1979).

42. Beth Richie, *Compelled to Crime: Gender Entrapment of Battered Black Women* (New York: Routledge, 1996); Beth Richie, "Gender Entrapment and African-American Women: An Analysis of Race, Ethnicity, Gender, and Intimate Violence," in *Violence and Crime: Assessing Race and Ethnic Differences*, ed. Darnell F. Hawkins (Cambridge: Cambridge University Press, 1994), pp. 198–212.

43. Heidi Hartmann, "Capitalism, Patriarchy, and Job Segregation by Sex," *Signs* 1 (Spring 1976): 137–169.

44. Lundy Bancroft, *Why Does He Do That? Inside the Minds of Angry and Controlling Men* (New York: Putnam's, 2002), pp. 156–157.

45. R. E. Connell, *The Men and the Boys* (San Francisco: University of California Press, 2000); Jeff Hearn, *The Violences of Men: How Men Talk About and How Agencies Respond to Men's Violence Against Women* (Thousand Oaks, CA: Sage, 1998).

Chapter 5

1. Donald Downs, *More Than Victims: Battered Women, the Syndrome Society, and the Law* (Chicago: University of Chicago Press, 1996).

2. Elizabeth Schneider, *Battered Women and Feminist Lawmaking* (New Haven, CT: Yale University Press, 2000).

3. Angela Browne, *When Battered Women Kill* (New York: Free Press, 1987), p. 10.

4. Of these, 41 allow women to obtain temporary custody of their children through a civil order of protection. Others allow visitation conditions to be set to protect the domestic violence victim, modifying the best interest of the child standard. Existing state legislation can be divided into three categories: (1) statutes that require courts to consider domestic violence before joint custody is awarded; (2) statutes that add domestic violence as a factor in the best interest of the child standard; and (3) statutes that direct that domestic violence influence other decisions, such as whether a parent has abandoned her children by fleeing domestic violence. Hart, *State Codes*; NCJFCJ, *Model State Code on Domestic and Family Violence* (1994).

5. Parish, "Trend Analysis." By 1993, courts in approximately half of the states had allowed persecutors or criminal defense lawyers to use expert testimony on the battered woman's syndrome. *State v. Hickson*, 630 So.2d 172 (Fla. 1993).

6. Stark, "Preparing for Expert Testimony."

7. In *Curtis v. Firth*, 850 P. 2d 749 (Idaho, 1993), substantial punitive damages were granted after psychologist Lenore Walker testified that her client suffered

from battered woman's syndrome. S. Shepard, "Suing the Abuser" (unpublished paper cited by Fredrica L. Lehrman, "Developments in Domestic Violence Litigation," available from the author at Shaw, Pittman, Potts & Trowbridge, 2300 N. Street NW, Washington, DC 20037). For use of expert testimony on abuse in custody cases, see *Knock v. Knock*, 224 Conn. 776, 783–86 (1993). In disability cases, see Patricia Murphy, *Making the Connections: Women, Work, and Abuse* (Orlando, FL: Paul M. Deutsch Press, 1993).

8. Cynthia Gillespie, *Justifiable Homicide: Battered Women, Self Defense and the Law* (Columbus: Ohio University Press, 1989).

9. This was the view of William Blackstone, *Commentaries on the Laws of England*, p. 1602; cited by Downs, *More than Victims*, p. 139.

10. Ann Jones, *Women Who Kill; Gillespie, Justifiable Homicide.*

11. Browne, *When Battered Women Kill.*

12. Holly Maguigan, "Battered Women And Self-Defense: Myths and Misconceptions in Current Reform Proposals," *University of Pennsylvania Law Review* 140 (1991): 397. Maguigan reviewed 223 cases heard on appeal and found that 75% involved confrontations, 4% were contract cases, 5% involved sleeping men, and 8% had the woman as the aggressor during a lull in the violence.

13. Sandra Davis Westervelt, *Shifting the Blame: How Victimization Became a Criminal Defense* (New Brunswick, NJ: Rutgers University Press, 1998).

14. Stephen J. Schulhofer, "The Gender Question in Criminal Law," *Social Philosophy and Policy* 7 (1990) 105–137, 120.

15. Dershowitz, *The Abuse Excuse.*

16. Lon Fuller, *Legal Fictions* (Stanford, CA: Stanford University Press, 1967). This discussion draws heavily on similar points made by Downs, *More Than Victims*, p. 114–116.

17. Downs, *More Than Victims*, p. 106.

18. James C. Scott, *Seeing Like a State: How Certain Schemes to Improve the Human Condition Have Failed* (New Haven, CT: Yale University Press, 1998).

19. In October 1994, a "hot blood" explanation was cited by Baltimore County Circuit Judge Robert Cahill in sentencing Kenneth Peacock to only 18 months in jail for killing his wife after finding her in bed with another man. Apparently, "hot" blood takes some time to cool, because Peacock argued with his wife for 2 hours before he shot her. Tamar Lewin, "Outrage Over 18 Months for a Killing," *New York Times*, October 21, 1994.

20. To some extent, Dr. Clark shared this view of his experiment. See Kenneth B. Clark, "The Desegregation Case: Criticism of the Social Scientist's Role," *Villanova Law Review* 5 (1959): 224, 231.

21. Quoted in Pleck, *Domestic Tyranny*, p. 156, citing *Annual Report of the American Bar Association* (Chicago: American Bar Association, 1938) 63:588. Also see Elizabeth Pleck, "Criminal Approaches to Family Violence, 1640–1980," in *Crime and Justice: A Biannual Review of Research*, eds. Lloyd Ohlin and Michael Tonry (Chicago: University of Chicago Press, 1989), pp. 19–57.

22. *People v. Bledsoe* (1984) 681p.2d 291 (Cal 1984) at 298.

23. This historical summary relies heavily on Pleck, *Domestic Tyranny*, pp. 17–108 and Pleck, "Criminal Approaches to Family Violence."

24. Pleck, *Domestic Tyranny*, p. 63.

25. Pleck, *Domestic Tyranny*, pp. 63–64.

26. John Stuart Mill, in *The Subjection of Women*, ed. Susan Okin (Indianapolis: Hackett, 1988); Cobbe, "Wife-Torture in England"; Francis Power Cobbe,

"Criminals, Idiots, Women, and Minors. Is the Classification Sound? A Discussion on the Laws Concerning the Property of Married Women" [reprinted, by Messrs. Longmans' Permission, From Fraser's Magazine, December 1868.] (Manchester: Ireland and Co. Pall Mall), available online at http://www.indiana.edu/~letrs/vwwp/cobbe/criminal.html (April 12, 2006); Harriet Taylor Mill, "Violence and Domestic Violence," in *The Complete Works of Harriet Taylor Mill*, Jo Ellen Jacobs, ed. (University of Indiana Press, 1998), pp. 75–134.

27. The Massachussets Body of Liberties provided that "everie marryed woeman shall be free from bodilie correction or stripes by her husband, unless it be in his own defence upon her assault." Cited in Pleck, *Domestic Tyranny*, p. 22. By contrast, the husband's right to chastisement was abolished in England in 1829 and wife beating was first outlawed in Britain by an 1853 act for "the Better Prevention of Aggravated Assaults Upon Women and Children." Schechter, *Women and Male Violence*; Pleck, *Domestic Tyranny*, p. 21–22.

28. Margaret May, "Violence in the Family: An Historical Perspective," in *Violence and the Family*, ed. John Martin (London: Wiley, 1978), p. 135, 138–149.

29. Pleck, *Domestic Tyranny*, pp. 49–69, 88–107.

30. In 1871, Alabama became the first state to rescind the legal right of men to beat their wives (*Fulgrahm v. State*). Although Massachusetts also declared wife beating illegal, Maryland was the first state to pass a law that made wife beating a crime, punishable by 40 lashes or a year in jail. Nancy Lemon, *Domestic Violence Law: A Comprehensive Overview of Cases and Sources* (San Francisco, CA:. Austin & Winfield, 1996). An interesting if imperfect record of key dates in the domestic violence revolution is *Herstory of Domestic Violence: A Timeline of the Battered Women's Movement* (SafeNetwork, California's Domestic Violence Resource, 1999), available online at http://www.mincava.umn.edu/documents/herstory/herstory.html.

31. Bills to flog wife beaters passed in Delaware (1901), Maryland (1882), and Oregon (1905), whereas in Nevada an 1877 bill allowed for wife beaters to be tied to a post for 2 to 10 hours. According to Pleck (*Domestic Tyranny*, p. 120), 6 whites and 15 blacks were flogged for wife beating in Delaware between 1901 and 1942. Baldwin argued that prisons perpetuated crime by confining men to foul atmosphere and believed, because wife beaters dreaded pain, it was best to do to them what they had done to others.

32. Cobbe, "Wife Torture," pp. 67–70; see also Pleck, *Domestic Tyranny*, pp. 55–87. A similar distinction between deserving victims and women who are "violence prone" and "bully other women at the shelter" was urged on Parliament by Erin Pizzey, founder of Chiswick House, in the 1970s. Evan Stark and Anne H. Flitcraft, "Social Knowledge, Social Therapy, and the Abuse of Women: The Case Against Patriarchal Benevolence," in *The Dark Side of Families*, eds. David Finkelhor, Richard Gelles, Gerald Hotaling, and Murray A. Straus (Beverly Hills, CA: Sage, 1983), pp. 330–348. Reprinted as chap. 2 in Stark and Flitcraft, *Women at Risk*.

33. Gordon, *Heroes of Their Own Lives*, pp. 59–81.

34. Karen Knox and Albert Roberts, "Police Social Work," in *Social Workers' Desk Reference*, eds. Albert Roberts and Gilbert Greene (New York: Oxford University Press, 2002), pp. 668–672.

35. Pleck, *Domestic Tyranny*, pp. 140–141.

36. Ernest Mowrer and Harriet Mowrer, *Domestic Discord: Its Analysis and Treatment* (Chicago: University of Chicago Press, 1928).

37. David L. Kirp, Mark G.Yudof, and Marlene Strong Franks, *Gender Justice* (Chicago: University of Chicago Press, 1986); Susan Atkins and Brends Hoggett, *Women and the Law* (London: Basil Blackwell, 1984).

38. The following discussion relies largely on Jones, *Women Who Kill*, pp. 140–209.

39. Jones, *Women Who Kill*, pp. 163–164. Linked to these "moral causes" were moral mania, moral insanity, or the "irresistible impulse" defense widely used by men to explain a defect of the will that drove a jealous husband to kill his wife though his reason and emotions told him this was wrong.

40. In 1870 Laura Fair, a twice-married and "shady" woman, shot her lover, the Honorable A. P. Crittenden, a prominent San Francisco judge and respectable family man, on the Oakland ferry. It was her view that a woman should stand up for herself. She wrote when "an American woman in justice avenges her outraged name, the act will strike terror to the hearts of sensualists and libertines. . . . By her act, her sex throughout the world will glorify the name of American women." Not only was Fair convicted and sentenced to death but when she proposed to set forth her views inciting wronged women to murder, thousands surrounded the lecture hall as well as her home, and she was almost lynched. Jones, *Women Who Kill*, pp. 173–174.

41. Ironically, even rough woman were expected to wear their best dress for their hanging. If a woman was too poor, clothes could be bought through private contributions or even, on several occasions, at the public's expense. A description of female hangings between 1600 and 1900 is available online at http://www.geocities.com/trctl11/femhang.htm.

42. Jones, *Women Who Kill*, p. 167.

43. The following description is based on McNulty, *The Burning Bed*, and Jones, *Next Time She'll be Dead*, pp. 101–105.

44. The presiding Judge, Ray C. Hotchkiss, shared this view. He told reporters that "self-defense is a real issue. But it had never really been covered in the trial" (quoted by Jones, *Women Who Kill*, p. 289).

45. Jones, *Women Who Kill*, p. 287. An insanity plea was also used in the case of Roxanne Gay, a black woman who had stabbed her husband, 225-pound Philadelphia Eagles lineman Blenda Gay, in the throat as he slept. Despite evidence of numerous calls for help and police testimony confirming a long history of beatings, Gay's defense attorney denied a history of abuse—fearing it would establish motive—and called on psychiatric testimony to establish that she was a paranoid schizophrenic. Murder charges were dropped. But, whereas Francine Hughes's insanity was apparently resolved with a few token psychiatric visits, Roxanne Gay was institutionalized in a state mental hospital.

46. *State v. Wanrow*, 88 Wash. 2d 221, 559 P. 2d 548 (1977). The instruction as given by the trial court is at *Wanrow* 558–559 and is quoted in Jones, *Women Who Kill*, p. 286.

47. Parrish, *Trend Analysis*; *People v. Dillard*, 53 Cal. Rptr. 2d 456 (1996).

48. Mary Ann Dutton, "Understanding Women's Response to Domestic Violence: A Redefinition of Battered Woman Syndrome," *Hofstra Law Review* 21 (1993): 1191–1242; Mary Ann Dutton, "Battered Women's Strategic Response to Violence: The Role of Context," in *Future Interventions With Battered Women and Their Families*, eds. Jeffrey Edleson and Zvi Eisikovitz (Thousand Oaks, CA: Sage, 1996), pp. 105–124; Mary Ann Dutton, *The Validity and Use of Evidence Concerning Battering and its Effects in Criminal Trials, a Report to Congress Under the Violence Against Women Act* (Washington, DC: U.S. Department of Justice and U.S. Department of Health and Human Services, 1996).

49. For the view that a history of violence by a partner can produce a reasonable fear that a current attack may put the defendant in serious danger, see *People v. Torres* (1985) 488 NY S. 2d at 338, Court of Appeals.

50. *State v. Hundley*, 693 P.2d 475 (1985), 479.

51. Mary Ann Dutton and Lisa A. Goodman, "Posttraumatic Stress Disorder Among Battered Women: Analysis of Legal Implications," *Behavioral Science and the Law* 12, no. 3 (1994): 215–234.

52. Herman, *Trauma and Recovery*.

53. Julie Blackman, *Intimate Violence: The Study of Injustice* (New York: Columbia University Press, 1989).

54. Katherine K. Baker, "Gender and Emotion in Criminal Law," *Harvard Journal of Law and Gender* 28 (2005): 457; Victoria Nourse, "Self-Defense and Subjectivity," *University of Chicago Law Review* 68 (2001): 1235–1282.

55. James Gilligan, *Violence: Our Deadly Epidemic and Its Causes* (New York: Grosset/Putnam Books, 1996).

56. Walker, *The Battered Woman Syndrome*.

57. The appellate court overturned the conviction, citing "ineffective assistance of counsel" resulting from the failure to introduce expert testimony. The case is described by Minouche Kandel, "Women Who Kill Their Batterers Are Getting Battered in Court," *Ms.* (July/August 1993): 88–89.

58. *State v. Kelly* (1984) (& N.J. 178, 478 A2d 364), 372.

59. *State v. Kelly*, 193.

60. *State v. Kelly*, 377.

61. *State v. Kelly*, 378.

62. *Cusseaux v. Pickett*, 279 NJ Super. 335, 652 A2nd 789 (Law Div. 1994), 344.

63. *Giovine v. Giovine*, 284 NJ Super.3 (App. Div) 1995.

64. A population-based study completed in Leon, Nicaragua identified severe partner violence with an extreme risk of "mental distress" and PTSD long after the physical abuse has ended. Mary Ellsberg, *Confites en el infierno: prevalencia y caracteristícas de la violencia conyugal hacia las mujeres en Nicaragua* (Managua: Asociación de Mujeres Profesionales por la Democracia en el Desarrollo, 1996); Mary Ellsberg, R. Peña, A. Herrera, et al., "Candies in Hell: Women's Experiences of Violence in Nicaragua," *Social Science and Medicine* 51 (2000): 1595–1610.

65. Suvi Keskinen, "Commitments and Contradictions: Linking Violence, Parenthood and Professionalism," in *Tackling Men's Violence in Families—Nordic Issues and Dilemmas*, eds. Maria Eriksson, Marianne Hester, Suvi Keskinen, and Keith Pringle (Bristol: Policy Press, 2005), p. 37.

66. Julie Blackman, "Emerging Images of Severely Battered Women and the Criminal Justice System," *Behavioral Sciences and the Law* 8, no. 2 (1990): 121–130.

67. Downs, *More Than Victims*, p. 7.

68. Walker, *Terrifying Love*, p. 7.

69. Coramae Mann,"Getting Even? Women Who Kill in Domestic Encounters," *Justice Quarterly* 5, no. 1 (March 1988): 33–51.

70. Coramae Mann, "Female Murderers and Their Motives: A Tale of Two Cities," in *Representing Battered Women Who Kill*, eds. Sara Lee Johann and Frank Osanka (Springfield, IL: Charles C. Thomas, 1992).

71. Charles Ewing, *Battered Women Who Kill: Psychological Self-Defense as Legal Justification* (Lexington, MA: Lexington Books, 1987), pp. 51–60.

72. Susan Osthoff, "Restoring Justice: Clemency for Battered Women," *Response* 14 (1991): 2–3.

73. Elizabeth Dermody Leonard, *Convicted Survivors: The Imprisonment of Battered Women Who Kill* (Stonybrook: State University of New York Press, 2002).

74. Karen Stout and Patricia Brown, "Legal and Social Differences Between Men and Women Who Kill Intimate Partners," *Affilia* 10 (1995): 194–205.

75. *Emick*, 103 AD2d 643, 481 NYS2d 552 (4th Dept 1984).

76. N.Y. Penal Law, Section 3515 (2) (a).

77. Mary Ann Dutton, *Empowering and Healing the Battered Woman: A Model for Assessment* (New York: Springer, 1992). I illustrate this in the case of Lavonne Lazarra summarized in Evan Stark, "A Failure to Protect: Unraveling the Battered Mother's Dilemma," *Western State University Law Review* 27 (Winter 2000): 101–183.

78. Maguigan, "Battered Women and Self-Defense."

79. Walker, *The Battered Woman Syndrome*, pp. 202–214. Walker's original description was based on "120 detailed stories of battered women," most of whom responded to newspaper ads, radio announcements, or came to Walker for therapy, and "fragments of over 300 more stories" (Walker, *The Battered Woman*, p. xiii). Her subsequent research project drew its 403 women from similar sources, though she provides no information on how many subjects came from which source.

80. *People v. Garcia*, Cr. No. 4259 (Superior Court, Monterey County, California, 1979); *State v. Little*, 74 Cr. No. 4176 (Superior Court, Beaufort County, North Carolina, 1975). The Karen Straw trial for murder is described in Jones, *Next Time She'll Be Dead*, pp. 132–135.

81. Ewing, *Battered Women Who Kill*, p. 65.

82. This idea originates in Michael Johnson and Kathleen J. Ferraro, "The Victimized Self: The Case of the Battered Woman," in *The Existential Self in Society*, eds. Joseph Kortarba and Andrea Fontana (Chicago: University of Chicago Press, 1984), p. 27.

Chapter 6

1. A good summary of these views is Catherine Eschle, *Global Democracy, Social Movements and Feminism* (Boulder, CO: Westview, 2001).

2. Women's status in the ancient world was by no means monolithic. By contrast with ancient Greece, some Egyptian women worked outside the home at their trades and at manual labor, and women of the commercial and properties classes had full rights of property, could testify at trials, and could guard against arbitrary divorce by means of prenuptial contracts. Women appear to have enjoyed even greater independence in ancient Babylon. Even in military Sparta, where women managed the land while men were fighting, they could inherit and retain landed estates as their own. Where there were no schools for girls in Athens, in Sparta women were admitted to the gymnasium. Women retained certain rights to inherited property in Rome as well.

3. Laurel Ulrich, *Good Wives: Image and Reality in the Lives of Women in Northern New England, 1650–1750* (New York: Vintage Books, 1991); Nancy Tomes, "A Torrent of Abuse: Crimes of Violence Between Working-Class Men and Women in London 1840–1875," *Journal of Social History* 11 (1978): 328–345.

4. Jürgen Habermas, *The Structural Transformation of the Public Sphere: An Inquiry Into a Category of Bourgeois Society*, trans. Thomas Burger with Frederick Lawrence (Cambridge, MA: MIT Press, 1991); Jürgen Habermas, "Further Reflections on the Public Sphere," in Craig Calhoun and Frederick Lawrence, trans., *Habermas and the Public Sphere* (Cambridge, MA: MIT Press, 1992).

5. In *The Sexual Contract* (Stanford, CA: Stanford University Press, 1988), Carole Pateman argues that the liberal formulation of free and equal men in civil society required the relocation of the patriarchy from the political to the private domain. Where the family had been conceived by Hobbes, Filmer, and other classic theorists as a miniature of the state, the family under nineteenth-century liberal regimes was reformulated in opposition to the state and civil society. Pateman and other feminist philosophers see this as a trade-off by which men presumably accept the social contract in exchange for the privatization of the sexual contract, that is, their right to rule the home like little kings. Though the argument is not completely convincing historically, it helps explain the legal credibility of "privacy" as a right of nonintrusion into patriarchal-like domestic arrangements.

6. See also Nancy Cott, *The Bonds of Womanhood: "Women's Sphere" In New England 1780–1835* (New Haven, CT: Yale University Press, 1977).

7. The struggle around the male wage within families is described in Jan Pahl, *Money and Marriage* (London: Macmillan,1989).

8. Cobbe, "Wife Torture," p. 61.

9. Cobbe, "Wife Torture," p. 62. Lest this be seen as idle rhetoric, consider the 1879 murder of Elizabeth Glover by William Hancock outside the Black Swan Tavern in London. Though Glover was repeatedly thrown to the ground in front of a crowd that included both a waiter from the tavern and a policeman, they had avoided intervening "because I thought (said the policeman) they were man and wife." Ellen Ross, *Love and Toil: Motherhood In Outcast London 1870–1918* (New York: Oxford University Press, 1993). p.85

10. Cobbe, *Criminals, Idiots, Women and Minors*, p. 18.

11. Mill's views on this issue are equivocal. He rejected the "separate sphere" assumption at the heart of sexism (that women's distinctive nature excluded them from the paid employment or public responsibility) and thought there was no basis for believing that women who are able to enjoy the free use of their faculties would do so in any different way than men. At the same time, in contrast to Cobbe and Harriet Taylor, he compared the woman's choice of marriage with the man's choice of a profession, arguing that married women, particularly with children, were already doing more than their fair share and would compromise their domestic responsibilities if they sought paid employment. Thus, even as he rejected the premise of the separate spheres principle, he accepted its conclusion, if only as a rule of thumb.

12. Mill, *The Subjection of Women* (1869), para 2.12c.

13. Stuart Ewen, *Captains of Consciousness: Advertising and the Social Roots of Consumer Culture* (New York: McGraw-Hill, 1976).

14. An exception is Cobbe's argument for a law that would have the state compensate battered wives for the income lost while their husbands were in jail. Still, the 1994 VAWA included economic sanctions on men who committed violence as mandatory restitution requirements.

15. These data are from U.S. Department of Commerce, Bureau of the Census, *Current Population Survey, Annual Social and Economic Supplement* (2003, rev. March 12, 2000), available online at http://www.census.gov/population/www/socdemo/school.html; U.S. Department of Commerce, Bureau of the Census, "Historical Income Tables—People: Full-Time, Year-Round Workers (All Races) by Median Earnings and Sex, 1960–2000, (2002), table P-37, Gender Wage Ratio (1960–2002), table P-40, rev. Feb. 22, 2006, both available online at http://www.census.gov/hhes/www/income/histinc/incpertoc.html; and the

Institute for Women's Policy Research (IWPR), *The Status of Women in the States*, 4th ed. (Washington, DC: IWPR, 2002–2003).

16. IWPR, *The Status of Women in the States*, also see table p. 31.

17. Jamie Maxner, *Women in the U.S. Labor Market: An Economic Analysis* (2003; rev. July 24, 1999), available online at "Women, Leadership, and Enerpreneurship" at http://instruct1.cit.cornell.edu/courses/aem425/Maxner.htm.

18. IWPR, *The Status of Women in the States*, p. 29. In the 2000 Census, the number of working mothers with infants had dropped slightly, particularly among married white mothers with at least 1 year of college, though not among single mothers or among African American or Hispanic women. This change may be a statistical quirk, a result of the economic downturn (for women who have a choice), the boom of the 1990s, or an effect of conservative and profamily sentiment.

19. Education data are from U.S. Department of Commerce, U.S. Census Bureau, *Current Population Survey*.

20. IWPR, *The Status of Women in the States*, pp. 14–17.

21. IWPR, *The Status of Women in the States*, pp. 14–17.

22. Jean Elshtain, "A Call to Civil Society," Society (July/August 1999): 1–8; Jean Elshtain, *Democracy on Trial* (New York: Basic Books, 1995); Seyla Benhabib, "From Identity Politics to Social Feminism: A Plea for the Nineties," available online at http://www.ed.uiuc.edu/EPS/PES-Yearbook/94_docs/BENHABIB.HTM.

23. Amy Caiazza, *Women's Community Involvement: The Effects of Money, Safety, Parenthood and Friends* (Washington, DC: IWPR, 2001).

24. Caiazza, Women's *Community Involvement*.

25. Martha H. Patterson, *Beyond the Gibson Girl: Reimagining the American New Woman, 1895–1915* (Champaign: Univesrity of Illinois Press, 2005).

26. The department stores and offices where increasing numbers of women found employment in the 1920s were new forms of work that served as way stations for the revolutions in consumer goods and information. But the "salesgirl" also became a symbol for the sexualization of consumption used in advertising to conceal the miserable conditions in which the largely female labor force produced the goods sold in department stores (Ewen, *Captains of Consciousness*). The romance enacted in a department store by Charlie Chaplin (as a night guard) and Paulette Goddard in *Modern Times* (1936) is a long way from the big store and bureaucratic rabbit warrens depicted in C. Wright Mills's classic on the American middle classes, *White Collar* (Oxford: New York, 1956).

27. Vachel Lindsay, *The Art of Making Movies* (1915; New York: Modern Library Edition, 2000).

28. The fate of other women in the film is similarly defined by pronatalist and profamily morality. Another secretary, impregnated by a rich lush, is saved because of her refusal to have an abortion. By contrast, a secretary-turned-actress dies in a fall after her affair with her director turns sour and a divorcée (Martha Hyer) finds her life as a single mother totally depressing.

29. Philip Slater, *The Pursuit of Loneliness: American Culture at the Breaking Point* (Boston: Beacon Press, 1970).

30. Margaret Hennig and Anne Jardim, *The Managerial Woman* (London: Pan Books, 1979).

31. A marked exception is Annie, the unambiguously happy mother in the TV show *Seventh Heaven*, who survives in an island of purity besieged by unwed fathers and a range of other contemporary problems. She is even popular among younger viewers, though primarily as a kitsch object of nostalgia.

32. Booker T. Washington, *Up From Slavery: An Autobiography* (New York: Thomas Nelson & Sons, 1901), p. 380.

33. IWPR, *The Status of Women in the States*, p. 5.

34. The source of these data is the U.S. Department of Labor, Bureau of Labor Statistics (2001a), tables 15 and 17. The data are extrapolated from the IWPR report *The Status of Women in the States*, table 4.5 and pp .21–27.

35. Catalyst, *The 2000 Catalyst Census of Women Corporate Officers and Top Earners* (New York: Catalyst, 2000).

36. IWPR, "Fact Sheet,"updated April 2006.

37. Stephen J. Rose and Heidi Hartman, *Still a Man's Labor Market: The Long-Term Earnings Gap* (Washington, DC: IWPR, 2004).

38. IWPR, *The Status of Women in the States*, p. 5.

39. Arlie Hochschild, *The Second Shift: Working Parents and the Revolution at Home* (New York: Viking, 1989), p. 18.

40. Hochschild, *The Second Shift.* Also see Arlie Hochschild, "Global Care Chains and Emotional Surplus Value," in *Global Capitalism*, eds. Will Hutton and Anthony Giddens (New York: New Press, 2000).

41. Jody Heymann, *The Widening Gap. Why America's Working Families Are in Jeopardy—And What Can Be Done About It* (New York: Basic Books, 2000).

42. Nancy Meyer-Emerick, "Policy Makers, Practitioners, Citizens: Perceptions of the Violence Against Women Act of 1994," *Administration and Society* 33 no. 6 (2002): 629–663.

43. Joan Huber and Glena Spitze, *Sex Stratification: Children, Housework, and Jobs* (New York: Academic Press, 1983).

44. Robert Putnam, *Bowling Alone: The Collapse and Revival of American Community* (New York: Simon & Schuster, 2000).

45. Gelertner writes, "They had jobs, but feminists weren't satisfied; every other woman had to get one too. So they opened fire on homemakers with a savagery that still echoes throughout our culture" (David Gelertner, *Drawing Life: Surviving the Unibomber* [New York: Free Press, 1997], p. 95). Meanwhile, according to Graglia, "Housewives, not men, were the prey in feminism's sights when Kate Millett decreed in 1969 that the family must go." Carolyn Graglia, *Domestic Tranquility, A Brief Against Feminism* (Dallas: Spence, 1998), p. 97.

46. Peggy Thoits, "Multiple Identities: Examining Gender and Marital Status Differences in Distress," *American Sociological Review* 51 (1986): 259–272; Peggy Thoits, "Social Support and Psychological Well-Being: Theoretical Possibilities," in *Social Support: Theory, Research and Applications*, eds. Irwin G. Sarason and Barbara Sarason (Boston: Martinus Nijhoff, 1985), pp. 51–72.

47. Iris Young, *Justice and the Politics of Difference* (Princeton, NJ: Princeton University Press, 1990).

48. Martha Fineman, "Preface," in Fineman and Mykitiuk, *Public Nature*, p. xv.

Chapter 7

1. Frantz Fanon, *Black Skin/White Masks* (London: Paladin, 1968).

2. Poco Kernsmith, "Exerting Power or Striking Back: A Gendered Comparison of Motivations for Domestic Violence Perpetration," *Violence and Victims* 20, no. 2 (2005): 173–186; Mary Beth Phelan, L. Kevin Hamberger, Clare Guse, Shauna Edwards, Suzanne Walczak, and Amy Zosel, "Domestic Violence

Among Male and Female Patients Seeking Emergency Medical Services," *Violence and Victims* 20, no. 2 (2005): 187–206.

3. Edgar Schein, Inga Schneier, and Curtis Barker, *Coercive Persuasion* (New York: Norton, 1961).

4. Camella Serum, "The Effects of Violent Victimization in the Family," Paper presented to the Michigan Coalition Against Domestic Violence, December 3, 1979; Margaret Singer, "The Nature of Coercive Control," Paper presented to the Michigan Coalition Against Domestic Violence, December 3. 1979, cited in Lewis Okun, *Woman Abuse: Facts Replacing Myths* (Albany: State University of New York Press, 1986), p. 258.

5. Stephen Morgan, *Conjugal Terrorism: A Psychology and Community Treatment Model of Wife Abuse* (Palo Alto, CA: R&E Research Associates, 1982).

6. Okun, *Woman Abuse*, pp. 86–89 and 113–140.

7. Jones, *Next Time She'll be Dead*, pp. 90–91.

8. David Adams, "Treatment Models of Men Who Batter: A Pro-Feminist Analysis," in *Feminist Perspectives on Wife Abuse*, eds. Kersti Yllo and Michele Bograd (Newbury Park, CA: Sage, 1988), p. 191. Also see David Adams and Andrew McCormick, "Men Unlearning Violence: A Group Approach Based on a Collective Model," in *The Abusive Partner: An Analysis of Domestic Battering*, ed. Maria Roy (New York: Van Nostrand Reinhold, 1982), pp. 170–197.

9. Bancroft, *Why Does He Do That?*, pp. 156–157.

10. Ann Jones and Susan Schechter, *When Love Goes Wrong* (New York: Harper Collins, 1992), p. 13.

11. Schneider, *Battered Women and Feminist Lawmaking*.

12. Gordon, *Heroes of Their Own Lives*.

13. Murray A. Straus, "Injury and Frequency of Assault and the 'Representative Sample Fallacy' in Measuring Wife-Beating and Child Abuse," in Straus and Gelles, *Physical Violence*.

14. Hugh Condon, *The Manchurian Candidate* (New York: Four Walls Eight Windows, 2003). The reality was somewhat less dramatic. During the Korean War, the North Koreans (and Chinese) played off the poor education received by American POWs by introducing them to alternative (Marxist) history lessons drawn from U.S. texts and American sociologists like C. Wright Mills and taught by North Korean and Chinese teachers who spoke perfect Chicago English.

15. Louise Story, "Many Women at Elite Colleges Set Career Path to Motherhood," *New York Times*, September 20, 2005, p. A-18.

16. Identifying home maintenance and child care as continuing sources of self-worth does not mean endorsing the quasi-genetic formulations of feminists who insist women are oriented toward "relationality," for example, Seyla Benhabib, *Situating the Self: Gender, Community and Postmodernism in Contemporary Ethics* (London: Routledge, 1992), or that these activities resonate with or elicit a generative impulse, a "different voice" or "maternal thinking" in the words of relational feminists like Carol Gilligan and Nancy Chodorow.

17. Richie, *Gender Entrapment*; Evan Stark and Anne H. Flitcraft, "Women and Children at Risk: A Feminist Perspective on Child Abuse," *International Journal of Health Services* 18, no. 1 (1988): 97–118. An edited version appears in Stark and Flitcraft, *Women at Risk*, pp. 73–98.

18. bell hooks, *Feminist Theory from Margin to Center*, cited in Mahoney, "Legal Images," p. 62.

19. Susan Okin, *Justice, Gender and the Family* (New York: Basic Books, 1989). See also Sally Goldfarb, "Violence Against Women and the Persistence of Privacy," *Ohio State Law Journal* 61, no. 1 (2000): 18–45.

20. John Hasnas, "Equal Opportunity, Affirmative Action, and the Anti-Discrimination Principle: The Philosophical Basis for the Legal Prohibition of Discrimination," *Fordham Law Review* 71 (November 2002): 423–542.

21. Cahterine MacKinnon, *Sexual Harassment of Working Women* (New Haven, CT: Yale University Press, 1979).

22. Donna Coker, "Transformative Justice: Anti-Subordination Processes in Cases of Domestic Violence," in *Restorative Justice and Family Violence*, eds. Heather Strang and John Braithwaite (Melbourne: Cambridge University Press, 2002), pp. 128–152.

23. Schechter, *Women and Male Violence*, pp. 318–319, cited in Schneider, *Feminist Law Making*, p. 22.

24. Michele E. Beasley and Dorothy Q. Thomas, "Domestic Violence as a Human Rights Issue," in *The Public Nature of Private Violence*, eds. Martha Fineman and Roxanne Mykitiuk (London: Routledge, 1994), pp. 323–348; Johanna Bond and Robin Phillips, "Violence Against Women as a Human Rights Violation: International Institutional Responses," in *Sourcebook on Violence Against Women*, eds. Jeffrey L. Edleson, Claire M. Renzetti, and Raquel Kennedy Bergen (Thousand Oaks, CA: Sage, 2001), pp. 481–500.

25. Amnesty International, *It's In Your Hands.*

26. Amnesty International, "Women on The Front Line: New Report Details 'Barbaric' Abuses of Women in More Than 40 Countries," AI Press Release, March 8, 1991(AI Index, ACT 77/04/9l)

27. UN Report 1989, p. 3., cited in Beasley and Thomas, "Domestic Violence," p. 329.

28. Cited in Bond and Phillips, "Violence Against Women," p. 490.

29. Bond and Phillips, "Violence Against Women," p. 489.

30. World Conference on Human Rights, *Vienna Declaration and Program of Action*, Article 18 (Vienna: World Conference on Human Rights, 1993), quoted by Bond and Philips, "Violence Against Women," p. 492.

31. Carin Benninger-Budel and Anne-Laurence Lacroix, *Violence Against Women: A Report* (Geneva: World Organization Against Torture, 1999), p. 43.

32. Cornell, *The Imaginary Domain.*

33. Mary Ann Glendon, *Rights Talk: The Impoverishment of Political Discourse* (New York: Free Press, 1993).

34. Duncan Kennedy, "Critical Labor Law Theory: A Comment," *Industrial Relations Law Journal* 4 (1981): 503, 506.

35. Wendy Brown, *States of Injury: Power and Freedom in Late Modernity* (Princeton, NJ: Princeton University Press, 1995).

36. Leon Chestang, "The Dilemma of Biracial Adoption," *Social Work* (May 1972): 400–405.

37. Donna Coker, "Enhancing Autonomy for Battered Women: Lessons From Navajo Peacemaking," *UCLA Law Review* 47, no. 1 (1999): 42–50.

38. *Griswold v. Connecticut*, 381 U.S. (1965), 479, 484; *Roe v. Wade*, 410 U.S. 113 (1973); *Doe v. Bolton*, 410 U.S., 179, 210–211(1972). A related point is made by Elizabeth Schneider, "The Violence of Privacy," in *The Public Nature of Private Violence*, eds. Martha A. Fineman and Roxanne Mykitiuk (New York: Routledge, 1994), pp. 36–58.

39. William O. Douglas, *Roe v. Wade* 410 U.S. 113 (1973), 209–219, cited in Cornell, *The Imaginary Domain*, pp. 60–61.

40. Douglas, *Roe v. Wade*.

41. Douglas, *Roe v. Wade*.

Chapter 8

1. Nia Parson, "Gendered Suffering and Social Transformations: Domestic Violence, Dictatorship and Democracy in Chile" (PhD diss., Rutgers University, 2004).

2. Lee Bowker, personal communication to author, September 20, 2005. Bowker makes a similar observation in Lee Bowker, "On Batterers and Dogs: An Investigation in Ethology and Sociology." *Domestic Violence Report* (October/November 2002): 1–2, 10.

3. Jan Stets and Murray A. Straus, "Gender Differences in Reporting Marital Violence and its Medical and Psychological Consequences," in *Physical Violence in American Families: Risk Factors and Adaptations to Violence in 8,145 Families*, ed. Murray A. Straus and Richard J. Gelles (New Brunswick, NJ: Transaction Press, 1990), pp. 151–166.

4. Barbara Morse, "Beyond the Conflict Tactics Scale: Assessing Gender Differences in Partner Violence," *Violence and Victims* 10, no. 4 (1995): 251–272.

5. Jean Baker-Miller, *Toward a New Psychology of Women* (Boston: Beacon Press, 1976), p. 14.

6. Daniel O'Leary, Julian Barling, Iaelna Arias, Alan Rosenbaum, A. Malone, and A. Tyree, "Prevalence and Stability of Physical Aggression Between Spouses: A Longitudinal Analysis," *Journal of Consulting and Clinical Psychology* 57 (1989): 263–268.

7. Piispa, "Complexity of Patterns of Violence."

8. Swan and Snow, "A Typology"; Swan, "Women Who Fight Back."

9. Suzanne Prescott and Carolyn Letko,"Battered Women: A Social Psychological Perspective," in *Battered Women: A Psycho-Sociological Study of Domestic Violence*, ed. Maria Roy (New York: Van Nostrand Reinhold, 1977); Okun, *Woman Abuse*; R. Emerson Dobash and Russell P. Dobash, "Wives: The 'Appropriate' Victims of Marital Violence," *Victimology* 2 (1978): 426–442.

10. Buzawa et al., *Response to Domestic Violence*; Johnson, "Patriarchal Terrorism"; Michael Johnson, "Conflict and Control: Gender Symmetry and Asymmetry in Domestic Violence," *Violence Against Women* 12, no. 11 (2006): 1003–1018.

11. Klein, "Re-Abuse in a Population of Court-Restrained Male Batterers"; Andrew Klein, *The Criminal Justice Response to Domestic Violence* (New York: Wadsworth, 2004); Hester, "Making it Through the Criminal Justice System."

12. Michael Rand, *Violence Related Injuries Treated in Hospital Emergency Departments*, Bureau of Justice Statistics: Special Report (Washington, DC: U.S. Department of Justice, 1997).

13. Piispa, "Complexity of Patterns of Violence."

14. Zorica Mrsevic and Donna Hughes, "Violence Against Women in Belgrade, Serbia: An S.O.S. Hotline 1990–1993," *Violence against Women* 3, no. 2 (1997): 123.

15. The actions of a few biased elders should not be confused with the official position of the church. *AWAKE*, the popular journal published by the Witnesses, has printed several well-informed articles outlining the nature of family violence

and the appropriate response. Still, high rates of domestic violence seem inevitable given attempts to sustain traditional sex hierarchies in a world where women's independence is so highly valued.

16. Anne Rees, Roxanne Agnew-Davies, and Michael Barkham, "Outcomes for Women Escaping Domestic Violence at Refuge," Paper presented at Society for Psychotherapy Research Annual Conference (Edinburgh, June 2006); Roxanne Agnew-Davies, personal communication of raw data tables shared via e-mail, June 2, 2006.

17. Rees, Agnew-Davies, and Barkham, "Outcomes for Women."

18. Neil Jacobson and John Gottman, *When Men Batter Women: New Insights Into Ending Abusive Relationships* (New York: Simon & Schuster, 1998).

19. Michael Shepherd, "Morbid Jealousy: Some Clinical and Social Aspects of a Psychiatric Symptom," in *Conceptual Issues in Psychological Medicine—Collected Papers of Michael Sherpherd* (Routledge: London 1990), pp. 39–68.

20. Gordon and Riger, *The Female Fear.*

21. Gelles, *The Violent Home.*

22. The English data in this section are abstracted from Davies, "Raw Data"; Rees, Agnew-Davies, and Barkham, "Outcomes for Women"; and Roxanne Agnew-Davies and Anne Rees, "Experience of Abuse Questionnaire (EAQ)," Paper presented at Society for Psychotherapy Research (2006): From Research to Practice, 37th Annual Meeting, June 21–24, Edinburgh. The U.S. data are from Richard Tolman, "The Development of a Measure of Psychological Maltreatment of Women by Their Male Partners," *Violence and Victims* 4, no. 3(1989): 159–177.

23. Evan Stark, "The Battered Mother in the Child Protective Service Caseload: Developing an Appropriate Response," *Women's Rights Law Reporter* 23, no. 2 (Spring 2002): 107–131.

24. Patricia Tjaden and Nancy Thoennes, *Stalking in America: Findings from the National Violence Against Women Survey* (Washington, DC: National Institute of Justice and Centers for Disease Control and Prevention, 1998).

25. Tjaden, and Thoennes, *Stalking*; Tjadden and Thoennes, "Extent, Nature and Consequences," p. 11. Interestingly, the strongest predictor of postseparation stalking is the length of time a woman has been out of the relationship. Mindy Mechanic, Terri Weaver, and Patricia Resick, "Intimate Partner Violence and Stalking Behavior: Exploration of Patterns and Correlates in a Sample of Acutely Battered Women," *Violence and Victims* 15, no. 1 (2000): 55–72.

26. Tjaden and Thoennes, *Stalking.*

27. Patricia Tjaden and Nancy Thoennes, "Stalking: Its Role in Serious Domestic Violence Cases," available online at http://www.ncjrs.gov/pdf-files1/nij/grants/187346.pdf (rev. November 17, 2006). See also Joan Zorza, "The Role of Stalking in Serious Domestic Violence Cases," *Domestic Violence Report* 8, no. 5 (June/July 2003): 68.

28. Tjaden and Thoennes. "Extent, Nature and Consequences," p. 36.

29. Cornell, *The Imaginary Domain*, pp. 8–10.

30. Rawls is quoted in Cornell, *The Imaginary Domain*, p. 9.

31. Face-to-Face Domestic Violence Project. A similar program is run in Connecticut by AmeriCares with the American Society for Dermatological Surgery.

32. James Forte, David Franks, Janett Forte, and Daniel Rigsby, "Asymmetrical Role Taking: Comparing Battered and Nonbattered Women," *Social Work* 41, no. 1 (1996): 59–74.

33. Marcelo Suarez-Orozco, "Speaking of the Unspeakable: Toward a Psychosocial Understanding of Responses to Terror," *Ethos* 18 (1990): 367.

34. Susan Lloyd and Nina Taluc, "The Effects of Violence on Women's Employment," *Violence Against Women* 5, no. 4 (1999): 370–392.

35. Richie, *Compelled to Crime*; Stark, "Race, Gender and Woman Battering."

36. Robert Hampton, "Family Violence and Homicide in the Black Community—Are They Linked?," in *Violence in the Black Family: Correlates and Consequences*, ed. Robert Hampton (Lexington, MA: Lexington Books, 1987); Jo-Ellen Asbury, "African American Women in Violent Relationships. An Exploration of Cultural Differences," in *Violence in the Black Family: Correlates and Consequences*, ed. Robert Hampton (Lexington, MA: Lexington Books, 1987).

37. Carol Stack, *All Our Kin: Strategies for Survival in a Black Community* (New York: Harper & Row, 1975); Richie, *Compelled to Crime*; Harriette McAdoo, "Black Kinship," *Psychology Today* 12 (May 1979): 67–70; Evan Stark, "Rethinking Homicide: Violence, Race and the Politics of Gender," *International Journal of Health Services* 20, no. 1 (1990): 3–26; Hampton, "Family Violence and Homicide"; Evan Stark, "Killing the Beast Within: Woman Battering and Female Suicidality," *International Journal of Health Services* 25 (1995): 43–64.

38. Available online at http://www.ketv.com/newsarchive/6783868/detail.html (rev. May 12, 2006).

39. A copy of the contract is available online at http://harrisspeakes.blogspot.com/2006/02/do-women-screen-men-they-marrie-any.html (rev. May 12, 2006).

40. Mrsevic and Hughes, "Violence Against Women in Belgrade."

41. Tolman, "The Development of a Measure."

42. Tolman, "The Development of a Measure."

43. Piispa, "Complexity of Patterns of Violence."

44. Buzawa et al., *Response to Domestic Violence*.

45. Allard, Albelda, Colten, and Cosenza, "In Harm's Way?"

46. Johnson, "Conflict and Control."

47. Nancy Glass, Jennifer Manganello, and Jacquelyn C. Campbell, "Risk for Intimate Partner Femicide in Violent Relationships," *DV Report* 9, no. 2, (December 2003/January 2004): 1, 2, 30–33.

48. Lischick, "Coping and Related Characteristics."

49. Piispa, "Complexity of Patterns of Violence."

50. John Locke, *Essay Concerning Human Understanding* [1690], abridged and edited by Kenneth Winkler (Indianapolis: Hackett, 1996).

51. See Barbara Hart, "Rule-Making and Enforcement/ Rule-Compliance and Resistance," in *I Am Not Your Victim: Anatomy of Domestic Violence*, eds. Beth Sipe and Evelyn J. Hall (Thousand Oaks, CA: Sage, 1996) pp. 258–263.

52. Lillian Rubin, *Worlds of Pain* (New York: Basic Books, 1992).

Chapter 9

1. Sharon La Franiere, "Entrenched Epidemic: Wife-Beatings in Africa," *New York Times*, August 11, 2005, A1 and A10.

2. Campbell, Rose, Kub, and Nedd, "Voices of Strength and Resistance"; Bachman and Salzman, "Violence Against Women"; Demi Kurz and Evan Stark, "Not So Benign Neglect: The Medical Response to Battering," in *Feminist Perspectives on Wife Abuse*, eds. Kersti Yllo and Michele Bograd (Newbury Park, CA: Sage, 1988), pp. 249–268.

3. I was consulted in an Illinois case where the woman who shot her husband wrapped him in a rug and went to a shoe sale before she returned to turn herself in. "Have you ever heard of anything more cold-blooded?" the prosecutor asked. I have had several clients whose lives were so restricted by their abusive partners that their first thought after he was dead was to exercise their newly won autonomy by shopping or doing something equally "irresponsible." Similar stories abound about how POWs spent their first hours of freedom. I suggested the prosecutor not make a point of the shoe sale to a jury that included women.

4. La Franiere, "Entrenched Epidemic."

5. Franiere, "Entrenched Epidemic." It may be even more remarkable that half of the women in Zambia do not accept a man's right to beat his wife in these circumstances.

Chapter 10

1. Connecticut Penal Code, Title 53a, p. 614.

2. Kristine Landry and John Brigham, "The Effect of Training in Criteria-Based Content Analysis on the Ability to Detect Deception in Adults," *Law and Human Behavior* 16 (1992): 663–676.

3. The classic description of this process remains Erving Goffman, *Asylums: Essays on the Social Situation of Mental Patients and Other Inmates* (New York: Doubleday Anchor, 1961).

Chapter 11

1. The following account is based on my interviews with Bonnie Foreshaw and an account of her experience written in her own words, Bonnie Jean Foreshaw, "Faith, Power and Pants," in *Couldn't Keep it to Myself*, eds. Wally Lamb and the Women of York Correctional Institution (New York: HarperCollins, 2003), pp. 186–209.

2. Foreshaw, "Faith, Power, and Pants," p. 188.

3. Blackman, *Intimate Violence*.

4. Foreshaw, "Faith, Power and Pants," p. 187.

5. Julie Blackman, "Potential Uses for Expert Testimony: Ideas Toward the Representation of Battered Women Who Kill," *Women's Rights Law Reporter* 9, nos. 3/4 (1986): 227–240; Blackman, *Intimate Violence*.

6. Foreshaw, "Faith, Power and Pants," p. 200.

7. In *Trauma and Recovery* (p. 134), psychiatrist Judy Hermann highlights the pathological dimensions of this process among traumatized victims and emphasizes the need in treatment to rebuild trust, autonomy, competence, identity, initiative, and intimacy.

8. Bonnie's heart-rending account of the fight over the prison uniform can be found in Foreshaw, "Faith, Power and Pants." Though she fought not to put on the pants and to keep her hair from being cut, Bonnie favored the dress code because it reduced competitiveness and inequality among the prisoners, even though it also reduced their opportunity for individual expression.

Chapter 12

1. Andrew Hacker, "How Are Women Doing?" *New York Review of Books*, April 11, 2002, pp. 63–66.

2. William Saletan, *Bearing Right: How Conservatives Won the Abortion War* (Berkeley: University of California Press, 2003).

3. Court Decisions, First Judicial Department, New York County Supreme Court, 217 *New York Law Journal* 26, no. 26 (1997).

4. Ruth Jones, "Guardianship for Coercively Controlled Battered Women: Breaking the Control of the Abuser," *Georgetown Law Review* 88 (2000): 605–657.

5. Susan Keilitz, "Improving Judicial System Responses to Domestic Violence: The Promises and Risks of Integrated Case Management and Technology Solutions," in Roberts, *Handbook*, pp. 147–172.

6. Hirschel and Hutchison, "Realities and Implications."

7. Sally Goldfarb, "Applying the Discrimination Model to Violence Against Women: Some Reflections on Theory and Practice," *American University Journal Of Gender, Social Policy & the Law* 11, no. 2 (2003): 251.

8. The dilemmas created by using a universal standard to assess a wide range of cultural practices are brilliantly dissected by Martha Nussbaum, *Sex and Social Justice* (New York: New York: Oxford, 1999), pp. 20–42.

9. Brown, States of Injury.

10. Audrey Mullender and Gill Hague, "Giving a Voice to Women Survivors of Domestic Violence Through Recognition as a Service User Group," *British Journal of Social Work* 35 (2005): 1321–1341.

11. Patricia Brownell and Albert Roberts, "National Organizational Survey of Domestic Violence Coalitions," in Roberts, *Handbook*, pp. 80–100.

12. John Braithwaite and Kathleen Daly, "Masculinities, Violence and Communitarian Control," in *Just Boys Doing Business? Men, Masculinities and Crime*, eds. Tim Newburn and Elizabeth Stanko (New York: Routledge, 1994); Donna Coker, "Enhancing Autonomy for Battered Women: Lessons from Navajo Peacemaking," *UCLA Law Review* 47, no. 1 (1999): 42–50.

13. Laura Shapiro, Perfection Salad: Women and Cooking at the Turn of the Century (New York: Modern Library, 2001).

14. Mo. Rev. Stat. sect. 565.074(5) or (6). Enacted in 2000, domestic assault in third degree. In 2001 North Carolina enacted a domestic assault statute to include continued harassment sufficient to inflict substantial emotional distress. The harassment includes written communications or transmissions that annoy, torment, or terrorize a specific person and serve no legitimate purpose. N.C. Gen Stat sect 50B-1(a).

15. *Feltmeier v. Feltmeier*, 207 Ill. 2d 263, 266 (2003).

16. Joyce McConnell, "Beyond Metaphor: Battered Women, Involuntary Servitude and the Thirteenth Amendment," *Yale Journal of Law and Feminism* 4 (1992): 207.

17. Sally Goldfarb, "The Supreme Court, the Violence Against Women Act, and the Use and Abuse of Federalism," *Fordham Law Review* 71 (2002): 57–147.

18. Goldfarb, "The Supreme Court," pp. 120–123; See also Julie Goldscheid, "Gender-Motivated Violence: Developing a Meaningful Paradigm for Civil Rights Enforcement," *Harvard Women's Law Journal* 22 (1999): 123.

19. Catharine MacKinnon, *Toward a Feminist Theory of the State* (Cambridge, MA: Harvard University Press, 1989), p. 194. See also Reva Siegal, "The Rule of Law: Wife Beating as Prerogative and Privacy," *Yale Law Journal* 105 (1996).

20. Hartmann, "Capitalism, Patriarchy, and Job Segregation by Sex."

21. *Nicholson v. Williams*, 203 F. Supp. 2d 153 (E.D.N.Y. 2002).

22. Sandra Day O'Connor, 1987, *United States v. Kosminski* 487 US 931, 942 (1988), [487 U.S. 931, 933].

23. Justice Brennan. 487 U.S. 931, 933.

24. Goldfarb, "Applying the Discrimination Model."

25. Marcia M. Clark (with T. Carpenter), *Without a Doubt* (New York: Viking, 1997).

26. *United States v. Morrison*, 529 U.S. 598, 627 (2000).

27. Versions of this argument can be found in John Leo, "Radical Feminism in the Senate," *U.S. News & World Report*, July 19, 1993, p. 19; Cathy Young, "Gender Poisoning: In the Bobbitt Era, Facing the Real Truth About Domestic Violence," *Washington Post*, January. 16, 1994, C5; and Somers, *Who Stole Feminism?*

28. Dutton, *The Domestic Assault of Women*; David Island and Patrick Letellier, *Men Who Beat the Men Who Love Them* (New York: Harrington Park Press, 1991); Mark Liddle, "Feminist Contributions to an Understanding of Violence Against Women—Three Steps Forward, Two Steps Back," *Canadian Review of Sociology & Anthropology* 26 (1989): 759–776.

29. Goldfarb, "Applying the Discrimination Model," p. 264. Also see Schneider, *Battered Women*, pp. 71–72.

30. Crenshaw, "Mapping the Margins."

31. Valerie Coleman, "Lesbian Battering: The Relationship Between Personality and the Perpetration of Violence," *Violence and Victims* 9, no. 2 (1994): 139–152; Kimberly Balsam, "Nowhere to Hide: Lesbian Battering, Homophobia, and Minority Stress," *Women & Therapy* 23, no. 3 (2001): 25–37; Janice Ricks, Carol (Jan) Vaughan, and Sophia Dziegielewski, "Domestic Violence Among Lesbian Couples," in Roberts, *Handbook*, pp. 451–463.

32. Paula Poorman and Sheila M. Seelau, "Lesbians Who Abuse Their Partners: Using the IRO-B to Assess Interpersonal Characteristics," *Women & Therapy* 23, no. 3 (2001): 87–105; Paula Poorman, "Forging Community Links to Address Abuse in Lesbian Relationships," *Women & Therapy* 23, no. 3 (2001): 7–24. Reports of same-sex violence estimate its prevalence as ranging from 17% to 73%. B. E. Carlson, "Questioning the Party Line on Family Violence," *Affilia* 7, no. 2 (1992): 94–110; Balsam, "Nowhere to Hide"; Ricks et al., "Domestic Violence Among Lesbian Couples."

33. Claire Renzetti, *Violent Betrayal: Partner Abuse in Lesbian Relationships* (Thousand Oaks, CA: Sage , 1992). It is far more likely that a lesbian than a male perpetrator will know the location of the shelter and even be acquainted with shelter staff, for instance, making a shelter stay far less safe for lesbian than for heterosexual victims. This was why Respond, Inc., a shelter in Massachusetts, developed special support groups for battered lesbians as well as a network of safe homes for lesbian victims. But few shelters have imitated this practice.

34. Claire Renzetti, "Studying Partner Abuse in Lesbian Relationships: A Case for the Feminist Participatory Research Model," in *Lesbian Social Services: Research Issues*, ed. Carol T. Tully (New York: Harrington Park Press/Haworth Press, 1995), pp. 29–42.

35. Renzetti, "Studying Partner Abuse."

36. Patricia Tjaden, Nancy Thoennes, Christine Allison, "Comparing Violence Over the Life Span in Samples of Same-Sex and Opposite-Sex Cohabitants," *Violence and Victims* 14 (1999): 413–425.

37. Poorman and Selau, "Lesbians Who Abuse Their Partners."

38. Jo-Ann Krestan and Claudia S. Bepko,"The Problem of Fusion in the Lesbian Relationship," *Family Process* 19 (1980): 277–289.

39. Personal communication with Gunner Scott, coordinator, Network/La Red: Ending Abuse in Lesbian, Bisexual Women, and Transgender Communities.

40. Barbara Hart, "Lesbian Battering: An Examination," in *Naming the Violence: Speaking Out About Lesbian Battering*, ed. Kerry Lobel (Seattle: Seal Press, 1986), p. 173.

41. Mills, *Insult to Injury*; Shamita Das Gupta, *Safety and Justice for All: Examining the Relationship Between the Women's Anti-Violence Movement and the Criminal Legal System* (New York: Ms. Foundation, 2003), available online at http://www.ms.foundation.org/user-assets/PDF/Program/safety_justice.pdf (June 23, 2004).

INDEX

abduction. *See* kidnapping
abortion rights, 364
abuse. *See also* battering/battery;
    domestic violence; violence;
    specific topics
    adapting a typology of, 375–97. *See
        also* batterers, typologies of
    boundary challenge, 384–85
    putting the typology to work in
        public law, 378–80
    technology of coercive control
        and, 234–41
    defining, 84–85, 202
        definitional stretching, 85–86
        the definition applied, 87–88
        gender and, 91–92
        and the politics of definitions,
            110–11
        violence definition of abuse,
            84–88, 110, 111, 121
    equated with physical force, 84–85
    estimating, 108–9
    explaining the duration of, 114–15
    proper measure of, 99–103
        relevance of a new typology for
            measurement, 106–8
        terminology, 107

toward a typology of force in
    relationships, 103–4
theories of, 117–20
    common theme among, 120–21
"abuse excuse," 9, 137–38
access
    to necessities, 271–74
    privileged, 207–8, 376
activism, 76
    and the law, 135–37
activist shelters, 74–76
Adams, David, 201
advocacy, 74
advocacy movements, 374–75, 399
African Americans. *See* racial
    differences in battered women
Against Our Will: Men, Women and Rape
    (Brownmiller), 26, 404n.5
agency and victimization, 215–16, 233.
    See also autonomy; freedom
Albanian culture, 293, 298, 299, 301–2,
    307, 310
alcohol, 356
All in the Family (TV show), 46–47
Allison, Marshall, 161
ameliorative hypothesis, 59
Amnesty International (AI), 220, 221

anal sex, forced, 261
Anderson, Rebecca, 268
anti-subordination principle, 367–68
apologies, 246
arrest(s), 61. *See also* police response
    dual, 378
    efficacy of, 62
    mandatory, 378, 379
Arzner, Dorothy, 185–86
Ashley, Marta Segovia, 29
Austen, Jane, 177
autonomy, 226, 227, 347–48. *See also*
    agency and victimization;
    freedom

"backlash" hypothesis, 59, 60
Baker-Miller, Jean, 234
Bancroft, Lundy, 130, 202, 207
Bard, Morton, 37
"battered data syndrome," 87
battered husbands. *See* female
    batterers
battered mother's dilemma, 253
Battered Wives (Martin), 118–19
Battered Woman, The (Walker), 119–20,
    200. *See also* Walker, Lenore
battered woman's defense, 134, 140,
    156, 303–5. *See also* battered
    woman's syndrome
    historical perspective on, 38–39
    judges, juries, and, 162
    legal strategies and, 151–53
    reframing the, 389–91
battered woman's syndrome (BWS),
    126, 151
    criteria for establishing, 158, 304
    expert testimony on, 135, 157, 160,
        161
    juries and, 163
    learned helplessness and, 114, 163
    Lenore Walker and, 120, 151, 152,
        160, 161, 163
battered women
    psychological characteristics of,
        112–13, 116, 120, 122–23, 127–29,
        330–31. *See also* trauma
    symptoms reported by, 128–29
Battered Women and Shelters (Loseke), 76
Battered Women's Directory, 30
batterer husband thesis, 97

batterer intervention programs (BIPs),
    7, 10, 39–40, 99, 201
    aims of counseling for perpetrators, 68
    drop-out rates of, 70
    effectiveness of, 69–72
    and paradox of treating a "normal"
        pathology, 66–73
    and treatability of "battering," 68–69
batterers
    childhoods of, 284
    female, 91–92, 97–98, 236–37
    psychological models and
        characteristics of, 59, 60, 68–69,
        93, 131, 157, 158, 236. *See also*
        battered woman's syndrome;
        domestic violence, causes of
    case material on, 331
    typologies of, 93–94, 103–4, 246. *See*
        also abuse, adapting a typology
        of
battering/battery. *See also specific topics*
    nonviolent dimensions of, 220–21.
        See also violence, physical *vs.*
        nonphysical
    reframed as a liberty crime, 380–82,
        387
battering experience, continuous
    nature of, 91–94, 99–101, 115
Benedek, Elisa, 151
Berkowitz, Sidney, 37
Biden, Joseph, 21, 22
Bigelow, Billy, 24
Blackman, Julie, 161, 345, 354
blacks. *See* Jamaican culture; racial
    differences in battered women
Bobbitt, Lorena, 141
Bograd, Michele, 119
Borderline Personality Organization
    (BPO), 69
boundary challenges and dilemmas,
    384–85
Bowman, Angela, 244–45
Bowker, Lee H., 232
Boychuk, Tascha, 65
Braden, Ann, 27
brainwashing, 12, 200, 201
Brandeis, Louis Dembitz, 226
Britain, 29, 143–45, 176–78, 181, 242
Brown, Steve, 156–157
Brown, Wendy, 223, 373

Browne, Angela, 136
Brownmiller, Susan, 26, 27, 404n.5
Bruno, Joseph, 101–2
Bruno v. Codd, 406n.33
Buell, Sara, 21, 48, 202
"burning bed," 148–49, 166
Burning Bed, The (film), 50

Campbell, Bonnie, 22
Campbell, Jacqueline, 109
Carousel (musical), 24
Casa de las Madres, La, 29, 35
"changing" (coerced persuasion), 200
Charlotte, North Carolina, 62–63
Chicago Hope (TV show), 47
child abuse as tangential spouse
    abuse, 251–53
Child Protective Services (CPS), 42–43
Childers, Ruth and Clifford, l51
children, 253
    abused women's enmeshment with
        their, 217
    protecting, 146
Chiswick Women's Aid, 28, 33
chronic offenders, 61
civic participation by women, 183–84
civil law, 383
Clark, Kenneth, 141–42
Clark, Marcia, 389
Clinton, Bill, 21, 48, 49, 61
Cobbe, Frances Power, 95, 143, 144,
    147, 160, 177–79
coerced persuasion, 200, 201
coercion, defined, 228
coercive control, 5, 11–14, 104, 155. *See
    also* control; terrorism; *specific
    topics*
    distinguishing fights, assaults, and,
        104–6
    experimental nature of, 206–7, 287
    fatality and, 276–77
    freedom and the unraveling of,
        310–13
    gendered nature of, 377–78
    generality of, 203–5, 332–34
    as indentured servitude, 385–88
    invisible in plain sight, 14–16
    moral justification for intervening
        in, 368–69
    naming the problem, 369–71

normalcy of, 210–11
particularity of, 205–11, 332–34
    frequency and routine nature of
        violence, 205–6. *See also*
        violence, as routine behavior
    privileged access and property
        rights, 207–8
    spatial and temporal extension of
        control, 208–10
    personal nature of, 206
    prevalence and social structure of,
        210
    specificity of, 193–97
    storying, 371
    technology of, 228, 241. *See also*
        intimidation
    dance of resistance and control,
        232–34
    defining terms, 228–30
    as gender strategy, 230–32
    structure and dynamics, 242–49
    typology of abuse, 234–41. *See also*
        abuse, adapting a typology of;
        batterers, typologies of
coercive control theory/model,
    198–99, 215. *See also* domesticity
    empirical support for, 274–76
    precursors to, 200–203
    toward a new theory of harms,
        218–21
Coercive Partner Profile (CPP), 100
Cohen, Jane Maslow, 9
Collins, Hazel, 96–97, 259, 269.
colonized people and victims of
    coercive control, 199–200
Committee on the Elimination of
    Discrimination Against Women
    (CEDAW), 220
common couple violence, 103. *See also*
    situational violence
Commonwealth Fund Survey of
    Women's Health, 90
Commonwealth Harris Poll, 88–90, 95,
    102,105
compensation hypothesis, 59
Comprehensive Employment and
    Training Act (CETA), 30, 34
confession, 204
confinement, 208. *See also* coercive
    control, particularity of

Conflict Tactics Scale (CTS), 53, 89, 100
"conjugal terrorism." *See* terrorism, "conjugal"
conspicuous subjugation, 133
Consultation on Battered Women, 27
control, 271. *See also* coercive control; *specific topics*
  dance of resistance and, 232–34
  defined, 229
  experimental nature of, 285–88
  freedom from, as human rights issue, 219–22
  irrational foundation of, 280–81
  material, 324–25
  power and, 278–88
  proportion of victimized women reporting, 276, 277
  separating the effects of, 278
  significance of, 308–10
  spatial dimensions, 326–28. 334
control tactics, 106
  lists, 317–320
  "beeper game," 326–28
controller's dilemma, 334–35
Cornell, Drucilla, 16, 222, 226, 232, 258
Costanza, Midge, 30
counseling for perpetrators. *See* batterer intervention programs
"couple violence," 104
Craig, Dorothy, 191
Craig's Wife (Kelly), 185–86
crimes, victims pressured to commit, 247, 248, 261, 325
criminalization of wife-beating, 25. *See also* legislation
criminal justice response, 36–37. *See also* arrest(s); legal response; police response
  from closed to evolving door, 60–66
crisis intervention, 37
cultural factors, 310. *See also* immigrant women; racial differences in battered women
cultural images and women's status, 184–88
"culture of victimization," 389
Curtis v. Firth, 423n.7
Cusseaux v. Pickett, 158, 427n.62
cycle model of violence, 245–48

Davis, Angela, 27
Davis v. Davis, 247
Day, Valoree, 156–57
Declaration on the Elimination of Violence Against Women, 220
Defense of Marriage Acts (DOMA), 396
defense strategies. *See* legal defense strategies
degradation, 155, 156, 258–60
"degradation prohibition," 258
DeKeseredy, Walter, 110
Dershowitz, Alan, 9, 137
deterrence, specific and general, 65–66
Diary of a Mad Housewife (film), 286–87
Dickens, Charles, 176
DiMedici, Danielle, 381
  murder of, 101–2
disguised betrayal, 127
Dobash, Emerson, 119
Dobash, Russell, 119
Doe v. Bolton, 226, 433n.38
Domestic Abuse Intervention Project (DAIP), 70, 202, 203
domesticity
  dialectics of, 211–16
  salience of, 212–13
domestic violence. *See also specific topics*
  causes of, 59. *See also* batterers, psychological models and characteristics of
  gender differences in, 98–99
  in couples not cohabitating, 90–91
  as decreasing, 51–60
  defined, 85–87. *See also* abuse, defining
  as discrete *vs.* continuous event, 91–94, 99–101, 115
  in historical context, 142–47. *See also* male dominance
  measuring harms from (limits of injury), 94–99
  prevalence and incidence of, 52–53, 87, 107, 117. *See also* violence, frequency and cumulative effects of
  data sources, 52–53, 88–90
  explaining trends, 56–57
  over the life course, 90
  why service research is unreliable, 88

rational/instrumental nature of
    abuse, 59
  reporting, 61–62
domestic violence assault, defined, 382
Domestic Violence Enhanced
    Response Team (DVERT), 256
domestic violence model, 10–12
domestic violence revolution, 6–7,
    21–22, 48–49, 193, 364, 399. See
    also feminism; shelters
  beginning of, 22–25
  changes in popular culture and,
    45–48
  and changing professional response,
    36. See also batterer intervention
    programs
    in child welfare, 42–43
    in criminal justice, 36–37
    in health care, 40–42
    in law and prosecution, 37–38
  expanded knowledge base and, 44
  goals of, 51
  and promise of emancipation, 31
  as stalled, 7–8, 50–51, 79–80
  why it is stalled, 8–10
dominance. See also male domination
  chain of, 229–30
Douglas, William O., 226, 227, 376, 380
Downs, Donald, 133, 139, 159
Dutton, Donald, 69–70
Dutton, Mary Ann, 127, 152
Dworkin, Andrea, 27

education for women, 182–83
egalitarianism, principle of, 222. See
    also sexual equality vs.
    inequality
Elshtain, Jean Bethke, 183, 184
Embezzlement scheme, 325
Emerge, 201–2
Emick, 161, 428n.75
Emick, Leslie, 161
employment, women's, 181–82,
    184–89, 269–70
empowerment. See under shelters
England. See Britain
enmeshment, 217
entrapment, 4–6, 205, 229, 278, 377. See
    also specific topics
  causes of, 8–12

discerning, 15
  meanings of, 370
  trauma theory and, 126–28
equal protection, 218–19
ER (TV show), 47, 187
Estate of Terry Traficonda v. the Town of
    Waterford, CT, 1–3
evidence-based prosecution, 21
Ewen, Stuart, 180
Ewing, Charles, 160, 161, 164, 165
expert testimony, 134, 135, 303. See also
    trauma theory/traumatization
    models; Walker, Lenore
  expert as storyteller, 141–42
  expert narratives, 134–35, 138–41

Fair, Laura, 426n.40
"false positives" (arrests), 64
Family Crisis Intervention Unit, 37
family ethos vs. self-interest, 223–24
Family Violence, Task Force on, 37
family violence school, 44–45, 121
Fanon, Frantz, 199
fatality. See homicide(s)
Federal Bureau of Investigation (FBI),
    52
Feltmeier v. Feltmeier, 383, 438n.15
female batterers, 91–92, 97–99, 236–37
"female fear," 249
female stereotypes, 60, 119, 146–47,
    213–14, 392
female subordination. See anti-
    subordination principle; male
    dominance
feminism. See also women's liberation
    movement
  battered woman's movement and,
    26–31
  shelters and, 75
  "social," 144
  "transformational," 79
feminist approach to intervention, 121
feminist arguments regarding gender
    differences in violence, 98–99
feminist influence on public policy,
    44–45
"feminist lawmakers," 134
feminist lawyers, 134
feminist model of domestic violence,
    118–20

feminist prequels to domestic violence revolution, 25–26
feminists, 9, 92, 234, 391
Ferraro, Kathleen J., 65
fights, couple, 234–35, 378, 379, 397
 vs. assaults, 104–6
film, 185–86, 211
 domestic violence in, 24, 45–48, 50, 135–36, 211, 254, 286–87
Fineman, Martha, 16, 196
Finland, 275–76, 278
Flitcraft, Anne, vii, x, 22, 40, 94, 121
force (in relationships)
 abuse equated with physical, 84–85
 toward a typology of, 103–4
 vs. violence, 84
Foreshaw, Bonnie Jean, 127, 128, 131, 224, 284, 339–41, 390, 437n.8
 an affirmative defense, 346–47
  Bonnie's credo, 355–61
  framing Bonnie's actions, 349–51
  reframing Bonnie's request for autonomy, 347–48
  reframing victimization, 351–52
  and the special reasonableness of battered women, 353–55
 appeal, 352–53
 background, 341–44
 traumatization *vs.* self-defense, 344–46
Frankl, Viktor E., 120
freedom. *See also* agency; autonomy; liberty
 from control, as human rights issue, 219–22
 and the unraveling of coercive control, 310–13
 "freedom is never free," 362
Frey, Travis, 273–74
Friedan, Betty, 26, 187
Friedman, Lucy, 22
Furman, Mark, 139

Garcia, Inez, 26, 149
Gaslight (film), 254
"gaslight" games, 255
Gay, Roxanne and Blenda, 426n.45
gay relationships. *See* same-sex relationships
Gelles, Richard, 52, 53, 56, 84, 86, 117

gendered nature of coercive control, 377–78
gendered standard of self-defense, 149–51
gender entrapment, 129–30, 211. *See also* domesticity
gender ideology, 232
gender roles. *See* sex roles
gender stereotypes, 60, 119, 146–47, 213–14, 392. *See also* domesticity; same-sex relationships
gender symmetry *vs.* asymmetry in partner violence, 91–92, 97–98
 feminist arguments regarding, 98–99
gender technology, 232
Gibson, Charles Dana, 184
Gilligan, James, 155
Giovine, Christina and Peter, 158
Giovine v. Giovine, 158, 427n.63
Gissing, George, 176
Giuliani, Rudolph, 101, 412n.40
Givens, Robin, 254
Glendon, Mary Ann, 223
Goldfarb, Sally, 391
Goldman, Ronald, 3
Gordon, Linda, 17, 144, 146, 205
Grambs, Marya, 29
Grapes of Wrath (Steinbeck), 46
Grayson, Dr., 340–41
Greydanus, Arron, 148–50, 166
Griswold v. Connecticut, 226. 433n.38

Habermas, Jürgen, 174
Hall-Smith, Paige, 100, 101
Hard Times (Dickens), 176
Hardy, Thomas, 174
harms. *See also under* domestic violence
 liberty, 380–82, 387
 toward a new theory of, 218–21
Harrell, Adele, 71–72
Hart, Barbara, 397
Hartmann, Hans, 269
Hartmann, Heidi, 189
Hatch, Orrin, 21
Hawkins, Darnell, 57–58
health care, 40–42
health consequences of entrapment, 121–24
helplessness. *See* learned helplessness

Herman, Judith L., 125–27, 152, 437n.7
heterosexism, 391, 394–97
High Noon (film), 135–36
Hochschild, Arlie, 190
homicide(s). *See also* self-defense;
    Women Who Kill
  coercive control and fatality, 276–77
  intimate, 136. *See also* "abuse
      excuse"; legal defense
      strategies; *specific cases*
    gender differences in, 54
    trends in gender and race
        differences in, 54–58
  partner and nonpartner, 53
  prison sentences for, 160–61
  sexual assault and, 149–50
homoeroticism, 249
homophobia, 213–15, 393, 395–97. *See
    also* heterosexism
homosexual relationships. *See* same-sex
    relationships
honeymoon phase, 245–46
"honor killings," 113
hostage analogy, 200–201, 204–8
"hot blood" defense, 141, 155
housework, shifts in, 190
housing, emergency, 23, 29. *See also*
    shelters
Hughes, Donna, 274
Hughes, Francine and Mickey, 50–51,
    138, 141, 148–49,155, 161, 166,
    259, 368, 381–82
human rights. *See also* rights
  freedom from control as issue of,
      219–22
  Hyde, Fanny, 146,148
  hypervigilance, 125, 354

identity, 262. *See also* self-respect
immigrant women, 265–66
Industrial Revolution, 174–75, 182
infidelity. *See* jealousy and violence
injuries, types of, 94–95, 242
insanity defense, 148, 149
insanity dilemma, 145–46, 158–59
Inter-American Convention on the
    Prevention, Punishment, and
    Eradication of Violence Against
    Women, 220
intersectionality, 392

intervention. *See also* arrest(s); batterer
    intervention programs; criminal
    justice response; legal response;
    police response
  challenges to, 365–71
    forging a story through talking
        and listening, 371–72
    moral justification for, 368–69
intimate terrorism. *See* terrorism, intimate
intimidation, 221, 249, 329. *See also*
    degradation; stalking; threats
  child abuse as tangential spouse
      abuse, 251–53
  surveillance, 255–58
invisibility. *See under* coercive control
"irresistible impulse" defense, 141. *See
    also* "hot blood" defense
Islamic societies, 113. *See also*
    Palestinian culture
isolation, 241, 262–70
  assessment of, 275
  in case of Donna Balis, 295–96,
      301–2, 307
  in case of Laura Ferrucci, 328–29
  defined, 382
  from family, 263–65
  from friends, 266–67
  from help, 271
  Lenore Walker on, 200
  proportion of victimized women
      reporting, 276, 277
  racial dynamics in, 270–71

Jamaican culture, 343, 349, 351, 358.
    See also Rastafarians
jealousy and violence, 229, 237, 248–49
Jehovah's Witnesses, 240–41
"Jezebel" stereotype, 60
Jimenez, Chris, 29
Johnson, Michael, 103–5
Jones, Ann, 136, 145–47, 201–3
Jones, Ruth, 366
Jurado, Katy, 135–36
justice
  law, services, and political change,
      397–401
  principles of, 218

Kelly, Gladys, 157, 158,160
Kelly, Liz, 110–11

Kennedy, Duncan, 223
Kerry, John F., 49
Kestinen, Suvi, 159
kidnapping, 101, 102, 204
"killing excuse," 149
Kipling, Rudyard, 176
Knock v. Knock, 424n.7

Laura X, 27
Law Enforcement Assistance
    Administration (LEAA), 30, 35
Lazarra, Lavonne and Miguel, 242,
    245, 251, 255, 264–65, 271, 283
learned helplessness, 114, 120, 124,
    127, 153, 157, 163
legal defense strategies, contemporary,
    136–37, 148–56. *See also* expert
    testimony; trauma
    theory/traumatization models
"legal fictions," 138–41
legal representation, dilemmas in, 145–48
    in historical context, 142–47
legal response. *See also* criminal justice
    response; intervention; police
    response
    crafting a new, 382–84, 397–401
legal services, women who call, 23
legislation, 25, 143–44, 385–86. *See also*
    political change; *specific legislation*
Leidholdt, Dorchen, 27
lesbian battering, 392–94, 397. *See also*
    same-sex relationships
liberal equity theory, 222
liberty, 226. *See also* freedom
liberty crime (battering as), 13, 363, 380
liberty harms and liberty rights,
    380–82, 387
"license to kill," 136
Lieberman, Joe, 370
Lindblom, Charles, 48
Lischick, Cynthia, viii–ix, 100, 101, 103,
    278
literature, domestic violence in, 46,
    176, 177
Locke, John, 279
Loseke, Donileen, 76–78

MacKinnon, Catharine, 218, 380
Mahoney, Betsy Marple (Warrior), 30
male dilemma, 194–96

male dominance, 229–30, 275
    construction of, 171–80
male domination, changing face of,
    192–93
Manchurian Candidate, The (Condon),
    208
Man with the Golden Arm (film), 46
Marcus, Isabel, 8, 204
marital rape, 50, 388. *See also* rape
marking, 260–61
"Married Women's Property Acts," 181
Martin, Del, 27, 118–19, 201
masculine, universal, 280–83
masculine imaginary, 232
masculinity and feminine stereotypes,
    213–14. *See also* gender
    stereotypes
"matriarch" stereotype, 60
McConnell, Joyce, 385, 386, 388
media. *See also* film
    domestic violence and, 24, 45–48
    women and, 184–87
mediation, 37
Mendez, Chris, 29
M (film), 251
micromanagement of everyday life,
    274, 275
microsurveillance, 257–58
Mill, John Stuart, 143, 178, 179, 369,
    429n.11
Morgan, Robin, 27
Morgan, Steven, 200
Morrison, Mary, 39
Mrsevic, Zorica, 274
mutual violence, 92
"myth of activism," 76

narcissism, 246–47
National Coalition Against Domestic
    Violence (NCADV), 29, 30, 35,
    39, 374
National Crime Victimization Survey
    (NCVS), 52, 56, 61, 88–93
National Family Violence Survey
    (NFVS), 53, 56, 61m 63, 88–93,
    97, 98, 103,105, 378
National Network to End Domestic
    Violence (NNEDV), 374
National Organization of Women
    (NOW), 28

National Violence Against Women
Survey (NVAWS), 88–93, 97,
108, 393–94
National Women's Aid Federation
(NWAF), 28–29, 31, 74
National Women's Liberation
Conference, 29
Nicholson v. Williams, ix, 438n.21
"no drop" prosecution, 21
nongovernmental organizations
(NGOs), 219–21
normalization, 95–97
NYPD Blue, 114–15

O'Connor, Sandra Day, 388
"Off our backs," 51
Okin, Susan, 218
Okun, Lewis, 200–202
Osthoff, Susan, 160
"ownership" contracts, 207–8

Palestinian culture, 238–39, 266
parental alienation syndrome (PAS),
252–53
Parker, James, 101–2. 381
Parkman, Nathaline (Nate), 17, 162–66
"parking lot syndrome," 72
partner assault(s), 235–36, 382. *See also*
specific topics
contexts of, 236–38
fights *vs.* assaults, 104–6
frequency of abusive assaults, 92–94,
205–6, 375–76
in immigrant and fundamentalist
communities, 238–41
"patriarchal mothering," 213
patriarchal terrorism, 103
patriarchy, traditional, 172–74
People v. Bledsoe, 424n.22
People v. Garcia, 428n.80
People v. Torres, 426n.49
perspecticide, 267–69
Peterson, Jan, 27, 30
Pizzey, Erin, 28, 33, 118–19, 425n.32
police, 2–3, 36, 37
police response, 62–65. *See also* arrest(s)
political change. *See also* legislation
law, services, and, 397–401
political control, personal violence in
the context of, 172–74

Polson, John, 144
population surveys, 88–90
pornography, 27
post-traumatic stress disorder (PTSD),
153
battered woman's syndrome and,
120, 152
case material on, 127, 304, 340, 341, 345
causes of, 124
complex, 125–26, 128
insanity defense and, 158–59
post- *vs.* "intra"-traumatic, 128
symptoms of, 125, 127, 304, 354
power, 279
control and, 278–88
preretreat duty, 154
presumption of intimacy, 104–5
Price, Dr., 341, 344, 353
prisoners of war (POWs), 200–201,
204–8, 333, 334
privacy, 376. *See also* safety zones;
surveillance
privacy rights, 226–27
privileged access, 207–8, 376
property rights, 207–8
protection orders (TROs), 66
psychiatric establishment, 112
psychological abuse, forms of, 202
psychological account of domestic
violence, 119–20. *See also*
battered women, psychological
characteristics of
psychological effects of domestic
violence, 100, 389–90. *See also*
battered women, psychological
characteristics of
psychological self-defense (PSD),
164–67
Public Enemy (film), 47

Quinn, Casey, 21

racial bias, 58
racial differences in battered women,
129
racial dynamics in isolation, 270–71
racial stereotypes, 351. *See also*
Jamaican culture
racial trends in partner homicide,
explaining, 54, 55, 57–58

Ramos, Sandy, 29
rape, 50, 243, 388, 404n.5. *See also*
    sexual coercion
  anal, 261
  criminal justice and, 22, 110–11, 142
  feminist movement and, 25–28
  incidence of, 242
rape defense, 26
rape trauma syndrome, 128
Rapid Intervention Program (RIP), 37
Rastafarians, 342, 349, 357–58
rationality, 281–83
Rawls, John, 258, 380
"reasonable man"/"reasonable
    person" standard, 137, 140, 150,
    151, 153, 156, 163, 360
reasonableness, 281–83
  "heightened," 345, 353–55
reform, dilemmas of, 363–65
"refreezing" (coerced persuasion), 200
religion, 214, 215, 239–41, 282. *See also*
    Rastafarians
Reno, Janet, 21
repeat offenders, 61
research on domestic violence, 44. *See*
    also domestic violence, prevalence
    and incidence of; *specific topics*
resistance and control, dance of, 232–34
"respectable woman," 144
"respectable woman" dilemma,
    146–47, 156
respect and disrespect, 155
restraining orders (TROs), 66
Richie, Beth, 129
Richmond, Mary, 144
righteousness, 281–83
rights. *See also* human rights
  concept of personal, informal, or
    "soft," 224–25
  framing, in personal life, 223–24
  privacy, 226–27
Roberts, Albert, 34
Roe v. Wade, 226, 376, 433n.38
role stripping, 333
Roper, Martha, 128
Rose, Stephen, 127, 189
routine behavior, violence as, 243–45,
    296–99
routine nature of violence, 205–6
Rubin, Lilian, 284

rules, 207, 268–69
  economy of, 283–86
Runkle, Mary, 147
Russell, Diana, 27
Ryan, Susan, 23

safety, limits of, 219
safety zones, 209, 216–18, 269, 374. *See*
    also zones of privacy
Saletan, William, 364
same-sex relationships, battering in,
    391–97
Schechter, Susan, 201–3, 219
Schneider, Elizabeth, 150, 157, 203, 353
Scott v. Hurt, 406n.33
Schulhofer, Stephen, 137
"search and destroy" missions, 217–18
"secondary battering," 119
self-defense, 141, 161. *See also* "abuse
    excuse"; expert testimony; legal
    defense strategies; trauma
    theory/traumatization models
  gendered standard of, 149–51
  psychological, 164–67
  vs. traumatization, 344–46
self-respect, 258
separation, 268
separation assault, 115–16, 239
Serum, Camella, 200
sex, control over, 273. *See also* sexual
    coercion
sex discrimination. *See also* sexual
    equality *vs.* inequality
  reframing the role of, 154–56
sexism, 429n.11. *See also* sexual
    equality *vs.* inequality
  banality of, 230
"sexism with a vengeance," 302–3, 392
sex roles, 26, 46–47, 119. *See also*
    domesticity; gender
    stereotypes; same-sex
    relationships
sexual coercion, 149–50, 238–39, 243.
    See also rape
sexual equality *vs.* inequality, 16,
    58–60, 105, 222, 223. *See also*
    male dominance; sex
    discrimination; sexism
  domestication of violence and,
    175–76

the fight for equality, 177–78
the great sexual transformation,
     181–88
understanding changes in women's
     status, 190–92
up to inequality, 188–93
"wife torture" and, 174–76
sexual harassment, 27
sexually assaulted women who kill
     perpetrators, 149–50
Shalala, Donna, 21
shaming, 260–61
Shapiro, Laura, 381
shelter movement, growth of, 33–36
shelters, 133–34, 364. *See also* housing
     and challenges to empowerment,
          73–80
     feminist organizations and, 28, 29
     first, 23–25
     functions of, 31–32
     law enforcement and, 35
     worth, unworthy victims, and, 76–80
shelter work, rethinking the politics of,
     372–75
Shepherd, Michael, 249
Simpson, O. J. and Nicole Brown, 3,
     139, 246, 402n.1
Simpsons, The (TV show), 47
Singer, Margaret, 200
situational violence, 103, 104
Slater, Philip, 187
slavery. *See* coercive control, as
     indentured servitude
Sleeping with the Enemy (film), 47–48,
     136, 254, 354
Soares, Girlene, 206, 245, 263, 265, 266
"social battering," 120
sociological account of domestic
     violence, 117–18
spatial and temporal extension of
     abuse, 377
spatial and temporal extension of
     control, 208–10, 326–28, 334–36
"special reasonableness of battered
     women," 161
stalking, 130–31, 256–57
Stanko, Elizabeth, 86
State v. Hickson, 423n.5
State v. Hundley, 427n.50
State v. Kelly, 157–59, 427nn.58–61

State v. Little, 428n.80
State v. Wanrow, 153–54, 156, 157, 163,
     368, 426n.46
*State of Connecticut v. Nathaline
     Parkman*, 162–64
State of Indiana v. Ruth Childers, 151
Steinmetz, Suzanne, 97, 117
Stockholm syndrome, 136, 335–36
Stone, Dr., 341, 344
Stone, Lucy, 143
Stop Violence Against Women (Amnesty
     International), 221
Straus, Murray, 97, 117
structural constraint, 376–77
subjugation, conspicuous, 133
subordination. *See* anti-subordination
     principle; male dominance
support groups, 133. *See also* shelters
surveillance, 255–58
survivor self, 305–7, 337–8
Symonds, Alexandra, 112, 116

tattoos, 260–61
Taylor, Harriet, 143, 178, 179
television, domestic violence on,
     45–48, 114–15, 136, 187
temporal extension of control. *See*
     spatial and temporal extension
     of control
tension buildup (phase), 245–46
terrorism, 200, 204–8, 210
     "conjugal," 200–201
     intimate, 103–5, 276
     patriarchal, 103
Thelma and Louise (film), 136
"therapeutic intervention," 41
"therapeutic" model (shelters), 74
Thomas v. Los Angeles, 406n.33
threats, 250–51
     active and passive, 253–54
     anonymous, 254–55
three Rs, 281–83, 302
Thurman, Tracy, 37
Thurman v. Torrington, 438n.15
Tolman, Richard, 274–76
"torture," 201, 204, 206–8, 220–21
Traficonda, Terry and Philip, 1–2, 273
"transformational" feminism, 79
transsexual victims, 393, 394
trauma, economy of, 124–30

trauma studies, Yale, 121–24
trauma theory/traumatization models,
      114, 116, 122, 152
  beyond, 128–29
    entrapment and, 126–28
    normalizing effect of, 159–64
    practical limits of, 138, 139, 156–67
    Stockholm syndrome, 136
  traumatization *vs.* self-defense, 344–46
Tyson, Mike, 254

"unfreezing" (coerced persuasion), 200
Uniform Crime Reporting System
      (UCR), 52
United Nations (UN), 219, 220
United States v. Kosminski, 438n.22
United States v. Morrison, 391

Vaughan, Sharon, 22–24, 29
victim blaming, 101, 102, 112–13, 130,
      153, 389
victimization. *See also* agency and
      victimization
  reframing, 351–52
violence. *See also* abuse;
      battering/battery; *specific topics*
  contradictory pretexts for, 245
  as cyclical, 245–48
  defined, 84–86. *See also* abuse, defining
  frequency and cumulative effects of,
      92–94, 205–6, 375–76. *See also*
      domestic violence, prevalence
      and incidence of
  physical *vs.* nonphysical, 85, 110,
      220–21
  as routine behavior, 205–6, 243–45,
      296–99
  types of, 242, 244
Violence Against Wives (Dobash and
      Dobash), 119
"violence against women," 370
Violence Against Women Act (VAWA),
      11, 21, 22, 48, 49, 61, 143, 391
"violence against women" approach, 44
Violence Against Women in the Family
      (United Nations), 220
violence approach, triumph of, 11
violence definition of abuse, 84–88,
      110, 111, 121
"violent brute" dilemma, 147–48

Walker, Lenore, 114, 124, 126–28,
      428n.79
  The Battered Woman, 119–20
  BWS model, 120, 151, 152, 160, 161,
      163
  cycle model, 245–46
  on isolation, 200
  testimony, 158, 160, 402n.1
Wanrow instruction, 137
Wanrow, Yvonne. 26, 137, 150, 151,
      153–54, 163, 368
Washington, Booker T., 188
Weinstein, Jack, 43, 388
Why Does He Do That? (Bancroft), 130
"wife beating," 143
"wife torture," 174–76
  coercive control and, 179–80
  as response to failure of domesticity,
      176–78
"Wife Torture in England" (Cobbe),
      177–78
woman battering, 55–56. *See also*
      specific topics
Woman House, 23, 28, 32, 33
woman-run refuges, 29
Woman Under the Influence, A (film), 286
women, anger toward, 283
Women Against Rape (WAR) groups,
      25–27
Women's Advocates, 23
Women's Aid, 74
Women's Aid Federation (WAFE),
      28–29, 74. *See also* National
      Women's Aid Federation
Women's Experience with Battering
      (WEB) Scale, 100
women's liberation movement, 25,
      143–45, 173. *See also* feminism
women who kill. *See* "abuse excuse";
      homicide(s); legal defense
      strategies
Women Who Kill (Jones), 136, 145–46,
      201
work. *See* employment

Yale trauma studies, 116, 121–24
Young, Iris, 192

zones of privacy, 226. *See also* safety
      zones

LaVergne, TN USA
11 January 2011
211821LV00002B/2/P